SECOND EDITION

Android Cookbook
Problems and Solutions for Android Developers

Ian Darwin

Beijing · Boston · Farnham · Sebastopo

Android Cookbook

by Ian F. Darwin

Copyright © 2017 O'Reilly Media, Inc. All rights reserved.

Printed in the United States of America.

Published by O'Reilly Media, Inc., 1005 Gravenstein Highway North, Sebastopol, CA 95472.

O'Reilly books may be purchased for educational, business, or sales promotional use. Online editions are also available for most titles (*http://www.oreilly.com/safari*). For more information, contact our corporate/institutional sales department: 800-998-9938 or *corporate@oreilly.com*.

Editors: Dawn Schanafelt and Meghan Blanchette	**Indexer:** Judith McConville
Production Editor: Colleen Lobner	**Interior Designer:** David Futato
Copyeditor: Kim Cofer	**Cover Designer:** Randy Comer
Proofreader: Rachel Head	**Illustrator:** Rebecca Demarest

May 2017: Second Edition

Revision History for the Second Edition

2017-05-05: First Release

See *http://oreilly.com/catalog/errata.csp?isbn=9781449374433* for release details.

978-1-449-37443-3

[LSI]

To Dennis M. Ritchie (1941–2011), language pioneer and co-inventor of Unix, who showed us all where the braces go, reminded us to keep it simple, and gave us so much more...

Table of Contents

Preface

Android is "the open source revolution" applied to cellular telephony and mobile computing. At least, part of the revolution. There have been many other attempts to provide open source cell phones, most of them largely defunct, ranging from the Openmoko Neo FreeRunner to QT Embedded, Moblin, LiMo, Debian Mobile, Maemo, Firefox OS, and Ubuntu Mobile to the open sourced Symbian OS and the now-defunct HP WebOS. And let's not forget the established closed source stalwart, Apple's iOS, and the two minor players (by market share), Microsoft's Windows Phone, and the now-abandoned BlackBerry OS 10.

Amongst all these offerings, two stand out as major players. Android is definitely here to stay! Due to its open source licensing, Android is used on many economy-model phones around the world, and indeed, Android has been estimated to be on as many as 90% of the world's smartphones (*http://money.cnn.com/2016/11/03/technol ogy/android-global-market-share-2016/index.html*). This book is here to help the Android developer community share the knowledge that will help make better apps. Those who contribute knowledge here are helping to make Android development easier for those who come after.

About Android

Android (*https://www.android.com/*) is a mobile technology platform that provides cell phones, tablets, and other handheld and mobile devices (even netbooks) with the power and portability of the Linux operating system, the reliability and portability of a standard high-level language and API, and a vast ecosystem of useful applications. Android apps are mostly written in the Java language (using tools such as Eclipse and Android Studio), compiled against the Android API, and translated into bytecode for an Android-specific VM.

Android is thus related by OS family to other Linux-based cell phone projects. Android is also related by programming language to BlackBerry's older Java ME phones, and to Java and the wider realm of Java Enterprise applications. Not to mention that all current BlackBerry devices can run Android applications, and, in fact, before it outsourced the remains of its smartphone business, BlackBerry's last devices only ran Android.

It's now generally believed that Android has almost three-quarters of the world smartphone market, although it has not displaced Apple's iPad in the tablet market. Sales figures change all the time, but it is clear that Android is, and will remain, one of the dominant players in the mobile space.

Android is also available for several specialized platforms. Android Wear (*https://developer.android.com/wear*) brings Android's programming model to the smartwatch and wearable environment for uses such as fitness trackers. Android Auto (*https://developer.android.com/auto*) is designed for controlling the entertainment units in automobiles. Android TV (*https://developer.android.com/tv*) runs in smart TVs and controllers for not-so-smart TVs. Finally, Android Things (*https://developer.android.com/things*) is designed for the embedded market, now known as "the internet of things" (IoT). Each of these platforms is fascinating, but to keep the book to a reasonable size, we focus primarily on "regular Android," Android for smartphone and tablet applications.

Who This Book Is By

This book was co-written by several dozen Android developers from the Android community at large. Development occurred in the open, on the Android Cookbook website (*https://androidcookbook.com/*), which I built (using Java, of course) to allow people to contribute, view, review, and comment on the recipes that would make up this book. A complete list can be found in "Acknowledgments" on page xxi. I am deeply grateful to all the contributors, who have helped move this book from a dream to the reality that you have in your hands (or onscreen if you are reading the ebook format). Thank you all!

Who This Book Is For

This book focuses on building Android applications using Java, the native language of Android applications. It is of course possible to package up a web application as a mobile app (see Recipe 19.10), but it will be difficult to get the all-important 100%-correct user experience with all the current features of Android that way.

So. Java. We assume you know the basics of the Java language. If not, see Recipe 1.4. We also assume you know the basics of the Java Standard Edition API (since this forms the basis of Android's runtime libraries) as well as the basics of Android. The terms *Activity*, *Intent*, *Service*, and *content provider*, while not necessarily being what you dream about at night, should at least be familiar to you. But if not, we've got you covered: see Recipe 1.2.

This book differs from the Samples associated with the Android SDK (*https://devel oper.android.com/samples/index.html*) in that it tries to focus more on how a given piece of technology works, rather than giving you (as many of the Samples do) a complete, working example that has both been simplified (to use very simple data) and complicated by adding in several "neat" features that are irrelevant to the problem at hand.

What's in This Book?

Chapter 1 takes you through the steps of setting up the Android development environment and building several simple applications of the well-known "Hello, World" type pioneered by Brian Kernighan.

Chapter 2 covers some of the differences in mobile computing that will hit developers coming from desktop and enterprise software environments, and talks about how mobile design (in particular, Android design) differs from those other environments.

Testing is often an afterthought for some developers, so we discuss this early on, in Chapter 3. Not so that you'll skip it, but so that you'll read and heed. We talk about unit testing individual components as well as testing out your entire application in a well-controlled way.

Android provides a variety of mechanisms for communicating within and across applications. In Chapter 4 we discuss Intents and broadcast receivers, Services, AsyncTasks, and handlers.

Chapter 5 covers a range of topics related to graphics, including use of the graphical drawing and compositing facilities in Android as well as using desktop tools to develop graphical images, textures, icons, and so on that will be incorporated into your finished application.

Every mobile app needs a GUI, so Chapter 6 covers the main ins and outs of GUI development for Android. Examples are given both in XML and, in a few cases, in Java-coded GUI development.

Chapter 7 covers all the pop-up mechanisms—menus, dialogs, and toasts—and one that doesn't pop up but is also for interaction outside your application's window, Android's notification mechanism.

Lists of items are very common in mobile applications on all platforms. Chapter 8 focuses on the "list" components in Android: the ListView and its newer replacement, the RecyclerView.

Android is rich in multimedia capabilities. Chapter 9 shows how to use the most important of these.

Chapter 10 shows how to save data into files, databases, and so on—and how to retrieve it later, of course. Another communication mechanism is about allowing controlled access to data that is usually in a SQL database. This chapter also shows you how to make application data available to other applications through something as simple but ubiquitous (in Android) as the URL, and how to use various cloud-based services to store data.

Android started out as an operating system for mobile telephones. Chapter 11 shows how to control and react to the telephony component that is in most mobile devices nowadays.

Mobile devices are, for the most part, always-on and always-connected. This has a major impact on how people use them and think about them. Chapter 12 shows the coding for traditional networked applications. This is followed by Chapter 13, which discusses gaming and animation, and Chapter 14, which discusses social networking.

The now-ubiquitous Global Positioning System (GPS) has also had a major impact on how mobile applications work. Chapter 15 discusses how to find a device's location, how to get map data from Google and OpenStreetMap, and how applications can be location-aware in ways that are just now being explored.

Chapter 16 talks about the sensors built into most Android devices and how to use them.

Chapter 17 talks about the low-energy very-local area networking that Bluetooth enables, going beyond connecting your Bluetooth headset to your phone.

Android devices are perhaps unique in how much control they give the developer. Some of these angles are explored in Chapter 18. Because Android is Linux-based, a few of the recipes in this chapter deal with traditional Unix/Linux commands and facilities.

In Chapter 19, we explore the use of other programming languages to write all or part of your Android application. Examples include C, Perl, Python, Lisp, and other languages.

While this edition of this book is in English, and English remains the number-one technical language worldwide, it is far from the only one. Most end users would rather have an application that has its text in their language and its icons in a form that is culturally correct for them. Chapter 20 goes over the issues of language and culture and how they relate to Android.

Finally, most Android developers hope other people will use their applications. But this won't happen if users can't find the applications. Chapter 21 shows how to prepare your application for distribution via the Google Play Store, and to use that as well as other markets to get your application out to the people who will use it.

Content Updates—Second Edition, March 2017

Major revision for Android Nougat (7.x). As befits a major revision, there are numerous new recipes to cover all the APIs that have been added or replaced over the past several releases of Android. Of necessity, a few older recipes were retired. Some recipes were moved around, which resulted in renumbering of most of the chapters.

The Android O Preview was released in the final week of this edition's proofing stage, and a few references are made to Android O; these should be regarded as "forward-looking statements," as "O" is still in a preview release.

Conventions Used in This Book

The following typographical conventions are used in this book:

Italic
> Indicates new terms, URLs, email addresses, filenames, and file extensions.

`Constant width`
> Used for program listings, as well as within paragraphs to refer to program elements such as variable or function names, databases, data types, environment variables, statements, and keywords.

`Constant width bold`
> Shows commands or other text that should be typed literally by the user.

`Constant width italic`
> Shows text that should be replaced with user-supplied values or by values determined by context.

 This element signifies a tip or suggestion.

 This element signifies a general note.

This element signifies a warning or caution.

 And here is our first warning: the term "I" used in a given recipe reflects the opinions or experience of that recipe's contributor, not necessarily of the book's editor.

Getting and Using the Code Examples

The code examples in this book vary from a few lines pasted from a complete application through to fully working apps. For those at the "few lines" end of the spectrum, you should not expect to be able to compile them from what we provide; these are intended to be merged into your application. All the examples that we have code for and that are compilable have been merged into a single GitHub repository, which is *the recommended way of getting the source code and keeping it up-to-date.* This repository can be accessed at *https://github.com/IanDarwin/Android-Cookbook-Examples.* Each directory in the repo contains one example program's project. As you will see if you visit this page, GitHub allows you to check out the source repository using the git clone command. As well, the web page offers the option to download the entire repository as a single (large) ZIP file as well as to browse portions of the repository in a web browser. Using Git will allow you to receive corrections and updates.

Contributors of each recipe also have the option to provide a download URL for their source code, hosted on some other public repository. These are listed as hyperlinks for ebook users to download from at the end of each recipe. In each case the archive file is expected to contain a complete Eclipse or Android Studio project. We have no control over these other repositories, so if one of them is incomplete, or stops working, please refer to the GitHub repository instead.

 Almost all code examples originally written for Eclipse now also contain a *build.gradle* file so they can be opened directly in Android Studio as well (see Recipe 1.12 to see how we did this). Code examples originally written for Android Studio can, in general, *not* be used by Eclipse without reorganizing the project structure.

How to Determine How a Project Can Be Built

If a project's top-level directory contains:

AndroidManifest.xml and *.project*
> It is openable with Eclipse.

build.gradle
> It is openable with Android Studio or buildable with command-line Gradle.

pom.xml
> It is buildable with command-line Maven (or using Maven inside an IDE).

build.xml
> It might still be buildable with the older Ant build tool.

See Figure P-1 for an example of a typical project layout.

The top level of the Git repository for the examples (*https://github.com/IanDarwin/Android-Cookbook-Examples*) contains a *README* file, viewable below the list of files and directories, which summarizes which projects can be built using which tools. Please pay attention to the Notes column, as there may at any time be some known issues with building the examples.

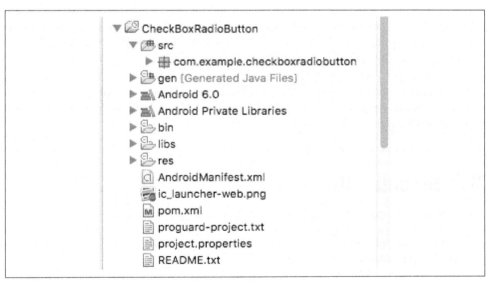

Figure P-1. Project layout for typical Eclipse and Studio projects

This book is here to help you get your job done. In general, you may use the code in this book in your programs and documentation. You do not need to contact us for permission unless you're reproducing a significant portion of the code. For example, writing a program that uses several chunks of code from this book does not require permission. Selling or distributing a CD-ROM of examples from O'Reilly books does require permission. Answering a question by citing this book and quoting example code does not require permission. Incorporating a significant amount of example code from this book into your product's documentation does require permission.

We appreciate, but do not require, attribution. An attribution usually includes the title, author, publisher, and ISBN. For example: "*Android Cookbook*, Second Edition, by Ian F. Darwin (O'Reilly). Copyright 2017 O'Reilly Media, Inc., 978-1-449-37443-3."

If you feel your use of code examples falls outside fair use or the permission given above, feel free to contact us at *permissions@oreilly.com*.

O'Reilly Safari

 *Safari* (formerly Safari Books Online) is a membership-based training and reference platform for enterprise, government, educators, and individuals.

Members have access to thousands of books, training videos, Learning Paths, interactive tutorials, and curated playlists from over 250 publishers, including O'Reilly Media, Harvard Business Review, Prentice Hall Professional, Addison-Wesley Professional, Microsoft Press, Sams, Que, Peachpit Press, Adobe, Focal Press, Cisco Press, John Wiley & Sons, Syngress, Morgan Kaufmann, IBM Redbooks, Packt, Adobe Press, FT Press, Apress, Manning, New Riders, McGraw-Hill, Jones & Bartlett, and Course Technology, among others.

For more information, please visit *http://oreilly.com/safari*.

How to Contact Us

Please address comments and questions concerning this book to the publisher:

O'Reilly Media, Inc.
1005 Gravenstein Highway North
Sebastopol, CA 95472
800-998-9938 (in the United States or Canada)
707-829-0515 (international or local)

707-829-0104 (fax)

We have a web page for this book, where we list errata, examples, and any additional information. You can access this page at *http://bit.ly/android-cookbook-2e*.

To comment or ask technical questions about this book, send email to *bookquestions@oreilly.com*.

For more information about our books, courses, conferences, and news, see our website at *http://www.oreilly.com*.

Find us on Facebook: *https://facebook.com/oreilly*

Follow us on Twitter: *https://twitter.com/oreillymedia*

Watch us on YouTube: *https://www.youtube.com/oreillymedia*

Acknowledgments

I would like to thank the dozens of people from the Android community at large who contributed so many of the recipes in the first edition of this book: Amir Alagic, Jim Blackler, Luis Vitorio Cargnini, Rupesh Chavan, Adrian Cowham, Wagied Davids, Nidhin Jose Davis, David Dawes, Enrique Diaz, Marco Dinacci, Claudio Esperanca, Kurosh Fallahzadeh, Daniel Fowler, Jonathan Fuerth, Sunit Katkar, Roger Kind Kristiansen, Vladimir Kroz, Alex Leffelman, Ulysses Levy, Thomas Manthey, Emaad Manzoor, Zigurd Mednieks, Keith Mendoza, Roberto Calvo Palomino, Federico Paolinelli, Johan Pelgrim, Catarina Reis, Mike Rowehl, Pratik Rupwal, Oscar Salguero, Ashwini Shahapurkar, Shraddha Shravagi, Rachee Singh, Saketkumar Srivastav, Corey Sunwold, Kailuo Wang, and Colin Wilcox.

Thanks to Mike Way, who contributed the permissions recipe (Recipe 2.2) for the second edition, and Daniel Fowler for updating several of his recipes for this second edition.

I must also mention the many people at O'Reilly who have helped shape this book, including my editors Mike Loukides, Courtney Nash, Meghan Blanchette, and Dawn Schanafelt; Adam Witwer and Sarah Schneider in production; production editor Teresa Elsey, who shepherded the whole production process; external copyeditor Audrey Doyle, who painstakingly read every word and phrase; Stacie Arellano, who proofread it all again; Lucie Haskins, who added index terms to all those recipes; designers Karen Montgomery and David Futato; illustrators Robert Romano and Rebecca Demarest; and anyone whom I've neglected to mention—you know who you are! For the second edition: Colleen Lobner, Kim Cofer, Rachel Head, and Judith McConville.

My late son Andrej Darwin (*https://darwinsys.com/andrej*) helped with some administrative tasks late in the recipe editing phase of the first edition. Thanks to all my family for their support.

Finally, a note of thanks to my two technical reviewers, Greg Ostravich and Zettie Chinfong, without whom there would be many more errors and omissions than the ones that doubtless remain. Not only that, they both came back for the second edition! Rick Isaacs made another pass and tested many recipes. Thanks also to the many people who pointed out minor errors and omissions in the first printing of the book, especially Anto Jurkovic and Joseph C. Eddy; most of these have been corrected at this time. The errors which surely remain are my own.

To all of the above, *thank you*!

## CHAPTER 1

Getting Started

The famous "Hello, World" pattern came about back in 1978 when Brian Kernighan and P.J. Plauger wrote a "recipe" on how to get started in any new programming language and environment. Their idea was that, if you could get a computer program to print out "Hello, World," then you had mastered how to use the system in general: how to create/edit a program's source code, compile/translate/process it into a runnable program as needed, and run it. And once you'd done that you could, with elaboration, make the computer do anything! This chapter is affectionately dedicated to these fine gentlemen, and to everyone who has ever struggled to *get started* in a new programming paradigm.

This chapter is a smorgasbord of "how to get started" recipes. We show you how to create and build an Android app using almost no tooling, using Apache Maven, using Eclipse, using Gradle, and using Android Studio. Nobody will regularly use all these techniques, but we chose to cover them all because some readers will like each way of doing things. Feel free to pick and choose, and try different ways of working on your application!

1.1 Understanding the Android Application Architecture

Ian Darwin

Problem

An Android application consists of many "moving parts" whose natures and interactions need to be understood in order to develop effectively.

Discussion

An Android application consists of one or more of the following components, written as Java classes:

- An *Activity* comprises the visual components ("views") for one screen as well as the code that displays data into that screen and can respond to user events on that screen. Almost every application has at least one Activity class.
- A *Service* is a component that has no user interface, and can run for a longer period of time than an Activity. Two main uses for Services are for long-running tasks (such as a music player), and running medium-length tasks without tying up the user-interface thread.
- *Broadcast receivers* are less common, and are used to respond to system-wide events such as the network losing or regaining connectivity, the battery running low, the system rebooting, and so on.
- *Content providers* are also relatively rare, and are used when one application needs to share its data with other applications; they can also be used with sync adapters.
- *Sync adapters* synchronize data with cloud services; the best-known examples are the Contacts and Calendar apps on the device, which can easily be synchronized to your Google account.

Your code does not create these objects using the new operator, as in conventional Java, but requests the invocation of Activities, Services, etc., using an *Intent*, an object that specifies your intention to have something done. Intents can start Activities within your application (by class name), start Activities in other applications (by specifying content type and other information), start Services, and request other operations. The interactions among these components are outlined in Figure 1-1.

Of these, the Activity is the most basic component, and the place you need to start when learning to develop Android applications.

Reference Documentation

Every Android developer should probably save at least these bookmarks or favorites in their browser for quick reference at any time:

- Introductory Documentation (*https://developer.android.com/guide/index.html*)
- Android API Reference (*https://developer.android.com/reference/*)

1.2 Understanding the Android Activity Life Cycle

Ian Darwin

Problem

Android apps do not have a "main" method; you need to understand how they get started and how they stop or get stopped.

Solution

The class `android.app.Activity` provides a number of well-defined life-cycle methods that are called when an application is started, suspended, restarted, and so on, as well as a method you can call to mark an Activity as finished.

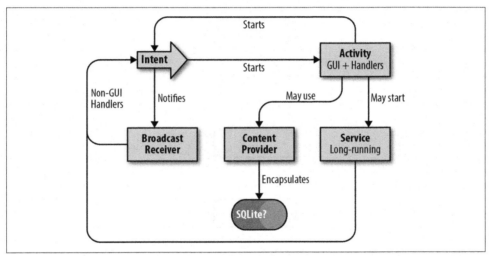

Figure 1-1. Android application components

Discussion

Your Android application runs in its own Unix process, so in general it cannot directly affect any other running application. The Android Runtime interfaces with the operating system to call you when your application starts, when the user switches to another application, and so on. There is a well-defined life cycle for Android applications.

An Android app can be in one of three states:

- Active, in which the app is visible to the user and is running.

- Paused, in which the app is partly obscured and has lost the input focus (e.g., when a dialog is in front of your Activity).
- Stopped, in which the app is completely hidden from view.

Your app will be transitioned among these states by Android calling the following methods on the current Activity at the appropriate time:

```
void onCreate(Bundle savedInstanceState)
void onStart()
void onResume()
void onRestart()
void onPause()
void onStop()
void onDestroy()
```

You can see the state diagram for this life cycle in Figure 1-2.

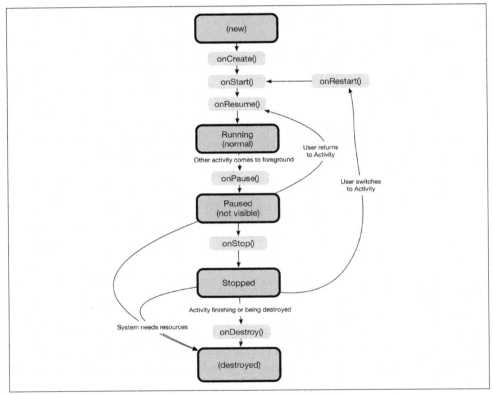

Figure 1-2. Android life-cycle states

The system's call to onCreate() is how you know that the Activity has been started. This is where you normally do constructor-like work such as setting up the "main window" with `setContentView()`, adding listeners to buttons to do work (including starting additional Activities), and so on. This is the one method that even the simplest Android Activity needs.

Note that most applications today base their UI on *Fragments*. A Fragment is a part of the UI for an Activity. For example, in the early days of Android a typical list-detail application would use two Activities, one for the list and one for the detail. This is still allowed, of course, but has the drawback that, on a tablet or a large-screen phone in landscape mode, it isn't possible to have both views side-by-side. An Activity can be divided into multiple Fragments (see Recipe 6.7), which solves this problem. A Fragment can only exist inside an Activity. The Fragment life cycle is similar to that of the Activity, but has a few additional methods.

You can see the invocations of the various life-cycle methods by creating a dummy project in Eclipse and overriding all the life-cycle methods with log "debug" statements (see also Recipe 3.11):

```
@Override
public void onPause() {
    Log.d(TAG, "In method onPause()");
}
```

1.3 Learning About Android Releases

Ian Darwin

Problem

You keep hearing about Ice Cream Sandwiches, Jelly Beans, Lollipops, KitKats, Marshmallows, and Nougats, and need to know what it all means.

Discussion

Android has gone through many versions in its lifetime. Each version has a version number, a code name, and an API level. The version number is a conventional versioning system like 2.1, 2.3.3, 3.0, 4.0, 4.1, 5.0, 6.0, and so on. When the first digit of the version changes, it's a big deal with lots of new APIs; when the second digit changes, it's more evolution than revolution (and occasionally a new code name); and if only the third digit changes, it's a minor change. The API levels are numbered monotonically. The code names are alphabetical and always refer to sweet foods. API levels 1 and 2 did not officially have code names.

Note that the Android system is backward-compatible in the usual sense: an app built for an older release will run on a newer version of Android, but not vice versa (unless special care is taken; see Recipe 1.21). An app built for 1.5 should run without recompilation on Android 7, for example. But an app written for and compiled on Android

7 will probably use API calls that don't exist on the 1.5 phone, so the phone will, in fact, refuse to install the newer app, unless you use some versioning and compatibility tricks that we'll touch on later (Recipe 1.21). The major versions of Android are summarized in Table 1-1.

Table 1-1. Android versions

Version number	API level	Name	Date	Major change/Notes	CM version
1.0	1		2008-09-23		
1.1	2		2009-02-09		
1.5	3	Cupcake	2009-04-30		3
1.6	4	Donut	2009-09-15		4
2.0	5	Eclair	2009-10-26		5
2.1	7	Eclair	2010-01-12		
2.2	8	Froyo	2010-05-20		6
2.3	9	Gingerbread	2010-12-06	Long the most widely-used version	7
2.3	10	Gingerbread			
3.0	11	Honeycomb	2011-02-22	Tablets only; source code release delayed	
3.1	12	Honeycomb	2011-05-10		
3.2	13	Honeycomb	2011-07-15		
4.0	14	Ice Cream Sandwich	2011-10-19	Merge tablet and phone support	9
4.0.3	15	Ice Cream Sandwich	2011-12-16		
4.1.2	16	Jelly Bean	2012-07-09		10
4.2.2	17	Jelly Bean	2012-11-13		10.1
4.3	18	Jelly Bean	2013-07-24		10.2
4.4	19	KitKat	2013-10-31	Co-marketing deal with Nestlé (makers of KitKat chocolate bar)	11
5.0	21	Lollipop	2014-11-10		12
6.0	23	Marshmallow	2015-10-05		13
7.0	24	Nougat	2016-08-22		14.0
7.1	25	Nougat			14.1

[a] Date information sourced from Wikipedia. (*https://en.wikipedia.org/wiki/Android_version_history*)

The final column, "CM version," shows the main version numbers of CyanogenMod (*https://en.wikipedia.org/wiki/CyanogenMod#Version_history*), long the leading "alternate distribution" or "community build" of Android. Based on the Android Open Source Project, "CM" was much beloved by many open source fans because it was independent of Google, allowed easier "root" access, and so on. As this edition of this book was going to press, CyanogenMod, Inc. decided to terminate its support for CyanogenMod, leading the community to fork the project and rename it to LineageOS (*https://LineageOS.org*). There are many other community builds of Android.

One focusing on security is CopperheadOS (*https://copperhead.co/android*). Several others are built by people frequenting XDA Developers (*https://www.xda-developers.com*) groups. Several commercial outfits claim to offer community builds, too; a web search will find these.

Of course, this table will continue to grow as new versions are released, and Android continues to grow.

1.4 Learning the Java Language

Ian Darwin

Problem

Android apps are written in the Java programming language before they are converted into Android's own class file format, DEX. If you don't know how to program in Java you will find it hard to write Android apps.

Solution

Lots of resources are available for learning Java. Most of them will teach you what you need, but will also mention some API classes that are not available for Android development. *Avoid* any sections in any resource that talk about topics listed in the left-hand column of Table 1-2.

Table 1-2. Parts of the Java API to ignore

Java API	Android equivalent
Swing, applets	Android's GUI; see Chapter 6.
Application entry point main()	See Recipe 1.2.
J2ME/Java ME	Most of android.* replaces the Java ME API.
Servlets/JSP/JSF, Java EE	Designed for server-side use.

Discussion

Here are some books and resources on Java programming:

- *Java in a Nutshell* by David Flanagan (O'Reilly). This is a good introduction for programmers, particularly those who are coming from C/C++. The book has grown from an acorn to a coconut in size through its various editions, to keep up with the growth of Java SE over its lifetime.

- *Head First Java* by Kathy Sierra and Bert Bates (O'Reilly). This provides a great visual-learner-oriented introduction to the language.

- *Thinking in Java* by Bruce Eckel (Prentice-Hall).

- *Learning Java* by Patrick Niemeyer and Jonathan Knudsen (O'Reilly).
- "Great Java: Level 1," by Brett McLaughlin (O'Reilly). This video provides a visual introduction to the language.
- *Java: The Good Parts* by Jim Waldo (O'Reilly).
- *Java Cookbook*, which I wrote and O'Reilly published. This is regarded as a good second book for Java developers. It has entire chapters on strings, regular expressions, numbers, dates and times, structuring data, I/O and directories, internationalization, threading, and networking, all of which apply to Android. It also has a number of chapters that are specific to Swing and to some EE-based technologies.
- Java Testing for Developers (*http://cjp.darwinsys.com/*), a video series I did on how to test out Java code as you develop it; covers both dynamic testing (with JUnit and many others) and static testing (with tools such as PMD and Find-Bugs).

Please understand that this list will probably never be completely up-to-date.

See Also

I maintain a list of Java resources online at *http://www.darwinsys.com/java/*.

O'Reilly has many of the best Java books around; there's a complete list at *http://oreilly.com/pub/topic/java*.

1.5 Creating a "Hello, World" Application from the Command Line

Ian Darwin

Problem

You want to create a new Android project without using any IDEs or plug-ins.

Solution

Use the Android Software Development Kit (SDK) tool android with the create project argument and some additional arguments to configure your project.

Discussion

This discussion assumes you have installed the Android SDK—one of the easiest ways to do so is to follow Recipe 1.8—and installed at least one platform version.

In addition to being the name of the platform, android is also the name of a command-line tool for creating, updating, and managing projects. To use it, you can either navigate into the *android-sdk-nnn* directory or set your PATH variable to include its *tools* subdirectory.

You have a choice of creating your project in the old format, which is the default, or the "new" Gradle-based format. We'll show the old way first, then the Gradle way. To create a new project, give the command android create project with some arguments. Example 1-1 shows running the command in a terminal window in a Microsoft environment.

Example 1-1. Creating a new project—old format

```
C:> PATH=%PATH%;"C:\Documents and Settings\Ian\My Documents\android-sdk-windows\tools"; \
    C:\Documents and Settings\Ian\My Documents\android-sdk-windows\platform-tools"
C:> android create project --target android-21 --package com.example.foo
    --name Foo --activity HelloWorldActivity --path .\MyAndroid
Created project directory: C:\Documents and Settings\Ian\My Documents\MyAndroid
Created directory C:\Documents and Settings\Ian\My Documents\MyAndroid\src\com\example\foo
Added file C:\Documents and Settings\Ian\My
Documents\MyAndroid\src\com\example\foo\HelloWorldActivity.java
Created directory C:\Documents and Settings\Ian\My Documents\MyAndroid\res
Created directory C:\Documents and Settings\Ian\My Documents\MyAndroid\bin
Created directory C:\Documents and Settings\Ian\My Documents\MyAndroid\libs
Created directory C:\Documents and Settings\Ian\My Documents\MyAndroid\res\values
Added file C:\Documents and Settings\Ian\My Documents\MyAndroid\res\values\strings.xml
Created directory C:\Documents and Settings\Ian\My Documents\MyAndroid\res\layout
Added file C:\Documents and Settings\Ian\My Documents\MyAndroid\res\layout\main.xml
Added file C:\Documents and Settings\Ian\My Documents\MyAndroid\AndroidManifest.xml
Added file C:\Documents and Settings\Ian\My Documents\MyAndroid\build.xml
C:>
```

On Unix or macOS you can use something like the following:

```
/Users/ian/android-sdk-macosx/tools/android create project --target android-21 \
    --package com.example.foo \
    --name Foo --activity HelloWorldActivity --path MyAndroid
```

Table 1-3 lists the arguments for the android create project command.

Table 1-3. List of android create project arguments

Name	Meaning	Example
--activity	Name of your "main class" and default name for the generated *.apk* file.	--activity HelloWorldActivity
--name	Name of the project and the generated *.apk* file.	--name MyProject
--package	Name of the Java package for your classes.	--package com.example.hello

Name	Meaning	Example
--path	Path to create the project in (does not create a subdirectory under this, so don't use /home/*you*/workspace, but rather / home / *you* / workspace / *NewProjectName*).	--path /home/ian/ workspace/MyProject (see Example 1-1 for Windows example)
--target	API level of the Android platform to target; use android list targets to see list of targets. A number is an "ID," not an API level; for that, use android- with the API level you want.	--target android-10
--gradle	Use Gradle format (requires --gradle-version).	--gradle
--gradle-version	Version of Gradle plug-in to use.	--gradle-version 3.3

If it cannot complete the requested operation, the android command presents a voluminous "command usage" message listing all the operations it can do and the arguments for them. If successful, the android create project command creates the files and directories listed in Table 1-4.

Table 1-4. Artifacts created by android create project

Name	Content
AndroidManifest.xml	Config file that tells Android about your project
bin	Generated binaries (compiled class files)
build.properties	Editable properties file
build.xml	Ant build control file
default.properties or *project.properties* (depending on tools version)	Stores SDK version and libraries used; maintained by plug-in
gen	Generated stuff
libs	Libraries, of course
res	Important resource files (*strings.xml*, layouts, etc.)
src	Source code for your application
src/packagename/ActivityName.java	Source of "main" starting Activity
test	Copies of most of the above

If we use the two Gradle-related arguments, we get a slightly different project structure, as shown in Example 1-2.

Example 1-2. Project creation—Gradle format

```
$ /Users/ian/android-sdk-macosx/tools/android create project \
    --target android-23 --package com.example.foo \
    --gradle --gradle-version 2.0.0 \
    --name Foo --activity HelloWorldActivity --path HelloGradle
Created project directory: HelloGradle
Created directory /home/ian/HelloGradle/src/main/java
Created directory /home/ian/HelloGradle/src/main/java/com/example/foo
```

```
Added file HelloGradle/src/main/java/com/example/foo/HelloWorldActivity.java
Created directory /home/ian/HelloGradle/src/androidTest/java
Created directory /home/ian/HelloGradle/src/androidTest/java/com/example/foo
Added file...
    HelloGradle/src/androidTest/java/com/example/foo/HelloWorldActivityTest.java
Created directory /home/ian/HelloGradle/src/main/res
Created directory /home/ian/HelloGradle/src/main/res/values
Added file HelloGradle/src/main/res/values/strings.xml
Created directory /home/ian/HelloGradle/src/main/res/layout
Added file HelloGradle/src/main/res/layout/main.xml
Created directory /home/ian/HelloGradle/src/main/res/drawable-xhdpi
Created directory /home/ian/HelloGradle/src/main/res/drawable-hdpi
Created directory /home/ian/HelloGradle/src/main/res/drawable-mdpi
Created directory /home/ian/HelloGradle/src/main/res/drawable-ldpi
Added file HelloGradle/src/main/AndroidManifest.xml
Added file HelloGradle/build.gradle
Created directory /home/ian/HelloGradle/gradle/wrapper
$
```

It is a normal and recommended Android practice to create your user interface in
XML using the layout file created under *res/layout*, but it is certainly possible to write
all the code in Java. To keep this example self-contained, we'll do it the "wrong" way
for now. Use your favorite text editor to replace the contents of the file *Hello-
World.java* with the contents of Example 1-3.

Example 1-3. HelloWorld.java

```java
import android.app.Activity;
import android.widget.*;

public class HelloWorld extends Activity {

    /**
     * This method gets invoked when the Activity is instantiated in
     * response to, e.g., clicking on the app's icon in the Home screen.
     * Reminder: this is NOT a best-practices way of creating the UI!
     */
    @Override
    public void onCreate(Bundle savedInstanceState) {
            super.onCreate(savedInstanceState);
            // Create a TextView for the current Activity
            TextView view = new TextView(this);
            // Make it say something
            view.setText("Hello World");
            // Put this newly created view into the Activity,
            // sort of like JFrame.getContentPane().add(view)
            setContentView(view);
    }
}
```

Although Google has moved from Eclipse to Android Studio, which uses the Gradle
build tool, the command-line version of generated projects still uses the Ant build

tool by default (i.e., if you omit the two Gradle-related arguments shown in Example 1-2). Assuming you have the Apache Software Foundation Ant build tool (*http://ant.apache.org/*) installed (and it is included with recent versions of the Android SDK), you can now (in a command-line window) change to the project directory (...MyDocuments\MyAndroid in Example 1-1) and issue the command:

```
$ ant debug
```

This will create an archive file named, for example, *MyAndroid.apk* (with "apk" standing for Android Package) in the *bin* directory.

If you are using the Gradle version, you can instead type:

```
gradlew build
```

The first time you run this, it may take a long time to complete. But it should work. If it doesn't, use the *HelloGradle* project in this book's GitHub repository (*https://github.com/IanDarwin/Android-Cookbook-Examples*).

If this is your first time here, you may need to create an Android Virtual Device (AVD), which is just a named configuration for the Android emulator specifying target resolution, API level, and so on. You can create an emulator using:

```
android create avd -n my_droid -t 21
```

The argument to -t is the target API level; see Recipe 1.3. For more details on creating an AVD, see Recipe 3.1.

You can then start the Android Debug Bridge (ADB) server for communication, and the emulator:

```
adb start-server
emulator -avd my_droid -t 19
```

Assuming you now have either the emulator running or your device plugged in and recognized via USB, you can issue a command similar to one of the following, depending on exactly what you built earlier. If you have both an emulator and a real device, add an argument of -e for *emulator* or -d for *device* between the adb command and the install operation:

```
$ adb install -r bin/HelloAndroid.apk # Ant build
```

```
$ adb install -r target/HelloAndroid-1.0-SNAPSHOT-debug.apk # Maven build
```

```
$ adb install -r build/outputs/apk/HelloAndroid-debug.apk # Gradle build
```

If you are handy with shell scripts or batch files, you'll want to create one called, say, *download*, to avoid having to type the adb invocation on every build cycle.

Finally, you can start your app! You can use the application list: tap the little icon that looks like a 5×5 row of dots, scroll to your application by name, and tap its icon.

You will probably find it convenient to create an icon for your app on the Home screen of the device or emulator; this icon will survive multiple `install -r` cycles, as long as you don't uninstall, so it's the easiest way to test the running of your application.

See Also

Recipe 1.10, Recipe 1.15.

1.6 Creating a "Hello, World" App with Apache Maven

Ian Darwin

Problem

The previous recipe used Android to create a project buildable with Apache Ant. However, many organizations are moving or have moved from Ant to Maven, due to Maven's dependency management. In fact, Maven is almost certainly the most widely used build tool in the Java environment. Ant doesn't handle dependencies on its own; although this can be grafted in (using Apache Ivy), Maven's shorter configuration files make direct use of Maven a better fit most of the time.

Solution

Use Apache Maven. Use a "Maven archetype" to generate your project, and use Maven to build and run it.

Discussion

There are several approaches to using Apache Maven to build Android projects. Here's one I've tested, based upon the akquinet `maven-android-archetypes`:

```
$ mvn archetype:generate \
-DarchetypeArtifactId=android-quickstart \
-DarchetypeGroupId=de.akquinet.android.archetypes \
-DarchetypeVersion=1.0.8 \
-DgroupId=com.androidcookbook \
-DartifactId=android-demo \
-Dplatform=17 \
-Dpackage=com.androidcookbook.hellomaven
```

Most of the `-D` arguments are obvious. `platform` is the API level. You can specify a number of other parameters and variations, including test projects.

Once you've created your project you can build it:

```
$ mvn clean package
```

Before the next step, you should plug in a device or start an emulator:

```
$ mvn android:deploy
# (not mvn deploy!) this will package and install, but not run, the app

$ mvn android:run # This will run the app
```

Maven and its Android plug-in offer support for other operations, including signing the APK for release.

There are also Eclipse plug-ins for Maven; these are included with the latest Eclipse builds, or see Recipe 1.16 and use the Marketplace to install M2E and M2E-Android. It is possible to "Eclipsify" a project such as the one you created using Maven. You can create minimal Eclipse project structures using `mvn eclipse:eclipse`, and make it into a full M2E project by right-clicking on the project in the Project Explorer and selecting Configure → Convert to Maven Project. This has been done to create many of the Eclipse files in the downloadable version of this project.

Incidentally, if you get an Eclipse error on your POM file stating "Plugin execution not covered by lifecycle configuration," you can turn this into a warning or even ignore it, under Eclipse Preferences → Maven → Errors/Warnings → Plugin execution not covered by lifecycle configuration → Warning, as shown in Figure 1-3.

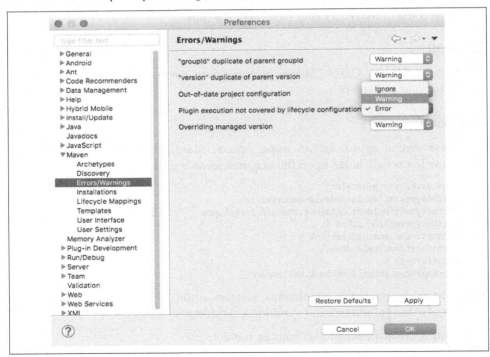

Figure 1-3. Maven: Plugin execution not covered by lifecycle configuration

See Also

Akquinet's guide to getting started with archetypes (*http://stand.spree.de/ wiki_details_maven_archetypes*); the source code for the artifacts (*https://github.com/ akquinet/android-archetypes*).

I have an experimental Maven archetype that creates a Maven project that should also work with Eclipse and Android Studio; you can try it out by referring to GitHub (*https://github.com/IanDarwin/mvn-archetype-android*).

1.7 Choosing an IDE for Android Development

Ian Darwin

Problem

Using build tools is OK, but coding with a plain-text editor is too slow to be your regular development stream. You want to choose an integrated development environment (IDE) to use for your Android projects: Android Studio, Eclipse, or "other."

Solution

Weigh the pros and cons of each, then roll the dice. Try each one on a reasonable-sized project.

Discussion

Whereas in the MS Windows world there is a single IDE that dominates, and in the Android world there is a single IDE that is "official," in the larger Java world there are several that are worth considering.

Eclipse (*http://eclipse.org*) was created by IBM in the early days of Java, once it was clear that its then-current IDE Visual Age was not going to live a long life (Visual Age was written in Smalltalk, not in Java). In my experience teaching Java courses, about 80% of Java developers use Eclipse, and that figure has been fairly steady over the years. Spring Tool Suite (STS) and various IBM developer studios are based on Eclipse and included in that figure.

Android Studio (*https://developer.android.com/tools/studio/index.html*) is the official Android IDE supported by Google. It is based on IntelliJ IDEA (*https:// www.jetbrains.com/idea*), a Java IDE that has long been around but had a relatively small usage level in the Java community until Google incorporated its plug-in into ItelliJ and renamed this version to "Android Studio."

NetBeans (*https://netbeans.org*) was written by a small company that Sun Microsystems acquired in 1999. Sun Microsystems was in turn acquired by Oracle in 2009.

NetBeans has been the "official" Java IDE for a long time, but its usage was "eclipsed" by Eclipse (remember: an eclipse occurs when another body passes in front of the Sun). Relatively few developers use NetBeans specifically for Android, so to keep the discussion focused, NetBeans will not be covered in this book.

For the first decade of Android's life, Google recommended use of Eclipse with its own plug-in, called Android Development Tools (ADT). Google offered it both as a standalone plug-in (for those who already had Eclipse up and running) and in a bundle already integrated with Eclipse. Around 2013 it announced the switch to Android Studio based on IntelliJ. Shortly thereafter, the Eclipse Foundation announced that a small team was picking up ADT (since it was open source) and merging in some additional tools. This new plug-in is called AndMore (*https://projects.eclipse.org/ projects/tools.andmore*). Eclipse with AndMore is equivalent to and forward-compatible with Eclipse with ADT, though some names in the project files have to be changed (see Recipe 1.11). Note that some organizations may choose to stay with ADT; if you're in that camp, you can (mostly) just substitute ADT where we say And-More.

Your project structure and accompanying build tool might also be a factor in choosing. Eclipse supports a single-level project, which is typically what you need for an application, with an optional second project for testing if you use the official Android unit testing framework (see Chapter 3). ADT (and thus AndMore) does not require an external build tool; the plug-in contains all the smarts to build any type of Android application. It has only two project files that need to be kept under source control: *.project* and *.classpath*. A directory *.settings* file can be controlled as well, but it changes a lot and can just as easily be ignored. There is even an API in Eclipse for manipulating project structure (*http://www.stateofflow.com/journal/66/creating-java-projects-programmatically*). Because there are only two files, hacking a project by editing configuration files is not out of the question. As well, Eclipse is well supported by the Maven build tool using the M2E (Maven Eclipse) and M2E-Android plug-ins (you'll want both). However, this setup can be a little bit quirky.

Android Studio, on the other hand, uses a maze of project files. Here is a list of the files (not including the source of your program!) in a project created by Android Studio 2.0:

```
./.gradle/2.4/taskArtifacts/cache.properties
./.gradle/2.4/taskArtifacts/cache.properties.lock
./.gradle/2.4/taskArtifacts/fileHashes.bin
./.gradle/2.4/taskArtifacts/fileSnapshots.bin
./.gradle/2.4/taskArtifacts/outputFileStates.bin
./.gradle/2.4/taskArtifacts/taskArtifacts.bin
./.idea/.name
./.idea/compiler.xml
./.idea/copyright/profiles_settings.xml
./.idea/encodings.xml
./.idea/gradle.xml
```

```
./.idea/libraries/appcompat_v7_23_0_1.xml
./.idea/libraries/design_23_0_1.xml
./.idea/libraries/hamcrest_core_1_3.xml
./.idea/libraries/junit_4_12.xml
./.idea/libraries/support_annotations_23_0_1.xml
./.idea/libraries/support_v4_23_0_1.xml
./.idea/misc.xml
./.idea/modules.xml
./.idea/runConfigurations.xml
./.idea/workspace.xml
./build/ - ignore
./build.gradle
./gradle/wrapper/gradle-wrapper.jar
./gradle/wrapper/gradle-wrapper.properties
./gradle.properties
./gradlew
./gradlew.bat
./local.properties
./MyApplication.iml
./settings.gradle
./mainapp/.gitignore
./mainapp/build.gradle
./mainapp/mainapp.iml
./mainapp/proguard-rules.pro
```

It appears to take Android Studio about 30 files to do what Eclipse does in just a few. Admittedly not all of those have to be kept under source control, but which ones do? To answer that, look in the *.gitignore* file in a project generated by Android Studio 2.x; this lists the files that should *not* be included in source control.

Android Studio also expects that every project have an extra level of directory structure, called *app* for the application, to cater to the relatively few applications that have multiple modules, such as a library. In Eclipse, you just make the project using the library depend on the library project. The extra directory structure put in by Studio encumbers pathnames, means the directory where a Studio project is created does not conform to the decade-old Maven project structure, and means that you can't use the old familiar grep -r *somePattern projectname*/src; you have to remember to type an extra "app/" every time. Seemingly harmless, but annoying. Of course people who commonly use multiple projects but forget to create them as such when they start will appreciate the way Studio does things.

You should also consider speed. Both are fairly quick at entering code you type. Because Studio is not a complete IDE but depends on Gradle to build, it used to be a lot slower, but Studio 2.x is supposed to be much improved in this regard. Different people have different ideas on how to measure speed, and different results have been claimed, so you should try this yourself on representative development hardware.

Eclipse provides a single window with a tree-based "Package Explorer," so you can easily move, copy, or compare files between projects. IntelliJ/Studio opens each project in a new window and, by default, closes the previous one.

So, there are many differences, but also many obvious similarities. It's sort of like buying a car: GM, Ford, Chrysler, Tesla, BMW, Toyota, and many more make automobiles, but you have to pick one of these to buy. With IDEs the choice is not as exclusive, though. What if you like both? You could use Eclipse for your regular Java work and IntelliJ/Android Studio for your Android work—especially if you need the latest Android support—although switching back and forth might be annoying. You could even set up your Android projects to be openable in both IDEs—we've done so for most of the projects in the samples repository. However, it's not a very profitable undertaking, and we don't recommend it as a general practice.

Oh, and if you do run both, be sure to configure them to share the same "SDK" folder —the actual Android tools, libraries, and emulator images—so you won't have to update everything twice.

As another path forward for the experienced Eclipse user, you could use Android Studio but tell it to use the Eclipse key-mappings, which will make it work somewhat like Eclipse—although many of the key sequence settings there are not quite right, and you'll need to fiddle with them a bit. And if you do so but another developer in your team is a "native" user of Studio or the underlying IntelliJ, you will both get frustrated when doing pair programming.

Summary

If you want the best support of new features, Android Studio may be a better choice. If you want an IDE that is widely used across the Java community, Eclipse may be a better choice. There is no hard and fast answer.

1.8 Setting Up Android Studio

Daniel Fowler, Ian Darwin

Problem

You want to develop your Android applications using Android Studio, so a concise guide to setting up that IDE would be useful.

Solution

The use of the Android Studio IDE is recommended by Google for developing Android apps. Configuring the IDE is not a single-shot install; several stages need to be completed. This recipe provides details on those stages.

Discussion

The Android Studio integrated development environment (IDE) is provided for free by Google to develop applications. Studio comes with the Android Software Development Kit (SDK), which provides essential programs to develop Android software. To set up a development system you will need to download and run the installers for:

- The Java Standard Edition Development Kit (JDK), if not already installed
- Android Studio

Installing the JDK, if necessary

Go to the Java download page (*http://www.oracle.com/technetwork/java/javase/down loads/index.html*). Click the Java icon to access the JDK downloads:

The list of JDK downloads will be shown. Click the Accept License Agreement radio button; otherwise, you will not be allowed to continue. You'll want to download and run one of the latest JDKs present; as of this writing, they are Java 8 builds whose version string ends in *8u121*, but that will surely change by the time you read this. Choose the download appropriate for your operating system: Windows x86 or 64-bit *.exe*, MacOS *.dmg*, Linux *.rpm* or *.tgz*, and so on. Accept any security warnings that appear, but only if you are downloading from the official Java download web page.

When the download has completed, run the installer and go through all the screens, clicking Next until the installer has finished. You should not need to change any options presented. When the JDK installer has completed, click the Finish button. A product registration web page may load; you can close this or you can choose to register your installation.

For Android use, you do not need to download any of the "demos or samples" from this site.

Install Android Studio

Go to the Android Studio download page (*https://developer.android.com/sdk/index.html*).

The installation process can take some time as the installer will download additional files. Click the Download Android Studio button, accept the terms and conditions, and begin the download by clicking a second Download Android Studio button. On MS Windows, the default is a file with a name like *android-studio-bundle-X.X-windows.exe*, which is over 1 GB and includes both the IDE and the Android SDK. If you already have the Android SDK installed, select Other Download Options and you will see the page in Figure 1-4, where you have a choice of that file or one without the SDK bundle, with a name like *android-studio-ide-X.X-windows.exe*. For macOS there is only the unbundled file, *android-studio-ide-X.X-mac.dmg*, where *X.X* is Studio's build number (this may not match the displayed version number; e.g., Android Studio 2.0 has a build number of 143.2739321). On Windows, accept the Windows User Account Control dialog.

On some 64-bit versions of Windows the installer may require the JAVA_HOME environment variable to be set. Use the Control Panel to access the System settings, and open the "Advanced systems settings" section. The Advanced tab on the System Properties dialog should be visible. Click the Environment Variables button to add a new JAVA_HOME system variable, and set it to the path of the Java JDK (e.g., *C:\Program Files \Java\jdk1.8.0*; enter the correct path for your system).

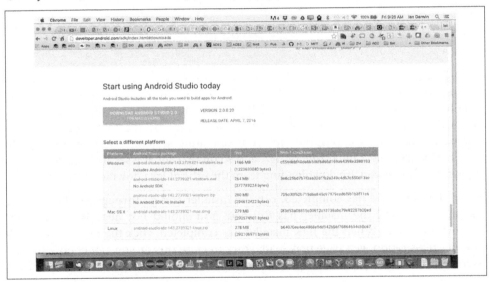

Figure 1-4. Android Studio download page

Proceed through the installer's dialogs. The installer configures Studio and the Android SDK (if you installed the bundle version), and downloads an initial Android Virtual Device (AVD). The default install location for the Android SDK is under the logged-in user's *AppData\Local* directory on Windows, or *$HOME/android-sdk-nnn* under macOS or Linux. You may want to select an easier-to-remember and shallower location (e.g., *C:\AndroidSDK*).

After installing Studio, further configuration (and downloading of the SDK if necessary) occurs when it is first run. Allow access through your desktop system's configuration if required. Further SDK packages will be downloaded. As well, each time Studio runs it checks for updates and may display a message if updates are needed. Aside from updates to Studio itself, the Android SDK and additional SDK packages are best updated via the Android SDK Manager program (see Recipe 1.9).

Once that's done, Studio is now configured to build and debug Android apps. See Recipe 3.1 to configure an Android emulator; then try a "Hello, World" app as a sanity check. Or plug a real Android device into the computer's USB port and use its settings to turn on USB Debugging.

 For a few Windows users Studio may not start the first time, and a DLL error is displayed. Installing the Microsoft Visual C++ 2010 SP1 Redistributable Package has been known to clear the error.

See Also

Recipe 3.1, Recipe 1.9.

1.9 Installing Platform Editions and Keeping the SDK Updated

Daniel Fowler

Problem

Whether using Android Studio, Eclipse, or command-line tools, you must install at least one Platform Edition before you can compile applications. The SDK should be kept updated so you can work with the latest APIs on the evolving Android platform.

Solution

Use the Android *SDK Manager* program to install, and later to update, the installed SDK packages and to install new SDK packages.

Discussion

Android itself is constantly evolving, and therefore so is the Android Software Development Kit. The ongoing development of Android is driven by:

- Google's research and development

- Phone manufacturers developing new and improved handsets
- Addressing security issues and possible exploits
- The need to support new devices
- Support for new hardware interfaces
- Fixing bugs
- Improvements in functionality (e.g., a new JavaScript engine)
- Changes in the underlying Linux kernel
- Deprecation of redundant programming interfaces
- New uses (e.g., Android Wear, Android Auto)
- The wider Android development community

 The following discussion is illustrated with screenshots from Android Studio, but the same tooling can be invoked from within Eclipse or by invoking the command-line tool named simply android.

Installation of the IDEs and the Android SDK has been covered elsewhere; see Recipe 1.8 or the developer documentation (*https://developer.android.com/sdk/installing/index.html*). When Android Studio is run it will check for updates to both Studio and the SDK. A message is displayed when updates are available. Most updates will be performed via the SDK Manager program. If you OK the update, Studio will close and the SDK Manager will run. If you don't want to update when the upgrade is offered, you can access the SDK Manager later from within Studio (see Figure 1-5) or directly from the Android SDK install location.

Figure 1-5. SDK Manager toolbar icon

The following steps work through the update process.

In Studio, selecting SDK Manager from the toolbar or via the Tools → Android menu shows the Android SDK settings, which shows what packages are installed or available (see Figure 1-6).

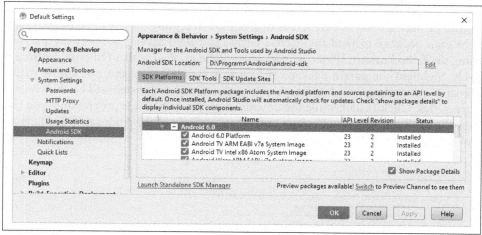

Figure 1-6. Android SDK settings, showing current installation status

To actually make changes, click the Launch Standalone SDK Manager link, which runs the external SDK Manager program shown in Figure 1-7. The Android SDK is divided into several packages. The SDK Manager automatically scans for updates to existing packages and will list new packages. Available updates will be shown in a list (alongside available optional packages).

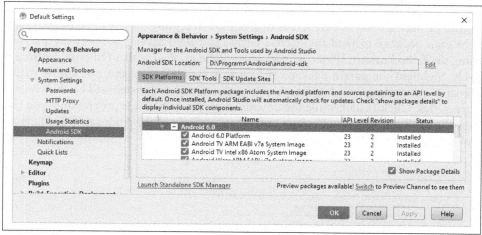

Figure 1-7. Standalone SDK Manager

Available updates will be checked ready for download and installation; uncheck the ones not required. (Unless you're short on disk space, you can have as many of the

API packages installed as you wish.) Then click the "Install *x* packages" button. If an update or package has license terms that require accepting, they will be listed. Highlight each package to read the license terms, and then accept or reject the package using the radio buttons. (Rejected packages will be marked with a red cross.) Alternatively, highlight the parent package and click Accept All to accept everything that is available. All packages and updates ready to download and install will be shown with a green tick. Click Install; while the download and installation is progressing, you can view the log by clicking the log icon in the bottom right of the Android SDK Manager dialog (see Figure 1-8).

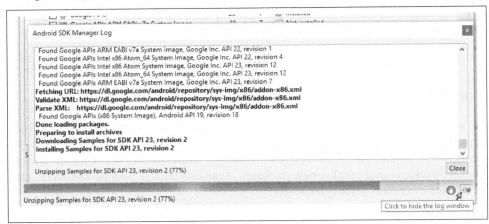

Figure 1-8. Android SDK update log

Any errors during the download and installation will be shown in red in the log dialog. Updates that affect the Android Debug Bridge (ADB) will result in a request to restart ADB; click Yes to restart it. Obsolete packages will have been deleted during the download and installation. When all packages have been updated and you've had a chance to inspect the log, you can close the log dialog, if open, and the Android SDK Manager dialog.

Android is an evolving platform, so checking for updates every few weeks allows you to work with the latest tools and APIs.

See Also

Recipe 1.8, The Android Studio User Guide documentation on installation (*https://developer.android.com/sdk/installing/index.html*).

1.10 Creating a "Hello, World" App Using Android Studio

Ian Darwin

Problem

You want to use Android Studio to develop your Android application.

Solution

Install Java, Android Studio, and one or more SDK versions. Create your project and start writing your app. Build it and test it under the emulator, all from within the IDE.

Discussion

Before you can create your application with Android Studio, you have to install these two packages:

- Android Studio itself
- One or more Android SDK versions (*https://developer.android.com/sdk/*)

For details on installing these items, please refer to Recipe 1.8.

Once you've done that, click on "Start a new Android Studio project" from the Welcome screen (Figure 1-9), which appears when you don't have any projects open.

Figure 1-9. Studio Welcome screen

On the Create New Project screen (Figure 1-10), choose the application name and Java code package.

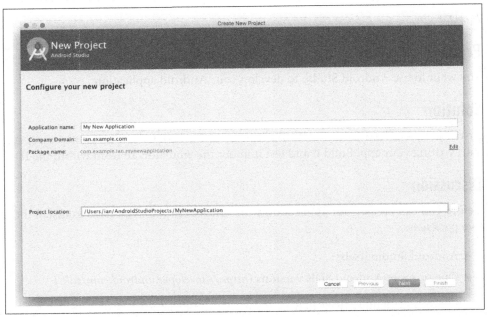

Figure 1-10. Studio New Project screen

On the next page of the same dialog, you can specify what kinds of devices (phone/tablet, Android Wear, Android TV, etc.) your project is going to target and, for mobile devices, the minimum and target SDK API levels (Figure 1-11).

Almost every Android application has at least one Activity class defined, and the "Hello, World" app is no exception. You can either pick Empty Activity (in which case you'll have to add some code) or Basic Activity; we went with the latter (Figure 1-12).

The next page asks you to pick names for your Activity and its layout file (Figure 1-13). For a single-Activity app, the defaults are fine.

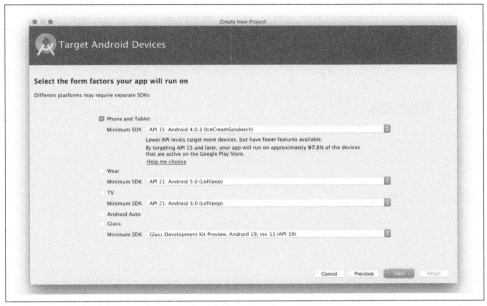

Figure 1-11. Studio device and target APIs

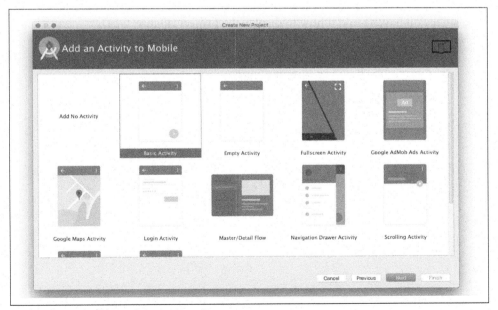

Figure 1-12. Defining the Activity class

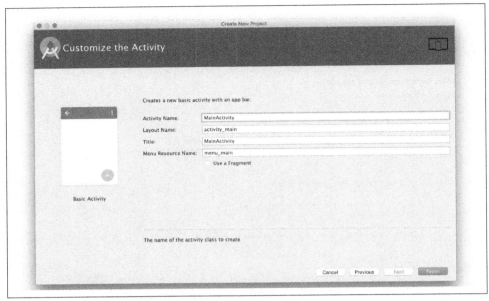

Figure 1-13. Studio customizing the Activity

After chugging for a while, Studio will create your project and give you a blank view of it, since you haven't told it how to display the project (Figure 1-14).

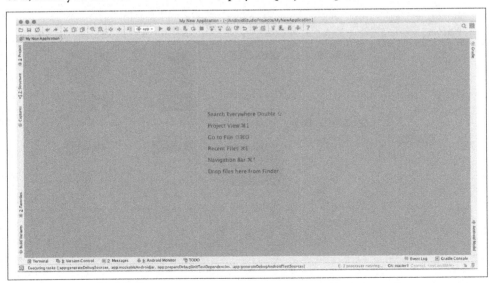

Figure 1-14. Studio blank view

Click the sideways label *1. Project* at the upper left of the main window. Drill down into App → Java → *package-name*/MainActivity, or whatever you called the Activity. Have a brief look at the provided Java code (Figure 1-15).

Figure 1-15. Studio-generated Activity

If you don't see a graphic representation of your Activity soon, expand Res → Layout and double-click *content_main.xml*. You should see a visual UI editor (Figure 1-16).

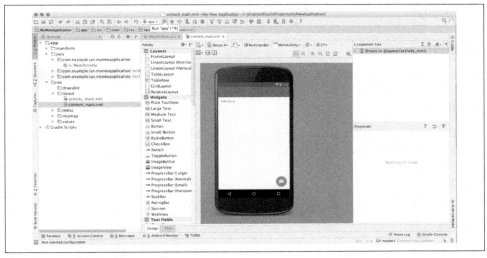

Figure 1-16. Studio layout editor

Note that the Studio Layout Editor isn't really running your application, just interpreting the user interface layout. To actually run it, click the Run button in the middle of the top toolbar. In the process of starting the app, Studio will ask you which AVD (emulator) to use. Eventually the application should appear in its own emulator window (Figure 1-17).

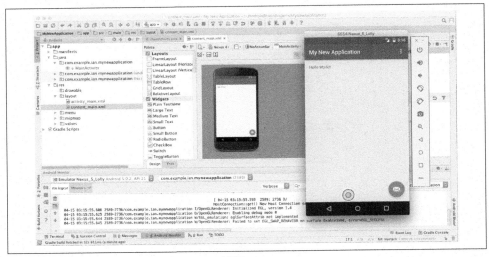

Figure 1-17. Studio running an app in AVD

1.11 Converting an Eclipse ADT Project to Android Studio

Ian Darwin

Problem

You have existing Eclipse/ADT projects but want to or have to use Android Studio.

Solution

Use the Android Studio *Import project* feature. This will make a copy of the files it needs in a new location, allowing you to build the project under Android Studio.

Discussion

Note that, at the time of writing, this works for ADT projects but not for AndMore projects.

To convert an ADT project to Studio, close any previous projects, or start Android Studio if it's not running. Select "Import project" from the Welcome screen (Figure 1-18).

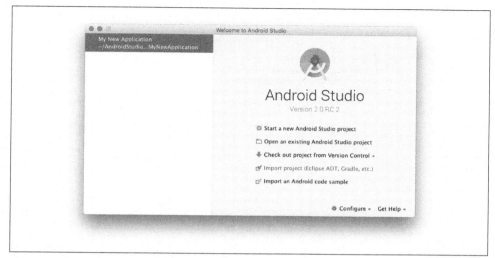

Figure 1-18. Studio: Starting to convert a project

In the dialog that pops up, navigate to the root of the Eclipse folder. This will normally have *res* and *src* folders underneath it, assuming that standard ADT layout was used (Figure 1-19).

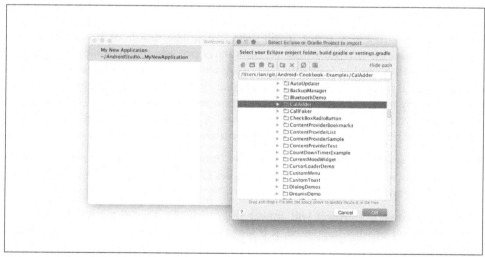

Figure 1-19. Studio: Location of project to convert

Now you get to pick a new location for the converted project (Figure 1-20). The default is good for starting, unless you or your organization has a policy on where to place projects.

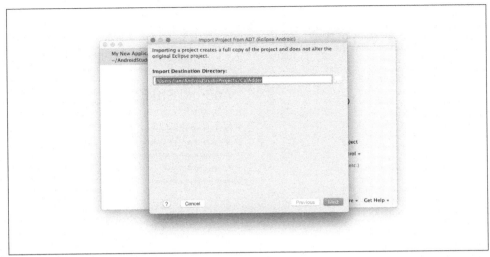

Figure 1-20. Studio: Location to convert the project into

Note that you must pick a different location from where the Android project exists, which totally destroys the project history—your Git or CVS or Subversion history ends at the current state of the application under Eclipse, and a new history will begin with it under Studio. For people who think Studio is the best thing since the motor car, this will seem like a good thing. For those of us who understand that Studio is just another tool in a long series, it will seem like an aberration, or at least an annoyance. I have files on GitHub whose revision dates precede the existence of both Java IDEs and GitHub (and at least one repository whose creation predates the existence of Java), and I wouldn't want to lose that history. It's annoying because it could be done better, by more comprehensive integration with tools such as Git. However, it is what it is. If you want to keep the history, you can work around this as described in Recipe 1.12, instead of following the recipe you are now reading.

After you've specified the import directory more options will appear, related to replacing JARs with references to standard ones (Figure 1-21). Again, the defaults are usually what you want.

Finally, the converted project will appear (Figure 1-22). The editor window is filled with a summary of what happened. If it looks similar to the one here, it has probably succeeded.

You should now be able to run the project by selecting the "app" module and pressing the green Run button.

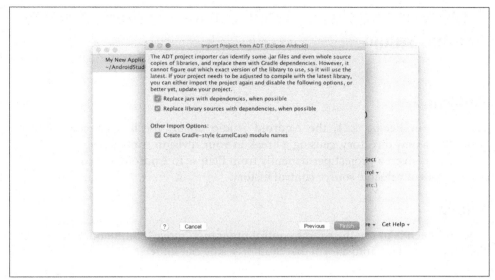

Figure 1-21. Studio: Options for converting the project

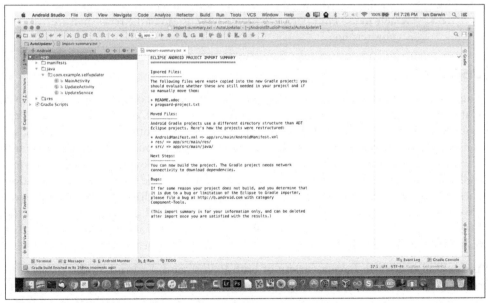

Figure 1-22. Studio: The converted project

1.12 Preserving History While Converting from Eclipse to Android Studio

Ian Darwin

Problem

As shown in Recipe 1.11, the Android Studio *import* mechanism creates a new project in a new directory, causing a break in your revision control history. You want instead to convert a project permanently from Eclipse to Android Studio, but without losing years of valuable source control history.

Solution

One approach is to use the source control program's "move" command to restructure the project in place, into a form that Studio/Gradle can understand.

 Eclipse can no longer process the project after it's been rearranged this much; there doesn't seem to be a way to tell it the new location for the Android manifest and the resource files. If you want to be able to use both IDEs, see Recipe 1.13 instead of the recipe you are now reading.

Discussion

The process will vary greatly depending on which source code management (SCM) system you use. One of the oldest widely used SCMs was CVS, the Concurrent Versions System. CVS did not support moving of files, so if your project is still in CVS (or RCS or SCCS, two even older SCMs) you will want to convert it into Git first, and learn to use Git, if you really want to preserve history. I know this process can work well because my public GitHub repositories contain some files with modification dates a full 10 years before Git was written. Accordingly, this example assumes you have your Eclipse Android project in the Git SCM. And I'll describe the steps in the form of Unix/Linux/macOS command-line steps because that's the most concise format. Understand that this is only general guidance; your mileage will certainly vary!

You will also want to have a variety of both Eclipse and Android Studio projects to compare with and to copy missing bits from; the examples from this book (see "Getting and Using the Code Examples" on page 18, or git clone *https://github.com/IanDarwin/Android-Cookbook-Examples*) would be a good resource to have at hand.

Plan A: Moving files around

I used this approach to convert a privately funded Android app, consisting of 30 Java files and numerous resource files, from Eclipse format to Android Studio format; I got it going in an hour or two, with its revision history intact.

First, create a copy, so that if the conversion messes up too badly you can delete the whole thing and start over (a Git purist might argue that you should just use a branch, but this is my way of doing it):

```
$ cp -r ~/git/myproject /tmp/myproject
$ cd /tmp/myproject
```

Now you need to convert the structure of the project. Eclipse used a simple *src* folder, whereas modern build tools like Maven (Recipe 1.6) and Gradle (Recipe 1.10) use a structure like *src/main/java*. If you have standalone (pure Java, non-Android) unit tests, they may be in a folder called *test*, which has to become *src/test/java*. Also, the resources folder (*res*) and the Android manifest file have to move to *src/main*:

```
$ rm -fr bin build gen target # Start with a cleanup
$ mkdir -p src/main/java
$ mkdir -p src/test/java
$ git mv src/com src/main/java
$ git mv test/com src/test/java/
$ git mv res src/main/
$ git mv AndroidManifest.xml src/main/
$ rmdir test
```

The next step is to convert the dependency information in your *.classpath* or *pom.xml* file into the *build.gradle* file:

```
$ cat ../__SomeExistingStudioProject__/build.gradle pom.xml > build.gradle
$ vi build.gradle # Merge the dependencies by hand
$ git rm -f pom.xml
$ git add build.gradle
```

Create a *local.properties* file containing the path to the Android SDK on your dev machine, using a command like one of the following:

```
$ cp ../__SomeExistingStudioProject__/local.properties .

$ echo 'sdk.dir=/Users/ian/android-sdk-macosx' > local.properties
```

Now you will need to copy a few files from an existing Android Studio project: at least *gradlew* (for Unix/Linux/macOS) and/or *gradlew.bat* (for Windows *cmd.exe*).

If your project doesn't have a *.gitignore* file, create one, and add the *local.properties* file to it:

```
$ echo local.properties >> .gitignore
```

Now try building the project, either by typing `gradlew build` or by opening it in Android Studio. Then hack at it until it works. When you're comfortable, `git commit`. When you're really happy, `git push`.

Plan B: Moving files into a new project

An alternative approach would be as follows. I have not tested this myself, but it seems simpler:

1. Create a new project using the Studio New Project wizard.

2. Copy files from your existing project into the new project, using the earlier move commands as a guide.

3. Copy your revision history into the new project, which won't have one yet:

   ```
   $ cp -r oldProject/.git newProject/.git
   ```

4. After verifying that the project is reasonably sane, save the changes, assuming that Git will recognize the moved files (it usually will):

   ```
   $ git commit -m "Reorganize project for Android Studio"
   ```

5. Hack at it as needed until it works properly.

6. `git commit` any last-minute changes, and `git push`.

See Also

Recipe 1.13.

1.13 Building an Android Application with both Eclipse and Android Studio

Ian Darwin

Problem

Your project team may have some developers who want to stay on Eclipse and some who want to work with Android Studio.

Solution

Make your project work with both major IDEs, by providing both Eclipse and Gradle build files.

Discussion

Assume you have a project that is working with Eclipse. It is possible to create a *build.gradle* file with all the file and directory paths set to the locations that Eclipse uses, and thus allow coexistence. This way you can edit and build the project using

---

either Eclipse or Android Studio! I did this several years ago, when Studio was still in Alpha or Beta status, and it can still be done. The basic steps are:

1. Copy the sample *build.gradle* file shown in Example 1-4 to the root of your Eclipse project.

2. Edit the file, uncommenting and changing the string *YOUR.PACKAGE.NAME.HERE* to your package name (as per *AndroidManifest.xml*) in the +applicationId line.

3. Either move the *src* folder to "Maven standard" *src/main/java* (and update your *.classpath*), or add a *java.src* entry to *build.gradle*. I recommend the first way because it's more commonplace to use this structure today.

4. Create the directory structure *gradle/wrapper* and copy the files *gradle-wrapper.jar* and *gradle-wrapper.properties* into the new directory.

5. Tell your revision control system (e.g., Git) to ignore *build*, *.gradle*, *.idea*, and *local.properties*.

6. Start Android Studio, choose "Open an existing Android Studio project," and select the root of your project!

Example 1-4. Sample build.gradle starter file

```
apply plugin: 'com.android.application'

buildscript {
    repositories {
        jcenter()
    }
    dependencies {
        classpath 'com.android.tools.build:gradle:+'
    }
}

android {
    compileSdkVersion 24
    buildToolsVersion "24"

    defaultConfig {
        applicationId "YOUR.PACKAGE.NAME.HERE"
        minSdkVersion 15
        targetSdkVersion 23
        versionCode 1
        versionName "1.0"
    }

    sourceSets {
        main {
            // Comment next line out if using maven/gradle str src/main/java
            java.srcDirs = ['src']
            res.srcDirs = ['res']
```

```
            assets.srcDirs = ['assets']
            manifest.srcFile 'AndroidManifest.xml'
        }

        androidTest.setRoot('tests')
    }
}

dependencies {
    compile fileTree(dir: 'libs', include: ['*.jar'])
    compile 'com.android.support:appcompat-v7:+'
}
```

A sample Unix/Linux/macOS shell script called *add-gradle-to-eclipse* that implements this (adapting the *build.gradle* to your *src* structure), as well as the files just mentioned, is provided in the Android Cookbook repository (*https://github.com/IanDar win/Android-Cookbook-Examples*), in the subdirectory *duellingIDEs* (see "Getting and Using the Code Examples" on page 18).

Android Studio may need to "synchronize the project" and set up a few files the first time it opens this project, but you should eventually wind up with a working project structure like Figure 1-23.

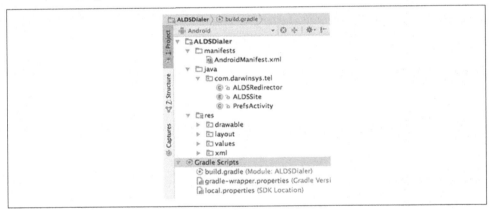

Figure 1-23. Android Studio editing an Eclipse project

Of course, if you have any extra JAR files you will need to tell Android Studio about them; if they are not already picked up by the reference to *libs* in the compile fileTree statement, you can either adjust that to refer to a different directory—older Eclipse projects used *lib* (singular), for example—or use the module settings as described in "Depend on a module or project" on page 63.

At this point your project should build and run under Android Studio (you may have to build it manually the first time, using the Build menu, to enable the green Run button). You will probably want to add the new files to your source repository.

Finally, commit (and push) your changes, and you should now have a working "bilingual" project!

1.14 Setting Up Eclipse with AndMore (Replacing ADT)

Daniel Fowler, Ian Darwin

Problem

You want to develop your Android applications using Eclipse, so a concise guide to setting up that IDE would be useful.

Solution

Many people use Eclipse for editing "standard Java" and Java Enterprise Edition (EE) projects. Some people would like to keep using the Eclipse IDE for developing Android apps. Configuring Eclipse is not a single-shot install; several stages need to be completed. This recipe provides details on those stages.

Discussion

The Eclipse integrated development environment for Java is one option for developing applications for Android. The formerly available Android Development Tools (ADT) plug-in has been discontinued by Google—it recommends switching to Android Studio (Recipe 1.8)—but ADT has arisen phoenix-like under the new name *AndMore*, from the Eclipse foundation. Like ADT (as well as the newer Android Studio), AndMore uses the Android Software Development Kit, which contains essential programs for developing Android software. To set up a development system you will need to download and install the following:

- The Java Standard Edition Development Kit (JDK, not JRE)
- The Eclipse IDE for Java Developers
- The Android Software Development Kit
- The AndMore Android plug-in (install from within Eclipse)

In the subsections that follow, we will cover these stages in detail for a PC running Windows. These steps have been tested on Windows 7 and 10 and on Mac OS X (though most of the screenshots and directory paths are Windows-based examples). Installing on Linux is similar but we haven't tested these steps in current versions of Linux.

Installing the JDK, if necessary

Go to the Java download page (*http://www.oracle.com/technetwork/java/javase/down loads/index.html*). Click the Java icon to access the JDK downloads:

The list of JDK downloads will be shown. Click the Accept License Agreement radio button; otherwise, you will not be allowed to continue. You'll want to download and run one of the latest JDKs present; as of this writing, they are Java 8 builds whose version string ends in *8u121*, but that will surely change by the time you read this. Choose the download appropriate for your operating system: Windows x86 or 64-bit *.exe*, MacOS *.dmg*, Linux *.rpm* or *.tgz*, and so on. Accept any security warnings that appear, but only if you are downloading from the official Java download web page.

When the download has completed, run the installer and go through all the screens, clicking Next until the installer has finished. You should not need to change any options presented. When the JDK installer has completed, click the Finish button. A product registration web page may load; you can close this or you can choose to register your installation.

For Android use, you do not need to download any of the "demos or samples" from this site.

Installing Eclipse for Java development

Go to the Eclipse Downloads web page (*http://www.eclipse.org/downloads*). The web page will usually autodetect your operating system (and 32- or 64-bit variant on systems that have this distinction); select the relevant (usually the latest) Eclipse IDE for Java Developers download link (see Figure 1-24).

On the next page you will be prompted to make a donation to the providers, the Eclipse Software Foundation, which is always a good thing to do when using open source software. The next step will download and run a typical software installer program. Then you will be prompted to specify the install location; the default is usually good (Figure 1-25).

Figure 1-24. Choosing an Eclipse download

Figure 1-25. Setting the Eclipse install location

You will eventually wind up with a lot of files in an Eclipse folder at that location, as shown in Figure 1-26 (obviously the exact list will vary from one release to the next). Enable the checkboxes to add a desktop icon, start menu entry, etc., as you prefer.

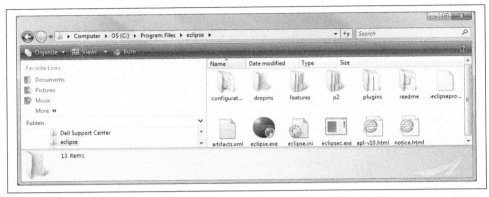

Figure 1-26. Contents of the Eclipse folder

Run Eclipse so that it sets up a workspace. This will also check that both Java and Eclipse were installed correctly. When you run Eclipse a security warning may be displayed; select Run to continue. Accept the default workspace location or use a different directory.

You should install the SDK next, if you don't already have it on your system.

Installing the Android SDK

Go to the Android Studio download page (*https://developer.android.com/studio/ index.html*). The goal of this web page is to convince you to use Android Studio, but we just need the SDK. If you think you might want to use both Studio and Eclipse (see Recipe 1.13), you can install the "Studio and SDK" package here and share that SDK between the two IDEs—there is no need to download the SDK and all the add-ins twice! However, if you're a dedicated Eclipse user, you can scroll to the very bottom of the page and get the "command line tools" (which are what both AndMore and Studio use). See Figure 1-27.

Choose the latest installer package for your operating system and run it. The Android SDK Tools installer will show some screens. Select the Next button on each screen; you should not need to change any options. Since *C:\Program Files* is a protected directory on some versions of MS Windows, you can either get permission to install there ("Run As Administrator") or, as some developers do, install to your user folder or another directory—for example, *C:\Android\android-sdk*.

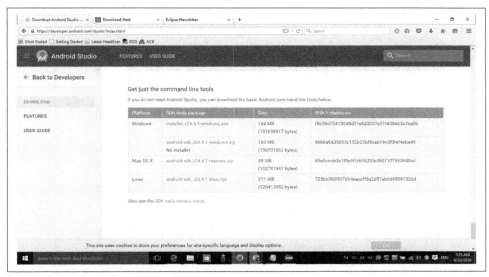

Figure 1-27. Downloading the standalone SDK

When you click the Install button, a progress screen will briefly display while the Android files are copied. Click the final Next button and the Finish button at the end of the installation. If you left the Start SDK Manager checkbox ticked the SDK Manager will run. Otherwise, select SDK Manager from the Android SDK Tools program group (Start → All Programs → Android SDK Tools → SDK Manager). When the SDK Manager starts, the Android packages available to download are checked. Then a list of all available packages is shown, with some preselected for download. A Status column shows whether a package is installed or not. In Figure 1-28, you can see that the Android SDK Tools have just been installed but there is already an update available, as reflected in the Status column.

Check each package that needs to be installed. Multiple packages are available. These include SDK platform packages for each application programming interface (API) level, application samples for most API levels, Google Maps APIs, manufacturers' device-specific APIs, documentation, source code, and a number of Google extra packages. From the "Extras," you should install the Android Support Repository, Google Play Services, Google USB Driver if offered, and Intel X86 Emulator Accelerator (HAXM) if offered, and anything else that looks interesting.

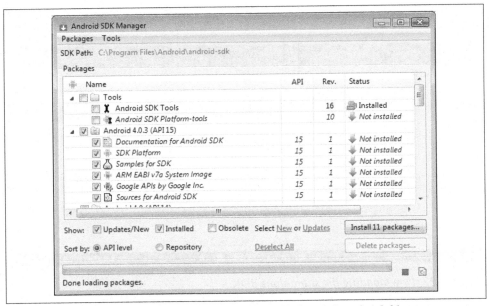

Figure 1-28. Android SDK Manager, showing installed and downloadable components

It is recommended that you download several SDK platforms to allow testing of apps against various device configurations. If in doubt about what to download, either accept the initial choices and rerun the SDK Manager to get other packages as and when required, or select all packages to download everything (the download may take a while). Click the "Install *x* packages" button.

The selected packages will be shown in a list; if a package has licensing terms that require acceptance, it is shown with a question mark. Highlight each package that has a question mark to read the licensing terms. You can accept or reject the package using the radio buttons. Rejected packages are marked with a red ×. Alternatively, click Accept All to accept everything that is available. Click the Install button and a progress log will show the packages being installed, as well as any errors that occur. On Windows a common error occurs when the SDK Manager is unable to access or rename directories. If this happens, rerun the SDK Manager as administrator and check that the directory does not have any read-only flags or files. When complete, close the SDK Manager by clicking the × button in the top corner of the window.

Note that, when updates to these packages become available, the SDK will notify you.

Installing the Android Tools (AndMore) plug-in

You install the ADT plug-in via Eclipse. Depending on where you installed Eclipse and/or the account you are using, you may need to run Eclipse with administrator privileges. If so, bring up the context menu (usually via a right-click), select "Run as administrator," and accept any security warnings. On newer versions of Windows, and on macOS, you will get a prompt that the installer wants to make changes to your system. Say yes, as long as you're installing from the official location.

If your Eclipse installation is so old that it lacks the "Eclipse Marketplace Client," install it as per the instructions in Recipe 1.16. Start the Marketplace Client from the Help menu.

Type "andmore" in the search box on the left side of the Marketplace Client window, and press the Go button at the right side. Select AndMore in the search results. Click Install.

A screen displays the licenses; ensure that each license has been accepted (select the "I accept the terms of the license agreements" radio button). Then click the Finish button. A security warning may need to be accepted to complete the installation; select OK when you see this warning. Eclipse will ask you for a restart. Select the Restart Now button and Eclipse will close and reload, and then a "Welcome to Android Development" dialog will appear. Set the SDK location in the Existing Location box (since the SDK Manager will have already run), browse to the Android SDK folder (if you installed it somewhere other than the default location), and click Next (see Figure 1-29).

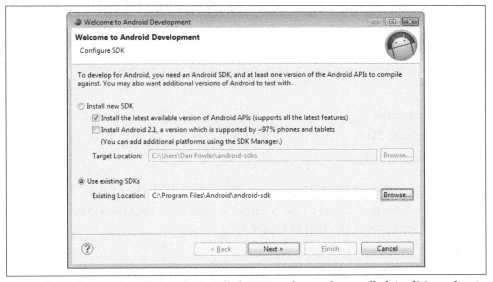

Figure 1-29. Connecting the newly installed SDK to the newly installed AndMore plug-in

A Google Android SDK usage monitoring question will appear; change the option if required and click Finish. Eclipse is now configured to build and debug Android apps. See Recipe 3.1 to configure an Android emulator; then try Recipe 1.15 as a sanity check. Plug a physical device into the computer and use its settings to turn on USB Debugging (under Development in Applications).

See Also

Recipe 1.9, Recipe 1.15, Recipe 3.1.

1.15 Creating a "Hello, World" Application Using Eclipse

Ian Darwin

Problem

You want to use Eclipse to develop your Android application.

Solution

Install Eclipse and the AndMore plug-in. Then, create your project and start writing your app. Build it and test it under the emulator, from within Eclipse.

Discussion

Before you can start creating an app with Eclipse, you need to install these three items:

- The Eclipse IDE
- The Android SDK
- The AndMore plug-in

For details on installing these items, please refer to Recipe 1.14.

Once you've done that, create a new Android project from the File → New menu, and you should see a screen like that in Figure 1-30.

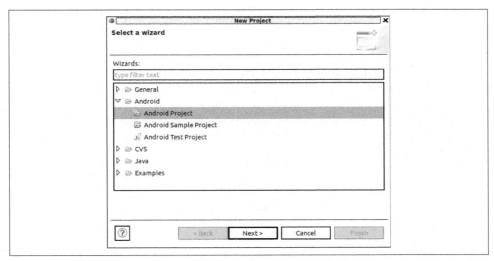

Figure 1-30. Starting to create an Eclipse project

Click Next. Give your new project a name (Figure 1-31), and click Next again.

Figure 1-31. Setting parameters for a new Eclipse project

Select an SDK version to target (Figure 1-32). Version 4.0 gives you almost all the devices in use today; later versions give you more features. You decide.

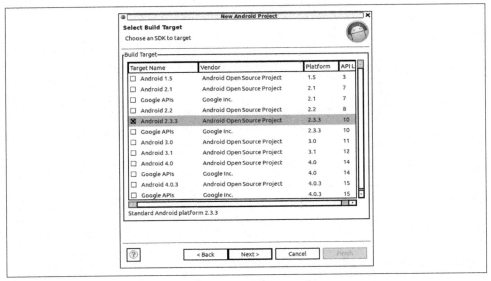

Figure 1-32. Setting SDK to target for a new Eclipse project

Figure 1-33 shows the project structure expanded in the Project panel on the right. It also shows the extent to which you can use Eclipse auto-completion within Android —I added the gravity attribute for the label, and Eclipse is offering a full list of possible attribute values. I chose center-horizontal, so the label should be centered when we get the application running.

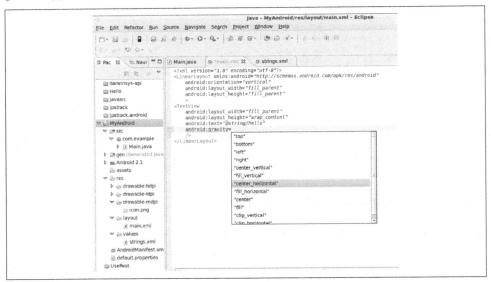

Figure 1-33. Using the Eclipse editor to set gravity on a TextView

In fact, if you set gravity to center_vertical on the LinearLayout *and* set it to center_horizontal on the TextView, the text will be centered both vertically and horizontally. Example 1-5 is the layout file *main.xml* (located under *res/layout*) that achieves this.

Example 1-5. The XML layout

```xml
<?xml version="1.0" encoding="utf-8"?>
<LinearLayout xmlns:android="http://schemas.android.com/apk/res/android"
    android:orientation="vertical"
    android:layout_width="fill_parent"
    android:layout_height="fill_parent"
    android:gravity="center_vertical"
    >
<TextView
    android:layout_width="fill_parent"
    android:layout_height="wrap_content"
    android:text="@string/hello"
    android:gravity="center_horizontal"
    />
</LinearLayout>
```

As always, Eclipse generates a compiled version whenever you save a source file. In an Android project it also creates the compiled, packaged APK that is ready to run, so you only need to run it. Right-click the project itself and select Run As → Android Application. (See Figure 1-34.)

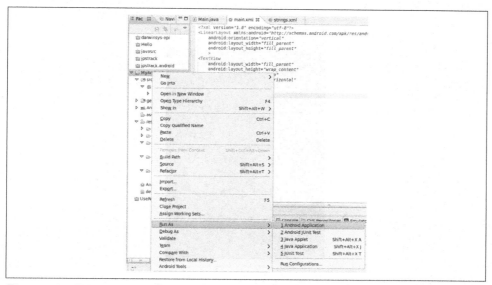

Figure 1-34. Running an Eclipse Android project

This will start the Android emulator if it's not already running. The emulator window will start with the word *Android* by itself on the screen (Figure 1-35), then after a while, you'll see the Android home screen.

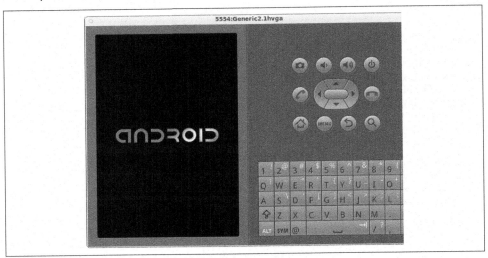

Figure 1-35. The Android project starting up in the emulator

After a little longer, your application should start up (Figure 1-36 only shows a screenshot of the application itself, since the rest of the emulator view is redundant).

Figure 1-36. The Eclipse project running in the emulator

See Also

Recipe 1.5.

While a little dated, the blog "a little madness" has a detailed example of setting up an Eclipse project (*http://www.alittlemadness.com/2010/05/31/setting-up-an-android-project-build*).

1.16 Installing the Eclipse Marketplace Client in Your Eclipse

Ian Darwin

Problem

The Eclipse Marketplace Client (MPC) is the best way to find and install Eclipse plug-ins. Some installations of Eclipse include the MPC, but some do not. Since the MPC is the easiest way to install new plug-ins into Eclipse, we document how to install it here.

Solution

If you don't have the MPC in your Eclipse installation, use the traditional Install New Software mechanism to *bootstrap* the Marketplace Client.

Discussion

First, see if your Eclipse installation already has the Marketplace Client. Near the bottom of the Help menu, in the section with "Check for Updates," you may or may not see an entry for "Eclipse Marketplace." If you do, you are done. If not, continue.

To install the Marketplace, select "Install New Software" from the above-mentioned Eclipse menu. To see what versions of Marketplace Client are available, switch to a web browser and visit *http://www.eclipse.org/mpc* (see Figure 1-37).

Mouse over the link for the version of Eclipse you are running (e.g., Mars, which also works in Neon). Right-click, and select "copy link location" or whatever your browser calls that function. Switch back to Eclipse, and paste the URL in the "Work with" field on the Install dialog as shown in Figure 1-38. Click Add.

After a moment you will see some items to install. You probably don't need the source code for the Marketplace Client, so you can deselect that, as in Figure 1-38. Click Next, Finish, Accept, and whatever it takes to complete this operation—remember that it will wake up part way through to remind you that you're installing unsigned software.

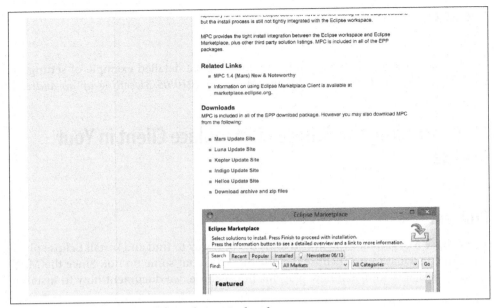

Figure 1-37. Download site for Eclipse Marketplace

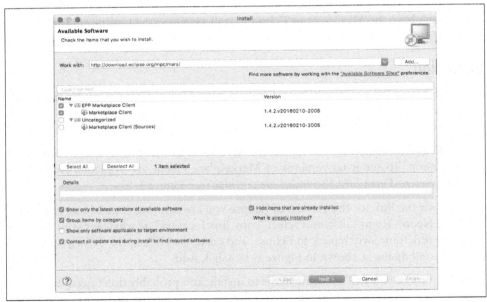

Figure 1-38. Install dialog for Eclipse Marketplace

When it's done, and Eclipse has restarted, go back to the Help menu, and you should now see a menu item for the Eclipse Marketplace (see Figure 1-39). Click this, and you should see the market, looking something like Figure 1-40.

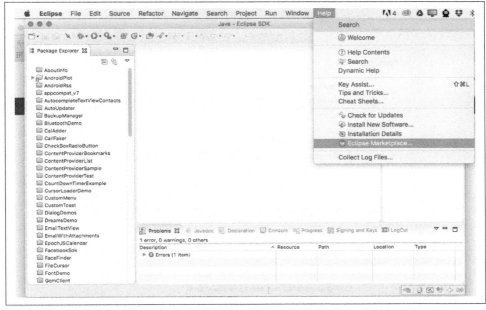

Figure 1-39. Eclipse Marketplace now in menu

1.17 Upgrading a Project from Eclipse ADT to Eclipse AndMore

Ian Darwin

Problem

You have projects that were based on Eclipse ADT and want to use them with Eclipse AndMore.

Solution

Convert the projects by changing some strings in two config files, or use the AndMore "convert project" feature.

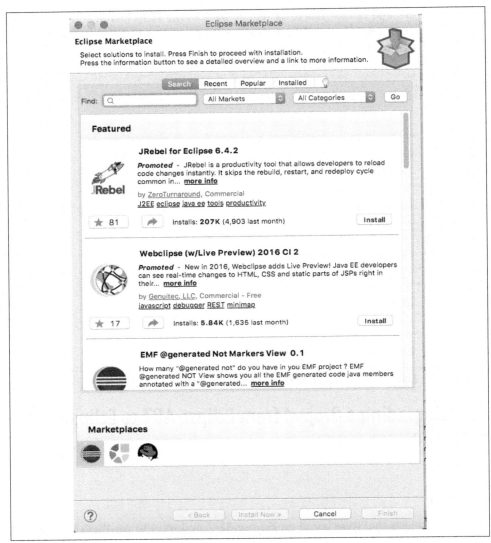

Figure 1-40. Eclipse Marketplace in action

Discussion

Editing config files

In the *.project* file you will see lines referring to *com.android.ide.eclipse.adt*, like:

```
<projectDescription>
    <buildSpec>
        <buildCommand>
```

```
        <name>com.android.ide.eclipse.adt.ResourceManagerBuilder</name>
        ...
      </buildCommand>
    </buildSpec>
    <natures>
        <nature>com.android.ide.eclipse.adt.AndroidNature</nature>
        <nature>org.eclipse.jdt.core.javanature</nature>
    </natures>
</projectDescription>
```

Change these to, for example, this:

```
<name>org.eclipse.andmore.ResourceManagerBuilder</name>
```

Similarly, in your *.classpath* you will see lines like:

```
<classpathentry kind="con" path="com.android.ide.eclipse.adt.ANDROID_FRAMEWORK"/>
```

Change them to, for example, this:

```
<classpathentry kind="con" path="org.eclipse.andmore.ANDROID_FRAMEWORK"/>
```

You can also make these changes globally. If you are experienced with command-line work you may have written a script like Brian Kernighan's *replace*, which changes lines in a large number of files without your having to open each one in an editor. You can find this script (and its helpers) in my *scripts* project (*https://github.com/IanDarwin/scripts*). Then you can change into the workspace root folder and convert tens or hundreds of projects with one command (be sure you have a backup, in case it goes wrong!):

```
$ cd workspace
$ replace com.android.ide.eclipse.adt org.eclipse.andmore */.classpath */.project
```

I in fact used that command to bulk-convert the Eclipse projects in the book's GitHub repository. If you don't like that approach, use the built-in AndMore converter to convert one project at a time.

Using the AndMore converter

Once you have installed AndMore as per Recipe 1.14, you can convert projects in your workspace. Open each project in Eclipse, with AndMore but not ADT installed, and you will see several errors, mainly to the effect that the class file for `java.lang.Object` cannot be found—a clear indication that the classpath is totally hosed (Figure 1-41).

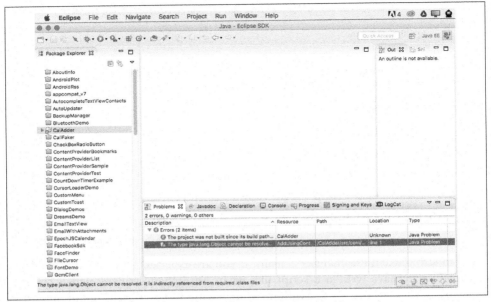

Figure 1-41. AndMore converter: Before, with classpath errors

To convert a project from ADT to AndMore, right-click the project in the Package Explorer and select Configure → Convert Android ADT Configuration (Figure 1-42).

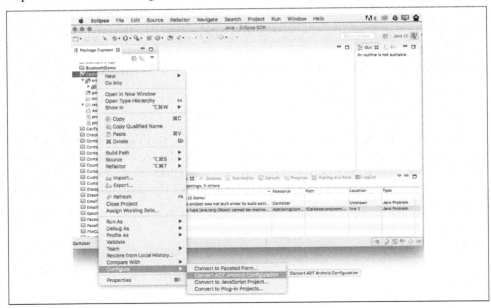

Figure 1-42. AndMore converter: Starting the conversion

Then just sit back and relax while the converter does its work and Eclipse rebuilds the project. It should wind up with no errors (Figure 1-43).

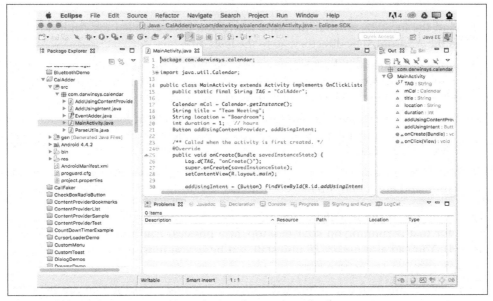

Figure 1-43. AndMore converter: After, with errors resolved

You can repeat this for as many projects as you have.

1.18 Controlling Emulators/Devices Using Command-Line ADB

Rachee Singh

Problem

You have an application's *.apk* file, and you want to install it on the emulator or a real device to check out the application, or because an application you are developing requires it.

Solution

Use the ADB command-line tool to install the *.apk* file onto the running emulator; you can also use this tool to install an *.apk* file onto a connected Android device, uninstall an *.apk* from such a device, list running/connected devices, etc.

Discussion

To install the *.apk* file, follow these steps:

1. Find the location on your machine where you have installed the Android SDK. In the Android SDK directory, go to the *tools* directory.

2. In the *tools* directory, look for an executable named *adb*. If it is not present, there should be an *adb_has_moved.txt* file. The contents of this file merely state that *adb* is present in the *platform-tools* directory instead of the *tools* directory.

3. Once you have located the *adb* program, either `cd` to that location in a terminal (Linux) or command prompt (Windows), or, add that directory to your PATH, however that's done on your operating system.

4. Use the command `adb install` *location of the .apk you want to install*. If you get "command not found" on macOS or Linux, try using `./adb` instead of just `adb`.

This should start the installation on the device that is currently running (either an emulator that is running on your desktop, or a physical Android device that is connected). You can also use `adb` to uninstall, but here, you must use the package name: e.g., `adb uninstall com.example.myapp`.

If you have more than one connected device or running emulator, you can list them with `adb devices`:

```
$ adb devices
List of devices attached
emulator-5554    device
ZX1G000BXB       device

$
```

In this listing, the ZX entry is a Nexus device, and one emulator is running.

When you only have one device connected or one emulator running, you can simply use `adb -d ...` or `adb -e ...`, respectively. There are also command-line options that let you refer to an emulator by its port number (port numbers are displayed at the top of the emulator window; they are the TCP/IP communications ports that start at 5554 and increment by 2 for each running emulator) or by its device serial number for a real device. The emulator in the preceding `adb devices` output is listening on TCP port 5554 for connections from `adb`.

One more thing you can do: `adb shell` gets you a Unix command-line shell *on the device*, which can be useful for developers to have access to. Unless your device is "rooted" it will run as a nonprivileged user, but at least you can look around, copy public files, etc.

After the installation finishes, you should see the icon of the application you just installed in the application drawer of the Android device/emulator. In this example we installed the HelloMaven application from Recipe 1.6, so the HelloMaven app icon appears near the lower left of Figure 1-44.

Figure 1-44. The HelloMaven app icon in the app drawer after installation completes

The adb command with no arguments, or invalid arguments, prints a very long "help text," which lists all its options.

1.19 Sharing Java Classes from Another Eclipse Project

Ian Darwin

Problem

You want to use a class from another project, but you don't want to copy and paste.

Solution

Add the project as a "referenced project," and Eclipse (and DEX) will do the work.

Discussion

Developers often need to reuse classes from another project. In my JPSTrack GPS tracking program, the Android version borrows classes such as the file I/O module from the Java SE version. You surely do not want to copy and paste classes willy-nilly from one project into another, because this makes maintenance improbable.

In the simplest case, when the library project contains the source of the classes you want to import, all you have to do is declare the project containing the needed classes (the Java SE version in my case) as a referenced project on the build path. Select Project → Properties → Java Build Path, select Projects, and click Add. In Figure 1-45, I am adding the SE project "jpstrack" as a dependency on the Android project "jpstrack.android."

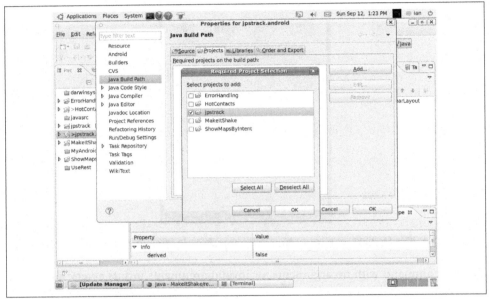

Figure 1-45. Making one Eclipse project depend on another—using standard Eclipse

Alternatively, create a JAR file using either Ant or the Eclipse wizard. Have the other project refer to it as an external JAR in the classpath settings, or physically copy it into the *libs* directory and refer to it from there.

A newer method that is often more reliable and is now officially recommended, but is only useful if both projects are Android projects, is to declare the library one as a library project, under Project → Properties → Android → Library tab, and use the Add button on the other project on the same screen to list the library project as a dependency on the main project (see Figure 1-46).

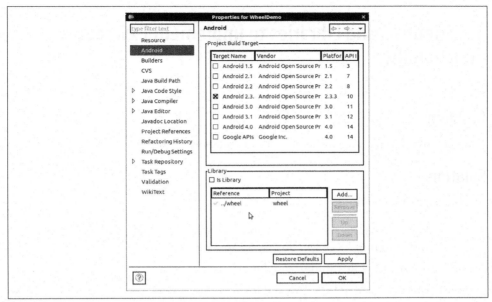

Figure 1-46. Making one project depend on another—using AndMore

For command-line fans, the first method involves editing the *.classpath* file, while the second method simply creates entries in the *project.properties* file. For example:

```
# Project target
target=android-7
android.library=false
android.library.reference.1=../wheel
```

Since you are probably keeping both projects under source control (and if these are programs you ever intend to ship, you should be!), remember to "tag" both projects when you release the Android project—one of the points in favor of source control is that you are able to re-create exactly what you shipped.

See Also

The Android Studio User Guide documentation on library projects (*https://devel oper.android.com/guide/developing/projects/index.html#LibraryProjects*).

1.20 Referencing Libraries to Implement External Functionality

Rachee Singh

Problem

You need to reference an external library in your source code.

Solution

There are several solutions:

- Use Maven or Gradle to build your project. Just list a Maven or Gradle dependency, and your build tool will download and verify it.
- Depend on a module (Studio) or a library project.
- (last resort) Download the JAR file for the library that you require and add it to your project.

Discussion

We describe here various mechanisms for downloading and including JAR files into your projects. We do not discuss the burden of responsibility for licensing issues when including third-party JAR files; that's between you and your organization's legal department. Please be aware of, and comply with, the license requirements of JAR files that you use!

List the dependency

Few developers want to download JAR files explicitly, when tools like Maven and Gradle will handle dependency management for them. To use an external API, you need only find the correct "coordinates" and list them. The coordinates consist of three parts:

- A group ID, which is often based on the JAR developer's domain name and project name, such as com.darwinsys, org.apache.commons, etc.
- An artifact ID, which is the name of the particular project from the developer, such as darwinsys-api, commons-logging-api, etc.
- A version number/string, such as 1.0.1, 1.2.3-SNAPSHOT, 8.1.0-Stable, etc.

These three parts are combined into a form like this for Maven in *build.xml*:

```
<dependency>
    <groupId>commons-logging</groupId>
    <artifactId>commons-logging-api</artifactId>
    <version>1.1</version>
</dependency>
```

For Gradle you use a shorter form in *build.gradle*:

```
compile 'commons-logging:commons-logging-api:1.1'
```

This shorter form of the coordinates is often used in documentation, even when working with other tools like Maven!

How do you find this information for a particular API? If you know the name of the API, you can use the ever-popular Maven Central site (*https://search.maven.org*). Type the API name (e.g., commons-logging) into the search box, pick a match from the list, select the default version number (unless you know you need an older version), pick your build tool if it's other than Maven (Maven is the default because the Maven people built up this entire wonderful infrastructure!), and copy and paste the dependency into your build tool. Alternatively, you can use your IDE (Studio, or Eclipse with the M2E plug-in) to explicitly add the dependency.

Once the dependency is in your build file, just build your project! If the JAR you need hasn't been downloaded already, the build tool will download it and save it in a private repository (e.g., for Maven, in *$USER_HOME/.m2/repository*), so you never have to download it again until you change the version number you're depending on.

For more on Apache Maven, see *https://maven.apache.org*. For more on Gradle, see *https://gradle.org*. The Gradle people are pretty zealous propagandists about their tool; the Maven people are a bit more laid back.

Note that in the future, if you develop an API that might be useful to others and are willing to make it available, and have a community around it or other ways of getting the word out about it, you are encouraged to give back to this pool of software; see *http://central.sonatype.org* to contribute your JAR.

Depend on a module or project

In Android Studio, right-click in the Project pane (upper left of screen) and select Open Module Settings. Choose the Dependencies tab. Click the Add button (the "+" sign in the lower left). Choose Library to use an existing library, File for a JAR file, or Module for a module in your project. Suppose you want to depend on my *darwinsys-api* JAR file, and have it downloaded from Maven Central so you don't have to keep track of the file. Select the Library choice. Enter darwinsys in the search box, and press Enter. After a second or two, you should see the list of darwinsys projects. Click the darwinsys-api entry (the first one in Figure 1-47). If you need to add more libraries, repeat the Add process. When done, click OK. The build files will be updated and the dependency downloaded, and it will be available on your classpath.

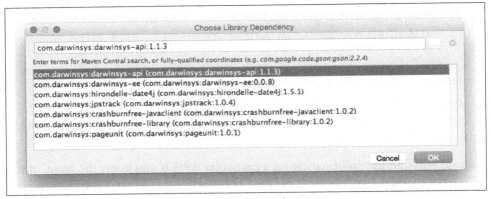

Figure 1-47. Adding a dependency in Android Studio

For Eclipse:

- If you are using Maven and the M2E plug-in, you can add a Maven dependency by editing your *pom.xml* file, then right-click the project and select Maven → Update Project.

- If you are not using Maven, use the following steps to download a JAR file manually.

Download a JAR file manually

Suppose you need to use AndroidPlot, a library for plotting charts and graphs in your application, or OpenStreetMap, a wiki project that creates and provides free geographic data and mapping. If so, your application needs to reference these libraries. You can do this in Eclipse in a few simple steps:

1. Download the JAR file corresponding to the library you wish to use.

2. With your Android project open in Eclipse, right-click the project name and select Properties in the menu (Figure 1-48).

3. From the list on the left side, select Java Build Path and click the Libraries tab (Figure 1-49).

4. Click the Add External JARs button (Figure 1-50).

5. Provide the location where you downloaded the JAR file for the library you wish to use.

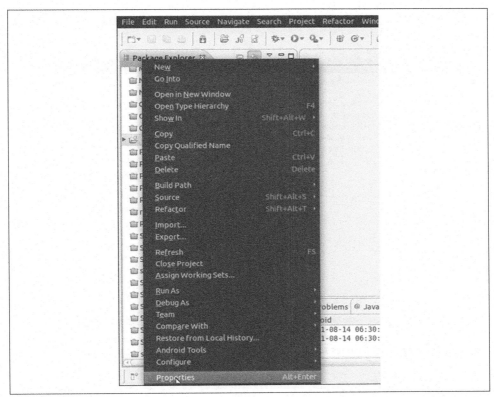

Figure 1-48. Selecting project properties

At this point you will see a *Referenced Libraries* directory in your project. The JARs you added will appear.

An alternative approach is to create a *libs* folder in your project, physically copy the JAR files there, and add them individually as you did earlier, but instead clicking the Add JARs button. This keeps everything in one place (especially useful if your project is shared via a version control system with others who might use a different operating system and be unable to locate the external JARs in the same place).

Whichever way you do it, it's pretty easy to add libraries to your project.

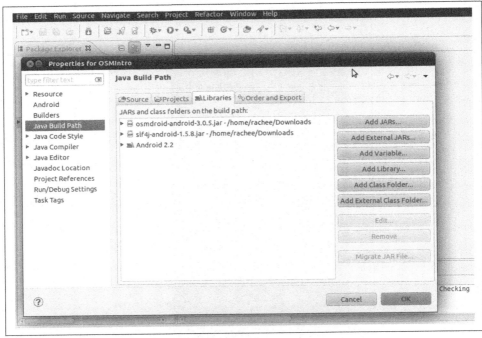

Figure 1-49. Adding libraries to an Eclipse project

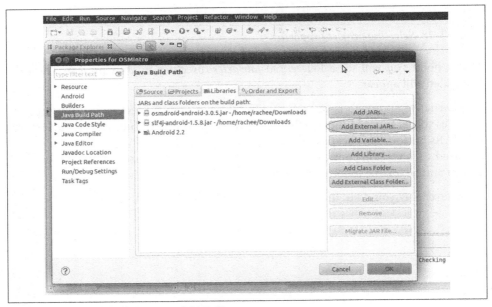

Figure 1-50. Adding the external JAR file

1.21 Using New Features on Old Devices via the Compatibility Libraries

Ian Darwin

Problem

You want to use new features of Android but have your application run correctly on older versions.

Solution

Use the compatibility libraries—that's what they're there for.

Discussion

Android is a wonderful system for users—new features are added with every release. But there's a problem—older devices don't get the latest version of Android. Manufacturers at the low end (low-budget devices) might not ever issue an update to their devices. At the higher end (so-called "flagship" devices), users usually get 2 or 3 years of updates from the manufacturer. But manufacturers (and cell phone carriers) expect users to update often, like car manufacturers who come out with new models every year to embarrass owners into buying upgrades they don't really need.

The downside of this for us as developers is that some features that have been added in modern versions, such as Android 7, will not exist on some users' devices. If you don't take this into account, you may wind up calling methods that exist in modern versions but not in the library on every user's device. This will, of course, end badly.

The solution is the compatibility libraries. These provide replacement versions of common classes (such as `Activity`) that use only features found on the older Android version, but provide the functionality of newer versions.

Now, you might think that old versions fade away quickly, but a look at the Android Versions dashboard (*https://developer.android.com/about/dashboards/index.html*) reveals this to be true only from a certain point of view (Figure 1-51).

Notice that Froyo, API 8, is at 0.1%, which is the threshold for inclusion. Thus you'd expect it to disappear any day now, but in fact, it's been at 0.1% for several months. There are an estimated 1.5 billion Android devices. So 0.1% of that means there are still a million and a half active users of Froyo devices. For Gingerbread there are still 25 million active devices. If you're prepared to overlook 26 million potential customers, fine. But even then it's not that simple—there are features that were added in Android 4, 5, 6, … How do you keep track of what features are in what versions? For the most part, you don't need to. That is, if you use the compatibility libraries!

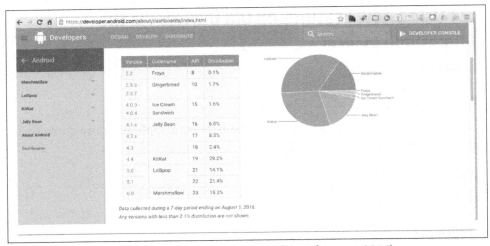

Figure 1-51. Android Platform Versions dashboard (as of August 2016)

If you create a new project using Android Studio, the project will by default use the compatibility library. If you are working on a project that doesn't have "compat" support, you can add it easily. One way is to add the library manually by editing your build file to include the library with coordinates (see Recipe 1.20) `com.android.support:design:24.1.1`; add this to *pom.xml* for Maven or *app/build.gradle* for Android Studio (you may have to do a "Refresh" or "Project Sync" afterward). In Android Studio you can also select the "app" module and select Module Properties → Dependencies, click Add, and select the latest version of the compatibility library.

Then, the most important change is to ensure that your Activities—any that will need the latest facilities—are based on `AppCompatActivity` rather than the regular `Activity`:

```
public class MainActivity extends AppCompatActivity {
    ...
}
```

There are some other places where the "appcompat" libraries enter into the view of the coder; we will mostly call these out in place in the rest of this book.

1.22 Using SDK Samples to Help Avoid Head Scratching

Daniel Fowler

Problem

Sometimes it is a struggle to code up some functionality, especially when the documentation is sketchy or does not provide any examples.

Solution

Looking at existing working code will help. The Android SDK has sample programs that you can pick apart to see how they work.

Discussion

The Android SDK comes with many sample applications that can be useful when trying to code up some functionality. Looking through the sample code can be instructive. Once you have installed the Android SDK, several samples become available. In Android Studio, you can examine the list, and make a runnable copy of one, using the Import Sample wizard (File → Import Sample). The available samples change over time; part of the list as of late 2016 is shown in Figure 1-52. Some of the samples feature screenshot previews, as does the Camera app currently selected. All the samples are individual repositories that can also be directly downloaded from Google Samples (*https://github.com/googlesamples*).

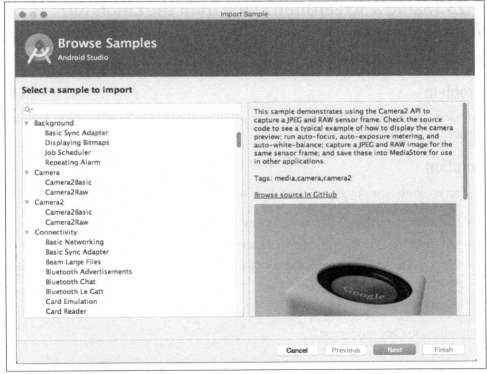

Figure 1-52. Google Android samples

To open a sample project, just select it in the list, and click Next. You will be given the option to change the application's name and where it is stored. Click Finish and the project will be created.

After a short time, the sample will open as a project, and you will be able to browse the source code to see how it is all done.

See Also

The samples at Google Samples (*https://github.com/googlesamples*); Android Developers (*https://developer.android.com/index.html*); and this cookbook, of course.

You can also search the web for additional programs or examples. If you still can't find what you need, you can seek help from Stack Overflow (*http://www.stackoverflow.com*), using "android" as the tag, or from the Internet Relay Chat (IRC) channel *#android-dev* on Freenode.

1.23 Taking a Screenshot/Video from the Emulator/Android Device

Rachee Singh, Ian Darwin

Problem

You want to take a screenshot or video of an application running on an Android device.

Solution

For screenshots, use any one of the following:

- The camera button in the toolbar of modern emulators
- On a physical device, your device's hardware buttons
- The Device Screen Capture feature of the Dalvik Debug Monitor Server (DDMS) view
- `adb screencap`

For videos, use `adb screenrecord`.

Discussion

Capturing screenshots

There are several methods of recording screen captures. Modern versions of the Android emulator or AVD feature a toolbar with a camera button, which works as long as the emulated device is based on API 14 or higher. This is shown in Figure 1-53.

Figure 1-53. Android emulator camera button

Pictures taken with this technique are stored *on your desktop computer* rather than on the device:

```
$ ls -lt ~/Desktop | head -2
total 12345
-rw-r--r--   1 ian  staff    254317 Nov  6 10:05 Screenshot_1478444709.png
open ~/Desktop/Screenshot_1478444709.png
$
```

On a Mac, the `open` command will normally cause the file to be opened (obvious, eh?) in the user's chosen image handling application (Preview by default).

If you are running on a real device, use the built-in hardware feature for screen capture. This varies per device, but on many commercial devices long-pressing both the

---

Power and Volume Down (or Volume Up and Volume Down), buttons at the same time will work—you'll hear a camera sound, and on modern devices you'll see a notification. You then have to locate and pull the file from your device, either using the Android Device Monitor in the IDE or from the command line, as shown here:

```
$ adb -d ls /sdcard/Pictures/Screenshots
$ adb -d pull /sdcard/Pictures/Screenshots/Screenshot_20160820-104327.png x.png
copy it someplace safe
$ adb -d shell rm /sdcard/Pictures/Screenshots/Screenshot_20160820-104327.png
```

This gets a listing (ls) of files in the *Screenshots* folder (whose location may vary slightly on different devices or versions) from the physical device (-d). Using -d avoids you having to shut down your running emulators or specify the device's long name. Then we pull the file from the device to the desktop machine, picking a meaningful name for it in the process. After backing it up, we return here and remove (rm) the file from the device. You don't have to do this, but if you don't it will get harder and harder to find the images, as the ls output will get longer and longer, and it's not displayed in any useful order.

It is believed that Android 7.1 will allow you to take a "partial screenshot" by starting in a similar fashion (perhaps pressing Power + Volume Up?), then dragging to select a region on the screen; the code exists but this is an unannounced feature, so we'll have to see whether it becomes available.

To use the DDMS Device Screen Capture feature, follow these steps:

1. Run the application in the IDE and go to the DDMS view (Window menu → Open Perspective → Other → DDMS or Window menu → Show View → Other → Android → Devices); the former is shown in Figure 1-54).

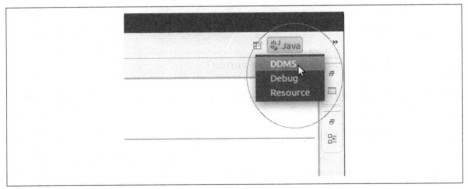

Figure 1-54. Starting DDMS view

2. In the DDMS view, select the device or emulator whose screen you want to capture.

3. In the DDMS view, click the Screen Capture icon (see Figure 1-55).

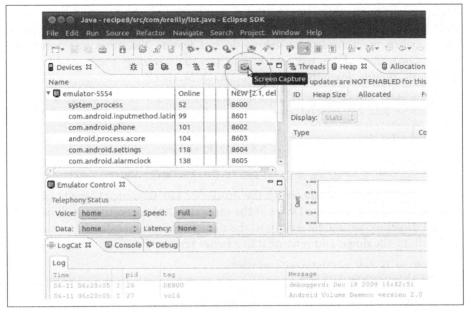

Figure 1-55. Device Screen Capture

4. A window showing the current screen of the emulator/Android device will pop up. It should look like Figure 1-56. You can save the screenshot and use it to document the app.

Figure 1-56. The screenshot

Alternatively, to do this at a command-line level, use adb. You will have to use adb shell to run the "mount" command to find a writable directory on your particular device, since most Android versions do not feature the otherwise-universal */tmp* folder. Once that's done, use adb shell to run the *screencap* program on the device, then "pull" the file down to your desktop, as shown here:

```
$ adb shell screencap -p /mnt/asec/pic.png  # Now in a file on the device
$ adb -e pull /mnt/asec/pic.png              # Now in a file on my dev machine
[100%] /mnt/asec/pic.png
$ ls -l pic.png                              # Make sure!
-rw-r--r--@ 1 ian  staff  59393 Jun 21 17:30 pic.png
$ adb shell rm /mnt/asec/pic.png             # Free up storage on the device
$ # ... now do something with pic.png on the developer machine
```

If you create your screenshot with the on-device key sequence (usually pressing and holding Power and Volume Down at the same time), the screenshot will be created in a fixed directory with a datestamp in the name; you can then "list" (ls) the directory and pull the file down and rename it to a better name:

```
$ adb -d ls /sdcard/Pictures/Screenshots
000041f9 00001000 57c62dd8 .
000041f9 00001000 578f7813 ..
000081b0 000a231c 55760303 Screenshot_20150608-170256.png
000081b0 0001176d 55760308 Screenshot_20150608-170303.png
000081b0 0006b9b4 557a1619 Screenshot_20150611-191328.png
000081b0 0001968a 55869982 Screenshot_20150621-070121.png
... and a bunch more ...
$ adb -d pull /sdcard/Pictures/Screenshots/Screenshot_20160714-093303.png
[100%] /sdcard/Pictures/Screenshots/Screenshot_20160714-093303.png
$ mv Screenshot_2016-07-14-09-33-03.png SomeBetterName.png
$
```

The datestamp portion of the filenames is, in case it isn't obvious, in the ISO international standard order—year, month, and day, then a dash (-), then hour, minute, and second—though not quite in the ISO format.

Capturing screen video

To record your device's screen for documentation or screencast purposes, you need to run the *screenrecord* program on the device, which creates a file there, then use adb pull or other means to bring the file over to your desktop system. Remember that both your desktop computer and your device have a similar hierarchical filesystem (if you run Unix, including macOS, or Linux, the filesystem structure is almost identical, since Android is based on Linux, and Linux began as a copy of Unix). Just keep in mind which filenames are on which computer! The adb command communicates with the device and runs a "shell" or command interpreter, which we use to run the screenrecord command on the device, capturing output into a temporary file in the */sdcard* directory:

```
$ adb shell screenrecord /sdcard/tmpFileName.mp4
```

Now you can interact with the application to show the bug or feature that you want to document. When you are done, stop the adb command, e.g., with Ctrl-C in the terminal window. Then pull the temporary file from the */sdcard* folder on the device to some convenient place on your desktop (you can assign it a better name at the same time if you like, such as *myScreencastSegment.mp4*):

```
$ adb pull /sdcard/tmpFileName.mp4 myScreencastSegment.mp4
```

You can then view or post-process the video using whatever tools you have on your desktop system. Figure 1-57 shows a simple video, recorded and downloaded in this way, playing on my desktop.

Once the video is safely on your desktop (and backed up!), you'll probably want to remove the file from your device so you don't run out of disk space:

```
$ adb rm /sdcard/tmpFileName.mp4
```

Figure 1-57. Captured video playing

See Also

The Android Studio User Guide documentation on the screencap tool (*https://devel oper.android.com/studio/command-line/adb.html#screencap*) and screenrecord tool (*https://developer.android.com/studio/command-line/adb.html#screenrecord*).

1.24 Program: A Simple CountDownTimer Example

Wagied Davids

Problem

You want a simple countdown timer, a program that will count down a given number of seconds until it reaches zero.

Solution

Android comes with a built-in class for constructing CountDownTimers. It's easy to use, it's efficient, and it works (that goes without saying!).

Discussion

The steps to provide a countdown timer are as follows:

1. Create a subclass of CountDownTimer. This class's constructor takes two arguments: CountDownTimer(long millisInFuture, long countDownInterval). The first is the number of milliseconds from now when the interval should be done; at this point the subclass's onFinish() method will be called. The second is the frequency in milliseconds of how often you want to get notified that the timer is still running, typically to update a progress monitor or otherwise communicate with the user. Your subclass's onTick() method will be called with each passage of this many milliseconds.

2. Override the onTick() and onFinish() methods.

3. Instantiate a new instance in your Android Activity.

4. Call the start() method on the new instance created!

The example Countdown Timer program consists of an XML layout (shown in Example 1-6) and some Java code (shown in Example 1-7). When run, it should look something like Figure 1-58, though the times will probably be different.

Example 1-6. main.xml

```xml
<?xml version="1.0" encoding="utf-8"?>
<LinearLayout
    xmlns:android="http://schemas.android.com/apk/res/android"
    android:orientation="vertical"
    android:layout_width="fill_parent"
    android:layout_height="fill_parent">
    <Button
        android:id="@+id/button"
        android:text="Start"
        android:layout_width="fill_parent"
        android:layout_height="wrap_content" />
    <TableLayout
        android:padding="10dip"
        android:layout_gravity="center"
        android:layout_width="fill_parent"
        android:layout_height="wrap_content">
        <TableRow>
            <TextView
                android:id="@+id/timer"
                android:text="Time: "
                android:paddingRight="10dip"
                android:layout_width="wrap_content"
                android:layout_height="wrap_content" />

            <TextView
                android:id="@+id/timeElapsed"
                android:text="Time elapsed: "
                android:paddingRight="10dip"
                android:layout_width="wrap_content"
                android:layout_height="wrap_content" />
        </TableRow>
    </TableLayout>
</LinearLayout>
```

Example 1-7. Main.java

```java
package com.examples;

import android.app.Activity;
import android.os.Bundle;
import android.os.CountDownTimer;
import android.view.View;
import android.view.View.OnClickListener;
import android.widget.Button;
import android.widget.TextView;

public class Main extends Activity implements OnClickListener {
        private MalibuCountDownTimer countDownTimer;
        private long timeElapsed;
        private boolean timerHasStarted = false;
        private Button startB;
```

```java
private TextView text;
private TextView timeElapsedView;

private final long startTime = 50 * 1000;
private final long interval = 1 * 1000;

/** Called when the Activity is first created. */
@Override
public void onCreate(Bundle savedInstanceState) {
        super.onCreate(savedInstanceState);
        setContentView(R.layout.main);
        startB = (Button) this.findViewById(R.id.button);
        startB.setOnClickListener(this);

        text = (TextView) this.findViewById(R.id.timer);
        timeElapsedView = (TextView) this.findViewById(R.id.timeElapsed);
        countDownTimer = new MalibuCountDownTimer(startTime, interval);
        text.setText(text.getText() + String.valueOf(startTime));
    }

@Override
public void onClick(View v) {
        if (!timerHasStarted) {
                countDownTimer.start();
                timerHasStarted = true;
                startB.setText("Start");
            }
        else {

                countDownTimer.cancel();
                timerHasStarted = false;
                startB.setText("RESET");
            }
    }

// CountDownTimer class
public class MalibuCountDownTimer extends CountDownTimer {

        public MalibuCountDownTimer(long startTime, long interval) {
                super(startTime, interval);
            }

        @Override
        public void onFinish() {
                text.setText("Time's up!");
                timeElapsedView.setText("Time Elapsed: " +
                    String.valueOf(startTime));
            }

        @Override
        public void onTick(long millisUntilFinished) {
                text.setText("Time remain:" + millisUntilFinished);
                timeElapsed = startTime - millisUntilFinished;
                timeElapsedView.setText("Time Elapsed: " +
                    String.valueOf(timeElapsed));
            }
```

```
        }
    }
```

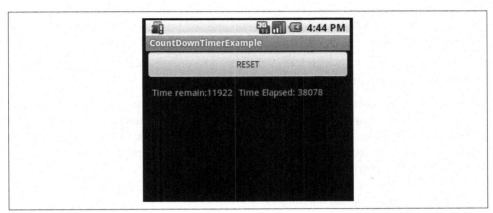

Figure 1-58. Timer reset

Source Download URL

The source code for this example is in the Android Cookbook repository (*https://github.com/IanDarwin/Android-Cookbook-Examples*), in the subdirectory *CountDownTimerExample* (see "Getting and Using the Code Examples" on page 18).

1.25 Program: Tipster, a Tip Calculator for the Android OS

Sunit Katkar

Problem

When you go with friends to a restaurant and wish to divide the check and tip, you can get into a lot of manual calculations and disagreements. Instead, you want to use an app that lets you simply add the tip percentage to the total and divide by the number of diners. Tipster is an implementation of this in Android, to show a complete application.

Solution

This is a simple exercise that uses the basic GUI elements in Android, with some simple calculations and some event-driven UI code to tie it all together.

Discussion

Android uses XML files for the layout of widgets. In our example project, the Android plug-in for Eclipse generates a *main.xml* file for the layout. This file has the XML-based definitions of the different widgets and their containers.

There is a *strings.xml* file, which has all the string resources used in the application. A default *icon.png* file is provided for the application icon.

Then there is the *R.java* file, which is automatically generated (and updated when any changes are made to any XML resource file). This file has the constants defined for each layout and widget. Do not edit this file manually; the SDK tooling does it for you when you make any changes to your XML files. In our example we have *Tipster.java* as the main Java file for the Activity.

Creating the layout and placing the widgets

The end goal is to create a layout similar to the one shown in Figure 1-59. For this screen layout we will use the following layouts and widgets:

TableLayout
> THis lays out View components in tabular form. Analogous to the HTML Table tag paradigm.

TableRow
> This defines a row in the TableLayout. It's like the HTML TR and TD tags combined.

TextView
> This View provides a label for displaying static text on the screen.

EditText
> This View provides a text field for entering values.

RadioGroup
> This groups together "radio buttons," only one of which can be pressed at a time (named by analogy with the station selection button on a car radio).

RadioButton
> This provides a radio button, for use in a group.

Button
> This is a regular button.

View
> We will use a View to create a visual separator with certain height and color attributes.

Familiarize yourself with these widgets, as you will be using these quite a lot in applications you build. When you go to the Javadocs for the given layout and widget components, look up the XML attributes. This will help you correlate the usage in the *main.xml* layout file and the Java code (*Tipster.java* and *R.java*) where these are accessed.

Also available is a visual layout editor in the IDE, which lets you create a layout by dragging and dropping widgets from a palette, like any form designer tool. However, it's probably a good exercise for you to create the layout by hand in XML, at least in your initial stages of learning Android. Later on, as you learn all the nuances of the XML layout API, you can delegate the task to such tools.

The layout file, *main.xml*, has the layout information (see Example 1-8). A TableRow widget creates a single row inside the TableLayout, so you use as many TableRows as the number of rows you want. In this tutorial we will use eight TableRows—five for the widgets up to the visual separator below the buttons, and three for the results area below the buttons and separator.

Example 1-8. /res/layout/main.xml

```
<?xml version="1.0" encoding="utf-8"?>
<!-- Using TableLayout to have HTML table-like control over layout -->
<TableLayout
        android:id="@+id/TableLayout01"
        android:layout_width="fill_parent"
        android:layout_height="fill_parent"
        android:stretchColumns="1"
        xmlns:android="http://schemas.android.com/apk/res/android">
    <!-- Row 1: Text label placed in column zero,
         text field placed in column two and allowed to
         span two columns. So a total of 4 columns in this row -->
    <TableRow>
    <TextView
            android:id="@+id/txtLbl1"
            android:layout_width="wrap_content"
            android:layout_height="wrap_content"
            android:layout_column="0"
            android:text="@string/textLbl1"/>
    <EditText ❶
            android:id="@+id/txtAmount"
            android:layout_width="wrap_content"
            android:layout_height="wrap_content"
            android:numeric="decimal"
            android:layout_column="2"
            android:layout_span="2"
            />
    </TableRow>
    <!-- Row 2: Text label placed in column zero,
         text field placed in column two and allowed to
         span two columns. So a total of 4 columns in this row -->
    <TableRow>
    <TextView
            android:id="@+id/txtLbl2"
```

```
                    android:layout_width="wrap_content"
                    android:layout_height="wrap_content"
                    android:layout_column="0"
                    android:text="@string/textLbl2"/>
            <EditText ❷
                    android:id="@+id/txtPeople"
                    android:layout_width="wrap_content"
                    android:layout_height="wrap_content"
                    android:numeric="integer"
                    android:layout_column="2"
                    android:layout_span="2"/>
        </TableRow>
<!-- Row 3: This has just one text label placed in column zero  -->
        <TableRow>
        <TextView
                    android:id="@+id/txtLbl3"
                    android:layout_width="wrap_content"
                    android:layout_height="wrap_content"
                    android:text="@string/textLbl3"/>
        </TableRow>
<!-- Row 4: RadioGroup for RadioButtons placed at column zero
     with column span of three, thus creating one radio button
     per cell of the table row. Last cell number 4 has the
     textfield to enter a custom tip percentage -->
        <TableRow>
        <RadioGroup
                    android:id="@+id/RadioGroupTips"
                    android:orientation="horizontal"
                    android:layout_width="wrap_content"
                    android:layout_height="wrap_content"
                    android:layout_column="0"
                    android:layout_span="3"
                    android:checkedButton="@+id/radioFifteen">
                <RadioButton android:id="@+id/radioFifteen"
                        android:layout_width="wrap_content"
                        android:layout_height="wrap_content"
                        android:text="@string/rdoTxt15"
                        android:textSize="15sp" />
                <RadioButton android:id="@+id/radioTwenty"
                        android:layout_width="wrap_content"
                        android:layout_height="wrap_content"
                        android:text="@string/rdoTxt20"
                        android:textSize="15sp" />
                <RadioButton android:id="@+id/radioOther"
                        android:layout_width="wrap_content"
                        android:layout_height="wrap_content"
                        android:text="@string/rdoTxtOther"
                        android:textSize="15sp" />
        </RadioGroup>
                <EditText
                        android:id="@+id/txtTipOther"
                        android:layout_width="fill_parent"
                        android:layout_height="wrap_content"
                        android:numeric="decimal"/>
        </TableRow>
```

```xml
<!-- Row for the Calculate and Rest buttons. The Calculate button
     is placed at column two, and Reset at column three -->
<TableRow>
<Button
        android:id="@+id/btnReset"
        android:layout_width="wrap_content"
        android:layout_height="wrap_content"
        android:layout_column="2"
        android:text="@string/btnReset"/>
<Button
        android:id="@+id/btnCalculate"
        android:layout_width="wrap_content"
        android:layout_height="wrap_content"
        android:layout_column="3"
        android:text="@string/btnCalculate"/>
</TableRow>

<!-- TableLayout allows any other views to be inserted between
     the TableRow elements. So insert a blank view to create a
     line separator. This separator view is used to separate
     the area below the buttons which will display the
     calculation results -->
<View
        android:layout_height="2px"
        android:background="#DDFFDD"
        android:layout_marginTop="5dip"
        android:layout_marginBottom="5dip"/>

<!-- Again TableRow is used to place the result textviews
     at column zero and the result in textviews at column two -->
<TableRow android:paddingBottom="10dip" android:paddingTop="5dip">
<TextView
        android:id="@+id/txtLbl4"
        android:layout_width="wrap_content"
        android:layout_height="wrap_content"
        android:layout_column="0"
        android:text="@string/textLbl4"/>
<TextView
        android:id="@+id/txtTipAmount"
        android:layout_width="wrap_content"
        android:layout_height="wrap_content"
        android:layout_column="2"
        android:layout_span="2"/>
</TableRow>

<TableRow android:paddingBottom="10dip" android:paddingTop="5dip">
<TextView
        android:id="@+id/txtLbl5"
        android:layout_width="wrap_content"
        android:layout_height="wrap_content"
        android:layout_column="0"
        android:text="@string/textLbl5"/>
<TextView
        android:id="@+id/txtTotalToPay"
        android:layout_width="wrap_content"
        android:layout_height="wrap_content"
```

```
                android:layout_column="2"
                android:layout_span="2"/>
        </TableRow>

        <TableRow android:paddingBottom="10dip" android:paddingTop="5dip">
        <TextView
                android:id="@+id/txtLbl6"
                android:layout_width="wrap_content"
                android:layout_height="wrap_content"
                android:layout_column="0"
                android:text="@string/textLbl6"/>
        <TextView
                android:id="@+id/txtTipPerPerson"
                android:layout_width="wrap_content"
                android:layout_height="wrap_content"
                android:layout_column="2"
                android:layout_span="2"/>
        </TableRow>
    <!-- End of all rows and widgets -->
</TableLayout>
```

TableLayout and TableRow

After examining *main.xml,* you can gather that `TableLayout` and `TableRow` are straight-forward to use. You create the `TableLayout` once, then insert a `TableRow`. Now you are free to insert any other widgets, such as `TextView`, `EditView`, and so on, inside this `TableRow`.

Do look at the attributes, especially `android:stretchColumns`, `android:layout_column`, and `android:layout_span`, which allow you to place widgets the same way you would use a regular HTML table. I recommend that you follow the links to these attributes and read up on how they work for a `TableLayout`.

Controlling input values

Look at the `EditText` widget in the *main.xml* file at ❶. This is the first text field for entering the "Total Amount" of the check. We want only numbers here. We can accept decimal numbers because real restaurant checks can be for dollars and cents—not just dollars, so we use the `android:numeric` attribute with a value of `decimal`. This will allow whole values like 10 and decimal values like 10.12, but will prevent any other type of entry.

Similarly, ❷ uses `android:integer` because you can't eat dinner with half a guest!

This is a simple and concise way to control input values, thus saving us the trouble of writing validation code in the *Tipster.java* file and ensuring that the user does not enter nonsensical values. This XML-based constraints feature of Android is quite powerful and useful. You should explore all the possible attributes that go with a particular widget to extract the maximum benefit from this XML shorthand way of setting constraints. In a future release, unless I have missed it completely in this release,

I hope that Android allows for entering ranges for the android:numeric attribute so that we can define what range of numbers we wish to accept.

Since ranges are not currently available (to the best of my knowledge), you will see later on that we do have to check for certain values like zero or empty values to ensure that our tip calculation arithmetic does not fail.

Examining Tipster.java

Now we will look at the *Tipster.java* file, which controls our application. This is the main class that does the layout and event handling and provides the application logic. The Android Eclipse plug-in creates the *Tipster.java* file in our project with the default code shown in Example 1-9.

Example 1-9. Code snippet 1 of TipsterActivity.java

```
package com.examples.tipcalc;

import android.app.Activity;

public class Tipster extends Activity {
    /** Called when the Activity is first created. */
    @Override
    public void onCreate(Bundle savedInstanceState) {
        super.onCreate(savedInstanceState);
        setContentView(R.layout.main);
    }
}
```

The Tipster class extends the android.app.Activity class. An Activity is a single, focused thing that the user can do. The Activity class takes care of creating the window and then laying out the UI. You have to call the setContentView(View view) method to put your UI in the Activity, so think of Activity as an outer frame that is empty and that you populate with your UI.

Now look at the snippet of the *Tipster.java* class shown in Example 1-10. First we define the widgets as class members. (Look at ❶ through ❷ in particular for reference.) Then we use the findViewById(int id) method to locate the widgets. The ID of each widget, defined in your *main.xml* file, is automatically defined in the *R.java* file when you clean and build the project in Eclipse. (By default, Eclipse is set to build automatically, so the *R.java* file is instantaneously updated when you update *main.xml*.)

Each widget is derived from the View class and provides special GUI features, so a TextView provides a way to put labels on the UI, while EditText provides a text field. Look at ❸ through ❻ in Example 1-10. You can see how findViewById() is used to locate the widgets.

Example 1-10. Code snippet 2 of TipsterActivity.java

```java
public class Tipster extends Activity {
    // Widgets in the application
    private EditText txtAmount;           ❶
    private EditText txtPeople;
    private EditText txtTipOther;
    private RadioGroup rdoGroupTips;
    private Button btnCalculate;
    private Button btnReset;

    private TextView txtTipAmount;
    private TextView txtTotalToPay;
    private TextView txtTipPerPerson;     ❷

    // For the ID of the radio button selected
    private int radioCheckedId = -1;

    /** Called when the Activity is first created. */
    @Override
    public void onCreate(Bundle savedInstanceState) {
        super.onCreate(savedInstanceState);
        setContentView(R.layout.main);

        // Access the various widgets by their ID in R.java
        txtAmount = (EditText) findViewById(R.id.txtAmount);    ❸
        // On app load, the cursor should be in the Amount field
        txtAmount.requestFocus();                                ❹

        txtPeople = (EditText) findViewById(R.id.txtPeople);
        txtTipOther = (EditText) findViewById(R.id.txtTipOther);

        rdoGroupTips = (RadioGroup) findViewById(R.id.RadioGroupTips);

        btnCalculate = (Button) findViewById(R.id.btnCalculate);
        // On app load, the Calculate button is disabled
        btnCalculate.setEnabled(false);                          ❺

        btnReset = (Button) findViewById(R.id.btnReset);

        txtTipAmount = (TextView) findViewById(R.id.txtTipAmount);
        txtTotalToPay = (TextView) findViewById(R.id.txtTotalToPay);
        txtTipPerPerson = (TextView) findViewById(R.id.txtTipPerPerson);  ❻

        // On app load, disable the Other Tip Percentage text field
        txtTipOther.setEnabled(false);                           ❼
```

Addressing ease of use or usability concerns

Our application must try to be as usable as any other established application or web page. In short, adding usability features will result in a good user experience. To address these concerns, look at Example 1-10 again.

First, look at ❹ where we use the `requestFocus()` method of the `View` class. Since the `EditText` widget is derived from the `View` class, this method is applicable to it. This is done so that when our application loads, the Total Amount text field will receive focus and the cursor will be placed in it. This is similar to popular web application login screens where the cursor is present in the Username text field.

Now look at ❺ where the Calculate button is disabled by calling the `setEnabled(boolean enabled)` method on the `Button` widget. This is done so that the user cannot click on it before entering values in the required fields. If we allowed the user to click Calculate without entering values in the Total Amount and No. of People fields, we would have to write validation code to catch these conditions. This would entail showing an alert pop-up warning the user about the empty values. This adds unnecessary code and user interaction. When the user sees the Calculate button disabled, it's quite obvious that unless all values are entered, the tip cannot be calculated.

Now look at ❼ in Example 1-10. Here, the Other Tip Percentage text field is disabled. This is done because the "15% tip" radio button is selected by default when the application loads. This default selection on application load is done via the *main.xml* file, in the following statement:

```
android:checkedButton="@+id/radioFifteen"
```

The `RadioGroup` attribute `android:checkedButton` allows you to select one of the `RadioButton` widgets in the group by default.

Most users who have used popular applications on the desktop as well as the web are familiar with the "disabled widgets enabled in certain conditions" paradigm. Adding such small conveniences always makes an application more usable and the user experience richer.

Processing UI events

Like popular Windows, Java Swing, Flex, and other UI frameworks, Android provides an event model that allows you to listen to certain events in the UI caused by user interaction. Let's see how we can use the Android event model in our application.

First let's focus on the radio buttons in the UI. We want to know which radio button the user selected, as this will allow us to determine the tip percentage in our calculations. To "listen" to radio buttons, we use the static interface `OnCheckedChangeListener()`. This will notify us when the selection state of a radio button changes.

In our application, we want to enable the Other Tip Percentage text field only when the Other radio button is selected. When the "15% tip" or "20% tip" button is selected, we want to disable this text field. Besides this, we want to add some more logic for the sake of usability. As we discussed before, we should not enable the Calculate button until all the required fields have valid values. In terms of the three radio buttons, we want to ensure that the Calculate button gets enabled for the following two conditions:

- The Other radio button is selected and the Other Tip Percentage text field has a valid value.
- The "15% tip" or "20% tip" radio button is selected and the Total Amount and No. of People text fields have valid values.

Look at Example 1-11, which deals with the radio buttons. The source code comments are quite self-explanatory.

Example 1-11. Code snippet 3 of TipsterActivity.java

```
/*
 * Attach an OnCheckedChangeListener to the
 * radio group to monitor radio buttons selected by user
 */
rdoGroupTips.setOnCheckedChangeListener(new OnCheckedChangeListener() {

    @Override
    public void onCheckedChanged(RadioGroup group, int checkedId) {
        // Enable/disable Other Tip Percentage field
        if (checkedId == R.id.radioFifteen
                || checkedId == R.id.radioTwenty) {
            txtTipOther.setEnabled(false);
            /*
             * Enable the Calculate button if Total Amount and No. of
             * People fields have valid values.
             */
            btnCalculate.setEnabled(txtAmount.getText().length() > 0
                    && txtPeople.getText().length() > 0);
        }
        if (checkedId == R.id.radioOther) {
            // Enable the Other Tip Percentage field
            txtTipOther.setEnabled(true);
            // Set the focus to this field
            txtTipOther.requestFocus();
            /*
             * Enable the Calculate button if Total Amount and No. of
             * People fields have valid values. Also ensure that user
             * has entered an Other Tip Percentage value before enabling
             * the Calculate button.
             */
            btnCalculate.setEnabled(txtAmount.getText().length() > 0
                    && txtPeople.getText().length() > 0
                    && txtTipOther.getText().length() > 0);
        }
        // To determine the tip percentage choice made by user
        radioCheckedId = checkedId;
    }
});
```

Monitoring key activity in text fields

As I mentioned earlier, the Calculate button must not be enabled unless the text fields have valid values. So we have to ensure that the Calculate button will be enabled only if the Total Amount, No. of People, and Other Tip Percentage text fields have valid values. The Other Tip Percentage text field is enabled only if the Other radio button is selected.

We do not have to worry about the type of values—that is, whether the user entered negative values or letters—because the android:numeric attribute has been defined for the text fields, thus limiting the types of values that the user can enter. We just have to ensure that the values are present.

So, we use the static interface OnKeyListener(). This will notify us when a key is pressed. The notification reaches us before the actual key pressed is sent to the EditText widget.

Look at the code in Examples 1-12 and 1-13, which deal with key events in the text fields. As in Example 1-11, the source code comments are quite self-explanatory.

Example 1-12. Code snippet 4 of TipsterActivity.java

```
/*
 * Attach a KeyListener to the Tip Amount, No. of People, and Other Tip
 * Percentage text fields
 */
txtAmount.setOnKeyListener(mKeyListener);
txtPeople.setOnKeyListener(mKeyListener);
txtTipOther.setOnKeyListener(mKeyListener);
```

Notice that we create just one listener instead of creating anonymous/inner listeners for each text field. I am not sure if my style is better or recommended, but I always write in this style if the listeners are going to perform some common actions. Here the common concern for all the text fields is that they should not be empty, and only when they have values should the Calculate button be enabled.

Example 1-13. Code snippet 5 from KeyListener of TipsterActivity.java

```
/*
 * KeyListener for the Total Amount, No. of People, and Other Tip Percentage
 * text fields. We need to apply this key listener to check for the following
 * conditions:
 *
 * 1) If the user selects Other Tip Percentage, then the Other Tip Percentage text
 * field should have a valid tip percentage entered by the user. Enable the
 * Calculate button only when the user enters a valid value.
 *
 * 2) If the user does not enter values in the Total Amount and No. of People fields,
 * we cannot perform the calculations. Hence we enable the Calculate button
 * only when the user enters valid values.
 */
```

```
private OnKeyListener mKeyListener = new OnKeyListener() {
    @Override
    public boolean onKey(View v, int keyCode, KeyEvent event) {

        switch (v.getId()) { ❶
        case R.id.txtAmount: ❷
        case R.id.txtPeople: ❸
            btnCalculate.setEnabled(txtAmount.getText().length() > 0
                    && txtPeople.getText().length() > 0);
            break;
        case R.id.txtTipOther: ❹
            btnCalculate.setEnabled(txtAmount.getText().length() > 0
                    && txtPeople.getText().length() > 0
                    && txtTipOther.getText().length() > 0);
            break;
        }
        return false;
    }
};
```

At ❶ in Example 1-13, we examine the ID of the View. Remember that each widget has a unique ID, defined in the *main.xml* file. These values are then defined in the generated *R.java* class.

At ❷ and ❸, if the key event occurred in the Total Amount or No. of People field, we check for the value entered in the field. We are ensuring that the user has not left both fields blank.

At ❹ we check if the user has selected the Other radio button, and then we ensure that the Other text field is not empty. We also check once again if the Total Amount and No. of People fields are empty.

So, the purpose of our KeyListener is now clear: ensure that all text fields are not empty and only then enable the Calculate button.

Listening to button clicks

Now we will look at the Calculate and Reset buttons. When the user clicks these buttons, we use the static interface OnClickListener(), which will let us know when a button is clicked.

As we did with the text fields, we create just one listener and within it we detect which button was clicked. Depending on the button that was clicked, the calculate() or reset() method is called. Example 1-14 shows how the click listener is added to the buttons.

Example 1-14. Code snippet 6 of TipsterActivity.java

```
/* Attach listener to the Calculate and Reset buttons */
btnCalculate.setOnClickListener(mClickListener);
btnReset.setOnClickListener(mClickListener);
```

Example 1-15 shows how to detect which button is clicked by checking for the ID of the View that receives the click event.

Example 1-15. Code snippet 7 of TipsterActivity.java

```
/**
 * ClickListener for the Calculate and Reset buttons.
 * Depending on the button clicked, the corresponding
 * method is called.
 */
private OnClickListener mClickListener = new OnClickListener() {

    @Override
    public void onClick(View v) {
        if (v.getId() == R.id.btnCalculate) {
            calculate();
        } else {
            reset();
        }
    }
};
```

Resetting the application

When the user clicks the Reset button, the input text fields should be cleared, the default "15% tip" radio button should be selected, and any results calculated should be cleared. Example 1-16 shows the reset() method.

Example 1-16. Code snippet 8 of TipsterActivity.java

```
/**
 * Resets the results text views at the bottom of the screen and
 * resets the text fields and radio buttons.
 */
private void reset() {
    txtTipAmount.setText("");
    txtTotalToPay.setText("");
    txtTipPerPerson.setText("");
    txtAmount.setText("");
    txtPeople.setText("");
    txtTipOther.setText("");
    rdoGroupTips.clearCheck();
    rdoGroupTips.check(R.id.radioFifteen);
    // Set focus on the first field
    txtAmount.requestFocus();
}
```

Validating the input to calculate the tip

As I said before, we are limiting what types of values the user can enter in the text fields. However, the user could still enter a value of zero in the Total Amount, No. of People, or Other Tip Percentage text fields, thus causing error conditions like divide by zero in our tip calculations.

If the user enters zero, we must show an alert pop-up asking the user to enter a non-zero value. We handle this with a method called showErrorAlert(String errorMessage, final int fieldId), which we will discuss in more detail later.

First, look at Example 1-17, which shows the calculate() method. Notice how the values entered by the user are parsed as double values. Now notice ❶ and ❷ where we check for zero values. If the user enters zero, we show a pop-up requesting a valid value. Next, look at ❸, where the Other Tip Percentage text field is enabled because the user selected the Other radio button. Here, too, we must check for the tip percentage being zero.

Example 1-17. Code snippet 9 of TipsterActivity.java

```java
/**
 * Calculate the tip as per data entered by the user.
 */
private void calculate() {
    Double billAmount = Double.parseDouble(
        txtAmount.getText().toString());
    Double totalPeople = Double.parseDouble(
        txtPeople.getText().toString());
    Double percentage = null;
    boolean isError = false;
    if (billAmount < 1.0) { ❶
        showErrorAlert("Enter a valid Total Amount.",
            txtAmount.getId());
        isError = true;
    }

    if (totalPeople < 1.0) { ❷
        showErrorAlert("Enter a valid value for No. of People.",
            txtPeople.getId());
        isError = true;
    }

    /*
     * If the user never changes the radio selection, then it means
     * the default selection of 15% is in effect. But it's
     * safer to verify
     */
    if (radioCheckedId == -1) {
        radioCheckedId = rdoGroupTips.getCheckedRadioButtonId();
    }
    if (radioCheckedId == R.id.radioFifteen) {
        percentage = 15.00;
```

```
        } else if (radioCheckedId == R.id.radioTwenty) {
            percentage = 20.00;
        } else if (radioCheckedId == R.id.radioOther) {
            percentage = Double.parseDouble(
                txtTipOther.getText().toString());
            if (percentage < 1.0) { ❸
                showErrorAlert("Enter a valid Tip percentage",
                    txtTipOther.getId());
                isError = true;
            }
        }

        /*
         * If all fields are populated with valid values, then proceed to
         * calculate the tip
         */
        if (!isError) {
            Double tipAmount = ((billAmount * percentage) / 100); ❹
            Double totalToPay = billAmount + tipAmount;
            Double perPersonPays = totalToPay / totalPeople; ❺

            txtTipAmount.setText(tipAmount.toString()); ❻
            txtTotalToPay.setText(totalToPay.toString());
            txtTipPerPerson.setText(perPersonPays.toString()); ❼
        }
}
```

When the application loads, the "15% tip" radio button is selected by default. If the user changes the selection, we assign the ID of the selected radio button to the member variable radioCheckedId, as we saw in Example 1-11, in OnCheckedChangeListener.

But if the user accepts the default selection, radioCheckedId will have the default value of -1. In short, we will never know which radio button was selected. Of course, we know which one is selected by default and could have coded the logic slightly differently, to assume 15% if radioCheckedId has the value -1. But if you refer to the API, you will see that we can call the method getCheckedRadioButtonId() only on the RadioGroup and not on individual radio buttons. This is because OnCheckedChangeListener readily provides us with the ID of the radio button selected.

Showing the results

Calculating the tip is simple. If there are no validation errors, the Boolean flag isError will be false. Look at ❹ through ❺ in Example 1-17 for the simple tip calculations. Next, the calculated values are set to the TextView widgets from ❻ to ❼.

Showing the alerts

Android provides the AlertDialog class to show alert pop-ups. This lets us show a dialog with up to three buttons and a message.

Example 1-18 shows the showErrorAlert() method, which uses this AlertDialog to show the error messages. Notice that we pass two arguments to this method: String errorMessage and int fieldId. The first argument is the error message we want to show to the user. The fieldId is the ID of the field that caused the error condition. After the user dismisses the alert dialog, this fieldId will allow us to request the focus on that field, so the user knows which field has the error.

Example 1-18. Code snippet 10 of TipsterActivity.java

```
/**
 * Shows the error message in an alert dialog
 *
 * @param errorMessage
 *            String for the error message to show
 * @param fieldId
 *            ID of the field which caused the error.
 *            This is required so that the focus can be
 *            set on that field once the dialog is
 *            dismissed.
 */
private void showErrorAlert(String errorMessage,
    final int fieldId) {
    new AlertDialog.Builder(this).setTitle("Error")
    .setMessage(errorMessage).setNeutralButton("Close",
            new DialogInterface.OnClickListener() {
                @Override
                public void onClick(DialogInterface dialog,
                        int which) {
                    findViewById(fieldId).requestFocus();
                }
        }).show();
}
```

When all this is put together, it should look like Figure 1-59.

Conclusion

Developing for the Android OS is not too different from developing for any other UI toolkit, including Microsoft Windows, X Windows, or Java Swing. Of course Android has its difference, and, overall, a very good design. The XML layout paradigm is quite cool and useful for building complex UIs using simple XML. In addition, the event handling model is simple, feature-rich, and intuitive to use in code.

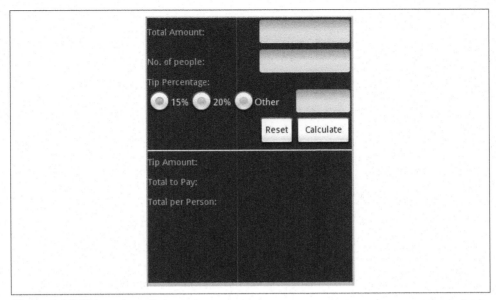

Figure 1-59. Tipster in action

See Also

"Reference Documentation" on page 2.

Source Download URL

The source code for this example is in the Android Cookbook repository (*https://github.com/IanDarwin/Android-Cookbook-Examples*), in the subdirectory *Tipster* (see "Getting and Using the Code Examples" on page 18).

## CHAPTER 2

Designing a Successful Application

This chapter is about design guidelines for writing imaginative and useful Android applications. Several recipes describe specific aspects of successful design. This section will list some others.

One purpose of this chapter is to explain the benefits of developing native Java Android applications over other methods of delivering rich content on mobile devices.

Requirements of a native handset application

There are a number of key requirements for successfully delivering any mobile handset application, regardless of the platform onto which it will be deployed:

- The application should be easy to install, remove, and update on a device.
- It should address the user's needs in a compelling, unique, and elegant way.
- It should be feature-rich while remaining usable by both novice and expert users.
- It should be familiar to users who have accessed the same information through other routes, such as a website.
- Key areas of functionality should be readily accessible.
- It should have a common look and feel with other native applications on the handset, conforming to the target platform's standards and style guidelines.
- It should be stable, scalable, usable, and responsive.
- It should use the platform's capabilities tastefully, when it makes the user's experience more compelling.

Android application design

Colin Wilcox

The Android application we will design in this chapter will exploit the features and functions unique to the Android OS platform. In general, the application will be an Activity-based solution allowing independent and controlled access to data on a screen-by-screen basis. This approach helps to localize potential errors and allows sections of the flow to be readily replaced or enhanced independently of the rest of the application.

Navigation will use a similar approach to that of the Apple iPhone solution in that all key areas of functionality will be accessed from a single navigation bar control. The navigation bar will be accessible from anywhere within the application, allowing the user to freely move around the application.

The Android solution will exploit features inherent to Android devices, supporting the devices' touch-screen features, the hardware button that allows users to switch the application to the background, and application switching capability.

Android provides the ability to jump back into an application at the point where it was switched out. This will be supported, when possible, within this design.

The application will use only standard Android user interface controls to make it as portable as possible. The use of themes or custom controls is outside the scope of this chapter.

The application will be designed such that it interfaces to a thin layer of RESTful web services that provide data in a JSON format. This interface will be the same as the one used by the Apple iPhone, as well as applications written for other platforms.

The application will adopt the Android style and design guidelines wherever possible so that it fits in with other Android applications on the device.

Data that is local to each view will be saved when the view is exited and automatically restored with the corresponding user interface controls repopulated when the view is next loaded.

A number of important device characteristics should be considered, as discussed in the following subsections.

Screen size and density.   In order to categorize devices by their screen type, Android defines two characteristics for each device: screen size (the physical dimensions of the screen) and screen density (the physical density of the pixels on the screen, or dpi [dots per inch]). To simplify all the different types of screen configurations, the Android system generalizes them into select groups that make them easier to target.

The designer should take into account the most appropriate choices for screen size and screen density when designing the application.

By default, an application is compatible with all screen sizes and densities, because the Android system makes the appropriate adjustments to the UI layout and image resources. However, you should create specialized layouts for certain screen sizes and provide specialized images for certain densities, by using alternative layout resources and by declaring in your manifest exactly which screen sizes your application supports.

Input configurations. Many devices provide a different type of user input mechanism, such as a hardware keyboard, a trackball, or a five-way navigation pad. If your application requires a particular kind of input hardware, you must declare it in the *AndroidManifest.xml* file, and be aware that the Google Play Store will not display your app on devices that lack this feature. However, it is rare for an application to require a certain input configuration.

Device features. There are many hardware and software features that may or may not exist on a given Android-powered device, such as a camera, a light sensor, Bluetooth capability, a certain version of OpenGL, or the fidelity of the touch screen. You should never assume that a certain feature is available on all Android-powered devices (other than the availability of the standard Android library).

A sophisticated Android application will use both types of menus provided by the Android framework, depending on the circumstances:

- *Options menus* contain primary functionality that applies globally to the current Activity or starts a related Activity. An options menu is typically invoked by a user pressing a hard button, often labeled Menu, or a soft menu button on an Action Bar (a vertical stack of three dots).

- *Context menus* contain secondary functionality for the currently selected item. A context menu is typically invoked by a user performing a long-press (press and hold) on an item. Like on the options menu, the selected operation can run in either the current or another Activity. A context menu is for any commands that apply to the current selection.

The commands on the context menu that appear when you long-press on an item should be duplicated in the Activity you get to by a normal press on that item.

As very general guidance:

- Place the most frequently used operations first in the menu.

- Only the most important commands should appear as buttons on the screen; delegate the rest to the menu.
- Consider moving menu items to the action bar if your application uses one.

The system will automatically lay out the menus and provide standard ways for users to access them, ensuring that the application will conform to the Android user interface guidelines. In this sense, menus are familiar and dependable ways for users to access functionality across all applications.

Our Android application will make extensive use of Google's Intent mechanism for passing data between Activity objects. Intents not only are used to pass data between views within a single application, but also allow data, or requests, to be passed to external modules. As such, much functionality can be adopted by the Android application by embedded functionality from other applications invoked by Intent calls. This reduces the development process and maintains the common look and feel and functionality behavior across all applications.

Data feeds and feed formats.   It is not a good idea to interface directly to any third-party data source; for example, it would be a bad idea to use a Type 3 JDBC driver in your mobile application to talk directly to a database on your server. The normal approach would be to mediate the data, from several sources in potentially multiple data formats, through middleware, which then passes data to an application through a series of RESTful web service APIs in the form of JSON data streams.

Typically, data is provided in such formats as XML, SOAP, or some other XML-derived representation. Representations such as SOAP are heavyweight, and as such, transferring data from the backend servers in this format increases development time significantly as the responsibility of converting this data into something more manageable falls on either the handset application or an object on the middleware server.

Mitigating the source data through a middleware server also helps to break the dependency between the application and the data. Such a dependency has the disadvantage that if, for some reason, the nature of the data changes or the data cannot be retrieved, the application may be broken and become unusable, and such changes may require the application to be republished. Mitigating the data on a middleware server ensures that the application will continue to work, albeit possibly in a limited fashion, regardless of whether the source data exists. The link between the application and the mitigated data will remain.

2.1 Exception Handling

Ian Darwin

Problem

Java has a well-defined exception handling mechanism, but it takes some time to learn to use it effectively without frustrating either users or tech support people.

Solution

Java offers an exception hierarchy that provides considerable flexibility when used correctly. Android offers several mechanisms, including dialogs and toasts, for notifying the user of error conditions. The Android developer should become acquainted with these mechanisms and learn to use them effectively.

Discussion

Java has had two categories of exceptions (actually of Exception's parent, Throwable) since it was introduced: checked and unchecked. In Java Standard Edition, apparently the intention was to force the programmer to face the fact that, while certain things could be detected at compile time, others could not. For example, if you were installing a desktop application on a large number of PCs, it's likely that the disk on some of those PCs would be near capacity, and trying to save data on them could fail; meanwhile, on other PCs some file that the application depended upon might have gone missing, not due to programmer error but to user error, filesystem happenstance, gerbils chewing on the cables, or whatever. So the category of IOException was created as a "checked exception," meaning that the programmer would have to check for it, either by having a try-catch clause inside the file-using method or by having a throws clause on the method definition. The general rule, which all well-trained Java developers memorize, is the following:

> Throwable is the root of the throwable hierarchy. Exception, and all of its subclasses other than RuntimeException or any subclass thereof, is checked. All else is unchecked.

This means that Error and all of its subclasses are unchecked (see Figure 2-1). If you get a VMError, for example, it means there's a bug in the runtime. There's nothing you can do about this as an application programmer. RuntimeException subclasses include things like the excessively long-named ArrayIndexOutOfBoundsException; this and friends are unchecked because it is your responsibility to catch these exceptions at development time, by testing for them (see Chapter 3).

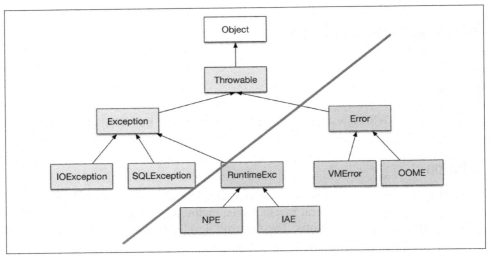

Figure 2-1. Throwable hierarchy

Where to catch exceptions

The (over)use of checked exceptions led a lot of early Java developers to write code that was sprinkled with try-catch blocks, partly because the use of the throws clause was not emphasized early enough in some training programs and books. As Java itself has moved more to enterprise work, and newer frameworks such as Spring, Hibernate, and JPA have come along and are emphasizing the use of unchecked exceptions, this early position has shifted. It is now generally accepted that you want to catch exceptions as close to the user as possible. Code that is meant for reuse—in libraries or even in multiple applications—should not try to do error handling. What it can do is what's called *exception translation*; that is, turning a technology-specific (and usually checked) exception into a generic, unchecked exception. Example 2-1 shows the basic pattern.

Example 2-1. Exception translation

```
public class ExceptionTranslation {
    public String readTheFile(String f) {
        try (BufferedReader is = new BufferedReader(new FileReader(f))) {
            String line = is.readLine();
            return line;
        } catch (FileNotFoundException fnf) {
            throw new RuntimeException("Could not open file " + f, fnf);
        } catch (IOException ex) {
            throw new RuntimeException("Problem reading file " + f, ex);
        }
    }
}
```

Note that prior to Java 7, you'd have had to write an explicit `finally` clause to close the file:

```
        } finally {
            if (is != null) {
                try {
                    is.close();
                } catch(IOException grr) {
                    throw new RuntimeException("Error on close of " + f, grr);
                }
            }
        }
    }
```

Note how the use of checked exceptions clutters even that code: it is virtually impossible for the `is.close()` to fail, but since you want to have it in a `finally` block (to ensure that it gets tried if the file was opened but then something went wrong), you have to have an additional `try-catch` around it. So, checked exceptions are (more often than not) an annoyance, should be avoided in new APIs, and should be paved over with unchecked exceptions when using code that requires them.

There is an opposing view, espoused by the official Oracle website and others. In a comment on the website from which this book was produced (*http://androidcook book.com/r/75*), reader Al Sutton points out the following:

> Checked exceptions exist to force developers to acknowledge that an error condition can occur and that they have thought about how they want to deal with it. In many cases there may be little that can be done beyond logging and recovery, but it is still an acknowledgment by the developer that they have considered what should happen with this type of error. The example shown ... stops callers of the method from differentiating between when a file doesn't exist (and thus may need to be re-fetched), and when there is a problem reading the file (and thus the file exists but is unreadable), which are two different types of error conditions.

Android, wishing to be faithful to the Java API, has a number of these checked exceptions (including the ones shown in the example), so they should be treated the same way.

What to do with exceptions

Exceptions should almost always be reported. When I see code that catches exceptions and does nothing at all about them, I despair. They should, however, be reported only once (do not both log and translate/rethrow!). The point of all normal exceptions is to indicate, as the name implies, an exceptional condition. Since on an Android device there is no system administrator or console operator, exceptional conditions need to be reported to the user.

You should think about whether to report exceptions via a dialog or a toast. The exception handling situation on a mobile device is different from that on a desktop computer. The user may be driving a car or operating other machinery, interacting with people, and so on, so you should not assume you have her full attention.

I know that most examples, even in this book, use a toast, because it involves less coding than a dialog. But remember that a toast will only appear on the screen for a few seconds; blink and you may miss it. If the user needs to do something to correct the problem, you should use a dialog.

Toasts simply pop up and then obliviate. Dialogs require the user to acknowledge an exceptional condition, and either do, or give the app permission to do, something that might cost money (such as turning on internet access in order to run an application that needs to download map tiles).

 Use toasts to "pop up" unimportant information; use dialogs to display important information and to obtain confirmation.

See Also

Recipe 3.9.

2.2 Requesting Android Permissions at Runtime

Mike Way

Problem

In Android 6 and later, you must check permissions at runtime in addition to specifying them in the manifest.

Solution

"Dangerous" resources are those that could affect the user's stored information, or privacy, etc. To access resources protected by "dangerous" permissions you must:

- Check if the user has already granted permission before accessing a resource.
- Explicitly request permissions from the user if the permissions have not previously been granted.
- Have an alternate course of action so the application does not crash if the permission is not granted.

Discussion

Before accessing a resource that requires permission, you must first check if the user has already granted permission. To do this, call the `Activity` method `checkSelfPermission(permission)`. It will return either `PERMISSION_GRANTED` or `PERMISSION_DENIED`:

```
if (ActivityCompat.checkSelfPermission(this,
    Manifest.permission.WRITE_EXTERNAL_STORAGE) ==
        PackageManager.PERMISSION_GRANTED) {
    // If you get here then you have the permission and can do some work
} else {
    // See below
}
```

If the preceding check indicates that the permission has not been granted, you must explicitly request it by calling the `Activity` method `requestPermissions()`:

```
void requestPermissions (String[] permissions, int requestCode)
```

As this will interact with the user, it is an asynchronous request. You must override the `Activity` method `onRequestPermissionsResult()` to get notified of the response:

```
public void onRequestPermissionsResult(
    int requestCode, String[] permissions, int[] grantResults);
```

For example:

```
// Unique request code for the particular permissions request
private static int REQUEST_EXTERNAL_STORAGE = 1;
...
// Request the permission from the user
ActivityCompat.requestPermissions(this,
    new String[]{Manifest.permission.WRITE_EXTERNAL_STORAGE },
    REQUEST_EXTERNAL_STORAGE);

// Callback handler for the eventual response
@Override
public void onRequestPermissionsResult(
    int requestCode, String[] permissions, int[] grantResults) {

  boolean granted = true;
  if (requestCode == REQUEST_EXTERNAL_STORAGE) {
        // Received permission result for external storage permission.
        Log.i(TAG, "Got response for external storage permission request.");

            // Check if all the permissions have been granted
            if (grantResults.length > 0 ) {
                for (int result : grantResults) {
                    if (result != PackageManager.PERMISSION_GRANTED) {
                        granted = false;
                    }
                }
            } else {
                granted = false;
```

```
        }
    }
    ...
    // If granted is true: carry on and perform the action. Calling
    // checkSelfPermission() will now return PackageManager.PERMISSION_GRANTED
```

It is usually a good idea to provide the user with information as to why the permissions are required. To do this you call the Activity method boolean shouldShowRequestPermissionRationale(String permission). If the user has previously refused to grant the permissions this method will return true, giving you the opportunity to display extra information as to why they should be granted:

```
if (ActivityCompat.shouldShowRequestPermissionRationale(this,
        Manifest.permission.WRITE_EXTERNAL_STORAGE)) {
    // Provide additional info if the permission was not granted
    // and the user would benefit from additional
    // context for the use of the permission
    Log.i(TAG, "Displaying permission rationale to provide additional context.");
    Snackbar.make(mLayout, R.string.external_storage_rationale,
            Snackbar.LENGTH_INDEFINITE)
        .setAction(R.string.ok, new View.OnClickListener() {
            @Override
            public void onClick(View view) {
                    ActivityCompat.requestPermissions(MainActivity.this,
                        new String[]{
                                Manifest.permission.WRITE_EXTERNAL_STORAGE,
                                Manifest.permission.READ_EXTERNAL_STORAGE},
                        REQUEST_EXTERNAL_STORAGE);
            }
    }).show();
```

This uses a Snackbar (see Recipe 7.1) to display the rationale, until the user clicks the Snackbar to dismiss it.

See Also

This permission checking technique is also used in the example project in Recipe 14.1. There is more documention at the official documentation site (*https://devel oper.android.com/training/permissions/requesting.html*).

Source Download URL

The source code for this example is in the Android Cookbook repository (*https:// github.com/IanDarwin/Android-Cookbook-Examples*), in the subdirectory *Permission-Request* (see "Getting and Using the Code Examples" on page 18).

2.3 Accessing Android's Application Object as a "Singleton"

Adrian Cowham

Problem

You need to access "global" data from within your Android app.

Solution

The best solution is to subclass `android.app.Application` and treat it as a singleton with static accessors. Every Android app is guaranteed to have exactly one `android.app.Application` instance for the lifetime of the app. If you choose to subclass `android.app.Application`, Android will create an instance of your class and invoke the `android.app.Application` life-cycle methods on it. Because there's nothing preventing you from creating another instance of your subclassed `android.app.Application`, it isn't a genuine singleton, but it's close enough.

Having global access to such objects as session handlers, web service gateways, or anything that your application only needs a single instance of will dramatically simplify your code. Sometimes these objects can be implemented as singletons, and sometimes they cannot because they require a `Context` instance for proper initialization. In either case, it's still valuable to add static accessors to your subclassed `android.app.Application` instance so that you can consolidate all globally accessible data in one place, have guaranteed access to a `Context` instance, and easily write "correct" singleton code without having to worry about synchronization.

Discussion

When writing your Android app you may find it necessary to share data and services across multiple Activities. For example, if your app has session data, such as the identity of the currently logged-in user, you will likely want to expose this information. When developing on the Android platform, the pattern for solving this problem is to have your `android.app.Application` instance own all global data, and then treat your `Application` instance as a singleton with static accessors to the various data and services.

When writing an Android app you're guaranteed to only have one instance of the `android.app.Application` class, so it's safe (and recommended by the Google Android team) to treat it as a singleton. That is, you can safely add a static `getInstance()` method to your `Application` implementation. Example 2-2 provides an example.

Example 2-2. The Application implementation

```
public class AndroidApplication extends Application {

    private static AndroidApplication sInstance;

    private SessionHandler sessionHandler; // Generic your-application handler
```

```
    public static AndroidApplication getInstance() {
      return sInstance;
    }

    public Session Handler getSessionHandler()
        return sessionHandler;
    }

    @Override
    public void onCreate() {
      super.onCreate();
      sInstance = this;
      sInstance.initializeInstance();
    }

    protected void initializeInstance() {
        // Do all your initialization here
        sessionHandler = new SessionHandler(
            this.getSharedPreferences( "PREFS_PRIVATE", Context.MODE_PRIVATE ) );
    }

    /** This is a stand-in for some application-specific session handler;
     * would normally be a self-contained public class.
     */
    private class SessionHandler {
        SharedPreferences sp;
        SessionHandler(SharedPreferences sp) {
            this.sp = sp;
        }
    }
  }
}
```

This isn't the classical singleton implementation, but given the constraints of the Android framework it's the closest thing we have; it's safe, and it works.

The notion of the "session handler" is that it keeps track of per-user information such as name and perhaps password, or any other relevant information, across different Activities and the same Activity even if it gets destroyed and re-created. Our SessionHandler class is a placeholder for you to compose such a handler, using whatever information you need to maintain across Activities!

Using this technique in this app has simplified and cleaned up the implementation. Also, it has made it much easier to develop tests. Using this technique in conjunction with the Robolectric testing framework (see Recipe 3.5), you can mock out the entire execution environment in a straightforward fashion.

Also, don't forget to add the application class's android:"name" declaration to the existing application element in your *AndroidManifest.xml* file:

```
<application android:icon="@drawable/app_icon"
    android:label="@string/app_name"
    android:name=".AndroidApplication">
```

See Also

My blog post (*http://mytensions.blogspot.com/2011/03/androids-application-object-as.html*).

Source Download URL

The source code for this project is in the Android Cookbook repository (*https://github.com/IanDarwin/Android-Cookbook-Examples*), in the subdirectory *AppSingleton* (see "Getting and Using the Code Examples" on page 18).

2.4 Keeping Data When the User Rotates the Device

Ian Darwin

Problem

When the user rotates the device, Android will normally destroy and re-create the current Activity. You want to keep some data across this cycle, but all the fields in your Activity are lost during it.

Solution

There are several approaches. If all your data comprises primitive types, consists of `Strings`, or is `Serializable`, you can save it in `onSaveInstanceState()` in the `Bundle` that is passed in.

Another solution lets you return a single arbitrary object. You need only override `onRetainNonConfigurationInstance()` in your Activity to save some values, call `getLastNonConfigurationInstance()` near the end of your `onCreate()` method to see if there is a previously saved value, and, if so, assign your fields accordingly.

Discussion

Using onSaveInstanceState()

See Recipe 1.2.

Using onRetainNonConfigurationInstance()

The `getLastNonConfigurationInstance()` method's return type is `Object`, so you can return any value you want from it. You might want to create a `Map` or write an inner class in which to store the values, but it's often easier just to pass a reference to the current Activity, for example, using `this`:

```
public class MyActivity extends Activity {
    ...
```

```
/** Returns arbitrary single token object to keep alive across
 * the destruction and re-creation of the entire Enterprise.
 */
@Override
public Object onRetainNonConfigurationInstance() {
        return this;
}
```

The preceding method will be called when Android destroys your main Activity. Suppose you wanted to keep a reference to another object that was being updated by a running service, which is referred to by a field in your Activity. There might also be a Boolean to indicate whether the service is active. In the preceding code, we return a reference to the Activity from which all of its fields can be accessed (even private fields, since the outgoing and incoming Activity objects are of the same class). In my geotracking app JPSTrack, for example, I have a FileSaver class that accepts data from the location service; I want it to keep getting the location, and saving it to disk, in spite of rotations, rather than having to restart it every time the screen rotates. Rotation is unlikely if the device is anchored in a car dash mount (we hope), but quite likely if a passenger, or a pedestrian, is taking pictures or typing notes while geotracking.

After Android creates the new instance, it calls onCreate() to notify the new instance that it has been created. In onCreate() you typically do constructor-like actions such as initializing fields and assigning event listeners. You still need to do those, so leave them alone. Near the end of onCreate(), however, you will add some code to get the old instance, if there is one, and get some of the important fields from it. The code should look something like Example 2-3.

Example 2-3. The onCreate() method

```
@Override
public void onCreate(Bundle savedInstanceState) {
    super.onCreate(savedInstanceState);
    setContentView(R.layout.main);

    saving = false;
    paused = false;

    // Lots of other initializations...

    // Now see if we just got interrupted by, e.g., rotation
        Main old = (Main) getLastNonConfigurationInstance();
        if (old != null) {
            saving = old.saving;
            paused = old.paused;

            // This is the most important line: keep saving to same file!
            fileSaver = old.fileSaver;
            if (saving) {
```

```
                    fileNameLabel.setText(fileSaver.getFileName());
        }
    return;
    }

    // I/O helper
    fileSaver = new GPSFileSaver(...);
}
```

The `fileSaver` object is the big one, the one we want to keep running and not re-create every time. If we don't have an old instance, we create the `fileSaver` only at the very end of `onCreate()`, since otherwise we'd be creating a new one just to replace it with the old one, which is (at the least) bad for performance. When the `onCreate()` method finishes, we hold no reference to the old instance, so it should be eligible for Java garbage collection. The net result is that the Activity appears to keep running nicely across screen rotations, despite the re-creation.

An alternative possibility is to set `android:configChanges="orientation"` in your *Android-Manifest.xml*. This approach prevents the Activity from being destroyed and re-created, but typically also prevents the application from displaying correctly in landscape mode, and is officially regarded as not good practice—see the following reference.

See Also

Recipe 2.3, the developer documentation on handling configuration changes (*https:// developer.android.com/guide/topics/resources/runtime-changes.html*).

Source Download URL

You can download the source code for this example from GitHub (*https://github.com/ IanDarwin/jpstrack.android*). Note that if you want it to compile, you will also need the jpstrack project, from the same GitHub account.

2.5 Monitoring the Battery Level of an Android Device

Pratik Rupwal

Problem

You want to detect the battery level on an Android device so that you can notify the user when the battery level goes below a certain threshold, thereby avoiding unexpected surprises.

Solution

A broadcast receiver that receives the broadcast message sent when the battery status changes can identify the battery level and can issue alerts to users.

Discussion

Sometimes we need to show an alert to the user when the battery level of an Android device goes below a certain limit. The code in Example 2-4 sets the broadcast message to be sent whenever the battery level changes and creates a broadcast receiver to receive the broadcast message, which can alert the user when the battery gets discharged below a certain level.

Example 2-4. The main Activity

```java
public class MainActivity extends Activity {

  /** Called when the Activity is first created. */
  @Override
  public void onCreate(Bundle savedInstanceState) {
      super.onCreate(savedInstanceState);
      setContentView(R.layout.main);

    /** This registers the receiver for a broadcast message to be sent
    * to when the battery level is changed. */

      this.registerReceiver(this.myBatteryReceiver,
        new IntentFilter(Intent.ACTION_BATTERY_CHANGED));

    /** Intent.ACTION_BATTERY_CHANGED can be replaced with
      * Intent.ACTION_BATTERY_LOW for receiving
      * a message only when battery level is low rather than sending
      * a broadcast message every time battery level changes.
      * There is also ACTION_BATTERY_OK for when the battery
      * has been charged a certain amount above the level that
      * would trigger the low condition.
      */
  }

  private BroadcastReceiver myBatteryReceiver =
      new BroadcastReceiver() {

    @Override
    public void onReceive(Context ctx, Intent intent) {
    // bLevel is battery percent-full as an integer
    int bLevel = intent.getIntExtra("level", 0);
    Log.i("BatteryMon", "Level now " + bLevel);
    }
  };
}
```

The `ACTION_BATTERY_LOW` and `ACTION_BATTERY_OK` levels are not documented, and are settable only by rebuilding the operating system, but they may be around 10 and 15, or 15 and 20, respectively.

2.6 Creating Splash Screens in Android

Rachee Singh and Ian Darwin

Problem

You want to create a splash screen that will appear while an application is loading.

Solution

You can construct a splash screen as an Activity or as a dialog. Since its purpose is accomplished within a few seconds, it can be dismissed after a short time interval has elapsed or upon the click of a button in the splash screen.

Discussion

The splash screen was invented in the PC era, initially as a cover-up for slow GUI construction when PCs were slow. Vendors have kept them for branding purposes. But in the mobile world, where the longest app start-up time is probably less than a second, people are starting to recognize that splash screens have become somewhat anachronistic. When I (Ian Darwin) worked at eHealth Innovation (*https://ehealthin novation.org*), we recognized this by making the splash screen for our BANT application disappear after just one second. The question arises whether we still need splash screens at all. With most mobile apps, the name and logo appear in the app launcher, and on lots of other screens within the app. Is it time to make the splash screen disappear altogether?

The answer to that question is left up to you and your organization. For completeness, here are two methods of handling the application splash screen.

The first version uses an Activity that is dedicated to displaying the splash screen. The splash screen displays for two seconds or until the user presses the Menu key, and then the main Activity of the application appears. First we use a thread to wait for a fixed number of seconds, and then we use an Intent to start the real main Activity. The one downside to this method is that your "main" Activity in your *AndroidManifest.xml* file is the splash Activity, not your real main Activity. Example 2-5 shows the splash Activity.

Example 2-5. The splash Activity

```java
public class SplashScreen extends Activity {
    private long ms=0;
    private long splashTime=2000;
    private boolean splashActive = true;
    private boolean paused=false;
    @Override
    protected void onCreate(Bundle savedInstanceState) {

        super.onCreate(savedInstanceState);
        setContentView(R.layout.splash);
        Thread mythread = new Thread() {
            public void run() {
                try {
                    while (splashActive && ms < splashTime) {
                        if(!paused)
                            ms=ms+100;
                        sleep(100);
                    }
                } catch(Exception e) {}
                finally {
                    Intent intent = new Intent(SplashScreen.this, Main.class);
                    startActivity(intent);
                }
            }
        };
        mythread.start();
    }

}
```

Example 2-6 shows the layout of the splash Activity, *splash.xml*.

Example 2-6. The splash layout

```xml
<?xml version="1.0" encoding="utf-8"?>
<LinearLayout xmlns:android="http://schemas.android.com/apk/res/android"
    android:orientation="vertical" android:layout_width="fill_parent"
    android:layout_height="fill_parent">

    <ImageView android:src="@drawable/background"
    android:id="@+id/image"
    android:layout_width="wrap_content"
    android:layout_height="wrap_content" />

    <ProgressBar android:id="@+id/progressBar1"
    android:layout_width="wrap_content"
    android:layout_height="wrap_content"
    android:layout_gravity="center_horizontal">
    </ProgressBar>
</LinearLayout>
```

One additional requirement is to put the attribute `android:noHistory="true"` on the splash Activity in your *AndroidManifest.xml* file so that this Activity will not appear in the history stack, meaning if the user uses the Back button from the main app he will go to the expected Home screen, not back into your splash screen (see Figure 2-2).

Figure 2-2. Splash screen

Two seconds later, this Activity leads to the next Activity, which is the standard "Hello, World" Android Activity, as a proxy for your application's main Activity (see Figure 2-3).

Figure 2-3. "Main" Activity

In the second version (Example 2-7), the splash screen displays until the Menu key on the Android device is pressed, then the main Activity of the application appears. For this, we add a Java class that displays the splash screen. We check for the pressing of the Menu key by checking the `KeyCode` and then finishing the Activity (see Example 2-7).

Example 2-7. Watching for KeyCodes

```java
public class SplashScreen extends Activity {
    private long ms=0;
    private long splashTime=2000;
    private boolean splashActive = true;
    private boolean paused=false;
    @Override
    protected void onCreate(Bundle savedInstanceState) {
        super.onCreate(savedInstanceState);
        setContentView(R.layout.splash);
    }

    public boolean onKeyDown(int keyCode, KeyEvent event) {
        super.onKeyDown(keyCode, event);
        if (KeyEvent.KEYCODE_MENU == keyCode) {
            Intent intent = new Intent(SplashScreen.this, Main.class);
            startActivity(intent);
        }
        if (KeyEvent.KEYCODE_BACK == keyCode) {
            finish();
        }
        return false;
    }
}
```

The layout of the splash Activity, *splash.xml*, is unchanged from the earlier version.

As before, after the button press this Activity leads to the next Activity, which represents the main Activity.

The other major method involves use of a dialog, started from the `onCreate()` method in your main method. This has a number of advantages, including a simpler Activity stack and the fact that you don't need an extra Activity that's only used for the first few seconds. The disadvantage is that it takes a bit more code, as you can see in Example 2-8.

Example 2-8. The splash dialog

```java
public class SplashDialog extends Activity {
    private Dialog splashDialog;

    /** Called when the Activity is first created. */
    @Override
    public void onCreate(Bundle savedInstanceState) {
        super.onCreate(savedInstanceState);

        StateSaver data = (StateSaver) getLastNonConfigurationInstance();
        if (data != null) { // "All this has happened before"
```

```
        if (data.showSplashScreen ) { // And we didn't already finish
            showSplashScreen();
        }
        setContentView(R.layout.main);
        // Do any UI rebuilding here using saved state
    } else {
        showSplashScreen();
        setContentView(R.layout.main);
        // Start any heavy-duty loading here, but on its own thread
    }
}
```

The basic idea is to display the splash dialog at application startup, but also to redisplay it if you get, for example, an orientation change while the splash screen is running, and to be careful to remove it at the correct time if the user backs out or if the timer expires while the splash screen is running.

See Also

Ian Clifton's blog post (*http://blog.iangclifton.com/2011/01/01/android-splash-screens-done-right/*) titled "Android Splash Screens Done Right" argues passionately for the dialog method.

Source Download URL

The source code for this example is in the Android Cookbook repository (*https://github.com/IanDarwin/Android-Cookbook-Examples*), in the subdirectory *SplashDialog* (see "Getting and Using the Code Examples" on page 18).

2.7 Designing a Conference/Camp/Hackathon/Institution App

Ian Darwin

Problem

You want to design an app for use at a conference, BarCamp, or hackathon, or inside a large institution such as a hospital.

Solution

Provide at least the required functions listed in this recipe's "Discussion" section, and as many of the optional ones as you think make sense.

Discussion

A good app of this type requires some or most of the following functions, as appropriate:

- A map of the building, showing the locations of meetings, food services, washrooms, emergency exits, and so on. You get extra points if you provide a visual slider for moving up or down levels if your conference takes place on more than one floor or level in the building (think about a 3D fly-through of San Francisco's Moscone Center, including the huge escalators). Remember that some people may know the building, but others will not. Consider having a "where am I" function (the user will type in the name or number of a room he sees; you get extra points if you offer visual matching or use the GPS instead of making the user type) as well as a "where is" function (the user selects from a list and the application jumps to the map view with a pushpin showing the desired location). Turn-by-turn walking directions through a maze of twisty little passages?

- A map of the exhibit hall (if there is a show floor, have a map and an easy way to find a given exhibitor). Ditto for poster papers if your conference features these.

- A schedule view. Highlight changes in red as they happen, including additions, last-minute cancellations, and room changes.

- A sign-up button if your conference has Birds of a Feather (BOF) gatherings; you might even want a "Suggest a new BOF" Activity.

- A local area map. This could be OpenStreetMap or Google Maps, or maybe something more detailed than the standard map. Add folklore, points of interest, navigation shortcuts, and other features. Limit it to a few blocks so that you can get the details right. A university campus is about the right size.

- An overview map of the city. Again, this is not the Google map, but an artistic, neighborhood/zone view with just the highlights.

- Tourist attractions within an hour of the site. Your mileage may vary.

- A food finder. People always get tired of convention food and set out on foot to find something better to eat.

- A friend finder. If Google's Latitude app were open to use by third-party apps, you could tie into Google's data. If it's a security conference, implement this functionality yourself.

- Private voice chat. If it's a small security gathering, provide a Session Initiation Protocol (SIP) server on a well-connected host, with carefully controlled access; it should be possible to have almost walkie talkie–like service.

- Sign-ups for impromptu group formation for trips to tourist attractions or any other purpose.

- Functionality to post comments to Twitter, Facebook, and LinkedIn.

- Note taking! Many people will have Android on large-screen tablets, so a "Notepad" equivalent, ideally linked to the session the notes are taken in, will be useful.

- A way for users to signal chosen friends that they want to eat (at a certain time, in so many minutes, *right now*), including the type of food or restaurant name and seeing if they're also interested.

See Also

The rest of this book shows how to implement most of these functions.

Google Maps has recently started serving building maps (*https://googleblog.blog spot.com/2011/11/new-frontier-for-google-maps-mapping.html*). The article shows who to contact to get your building's internal locations added to the map data; if appropriate, consider getting the venue operators to give Google their building's data.

2.8 Using Google Analytics in an Android Application

Ashwini Shahapurkar

Problem

Developers often want to track their applications in terms of features used by users. How can you determine which feature is most used by your app's users?

Solution

Use Google Analytics to track the app based on defined criteria, similar to Google Analytics's website-tracking mechanism.

Discussion

Before we use Google Analytics in our app, we need an analytics account which you can get for free from Google using one of two approaches to getting the Google Analytics SDK running:

Automated Approach

For Android Studio only, you can follow the steps to get the Analytics SDK given at *https://developers.google.com/analytics/devguides/collection/android/resources*, which involve having Google generate a simple configuration file containing your Analytics account, then adding two classpath dependencies and a Gradle plugin in your Gradle build scripts. The plugin will read your downloaded configuration file and apply the information to your code.

Hands-On Approach

A more hands-on approach involves creating your account directly at *https://accounts.google.com/SignUp?continue=https%3A%2F%2Fwww.google.com%2Fanalytics%2Fmobile%2F&hl=en*, then adding two dependencies and providing the analytics account to the SDK. The two dependencies are `com.google.gms:google-services:3.0.0` and `com.google.android.gms:play-services-analytics:10.0.1`.

Now, sign in to your analytics account and create a website profile for the app. The website URL can be fake but should be descriptive. I recommend that you use the reverse package name for this. For example, if the application package name is `com.example.analytics.test`, the website URL for this app can be *http://test.analytics.example.com*. After you create the website profile, a web property ID is generated for that profile. Jot it down - save it in a safe place-as we will be using this ID in our app. The ID, also known as the UA number of the tracking code, uniquely identifies the website profile.

Common Steps

Next, ensure you have the following permissions in your project's *AndroidManifest.xml* file:

```
<uses-permission android:name="android.permission.INTERNET" />
<uses-permission android:name="android.permission.ACCESS_NETWORK_STATE" />
```

 For both legal and licensing reasons, you *must* inform your users that you are collecting anonymous user data in your app. You can do so via a policy statement, in the end-user license agreement, or somewhere else where users will see this information. See Recipe 2.9.

Now we are ready to track our application. Obtain the singleton instance of the tracker by calling the `GoogleAnalytics.getInstance().newTracker()` method. Usually, you will want to track more than Activities in the app. In such a scenario, it's a good idea to have this tracker instance in the `onCreate()` method of the `Application` class of the app (see Example 2-9).

Example 2-9. The application implementation for tracking

```
public class GADemoApp extends Application {
    /*
     * Define web property ID obtained after creating a profile for the app. If
     * using the Gradle plugin, this should be available as R.xml.global_tracker.
     */
    private String webId = "UA-NNNNNNNN-Y";

    /* Analytics tracker instance */
```

```
Tracker tracker;

/* This is the getter for the tracker instance. This is called from
 * within the Activity to get a reference to the tracker instance.
 */
public synchronized Tracker getTracker() {
    if (tracker == null) {
        // Get the singleton Analytics instance, get Tracker from it
        GoogleAnalytics instance = GoogleAnalytics.getInstance(this);

        // Start tracking the app with your web property ID
        tracker = instance.newTracker(webId);

        // Any app-specific Application setup code goes here...
    }
    return tracker;
    }
}
```

You can track page views and events in the Activity by calling the setScreenName() and
send() methods on the tracker instance (see Example 2-10).

Example 2-10. The Main Activity with tracking

```
public class MainActivity extends Activity {
    public void onCreate(Bundle savedInstanceState) {
        super.onCreate(savedInstanceState);
        setContentView(R.layout.main);

        // Track the page view for the Activity
        Tracker tracker =
            ((GADemoApp)getApplication()).getTracker();
        tracker.setScreenName("MainActivity");
        tracker.send(new HitBuilders.ScreenViewBuilder().build());

        /* You can track events like button clicks... */
        findViewById(R.id.actionButton).setOnClickListener(v -> {
                Tracker tracker =
                    ((GADemoApp)getApplication()).getTracker();
                tracker.send(new HitBuilders.EventBuilder(
                    "Action Event", "Button Clicked").build());
        });
    }
}
```

Using this mechanism, you can track all the Activities and events inside them. You
then visit the Analytics web site to see how many times each Activity or other event
has been invoked.

See Also

The main page for the Android Analytics API[*https://developer.android.com/distrib ute/analyze/start.html*].

Source Download URL

The source code for this example is in the Android Cookbook repository (*https:// github.com/IanDarwin/Android-Cookbook-Examples*), in the subdirectory *Analytics* (see "Getting and Using the Code Examples" on page 18).

2.9 Setting First-Run Preferences

Ashwini Shahapurkar

Problem

You have an application that collects app usage data anonymously, so you are obligated to make users aware of this the first time they run your application.

Solution

Use shared preferences as persistent storage to store a value, which gets updated only once. Each time the application launches, it will check for this value in the preferences. If the value has been set (is available), it is not the first run of the application; otherwise it is the first run.

Discussion

You can manage the application life cycle by using the `Application` class of the Android framework. We will use shared preferences as persistent storage to store the first-run value.

We will store a Boolean flag in the preferences if this is the first run. When the application is installed and used for the first time, there are no preferences available for it. They will be created for us. In that case the flag will return a value of `true`. After getting the `true` flag, we can update this flag with a value of `false` as we no longer need it to be `true`. See Example 2-11.

Example 2-11. First-run preferences

```
public class MyApp extends Application {

    SharedPreferences mPrefs;

    @Override
```

```
public void onCreate() {
    super.onCreate();

    Context mContext = this.getApplicationContext();
    // 0 = mode private. Only this app can read these preferences.
    mPrefs = mContext.getSharedPreferences("myAppPrefs", 0);


    // Your app initialization code goes here
}
public boolean getFirstRun() {
    return mPrefs.getBoolean("firstRun", true);
}

public void setRunned() {
    SharedPreferences.Editor edit = mPrefs.edit();
    edit.putBoolean("firstRun", false);
    edit.commit();
}
}
```

This flag from the preferences will be tested in the launcher Activity, as shown in Example 2-12.

Example 2-12. Checking whether this is the first run of this app

```
if(((MyApp) getApplication()).getFirstRun()) {
    // This is the first run
    ((MyApp) getApplication()).setRunned();

    // Your code for the first run goes here

    }
else {
    // This is not the first run on this device
}
```

Even if you publish updates for the app and the user installs the updates, these preferences will not be modified; therefore, the code will work for only the first run after installation. Subsequent updates to the app will not bring the code into the picture, unless the user has manually uninstalled and reinstalled the app.

 You could use a similar technique for distributing shareware versions of an Android app (i.e., limit the number of trials of the application). In this case, you would use an integer count value in the preferences to indicate the number of trials. Each trial would update the preferences. After the desired value is reached, you would block the usage of the application until the user pays the usage fee.

2.10 Formatting Numbers

Ian Darwin

Problem

You need to format numbers, because the default formatting of `Double.toString()` and friends does not give you enough control over how the results are displayed.

Solution

Use `String.format()` or one of the `NumberFormat` subclasses.

Discussion

The `printf()` function was first included in the C programming language in the 1970s, and it has been used in many other languages since, including Java. Here's a simple `printf()` example in Java SE:

```
System.out.printf("Hello %s at %s%n", userName, time);
```

The preceding example could be expected to print something like this:

```
Hello Robin at Wed Jun 16 08:38:46 EDT 2010
```

Since we don't use `System.out` in Android, you'll be relieved to note that you can get the same string that would be printed, for putting it into a view, by using:

```
String msg = String.format("Hello %s at %s%n", userName, time);
```

If you haven't seen `printf()` before, the first argument is obviously the format code string, and any other arguments here, (`userName` and `time`) are values to be formatted. The format codes begin with a percent sign (%) and have at least one "type" code; Table 2-1 shows some common type codes.

Table 2-1. Some common format codes

Character	Meaning
s	String (convert primitive values using defaults; convert objects by `toString`)
d	Decimal integer (`int`, `long`)
f	Floating point (`float`, `double`)
n	Newline
t	Time/date formats, Java-specific; see the discussion referred to in the "See Also" section at the end of the recipe

The default date formatting is pretty ugly, so we often need to expand on it. The `printf()` formatting capabilities are actually housed in the `java.util.Formatter` class, to which reference should be made for the full details of its formatting language.

Unlike `printf()` in other languages you may have used, all these format routines optionally allow you to refer to arguments by their number, by putting a number plus a dollar sign after the % lead-in but before the formatting code proper; for example, `%2$3.1f` means to format the second argument as a decimal number with three characters and one digit after the decimal place. This numbering can be used for two purposes: to change the order in which arguments print (often useful with internationalization), and to refer to a given argument more than once. The date/time format character t requires a second character after it, such as Y for the year, m for the month, and so on. Here we take the `time` argument and extract several fields from it:

```
msg = String.format("Hello at %1$tB %1$td, %1$tY%n", time);
```

This might format as July 4, 2010.

To print numbers with a specific precision, you can use f with a width and a precision, such as:

```
msg = String.format("Latitude: %10.6f", latitude);
```

This might yield:

```
Latitude:  -79.281818
```

While such formatting is OK for specific uses such as latitudes and longitudes, for general use such as currencies, it may give you too much control.

General formatters

Java has an entire package, `java.text`, that is full of formatting routines as general and flexible as anything you might imagine. Like `printf()`, it has an involved formatting language, described in the online documentation page. Consider the presentation of numbers. In North America, the number "one thousand twenty-four and a quarter" is written 1,024.25; in most of Europe it is 1 024,25, and in some other parts of the world it might be written 1.024,25. The formatting of currencies and percentages is equally varied. Trying to keep track of this yourself would drive the average software developer around the bend rather quickly.

Fortunately, the `java.text` package includes a `Locale` class. Furthermore, the Java or Android runtime automatically sets a default `Locale` object based on the user's environment; this code works the same on desktop Java as it does in Android. To provide formatters customized for numbers, currencies, and percentages, the `NumberFormat` class has static factory methods that normally return a `DecimalFormat` with the correct pattern already instantiated. A `DecimalFormat` object appropriate to the user's locale can be obtained from the factory method `NumberFormat.getInstance()` and manipulated using set methods. Surprisingly, the method `setMinimumIntegerDigits()` turns out to be the easy way to generate a number format with leading zeros. Example 2-13 is an example.

Example 2-13. Number formatting demo

```java
import java.text.NumberFormat;

/*
 * Format a number our way and the default way.
 */
public class NumFormat2 {
    /** A number to format */
    public static final double data[] = {
        0, 1, 22d/7, 100.2345678
    };

    public static void main(String[] av) {
        // Get a format instance
        NumberFormat form = NumberFormat.getInstance();

        // Tailor it to look like 999.99[99]
        form.setMinimumIntegerDigits(3);
        form.setMinimumFractionDigits(2);
        form.setMaximumFractionDigits(4);

        // Now print using it
        for (int i=0; i<data.length; i++)
            System.out.println(data[i] + "\tformats as " +
                form.format(data[i]));
    }
}
```

This prints the contents of the array using the NumberFormat instance form. We show running it as a main program instead of in an Android application just to isolate the effects of the NumberFormat.

For example, $ java NumFormat2 0.0 formats as 000.00; with the argument 1.0 it formats as 001.00, with 3.142857142857143 it formats as 003.1429, and with 100.2345678 it formats as 100.2346.

You can also construct a DecimalFormat with a particular pattern or change the pattern dynamically using applyPattern(). Table 2-2 shows some of the more common pattern characters.

Table 2-2. Common DecimalFormat pattern characters

Character	Explanation
#	Numeric digit (leading zeros suppressed)
0	Numeric digit (leading zeros provided)
.	Locale-specific decimal separator (decimal point)
,	Locale-specific grouping separator (comma in English)
-	Locale-specific negative indicator (minus sign)
%	Shows the value as a percentage

Character	Explanation
;	Separates two formats: the first for positive and the second for negative values
'	Escapes one of the preceding characters so that it appears as itself
Anything else	Appears as itself

The NumFormatTest program uses one DecimalFormat to print a number with only two decimal places and a second to format the number according to the default locale, as shown in Example 2-14.

Example 2-14. NumberFormat demo Java SE program

```java
import java.text.DecimalFormat;
import java.text.NumberFormat;

public class NumFormatDemo {
    /** A number to format */
    public static final double intlNumber = 1024.25;
    /** Another number to format */
    public static final double ourNumber = 100.2345678;

    public static void main(String[] av) {

        NumberFormat defForm = NumberFormat.getInstance();
        NumberFormat ourForm = new DecimalFormat("##0.##");
        // toPattern() will reveal the combination of #0., etc.
        // that this particular Locale uses to format with
        System.out.println("defForm's pattern is " +
            ((DecimalFormat)defForm).toPattern());
        System.out.println(intlNumber + " formats as " +
            defForm.format(intlNumber));
        System.out.println(ourNumber + " formats as " +
            ourForm.format(ourNumber));
        System.out.println(ourNumber + " formats as " +
            defForm.format(ourNumber) + " using the default format");
    }
}
```

This program prints the given pattern and then formats the same number using several formats:

```
$ java NumFormatTest
defForm's pattern is #,##0.###
1024.25 formats as 1,024.25
100.2345678 formats as 100.23
100.2345678 formats as 100.235 using the default format
```

See Also

Chapter 10 of my book *Java Cookbook* and Part VI of [*Java I/O*] by Elliotte Rusty Harold (both from O'Reilly).

2.11 Formatting with Correct Plurals

Ian Darwin

Problem

You're displaying something like `"Found "+ n +" reviews"`, but in English, "Found 1 reviews" is ungrammatical. You want `"Found 1 review"` for the case `n==1`.

Solution

For simple, English-only results, use a conditional statement. For better results that can be internationalized, use a `ChoiceFormat`. On Android, you can use `<plural>` in an XML resources file.

Discussion

The "quick and dirty" method is to use Java's ternary operator (`cond ? trueval : falseval`) in a string concatenation. Since in English, for most nouns, both zero and plurals get an *s* appended to the noun ("no books, one book, two books"), we need only test for `n==1`:

```
// FormatPlurals.java
public static void main(String argv[]) {
 report(0);
 report(1);
 report(2);
}
/** report -- using conditional operator */
public static void report(int n) {
  System.out.println("Found " + n + " item" + (n==1?"":"s"));
}
```

Running this on Java SE as a main program shows the following output:

```
$ java FormatPlurals
Found 0 items
Found 1 item
Found 2 items
```

The final `println()` statement is short for:

```
if (n==1)
  System.out.println("Found " + n + " item");
else
  System.out.println("Found " + n + " items");
```

This is longer, so Java's ternary conditional operator is worth learning.

Of course, you can't use this arbitrarily, because English is a strange and somewhat idiosyncratic language. Some nouns, such as *bus*, require "es" at the end, while others, such as *cash*, are collective nouns with no plural (you can have two flocks of geese or two stacks of cash, but you cannot have "two geeses" or "two cashes"). Still other nouns, such as *fish*, can be considered plural as they are, although *fishes* is also a correct plural.

A better way

The ChoiceFormat class from java.text is ideal for handling plurals; it lets you specify singular and plural (or, more generally, range) variations on the noun. It is capable of more, but in Example 2-15 I'll show only a couple of the simpler uses. I specify the values 0, 1, and 2 (or more), and the string values to print corresponding to each number. The numbers are then formatted according to the range they fall into.

Example 2-15. Formatting plurals using ChoiceFormat

```java
import java.text.*;

/**
 * Format a plural correctly, using a ChoiceFormat.
 */
public class FormatPluralsChoice extends FormatPlurals {

    // ChoiceFormat to just give pluralized word
    static double[] limits = { 0, 1, 2 };
    static String[] formats = { "reviews", "review", "reviews"};
    static ChoiceFormat pluralizedFormat =
        new ChoiceFormat(limits, formats);

    // ChoiceFormat to give English text version, quantified
    static ChoiceFormat quantizedFormat = new ChoiceFormat(
        "0#no reviews|1#one review|1<many reviews");

    // Test data
    static int[] data = { -1, 0, 1, 2, 3 };

    public static void main(String[] argv) {
        System.out.println("Pluralized Format");
        for (int i : data) {
            System.out.println("Found " + i + " " +
                pluralizedFormat.format(i));
        }

        System.out.println("Quantized Format");
        for (int i : data) {
            System.out.println("Found " +
                quantizedFormat.format(i));
        }
    }
}
```

Either of these loops generates output similar to the basic version. The code using the `ChoiceFormat` is slightly longer, but more general, and lends itself better to internationalization. Put the string for the "quantized" form constructor into *strings.xml* and it will be part of your localization actions.

The best way (Android only)

Create a file in */res/values$$/* containing something like this:

```
<?xml version="1.0" encoding="utf-8"?>
<resources>
  <plurals name="numberOfSongsAvailable">
  <item quantity="one">One item found.</item>
  <item quantity="other">%d items found.</item>
  </plurals>
</resources>
```

In your code, you can then use the following:

```
int count = getNumberOfsongsAvailable();
Resources res = getResources();
String songsFound =
    res.getQuantityString(R.plurals.numberOfSongsAvailable, count);
```

This use of XML resources was suggested by Tomas Persson.

See Also

For the Android-specific way, see the developer documentation on quantity strings (*https://developer.android.com/guide/topics/resources/string-resource.html#Plurals*).

Source Download URL

You can download the source code for this example from GitHub (*https://github.com/ IanDarwin/javasrc/blob/master/src/main/java/numbers/FormatPluralsChoice.java*).

2.12 Formatting the Time and Date for Display

Pratik Rupwal

Problem

You want to display the time and date in different standard formats.

Solution

The `DateFormat` class provides APIs for formatting time and date in a custom format. Using these APIs requires minimal effort.

Discussion

Example 2-16 adds five different `TextViews` for showing the time and date in different formats.

Example 2-16. The TextView layout

```xml
<?xml version="1.0" encoding="utf-8"?>
<LinearLayout xmlns:android="http://schemas.android.com/apk/res/android"
    android:orientation="vertical"
    android:layout_width="fill_parent"
    android:layout_height="fill_parent"
    >
<TextView
    android:layout_width="fill_parent"
    android:layout_height="wrap_content"
    android:id="@+id/textview1"
    />
<TextView
    android:layout_width="fill_parent"
    android:layout_height="wrap_content"
    android:id="@+id/textview2"
    />
    <TextView
    android:layout_width="fill_parent"
    android:layout_height="wrap_content"
    android:id="@+id/textview3"
    />
    <TextView
    android:layout_width="fill_parent"
    android:layout_height="wrap_content"
    android:id="@+id/textview4"
    />
    <TextView
    android:layout_width="fill_parent"
    android:layout_height="wrap_content"
    android:id="@+id/textview5"
    />

</LinearLayout>
```

Example 2-17 obtains the current time and date using the `java.util.Date` class and then displays it in different formats (please refer to the comments for sample output).

Example 2-17. The date formatter Activity

```java
package com.sym.dateformatdemo;

import java.util.Date;
import android.app.Activity;
import android.os.Bundle;
import android.text.format.DateFormat;
import android.widget.TextView;
```

```
public class TestDateFormatterActivity extends Activity {
    /** Called when the Activity is first created. */
    @Override
    public void onCreate(Bundle savedInstanceState) {
        super.onCreate(savedInstanceState);
        setContentView(R.layout.main);
        TextView textView1 = (TextView) findViewById(R.id.textview1);
        TextView textView2 = (TextView) findViewById(R.id.textview2);
        TextView textView3 = (TextView) findViewById(R.id.textview3);
        TextView textView4 = (TextView) findViewById(R.id.textview4);
        TextView textView5 = (TextView) findViewById(R.id.textview5);

        String delegate = "MM/dd/yy hh:mm a"; // 09/21/2011 02:17 pm
        Date noteTS = new Date();
        textView1.setText("Found Time :: "+DateFormat.format(delegate,noteTS));

        delegate = "MMM dd, yyyy h:mm aa"; // Sep 21,2011 02:17 pm
        textView2.setText("Found Time :: "+DateFormat.format(delegate,noteTS));

        delegate = "MMMM dd, yyyy h:mmaa"; // September 21,2011 02:17pm
        textView3.setText("Found Time :: "+DateFormat.format(delegate,noteTS));

        delegate = "E, MMMM dd, yyyy h:mm:ss aa";//Wed, September 21,2011 02:17:48 pm
        textView4.setText("Found Time :: "+DateFormat.format(delegate,noteTS));

        delegate =
            "EEEE, MMMM dd, yyyy h:mm aa"; //Wednesday, September 21,2011 02:17:48 pm
        textView5.setText("Found Time :: "+DateFormat.format(delegate,noteTS));
    }
}
```

See Also

Recipe 2.13. Also, the classes shown in the following table, in the package android.text.format, may be of use in this type of application.

Name	Usage
DateUtils	This class contains various date-related utilities for creating text for things like elapsed time and date ranges, strings for days of the week and months, and a.m./p.m. text.
Formatter	This is a utility class to aid in formatting common values that are not covered by java.util.Formatter.
Time	This class is a faster replacement for the java.util.Calendar and java.util.GregorianCalendar classes.

Source Download URL

The source code for this example is in the Android Cookbook repository (*https://github.com/IanDarwin/Android-Cookbook-Examples*), in the subdirectory *DateFormatDemo* (see "Getting and Using the Code Examples" on page 18).

2.13 Simplifying Date/Time Calculations with the Java 8 java.time API

Ian Darwin

Problem

You've heard that the JSR-310 date/time API, included in Java SE 8, simplifies date and time calculations, and you'd like to use it in Android.

Solution

You can use the new java.time API in Android O and later. Since Android did not become fully compliant with JDK 8 even in Android Nougat, despite being "based on" OpenJDK 8, for Android Nougat and earlier, you must use a third-party library such as the JSR-310 "backport" to access the java.time facilities, albeit with a different package name.

Discussion

There is a long history to the java.time API that I won't bore you with here; suffice it to say that we are all indebted to Steven Colbourne for inventing it and for his constancy in urging first Sun, then Oracle, to incorporate it into Java, which finally happened in Java 8. For licensing reasons, the backport of JSR-310—by its original author —to Java 6/7 was placed in a non-Java package, org.threeten.bp.

Since Android N didn't provide full compatibility with Java 8, we use an external library. We'll use an Android-specific version of this "backport" library, by Jake Wharton, is available on GitHub (*https://github.com/JakeWharton/ThreeTenABP*). You can add it to any Gradle or Maven project just by adding the coordinates compile 'com.jakewharton.threetenabp:threetenabp:1.0.3' to your build script (the version number may change over time, of course).

Here is an example to show you the level of complexity of the kinds of calculations that are built in. I've omitted the imports because they differ from the backport libraries and "standard Java" and Android O. The example shows how little code is needed to figure out the day of the month on which the next weekly and monthly paydays occur:

```
LocalDateTime now = LocalDateTime.now();
LocalDateTime weeklyPayDay =
    now.with(TemporalAdjusters.next(DayOfWeek.FRIDAY));
weekly.setText("Weekly employees' payday is Friday " +
    weeklyPayDay.getMonth() + " " +
    weeklyPayDay.getDayOfMonth());
LocalDateTime monthlyPayDay =
    now.with(TemporalAdjusters.lastInMonth(DayOfWeek.FRIDAY));
```

```
monthly.setText("Monthly employees are paid on " +
    monthlyPayDay.getMonth() + " " +
    monthlyPayDay.getDayOfMonth());
```

The API includes LocalDate objects, which just represent one particular day; LocalTime objects, which represent a time of day; and LocalDateTime objects, which represent a date and a time. As the names imply, all three are local, not meant to represent time across the world's time zones. For that, you want to use one of several classes that represent time zones. See the java.time documentation (*https://developer.android.com/reference/java/time/package-summary.html*) for details of all the classes.

To use the backport library on Android N and earlier, you need one extra call to initialize it, either in your Application class (see Recipe 2.3) or in your Activity. In the main Activity's onCreate() method you'd say:

```
AndroidThreeTen.init(getApplication());
```

The result should look like Figure 2-4.

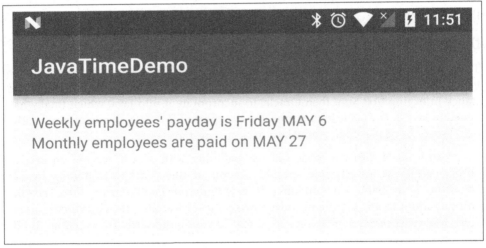

Figure 2-4. Java time example

See Also

The new API is covered in Chapter 6 of my *Java Cookbook* (*http://javacook.darwin sys.com*) and in some tutorials on the web. Make sure you use the version of the tutorial corresponding to the API you are using. The Java 8 version differs slightly from "ThreeTen" versions, and these both differ from the original Joda Time versions.

Source Download URL

The source code for this example is in the Android Cookbook repository (*https://github.com/IanDarwin/Android-Cookbook-Examples*), in the subdirectory *JavaTime-Demo* (see "Getting and Using the Code Examples" on page 18).

2.14 Controlling Input with KeyListeners

Pratik Rupwal

Problem

Your application contains text boxes in which you want to restrict users to entering only numbers; also, in some cases you want to allow only positive numbers, or integers, or dates.

Solution

Android provides `KeyListener` classes to help you restrict users to entering only numbers, positive numbers, integers, positive integers, and much more.

Discussion

The `Android.text.method` package includes a `KeyListener` interface, along with some classes such as `DigitsKeyListener` and `DateKeyListener` that implement this interface.

Example 2-18 is a sample application that demonstrates a few of these classes. This layout file creates five `TextViews` and five `EditTexts`; the `TextViews` display the input type allowed for their respective `EditTexts`.

Example 2-18. Layout with TextViews and EditTexts

```xml
<?xml version="1.0" encoding="utf-8"?>
<LinearLayout xmlns:android="http://schemas.android.com/apk/res/android"
    android:orientation="vertical"
    android:layout_width="fill_parent"
    android:layout_height="fill_parent"
    >

    <TextView
    android:layout_width="fill_parent"
    android:layout_height="wrap_content"
    android:id="@+id/textview1"
    android:text="digits listener with signs and decimal points"
    />
    <EditText
    android:layout_width="fill_parent"
    android:layout_height="wrap_content"
    android:id="@+id/editText1"
```

```
    />
    <TextView
    android:layout_width="fill_parent"
    android:layout_height="wrap_content"
    android:id="@+id/textview2"
    android:text="digits listener without signs and decimal points"
    />
    <EditText
    android:layout_width="fill_parent"
    android:layout_height="wrap_content"
    android:id="@+id/editText2"
    />

    <TextView
    android:layout_width="fill_parent"
    android:layout_height="wrap_content"
    android:id="@+id/textview3"
    android:text="date listener"
    />
    <EditText
    android:layout_width="fill_parent"
    android:layout_height="wrap_content"
    android:id="@+id/editText3"
    />

    <TextView
    android:layout_width="fill_parent"
    android:layout_height="wrap_content"
    android:id="@+id/textview4"
    android:text="multitap listener"
    />
    <EditText
    android:layout_width="fill_parent"
    android:layout_height="wrap_content"
    android:id="@+id/editText4"
    />

    <TextView
    android:layout_width="fill_parent"
    android:layout_height="wrap_content"
    android:id="@+id/textview5"
    android:text="qwerty listener"
    />
    <EditText
    android:layout_width="fill_parent"
    android:layout_height="wrap_content"
    android:id="@+id/editText5"
    />
</LinearLayout>
```

Example 2-19 is the code for the Activity that restricts the EditText inputs to numbers, positive integers, and so on (refer to the comments for groups of keys allowed).

Example 2-19. The main Activity

```
import android.app.Activity;
import android.os.Bundle;
import android.text.method.DateKeyListener;
import android.text.method.DigitsKeyListener;
import android.text.method.MultiTapKeyListener;
import android.text.method.QwertyKeyListener;
import android.text.method.TextKeyListener;
import android.widget.EditText;

public class KeyListenerDemo extends Activity {
    /** Called when the Activity is first created. */
    @Override
    public void onCreate(Bundle savedInstanceState) {
        super.onCreate(savedInstanceState);
        setContentView(R.layout.main);
        // Allows digits with positive/negative signs and decimal points
        EditText editText1=(EditText)findViewById(R.id.editText1);
        DigitsKeyListener digkl1=DigitsKeyListener.getInstance(true,true);
        editText1.setKeyListener(digkl1);

        // Allows positive integers only (no decimal values allowed)
        EditText editText2=(EditText)findViewById(R.id.editText2);
        DigitsKeyListener digkl2=DigitsKeyListener.getInstance();
        editText2.setKeyListener(digkl2);

        // Allows dates only
        EditText editText3=(EditText)findViewById(R.id.editText3);
        DateKeyListener dtkl=new DateKeyListener();
        editText3.setKeyListener(dtkl);

        // Allows multitap with 12-key keypad layout
        EditText editText4=(EditText)findViewById(R.id.editText4);
        MultiTapKeyListener multitapkl =
            new MultiTapKeyListener(TextKeyListener.Capitalize.WORDS,true);
        editText4.setKeyListener(multitapkl);

        // Allows qwerty layout for typing
        EditText editText5=(EditText)findViewById(R.id.editText5);
        QwertyKeyListener qkl =
            new QwertyKeyListener(TextKeyListener.Capitalize.SENTENCES,true);
        editText5.setKeyListener(qkl);
    }
}
```

To use `MultiTapKeyListener`, your phone should support the 12-key layout and it needs to be activated. To activate the 12-key layout, go to Settings → Language and Keyboard → On-screen Keyboard Layout and then select the "Phone layout" options.

See Also

The `Listener` types in the following table will be of use in writing this type of application.

Name	Usage
BaseKeyListener	This is an abstract base class for key listeners.
DateTimeKeyListener	This is for entering dates and times in the same text field.
MetaKeyKeyListener	This base class encapsulates the behavior for tracking the state of meta keys such as SHIFT, ALT, and SYM, as well as the pseudo-meta state of selecting text.
NumberKeyListener	This is for numeric text entry.
TextKeyListener	This is the key listener for typing normal text.
TimeKeyListener	This is for entering times in a text field.

2.15 Backing Up Android Application Data

Pratik Rupwal

Problem

When a user performs a factory reset or converts to a new Android-powered device, the application loses stored data or application settings.

Solution

Android's Backup Manager helps to automatically restore backup data or application settings when the application is reinstalled.

Discussion

Android's Backup Manager basically operates in two modes: backup and restore. During a backup operation, the Backup Manager (BackupManager class) queries your application for backup data, then hands it to a backup transport, which then delivers the data to cloud-based storage. During a restore operation, the Backup Manager retrieves the backup data from the backup transport and returns it to your application so that your application can restore the data to the device. It's possible for your application to request a restore, but not necessary because Android performs a restore operation when your application is installed and backup data associated with the user exists. The primary scenario in which backup data is restored happens when a user resets her device or upgrades to a new device and her previously installed applications are reinstalled.

Example 2-20 shows how to implement the Backup Manager for your application so that you can save the current state of your application.

Example 2-20. The backup/restore layout

```
<LinearLayout xmlns:android="http://schemas.android.com/apk/res/android"
    android:orientation="vertical"
```

```
android:layout_width="match_parent"
android:layout_height="wrap_content">

<ScrollView
    android:orientation="vertical"
    android:layout_width="fill_parent"
    android:layout_height="fill_parent"
    android:layout_weight="1">

    <LinearLayout
        android:orientation="vertical"
        android:layout_width="match_parent"
        android:layout_height="wrap_content">

        <TextView android:text="@string/filling_text"
            android:textSize="20dp"
            android:layout_marginTop="20dp"
            android:layout_marginBottom="10dp"
            android:layout_width="match_parent"
            android:layout_height="wrap_content"/>

        <RadioGroup android:id="@+id/filling_group"
            android:layout_width="match_parent"
            android:layout_height="wrap_content"
            android:layout_marginLeft="20dp"
            android:orientation="vertical">

            <RadioButton android:id="@+id/bacon"
                android:text="@string/bacon_label"/>
            <RadioButton android:id="@+id/pastrami"
                android:text="@string/pastrami_label"/>
            <RadioButton android:id="@+id/hummus"
                android:text="@string/hummus_label"/>

        </RadioGroup>

        <TextView android:text="@string/extras_text"
            android:textSize="20dp"
            android:layout_marginTop="20dp"
            android:layout_marginBottom="10dp"
            android:layout_width="match_parent"
            android:layout_height="wrap_content"/>

        <CheckBox android:id="@+id/mayo"
            android:text="@string/mayo_text"
            android:layout_marginLeft="20dp"
            android:layout_width="match_parent"
            android:layout_height="wrap_content"/>

        <CheckBox android:id="@+id/tomato"
            android:text="@string/tomato_text"
            android:layout_marginLeft="20dp"
            android:layout_width="match_parent"
            android:layout_height="wrap_content"/>

    </LinearLayout>
```

```
        </ScrollView>

</LinearLayout>
```

Here is a basic description of the procedure in step-by-step form:

1. Create a `BackupManagerExample` project in Eclipse.
2. Open the *layout/backup_restore.xml* file and insert the code in Example 2-20 into it.
3. Open the *values/string.xml* file and insert into it the code shown in Example 2-21.
4. Your manifest file will look like the code shown in Example 2-22.
5. The code in Example 2-23 completes the implementation of the Backup Manager for your application.

Example 2-21. Strings for the example

```
<resources>
  <string name="hello">Hello World, BackupManager!</string>
  <string name="app_name">BackupManager</string>
  <string name="filling_text">Choose Settings for your application:</string>
  <string name="bacon_label">Sound On</string>
  <string name="pastrami_label">Vibration On</string>
  <string name="hummus_label">Backlight On</string>
  <string name="extras_text">Extras:</string>
  <string name="mayo_text">Use Orientation?</string>
  <string name="tomato_text">Use Camera?</string>
</resources>
```

Example 2-22. AndroidManifest.xml

```
<?xml version="1.0" encoding="utf-8"?>
<manifest xmlns:android="http://schemas.android.com/apk/res/android"
    package="com.sym.backupmanager"
    android:versionCode="1"
    android:versionName="1.0">
  <uses-sdk android:minSdkVersion="9" />

  <application android:label="Backup/Restore" android:icon="@drawable/icon"
      android:backupAgent="ExampleAgent"> <!--Here you specify the backup agent-->

    <!--Some backup transports may require API keys or other metadata-->
    <meta-data android:name="com.google.android.backup.api_key"
            android:value="INSERT YOUR API KEY HERE" />

    <activity android:name=".BackupManagerExample">
            <intent-filter>
                    <action android:name="android.intent.action.MAIN" />
                    <category android:name="android.intent.category.LAUNCHER" />
```

```
            </intent-filter>
        </activity> </application>

</manifest>
```

Example 2-23. The backup/restore Activity

```
package com.sym.backupmanager;

import android.app.Activity;
import android.app.backup.BackupManager;
import android.os.Bundle;
import android.util.Log;
import android.widget.CheckBox;
import android.widget.CompoundButton;
import android.widget.RadioGroup;
import java.io.File;
import java.io.IOException;
import java.io.RandomAccessFile;

public class BackupManagerExample extends Activity {
    static final String TAG = "BRActivity";

    static final Object[] sDataLock = new Object[0];

    static final String DATA_FILE_NAME = "saved_data";

    RadioGroup mFillingGroup;
    CheckBox mAddMayoCheckbox;
    CheckBox mAddTomatoCheckbox;

    File mDataFile;

    BackupManager mBackupManager;

    @Override
    public void onCreate(Bundle savedInstanceState) {
        super.onCreate(savedInstanceState);

        setContentView(R.layout.backup_restore);

        mFillingGroup = (RadioGroup) findViewById(R.id.filling_group);
        mAddMayoCheckbox = (CheckBox) findViewById(R.id.mayo);
        mAddTomatoCheckbox = (CheckBox) findViewById(R.id.tomato);

        mDataFile = new File(getFilesDir(), BackupManagerExample.DATA_FILE_NAME);

        mBackupManager = new BackupManager(this);

        populateUI();
    }

    void populateUI() {
        RandomAccessFile file;
```

```
        int whichFilling = R.id.pastrami;
        boolean addMayo = false;
        boolean addTomato = false;

        synchronized (BackupManagerExample.sDataLock) {
            boolean exists = mDataFile.exists();
            try {
                file = new RandomAccessFile(mDataFile, "rw");
                if (exists) {
                    Log.v(TAG, "datafile exists");
                    whichFilling = file.readInt();
                    addMayo = file.readBoolean();
                    addTomato = file.readBoolean();
                    Log.v(TAG, "  mayo=" + addMayo
                            + " tomato=" + addTomato
                            + " filling=" + whichFilling);
                } else {
                    Log.v(TAG, "creating default datafile");
                    writeDataToFileLocked(file,
                            addMayo, addTomato, whichFilling);

                    mBackupManager.dataChanged();
                }
            } catch (IOException ioe) {
                // Do some error handling here!
            }
        }

        mFillingGroup.check(whichFilling);
        mAddMayoCheckbox.setChecked(addMayo);
        mAddTomatoCheckbox.setChecked(addTomato);

        mFillingGroup.setOnCheckedChangeListener(
                new RadioGroup.OnCheckedChangeListener() {
                    public void onCheckedChanged(RadioGroup group,
                            int checkedId) {
                        Log.v(TAG, "New radio item selected: " + checkedId);
                        recordNewUIState();
                    }
                });

        CompoundButton.OnCheckedChangeListener checkListener
                = new CompoundButton.OnCheckedChangeListener() {
            public void onCheckedChanged(CompoundButton buttonView,
                    boolean isChecked) {
                Log.v(TAG, "Checkbox toggled: " + buttonView);
                recordNewUIState();
            }
        };
        mAddMayoCheckbox.setOnCheckedChangeListener(checkListener);
        mAddTomatoCheckbox.setOnCheckedChangeListener(checkListener);
    }

    void writeDataToFileLocked(RandomAccessFile file,
            boolean addMayo, boolean addTomato, int whichFilling)
        throws IOException {
```

```
            file.setLength(OL);
            file.writeInt(whichFilling);
            file.writeBoolean(addMayo);
            file.writeBoolean(addTomato);
            Log.v(TAG, "NEW STATE: mayo=" + addMayo
                    + " tomato=" + addTomato
                    + " filling=" + whichFilling);
    }

    void recordNewUIState() {
        boolean addMayo = mAddMayoCheckbox.isChecked();
        boolean addTomato = mAddTomatoCheckbox.isChecked();
        int whichFilling = mFillingGroup.getCheckedRadioButtonId();
        try {
            synchronized (BackupManagerExample.sDataLock) {
                RandomAccessFile file = new RandomAccessFile(mDataFile, "rw");
                writeDataToFileLocked(file, addMayo, addTomato, whichFilling);
            }
        } catch (IOException e) {
            Log.e(TAG, "Unable to record new UI state");
        }

        mBackupManager.dataChanged();
    }
}
```

Data backup is not guaranteed to be available on all Android-powered devices. However, your application is not adversely affected in the event that a device does not provide a backup transport. If you believe that users will benefit from data backup in your application, you can implement it as described in this recipe, test it, and then publish your application without any concern about which devices actually perform backups. When your application runs on a device that does not provide a backup transport, the application will operate normally but will not receive callbacks from the Backup Manager to back up data.

Although you cannot know what the current transport is, you are always assured that your backup data cannot be read by other applications on the device. Only the Backup Manager and backup transport have access to the data you provide during a backup operation.

Because the cloud storage and transport services can differ among devices, Android makes no guarantees about the security of your data while using backup. You should always be cautious about using backup to store sensitive data, such as usernames and passwords.

Testing your backup agent

Once you've implemented your backup agent, you can use the bmgr command to test the backup and restore functionality by following these steps:

1. Install your application on a suitable Android system image, running any current emulator or device with Google Play Services.

2. Ensure that backup capability is enabled. If you are using the emulator, you can enable backup with the following command from your SDK tools/path:

```
$ adb shell bmgr enable true
```

3. If you are using a device, open the system settings, select Privacy, and then enable "Back up my data" and "Automatic restore."

4. Open your application and initialize some data.

If you've properly implemented backup capability in your application, it should request a backup each time the data changes. For example, each time the user changes some data, your app should call dataChanged(), which adds a backup request to the Backup Manager queue. For testing purposes, you can also make a request with the following ++bmgr++ command:

```
$ adb shell bmgr backup your.package.name
```

5. Initiate a backup operation:

```
$ adb shell bmgr run
```

This forces the Backup Manager to perform all backup requests that are in its queue.

6. Uninstall your application:

```
$ adb uninstall your.package.name
```

7. Reinstall your application.

If your backup agent is successful, all the data you initialized in step 4 is restored.

2.16 Using Hints Instead of Tool Tips

Daniel Fowler

Problem

Android devices can have small screens, so there may not be room for help text, and tool tips are not part of the platform.

Solution

Android provides the hint attribute for Views.

Discussion

Sometimes an input field needs clarification with regard to the value that should be entered. For example, a stock-ordering application asking for item quantities may need to state the minimum order size. In desktop programs, with large screens and the use of a mouse, extra messages can be displayed in the form of tool tips (a pop-up label over a field when the mouse moves over it). Alternatively, long descriptive labels may be used. With Android devices, the screen may be small and no mouse is generally used. The alternative here is to use the android:hint attribute on a View. This causes a "watermark" containing the hint text to be displayed in the input field when it is empty; this disappears when the user starts typing in the field. The corresponding function for android:hint is setHint(int resourceId). Figure 2-5 shows an example hint.

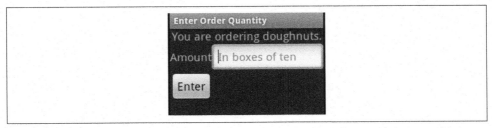

Figure 2-5. An example with hints

You can set the color of the hint text with android:textColorHint, with setHintTextColor(int color) being the associated function.

Using hints can also help with screen layouts when space is tight. A screen design can sometimes be improved by removing a label and using a hint, as shown in Figure 2-6.

The EditText definition in Figure 2-6 is shown in the following code so that you can see android:hint in use:

```
<EditText android:id="@+id/etQuantity"
    android:layout_width="fill_parent"
    android:layout_height="wrap_content"
    android:hint="Number of boxes of ten"
    android:textSize="18sp"/>
```

Figure 2-6. A hint and no label

Hints can guide users as they are filling in app fields, though as with any feature over-use is possible. Hints should not be used when it is obvious what is required; a field with a label of "First Name" would not need a hint such as "Enter your first name here," for example. Figure 2-6 shows our hypothetical ordering application improved somewhat by removing the redundant label.

## CHAPTER 3

Application Testing

"Test early and often" is a common cry among advocates of testing, as is the all-important question, "If you don't have a test, how do you know your code works?"

There are many types of testing. *Unit testing* checks out individual components ("units" such as methods) in isolation (not hitting the network or the database), whereas *integration testing* tests the entire system, or at least large swaths of it. JUnit and TestNG are the leading unit testing frameworks for Java. *Mock objects* are used where interaction with other components is required; there are several good mocking frameworks for Java. Android provides a number of specific testing techniques, many of which are discussed in this chapter.

In the broader scheme of things, software verification tools can be categorized as static or dynamic. JUnit is one example of a widely used method of dynamic testing, as is integration testing. Static code analysis works by examining the code rather than running it. Two well-known static analysis tools are FindBugs and PMD, which are covered in my book and my video series on testing (*http://cjp.darwinsys.com/*). This site also has a bibliography of testing books/papers and a list of Java-specific testing tools. Android has its own static analysis tool, Android Lint, covered in Recipe 3.13.

Android apps can be run on a vast array of devices, including small phones, mid-sized tablets, large phones, large tablets, and (as of ChromeOS Release 53) most Chromebooks. They also run on many proprietary readers such as the Amazon Kindle Fire tablets. Although we show how to test using the emulator in Recipe 3.1, you will want to have several real devices for testing, because the emulator is, after all, an emulator.

The terms *NPE*, *ANR*, and *FC* are used throughout this chapter. NPE is a "traditional Java" acronym for Null Pointer Exception. ANR is an Android-specific acronym; it stands for Application Not Responding, the first few words of a dialog you get when your application is judged to be taking too long to respond to a request. FC stands for Force Close, which occurs when Android requests that you close a failed application.

Entering Developer Mode on a real device

To put a real device into "developer mode," go into Settings → "About phone" (or tablet). At the bottom you will see a "Build number" entry. Tap seven times on "Build number" and it will say something like "Congratulations, you are now a developer!" and will enable the developer options in the main Settings screen.

3.1 Setting Up an Android Virtual Device (AVD) for App Testing

Daniel Fowler

Problem

Successful apps must run on a wide range of Android devices and versions, so you need to test them on a range of devices.

Solution

Use the Android SDK's device emulation toolkit to configure combinations of devices and operating systems. Testing on various combinations reduces issues related to hardware differences in devices.

Discussion

Android devices are manufactured to cover a wide market, from low cost to high specification and high value. Android has also been in the marketplace for more than a couple of years. For these reasons, a wide range of devices with a wide range of hardware options and operating system versions are in use. A successful application will be one that can run on a broad array of devices. An app developer will usually only be able to test on a very small range of physical devices, but fortunately, a developer can boost the confidence he has in his app by using an Android Virtual Device.

A compiled app can be tested on a physical device or on a virtual device. An AVD is an emulation of an Android platform on a host machine, usually the development machine. AVDs simplify testing for these reasons:

- Multiple AVD configurations can be created to test an app on different versions of Android.

- Different (emulated) hardware configurations can be used—for example, GPS or no GPS.

- An AVD is automatically launched and your compiled app is installed onto it when the Run button is clicked in your IDE.

- You can test your app on many more combinations of Android versions and hardware versions than physical devices you possess.

- Testing on AVDs greatly reduces the amount of testing required on physical devices.

- AVDs can be used alongside a physical device.

- You don't need to handicap your physical device to induce error conditions—for example, to test on a device with no Secure Digital (SD) card, just set up an AVD with no SD card.

- An AVD can simulate network events without the costs involved in using a physical device; for example, you can simulate phone calls or send an SMS message between two AVDs.

- You can simulate GPS data from an AVD from different physical locations without moving from your desk.

- When app users report bugs you can try to mimic their hardware configurations using AVDs.

- Testing on an AVD can avoid messing up your real device.

Please note that on underconfigured development machines and when emulating larger Android devices the performance of an AVD will often be less than that of a physical device.

You can configure an AVD using the SDK Manager program (opened directly from the filesystem or from within Eclipse). It is also possible to create AVDs from the command line. Note that the screenshots in this recipe, and the options they carry, will vary depending on what release of the Android SDK tools you have installed.

To create an AVD with the SDK Manager, you must first load the program. When using most IDEs, there is an AVD Manager icon, the Studio version of which is shown in Figure 3-1.

Figure 3-1. Selecting the AVD Manager

You can also start the program directly from the filesystem. For example, in Windows, open *C:\Program Files\Android\android-sdk\SDK Manager.exe*. If you started the program directly from the filesystem, the SDK Manager will check for SDK updates, in which case select Cancel to go to the main window, titled "Android SDK and AVD Manager." If you opened the program from your IDE, the main window will appear without the check for updates to the SDK.

The Virtual Device Configuration wizard loads. Choose an existing profile or create a new one (Figure 3-2).

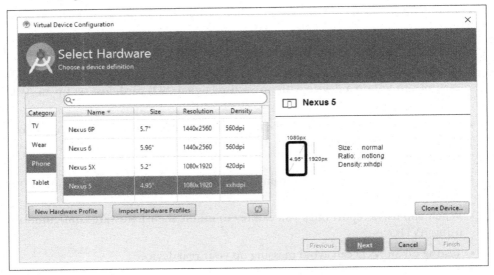

Figure 3-2. Creating an AVD—Part 1

The following fields are used to define an AVD:

Name

Give a name to the new Android device that is to be emulated. Make the name descriptive—for example, if you're emulating a device with a version 5.1 operating system and medium-resolution screen (HVGA), a name such as *Android-v5.1-HVGA* is better than *AndroidDevice*. The name may not contain spaces.

Target

This is the version of the Android operating system that will be running on the emulated device. As an example, for a device running version 6.0 this will be set to "Android 6.0-API Level 23."

SD Card

Here you specify the size of the device's emulated SD card, or select an existing SD card image (allowing the ability to share SD card data among different AVD emulations). To specify a new SD card, enter the size in megabytes (MB). Remember: the bigger the number, the bigger the file created on the host computer system to mimic the SD card. Alternatively, select the File option and browse to an existing SD card image (on a Windows machine the *sdcard.img* files will be found in the subfolders of the *avd* directory under the *.android* directory in the logged-on user's folder).

Snapshot

Check the Enabled box if you want the runtime state of the emulated device to persist between sessions, which is useful if a long-running series of tests is being performed and when the AVD is closed you do not want to have to start the tests from the beginning. It also speeds up the start-up time of an AVD.

Skin

Here you select the screen size for the device; a list of common screen sizes is presented (e.g., HVGA, QVGA, etc.). The list will vary depending on the operating system version. Alternatively, a custom resolution can be entered.

The following table lists the major choices you have to make in creating an AVD.

Name	Data type	Value	Description
Device	Choice	One of listed	List of known devices
Target	Choice	One of listed	List of API levels
CPU/ABI	Choice	One of listed	List of CPUs: ARM, Intel, etc.
Keyboard	Boolean	Yes or no	Controls emulation of a physical keyboard (as opposed to an onscreen one)
Skin	Choice	One of listed	Size of screen, e.g., QVGA, WVGA, etc.
Front Camera	Choice	One of None, Emulated, Webcam	User-facing camera
Back Camera	Choice	One of None, Emulated, Webcam	Outward-facing camera
Memory Options: RAM	Integer	Megabytes	Determines the size of the AVD's total main memory
Memory Options: VM Heap	Integer	Megabytes	Determines the size of the AVD's heap memory, for allocations
Internal Storage	Integer	Megabytes	Determines the size of the AVD's internal memory, for running applications
SD card support	Size or File	-	SD card allocated (if MB specified) or existing file used
Emulation options	Radio	Snapshot or Use Host GPU	Enable one of two performance options

When you have selected a device and pressed Next, you will see the System Image selection screen (Figure 3-3). Choose your operating system version here, and click the Finish button to generate the AVD. The AVD will now be listed in the "Android SDK and AVD Manager" window (see Figure 3-4).

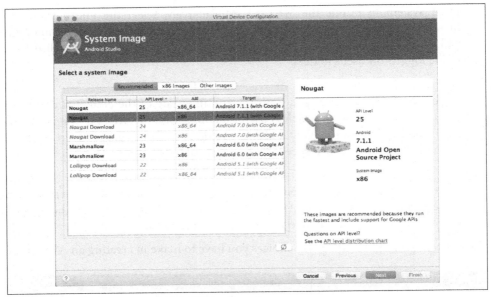

Figure 3-3. Creating an Android AVD—Part 2

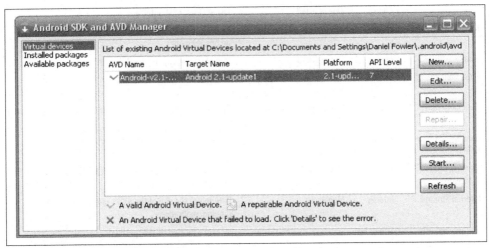

Figure 3-4. Starting the new AVD

The AVD is ready to be launched using the Start button. It is also ready to be selected in a project configuration to test an app under development. When the Start button is clicked, the Launch Options window is shown (see Figure 3-5).

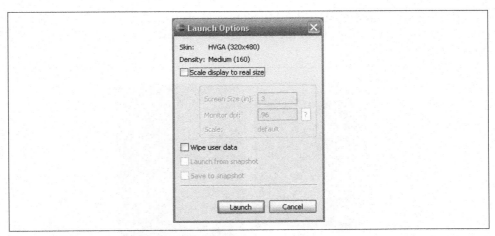

Figure 3-5. Launch options for the AVD

The options at launch are:

Scale display to real size
> On larger computer monitors you will not normally need to change the AVD scale. The dpi of the Android screen is greater than the standard dpi on computer monitors; therefore, the AVD screen will appear larger than the physical device. If necessary this can be scaled back to save screen space. Use this option to get the AVD to display at an approximate real size on the computer monitor. The values need to be set so that the AVD screen and keyboard are not too small to be used.

Wipe user data
> When the AVD is started the user data file is reset and any user data generated from previous runs of the AVD is lost.

Launch from snapshot
> If Snapshot has been enabled for an AVD, after it has been first launched subsequent launches are quicker. The AVD is loaded from a snapshot and the Android operating system does not need to start up again. However, when the AVD is closed the shutdown takes longer because the snapshot has to be written to disk.

Save to snapshot
> When the AVD is closed the current state is saved for quicker launching next time; the downside is that it takes longer to close as the snapshot is written to disk. Once you have a snapshot you can uncheck this option so that closing an AVD is quick as well, though any changes since the last snapshot will be lost.

Use the Launch button to start the AVD. Once loaded it can be used like any other Android device and driven from the keyboard and mouse of the host computer. See Figure 3-6.

Figure 3-6. The AVD in action

AVDs combined with physical devices are a useful combination for testing apps in a variety of scenarios.

See Also

The developer documentation on running apps on the emulator (*https://devel oper.android.com/studio/run/emulator.html*).

3.2 Testing on a Wide Range of Devices with Cloud-Based Testing

Ian Darwin

Problem

You need to test your app on a wide variety of devices.

Solution

Use one of several web-based or cloud-based app testing services.

Discussion

When Android was young, it was perhaps feasible to own one of each kind of device, to be able to say you had tested it on everything. I have half a dozen Android devices, most of them semiexpired, for this purpose. Yet today there are hundreds of different devices to test on, some with two or three different OS versions, different cell radios, and so on. It's just not practical for each developer to own enough devices to test on everything. That leaves two choices: either set up a hundred different AVDs, as discussed elsewhere in this chapter, or use a cloud-based or web-based testing service.

The basic idea is that these test-hosting companies buy lots of devices, and put them in server rooms with a webcam pointed at the screen and USB drivers that transfer keystrokes and touch gestures from your web browser–based control program to the real devices. These devices are in cities around the world, so you can test while online with various mobile service providers, get GPS coordinates from the real location, and so on.

Here are some of the providers in this space, listed in alphabetical order. Some are Android-specific while some also cover iOS, BlackBerry, and other devices. Listing them here does not constitute an endorsement of their products or services; caveat emptor!

- Bitbar TestDroid (*http://bitbar.com/*)
- Bsquare (*http://www.bsquare.com/*)
- Experitest (*https://experitest.com/*)
- Jamo Solutions (*http://www.jamosolutions.com/*)
- Perfecto Mobile (*https://www.perfectomobile.com*)

3.3 Testing with Eclipse and JUnit

Adrián Santalla

Problem

You need to create and use a new Eclipse test project to test your Android application.

Solution

Here's how to create and use a test project:

1. Within Eclipse, create a new Android project associated with your Android application project.
2. Configure the *AndroidManifest.xml* file of your test project with the necessary lines to test your Android application.
3. Write and run your tests.

Discussion

The following subsections describe the preceding steps in more detail.

Step 1: Create a new Android test project alongside your Android application project

First of all, you need to create a new Android project alongside the main application project to store your tests. This new Eclipse project should have an explicit dependency on your main application project. The Eclipse New Android Project wizard will create this and set it up correctly when you create the original project, if you remember to click the "Create Test Project" checkbox. Figure 3-7 shows the Eclipse project structure: two projects.

Figure 3-7. Target and Test projects in Eclipse

`HelloTestingTarget` is the target of our tests; that is, the main application. `HelloTestingTestProject` is, of course, the test project.

Step 2: Configure the AndroidManifest.xml file of the test project

Once you have created your new test project, you should properly set all the values of the project's *AndroidManifest.xml* file. It's necessary to set the package name of the main source of the application that you would like to test.

Imagine that you are testing an application whose package name is `my.pkg.app`. You should create a test project, and your *AndroidManifest.xml* file should look like the code in Example 3-1.

Example 3-1. The AndroidManifest.xml file for testing

```xml
<?xml version="1.0" encoding="utf-8"?>

<manifest xmlns:android="http://schemas.android.com/apk/res/android"
    package="my.pkg.app.tests"
    android:versionCode="1"
    android:versionName="1.0">

    <application>
        <uses-library android:name="android.test.runner" />
    </application>

    <instrumentation android:name="android.test.InstrumentationTestRunner"
        android:targetPackage="my.pkg.app"
        android:label="Tests for my.pkg.app"/>
</manifest>
```

The `package` attribute of the `manifest` tag stores the package name of the test project; more importantly, the `android:targetPackage` attribute of the `instrumentation` tag stores the package name that you would like to test. Again, the Eclipse wizard will set this up if you create the main and test projects at the same time. The resulting structure was shown in Figure 3-7.

Step 3: Write and run your tests

Now you can write your tests. The Android testing API has traditionally been based on the JUnit 3.8 API (although it is now possible to use JUnit 4, as in Recipe 3.4) and provides several types of test classes, including `AndroidTestCase`, `ActivityInstrumentationTestCase2`, `ApplicationTestCase`, and `InstrumentationTestCase`.

When you create your first test case with your IDE, it is useful to create a test case that inherits from `ActivityInstrumentationTestCase2`. This kind of test class allows you to create functional tests. Example 3-2 shows a simple functional test.

Example 3-2. A test case

```
public class MainTest extends ActivityInstrumentationTestCase2 <Main> {

    public MainTest() {
        super("my.pkg.app", Main.class);
        }

    public void test() {
        TextView textView = (TextView) getActivity().findViewById(R.id.textView);

        assertEquals("Hello World!", textView.getText());
    }
}
```

The Main class that appears as a type parameter in the test class is the main Activity of the main application project. The test constructor uses the main application package name and the class of the main Activity. From now on, you can create test cases using the standard methods of the Android API to get references to the Activity elements. In the preceding test we are testing that the main Activity has a TextView with the text "Hello World!" associated with it.

Source Download URL

The source code for this project is in the Android Cookbook repository (*https://github.com/IanDarwin/Android-Cookbook-Examples*), in the subdirectory *HelloTestingTarget* (see "Getting and Using the Code Examples" on page 18); the test project is in *HelloTestingTestProject*.

3.4 Testing with Android Studio and JUnit

Ian Darwin

Problem

You want to use JUnit to test your Android Studio–based application.

Solution

For standalone unit testing, use the *test* folder; for full Android unit testing, use the *androidTest* folder.

Discussion

For the purposes of this exercise, we'll create a new Android Studio project (see Recipe 1.10). Name the project "HelloStudioTesting" and use a package name like com.example. On the next screen, select "Phone and Tablet" and pick your favorite API level. After Gradle gets through grinding, you will see a project structured rather like Figure 3-8.

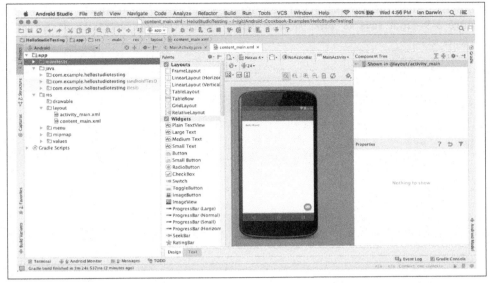

Figure 3-8. Android Studio project structure

Note in particular the presence of two test folders, with the same package name, labeled *test* and *androidTest*. The project is set up to support the two most common types of testing: plain Java JUnit testing and Android-specific testing. The latter uses JUnit but is more like an integration test than a unit test. Unit tests test code in isolation; the *androidTest* mechanism supports testing the common Android components, and runs them in a test application running on an AVD emulator or on a real device. We'll use both in this recipe.

Out of the box, the *test* folder contains an example test. We'll replace that with this test case:

```
public class DataModelTest {
    @Test
    public void NameCorrect() throws Exception {
        assertEquals("Robin Good", new DataModel().getName());
    }
}
```

Note the modern JUnit conventions: use of arbitrary method names and the `@Test` annotation to mark test methods. To make this test work we've created a class called `DataModel` with a hardcoded `getName()` method. The key thing to understand is that this test methodology uses standard JUnit and runs it in a standard Java Virtual Machine (JVM), so you can test any "normal" Java component, but you cannot test anything that depends on the Android framework! We'll cover that type of testing in a few paragraphs.

Note first that the sample JUnit test has a code comment—which I left in in Figure 3-9—that says `To work on unit tests, switch the Test Artifact in the Build Variants view`.

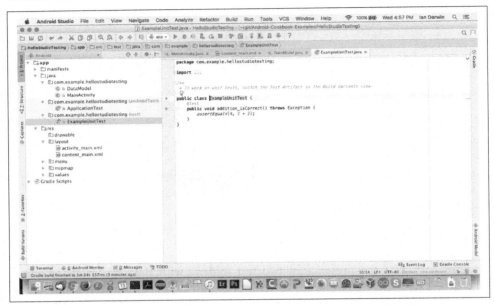

Figure 3-9. A non-example test in test

In practice, I find it easier just to right-click the *test* module, as in Figure 3-10.

At this stage of trivial examples you should expect your test to pass the first time, but it's still reassuring to see the green bar appear (see Figure 3-11), which indicates that 100% of the tests passed.

The *androidTest* package is for testing Android-specific functionality, such as `Activity` code. This testing mechanism is based on JUnit 3.8, where inheritance from `TestCase` is required and annotations are not used. You could use JUnit 4 here by adding a test runner and creating an alternate test configuration; we'll use this approach in Recipe 3.6. There are several base test classes, some of which are now deprecated. We'll use the `ActivityInstrumentationTestCase2` class and ignore the deprecation warnings.

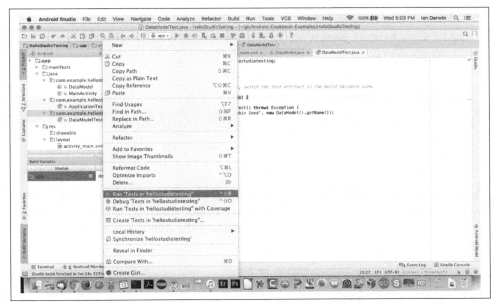

Figure 3-10. Running tests in test

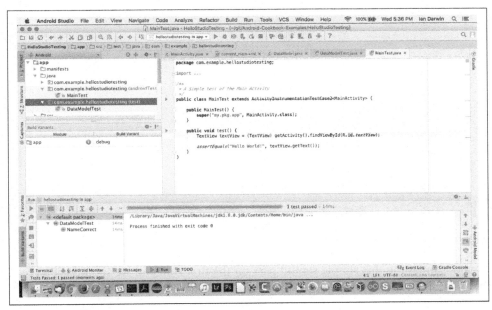

Figure 3-11. Unit tests—success

Our example test looks like this:

```
public class MainTest extends ActivityInstrumentationTestCase2<MainActivity> {

    public MainTest() {
        super("my.pkg.app", MainActivity.class);
    }

    public void test() {
        TextView textView = (TextView) getActivity().findViewById(R.id.textView);

        assertEquals("Hello World!", textView.getText());
    }
}
```

This code is creating the main Activity, finding the TextView, and asserting that the TextView contains the correct text. We run this by right-clicking the *androidTest* folder (not the *test* folder as in Figure 3-10) and selecting the Run menu item, as shown in Figure 3-12.

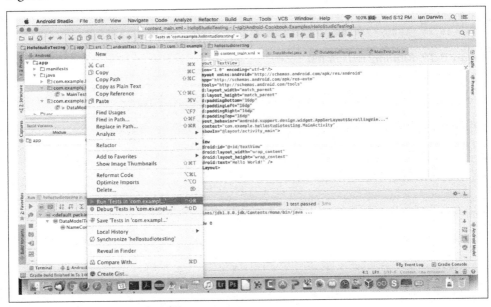

Figure 3-12. Running androidTest tests

Again, something this simple should pass on the first run, and we should get a green bar as in Figure 3-13.

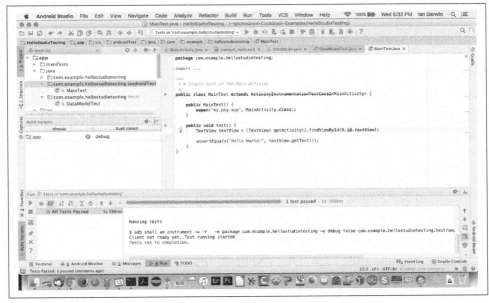

Figure 3-13. Android tests—success

These are both trivial tests of the "Hello, World" variety, but they show what you need to build up and run tests of greater complexity of both types: plain JUnit and Android-specific tests.

Source Download URL

The source code for this example is in the Android Cookbook repository (*https:// github.com/IanDarwin/Android-Cookbook-Examples*), in the subdirectory *HelloStudioTesting* (see "Getting and Using the Code Examples" on page 18).

See Also

The Android Studio User Guide documentation on testing (*https://devel oper.android.com/tools/testing/testing_android.html*).

3.5 Testing with Robolectric and JUnit 4

Ian Darwin

Problem

You like unit testing, but Android's original test framework was based on the ancient Android 3.8, and it runs in the emulator so it's slow.

Solution

Use Robolectric, a fast JUnit 4 test runner.

Discussion

These instructions are set up for Eclipse.

Assuming you have your "main" project set up as a normal Android project, create a folder called, e.g., *test* in this project (do not mark it as as source folder), and then do the following:

1. Create a separate project using the New Project wizard (*not* using the New Android Test Project wizard).

2. Make this project depend on your main project (Build Path → Configure).

3. Remove the default source folder, *src*, from the new project's build path.

4. Still in the build path, click "Link additional source"; browse to and select */Main-Project/test*.

5. Add *Robolectric-3.1.jar* to the new project's classpath, either by copying it into *libs* or by specifying it in your build script (Maven or Gradle).

6. Add JUnit 4 (not 3.8!) to your new project's classpath, either explicitly, or implicitly by choosing JUnit 4 from the "New Class → JUnit Test" wizard.

7. Annotate your JUnit 4 tests to run with the Robolectric test runner (see the following example).

8. Use Robolectric "shadow" classes where needed.

Next, create an Eclipse run configuration with the following special attributes (this section is adapted from the Robolectric website (*http://robolectric.org*)):

1. Choose Run → Run Configurations.

2. Double-click JUnit (not Android JUnit Test).

3. Name the project "MyProjectTestConfiguration."

4. Select the "Run all tests in the selected project, package or source folder" radio button.

5. Click the Search button.

6. Select MyProjectTest.

7. Choose JUnit 4 as the test runner.

8. Click the link "Multiple launchers available Select one" at the bottom of the dialog.

---

9. Check the "Use configuration specific settings" box.

10. Select Eclipse JUnit Launcher.

11. Click OK.

12. Click the Arguments tab.

13. Under "Working directory," select the Other radio button.

14. Click Workspace.

15. Select MyProject (not MyProjectTest; the value inside the Other edit box should be ${workspace_loc:MyProject}).

16. Click OK.

17. Click Close.

Now run your new run configuration. Example 3-3 is a sample Robolectric unit test.

Example 3-3. Robolectric test

```
@RunWith(RobolectricTestRunner.class)
public class HistoryActivityTest {

    private HistoryActivity activity;
    private Button listButton;

    @Before
    public void setup() {
        activity = new HistoryActivity();
        activity.onCreate(null);
        listButton = (Button) activity.findViewById(R.id.listButton);
    }

    @Test
    public void didWeGetTheRightButton() {
        assertEquals("History Log (Morning)", (String) listButton.getText());
    }

    @Test
    public void listButtonShouldLaunchListActivity() throws InterruptedException {

        assertNotNull(listButton);
        boolean clicked = listButton.performClick();
        assertTrue("performClick", clicked);

        ShadowActivity shadowActivity = Robolectric.shadowOf(activity);
        Intent startedIntent = shadowActivity.getNextStartedActivity();
        assertNotNull("shadowActivity.getNextStartedActivity == null?",
            startedIntent);
        ShadowIntent shadowIntent = Robolectric.shadowOf(startedIntent);
        assertEquals(WeightListActivity.class.getName(),
            shadowIntent.getComponent().getClassName());
```

```
    }
}
```

See Also

Robolectric (*http://robolectric.org/*).

3.6 Testing with ATSL, Espresso, and JUnit 4

Ian Darwin

Problem

You want to use the latest official testing software.

Solution

Use *Espresso*, part of the Android Testing Support Library (ATSL) (*https://devel oper.android.com/tools/testing-support-library/index.html*). Espresso uses JUnit 4 (as does Robolectric), but still requires that the tests be packaged and run on an emulator or device.

Discussion

Espresso is a relatively new testing framework that's designed to bring the advantages of JUnit 4 and Hamcrest matching styles to Android testing. As with the previous generation of Android tests, Espresso tests are packaged into an APK and sent to an emulator or real device. Robolectric (Recipe 3.5) may be faster since it runs on a specialized JVM on the development machine, but Espresso is usually easier to use. And since (as the name ATSL implies) it is a support library, Espresso tests can run on devices as old as API 8. The official documentation emphasizes UI interaction examples, but Espresso is not limited to this use.

To configure Espresso, you need to add some entries to the *build.gradle* for your application (usually this is in the *app* folder). Typically, you need to add the `testInstrumentationRunner`, `compile`, and `androidTestCompile` settings shown in Example 3-4.

Example 3-4. Gradle setup for Espresso

```
apply plugin: 'com.android.application'

android {
    compileSdkVersion 22
    buildToolsVersion "22"

    defaultConfig {
```

```
            applicationId "com.example.myapp"
            minSdkVersion 10
            targetSdkVersion 22.0.1
            versionCode 1
            versionName "1.0"

            testInstrumentationRunner "android.support.test.runner.AndroidJUnitRunner"
        }
    }

    dependencies {
        compile 'com.android.support:support-annotations:22.2.0'

        androidTestCompile 'com.android.support.test:runner:0.5'
        androidTestCompile 'com.android.support.test.espresso:espresso-core:2.2.2'
    }
```

Now you can write your tests. Every test class will need the
`@RunWith(AndroidJUnit4.class)` annotation.

For our "Hello, World" test, we are going to test a simple application that displays a
text field, a button, and a second text field. When you click the button, the text from
the first text field is copied to the second, to simulate starting some long-running
Activity. Here is the core of the Activity:

```java
protected void onCreate(Bundle savedInstanceState) {
    super.onCreate(savedInstanceState);
    setContentView(R.layout.activity_main);
    TextView tv = (TextView) findViewById(R.id.tvTarget);
    EditText et = (EditText) findViewById(R.id.tf);
    Button b = (Button) findViewById(R.id.startButton);
    b.setOnClickListener(v -> {
        tv.setText(et.getText());
    });
}
```

To test this, we will simulate the user typing something in the text field and clicking
the button. We also need to close the soft keyboard to ensure that it doesn't remain on
screen, hiding the target text field. Then we check to ensure that the text in the target
has changed. Example 3-5 shows the complete test code, including imports—unusual
for this book, but these are a bit complex to guess at. The `@Rule` is explained shortly.

Example 3-5. Espresso test case

```java
package com.example.helloespressotesting;

import android.support.test.rule.ActivityTestRule;
import android.support.test.runner.AndroidJUnit4;

import org.junit.Rule;
import org.junit.Test;
import org.junit.runner.RunWith;
```

```
import static android.support.test.espresso.Espresso.closeSoftKeyboard;
import static android.support.test.espresso.Espresso.onView;
import static android.support.test.espresso.action.ViewActions.click;
import static android.support.test.espresso.action.ViewActions.typeText;
import static android.support.test.espresso.assertion.ViewAssertions.matches;
import static android.support.test.espresso.matcher.ViewMatchers.withId;
import static android.support.test.espresso.matcher.ViewMatchers.withText;

/**
 * Demonstrate use of Espresso testing.
 */
@RunWith(AndroidJUnit4.class)
public class MainActivityTest {

    @Rule
    public ActivityTestRule<MainActivity> mActivityRule =
        new ActivityTestRule<>(MainActivity.class);

    @Test
    public void changeText_sameActivity() {
        final String MESG = "Hello Down There!";

        // Simulate typing text into 'tf'
        onView(withId(R.id.tf))
                .perform(typeText(MESG));
        closeSoftKeyboard();

        // Simulate clicking the Button 'startButton'
        onView(withId(R.id.startButton)).perform(click());

        // Find the target, and check that the text was changed
        onView(withId(R.id.tvTarget))
                .check(matches(withText(MESG)));
    }
}
```

Most Activity-testing classes will need a @Rule (a JUnit annotation) to specify the ActivityTestRule rule and to identify which Activity is needed. This rule handles all the grunt work of setting up the Activity, running on the correct thread, etc. It is run before the @Before (if any) and each @Test-annotated method so you get a clean Activity instance for each test:

```
@Rule
public ActivityTestRule<MainActivity> mActivityRule =
    new ActivityTestRule(MainActivity.class);
```

In your test method you can do the expected operations: find a view, click a button, and check the results. To run your test, you have to configure the AVD and create a test runner configuration. On the AVD or device you want to test, go into Settings → "Developer options" and turn off the following three options:

- Window animation scale

- Transition animation scale
- Animator duration scale

If you want to run the tests from the command line, you can just type ./gradlew connectedAndroidTest, which will run all the tests in *androidTest*. To run under Android Studio, you need to create a test runner configuration (see Figure 3-14):

1. Select Run → Edit Configurations.
2. Add a new Android Tests configuration (click the + button in the upper left).
3. Assign a meaningful name such as "Espresso Tests."
4. Choose a module (usually it's just "app").
5. Add android.support.test.runner.AndroidJUnitRunner as an instrumentation test runner.

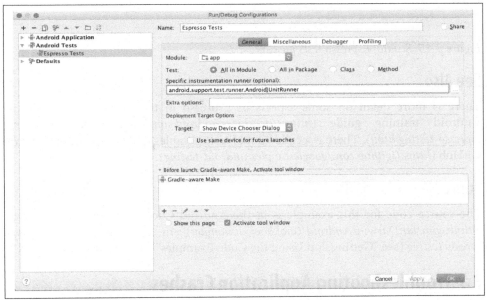

Figure 3-14. Studio: Creating an Espresso test/run configuration

Now you can run your tests using this configuration. As always, you should get a green bar, as shown in Figure 3-15.

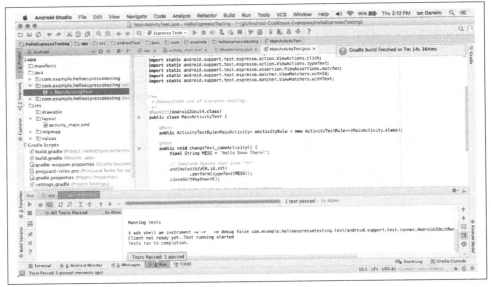

Figure 3-15. Studio: Espresso tests passing

See Also

There is more detail on some aspects of Espresso in the "Automating UI Tests" Android training guide (*https://developer.android.com/training/testing/ui-testing/ espresso-testing.html*). There is a collection of test examples in different styles at the on GitHub (*https://github.com/googlesamples/android-testing*).

Source Download URL

The source code for this example is in the Android Cookbook repository (*https:// github.com/IanDarwin/Android-Cookbook-Examples*), in the subdirectory *HelloE-spressoTesting* (see "Getting and Using the Code Examples" on page 18).

3.7 Troubleshooting Application Crashes

Ulysses Levy

Problem

Your app crashes and you are not sure why (see Figure 3-16).

Solution

Begin by viewing the log.

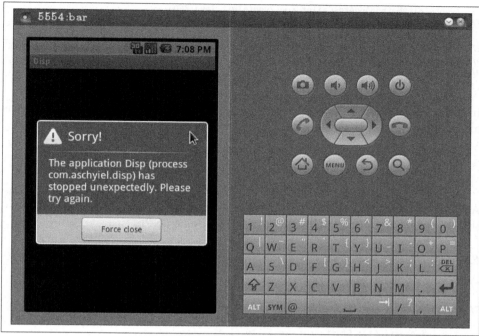

Figure 3-16. What an app crash looks like

Discussion

We can use the `adb logcat` command or the IDE LogCat window to view our AVD's log. Example 3-6 shows how to find the failure location by looking in the stack trace using `adb logcat`.

Example 3-6. The permission denied stack trace

```
E/DatabaseUtils( 53): Writing exception to `parcel
E/DatabaseUtils( 53): java.lang.SecurityException: Permission Denial: writing
    com.android.providers.settings.SettingsProvider uri content://settings/system
    from pid=430, uid=10030 requires android.permission.WRITE_SETTINGS
E/DatabaseUtils( 53): at android.content.ContentProvider$Transport.
    enforceWritePermission(ContentProvider.java:294)
E/DatabaseUtils( 53): at android.content.ContentProvider$Transport.
    insert(ContentProvider.java:149)
E/DatabaseUtils( 53): at android.content.ContentProviderNative.
    onTransact(ContentProviderNative.java:140)
E/DatabaseUtils( 53): at android.os.Binder.execTransact(Binder.java:287)
E/DatabaseUtils( 53): at com.android.server.SystemServer.init1(Native Method)
E/DatabaseUtils( 53): at com.android.server.SystemServer.main(SystemServer.java:497)
E/DatabaseUtils( 53): at java.lang.reflect.Method.invokeNative(Native Method)
E/DatabaseUtils( 53): at java.lang.reflect.Method.invoke(Method.java:521)
E/DatabaseUtils( 53): at com.android.internal.os.
```

```
          ZygoteInit$MethodAndArgsCaller.run(ZygoteInit.java:860)
E/DatabaseUtils( 53): at com.android.internal.os
    .ZygoteInit.main(ZygoteInit.java:618)
E/DatabaseUtils( 53): at dalvik.system.NativeStart.main(Native Method)
D/AndroidRuntime( 430): Shutting down VM
W/dalvikvm( 430): threadid=3: thread exiting with uncaught exception
...
```

In Example 3-6, we have a permission issue. The solution in this particular instance is to add the WRITE_SETTINGS permission to our *AndroidManifest.xml* file:

```
<manifest ... >
    <application ... />
    <uses-permission android:name="android.permission.WRITE_SETTINGS" />
</manifest>
```

Another fairly common error is the Null Pointer Exception (NPE). Example 3-7 shows the LogCat output you might see when getting an NPE.

Example 3-7. LogCat output

```
I/ActivityManager( 53): Displayed activity com.android.launcher/.Launcher:
    28640 ms (total 28640 ms)
I/ActivityManager( 53): Starting activity: Intent { act=android.intent.action.MAIN
    cat=[android.intent.category.LAUNCHER] flg=0x10200000 cmp=com.aschyiel.disp/.Disp }
I/ActivityManager( 53): Start proc com.aschyiel.disp for
    activity com.aschyiel.disp/.Disp: pid=214 uid=10030 gids={1015}
I/ARMAssembler( 53): generated scanline__00000177:03515104_00000001_00000000 [ 73 ipp]
    (95 ins) at [0x47c588:0x47c704] in 2087627 ns
I/ARMAssembler( 53): generated scanline__00000077:03545404_00000004_00000000 [ 47 ipp]
    (67 ins) at [0x47c708:0x47c814] in 1834173 ns
I/ARMAssembler(    53): generated scanline__00000077:03010104_00000004_00000000 [ 22 ipp]
    (41 ins) at [0x47c818:0x47c8bc] in 653016 ns
D/AndroidRuntime( 214): Shutting down VM
W/dalvikvm( 214): threadid=3: thread exiting with uncaught exception (group=0x4001b188)
E/AndroidRuntime( 214): Uncaught handler: thread main exiting due to uncaught exception
E/AndroidRuntime( 214): java.lang.RuntimeException: Unable to start activity
    ComponentInfo{com.aschyiel.disp/com.aschyiel.disp.Disp}:java.lang.NullPointerException
E/AndroidRuntime( 214): at android.app.ActivityThread.performLaunchActivity(
    ActivityThread.java:2496)
E/AndroidRuntime( 214): at android.app.ActivityThread.handleLaunchActivity(
    ActivityThread.java:2512)
E/AndroidRuntime( 214): at android.app.ActivityThread.access$2200(
    ActivityThread.java:119)
E/AndroidRuntime( 214): at android.app.ActivityThread$H.handleMessage(
    ActivityThread.java:1863)
E/AndroidRuntime( 214): at android.os.Handler.dispatchMessage(Handler.java:99)
E/AndroidRuntime( 214): at android.os.Looper.loop(Looper.java:123)
E/AndroidRuntime( 214): at android.app.ActivityThread.main(ActivityThread.java:4363)
E/AndroidRuntime( 214): at java.lang.reflect.Method.invokeNative(Native Method)
E/AndroidRuntime( 214): at java.lang.reflect.Method.invoke(Method.java:521)
E/AndroidRuntime( 214): at com.android.internal.os.ZygoteInit$MethodAndArgsCaller.run(
    ZygoteInit.java:860)
E/AndroidRuntime( 214): at com.android.internal.os.ZygoteInit.main(ZygoteInit.java:618)
```

```
E/AndroidRuntime(  214): at dalvik.system.NativeStart.main(Native Method)
E/AndroidRuntime(  214): Caused by: java.lang.NullPointerException
E/AndroidRuntime(  214): at com.aschyiel.disp.Disp.onCreate(Disp.java:66)
E/AndroidRuntime(  214): at android.app.Instrumentation.callActivityOnCreate(
    Instrumentation.java:1047)
E/AndroidRuntime(  214): at android.app.ActivityThread.performLaunchActivity(
    ActivityThread.java:2459)
E/AndroidRuntime(  214): ... 11 more
```

The example code with the error looks like this:

```java
public class Disp extends Activity {
    private TextView foo;
    @Override
    public void onCreate( Bundle savedInstanceState ) {
        ...
        foo.setText("bar");
    }
}
```

The preceding code fails because we forgot to call `findViewById()` to assign "foo" a reference to the `TextView` instance. Here is the example code with the fix:

```java
public class Disp extends Activity {
    private TextView foo;
    @Override
    public void onCreate( Bundle savedInstanceState ) {
        ...
        foo = (TextView) findViewById(R.id.id_foo);
        foo.setText("bar");
    }
}
```

This code should make the error go away.

See Also

Justin Mattson's Google I/O 2009 presentation (*https://www.youtube.com/watch?v=Dgnx0E7m1GQ*) "Debugging Arts of the Ninja Masters," Android Developers discussion on processes stopping unexpectedly (*https://groups.google.com/d/topic/android-developers/kup3bP1CqkU*).

3.8 Debugging Using Log.d() and LogCat

Rachee Singh

Problem

Usually the Java code compiles without errors, but sometimes a running application crashes, giving a "Force Close" (or similar) error message.

Solution

Debugging the code using LogCat messages is a useful technique for developers who find themselves in such a situation.

Discussion

Those who are familiar with traditional Java programming have probably used `System.out.println` statements while debugging their code. Similarly, debugging an Android application can be facilitated by using the `Log.d()` method. This enables you to print necessary values and messages in the LogCat window. Start by importing the `Log` class:

```
import android.util.Log;
```

Then, insert the following line at places in the code where you wish to check the status of the application:

```
Log.d("Testing", "Checkpoint 1");
```

`Testing` is the tag that appears in the "tag" column in the LogCat window, as shown in Figure 3-17; normally this would be defined as a constant in the main class to ensure consistent spelling. `Checkpoint 1` is the message that appears in the Message column in the LogCat window. `Log.d()` takes these two arguments. Corresponding to these, an appropriate message is displayed in the LogCat window. So, if you have inserted this `Log.d` statement as a checkpoint and you get the `Checkpoint 1` message displayed in the LogCat window, it implies that the code works fine up to that point.

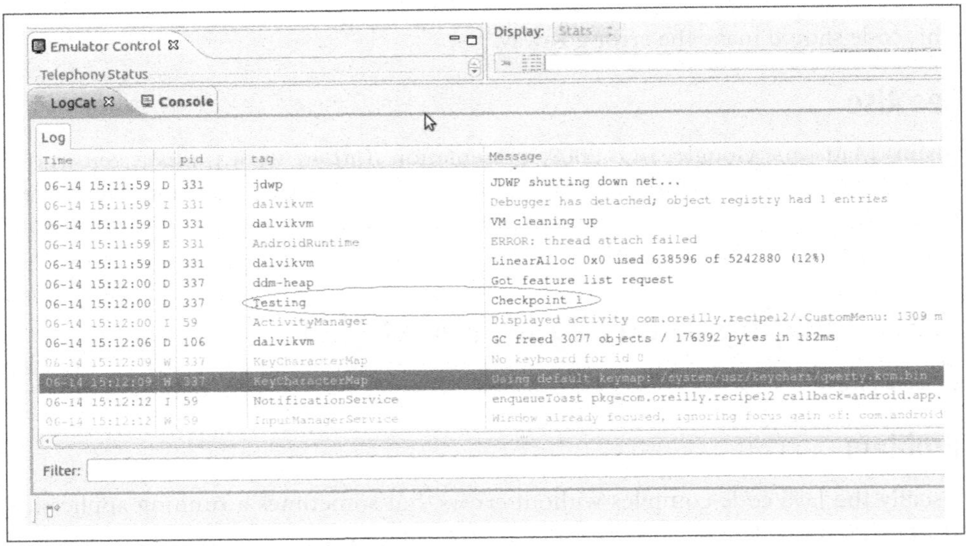

Figure 3-17. Debugging output

The `Log.d()` method does not accept variable arguments, so if you wish to format more than one item, use string concatenation or `String.format()` (but omit the trailing %n):

```
Log.d("Testing", String.format("x0 = %5.2f, x1=%5.2f", x0, x1));
```

3.9 Getting Bug Reports Automatically with Crash Reporting

Ian Darwin

Problem

Users don't necessarily inform you every time your app crashes, and when they do, often important details are omitted. You'd like a service that catches every exception and reports it in detail.

Solution

There are both open source and commercial technologies for reporting application crashes. One of the widely used open source ones is Application Crash Reports for Android (ACRA). ACRA provides its own backend reporting tool (*https:// github.com/ACRA/acralyzer*) but also supports Google Docs and many other backends. If you have your own Java EE server, you can use the author's own CrashBurn-Free service, which also works on non-Android implementations of Java. Alternatively, you can sign up for one of the commercial services. With most of these, you just add one JAR file and one call to your app. Then sit back and await notifications, or view the appropriate web dashboard for lists of errors and detail pages.

Discussion

There is no magic to crash reporting, and it doesn't provide anything that you can't do yourself. But it's already done for you, so just use it!

The basic steps to use ACRA are:

1. Decide on which server/backend you're going to use.

2. Add one JAR file to your project.

3. Annotate your `Application` class (see Recipe 2.3) to indicate that it's an ACRA-enabled application.

The basic steps to use CrashBurnFree are:

1. Download the server JAR, or, build it (*https://github.com/IanDarwin/CrashBurn Free*), or deploy it to your server.

2. Configure a security key for your own use on the server.

3. Add one JAR file to your project.

4. Add one call (using the security key) into your `Application` class or main Activity's `onCreate()` method.

Step 1 is out of scope for this book; if you have a Java EE server you can probably handle it.

To use one of the commercial services, use these steps (for example, Splunk MINT (*https://mint.splunk.com*), formerly BugSense—the process is similar):

1. Create an account.

2. Register your app and retrieve its unique key from the service's website.

3. Download a JAR file from the website and add it to your project.

4. Add one call (using the app's unique key) into your `Application` class or main Activity's `onCreate()` method.

After these steps are done, you can distribute your app to users. The first one or two steps are straightforward, so we won't discuss them further. The remaining steps require a little more detail, and we discuss them in the following subsections.

Project setup

The JAR file for ACRA can be added using the following Maven coordinates (if you use Gradle, you know how to trim this down):

```
<dependency>
    <groupId>ch.acra</groupId>
    <artifactId>acra</artifactId>
    <version>v4.9.0</version>
</dependency>
```

Similarly, for CrashBurnFree:

```
<dependency>
    <groupId>com.darwinsys</groupId>
    <artifactId>crashburnfree-javaclient</artifactId>
    <version>1.0.2</version>
</dependency>
```

The JAR file for Splunk MINT is *mint-5.2.1.jar* (*https://docs.splunk.com/Documenta tion/MintAndroidSDK/5.2.x/DevGuide/Requirementsandinstallation*). You probably know how to add JARs to your project; if not, see Recipe 1.20.

Because this mechanism reports errors via the internet, the following should go without saying (but let me say it anyway): you need internet permission to use it! Add the following code to your *AndroidManifest.xml* file:

```
<uses-permission android:name="android.permission.INTERNET" />
```

Requesting crash reporting at app start

You usually only need to make one call, in your `Application` class or Activity's `onCreate()` method.

For ACRA, you annotate your `Application` class:

```java
import org.acra.*;
import org.acra.annotation.*;

@ReportsCrashes(formUri = "http://somereportingbackend.com/somereportpath")
public class MyApplication extends Application {
  @Override
  public void onCreate() {
    super.onCreate();
    ACRA.init(this);
    ...
  }
}
```

Here is the code in the `onCreate()` method for CrashBurnFree:

```java
final long KEY = 12345;
final String PASS = "some enchanted evening";
final String url = "https://REST URL to your server";
@Override
public void onCreate() {
    super.onCreate();
    setContentView(R.layout.main);
    CrashBurnFree.register(url, key, pass);
    ...
}
```

And here is the code in the `onCreate()` method for BugSense:

```java
private static final String KEY = "... your key here ...";

@Override
public void onCreate() {
    super.onCreate();
    setContentView(R.layout.main);
    Mint.setApplicationEnvironment(Mint.appEnvironmentStaging);
    Mint.initAndStartSession(this.getApplication(), "YOUR_API_KEY");
    ...
}
```

See Also

To learn how these programs catch uncaught exceptions, see Recipe 14.10 in *Java Cookbook*, Third edition, "Catching and Formatting GUI Exceptions," where the technique is used for similar reporting in desktop applications. See also the source code for CrashBurnFree, available on GitHub (*https://github.com/IanDarwin/CrashBurnFree*).

You can get some crash reports using only the Google Play Console web reporting page, which is accessible after you log in. There are other tools in the same problem space, listed in the online version of this book (*http://androidcookbook.com/r/5139*).

3.10 Using a Local Runtime Application Log for Analysis of Field Errors or Situations

Atul Nene

Problem

Users reported something about your app that you don't think should happen, but now that the release mode app is on the market, you have no way to find out what's going on in the users' environment, and bug reports end up in a "cannot reproduce" scenario.

Solution

LogCat output is great as far as it goes, but a longer-term logging mechanism will be more useful in some circumstances. Design a built-in mechanism for your app that will give additional insight in such cases. You know the important events or state changes and resource needs of your app, and if you log them in a runtime application log from the app, the log becomes an additional much-needed resource that goes to the heart of the issue being reported and investigated. This simple preventive measure and mechanism goes a long way toward reducing low user ratings caused by unforeseen situations, and improves the quality of the overall user experience.

One solution is to use the Java standard `java.util.logging` package. This recipe provides an example `RuntimeLog`, which uses `java.util.logging` to write to a logfile on the device, and gives the developer extensive control over what level of detail is recorded.

Discussion

You have designed, developed, and tested your application and released it on the Google Play Store, so now you think you can take a vacation. Not so fast! Apart from the simplest cases, one cannot take care of all possible scenarios during app testing, and users are bound to report some unexpected app behavior. It doesn't have to be a bug; it might simply be a runtime situation you didn't encounter in your testing. Prepare for this in advance by designing a runtime application log mechanism into your app.

Log the most important events from your app—for example, a state change, a resource timeout (internet access, thread wait), or a maxed-out retry count. It might even be worthwhile to defensively log an unexpected code path execution in a strange scenario, or some of the most important notifications that are sent to the user.

 Only create log statements that will provide insight into how the app is working. Otherwise, the large size of the log itself may become a problem, and while Log.d() calls are ignored at runtime in signed apps, too many log statements may still slow down the app.

You may be wondering why we don't use LogCat, or tools like BugSense and ACRA (see Recipe 3.9), to handle this task. These solutions do not suffice in all cases, for the following reasons:

- The standard LogCat mechanism isn't useful in end-user runtime scenarios since the user is unlikely to have the ability to attach a debugger to her device. Too many Log.d and Log.i statements in your code may negatively impact app performance. In fact, for this reason, you shouldn't have Log.* statements compiled into the released app.

- Tools like ACRA and BugSense work well when the device is connected to the internet, but it may not always have a connection, and some classes of applications may not require one at all except for ACRA. Also, the ACRA stack trace provides only the details (in the stack trace) at the instant the exception was thrown, while this recipe provides a longer-term view while the app is running.

The RuntimeLog class is shown in Example 3-8.

Example 3-8. The RuntimeLog class

```
import java.util.logging.*;

/** Runtime file-based logging, using standard java.util.logging (JUL).
 * It is REALLY too bad that JUL was added before Java enums!
 */
public class RuntimeLog {
    // The JUL log levels are:
    // SEVERE (highest value)
    // WARNING
    // INFO
    // CONFIG
```

```
// FINE
// FINER
// FINEST (lowest value)

// Change this to MODE_DEBUG to use for in-house debugging
enum Mode {
    MODE_DEBUG,
    MODE_RELEASE
}
private static final Mode mode = Mode.MODE_RELEASE;
private static String logfileName = "/sdcard/YourAppName.log";
private static Logger logger;

// Initialize the log on first use of the class and
// create a custom log formatter

static {
    try {
        FileHandler fh = new FileHandler(logfileName, true);
        fh.setFormatter(new Formatter() {
            public String format(LogRecord rec) {
                java.util.Date date = new java.util.Date();
                return new StringBuffer(1000)
                        .append((date.getYear())).append('/')
                        .append(date.getMonth()).append('/')
                        .append(date.getDate())
                        .append(' ')
                        .append(date.getHours())
                        .append(':')
                        .append(date.getMinutes()).append(':')
                        .append(date.getSeconds())
                        .append('\n')
                        .toString();
            }
        });
        logger = Logger.getLogger(logfileName);
        logger.addHandler(fh);
    }
    catch (IOException e) {
        e.printStackTrace();
    }
}

// The log method
public static void log(Level logLevel, String msg) {
    // Don't log DEBUG and VERBOSE statements in release mode
    if (mode == Mode.MODE_RELEASE &&
            logLevel.intValue() >= Level.FINE.intValue())
        return;
    final LogRecord record = new LogRecord(logLevel, msg);
    record.setLoggerName(logfileName);
    logger.log(record);
}

/**
 * Reveal the logfile path, so part of your app can read the
```

```
 * logfile and either email it to you, or
 * upload it to your server via REST
 * @return
 */
public static String getFileName() {
    return logfileName;
}
}
```

This code has the advantage of automatically dropping verbose-level log calls when in production mode. There are, of course, variations that could be used:

- You can use the same mechanism to uncover complex runtime issues while you are developing the app. To do so, set the Mode variable to MODE_DEBUG.

- For a complex app with many modules, it might be useful to add the module name to the log call, as an additional parameter.

- You can also extract the ClassName and MethodName from the LogRecord and add them to the log statements; however, it is not recommended that you do this for runtime logs.

Example 3-9 shows that basic use of this facility is as simple as regular Log.d() calls.

Example 3-9. Using the RuntimeLog class

```
RuntimeLog.log(Level.ERROR, "Network resource access request failed");
RuntimeLog.log(Level.WARNING, "App changed state to STRANGE_STATE");
...
```

The filename shouldn't be hardcoded, but should be obtained as in Recipe 10.1. Even better, create a directory, with logfile rotation (delete logfiles that are older than a certain age deemed no longer useful) to limit the disk storage of the logfiles.

To allow users to send the logfile(s) from their devices to your support team, you would certainly want to write code to automate this, using the getLogfileName() method to access the file. Or you could use the same Java language hooks as the crash recorders (see Recipe 3.9) use, and send the file automatically upon detecting an application crash.

This mechanism does not have to be in an "always on" state. You can log based on a user-settable configuration option and enable it only when end users are trying to reproduce problem scenarios.

See Also

Recipe 3.8, Recipe 3.9.

3.11 Reproducing Activity Life-Cycle Scenarios for Testing

Daniel Fowler

Problem

Apps should be resilient to the Activity life cycle. Developers need to know how to reproduce different life-cycle scenarios.

Solution

Use logging to get a good understanding of the Activity life cycle. Life-cycle scenarios are then easier to reproduce for app testing.

Discussion

Android is designed for life on the go, where a user is engaged in multiple tasks: taking calls, checking email, sending SMS messages, engaging in social networking, taking pictures, accessing the internet, running apps—maybe even getting some work done! As such, a device can have multiple apps, and hence many Activities, loaded in memory.

The foreground app and its current Activity can be interrupted and paused at any moment. Apps, and hence Activities, that are paused can be removed from memory to free up space for newly started apps. An app has a life cycle that it cannot control, as it is the Android operating system that starts, monitors, pauses, resumes, and destroys the app's Activities. Yet an Activity does know what is going on, because as Activities are instantiated, hidden, and destroyed, various functions are called. This allows the Activity to keep track of what the operating system is doing to the app, as discussed in Recipe 1.2.

Because of all this, app developers become familiar with the functions invoked when an Activity starts:

- `onCreate(Bundle savedInstanceState){…};`
- `onStart(){…};`
- `onResume(){…};`

and with the functions called when an Activity is paused and then removed from memory (destroyed):

- `onPause(){…};`
- `onStop(){…};`

- onDestroy(){…};

It is easy to see these functions in action. Create a simple app in Android Studio and, in the first loaded Activity, override the preceding functions, calling through to the superclass versions. Add a call to Log.d() to pass in the name of the app and the function being invoked. (Here, for a basic app, the application name is set to MyAndroid and an empty Activity is used. Note that by default Studio uses the AppCompatActivity class, which is derived from Activity.) The MainActivity code will look like Example 3-10.

Example 3-10. Life-cycle logging

```
public class Main extends Activity {
    @Override
    public void onCreate(Bundle savedInstanceState) {
        super.onCreate(savedInstanceState);
        setContentView(R.layout.main);
        Log.d("MyAndroid", "onCreate");
    }
    @Override
    public void onStart() {
        super.onStart();
        Log.d("MyAndroid", "onStart");
    }
    @Override
    public void onResume() {
        super.onResume();
        Log.d("MyAndroid","onResume");
    }
    @Override
    public void onPause() {
        super.onPause();
        Log.d("MyAndroid","onPause");
    }
    public void onStop() {
        super.onStop();
        Log.d("MyAndroid","onStop");
    }
    public void onDestroy() {
        super.onDestroy();
        Log.d("MyAndroid","onDestroy");
    }
}
```

(There are other ways to print the program name and function name in Java, but hardcoded strings are used here for convenience and simplicity.)

Run the program on a device (virtual or physical) to see the debug messages in Logcat. If Logcat isn't visible, open the Android Monitor (click the button at the bottom of the main Studio window, or use the View → Tool Windows menu, or press Alt-6). When the Back button is pressed, the three teardown messages are seen, as in Figure 3-18.

To see only the messages from the app, add a Logcat filter: use the last drop-down above the Logcat display area to select Edit Filter Configuration. In the Create New Logcat Filter dialog, give the filter a name; here we used "MyAndroid." The Log Tag is used for filtering (the first parameter of the Log.d() call; again set to "MyAndroid"). Logcat will now show only the messages explicitly sent from the app (see Figure 3-19).

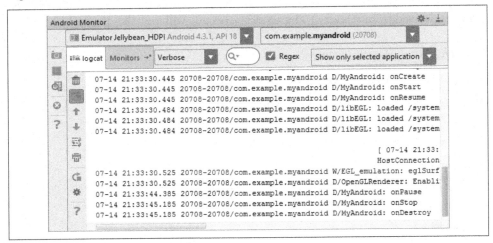

Figure 3-18. The Android Monitor

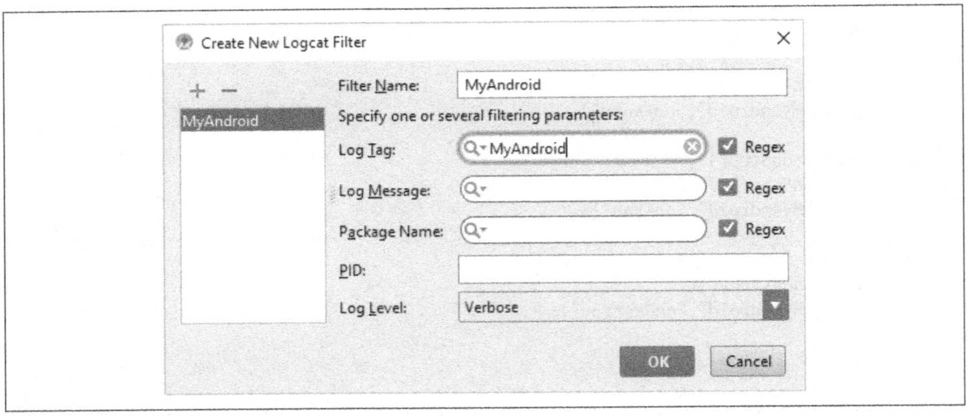

Figure 3-19. Filtering with Logcat

The Logcat output can be further simplified by changing the header configuration (use the gear icon to the left of the Logcat area). The LogCat output can be cleared by clicking the trash can icon to the left of the Logcat area. It is useful to have a clean sheet before performing an action to watch for more messages.

To see the functions called when a program is paused, open another application while the MyAndroid program is running. The code for the onRestart() method is key here. Create the function for onRestart(), and this debug message:

```
@Override
public void onRestart() {
    super.onRestart();
    Log.d("MyAndroid","onRestart");
}
```

Run the program, click the Home button, and then launch the program again from the device (or emulator). You should see output similar to that in Figure 3-20.

Figure 3-20. Filtered, with onRestart()

Logcat shows the usual start-up function sequence; then, when the Home button is clicked, onPause() and onStop() run, but not onDestroy(). The program is not ending but effectively sleeping. When the program is run again it isn't reloaded, so no onCreate() executes; instead, onRestart() is called.

Run the program again, then swipe it from the screen in tiled view to kill it (or go into Apps via Settings, select the program, and then press the Force Close button). Then start the app again.

The usual start-up functions (onStart() and onResume()) are invoked, and then the Activity "sleeps." No onDestroy() is seen as the second instance is run (see Figure 3-21).

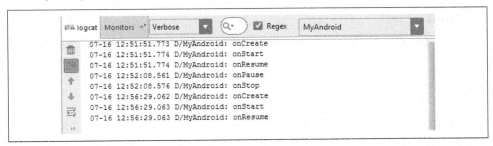

Figure 3-21. Force-stop messages

In this recipe, we discussed the following different life-cycle scenarios:

- Normal start-up and then finish
- Start-up, pause, and then restart
- Start-up, pause, forced removal from memory, and then start-up again

These scenarios result in different sequences of life-cycle functions being executed. Using these scenarios when testing ensures that an app performs correctly for a user. You can extend the techniques described here when implementing additional over-ridden functions. These techniques also apply to using Fragments in an Activity and testing their life cycle.

See Also

Recipe 1.2, Recipe 1.15, and the developer documentation on the `Activity` class (*https://developer.android.com/reference/android/app/Activity.html*), the `Log` class (*https://developer.android.com/reference/android/util/Log.html*), and Fragments (*https://developer.android.com/guide/topics/fundamentals/fragments.html*).

Source Download URL

The code for this recipe can be downloaded from Tek Eye (*http://tekeye.uk/android/examples/download/lifecycletesting.zip*).

3.12 Keeping Your App Snappy with StrictMode

Adrian Cowham

Problem

You want to make sure your app's GUI is as snappy as possible.

Solution

Android has a tool called `StrictMode` that will detect all cases where an "Application Not Responding" (ANR) error might occur. For example, it will detect and log to Logcat all database reads and writes that happen on the main thread (i.e., the GUI thread).

Discussion

I wish I could have used a tool like `StrictMode` back when I was doing Java Swing desk-top development. Making sure our Java Swing app was snappy was a constant chal-lenge: green and seasoned engineers alike would invariably perform database operations on the UI thread that would cause the app to hiccup. Typically, we found these hiccups when QA (or customers) used the app with a larger data set than the engineers were testing with. Having QA find these little defects was unacceptable, and ultimately a waste of everyone's time (and the company's money). We eventually solved the problem by investing more heavily in peer reviews, but having a tool like StrictMode would have been comparatively cheaper.

The following example code illustrates how easy it is to turn on StrictMode in your app:

```
// Make sure you import StrictMode
import android.os.StrictMode;

// In your app's Application or Activity instance, add the following
// lines to the onCreate() method
if (Build.VERSION.SDK_INT >= 9 && isDebug() ) {
  StrictMode.enableDefaults();
}
```

Please note that I have intentionally omitted the isDebug() implementation, as the logic of that depends on your application. I recommend only enabling StrictMode when your app is in debug mode; it's unwise to put your app in the Google Play Store with StrictMode running in the background and consuming resources unnecessarily.

See Also

StrictMode is highly configurable, allowing you to customize what problems to look for. For detailed information on customizing StrictMode policies, see the developer documentation (*https://developer.android.com/reference/android/os/StrictMode.html*).

3.13 Static Code Testing with Android Lint

Ian Darwin

Problem

Your code looks OK, but you want to see if it passes muster when subjected to expert scrutiny.

Solution

Run your code through Android Lint (included with modern versions of the Android SDK and supported by the relevant versions of the IDE plug-ins). Examine the warnings, and improve the code where it needs it.

Discussion

The first "lint" program originated at Bell Laboratories, in Seventh Edition Unix. Steve Johnson wrote it as an offshoot of his development of the first Portable C Compiler, in the late 1970s. It was covered in my little book *Checking C Programs with Lint* (O'Reilly). Ever since, people have been writing lint-like tools. Some well-known ones for Java code include PMD, FindBugs, and Checkstyle. The first two, plus a number of other tools, are covered in my 2007 book *Checking Java Programs* (O'Reilly). The most recent one that's relevant to us is, of course, Android Lint, a part of the standard Android SDK.

What each of these tools does is examine your code, and offer opinions based on expert-level knowledge of the language and libraries. The hard part is to bear in mind that they are only opinions. There will be cases where you think you know better than the tool, and you later find out that you're wrong. But there will be cases where you're right. And, of course, it's impossibly hard for the computer to know which, so there is no substitute for the judgment of an experienced developer!

These tools typically find a lot of embarrassing issues in your code the first time you run them. One very common error is to create a toast by calling makeText(), and forget to call the new toast's show() method; the toast is created but never pops up! The standard compiler cannot catch this kind of error, but Android Lint can, and that is just one of its many capabilities. After laughing at yourself for a minute, you can edit (and test!) your code, and run lint again. You repeat this process until you no longer get any messages that you care about.

To run Android Lint, you can use the command-line version in *$SDK_HOME/tools/lint*. Under Eclipse, you invoke Android Lint by right-clicking the project in the Project Explorer and selecting Android Tools → Run Lint. The warnings appear as code markers just like the ones from Eclipse itself. Since they are not managed by the Eclipse compiler, you may need to run lint again after editing your code. If you get tired of the game, you can use the same menu to remove the lint markers. Under Android Studio, the Analyze → Inspect Code tool actually runs Android Lint. Example 3-11 shows the command-line version of lint since that's the clearest way to show in print some examples of the errors it catches; rest assured it will catch the same errors when run under an IDE, though the messages may be less verbose.

Example 3-11. Running lint from the command line

```
$ cd MyAndroidProject
$ lint .
Scanning .: ......
Scanning . (Phase 2): ..
AndroidManifest.xml:16: Warning: <uses-sdk> tag should specify a target API level
  (the highest verified version; when running on later versions, compatibility
  behaviors may be enabled) with android:targetSdkVersion="?" [UsesMinSdkAttributes]
```

```
    <uses-sdk android:minSdkVersion="7" />

AndroidManifest.xml:16: Warning: <uses-sdk> tag appears after <application> tag
[ManifestOrder]
    <uses-sdk android:minSdkVersion="7" />

AndroidManifest.xml:6: Warning: Should explicitly set android:allowBackup to true or
false (it's true by default, and that can have some security implications for the
application's data) [AllowBackup]
    <application android:icon="@drawable/icon" android:label="@string/app_name">
    ^
res/values/strings.xml:5: Warning: The resource R.string.addAccounrSuccess appears to
  be unused [UnusedResources]
    <string name="addAccounrSuccess">Account created</string>

res/values/strings.xml:6: Warning: The resource R.string.addAccounrFailure appears to
  be unused [UnusedResources]
    <string name="addAccounrFailure">Account creation failed</string>

res: Warning: Missing density variation folders in res: drawable-xhdpi
[IconMissingDensityFolder]
0 errors, 6 warnings
$
```

Nothing serious was found in this project, but several things can be cleaned up
quickly and easily. Of course the unused string resources don't need any action if they
are intended for future use, but if they are old and have fallen out of use, you should
remove them to keep your app clean. As with any automated tool, you know your app
better than the tool does, at least for making such decisions.

See Also

The developer documentation on checking code with lint (*https://devel
oper.android.com/tools/debugging/improving-w-lint.html*), my book *Checking Java Programs*, my video training series Java Testing for Developers, and my older book
Checking C Programs with Lint (all from O'Reilly Media).

3.14 Dynamic Testing with the Monkey Program

Adrian Cowham

Problem

You want some good random usage testing of your application.

Solution

Use the Android Monkey command-line tool to test applications you are developing.

Discussion

Testing is so easy a monkey can do it, literally. Despite the limitations of testing tools for Android, I have to admit that the Monkey is pretty cool. The Android Monkey is a testing tool (included with the Android SDK) that simulates a monkey (or perhaps a child) using an Android device. Imagine a monkey sitting at a keyboard and flailing away—get the idea? What better way to flush out those hidden ANR messages?

Running the Monkey is as simple as starting the emulator (or connecting your development device to your development machine) and launching the Monkey script. I hate to admit this, but by running the Monkey on a daily basis, we've repeatedly found defects that probably would've escaped a normal QA pass and would've been very challenging to troubleshoot if found in the field—or, worse yet, caused users to stop using our app.

Here are a few best practices for using the Monkey in your development process:

- Create your own Monkey script that wraps Android's Monkey script. This is to ensure that all the developers on your team are running the Monkey with the same parameters. If you're a team of one, this helps with predictability (discussed shortly).

- Configure the Monkey so that it runs long enough to catch defects but not so long that it's a productivity killer. In our development process, we configured the Monkey to run for a total of 50,000 events. This took about 40 minutes on a Samsung Galaxy Tab. Not too bad, but I would've liked it to be in the 30-minute range. Obviously, faster tablets will have a higher throughput.

- The Monkey is random, so when we first started running it, every developer was getting different results and we were unable to reproduce defects. We then figured out that the Monkey allows you to set the seed for its random number generator. So, configure your wrapper script to set the Monkey's seed. This will ensure uniformity and predictability across Monkey runs in your development team.

- Once you gain confidence in your app with a specific seed value, change it, because you'll never know what the Monkey will find.

- Never run the Monkey on your production ("daily driver") phone, as it will occasionally escape from the program under test and "creatively" alter settings in other apps!

Here is a Monkey script wrapper, followed by a description of its arguments:

```
#!/bin/bash
# Utility script to run monkey
#
# See: https://developer.android.com/studio/test/monkey.html
```

```
rm tmp/monkey.log
adb shell monkey -p package_name --throttle 100 -s 43686 -v 50000 |
    tee tmp/monkey.log
```

- -p *package_name* will ensure that the Monkey only targets the package specified.
- --throttle is the delay between events.
- -s is the seed value.
- -v is the VERBOSE option.
- 50000 is the number of events the Monkey will simulate.

Many more configuration options are available for the Monkey; we deliberately chose not to mess around with what types of events the Monkey generates because we appreciate the pain. For example, the seed value we chose causes the Monkey to disable WiFi about halfway through the run. This was really frustrating at first because we felt like we weren't getting the coverage we wanted. It turns out that the Monkey did us a favor by disabling WiFi and then relentlessly playing with our app. After discovering and fixing a few defects, we soon had complete confidence that our app operated as expected without a network connection.

Good Monkey.

See Also

The developer documentation on the Monkey (*https://developer.android.com/studio/test/monkey.html*).

3.15 Sending Text Messages and Placing Calls Between AVDs

Johan Pelgrim

Problem

You have developed an app that needs to place or listen for calls or send or receive text messages, and you want to test this behavior.

Solution

Fire up two Android Virtual Devices and use the port number to send text messages and place calls.

Discussion

When you create an app that listens for incoming calls or text messages—similar to the one in Recipe 11.1—you can, of course, use the DDMS perspective in Eclipse to simulate placing calls or sending text messages. But you can also fire up another AVD!

If you look at the AVD window's title, you will see a number before your AVD's name. This is the port number that you can use to telnet to your AVD's shell (e.g., telnet localhost 5554). Fortunately, for testing purposes this number is your AVD's *phone number* as well, so you can use this number to place calls (see Figure 3-22) or to send a text (Figure 3-23).

See Also

Recipe 11.1.

Figure 3-22. Calling from one AVD to another

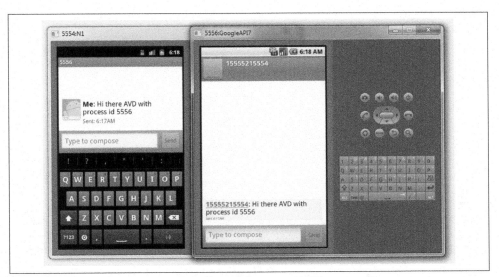

Figure 3-23. Sending a text message (SMS) from one AVD to another

## CHAPTER 4

Inter-/Intra-Process Communication

Android offers a unique collection of mechanisms for inter-application (and intra-application) communication. This chapter discusses the following:

Intents

Specify what you intend to do next: either to invoke a particular class within your application, or to invoke whatever application the user has configured to process a particular request on a particular type of data

Broadcast receivers

In conjunction with Intent filters, allow you to define an application as able to process a particular request on a particular type of data (i.e., the target of an Intent)

AsyncTasks

Allow you to specify long-running code that should not be on the "GUI thread" or "main event thread" to avoid slowing the app to the point that it gets ANR ("Application Not Responding") errors

Handlers

Allow you to queue up messages from a background thread to be handled by another thread such as the main Activity thread, usually to cause information to update the screen safely

4.1 Opening a Web Page, Phone Number, or Anything Else with an Intent

Ian Darwin

Problem

You want one application to have some entity processed by another application without knowing or caring what that other application is.

Solution

Invoke the `Intent` constructor; then invoke `startActivity()` on the constructed `Intent`.

Discussion

The `Intent` constructor takes two arguments: the action to take and the entity to act on. Think of the first as the verb and the second as the object of the verb. The most common action is `Intent.ACTION_VIEW`, for which the string representation is `android.intent.action.VIEW`. The second will typically be a URL or, in Android, a URI (uniform resource identifier). URI objects can be created using the static `parse()` method in the `Uri` class (note the two lowercase letters in the class name do not use the `URI` class from `java.net`). Assuming that the string variable `data` contains the location we want to view, the code to create an `Intent` for it might be something like the following:

```
Intent intent = new Intent(Intent.ACTION_VIEW, Uri.parse(data));
```

That's all! The beauty of Android is shown here—we don't know or care if `data` contains a web page URL with `http:`, a phone number with `tel:`, or even something we've never seen. As long as there is an application registered to process this type of Intent, Android will find it for us, after we invoke it. How do we invoke the Intent? Remember that Android will start a new Activity to run the Intent. Assuming the code is in an Activity, we just call the inherited `startIntent()` method. For example:

```
startActivity(intent);
```

If all goes well, the user will see the web browser, phone dialer, maps application, or whatever.

Google defines many other actions, such as `ACTION_OPEN` (which tries to open the named object). In some cases `VIEW` and `OPEN` will have the same effect, but in other cases the former may display data and the latter may allow the user to edit or update the data.

If the request fails because your particular device doesn't have a single Activity in all its applications that has said it can handle this particular Intent, the user will not see another Activity, but instead the `startActivity()` call will throw the unchecked `ActivityNotFoundException`.

And even if things do work, we won't find out about it. That's because we basically told Android that we don't care whether the Intent succeeds or fails. To get feedback, we would instead call `startActivityForResult()`:

```
startActivityForResult(intent, requestCode);
```

The `requestCode` is an arbitrary number used to keep track of multiple Intent requests; you should generally pick a unique number for each Intent you start, and keep track of these numbers to track the results later (if you only have one Intent whose results you care about, just use the number 1).

Just making this change will have no effect, however, unless we also override an important method in `Activity`:

```
@Override
public void onActivityResult(int requestCode, int resultCode, Intent data) {
    // Do something with the results...
}
```

It may be obvious, but it is important to note that you cannot know the result of an Intent until the Activity that was processing it is finished, which may be an arbitrary time later. However, `onActivityResult()` will eventually be called.

The `resultCode` is, of course, used to indicate success or failure. There are defined constants for these, notably `Activity.RESULT_OK` and `Activity.RESULT_CANCELED`. Some Intents provide their own, more specific result codes; for one example, see Recipe 9.7. For information on use of the passed Intent, please refer to recipes on passing extra data, such as Recipe 4.4.

The sample program attached to this recipe allows you to type in a URL and either OPEN or VIEW it, using the actions defined previously. Some example URLs that you might try are shown in the following table.

URL	Meaning	Note
http://www.google.com/	Web page	
content://contacts/people/	List of contacts	
content://contacts/people/1	Contact details for one person	
geo:50.123,7.1434?z=10	Location and zoom	Need Google API
geo:39.0997,-94.5783	Location	Need Google API

Source Download URL

The source code for this example is in the Android Cookbook repository (*https://github.com/IanDarwin/Android-Cookbook-Examples*), in the subdirectory *Intents-Demo* (see "Getting and Using the Code Examples" on page 18).

4.2 Emailing Text from a View

Wagied Davids

Problem

You want to send an email containing text or images from a view.

Solution

Pass the data to be emailed to the mail app as a parameter using an Intent.

Discussion

The steps for emailing text from a view are pretty straightforward:

1. Modify the *AndroidManifest.xml* file to allow for an internet connection so that email can be sent. This is shown in Example 4-1.

2. Create the visual presentation layer with an Email button that the user clicks. The layout is shown in Example 4-2, and the strings used to populate it are shown in Example 4-3.

3. Attach an OnClickListener to allow the email to be sent when the user clicks the Email button. The code for this is shown in Example 4-4.

Example 4-1. AndroidManifest.xml

```
<?xml version="1.0" encoding="utf-8"?>
<manifest
    xmlns:android="http://schemas.android.com/apk/res/android"
    package="com.examples"
    android:versionCode="1"
    android:versionName="1.0">

    <uses-permission
            android:name="android.permission.INTERNET" />

    <application
        android:icon="@drawable/icon"
        android:label="@string/app_name">
        <activity
```

```
            android:name=".Main"
            android:label="@string/app_name">
            <intent-filter>
                <action
                    android:name="android.intent.action.MAIN" />
                <category
                    android:name="android.intent.category.LAUNCHER" />
            </intent-filter>
        </activity>

    </application>
</manifest>
```

Example 4-2. Main.xml

```
<?xml version="1.0" encoding="utf-8"?>
<LinearLayout
    xmlns:android="http://schemas.android.com/apk/res/android"
    android:orientation="vertical"
    android:layout_width="fill_parent"
    android:layout_height="fill_parent">

    <Button
        android:id="@+id/emailButton"
        android:text="Email Text!"
        android:layout_width="fill_parent"
        android:layout_height="wrap_content">
    </Button>

    <TextView
        android:id="@+id/text_to_email"
        android:layout_width="fill_parent"
        android:layout_height="wrap_content"
        android:text="@string/my_text" />

</LinearLayout>
```

Example 4-3. Strings.xml

```
<?xml version="1.0" encoding="utf-8"?>
<resources>
    <string
        name="hello">Hello World, Main!</string>
    <string
        name="app_name">EmailFromView</string>
    <string
        name="my_text">
        Lorem Ipsum is simply dummy text of the printing and typesetting industry.
        Lorem Ipsum has been the industry's standard dummy text ever since the 1500s,
        when an unknown printer took a galley of type and scrambled it to make a
        type specimen book. It has survived not only five centuries, but also the
        leap into electronic typesetting, remaining essentially unchanged. It was
        popularized in the 1960s with the release of Letraset sheets containing Lorem
        Ipsum passages, and more recently with desktop publishing software like
```

```
            Aldus PageMaker including versions of Lorem Ipsum.
</string>
</resources>
```

Example 4-4. Main.java

```java
import android.app.Activity;
import android.content.Intent;
import android.os.Bundle;
import android.view.View;
import android.view.View.OnClickListener;
import android.widget.Button;

public class Main extends Activity implements OnClickListener {
        private static final String TAG = "Main";
        private Button emailButton;

        /** Called when the Activity is first created. */
        @Override
        public void onCreate(Bundle savedInstanceState) {
                super.onCreate(savedInstanceState);

                // Set the view layer
                setContentView(R.layout.main);

                // Get reference to Email button
                this.emailButton = (Button) this.findViewById(R.id.emailButton);

                // Set the onClick event listener
                this.emailButton.setOnClickListener(this);

        }

        @Override
        public void onClick(View view) {
            if (view == this.emailButton) {
                Intent emailIntent = new Intent(Intent.ACTION_SEND);
                emailIntent.setType("text/html");
                emailIntent.putExtra(Intent.EXTRA_TITLE, "My Title");
                emailIntent.putExtra(Intent.EXTRA_SUBJECT, "My Subject");

                // Obtain reference to String and pass it to Intent
                emailIntent.putExtra(Intent.EXTRA_TEXT,
                    getString(R.string.my_text));
                startActivity(emailIntent);
            }
        }
    }
```

Source Download URL

The source code for this example is in the Android Cookbook repository (*https://github.com/IanDarwin/Android-Cookbook-Examples*), in the subdirectory *EmailText-View* (see "Getting and Using the Code Examples" on page 18).

4.3 Sending an Email with Attachments

Marco Dinacci

Problem

You want to send an email with attachments.

Solution

Create an Intent, add extended data to specify the file you want to include, and start a new Activity to allow the user to send the email.

Discussion

The easiest way to send an email is to create an Intent of type ACTION_SEND:

```
Intent intent = new Intent(Intent.ACTION_SEND);
intent.putExtra(Intent.EXTRA_SUBJECT, "Test single attachment");
intent.putExtra(Intent.EXTRA_EMAIL, new String[]{recipient_address});
intent.putExtra(Intent.EXTRA_TEXT, "Mail with an attachment");
```

To attach a single file, we add some extended data to our Intent:

```
intent.putExtra(Intent.EXTRA_STREAM, Uri.fromFile(new File("/path/to/file")));
intent.setType("text/plain");
```

The MIME type can always be set as text/plain, but you may want to be more specific so that applications parsing your message will work properly. For instance, if you're including a JPEG image you should write image/jpeg.

To send an email with multiple attachments, the procedure is slightly different, as shown in Example 4-5.

Example 4-5. Multiple attachments

```
Intent intent = new Intent(Intent.ACTION_SEND_MULTIPLE);
intent.setType("text/plain");
intent.putExtra(Intent.EXTRA_SUBJECT, "Test multiple attachments");
intent.putExtra(Intent.EXTRA_TEXT, "Mail with multiple attachments");
intent.putExtra(Intent.EXTRA_EMAIL, new String[]{recipient_address});

ArrayList<Uri> uris = new ArrayList<Uri>();
uris.add(Uri.fromFile(new File("/path/to/first/file")));
uris.add(Uri.fromFile(new File("/path/to/second/file")));

intent.putParcelableArrayListExtra(Intent.EXTRA_STREAM, uris);
```

First, you need to use Intent.ACTION_SEND_MULTIPLE, which has been available since Android 1.6. Second, you need to create an ArrayList with the URIs of the files you want to attach to the mail and call `putParcelableArrayListExtra()`. If you are sending different types of files you may want to use `multipart/mixed` as the MIME type.

Finally, in both cases, don't forget to start the desired Activity with the following code:

```
startActivity(this, intent);
```

Which mail program will be used if there's more than one on the device? If the user has previously made a choice that will be respected, but if the user hasn't selected an application to handle this type of Intent a chooser will be launched.

The example in the source download shows both the single attachment and multiple attachment options, each connected to a `Button` with obvious labeling. The multiple attachment button looks like Figure 4-1 in my email client.

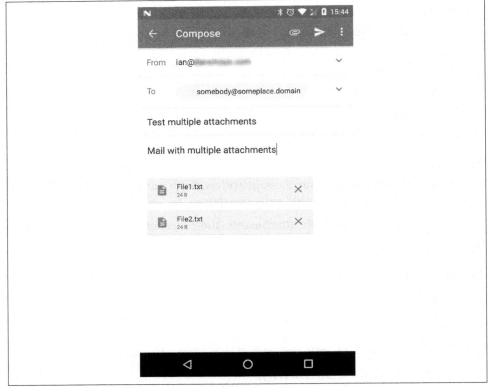

Figure 4-1. Email with multiple attachments

Source Download URL

The source code for this example is in the Android Cookbook repository (*https://github.com/IanDarwin/Android-Cookbook-Examples*), in the subdirectory *EmailWithAttachments* (see "Getting and Using the Code Examples" on page 18).

4.4 Pushing String Values Using Intent.putExtra()

Ulysses Levy

Problem

You need to pass some parameters into an Activity while launching it.

Solution

A quick solution is to use `Intent.putExtra()` to push the data. Then use `getIntent().getExtras().getString()` to retrieve it.

Discussion

Example 4-6 shows the code to push the data.

Example 4-6. The push data

```
import android.content.Intent;
    ...

    Intent intent =
        new Intent(
            this,
            MyActivity.class );
    intent.putExtra( "paramName", "paramValue" );
    startActivity( intent );
```

This code might be inside the main Activity. `MyActivity.class` is the second Activity we want to launch and it must be explicitly included in your *AndroidManifest.xml* file:

```
<activity android:name=".MyActivity" />
```

Example 4-7 shows the code to pull the data in the target (receiving) Activity.

Example 4-7. The code to pull the data

```
import android.os.Bundle;

    ...

    Bundle extras = getIntent().getExtras();
```

```
if (extras != null) {
    String myParam = extras.getString("paramName");
}
else {
    //Oops!
}
```

In this example, the code would be inside your main *Activity.java* file.

In addition to Strings, the Bundle (the "extras") can contain several other types of data; see the documentation for Bundle for a complete list.

See Also

The blog post "Playing with Intents" (*http://mylifewithandroid.blogspot.com/2007/12/playing-with-intents.html*), the developer documentation on `Intent.putExtra()` (*https://developer.android.com/reference/android/content/Intent.html#putExtra(java.lang.String,%20android.os.Bundle)*).

4.5 Retrieving Data from a Subactivity Back to Your Main Activity

Ulysses Levy

Problem

Your main Activity needs to retrieve data from another Activity, sometimes informally called a "subactivity."

Solution

Use `startActivityForResult()`, `onActivityResult()` in the main Activity, and `setResult()` in the subactivity.

Discussion

In this example, we return a string from a subactivity (`MySubActivity`) back to the main Activity (`MyMainActivity`). The first step is to "push" data from `MyMainActivity` via the `Intent` mechanism (see Example 4-8).

Example 4-8. The push data from the Activity

```
public class MyMainActivity extends Activity
{
    //For logging
    private static final String TAG = "MainActivity";
```

```
//The request code is supposed to be unique
public static final int MY_REQUEST_CODE = 123;

@Override
public void onCreate( Bundle savedInstanceState ) {
    ...
}

private void pushFxn() {
    Intent intent =
        new Intent(
            this,
            MySubActivity.class );

    startActivityForResult( intent, MY_REQUEST_CODE );
}

protected void onActivityResult(
        int requestCode,
        int resultCode,
        Intent pData) {
    if ( requestCode == MY_REQUEST_CODE ) {
        if (resultCode == Activity.RESULT_OK ) {
            final String zData = pData.getExtras().getString
                ( MySubActivity.EXTRA_STRING_NAME );

            //Do something with our retrieved value

            Log.v( TAG, "Retrieved Value zData is "+zData );
            //Logcats "Retrieved Value zData is returnValueAsString"

        }
    }

}
}
```

There will be a button with an event listener that calls the pushFxn() method; this starts the subactivity. In Example 4-8, the following occurs:

- The main Activity's onActivityResult() method gets called after MySubActivity.finish().

- The retrieved value is technically an Intent, and so we could use it for more complex data (such as a URI to a Google contact). However, in Example 4-8, we are only interested in a string value via Intent.getExtras().

- The requestCode (MY_REQUEST_CODE) is supposed to be unique, and is used to differentiate among multiple outstanding subactivity calls.

The second major step is to "pull" data back from MySubActivity to MyMainActivity (see Example 4-9).

Example 4-9. The pull data from the subactivity

```
public class MySubActivity extends Activity
{
    public static final String EXTRA_STRING_NAME = "extraStringName";

    @Override
    public void onCreate( Bundle savedInstanceState ) {
        ...
    }


    private void returnValuesFxn() {
        Intent iData = new Intent();
        iData.putExtra(
            EXTRA_STRING_NAME,
            "returnValueAsString" );

        setResult(
            android.app.Activity.RESULT_OK,
            iData );

        //Returns us to the parent "MyMainActivity"
        finish();
    }
}
```

Again, something in the `MySubActivity` will call the `returnValuesFxn()` method in Example 4-9. Note the following:

- Once again, Intents are used as data (i.e., `iData`).
- `setResult()` requires a result code such as `RESULT_OK`.
- `finish()` essentially pushes the result from `setResult()`.
- The data from `MySubActivity` doesn't get "pulled" until we're back on the other side with `MyMainActivity`, so arguably it is more similar to a second "push."
- We don't have to use a `public static final String` variable for our "extra" field name, but I chose to do so because I thought it was a good style.

Use case (informal)

In my app, I have a `ListActivity` with a `ContextMenu` (the user long-presses a selection to do something), and I wanted to let the `MainActivity` know which row the user had selected for the `ContextMenu` action (my app only has one action). I ended up using Intent extras to pass the selected row's index as a string back to the parent Activity; from there I could just convert the index back to an `int` and use it to identify the user's row selection via `ArrayList.get(index)`. This worked for me; however, I am sure there is another/better way.

See Also

Recipe 4.4, `resultCode` *"gotcha"* (*http://androidforums.com/application-development/ 102689-startactivityforresult.html*), `startActivityForResultExample` (under "Returning a Result from a Screen"); `Activity.startActivityForResult()` (*https://devel oper.android.com/reference/android/app/Activity.html#startActivityForRe sult(android.content.Intent, int))*.

4.6 Keeping a Background Service Running While Other Apps Are on Display

Ian Darwin

Problem

You want part of your application to continue running in the background while the user switches to interact with other apps.

Solution

Create a `Service` class to do the background work; start the Service from your main application. Optionally provide a Notification icon to allow the user either to stop the running Service or to resume the main application.

Discussion

A `Service` class (`android.app.Service`) runs as part of the same process as your main application, but keeps running even if the user switches to another app or goes to the Home screen and starts up a new app.

As you know by now, `Activity` classes can be started either by an Intent that matches their content provider or by an Intent that mentions them by class name. The same is true for Services. This recipe focuses on starting a Service directly; Recipe 4.1 covers starting a Service implicitly. The following example is taken from JPSTrack, a GPS tracking program for Android. Once you start tracking, you don't want the tracking to stop if you answer the phone or have to look at a map(!), so we made it into a Service. As shown in Example 4-10, the Service is started by the main Activity when you click the Start Tracking button, and is stopped by the Stop button. Note that this is so common that `startService()` and `stopService()` are built into the `Activity` class.

Example 4-10. The onCreate{} method

```
@Override
public void onCreate(Bundle savedInstanceState) {
    ...
```

```
        Intent theIntent = new Intent(this, TrackService.class);
        Button startButton = (Button) findViewById(R.id.startButton);
        startButton.setOnClickListener(new OnClickListener() {
                @Override
                public void onClick(View v) {
                    startService(theIntent);
                    Toast.makeText(Main.this, "Starting", Toast.LENGTH_LONG).show();
                }
        });
        Button stopButton = (Button) findViewById(R.id.stopButton);
        stopButton.setOnClickListener(new OnClickListener() {
                @Override
                public void onClick(View v) {
                    stopService(theIntent);
                    Toast.makeText(Main.this, "Stopped", Toast.LENGTH_LONG).show();
                }
        });
        ...
}
```

The `TrackService` class directly extends `Service`, so it has to implement the abstract
`onBind()` method. This is not used when the class is started directly, so it can be a stub
method. You will typically override at least the `onStartCommand()` and `onUnbind()` methods, to begin and end some Activity. Example 4-11 starts the GPS service sending us
notifications that we save to disk, and we do want that to keep running, hence this
`Service` class.

Example 4-11. The TrackService (GPS-using service) class

```
public class TrackService extends Service {
        private LocationManager mgr;
        private String preferredProvider;

        @Override
        public IBinder onBind(Intent intent) {
                return null;
        }

        @Override
        public int onStartCommand(Intent intent, int flags, int startId) {
                initGPS();       // Sets up the LocationManager mgr

                if (preferredProvider != null) {
                    mgr.requestLocationUpdates(preferredProvider, MIN_SECONDS * 1000,
                                MIN_METRES, this);
                        return START_STICKY;
                }
                return START_NOT_STICKY;
        }

        @Override
        public boolean onUnbind(Intent intent) {
                mgr.removeUpdates(this);
```

```
        return super.onUnbind(intent);
    }
```

You may have noticed the different return values from `onStartCommand()`. If you return `START_STICKY`, Android will restart your Service if it gets terminated. If you return `START_NOT_STICKY`, the Service will not be restarted automatically. These values are discussed in more detail in the online documentation for the `Service` class (*https://devel oper.android.com/reference/android/app/Service.html*). Remember to declare the `Service` subclass in the `Application` part of your *AndroidManifest.xml*:

```
<service android:enabled="true" android:name=".TrackService">
```

4.7 Sending/Receiving a Broadcast Message

Vladimir Kroz

Problem

You want to create an Activity that receives a simple broadcast message sent by another Activity.

Solution

Set up a broadcast receiver, instantiate the message receiver object, and create an `IntentFilter`. Then register your receiver with an Activity that must receive the broadcast message.

Discussion

The code in Example 4-12 sets up the broadcast receiver, instantiates the message receiver object, and creates the `IntentFilter`.

Example 4-12. Creating and registering the BroadcastReceiver

```
// Instantiate message receiver object. You should
// create this class by extending android.content.BroadcastReceiver.
// The method onReceive() of this class will be called when broadcast is sent.
MyBroadcastMessageReceiver _bcReceiver = new MyBroadcastMessageReceiver();

// Create IntentFilter
IntentFilter filter = new IntentFilter(MyBroadcastMessageReceiver.class.getName());

// Register your receiver with your Activity, which must receive broadcast messages.
// Now whenever this type of message is generated somewhere in the system the
// _bcReceiver.onReceive() method will be called within main thread of myActivity.
myActivity.registerReceiver(_bcReceiver, filter);
```

The code in Example 4-13 shows how to publish the broadcast event.

Example 4-13. Publishing the broadcast event

```
Intent intent = new Intent(MyBroadcastMessageReceiver.class.getName());
intent.putExtra("some additional data", choice);
someActivity.sendBroadcast(intent);
```

4.8 Starting a Service After Device Reboot

Ashwini Shahapurkar

Problem

You have a Service in your app and you want it to start after the phone reboots.

Solution

Listen to the Intent for boot events and start the Service when the event occurs.

Discussion

Whenever a platform boot is completed, an Intent is broadcast with the android.intent.action.BOOT_COMPLETED action. You need to register your application to receive this Intent, and to request permission for it. To do so, add the following code to your *AndroidManifest.xml* file:

```
<uses-permission android:name="android.permission.RECEIVE_BOOT_COMPLETED" />
<application>
    <receiver android:name=".ServiceManager">
            <intent-filter>
                <action android:name="android.intent.action.BOOT_COMPLETED" />
            </intent-filter>
    </receiver>
    ...
```

For ServiceManager to be the broadcast receiver that receives the Intent for the boot event, the ServiceManager class would be coded as shown in Example 4-14.

Example 4-14. The BroadcastReceiver implementation

```
public class ServiceManager extends BroadcastReceiver {

    Context mContext;
    private final String BOOT_ACTION = "android.intent.action.BOOT_COMPLETED";

    @Override
    public void onReceive(Context context, Intent intent) {
            // All registered broadcasts are received by this
        mContext = context;
        String action = intent.getAction();
        if (action.equalsIgnoreCase(BOOT_ACTION)) {
                    // Check for boot complete event & start your service
```

```
        startService();
    }
}

private void startService() {
    // Here, you will start your service
    Intent mServiceIntent = new Intent();
    mServiceIntent.setAction("com.bootservice.test.DataService");
    mContext.startService(mServiceIntent);
}
}
```

4.9 Creating a Responsive Application Using Threads

Amir Alagic

Problem

You have an application that performs long tasks, and you don't want your application to appear nonresponsive while these are ongoing.

Solution

By using threads, you can create an application that is responsive even when it is handling time-consuming operations.

Discussion

To make your application responsive while time-consuming operations are running on the Android OS you have a few options. If you already know Java, you know you can create a class that extends the `Thread` class and overrides the `public void run()` method and then call the `start()` method on that object to run the time-consuming process. If your class already extends another class, you can implement the `Runnable` interface. Another approach is to create your own class that extends Android's `AsyncTask` class, but we will talk about `AsyncTask` in Recipe 4.10.

In the early days of Java and Android, we were taught about direct use of the `Thread` class. This pattern was coded as follows:

```
Thread thread = new Thread(new Runnable() {          // Deprecated, do not use!
    public void run() {
        getServerData();
    }
});
thread.start();
```

There are many issues around this usage of threads, but the biggest strike against it is the overhead of creating threads. For all but the simplest cases, it is now recommended to use thread pools, which have been in Java for half of its lifetime. Example 4-15 shows the pool-based implementation of this class.

Example 4-15. The networked Activity implementation

```
public class NetworkConnection extends Activity {

    ExecutorService pool = Executors.newSingleThreadExecutor();

    /** Called when the Activity is first created. */
    @Override
    public void onCreate(Bundle savedInstanceState) {
        super.onCreate(savedInstanceState);
        setContentView(R.layout.main);

        pool.submit(new Runnable() {
            public void run() {
                getServerData();
            }
        });
    }
}
```

As you can see, when we start our Activity in the `onCreate()` method we create and submit a `Runnable` object. The `Runnable` method run() will be executed some time after we call the `submit()` method on the pool. From here you can call another method or a few other methods and operations that are time-consuming and that would otherwise block the main thread and make your application look unresponsive.

Often when we are done with the thread we get results that we want to present to the application user. If you try to update the GUI from the thread that you started (not the main thread) your application will crash. The Android UI is not thread safe—this was done deliberately, for performance reasons—so that if you try to change any UI component (even a single call to, e.g, `someTextView.setText()`) from a thread other than the main thread, your app will crash.

Of course, there are several ways to send data from background threads to the UI. One way is to use a `Handler` class; see Recipe 4.11. Alternatively, you can divide your code differently using `AsyncTask` (see Recipe 4.10).

4.10 Using AsyncTask to Do Background Processing

Johan Pelgrim

Problem

You have to do some heavy processing, or load resources from the network, and you want to show the progress and results in the UI.

Solution

Use AsyncTask and ProgressDialog.

Discussion

As explained in the Processes and Threads" section of the Android Developers API Guides (*https://developer.android.com/guide/topics/fundamentals/processes-and-threads.html*), you should *never* block the UI thread, or access the Android UI toolkit from outside the UI thread. Bad things will happen if you do.

You can run processes in the background and update the UI inside the UI thread (a.k.a. the main thread) in several ways, but using the AsyncTask class is very convenient and every Android developer should know how to do so.

The steps boil down to creating a class that extends AsyncTask. AsyncTask itself is abstract and has one abstract method, Result doInBackground(Params… params);. The AsyncTask simply creates a callable working thread in which your implementation of doInBackground() runs. Result and Params are two of the types we need to define in our class definition. The third is the Progress type, which we will talk about later.

Our first implementation will do everything in the background, showing the user a spinner in the title bar and updating the ListView once the processing is done. This is the typical use case, not interfering with the user's task at hand and updating the UI when we have retrieved the result.

The second implementation will use a *modal* dialog to show the processing progressing in the background. In some cases we want to prevent the user from doing anything else when some processing takes place, and this is a good way to do just that.

We will create a UI that contains three Buttons and a ListView. The first button is to start our first refresh process. The second is for the other refresh process and the third is to clear the results in the ListView (see Example 4-16).

Example 4-16. The main layout

```xml
<?xml version="1.0" encoding="utf-8"?>
<LinearLayout xmlns:android="http://schemas.android.com/apk/res/android"
    android:orientation="vertical" android:layout_width="fill_parent"
    android:layout_height="fill_parent">
    <LinearLayout xmlns:android="http://schemas.android.com/apk/res/android"
        android:orientation="horizontal" android:layout_width="fill_parent"
        android:layout_height="wrap_content">
        <Button android:text="Refresh 1" android:id="@+id/button1"
            android:layout_width="fill_parent" android:layout_height="wrap_content"
            android:layout_weight="1"></Button>
        <Button android:text="Refresh 2" android:id="@+id/button2"
            android:layout_width="fill_parent" android:layout_height="wrap_content"
            android:layout_weight="1"></Button>
```

```
        <Button android:text="Clear" android:id="@+id/button3"
            android:layout_width="fill_parent" android:layout_height="wrap_content"
            android:layout_weight="1"></Button>
    </LinearLayout>
    <ListView android:id="@+id/listView1" android:layout_height="fill_parent"
        android:layout_width="fill_parent"></ListView>
</LinearLayout>
```

We assign these UI elements to various fields in onCreate() and add some click listeners (see Example 4-17).

Example 4-17. The onCreate() and onItemClick() methods

```
ListView mListView;
Button mClear;
Button mRefresh1;
Button mRefresh2;

@Override
public void onCreate(Bundle savedInstanceState) {
    super.onCreate(savedInstanceState);
    setContentView(R.layout.main);

    mListView = (ListView) findViewById(R.id.listView1);
    mListView.setTextFilterEnabled(true);
    mListView.setOnItemClickListener(this);

    mRefresh1 = (Button) findViewById(R.id.button1);

    mClear = (Button) findViewById(R.id.button3);
    mClear.setOnClickListener(new OnClickListener() {
        @Override
        public void onClick(View v) {
            mListView.setAdapter(null);
        }
    });

}

public void onItemClick(AdapterView<?> parent, View view, int position, long id) {
    Datum datum = (Datum) mListView.getItemAtPosition(position);
    Uri uri = Uri.parse("http://androidcookbook.com/Recipe.seam?recipeId=" +
        datum.getId());
    Intent intent = new Intent(Intent.ACTION_VIEW, uri);
    this.startActivity(intent);
}
```

The following subsections describe two use cases: processing in the background and processing in the foreground.

Use case 1: Processing in the background

First we create an inner class that extends AsyncTask:

```
protected class LoadRecipesTask1 extends AsyncTask<String, Void, ArrayList<Datum>> {
...
}
```

As you can see, we must supply three types to the class definition. The first is the type of the parameter we will provide when starting this background task—in our case a String, containing a URL. The second type is used for progress updates (we will use this later). The third type is the type returned by our implementation of the doInBackground() method, and typically is something with which you can update a specific UI element (a ListView in our case).

Let's implement the doInBackground() method:

```
@Override
protected ArrayList<Datum> doInBackground(String... urls) {
    ArrayList<Datum> datumList = new ArrayList<Datum>();
    try {
        datumList = parse(urls[0]);
    } catch (IOException e) {
        e.printStackTrace();
    } catch (XmlPullParserException e) {
        e.printStackTrace();
    }
    return datumList;
}
```

As you can see, this is pretty simple. The parse() method—which creates a list of Datum objects—is not shown as it's related to a specific data format in one application. The result of the doInBackground() method is then passed as an argument to the onPostExecute() method in the same (inner) class. In this method we are allowed to update the UI elements in our layout, so we set the adapter of the ListView to show our result:

```
@Override
protected void onPostExecute(ArrayList<Datum> result) {
    mListView.setAdapter(new ArrayAdapter<Datum>(MainActivity.this,
        R.layout.list_item, result));
}
```

Now we need a way to start this task. We do this in mRefresh1's onClickListener() by calling the execute(Params… params) method of AsyncTask (execute(String… urls) in our case):

```
mRefresh1.setOnClickListener(new OnClickListener() {

    @Override
    public void onClick(View v) {
        LoadRecipesTask1 mLoadRecipesTask = new LoadRecipesTask1();
        mLoadRecipesTask.execute(
            "http://androidcookbook.com/seam/resource/rest/recipe/list");
    }
});
```

Now, when we start the app it indeed retrieves the recipes and fills the ListView, but the user has no idea that something is happening in the background. In order to notify the user of ongoing activity, we can set the window state to "indefinite progress"; this displays a small progress animation in the top right of our app's title bar. We request this feature by calling the following method in onCreate(): requestWindowFeature(Window.FEATURE_INDETERMINATE_PROGRESS). (Be aware that this feature is deprecated; we will show a better way to keep the user informed on progress in use case 2, next.)

Then we can start the progress animation by calling the setProgressBarIndeterminateVisibility(boolean visibility) method from within a new method in our inner class, the onPreExecute() method:

```
protected void onPreExecute() {
    MainActivity.this.setProgressBarIndeterminateVisibility(true);
}
```

We stop the spinning progress bar in our window title by calling the same method from within our onPostExecute() method, which will become:

```
protected void onPostExecute(ArrayList<Datum> result) {
    mListView.setAdapter(new ArrayAdapter<Datum>(MainActivity.this,
        R.layout.list_item, result));
    MainActivity.this.setProgressBarIndeterminateVisibility(false);
}
```

We're done! Take your app for a *spin* (pun intended). See Figure 4-2.

Figure 4-2. The AsyncTask demo in action

As you can see, this is a nifty feature for creating a better user experience!

Use case 2: Processing in the foreground

In this example, we show a modal dialog to the user that displays the progress of loading the recipes in the background. Such a dialog is called a ProgressDialog. First we add it as a field to our Activity:

```
ProgressDialog mProgressDialog;
```

Then we add the onCreateDialog() method to be able to answer showDialog() calls and create our dialog:

```
protected Dialog onCreateDialog(int id) {
        switch (id) {
        case DIALOG_KEY:                                                   ❶
            mProgressDialog = new ProgressDialog(this);
            mProgressDialog.setProgressStyle(ProgressDialog.STYLE_HORIZONTAL); ❷
            mProgressDialog.setMessage("Retrieving recipes...");          ❸
            mProgressDialog.setCancelable(false);                         ❹
            return mProgressDialog;
        }
        return null;
    }
```

❶ We should handle the request and creation of all dialogs here. The DIALOG_KEY is an int constant with an arbitrary value (we used 0) to identify this dialog.

❷ We set the progress style to STYLE_HORIZONTAL, which shows a horizontal progress bar. The default is STYLE_SPINNER.

❸ We set our custom message, which is displayed above the progress bar.

❹ By calling setCancelable() with the argument false we disable the Back button, making this dialog *modal*.

Our new implementation of AsyncTask is as shown in Example 4-18.

Example 4-18. The AsyncTask implementation

```
protected class LoadRecipesTask2 extends AsyncTask<String, Integer, ArrayList<Datum>>{

    @Override
    protected void onPreExecute() {
        mProgressDialog.show();                                          ❶
    }

    @Override
    protected ArrayList<Datum> doInBackground(String... urls) {
        ArrayList<Datum> datumList = new ArrayList<Datum>();
        for (int i = 0; i < urls.length; i++) {                         ❷
            try {
                datumList = parse(urls[i]);
                publishProgress((int) (((i+1) / (float) urls.length) * 100)); ❸
            } catch (IOException e) {
                e.printStackTrace();
            } catch (XmlPullParserException e) {
                e.printStackTrace();
            }
```

```
        }
        return datumList;
    }

    @Override
    protected void onProgressUpdate(Integer... values) {
        mProgressDialog.setProgress(values[0]);
    }

    @Override
    protected void onPostExecute(ArrayList<Datum> result) {
        mListView.setAdapter(new ArrayAdapter<Datum>(
            MainActivity.this, R.layout.list_item, result));
        mProgressDialog.dismiss();
    }
}
```
❹
❺

❻

We see a couple of new things here:

❶ Before we start our background process we show the modal dialog.

❷ In our background process we loop through all the URLs, expecting to receive more than one. This will give us a good indication of our progress.

❸ We can update the progress by calling publishProgress(). Notice that the argument is of type int, which will be auto-boxed to the second type defined in our class definition, Integer.

❹ The call to publishProgress() will result in a call to onProgressUpdate(), which again has arguments of type Integer. You could, of course, use String or something else as the argument type by simply changing the second type in the inner class definition to String and, of course, in the call to publishProgress().

❺ We use the first Integer to set the new progress value in our ProgressDialog.

❻ We dismiss the dialog, which removes it.

Now we can bind this all together by implementing our onClickListener() for our second refresh button.:

```
mRefresh2.setOnClickListener(new OnClickListener() {

    @Override
    public void onClick(View v) {
        LoadRecipesTask2 mLoadRecipesTask = new LoadRecipesTask2();
        String url =
            "http://androidcookbook.com/seam/resource/rest/recipe/list";
        showDialog(DIALOG_KEY);                                          ❶
        mLoadRecipesTask.execute(url, url, url, url, url);               ❷
```

```
    }
});
```

❶ We show the dialog by calling `showDialog()` with the `DIALOG_KEY` argument, which will trigger our previously defined `onCreateDialog()` method.

❷ We execute our new task with five URLs, simply to show a little bit of progress.

It will look something like Figure 4-3.

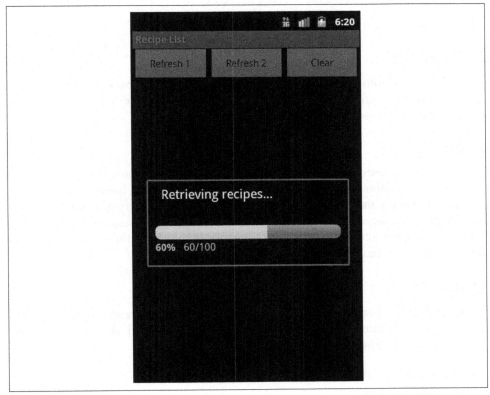

Figure 4-3. Retrieving recipes in the background

Implementing background tasks with `AsyncTask` is very simple and should be done for all long-running processes that also need to update your user interface.

See Also

The developer documentation on processes and threads (*https://devel oper.android.com/guide/topics/fundamentals/processes-and-threads.html*).

Source Download URL

The source code for this project is in the Android Cookbook repository (*https://github.com/IanDarwin/Android-Cookbook-Examples*), in the subdirectory *RecipeList* (see "Getting and Using the Code Examples" on page 18).

4.11 Sending Messages Between Threads Using an Activity Thread Queue and Handler

Vladimir Kroz

Problem

You need to pass information or data from a Service or other background task to an Activity. Because Activities run on the UI thread, it is not safe to call them from a background thread.

Solution

You can write a nested class that extends Android's `Handler` class, then override the `handleMessage()` method that will read messages from the thread queue. Pass this handler to the worker thread, usually via the worker class's constructor; in the worker thread, post messages using the various `obtainMessage()` and `sendMessage()` methods. This will cause the Activity to be called in the `handleMessage()` method, but on the event thread so that you can safely update the GUI.

Discussion

There are many situations in which you must have a thread running in the background and send information to the main Activity's UI thread. At the architectural level, you can take one of the following two approaches:

- Use Android's `AsyncTask` class.
- Start a new thread.

Though using `AsyncTask` is very convenient, sometimes you really need to construct a worker thread by yourself. In such situations, you likely will need to send some information back to the Activity thread. Keep in mind that Android doesn't allow other threads to modify any content of the main UI thread. Instead, you must wrap the data into messages and send the messages through the message queue.

To do this, you must first add an instance of the `Handler` class to, for example, your `MapActivity` instance (see Example 4-19).

Example 4-19. The handler

```java
public class MyMap extends MapActivity {
    .
    public Handler _handler = new Handler() {
        @Override
        public void handleMessage(Message msg) {
            Log.d(TAG, String.format("Handler.handleMessage(): msg=%s", msg));
            // This is where the main Activity thread receives messages
            // Put incoming message handling posted by other threads here
            super.handleMessage(msg);
        }

    };
    .
}
```

Now, in the worker thread, post a message to the Activity's main queue whenever you need to add the Handler class instance to your main Activity instance (see Example 4-20).

Example 4-20. Posting a Runnable to the queue

```java
/**
 * Performs background job
 */
class MyThreadRunner implements Runnable {
    // @Override
    public void run() {
        while (!Thread.currentThread().isInterrupted()) {
            // Dummy message -- real implementation
            // will put some meaningful data in it
            Message msg = Message.obtain();
            msg.what = 999;
            MyMap.this._handler.sendMessage(msg);
            // Dummy code to simulate delay while working with remote server
            try {
                Thread.sleep(5000);
            } catch (InterruptedException e) {
                Thread.currentThread().interrupt();
            }
        }
    }
}
```

4.12 Creating an Android Epoch HTML/JavaScript Calendar

Wagied Davids

Problem

You need a custom calendar written in JavaScript, and you want it to understand how to interact between JavaScript and Java.

Solution

Use a WebView component to load an HTML file containing the Epoch JavaScript calendar component.

 An *epoch* is a contiguous set of years, such as the years of recorded history BC or BCE, the years AD or CE, or the years since "time zero," the beginning of modern computer timekeeping (January 1, 1970 in Unix, macOS, Java 1.0's Date class, some MS Windows time functions, and so on). The "Epoch" discussed here is a JavaScript calendaring package that takes its name from the conventional meaning of epoch.

Briefly, here are the steps in creating this calendar app:

1. Download the Epoch DHTML/JavaScript calendar (*http://www.javascriptkit.com/ script/script2/epoch/index.shtml*).
2. Create an assets directory under your Android project folder (e.g., *TestCalendar/ assets/*).
3. Code your main HTML file for referencing the Epoch calendar.
4. Create an Android Activity for launching the Epoch calendar.

Files placed in the Android assets directory are referenced as *file:///android_asset/* (note the triple leading slash and the singular spelling of *asset*).

Discussion

To enable interaction between the JavaScript-based view layer and the Java-based logic layer, a Java–JavaScript bridge interface is required: the MyJavaScriptInterface inner class. The onDayClick() function, shown in Example 4-21, shows how to call a JavaScript function from an Android Activity—for example, webview.loadUrl("javascript: popup();");. The HTML/JavaScript component is shown in Example 4-21, and the Java Activity code is shown in Example 4-22.

Example 4-21. calendarview.html

```html
<html>
    <head>
        <title>My Epoch DHTML JavaScript Calendar</title>
        <style type="text/css">
            dateheader {
                -background-color: #3399FF;
                -webkit-border-radius: 10px;
                -moz-border-radius: 10px;
                -border-radius: 10px;
                -padding: 5px;
            }
        </style>

        <style type="text/css">
        html {height:100%;}
        body {height:100%; margin:0; padding:0;}
        #bg {position:fixed; top:0; left:0; width:100%; height:100%;}
        #content {position:relative; z-index:1;}
        </style>
        <!--[if IE 6]>
        <style type="text/css">
        html {overflow-y:hidden;}
        body {overflow-y:auto;}
        #page-background {position:absolute; z-index:-1;}
        #content {position:static;padding:10px;}
        </style>
        <![endif]-->

        <link rel="stylesheet" type="text/css" href="epoch_v106/epoch_styles.css" />
        <script type="text/javascript" src="epoch_v106/epoch_classes.js"></script>

        <script type="text/javascript">
            /*You can also place this code in a separate
              file and link to it like epoch_classes.js*/
            var my_cal;

            window.onload = function () {
                my_cal = new Epoch('epoch_basic','flat',
                    document.getElementById('basic_container'));
            };

            function popup() {
                var weekday=new Array("Sun","Mon","Tue","Wed","Thur","Fri","Sat");
                var monthname=new Array("Jan","Feb","Mar","Apr","May","Jun",
                    "Jul","Aug","Sep","Oct","Nov","Dec");
                var date = my_cal.selectedDates.length > 0 ?
                    my_cal.selectedDates[0] :
                    null;
                if ( date != null ) {
                        var day = date.getDate();
                        var dayOfWeek= date.getDay();
                        var month = date.getMonth();
                        var yy = date.getYear();
                        var year = (yy < 1000) ? yy + 1900 : yy;
```

```
                            /* Set the user-selected date in HTML form */
                            var dateStr= weekday[dayOfWeek]  + ", " + day + " " +
                                monthname[month] + " " + year;
                                document.getElementById("selected_date").value= dateStr;

                                /* IMPORTANT:
                                 * Call Android JavaScript->Java bridge setting a
                                 * Java-field variable
                                 */
                                window.android.setSelectedDate( date );
                                window.android.setCalendarButton( date );
                            }
                    }
            </script>
        </head>
        <body>
        <div id="bg"><img src="bg.png" width="100%" height="100%" alt=""></div>
            <div id="content">
                <div class="dateheader" align="center">
                    <form name="form_selected_date">
                            <span style="color:white">Selected day:</span>
                            <input id="selected_date" name="selected_date" type="text"
                                readonly="true">
                    </form>
                </div>
                <div id="basic_container" onClick="popup()"></div>
            </div>
        </body>
</head>>
```

Example 4-22. CalendarViewActivity.java

```java
import java.util.Date;

import android.app.Activity;
import android.content.Intent;
import android.os.Bundle;
import android.os.Handler;
import android.util.Log;
import android.view.View;
import android.view.View.OnClickListener;
import android.webkit.JsResult;
import android.webkit.WebChromeClient;
import android.webkit.WebSettings;
import android.webkit.WebView;
import android.widget.Button;
import android.widget.ImageView;
import android.widget.Toast;

import com.pfizer.android.R;
import com.pfizer.android.utils.DateUtils;
import com.pfizer.android.view.screens.journal.CreateEntryScreen;

public class CalendarViewActivity extends Activity {
```

```
private static final String tag = "CalendarViewActivity";
private ImageView calendarToJournalButton;
private Button calendarDateButton;
private WebView webview;
private Date selectedCalDate;

private final Handler jsHandler = new Handler();

/** Called when the Activity is first created. */
@Override
public void onCreate(Bundle savedInstanceState) {
        Log.d(tag, "Creating View ...");
        super.onCreate(savedInstanceState);

        // Set the view layer
        Log.d(tag, "Setting-up the View Layer");
        setContentView(R.layout.calendar_view);

        // Go to CreateJournalEntry
        calendarToJournalButton = (ImageView) this.findViewById
            (R.id.calendarToJournalButton);
        calendarToJournalButton.setOnClickListener(new OnClickListener() {
                @Override
                public void onClick(View v) {
                        Log.d(tag, "Re-directing -> CreateEntryScreen ...");
                        Intent intent = intent =
                            new Intent(getApplicationContext(),
                                CreateEntryScreen.class);
                        startActivity(intent);
                }
        });

        // User-selected calendar date
        calendarDateButton =
         (Button) this.findViewById(R.id.calendarDateButton);

        // Get access to the WebView holder
        webview = (WebView) this.findViewById(R.id.webview);

        // Get the settings
        WebSettings settings = webview.getSettings();

        // Enable JavaScript
        settings.setJavaScriptEnabled(true);

        // Enable ZoomControls visibility
        settings.setSupportZoom(true);

        // Add JavaScript interface
        webview.addJavaScriptInterface(new MyJavaScriptInterface(), "android");

        // Set the Chrome client
        webview.setWebChromeClient(new MyWebChromeClient());

        // Load the URL of the HTML file
        webview.loadUrl("file:///android_asset/calendarview.html");
```

```
        }

    public void setCalendarButton(Date selectedCalDate) {
            Log.d(tag, jsHandler.obtainMessage().toString());
            calendarDateButton.setText(
                DateUtils.convertDateToSectionHeaderFormat(
                    selectedCalDate.getTime())));
        }

    /**
     *
     * @param selectedCalDate
     */
    public void setSelectedCalDate(Date selectedCalDate) {
            this.selectedCalDate = selectedCalDate;
        }

    /**
     *
     * @return
     */
    public Date getSelectedCalDate() {
            return selectedCalDate;
        }

    /**
     * JAVA->JAVASCRIPT INTERFACE
     *
     * @author wagied
     *
     */
    final class MyJavaScriptInterface {
            private Date jsSelectedDate;
            MyJavaScriptInterface() {
                    // EMPTY;
            }

            public void onDayClick() {
                    jsHandler.post(new Runnable() {
                            public void run() {
                                    // Java telling JavaScript to do things
                                    webview.loadUrl("javascript: popup();");
                            }
                    });
                }

            /**
             * NOTE: THIS FUNCTION IS BEING SET IN JAVASCRIPT
             * User-selected date in WebView
             *
             * @param dateStr
             */
            public void setSelectedDate(String dateStr) {
                    Toast.makeText(getApplicationContext(), dateStr,
                        Toast.LENGTH_SHORT).show();
```

```
                        Log.d(tag, "User Selected Date: JavaScript -> Java : " + dateStr);

                        // Set the user-selected calendar date
                        setJsSelectedDate(new Date(Date.parse(dateStr)));
                        Log.d(tag, "java.util.Date Object: " +
                            Date.parse(dateStr).toString());
                    }
                private void setJsSelectedDate(Date userSelectedDate) {
                        jsSelectedDate = userSelectedDate;
                    }
                public Date getJsSelectedDate() {
                        return jsSelectedDate;
                    }
            }

        /**
         * Alert pop-up for debugging purposes
         *
         * @author wdavid01
         *
         */
        final class MyWebChromeClient extends WebChromeClient {
                @Override
                public boolean onJsAlert(WebView view, String url,
                    String message, JsResult result) {
                        Log.d(tag, message);
                        result.confirm();
                        return true;
                    }
            }

        @Override
        public void onDestroy() {
                Log.d(tag, "Destroying View!");
                super.onDestroy();
            }
    }
```

For debugging purposes, a `MyWebChromeClient` is created—this is the final inner class extending `WebChromeClient` defined near the end of the main class—and in particular the `onJsAlert()` method is overridden.

Source Download URL

The source code for this example is in the Android Cookbook repository (*https://github.com/IanDarwin/Android-Cookbook-Examples*), in the subdirectory *EpochJSCalendar* (see "Getting and Using the Code Examples" on page 18).

## CHAPTER 5

Graphics

Computer graphics are used for any kind of display for which there isn't a GUI component: charting, displaying pictures, and so on. Graphics tools are used to create GUI components as well as to draw shapes, lines, pictures, etc. Android is well provisioned for graphics, including a full implementation of OpenGL ES, a subset of OpenGL intended for smaller devices.

This chapter starts with a recipe for using a custom font for special text effects, followed by some recipes on OpenGL graphics and one on graphical "touch" input. From there we continue the input theme with various image capture techniques. Then we have some recipes on graphics files, and one to round out the chapter discussing "pinch to zoom," using user touch input to scale graphical output.

5.1 Using a Custom Font

Ian Darwin

Problem

The range of fonts on Android devices is pretty small. You want something better.

Solution

Install a TTF or OTF version of your font in *assets/fonts* (creating this directory if necessary). In your code, create a typeface from the "asset" and call the View's setTypeface() method. You're done!

Discussion

You can provide one or more fonts with your application. We have not yet discovered a documented way to install system-wide fonts. Beware of huge font files, as they will be downloaded with your application, increasing its size.

Your custom font's format should be TTF or OTF (TrueType or OpenType, a TTF extension). You need to create a *fonts* subdirectory under *assets* in your project, and install the font there.

While you can refer to the predefined fonts just using XML, you cannot refer to your own fonts using XML. This may change someday, but for now the content model of the android:typeface attribute is an XML enumeration containing only normal, sans, serif, and monospace—that's it! Therefore, you have to use code.

There are several Typeface.create() methods, including:

- create(String familyName, int style)
- create(TypeFace family, inst style)
- createFromAsset(AssetManager mgr, String path)
- createFromFile(File path)
- createFromFile(String path)

You can see how most of these should work. The parameter style is, as in Java, one of several constants defined on the class representing fonts, here Typeface. You can create representations of the built-in fonts, and variations on them, using the first two forms in the list. The code in Example 5-2 uses the createFromAsset() method, so we don't have to worry about font locations. If you have stored the file on internal or external storage (see Recipe 10.1), you could provide a File object or the font file's absolute path using the last two forms in the list. If the font file is on external storage, remember to request permission in *AndroidManifest.xml*.

I used the nice Iceberg font, from SoftMaker Software GmbH (*http://www.soft maker.de*). This font is copyrighted and I do not have permission to redistribute it, so when you download the project and want to run it, you will need to install a True-Type font file at *assets/fonts/fontdemo.ttf*. Note that if the font is missing, the createFromAsset() method will return null; the online version of the code provides error handling. If the font is invalid, Android will *silently ignore it* and use a built-in font.

In this demo we provide two text areas, one using the built-in serif font and one using a custom font. They are defined, and various attributes added, in *main.xml* (see Example 5-1).

Example 5-1. XML layout with font specification

```xml
<?xml version="1.0" encoding="utf-8"?>
<LinearLayout
    xmlns:android="http://schemas.android.com/apk/res/android"
    android:orientation="vertical"
    android:layout_width="fill_parent"
    android:layout_height="fill_parent"
    >
<TextView
    android:id="@+id/PlainTextView"
    android:layout_width="fill_parent"
    android:layout_height="wrap_content"
    android:text="@string/plain"
    android:textSize="36sp"
    android:typeface="serif"
    android:padding="10sp"
    android:gravity="center"
    />
<TextView
    android:id="@+id/FontView"
    android:layout_width="fill_parent"
    android:layout_height="wrap_content"
    android:text="@string/nicer"
    android:textSize="36sp"
    android:typeface="normal"
    android:padding="10sp"
    android:gravity="center"
    />
</LinearLayout>
```

Example 5-2 shows the source code.

Example 5-2. Setting a custom font

```java
public class FontDemo extends Activity {

    @Override
    public void onCreate(Bundle savedInstanceState) {
        super.onCreate(savedInstanceState);
        setContentView(R.layout.main);

        TextView v = (TextView) findViewById(R.id.FontView);   ❶
        Typeface t = Typeface.createFromAsset(getAssets(),      ❷
                "fonts/fontdemo.ttf");
        v.setTypeface(t, Typeface.BOLD_ITALIC);                 ❸
    }
}
```

❶ Find the View you want to use your font in.

❷ Create a Typeface object from one of the Typeface class's static create() methods.

❸ Message the `Typeface` into the `View`'s `setTypeface()` method.

If all is well, running the app should look like Figure 5-1.

Figure 5-1. Custom font

Source Download URL

The source code for this example is in the Android Cookbook repository (*https://github.com/IanDarwin/Android-Cookbook-Examples*), in the subdirectory *FontDemo* (see "Getting and Using the Code Examples" on page 18).

5.2 Drawing a Spinning Cube with OpenGL ES

Marco Dinacci

Problem

You want to create a basic OpenGL ES application.

Solution

Create a `GLSurfaceView` and a custom `Renderer` that will draw a spinning cube.

Discussion

Android supports 3D graphics via the OpenGL ES API, a flavor of OpenGL specifically designed for embedded devices. This recipe is not an OpenGL tutorial; it assumes the reader already has basic OpenGL knowledge. The final result will look like Figure 5-2.

Figure 5-2. OpenGL graphics sample

First we write a new Activity, and in the onCreate() method we create the two funda-
mental objects we need to use the OpenGL API: a GLSurfaceView and a Renderer (see
Example 5-3).

Example 5-3. OpenGL demo Activity

```
public class OpenGLDemoActivity extends Activity {

    @Override
    public void onCreate(Bundle savedInstanceState) {
        super.onCreate(savedInstanceState);

        // Go fullscreen
        requestWindowFeature(Window.FEATURE_NO_TITLE);
        getWindow().setFlags(WindowManager.LayoutParams.FLAG_FULLSCREEN,
                    WindowManager.LayoutParams.FLAG_FULLSCREEN);

        GLSurfaceView view = new GLSurfaceView(this);
        view.setRenderer(new OpenGLRenderer());
        setContentView(view);
    }
}
```

Example 5-4 is the code for our Renderer; it uses a simple Cube object we'll describe later
to display a spinning cube.

Example 5-4. The renderer implementation

```
class OpenGLRenderer implements Renderer {

        private Cube mCube = new Cube();
        private float mCubeRotation;

        @Override
        public void onSurfaceCreated(GL10 gl, EGLConfig config) {
            gl.glClearColor(0.0f, 0.0f, 0.0f, 0.5f);
```

```
        gl.glClearDepthf(1.0f);
        gl.glEnable(GL10.GL_DEPTH_TEST);
        gl.glDepthFunc(GL10.GL_LEQUAL);

        gl.glHint(GL10.GL_PERSPECTIVE_CORRECTION_HINT,
                GL10.GL_NICEST);

    }

    @Override
    public void onDrawFrame(GL10 gl) {
        gl.glClear(GL10.GL_COLOR_BUFFER_BIT | GL10.GL_DEPTH_BUFFER_BIT);
        gl.glLoadIdentity();

        gl.glTranslatef(0.0f, 0.0f, -10.0f);
        gl.glRotatef(mCubeRotation, 1.0f, 1.0f, 1.0f);

        mCube.draw(gl);

        gl.glLoadIdentity();

        mCubeRotation -= 0.15f;
    }

    @Override
    public void onSurfaceChanged(GL10 gl, int width, int height) {
        gl.glViewport(0, 0, width, height);
        gl.glMatrixMode(GL10.GL_PROJECTION);
        gl.glLoadIdentity();
        GLU.gluPerspective(gl, 45.0f, (float)width / (float)height, 0.1f, 100.0f);
        gl.glViewport(0, 0, width, height);

        gl.glMatrixMode(GL10.GL_MODELVIEW);
        gl.glLoadIdentity();
    }
}
```

Our onSurfaceChanged() and onDrawFrame() methods are basically the equivalent of the
GLUT glutReshapeFunc() and glutDisplayFunc(). The first is called when the surface is
resized—for instance, when the phone switches between landscape and portrait
modes. The second is called at every frame, and that's where we put the code to draw
our cube (see Example 5-5).

Example 5-5. The Cube class

```
class Cube {

    private FloatBuffer mVertexBuffer;
    private FloatBuffer mColorBuffer;
    private ByteBuffer  mIndexBuffer;

    private float vertices[] = {
                            -1.0f, -1.0f, -1.0f,
```

```
                               1.0f, -1.0f, -1.0f,
                               1.0f,  1.0f, -1.0f,
                              -1.0f,  1.0f, -1.0f,
                              -1.0f, -1.0f,  1.0f,
                               1.0f, -1.0f,  1.0f,
                               1.0f,  1.0f,  1.0f,
                              -1.0f,  1.0f,  1.0f
                              };
private float colors[] = {
                               0.0f,  1.0f,  0.0f,  1.0f,
                               0.0f,  1.0f,  0.0f,  1.0f,
                               1.0f,  0.5f,  0.0f,  1.0f,
                               1.0f,  0.5f,  0.0f,  1.0f,
                               1.0f,  0.0f,  0.0f,  1.0f,
                               1.0f,  0.0f,  0.0f,  1.0f,
                               0.0f,  0.0f,  1.0f,  1.0f,
                               1.0f,  0.0f,  1.0f,  1.0f
                          };

private byte indices[] = {
                               0, 4, 5, 0, 5, 1,
                               1, 5, 6, 1, 6, 2,
                               2, 6, 7, 2, 7, 3,
                               3, 7, 4, 3, 4, 0,
                               4, 7, 6, 4, 6, 5,
                               3, 0, 1, 3, 1, 2
                               };

public Cube() {
        ByteBuffer byteBuf = ByteBuffer.allocateDirect(vertices.length * 4);
        byteBuf.order(ByteOrder.nativeOrder());
        mVertexBuffer = byteBuf.asFloatBuffer();
        mVertexBuffer.put(vertices);
        mVertexBuffer.position(0);

        byteBuf = ByteBuffer.allocateDirect(colors.length * 4);
        byteBuf.order(ByteOrder.nativeOrder());
        mColorBuffer = byteBuf.asFloatBuffer();
        mColorBuffer.put(colors);
        mColorBuffer.position(0);

        mIndexBuffer = ByteBuffer.allocateDirect(indices.length);
        mIndexBuffer.put(indices);
        mIndexBuffer.position(0);
}

public void draw(GL10 gl) {
    gl.glFrontFace(GL10.GL_CW);

    gl.glVertexPointer(3, GL10.GL_FLOAT, 0, mVertexBuffer);
    gl.glColorPointer(4, GL10.GL_FLOAT, 0, mColorBuffer);

    gl.glEnableClientState(GL10.GL_VERTEX_ARRAY);
    gl.glEnableClientState(GL10.GL_COLOR_ARRAY);

    gl.glDrawElements(GL10.GL_TRIANGLES, 36, GL10.GL_UNSIGNED_BYTE,
```

```
                        mIndexBuffer);

        gl.glDisableClientState(GL10.GL_VERTEX_ARRAY);
        gl.glDisableClientState(GL10.GL_COLOR_ARRAY);
    }
}
```

The `Cube` uses two `FloatBuffer` objects to store vertex and color information and a `ByteBuffer` to store the face indexes. In order for the buffers to work it is important to set their order according to the endianness of the platform, using the `order()` method. Once the buffers have been filled with the values from the arrays, the internal cursor must be restored to the beginning of the data using `buffer.position(0)`.

See Also

OpenGL ES (*https://www.khronos.org/opengles*).

5.3 Adding Controls to the OpenGL Spinning Cube

Marco Dinacci

Problem

You want to interact with an OpenGL polygon using your device's keyboard.

Solution

Create a custom `GLSurfaceView` and override the `onKeyUp()` method to listen to the `KeyEvent` created from a directional pad (D-pad).

Discussion

This recipe builds on Recipe 5.2 to show how to control the cube using a D-pad. We're going to increment the speed rotation along the x-axis and y-axis using the D-pad's directional keys. The biggest change from that recipe is that we now have our custom class that extends the `SurfaceView`. We do this so that we can override the `onKeyUp()` method and be notified when the user uses the D-pad.

The `onCreate()` method of our Activity looks like Example 5-6.

Example 5-6. The spinning cube Activity

```
public class SpinningCubeActivity2 extends Activity {
    @Override
    public void onCreate(Bundle savedInstanceState) {
        super.onCreate(savedInstanceState);

        // go fullscreen
```

```
        requestWindowFeature(Window.FEATURE_NO_TITLE);
        getWindow().setFlags(WindowManager.LayoutParams.FLAG_FULLSCREEN,
                    WindowManager.LayoutParams.FLAG_FULLSCREEN);

        // create our custom view
        GLSurfaceView view = new OpenGLSurfaceView(this);
        view.setRenderer((Renderer)view);
        setContentView(view);
    }
}
```

Our new `GLSurfaceView` also implements the `Renderer` interface. The `onSurfaceCreated()` and `onSurfaceChanged()` methods are exactly the same as in Recipe 5.2; most of the changes occur in `onDrawFrame()` as we introduce four new parameters: `mXrot` and `mYrot` to control the rotation of the cube along the x-axis and y-axis, and `mXspeed` and `mYSpeed` to store the speed of the rotation along the x-axis and y-axis. Each time the user clicks a D-pad button we alter the speed of the cube by modifying these parameters.

Example 5-7 shows the full code of our new class.

Example 5-7. The GLSurfaceView implementation

```
class OpenGLSurfaceView extends GLSurfaceView implements Renderer {

    private Cube mCube;
    private float mXrot;
    private float mYrot;
    private float mXspeed;
    private float mYspeed;

    public OpenGLSurfaceView(Context context) {
        super(context);

        // give focus to the GLSurfaceView
        requestFocus();
        setFocusableInTouchMode(true);

        mCube = new Cube();
    }

    @Override
    public void onDrawFrame(GL10 gl) {
        gl.glClear(GL10.GL_COLOR_BUFFER_BIT | GL10.GL_DEPTH_BUFFER_BIT);
        gl.glLoadIdentity();

        gl.glTranslatef(0.0f, 0.0f, -10.0f);

        gl.glRotatef(mXrot, 1.0f, 0.0f, 0.0f);
        gl.glRotatef(mYrot, 0.0f, 1.0f, 0.0f);

        mCube.draw(gl);

        gl.glLoadIdentity();
```

```
        mXrot += mXspeed;
        mYrot += mYspeed;
    }

    @Override
    public boolean onKeyUp(int keyCode, KeyEvent event) {
        if(keyCode == KeyEvent.KEYCODE_DPAD_LEFT)
            mYspeed -= 0.1f;
        else if(keyCode == KeyEvent.KEYCODE_DPAD_RIGHT)
            mYspeed += 0.1f;
        else if(keyCode == KeyEvent.KEYCODE_DPAD_UP)
            mXspeed -= 0.1f;
        else if(keyCode == KeyEvent.KEYCODE_DPAD_DOWN)
            mXspeed += 0.1f;

        return true;
    }

    // unchanged
    @Override
    public void onSurfaceCreated(GL10 gl, EGLConfig config) {
        gl.glClearColor(0.0f, 0.0f, 0.0f, 0.5f);

        gl.glClearDepthf(1.0f);
        gl.glEnable(GL10.GL_DEPTH_TEST);
        gl.glDepthFunc(GL10.GL_LEQUAL);

        gl.glHint(GL10.GL_PERSPECTIVE_CORRECTION_HINT,
                GL10.GL_NICEST);
    }


    // unchanged
    @Override
    public void onSurfaceChanged(GL10 gl, int width, int height) {
        gl.glViewport(0, 0, width, height);
        gl.glMatrixMode(GL10.GL_PROJECTION);
        gl.glLoadIdentity();
        GLU.gluPerspective(gl, 45.0f, (float)width / (float)height, 0.1f, 100.0f);
        gl.glViewport(0, 0, width, height);

        gl.glMatrixMode(GL10.GL_MODELVIEW);
        gl.glLoadIdentity();
    }
}
```

The Cube is inherited from Recipe 5.2. Don't forget to call requestFocus() and setFocusableInTouchMode(true) in the constructor of the view, or else the key events will not be received.

See Also

Recipe 5.2.

Source Download URL

The source code for this example is in the Android Cookbook repository (*https:// github.com/IanDarwin/Android-Cookbook-Examples*), in the subdirectory *Spinning-CubeDemo* (see "Getting and Using the Code Examples" on page 18).

5.4 Freehand Drawing Smooth Curves

Ian Darwin

Problem

You want to allow the user to draw smooth curves, such as freehand Bezier curves, legal signatures, and so on.

Solution

Create a custom `View` with a carefully written `OnTouchListener` that handles the case where input arrives faster than your code can process it; save the results in an array, and draw them in `onDraw()`.

Discussion

This code was originally written by Eric Burke of Square Inc., for signatures when people use the Square app to capture credit card purchases. To be legally acceptable as proof of purchase, the captured signatures have to be of good quality. Square has graciously placed this code under the Apache Software License 2.0, but was not able to provide a description of it as part of this recipe.

I have since adapted the signature code for use in JabaGator, my very simple, general-purpose drawing program for the Java desktop and for Android (the fact that the name rhymes with a well-known illustration program from Adobe is, of course, purely coincidental).

Eric's initial "by the book" drawing code worked but was very jerky and very slow. Upon investigation, Square learned that Android's graphics layer sends touch events in "batches" when it cannot deliver them quickly enough individually. Each `MotionEvent` delivered to `onTouchEvent()` may contain a number of touch coordinates—as many as were captured since the last `onTouchEvent()` call. To draw a smooth curve, you must get all of the points. You do this using the number of coordinates from the `TouchEvent` method `getHistorySize()`, iterating over that count and calling `getHistoricalX(int)` and `getHistoricalY(int)` to get the point locations (see Example 5-8).

Example 5-8. Drawing all the points

```
// in onTouchEvent(TouchEvent):
for (int i=0; i < event.getHistorySize(); i++) {
    float historicalX = event.getHistoricalX(i);
    float historicalY = event.getHistoricalY(i);
    // add point (historicalX, historicalY) to your path...
}
// add point (eventX, eventY) to your path...
```

This provides significant improvements, but it still is too slow for people to draw with —many nongeeks will wait for the drawing code to catch up with their finger if it doesn't draw quickly enough! The problem is that this simple solution calls invalidate() after each line segment, which is correct but very slow as it forces Android to redraw the entire screen. The solution to this problem is to call invalidate() with just the region that you drew the line segment into, and it involves a bit of arithmetic to get the region correct; see the expandDirtyRect() method in Example 5-9. Here's Eric's description of the dirty-region algorithm:

1. Create a rectangle representing the dirty region.

2. Set the points for the four corners to the +X+ and +Y+ coordinates from the ACTION_DOWN event.

3. For ACTION_MOVE and ACTION_UP, expand the rectangle to encompass the new points. (Don't forget the historical coordinates!)

4. Pass just the dirty rectangle to invalidate(). Android won't redraw the rest.

This set of steps makes the drawing code responsive and the application usable.

Example 5-9 shows my version of the final code. I have several OnTouchListeners: one for drawing curves, one for selecting objects, one for drawing rectangles, and so on. That code is not complete at present, but the curve-drawing part works nicely.

Example 5-9. DrawingView.java

```
// This code is dual-licensed under Creative Commons and Apache Software License 2.0
public class DrawingView extends View {

    private static final float STROKE_WIDTH = 5f;

    /** Need to track this so the dirty region can accommodate the stroke. **/
    private static final float HALF_STROKE_WIDTH = STROKE_WIDTH / 2;

    private Paint paint = new Paint();
    private Path path = new Path();

    /**
     * Optimizes painting by invalidating the smallest possible area.
     */
    private float lastTouchX;
```

```java
private float lastTouchY;
private final RectF dirtyRect = new RectF();

final OnTouchListener selectionAndMoveListener = // not shown;

final OnTouchListener drawRectangleListener = // not shown;

final OnTouchListener drawOvalListener = // not shown;

final OnTouchListener drawPolyLineListener = new OnTouchListener() {

  @Override
  public boolean onTouch(View v, MotionEvent event) {
      // Log.d("jabagator", "onTouch: " + event);
      float eventX = event.getX();
      float eventY = event.getY();

      switch (event.getAction()) {
        case MotionEvent.ACTION_DOWN:
          path.moveTo(eventX, eventY);
          lastTouchX = eventX;
          lastTouchY = eventY;
          // No end point yet, so don't waste cycles invalidating.
          return true;

        case MotionEvent.ACTION_MOVE:
        case MotionEvent.ACTION_UP:
          // Start tracking the dirty region.
          resetDirtyRect(eventX, eventY);

          // When the hardware tracks events faster than
          // they can be delivered to the app, the
          // event will contain a history of those skipped points.
          int historySize = event.getHistorySize();
          for (int i = 0; i < historySize; i++) {
            float historicalX = event.getHistoricalX(i);
            float historicalY = event.getHistoricalY(i);
            expandDirtyRect(historicalX, historicalY);
            path.lineTo(historicalX, historicalY);
          }

          // After replaying history, connect the line to the touch point.
          path.lineTo(eventX, eventY);
          break;

        default:
          Log.d("jabagator", "Unknown touch event  " + event.toString());
          return false;
      }

      // Include half the stroke width to avoid clipping.
      invalidate(
          (int) (dirtyRect.left - HALF_STROKE_WIDTH),
          (int) (dirtyRect.top - HALF_STROKE_WIDTH),
          (int) (dirtyRect.right + HALF_STROKE_WIDTH),
          (int) (dirtyRect.bottom + HALF_STROKE_WIDTH));
```

```java
            lastTouchX = eventX;
            lastTouchY = eventY;

            return true;
    }

      /**
       * Called when replaying history to ensure the dirty region
       * includes all points.
       */
      private void expandDirtyRect(float historicalX, float historicalY) {
        if (historicalX < dirtyRect.left) {
          dirtyRect.left = historicalX;
        } else if (historicalX > dirtyRect.right) {
          dirtyRect.right = historicalX;
        }
        if (historicalY < dirtyRect.top) {
          dirtyRect.top = historicalY;
        } else if (historicalY > dirtyRect.bottom) {
          dirtyRect.bottom = historicalY;
        }
      }

      /**
       * Resets the dirty region when the motion event occurs.
       */
      private void resetDirtyRect(float eventX, float eventY) {

        // The lastTouchX and lastTouchY were set when the ACTION_DOWN
        // motion event occurred.
        dirtyRect.left = Math.min(lastTouchX, eventX);
        dirtyRect.right = Math.max(lastTouchX, eventX);
        dirtyRect.top = Math.min(lastTouchY, eventY);
        dirtyRect.bottom = Math.max(lastTouchY, eventY);
      }
};

/** DrawingView constructor */
public DrawingView(Context context, AttributeSet attrs) {
    super(context, attrs);

    paint.setAntiAlias(true);
    paint.setColor(Color.WHITE);
    paint.setStyle(Paint.Style.STROKE);
    paint.setStrokeJoin(Paint.Join.ROUND);
    paint.setStrokeWidth(STROKE_WIDTH);

    setMode(MotionMode.DRAW_POLY);
}

public void clear() {
    path.reset();

    // Repaints the entire view.
    invalidate();
```

```
    }

    @Override
    protected void onDraw(Canvas canvas) {
        canvas.drawPath(path, paint);
    }

    /**
     * Sets the DrawingView into one of several modes, such
     * as "select" mode (e.g., for moving or resizing objects),
     * or "draw polyline" (smooth curve), "draw rectangle", etc.
     */
    private void setMode(MotionMode motionMode) {
        switch(motionMode) {
        case SELECT_AND_MOVE:
            setOnTouchListener(selectionAndMoveListener);
            break;
        case DRAW_POLY:
            setOnTouchListener(drawPolyLineListener);
            break;
        case DRAW_RECTANGLE:
            setOnTouchListener(drawRectangleListener);
            break;
        case DRAW_OVAL:
            setOnTouchListener(drawOvalListener);
            break;
        default:
            throw new IllegalStateException("Unknown MotionMode " + motionMode);
        }
    }
}
```

Figure 5-3 shows JabaGator running, showing my attempt at legible handwriting (don't worry, that's not my legal signature).

Figure 5-3. Touch drawing sample

This gives good drawing performance and smooth curves. The code to capture the curves into the drawing data model is not shown as it is application-specific.

See Also

You can find the original code and Eric's description on the Square Corner blog (*https://medium.com/square-corner-blog/smooth-signatures-9d92df119ff8*).

Source Download URL

You can download the source code for this example from *https://github.com/IanDarwin/jabagator.android/*.

5.5 Taking a Picture Using an Intent

Ian Darwin

Problem

You want to take a picture from within your app and don't want to write a lot of code.

Solution

Create an `Intent` for `MediaStore.ACTION_IMAGE_CAPTURE`, tailor it a little, and call `startActivityForResult` on this `Intent`. Provide an `onActivityResult()` callback to get notified when the user is done with the camera.

Discussion

Example 5-10 shows code excerpted from the camera Activity in my JPSTrack application. Assuming that you want to save the image with your application's data (instead of in the Media Gallery location), you want to provide a file-based URI referring to the target location, using `intent.putExtra(MediaStore.EXTRA_OUTPUT, uri)`. Note that the Intent handler may give different results on different vendors' platforms.

Example 5-10. The camera capture Activity

```
public class MainActivity extends Activity {
    private static final String TAG = "CameraLaunchingActivity";
    private final static int ACTION_TAKE_PICTURE = 123;

    private File pictureFile;

    @Override
    protected void onCreate(Bundle savedInstanceState) {
        super.onCreate(savedInstanceState);
        setContentView(R.layout.activity_main);
```

```java
    }

    public void takePicture(View v) {
        Log.d(TAG, "Starting Camera Activity");
        try {
            // Use an Intent to get the Camera app going.
            Intent imageIntent = new Intent(MediaStore.ACTION_IMAGE_CAPTURE);
            // Set up file to save image into.
            File baseDir = Environment.getExternalStoragePublicDirectory(
                Environment.DIRECTORY_PICTURES);
            File pictureFile = new File(baseDir, "picture1234.jpg");
            imageIntent.putExtra(MediaStore.EXTRA_VIDEO_QUALITY, 1);
            imageIntent.putExtra(MediaStore.EXTRA_OUTPUT,
                    Uri.fromFile(pictureFile));
            // And away we go!
            startActivityForResult(imageIntent, ACTION_TAKE_PICTURE);
        } catch (Exception e) {
            Toast.makeText(this,
                    getString(R.string.cant_start_activity) + ": " + e,
                    Toast.LENGTH_LONG).show();
        }
    }

    /** Called when an Activity we started for Result is complete */
    @Override
    protected void onActivityResult(int requestCode, int resultCode, Intent data) {
        switch (requestCode) {
            case ACTION_TAKE_PICTURE:
                switch (resultCode) {
                    case Activity.RESULT_OK:
                        if (pictureFile.exists()) {
                            final String message =
                                getString(R.string.picture_saved) +
                                " " + pictureFile.getAbsoluteFile();
                            Log.d(TAG, message);
                            Toast.makeText(this, message, Toast.LENGTH_LONG).show();
                        } else {
                            final String message =
                                getString(R.string.picture_created_but_missing);
                            Toast.makeText(this, message, Toast.LENGTH_LONG).show();
                        }
                        break;
                    case Activity.RESULT_CANCELED:
                        Toast.makeText(this, "Done", Toast.LENGTH_LONG).show();
                        break;
                    default:
                        Toast.makeText(this, "Unexpected resultCode: " + resultCode,
                                                        Toast.LENGTH_LONG).show();
                        break;
                }
                break;
            default:
                Toast.makeText(
                    this, "Unexpected requestCode: " + requestCode,
                    Toast.LENGTH_LONG).show();
        }
```

```
        }
    }
```

 This code will fail if you set the target API to 24 or higher, since API 24 enforces a restriction on exporting URIs to another application via `ClipData` (the theory being that the other app might not have `READ_EXTERNAL_STORAGE` data). It is recommended to use a `content://` URI, which requires either a content provider (Recipe 10.15) or a file provider (Recipe 10.19), both of which are sort of overkill for this project.

See Also

Recipe 5.6.

Source Download URL

The source code for this project is in the Android Cookbook repository (*https://github.com/IanDarwin/Android-Cookbook-Examples*), in the subdirectory *CameraIntent* (see "Getting and Using the Code Examples" on page 18).

5.6 Taking a Picture Using android.media.Camera

Marco Dinacci

Problem

You want to have more control of the various stages involved when taking a picture.

Solution

Create a `SurfaceView` and implement the callbacks fired when the user takes a picture in order to have control over the image capture process.

Discussion

Sometimes you may want more control over the stages involved when taking a picture, or you may want to access and modify the raw image data acquired by the camera. In these cases, using a simple Intent to take a picture is not enough.

We're going to create a new Activity and customize the view to make it full-screen inside the `onCreate()` method (Example 5-11).

Example 5-11. The take picture Activity

```
public class TakePictureActivity extends Activity {
    private Preview mCameraView;

    @Override
    public void onCreate(Bundle savedInstanceState) {
        super.onCreate(savedInstanceState);

        // Force screen to landscape mode as showing a video in
        // portrait mode is not easily doable on all devices
        setRequestedOrientation(ActivityInfo.SCREEN_ORIENTATION_LANDSCAPE);

        // Hide window title and go fullscreen
        requestWindowFeature(Window.FEATURE_NO_TITLE);
        getWindow().addFlags(WindowManager.LayoutParams.FLAG_FULLSCREEN);

        mCameraView= new Preview(this);
        setContentView(mCameraView);
    }
}
```

The `Preview` class is the bulk of the recipe. It handles the `Surface` where the pixels are drawn, and the `Camera` object.

We define a `ClickListener` in the constructor so that the user can take a picture by just tapping once on the screen. Once we get the notification of the click, we take a picture, passing as parameters four (all optional) callbacks (see Example 5-12).

Example 5-12. The SurfaceView implementation

```
class Preview extends SurfaceView implements SurfaceHolder.Callback, PictureCallback
{

    private SurfaceHolder mHolder;
    private Camera mCamera;
    private RawCallback mRawCallback;

    public Preview(Context context) {
        super(context);

        mHolder = getHolder();
        mHolder.addCallback(this);
        mHolder.setType(SurfaceHolder.SURFACE_TYPE_PUSH_BUFFERS);
        mRawCallback = new RawCallback();

        setOnClickListener(new OnClickListener() {

            @Override
            public void onClick(View v) {
                mCamera.takePicture(mRawCallback, mRawCallback, null,
                                    Preview.this);
            }
```

```
        });
    }
```

The `Preview` class implements the `SurfaceHolder.Callback` interface in order to be notified when the underlying surface is created, changed, and destroyed. We'll use these callbacks to properly handle the `Camera` object (see Example 5-13).

Example 5-13. The surfaceChanged() method

```
@Override
public void surfaceChanged(SurfaceHolder holder, int format, int width,
        int height) {

    Camera.Parameters parameters = mCamera.getParameters();
    parameters.setPreviewSize(width, height);
    mCamera.setParameters(parameters);

    mCamera.startPreview();
}

@Override
public void surfaceCreated(SurfaceHolder holder) {
    mCamera = Camera.open();

    configure(mCamera);

    try {
        mCamera.setPreviewDisplay(holder);
    } catch (IOException exception) {
        closeCamera();
    }
}

@Override
public void surfaceDestroyed(SurfaceHolder holder) {
    closeCamera();
}
```

As soon as the camera is created we call `configure()` in order to set the parameters the camera will use to take a picture—things like flash mode, effects, picture format, picture size, scene mode, and so on (Example 5-14). Since not all devices support all kinds of features, always ask which features are supported before setting them.

Example 5-14. The configure() method

```
private void configure(Camera camera) {
    Camera.Parameters params = camera.getParameters();

    // Configure image format. RGB_565 is the most common format.
    List<Integer> formats = params.getSupportedPictureFormats();
    if (formats.contains(PixelFormat.RGB_565))
        params.setPictureFormat(PixelFormat.RGB_565);
```

```
    else
        params.setPictureFormat(PixelFormat.JPEG);

    // Choose the biggest picture size supported by the hardware
    List<Size> sizes = params.getSupportedPictureSizes();
    Camera.Size size = sizes.get(sizes.size()-1);
    params.setPictureSize(size.width, size.height);

    List<String> flashModes = params.getSupportedFlashModes();
    if (flashModes.size() > 0)
        params.setFlashMode(Camera.Parameters.FLASH_MODE_AUTO);

    // Action mode takes pictures of fast-moving objects
    List<String> sceneModes = params.getSupportedSceneModes();
    if (sceneModes.contains(Camera.Parameters.SCENE_MODE_ACTION))
        params.setSceneMode(Camera.Parameters.SCENE_MODE_ACTION);
    else
        params.setSceneMode(Camera.Parameters.SCENE_MODE_AUTO);

    // If you choose FOCUS_MODE_AUTO remember to call autoFocus() on
    // the Camera object before taking a picture
    params.setFocusMode(Camera.Parameters.FOCUS_MODE_FIXED);

    camera.setParameters(params);
}
```

When the surface is destroyed, we close the camera and free its resources (Example 5-15):

Example 5-15. The closeCamera() method

```
private void closeCamera() {
    if (mCamera != null) {
        mCamera.stopPreview();
        mCamera.release();
        mCamera = null;
    }
}
```

The jpeg callback is the last one called; this is where we restart the preview and save the file on disk (Example 5-16):

Example 5-16. Restarting the preview

```
@Override
public void onPictureTaken(byte[] jpeg, Camera camera) {
    // Now that all callbacks have been called it is safe to resume preview
    mCamera.startPreview();

    saveFile(jpeg);
}
```

Finally, we implement the `ShutterCallback` and we again implement the `PictureCallback` to receive the uncompressed raw image data (see Example 5-17).

Example 5-17. The ShutterCallback implementation

```
class RawCallback implements ShutterCallback, PictureCallback {

    @Override
    public void onShutter() {
        // Notify the user, normally with a sound, that the picture has
        // been taken
    }

    @Override
    public void onPictureTaken(byte[] data, Camera camera) {
        // Manipulate uncompressed image data
    }
}
```

See Also

Recipe 5.5.

5.7 Scanning a Barcode or QR Code with the Google ZXing Barcode Scanner

Daniel Fowler

Problem

You want your app to be able to scan a barcode or QR code ("QR" originally stood for Quick Response).

Solution

Use an Intent to access the scanning functionality exposed by the Google ZXing barcode scanner.

Discussion

One of the great features of Android is how easy it is to tap into existing functionality. Scanning barcodes and QR codes is a good example. Google has a free scanning app that you can access via an Intent; thus, an app can easily add scanning functionality, opening up new interface, communication, and feature possibilities.

The program in this recipe is an example of how to access the Google barcode scanner via an Intent. First, make sure the Google barcode scanner (*https://market.android.com/details?id=com.google.zxing.client.android*) is installed. In Figure 5-4 there are three buttons that let the user choose to scan either a QR code, a product barcode, or something else. There are two TextViews to display the type of barcode scanned and the data it contains. The layout is conventional, a vertical LinearLayout, so we don't need to reproduce it here.

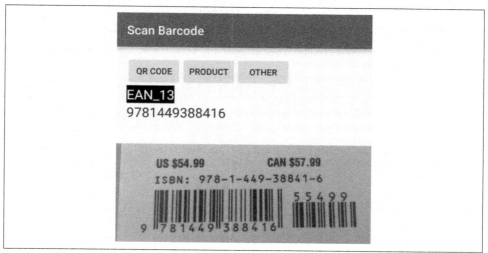

Figure 5-4. Barcode scanner application

The Activity code is shown in Example 5-18; depending on which button is pressed, the program puts the relevant parameters into the Intent before starting the ZXing Activity, and waits for the result.

Example 5-18. Scan program main Activity

```
public class MainActivity extends AppCompatActivity {

    @Override
    protected void onCreate(Bundle savedInstanceState) {
        super.onCreate(savedInstanceState);
        setContentView(R.layout.activity_main);
    }
    public void HandleClick(View arg0) {
        Intent intent = new Intent("com.google.zxing.client.android.SCAN");
        switch(arg0.getId()) {
            case R.id.butQR:
                intent.putExtra("SCAN_MODE", "QR_CODE_MODE");
                break;
            case R.id.butProd:
                intent.putExtra("SCAN_MODE", "PRODUCT_MODE");
```

```
                break;
            case R.id.butOther:
                intent.putExtra("SCAN_FORMATS",
                        "CODE_39,CODE_93,CODE_128,DATA_MATRIX,ITF,CODABAR");
                break;
        }
        try {
            startActivityForResult(intent, 0); // Barcode scanner to scan for us
        } catch (ActivityNotFoundException e)  {
            Toast.makeText(this, "Please install the ZXing Barcode Scanner app",
                                Toast.LENGTH_LONG).show();
        }
    }
    public void onActivityResult(int requestCode, int resultCode, Intent intent) {
        if (requestCode == 0) {
            TextView tvStatus=(TextView)findViewById(R.id.tvStatus);
            TextView tvResult=(TextView)findViewById(R.id.tvResult);
            if (resultCode == RESULT_OK) {
                tvStatus.setText(intent.getStringExtra("SCAN_RESULT_FORMAT"));
                tvResult.setText(intent.getStringExtra("SCAN_RESULT"));
            } else if (resultCode == RESULT_CANCELED) {
                tvStatus.setText("Press a button to start a scan.");
                tvResult.setText("Scan cancelled.");
            }
        }
    }
}
```

Notice, in the table that follows, how it's possible to scan for a family of barcodes (using SCAN_MODE) or for a specific type of barcode (using SCAN_FORMATS). If you know what type of barcode is being decoded, setting SCAN_FORMATS to that particular type may result in faster decoding (because the ZXing app won't try to run through all the barcode decoding algorithms). For example, you could use intent.putExtra("SCAN_FORMATS", "CODE_39"). To use multiple formats, you'd pass a comma-separated list; refer back to Example 5-18.

SCAN_MODE	SCAN_FORMATS
QR_CODE_MODE	QR_CODE
PRODUCT_MODE	EAN_13
	EAN_8
	RSS_14
	UPC_A
	UPC_E
ONE_D_MODE	As for PRODUCT_MODE, plus:
	CODE_39
	CODE_93
	CODE_128

SCAN_MODE	SCAN_FORMATS
	ITF
DATA_MATRIX_MODE	DATA_MATRIX
AZTEC_MODE	AZTEC (beta)
PDF417_MODE	PDF_417 (beta)

Now go and make that scanning inventory control or grocery list app you've been thinking of!

See Also

XZing (*https://github.com/zxing/zxing*), the developer documentation on intents and intent filters (*https://developer.android.com/guide/topics/intents/intents-filters.html*).

Source Download URL

The source code for this example is in the Android Cookbook repository (*https://github.com/IanDarwin/Android-Cookbook-Examples*), in the subdirectory *ScanBarcode* (see "Getting and Using the Code Examples" on page 18).

5.8 Using AndroidPlot to Display Charts and Graphs

Rachee Singh

Problem

You want to display data graphically in an Android application.

Solution

Use one of the many third-party graph libraries available for Android. In this example we will use AndroidPlot, an open source library, to depict a simple graph.

Discussion

You can either download the AndroidPlot library (*http://androidplot.com/wiki/Download*) and add it to your *libs* folder or, preferably, add the coordinates `com.androidplot:androidplot-core:jar:1.2.1` to your build scripts or add this as a module dependency in Android Studio.

In our sample application, we are hardcoding some data and showing the plot corresponding to the data in the application. So, we need to add an (*x,y*) plot to our XML layout (*main.xml*). Example 5-19 shows what *main.xml* looks like with an `XYPlot` component in a linear layout.

Example 5-19. The XML layout with XYPlot

```xml
<?xml version="1.0" encoding="utf-8"?>
<LinearLayout xmlns:android="http://schemas.android.com/apk/res/android"
    android:orientation="vertical"
    android:layout_width="fill_parent"
    android:layout_height="fill_parent"
    >
  <com.androidplot.xy.XYPlot
    android:id="@+id/mySimpleXYPlot"
    android:layout_width="fill_parent"
    android:layout_height="wrap_content"
    title="Stats"/>
</LinearLayout>
```

Now, in the application code, get a reference to the XYPlot defined in the XML:

```java
mySimpleXYPlot = (XYPlot) findViewById(R.id.mySimpleXYPlot);
```

Initialize two arrays of numbers for which the plot will be displayed:

```java
// Create two arrays of y-values to plot:
Number[] series1Numbers = {1, 8, 5, 2, 7, 4};
Number[] series2Numbers = {4, 6, 3, 8, 2, 10};
```

Turn the arrays into XYSeries:

```java
XYSeries series1 = new SimpleXYSeries(
    // SimpleXYSeries takes a List, so turn our array into a List
    Arrays.asList(series1Numbers),
    // Y_VALS_ONLY means use the element index as the x-value
    SimpleXYSeries.ArrayFormat.Y_VALS_ONLY,
    // Set the display title of the series
    "Series1");
```

Create a formatter to use for drawing a series using LineAndPointRenderer:

```java
LineAndPointFormatter series1Format = new LineAndPointFormatter(
    Color.rgb(0, 200, 0),            // line color
    Color.rgb(0, 100, 0),            // point color
    Color.rgb(150, 190, 150));       // fill color (optional)
```

Add series1 and series2 to the XYPlot:

```java
mySimpleXYPlot.addSeries(series1, series1Format);
mySimpleXYPlot.addSeries(series2,
    new LineAndPointFormatter(Color.rgb(0, 0, 200),
    Color.rgb(0, 0, 100), Color.rgb(150, 150, 190)));
```

And make it look cleaner:

```java
// Reduce the number of range labels
mySimpleXYPlot.setTicksPerRangeLabel(3);

// By default, AndroidPlot displays developer guides to aid in laying out
// your plot. To get rid of them call disableAllMarkup().
mySimpleXYPlot.disableAllMarkup();
```

```
mySimpleXYPlot.getBackgroundPaint().setAlpha(0);
mySimpleXYPlot.getGraphWidget().getBackgroundPaint().setAlpha(0);
mySimpleXYPlot.getGraphWidget().getGridBackgroundPaint().setAlpha(0);
```

Run the application! It should look like Figure 5-5.

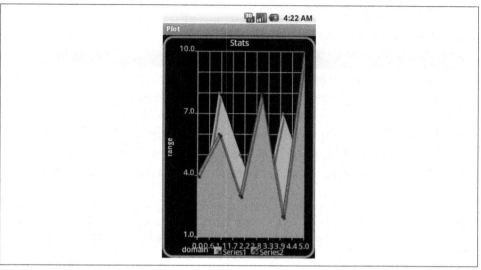

Figure 5-5. AndroidPlot display

Source Download URL

The source code for this project is in the Android Cookbook repository (*https://github.com/IanDarwin/Android-Cookbook-Examples*), in the subdirectory *Android-Plot* (see "Getting and Using the Code Examples" on page 18).

About Android Launcher Icons

One important step in getting an application ready for publishing is creating the launcher icon. The icon will usually be the most common graphical representation of the app that a user encounters. It will represent the app on the Applications screen, in Manage Applications, and as a shortcut if added to the Home screen. A good icon fosters a positive first impression of the app, and helps the app stand out in the crowd.

These files must be in the PNG (often pronounced "ping") or Portable Network Graphics file format, a format supported by most graphical applications nowadays. They also should be in a range of sizes, which we'll discuss here.

Android supports different screen densities, measured in dots per inch (dpi). These are grouped into densities such as medium density (mdpi), high density (hdpi), extra-high density (xhdpi), and so on. When a new project is created in Android Studio,

---

default launcher icons are generated in the *mipmap* folders; older projects used the *drawable* folder, which is still used for drawables other than the application's launcher icon. For best results (sharp images with no pixelation), a project should include an icon for all the possible screen densities that the app will encounter. To do this, place icon files of the correct size into the *mipmap* folders, as shown in Table 5-1.

Table 5-1. Launcher icon sizes

Size	Folder	Purpose
36×36-pixel icon	*res/mipmap-ldpi*	(optional) Low-density screens (approx. 120 dpi)
48×48-pixel icon	*res/mipmap-mdpi*	Medium-density screens (approx. 160 dpi)
72×72-pixel icon	*res/mipmap-hdpi*	High-density screens (approx. 240 dpi)
96×96-pixel icon	*res/mipmap-xhdpi*	Extra-high-density screens (approx. 320 dpi)
144×144-pixel icon	*res/mipmap-xxhdpi*	Extra-extra-high density screens (approx. 480 dpi)
192×192-pixel icon	*res/mipmap-xxxhdpi*	Extra-extra-extra-high-density screens (approx. 640 dpi)

Each icon must include a border around the central image, used for onscreen spacing and minor image protrusions (see Figure 5-6). The recommended border is one-twelfth of the icon size. This means that the space the actual icon image occupies is smaller than the icon pixel size:

- For a 36×36 icon, the image size is 30×30 pixels
- For a 48×48 icon, the image size is 40×40 pixels
- For a 72×72 icon, the image size is 60×60 pixels
- For a 96×96 icon, the image size is 80×80 pixels
- For a 144×144 icon, the image size is 120×120 pixels
- For a 192×192 icon, the image size is 160×160 pixels

Figure 5-6. Icon with border

We discuss programs that can be used to create launcher icons in Recipe 5.9 and Recipe 5.10.

5.9 Using Inkscape to Create an Android Launcher Icon from OpenClipArt.org

Daniel Fowler

Problem

You want to set your app apart from others and make it look professional with a good launcher icon.

Solution

Inkscape is a free and feature-rich graphics program that can export to a bitmap file; you can use it to create the variously sized icons needed for an app.

Discussion

You need a graphics program to design the graphical resources used in an Android application. Inkscape is a free, multiplatform graphics program with some very powerful features. You can use it to generate high-quality vector graphics that can then be exported to any required resolution. This is ideal for generating Android launcher icons (and other graphical resources). See the Inkscape website (*https://inkscape.org/ en/*) for more information on the program and to download the latest version.

The required sizes are described in "About Android Launcher Icons" on page 255. When designing an icon, it's better to work with images that are larger than the required size. A larger image is easier to work with in a graphics program and easily scaled down when completed. An image that is 576×576 pixels is divisible equally by all the icon sizes, and this is a reasonable size in which to design. For a vector-based graphics package such as Inkscape, the image size is irrelevant; it can be scaled up and down without losing quality. Inkscape uses the open Scalable Vector Graphics (SVG) format. Image detail is only lost when the final bitmap images are produced from the vector image.

If you want to learn how to design images in Inkscape, you can use the many tutorials that are available both via the Help menu and online; the Inkscape Tutorials Blog (*https://inkscapetutorials.org/*) is a good tutorial reference.

Once you have designed an image in Inkscape, you can export it to a PNG file for use as an app icon. In the following example, the image to be converted to icons came from the "Creating a Coffee Cup with Inkscape" tutorial (*http://vector.tutsplus.com/ tutorials/illustration/creating-a-coffee-cup-with-inkscape/*). If you follow the tutorial, you'll create the image shown in Figure 5-7.

Figure 5-7. A cup of java

If you don't want to follow the tutorial, you can obtain a coffee cup image from Openclipart (*https://openclipart.org/*), a great source of free images (see Figure 5-8). Search for "coffee" and you'll see various coffee-related images, including the one shown in Figure 5-7, uploaded by this recipe's author. Select the image, click the View SVG button, and then use your browser's File → Save menu to save the image.

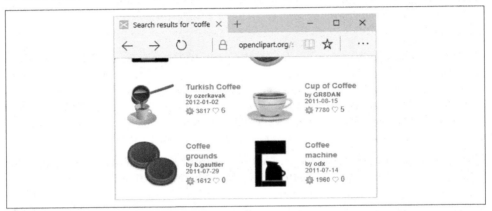

Figure 5-8. Searching for the perfect cup

You can now convert the image to an icon for whatever coffee-related app is currently in the pipeline. The required icon sizes are generated from the image using the Inkscape Export to PNG option. The image is opened and correctly proportioned for the export. This can be done for any image designed or opened in Inkscape. Remember that images should not be overly detailed or have too many colors (detail is reduced during resizing), and that they should try to fill (or fit) a square area. It's worth reading the Android Design guidelines (*https://developer.android.com/design/index.html*), including those on launcher icons (*https://developer.android.com/guide/practices/ui_guidelines/icon_design_launcher.html*).

With the image open, resize the document to 576×576 pixels. To do this, use the Document Properties option under the File menu (see Figure 5-9). In the "Custom size" section, set Width and Height to 576 and check that Units is set to "px" (for pixels). Also, make sure that the "Show page border" checkbox is ticked.

Close the Document Properties dialog, then drag two vertical and two horizontal guides from the rulers (click and drag from any part of the page ruler; if the rulers aren't visible, use the View → Show/Hide → Rulers menu option to display them.) Drag the guides inside each page border approximately one-twelfth of the width and height of the visible page border. You'll now set the accurate position of the guides using the guide properties. Double-click each guide and set the following positions:

Guide	x	y
Top horizontal	0	528
Bottom horizontal	0	48
Left vertical	48	0
Right vertical	528	0

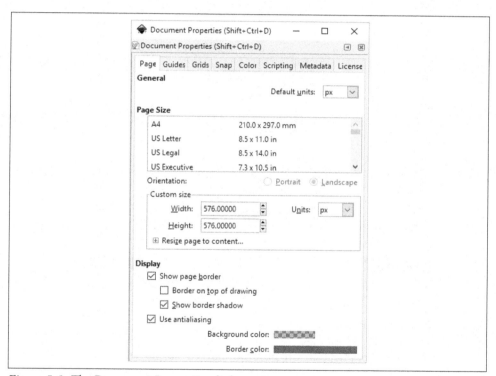

Figure 5-9. The Document Properties dialog

At this point, you should be able to easily adjust the image to fit within the guides. (Minor protrusions into the border area are allowed if required for image balance.) Use the Edit → Select All menu item or press Ctrl-A to select the image, drag the image into position, and then resize it as appropriate to fit within the box outlined by the guides (see Figure 5-10).

With the image created and correctly proportioned, you can now create the bitmaps for an Android project. In Inkscape, ensure that the image is *not* selected (click outside the image), and then use the File → Export PNG Image menu option to bring up the Export PNG Image dialog (see Figure 5-11). Select Page, then under "Image size" set Width and Height as per Table 5-1; you do not need to change the dpi setting (it will change as Width and Height are changed). Under Filename, browse to the project directory for the icon and enter *ic_launcher.png* for the filename. Finally, click the Export button to generate the icon. Repeat this process for all the icon resolutions.

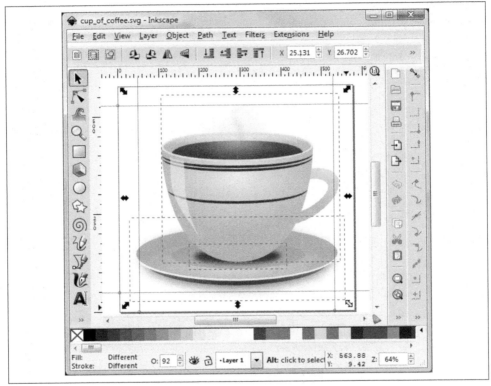

Figure 5-10. Resizing in Inkscape

You should test the application on physical and virtual devices to ensure that the icons display as expected (see Figure 5-12).

The icon files do not need to be called *ic_launcher.png*; see Recipe 5.10 for information on changing the launcher icon filename.

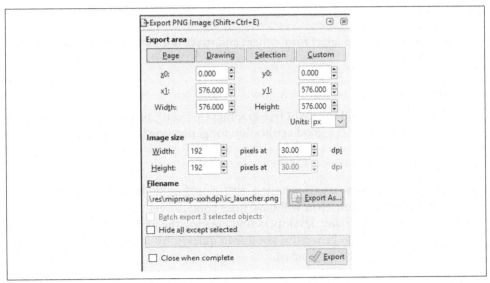

Figure 5-11. The Export PNG Image dialog

Figure 5-12. Icon in use

See Also

Recipe 5.10; Inkscape (*https://inkscape.org/en/*), Inkscape Tutorials Blog (*http://inksca petutorials.org/*), "Creating a Coffee Cup with Inkscape" tutorial (*https://design.tuts plus.com/tutorials/creating-a-coffee-cup-with-inkscape—vector-30*), Openclipart (*https://openclipart.org/*), Android design guidelines for launcher icons (*https://devel oper.android.com/guide/practices/ui_guidelines/icon_design_launcher.html*).

5.10 Using Paint.NET to Create Launcher Icons from OpenClipArt.org

Daniel Fowler

Problem

You want to set your app apart from others and make it look professional with a good launcher icon.

Solution

Openclipart.org is a good source of free graphics that you can adapt for use as an icon for your app. Paint.NET is a good application for generating launcher icons.

Discussion

Developers with access to a graphic artist, either professionally or through friends, or who are good artists themselves will have finer control over the graphics within their applications. However, many developers find creating the graphics in an app a chore. This recipe shows how to generate a good icon quickly, by compromising on the fine control provided by a dedicated artist.

Android Studio comes with the Image Asset utility, which is good for creating basic images at various densities, including launcher icons. To run the utility, with the app folder highlighted in Studio, use the File → New → Image Asset menu option. To use an existing clip art image as your starting point, click the tiny "Clip Art" icon in the left panel. In Figure 5-13 we have selected the Heart icon (about one-third of the way down in the All category), clicked OK, and changed the foreground and background colors.

For a more complex icon, a good source of free images is Openclipart (*https://opencli part.org/*). The graphics provided are in vector format, which makes them great for scaling to icon size. Icons are a raster format, so once a suitable graphic has been chosen it needs to be converted to the Android icon format, Portable Network Graphics (PNG).

For this recipe, we will add an icon to the example "Hello, World" app created in Recipe 1.15.

First, find a suitable free graphic as a starting point. Go to *https://openclipart.org/* and use the Search box. The search results may include graphics that don't seem logical. This is because the search not only includes the name of the graphic, but also tags and descriptions, as well as partial words; therefore, graphics unrelated to the major search term will appear, as will contributions with misspellings or whose names are in a different language. But this also means that you may find an unexpected but suitable graphic.

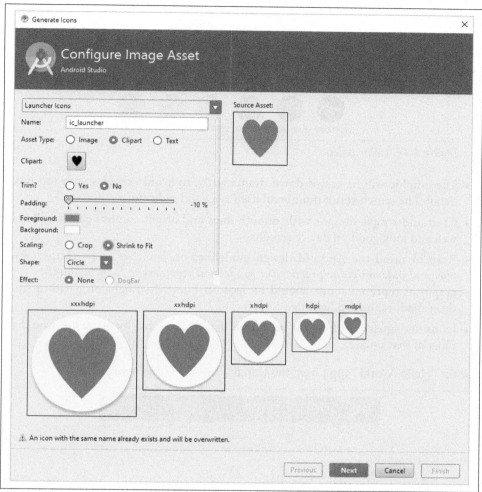

Figure 5-13. Studio Image Asset tool—Generate Icons

Page through the search results, which are provided as thumbnails with title, contributor name, date of submission, and number of downloads. When looking for a graphic to use as an icon, keep these pointers in mind:

- Figure 5-14 shows the recommended color palette to fit in with the Android theme; this is only a recommendation, but it is a useful guide. Avoid any color that is too extreme.

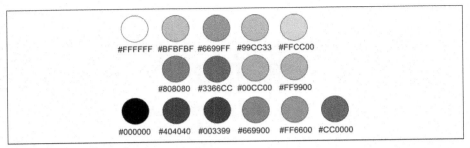

Figure 5-14. Color palette

- The graphic will be scaled down dramatically, so avoid graphics with too much detail. The search result thumbnail itself is a good indicator.

- Clear and simple designs with smooth lines and bright, neutral colors will scale well and look good on device screens.

- Keep in mind the Android design guidelines on launcher icons (*https://devel oper.android.com/guide/practices/ui_guidelines/icon_design_launcher.html*); graphical representations should be face on (viewed straight on), with a small drop shadow and top lighting.

- Icons are square, so look for an image that, if bounded by a square, would fill most of that square.

For the "Hello, World" app I used the search term *earth* (see Figure 5-15).

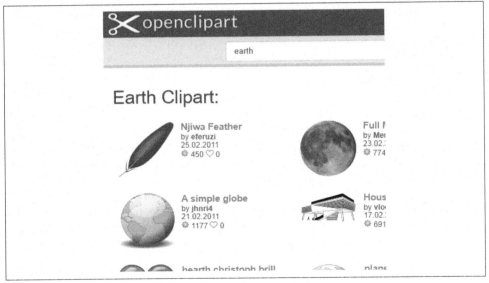

Figure 5-15. Clip art search results

I chose the graphic titled "A simple globe." Click the graphic to bring up its details. You can save the graphic to the local machine by clicking it (or clicking the View SVG button) and using the browser's File menu. However, using the browser's File → Save menu option or typing Ctrl-S will save the file as a vector file, which, as discussed earlier, is not a good format for an icon. Fortunately, the image's Openclipart page has an option to obtain the file as a PNG file; click the image you want, and the dialog in Figure 5-16 will appear.

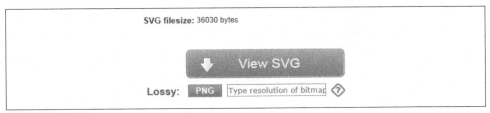

Figure 5-16. Convert to PNG with given size

On this page, we can use the PNG button to obtain PNG files in the image sizes required (refer back to "About Android Launcher Icons" on page 255 for details on sizes). In the box next to the PNG button type in the first image size required, 30 (for the low-density icon; see Figure 5-16). We cannot put in the full icon size, 36, because that would not leave any border.

Click the PNG button and then use the browser's File menu (or Ctrl-S) to save the generated PNG file. Then click the browser's Back button. Clear the box next to the PNG button and enter the size of the next icon graphic required: in this case, 40 for the medium-density icon. Again click the PNG button and save the generated file. Do the same for all the other sizes. When you are done, you should have five or six files, each containing the same image at a different resolution (Figure 5-17). The graphics files may not be perfectly square—for example, they may be 39×40 instead of 40×40 pixels—but the small difference does not matter.

Figure 5-17. Icons of Earth in some of the required sizes

You now need to resize the files to the correct icon sizes by adding the empty border. You can do this in a graphics application such as GIMP (*https://www.gimp.org/*), Inkscape (*http://inkscape.org/*), or Paint.NET (*http://www.getpaint.net*) (Windows only). For this recipe, we will use Paint.NET.

In Paint.NET, open the first graphics file. Set the secondary (background) color to transparent by selecting the Window menu option → Colors or pressing F8; in the Colors dialog, ensure that Secondary is selected in the drop-down, and then click the More button to see the advanced options. Set the Transparency option in the bottom right of the Colors dialog to zero (see Figure 5-18).

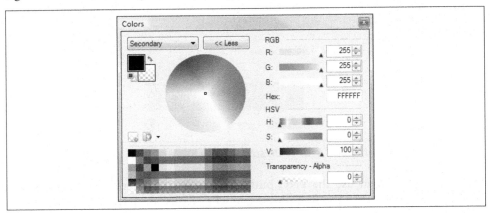

Figure 5-18. Color selection palette

Next, open the Canvas Size dialog by selecting the Image → Canvas Size menu option or pressing Ctrl-Shift-R. Select the "By absolute size" radio button, but ignore the "Maintain aspect ratio" checkbox (if the graphic is square, this checkbox can be checked, but if not it should be unchecked). In the "Pixel size" options, set the correct Width and Height for the icon for the given graphic—both 36 for the 30×30 graphic, both 48 for the 40×40 graphic, both 72 for the 60×60 graphic, and so on for the other sizes. Set the Anchor option to Middle. When you're done, click OK (see Figure 5-19). Save the resized image and repeat for the remaining sizes.

With a project open in Android Studio, under the *res* folder there will exist some *mipmap* folders for the launcher icon (the older *drawable* folders are used for all graphics other than the launcher icons). Copy the new PNG files into the correct density folders as *ic_launcher.png*, creating the required folder under *res* if needed. Table 5-2 provides a summary.

Table 5-2. Icon formatting summary

Folder	Icon size	Image size	dpi	Android density	Example screen	Notes
mipmap-ldpi	36×36	30×30	120	ldpi	Small QVGA	
mipmap-mdpi	48×48	40×40	160	mdpi	Normal HVGA	Default icon in absence of anything else
mipmap-hdpi	72×72	60×60	240	hdpi	Normal WVGA800	
mipmap-xhdpi	96×96	80×80	320	xhdpi	WXGA720	

Folder	Icon size	Image size	dpi	Android density	Example screen	Notes
mipmap-xxhdpy	144×144	120×120	160	xxdpi	Nexus 5	
mipmap-xxxhdpy	192×192	160×160	160	xxxhdpi	Nexus 6	

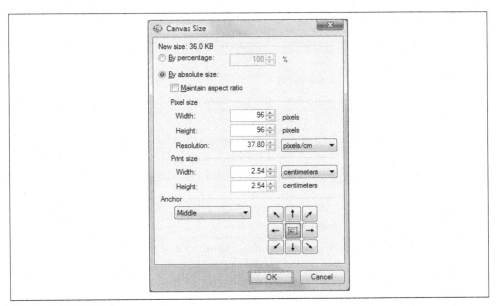

Figure 5-19. Setting canvas size

Figure 5-20 illustrates the effect of adding a border around the image by specifying the larger icon size; this allows for appropriate spacing between icons and accommodates any minor image protrusions.

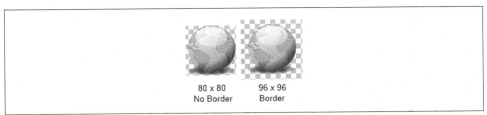

Figure 5-20. An 80x80-pixel icon, with and without the recommended border

Note that QVGA stands for "Quarter VGA" (VGA was the "advanced" 640×480 video on a model of the original IBM PC in the last century), HVGA is Half VGA, and so on.

The *AndroidManifest.xml* file references the icon file via the `application` element's `android:icon` attribute (here, `android:icon="@mipmap/ic_launcher"`). This is shown in Figure 5-21.

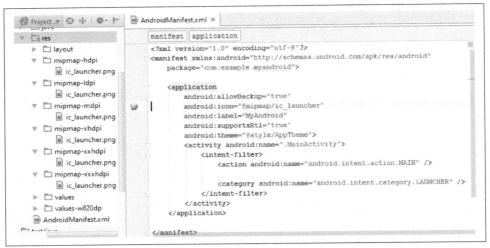

Figure 5-21. The icon file setting in the AndroidManifest.xml file

 The icon files do not need to be called *ic_launcher.png*. As long as all the filenames in all the resource folders are valid and the same, they can be named something else. For example, you might call these icon files *globe.png*. If you change the filename from the default, however, you will also need to change the value of the `android:icon` attribute in the application element in the manifest file (for example, from `android:icon="@mipmap/ic_launcher"` to `android:icon="@mipmap/globe"`).

Now you should be all set—you should see icons in each of the *mipmap* subdirectories. Be sure to test the icons on various devices to make sure they look okay.

Remember to give thanks for free stuff; in this case I thank Open Clipart Library contributor jhnri4.

See Also

Recipe 1.15; Android design guidelines for icons (*https://developer.android.com/guide/practices/ui_guidelines/icon_design_launcher.html*), Openclipart (*https://openclipart.org/*), Paint.NET (*http://www.getpaint.net/*), Inkscape (*http://inkscape.org/*), GIMP (*https://www.gimp.org/*).

5.11 Using Nine Patch Files

Daniel Fowler

Problem

When designing a user interface, you want to change the default view backgrounds to fit in with an app's overall style. The backgrounds must be able to scale correctly for variously sized views.

Solution

Use Android's NinePatch files to provide support for scaling of backgrounds as view sizes change.

Discussion

In the following picture, the word "Text" has a background that is a rounded rectangle (a black border with a gray background). The rectangle has then been uniformly scaled to fit "Longer Text." As a result of the scaling, the corners and vertical edges have been distorted, giving the rounded rectangle an unbalanced look. Compare that to the second "Longer Text," where the background has maintained its balance:

To correctly scale the background, selected parts of the image are scaled in a particular direction, or not scaled at all. Which parts are scaled and in which direction are shown in this diagram:

The Xs indicate that corners are not scaled, while the vertical edges are scaled vertically, the horizontal edges are scaled horizontally, and the central area is scaled in both directions. Hence the name NinePatch:

```
4 corners +
2 vertical edges +
2 horizontal edges +
1 central area
```

```
---------------------
9 areas (patches) in total
```

In the following example, the default black border and gray gradient background of an EditText is replaced with a solid turquoise background and a black border. The required rounded rectangle can be drawn in a graphics program such as GIMP or Paint.NET. The rectangle should be drawn as small as possible (resembling a circle) to support small views, with a 1-pixel border and a transparent background. I've also drawn a version of the rectangle with an orange border to support focus indication used with keypad navigation:

Android needs to know which proportions of the vertical and horizontal edges need to be scaled, as well as where the view content sits in relation to the background. These factors are determined from indicators drawn within the image. To apply these indicators, use the *draw9patch* program supplied with the Android SDK tools. Start the program and open the background image (drag and drop it onto the draw9patch dialog). The program will expand the image by one pixel all around, as per Figure 5-22. You're going to draw indicator lines on this extra 1-pixel edging. Enlarge the image using the Zoom slider. In the lefthand and top edges, draw the indicator lines to mark which of the vertical and horizontal pixels can be duplicated for scaling. In the righthand and bottom edges, draw the indicator lines to show where content can be positioned.

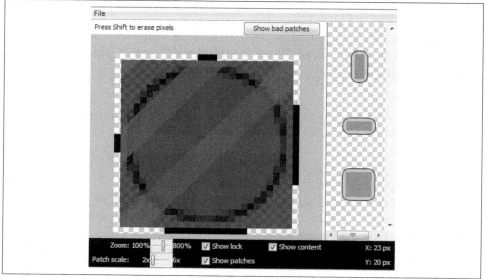

Figure 5-22. The draw9patch program in action

Figure 5-23 shows the right and bottom markers for content placement. If content does not fit in the indicated rectangle, the background image is stretched using the area shown by the left and top markers.

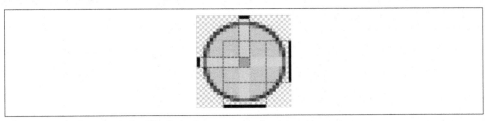

Figure 5-23. draw9patch: Markers for content placement

Save the marked-up file in the *res/drawable* folder for a project. Android determines whether an image is scaled using NinePatch scaling instead of uniform scaling via the filename; it must have *.9* before the *.png* file extension. For example, an image file named *turquoise.png* would be named *turquoise.9.png*. To use the background image, reference it in a layout with `android:background="@drawable/turquoise"`. If you are also using another image to indicate view focus, use a selector file—for example, save this XML file in the *drawable* folder as *selector.xml*:

```xml
<?xml version="1.0" encoding="utf-8"?>
<selector xmlns:android="http://schemas.android.com/apk/res/android">
    <item android:state_focused="true"
      android:drawable="@drawable/turqfocus" />
    <item android:drawable="@drawable/turquoise" />
</selector>
```

Then reference this as `android:background="@drawable/selector"`. Figure 5-24 shows the results.

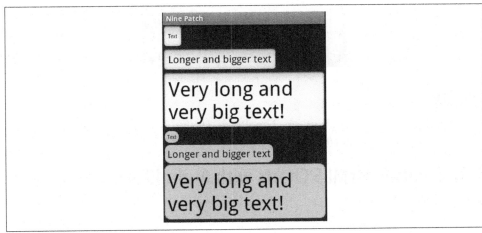

Figure 5-24. NinePatch file used as selector and background

Notice that the new view background is using a little less space than the default (this is useful to know if a project needs a little bit more screen area).

NinePatch files are not restricted to simple view backgrounds. This NinePatch file is used to frame a photograph:

Notice how the left and top scaling indicators are split where detail that must not be scaled (because it would distort) is located. Here's the result:

See Also

The developer documentation on NinePatch (*https://developer.android.com/guide/topics/graphics/2d-graphics.html#nine-patch*).

5.12 Creating HTML5 Charts with Android RGraph

Wagied Davids

Problem

You need to visualize data in a plot or chart and be able to interact with the chart via JavaScript.

Solution

As an alternative to creating Android charts in pure Java, create charts using RGraph, an HTML5 JavaScript charts library.

 RGraph will not work on Android prior to 2.1, but that shouldn't be a problem today.

Discussion

To create a chart with RGraph (*https://www.rgraph.net/*), follow these steps:

1. Create an assets directory for HTML files; Android internally maps it to *file:/// android_asset/* (note the triple slash and singular spelling of "asset").

2. Copy *rgraphview.html* (see Example 5-20) into it: *res/assets/rgraphview.html*.

3. Create a JavaScript directory: *res/assets/RGraph*.

4. Create the layout (Example 5-21) and the Activity (Example 5-22) as in any other Android project.

Example 5-20 shows the HTML using the RGraph library. Figure 5-25 shows the RGraph output.

Example 5-20. HTML using the RGraph library

```
<html>
<head>
<title>RGraph: HTML5 canvas graph library - pie chart</title>

    <script src="RGraph/libraries/RGraph.common.core.js" ></script>
    <script src="RGraph/libraries/RGraph.common.annotate.js" ></script>
    <script src="RGraph/libraries/RGraph.common.context.js" ></script>
    <script src="RGraph/libraries/RGraph.common.tooltips.js" ></script>
    <script src="RGraph/libraries/RGraph.common.zoom.js" ></script>
    <script src="RGraph/libraries/RGraph.common.resizing.js" ></script>
    <script src="RGraph/libraries/RGraph.pie.js" ></script>

    <script>
      window.onload = function () {
        /**
```

```
             * These are not angles - these are values.
             * The appropriate angles are calculated.
             */
            var pie1 = new RGraph.Pie('pie1', [41,37,16,3,3]); // Create pie object
            pie1.Set('chart.labels', ['MSIE 7 (41%)', 'MSIE 6 (37%)',
                                     'Firefox (16%)', 'Safari (3%)', 'Other (3%)']);
            pie1.Set('chart.gutter', 30);
            pie1.Set('chart.title', "Browsers (tooltips, context, zoom)");
            pie1.Set('chart.shadow', false);
            pie1.Set('chart.tooltips.effect', 'contract');
            pie1.Set('chart.tooltips', [
                                        'Internet Explorer 7 (41%)',
                                        'Internet Explorer 6 (37%)',
                                        'Mozilla Firefox (16%)',
                                        'Apple Safari (3%)',
                                        'Other (3%)'
                                       ]
                                      );
            pie1.Set('chart.highlight.style', '3d'); // 2d or 3d; defaults to 3d

            if (!RGraph.isIE8()) {
                pie1.Set('chart.zoom.hdir', 'center');
                pie1.Set('chart.zoom.vdir', 'up');
                pie1.Set('chart.labels.sticks', true);
                pie1.Set('chart.labels.sticks.color', '#aaa');
                pie1.Set('chart.contextmenu', [['Zoom in', RGraph.Zoom]]);
            }

            pie1.Set('chart.linewidth', 5);
            pie1.Set('chart.labels.sticks', true);
            pie1.Set('chart.strokestyle', 'white');
            pie1.Draw();

            var pie2 = new RGraph.Pie('pie2', [2,29,45,17,7]); // Create pie object
            pie2.Set('chart.gutter', 45);
            pie2.Set('chart.title', "Some data (context, annotatable)");
            pie2.Set('chart.linewidth', 1);
            pie2.Set('chart.strokestyle', '#333');
            pie2.Set('chart.shadow', true);
            pie2.Set('chart.shadow.blur', 3);
            pie2.Set('chart.shadow.offsetx', 3);
            pie2.Set('chart.shadow.offsety', 3);
            pie2.Set('chart.shadow.color', 'rgba(0,0,0,0.5)');
            pie2.Set('chart.colors', ['red', 'pink', '#6f6', 'blue', 'yellow']);
            pie2.Set('chart.contextmenu', [['Clear',
                function () {RGraph.Clear(pie2.canvas); pie2.Draw();}]]);
            pie2.Set('chart.key', ['John (2%)', 'Richard (29%)',
                'Fred (45%)', 'Brian (17%)', 'Peter (7%)']);
            pie2.Set('chart.key.background', 'white');
            pie2.Set('chart.key.shadow', true);
            pie2.Set('chart.annotatable', true);
            pie2.Set('chart.align', 'left');
            pie2.Draw();
        }
    </script>
</head>
```

```
<body>

    <div style="text-align: center">
        <canvas id="pie1" width="420" height="300">[No canvas support]</canvas>
        <canvas id="pie2" width="440" height="300">[No canvas support]</canvas>
    </div>

</body>
</html>
```

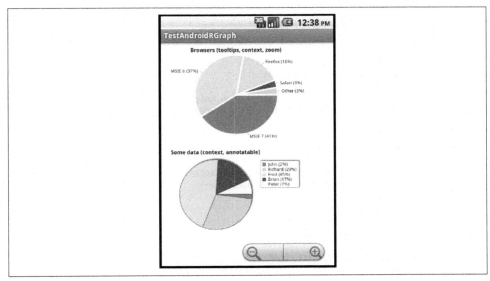

Figure 5-25. RGraph output

Example 5-21. The main.xml file

```
<?xml version="1.0" encoding="utf-8"?>
<LinearLayout
    xmlns:android="http://schemas.android.com/apk/res/android"
    android:orientation="horizontal"
    android:layout_width="fill_parent"
    android:layout_height="fill_parent"
    android:background="#FFFFFF">

    <WebView
        android:id="@+id/webview"
        android:layout_width="fill_parent"
        android:layout_height="fill_parent">
    </WebView>
</LinearLayout>
```

Example 5-22. The main Activity

```
import android.app.Activity;
import android.os.Bundle;
import android.webkit.WebChromeClient;
import android.webkit.WebSettings;
import android.webkit.WebView;
import android.webkit.WebViewClient;

public class Main extends Activity {

        /** Called when the Activity is first created. */
        @Override
        public void onCreate(Bundle savedInstanceState) {
                super.onCreate(savedInstanceState);
                setContentView(R.layout.main);

                // Obtain reference to the WebView holder
                WebView webview = (WebView) this.findViewById(R.id.webview);

                // Get the settings
                WebSettings webSettings = webview.getSettings();

                // Enable JavaScript for user interaction clicks
                webSettings.setJavaScriptEnabled(true);

                // Display zoom controls
                webSettings.setBuiltInZoomControls(true);
                webview.requestFocusFromTouch();

                // Set the client
                webview.setWebViewClient(new WebViewClient());
                webview.setWebChromeClient(new WebChromeClient());

                // Load the URL
                webview.loadUrl("file:///android_asset/rgraphview.html");
        }

}
```

Source Download URL

The source code for this example is in the Android Cookbook repository (*https://github.com/IanDarwin/Android-Cookbook-Examples*), in the subdirectory *RGraph-Demo* (see "Getting and Using the Code Examples" on page 18).

5.13 Adding a Simple Raster Animation

Daniel Fowler

Problem

You need to add an animated image to a screen.

Solution

Android has good support for user interface animation; it is easy to sequence images using the AnimationDrawable class.

Discussion

To create the animation, first generate the images to be sequenced, using a graphics program. Each image represents one frame of the animation; the images will usually be the same size, with changes between each frame as required.

This animation recipe will sequence some traffic light images. The images can be generated using the open source vector graphics program Inkscape (*http://inkscape.org*). A copy of the image used is available from the Open clipart library (*https://opencli part.org/*); search for "traffic lights turned off," select the image, click the View SVG button, and save the file from your browser. Then open the file in Inkscape.

The animation will comprise four images showing the sequence of traffic lights as used in the United Kingdom: red, red and yellow, green, yellow, and back to red. The SVG image has all the lights available—they are just hidden behind translucent circles. To generate the first image, select the circle covering the red light and delete it. Then use the Edit → Select All menu option to highlight the whole image. Select Export to PNG from the File menu. In the Export to PNG dialog, under "Bitmap size," enter 150 in the Height box, and choose a directory and filename for the file to be generated—for example, *red.png* (see Figure 5-26).

Click the Export button to export the bitmap. Delete the circle covering the yellow light, click Edit → Select All again, and export as before to a file; for example, *red_yel-low.png*. Use the Edit → Undo menu option (twice) to cover the red light and yellow light, and then delete the circle covering the green light. Export to *green.png*. Again use Undo to cover the green light, and delete the circle covering the yellow light. Export the bitmap to *yellow.png*.

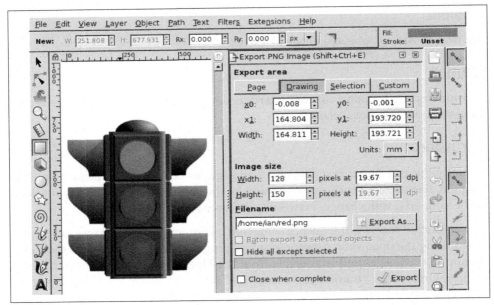

Figure 5-26. The Export to PNG dialog

The files are now ready for the animation:

Start an Android project. Copy the four generated files into the *res/drawable* direc-tory. An `animation-list` needs to be defined in the same directory. Create a new file in *res/drawable* called *uktrafficlights.xml*. In this new file, add the following:

```xml
<?xml version="1.0" encoding="utf-8"?>
<animation-list xmlns:android="http://schemas.android.com/apk/res/android"
    android:oneshot="false">
    <item android:drawable="@drawable/red" android:duration="2000" />
    <item android:drawable="@drawable/red_yellow" android:duration="2000" />
    <item android:drawable="@drawable/green" android:duration="2000" />
    <item android:drawable="@drawable/yellow" android:duration="2000" />
</animation-list>
```

This lists the images to be animated in the order of the animation and how long each one needs to be displayed (in milliseconds). If the animation needs to stop after run-ning through the images, set the attribute `android:oneshot` to `true`.

In the layout file for the program, add an `ImageView` whose source is given as `@drawable/uktrafficlights` (i.e., pointing to the created file):

```
<?xml version="1.0" encoding="utf-8"?>
<LinearLayout xmlns:android="http://schemas.android.com/apk/res/android"
    android:orientation="vertical"
    android:layout_width="fill_parent"
    android:layout_height="fill_parent">
    <ImageView android:id="@+id/imageView1"
        android:src="@drawable/uktrafficlights"
        android:layout_height="wrap_content"
        android:layout_width="wrap_content"/>
</LinearLayout>
```

In the Activity class, create an instance of AnimationDrawable (the Android class that performs the animation) called lightsAnimation. In onCreate(), assign it to the Drawable that the ImageView uses. Finally, start the animation by calling the AnimationDrawable start() method (there is a stop() method available to end the animation if required). We do this in onWindowFocusChanged to ensure that everything has loaded before the animation starts (it could easily have been started with a button or other type of input). Example 5-23 shows the code for the main Activity.

Example 5-23. The main Activity

```
public class main extends Activity {
    AnimationDrawable lightsAnimation;
    @Override
    public void onCreate(Bundle savedInstanceState) {
        super.onCreate(savedInstanceState);
        setContentView(R.layout.main);
        ImageView lights = (ImageView) findViewById(R.id.imageView1);
        lightsAnimation=(AnimationDrawable) lights.getDrawable();
    }
    @Override
    public void onWindowFocusChanged(boolean hasFocus) {
        super.onWindowFocusChanged(hasFocus);
        lightsAnimation.start();
    }
}
```

Image animations can be useful to add interest to screens and can be used in games or cartoons.

See Also

Inkscape (*http://inkscape.org*), Openclipart (*https://openclipart.org/*).

5.14 Using Pinch to Zoom

Pratik Rupwal

Problem

You want to use touch capability to change the position of an image viewed on the screen, and use pinch-in and pinch-out movements for zoom-in and zoom-out operations.

Solution

Scale the image as a matrix to apply transformations to it, to show different visual effects.

Discussion

First, add a simple `ImageView` inside a `FrameLayout` in *main.xml*, as shown here:

```xml
<?xml version="1.0" encoding="utf-8"?>
<FrameLayout
  xmlns:android="http://schemas.android.com/apk/res/android"
  android:layout_width="fill_parent"
  android:layout_height="fill_parent" >
<ImageView android:id="@+id/imageView"
    android:layout_width="fill_parent"
    android:layout_height="fill_parent"
    android:src="@drawable/nature"
    android:scaleType="matrix" >
</ImageView>
</FrameLayout>
```

Example 5-24 scales the `ImageView` as a matrix to apply transformations on it.

Example 5-24. Touch listener with scaling

```java
public class Touch extends Activity implements OnTouchListener {
private static final String TAG = "Touch";

// These matrixes will be used to move and zoom image
Matrix matrix = new Matrix();
Matrix savedMatrix = new Matrix();

// We can be in one of these 3 states
static final int NONE = 0;
static final int DRAG = 1;
static final int ZOOM = 2;
```

```
int mode = NONE;

// Remember some things for zooming
PointF start = new PointF();
PointF mid = new PointF();
float oldDist = 1f;

@Override
public void onCreate(Bundle savedInstanceState) {
    super.onCreate(savedInstanceState);
    setContentView(R.layout.main);
    ImageView view = (ImageView) findViewById(R.id.imageView);
    view.setScaleType(ImageView.ScaleType.FIT_CENTER);
    // Make the image fit to the center
    view.setOnTouchListener(this);
}

public boolean onTouch(View v, MotionEvent event) {
    ImageView view = (ImageView) v;
    // Make the image scalable as a matrix
    view.setScaleType(ImageView.ScaleType.MATRIX);
    float scale;

    // Handle touch events here...
    switch (event.getAction() & MotionEvent.ACTION_MASK) {

    case MotionEvent.ACTION_DOWN: // First finger down only
    savedMatrix.set(matrix);
    start.set(event.getX(), event.getY());
    Log.d(TAG, "mode=DRAG" );
    mode = DRAG;
    break;
    case MotionEvent.ACTION_UP: // First finger lifted
    case MotionEvent.ACTION_POINTER_UP: // Second finger lifted
    mode = NONE;
    Log.d(TAG, "mode=NONE" );
    break;
    case MotionEvent.ACTION_POINTER_DOWN: // Second finger down
    // Calculates the distance between two points where user touched
    oldDist = spacing(event);
    Log.d(TAG, "oldDist=" + oldDist);
    // Minimal distance between both the fingers
    if (oldDist > 5f) {
        savedMatrix.set(matrix);
        // Sets mid-point of line between two points where user touched
        midPoint(mid, event);
        mode = ZOOM;
        Log.d(TAG, "mode=ZOOM" );
    }
    break;

    case MotionEvent.ACTION_MOVE:
    if (mode == DRAG) { // Movement of first finger
        matrix.set(savedMatrix);
        if (view.getLeft() >= -392) {
            matrix.postTranslate(event.getX() - start.x, event.getY() - start.y);
```

```
            }
        }
        else if (mode == ZOOM) { // Pinch zooming
            float newDist = spacing(event);
            Log.d(TAG, "newDist=" + newDist);
            if (newDist > 5f) {
                matrix.set(savedMatrix);
                // Thinking I need to play around with this value to limit it
                scale = newDist/oldDist;
                matrix.postScale(scale, scale, mid.x, mid.y);
            }
        }
        break;
        }

        // Perform the transformation
        view.setImageMatrix(matrix);

        return true; // Indicate event was handled
    }

    private float spacing(MotionEvent event) {
        float x = event.getX(0) - event.getX(1);
        float y = event.getY(0) - event.getY(1);
         return FloatMath.sqrt(x * x + y * y);
    }

    private void midPoint(PointF point, MotionEvent event) {
        float x = event.getX(0) + event.getX(1);
        float y = event.getY(0) + event.getY(1);
        point.set(x / 2, y / 2);
    }
}
```

See Also

The reference documentation for Matrix (*https://developer.android.com/reference/android/graphics/Matrix.html*), used in the calculations.

Source Download URL

The source code for this example is in the Android Cookbook repository (*https://github.com/IanDarwin/Android-Cookbook-Examples*), in the subdirectory *PinchAndZoom* (see "Getting and Using the Code Examples" on page 18).

## CHAPTER 6

Graphical User Interface

When Android was being invented, its designers faced many choices whose outcome would determine the success or failure of their project. Once they had rejected all the other smartphone operating systems, both closed and open source, and decided to build their own atop the Linux kernel, they were faced with somewhat of a blank canvas. One important choice was which programming language to use; they wisely chose Java. But once that choice was made, there was the choice of user interface technology to deploy: Java ME, Swing, the Standard Widget Toolkit (SWT), or none of the above.

Java ME (*http://www.oracle.com/technetwork/java/javame/*) is the Java Micro Edition, Sun/Oracle's official standard API for cell phones and other small devices. Java ME was once a pretty big success story: tens if not hundreds of millions of cell phones have a Java ME runtime inside. Also, all BlackBerry devices made from around 2000 to around 2010, and all BlackBerry smartphone applications for BlackBerry OSes 5, 6 and 7 (but not including BlackBerry OS 10), were based on Java ME. But the Java ME GUI was regarded as too limiting by the Android team, having been designed for the days when cell phones had really tiny screens and limited functionality (it's noteworthy that BlackBerry came to a similar conclusion, dropping Java ME when it came time to produce BlackBerry 10).

Swing (*http://java.sun.com/javase/6/docs/technotes/guides/swing/index.html*) is the Java Standard Edition (desktop Java, Java SE, a.k.a. JDK or JRE) GUI. It is based on Java's earlier widget toolkit, the Abstract Window Toolkit (AWT). Swing can make some beautiful GUI music in the right hands (*https://java.net/projects/swinglabs/sour ces/svn/content/trunk/website/web/docs/presentations/2007/DesktopMatters/FilthyRich Clients.pdf?rev=340*), but is rather large and uses too much overhead for Android.

SWT is the GUI layer developed for use in the Eclipse IDE (*http://www.eclipse.org/*) itself and in Eclipse rich clients. It is an abstraction layer, and depends on the underlying operating system–specific toolkit (e.g., Win32 in the Microsoft arena, GTK under Unix/Linux, etc.).

The final option, and the one ultimately chosen, was to go it alone. The Android designers thus built their own GUI toolkit designed specifically for smartphones. But they took many good ideas from the other toolkits, and learned from the mistakes that had been made along the way.

To learn any new GUI framework is, necessarily, a lot of work. Making your apps work well in the community of apps for that UI is even more work. Recognizing this, Google has set up the Android Design site (*https://developer.android.com/design/index.html*). Another set of guidelines that can help is the Android Patterns site (*http://androidpatterns.com*), which is not about coding but about showing designers *how* the Android visual experience is supposed to work. Illustrated, crowdsourced, and recommended!

One word of terminological warning: the term "widget" has two distinct meanings. All GUI controls such as buttons, labels, and the like are widgets and appear in the `android.widget` package. This package also contains the "layout containers" (`ViewGroup` subclasses), which are rather like a combination of `JPanel` and `LayoutManager` in Swing. Simple widgets and layouts are subclassed from `View`, so collectively they are often referred to as a view. The other kind of widget is one that can appear on an Android Home screen; these are now called "app widgets" to distinguish them from the basic ones and are in their own package, `android.appwidget`. This type of widget is commonly used for status displays such as news and weather updates, updates from friends/social streams, and the like. We have a recipe on app widgets (Recipe 6.30), at the end of this chapter. While we'll try to use the terms *widget* and *app widget* correctly, you sometimes have to infer from the context which meaning is intended.

This chapter covers the main GUI elements in Android. The following chapter covers the "things that go bump in your device": menus, dialogs, toasts, and notifications. The one after that treats the all-important topic of list views (`ListView` and `RecyclerView`).

6.1 Understanding and Following User Interface Guidelines

Ian Darwin

Problem

Lots of developers, even good ones, are very bad at user interface design.

Solution

Use the user interface guidelines. But which ones?

Discussion

UI guidelines have been around almost since Xerox PARC invented GUIs in the 1980s and showed them to Microsoft and Apple. A given set of guidelines must be appropriate to the platform. General guidelines for mobile devices are available from several sources. Android.com publishes advice too.

The official Android UI Guidelines (*https://developer.android.com/guide/practices/ ui_guidelines/index.html*) are probably as good a starting place as any, especially if you already have some background in UI design. If not, some of the other works discussed in this recipe may help you understand UI design issues.

For some thoughtful UI pattern notes, see the Android Developers blog (*http:// android-developers.blogspot.com/2010/05/twitter-for-android-closer-look-at.html*).

One of the oldest GUI guides is Microsoft's *The Gui Guide: International Terminology for the Windows Interface*. This was less about UI design than about internationalization; it came with a floppy disk (remember those?) containing recommended translations for common Microsoft Windows GUI element names into a dozen or so common languages. This book is rather dated today.

In the 1980s and 1990s Sun's user interface development was heavily influenced by Xerox PARC, in XView, Sun's long-defunct Unix implementation of OPEN LOOK, and in the "Java Look and Feel," respectively. A classic but technology-specific work from this time and place is the *Java Look and Feel Design Guidelines* (Addison-Wesley).

A more general work is *Designing Visual Interfaces: Communication-Oriented Techniques* by Kevin Mullet and Darrell Sano (Prentice Hall). This is a thorough discussion of the design issues, mostly from a desktop perspective (Mac, Unix, Windows), but the principles spelled out here are useful in dealing with human–computer interaction issues.

Concluding the desktop front is the more recent Microsoft-oriented book *About Face: The Essentials of Interaction Design* (Wiley). Now in its third edition, this book was originally written by Alan Cooper, known as the "Father of Visual Basic."

6.2 Looking Good with Material Design

Ian Darwin

Problem

You want your app to look like a modern Android application.

Solution

Use *Material Design*, Android's new visual paradigm for application development—or, as Android puts it, "a comprehensive guide for visual, motion, and interaction design across platforms and devices." You can make your apps look great using this modern set of visual approaches.

Discussion

The main steps you need to implement in creating or updating an app for Material Design include the following:

- Read the official Material Design specification (*https://material.io/guidelines/*).
- Apply the material *theme* to your app.
- Create or update your layouts following Material Design guidelines.
- Add elevation to your View objects, causing them to cast shadows.
- Consider using new features, such as card widgets, and new versions of widgets such as the RecyclerView in place of the older ListView.
- Add or customize animations in your app.
- And do all this while maintaining backward compatibility!

Google introduced the material design approach in Android 50. It is also used in Google web applications, supported by a web toolkit called Material Design Lite (*https://getmdl.io/*). The name comes from the analogy with physical material, e.g., either "physical stuff" or "fabric." Material Design is a largely two-dimensional framework, except that objects (such as View objects in Android) have *elevation*, which causes them to cast shadows (drop-shadow effects have been with us for decades, but this formalizes them a bit), and can be animated on entry, activation, or exit.

The basic step in using a material theme is to base your application's theme on material rather than the older Holo-based themes. You will typically tailor the colors used in your theme. For example, in the *AndroidManifest.xml* file, you might have:

```
<application
        android:name=".AndroidApplication"
        android:icon="@drawable/icon"
        android:label="@string/app_name"
        android:theme="@style/AppTheme" >
        android:allowBackup="true">
        ...
</application>
```

You would then have a *styles.xml* file defining `AppTheme`, based on `android:Theme.Material`, as per Example 6-1. The five main colors you can set are shown in Figure 6-1.

Example 6-1. res/values/styles.xml

```
<resources>
    <style name="AppTheme" parent="android:Theme.Material">
        <item name="android:colorPrimary">@color/primary</item>
        <item name="android:colorPrimaryDark">@color/primary_dark</item>
        <item name="android:colorAccent">@color/accent</item>
    </style>
</resources>
```

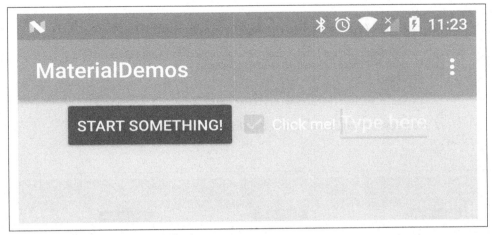

Figure 6-1. Material Design colors

The actual values of these colors must be defined in an XML file. We'll choose colors from the palettes listed in the specification (*https://www.google.com/design/spec/style/color.html*)—here we're using the 300, 500, and 700 colors of the Orange palette:

```
<resources>
    <color name="primary">#FF9800</color>
    <color name="primary_dark">#F57C00</color>
    <color name="accent">#FFCC80</color>
</resources>
```

Creating your layouts is a matter of applying the design prescriptions as you go along, paying attention to sizes, distances, and the like.

Adding elevation is partly a matter of using the new `android:elevation` attribute:

```
<Button
    ...
    android:elevation="5sp"/>
```

Elevation is used to represent the fact that material has thickness and, for example, if you place a book on a table, the book will cast a shadow. Material Design recommends that the action bar (see Recipe 6.5) always have an elevation of 4dp. Purely for demonstration purposes (we don't recommend ever doing this in a real app), Example 6-2 shows code that produces various elevations; this code allows you, by dragging the slider, to view the effects of different elevations on the drop shadow (see Figure 6-2).

Example 6-2. Elevation/displacement example

```
public void onCreate(Bundle b) {

    Button raisable = (Button) findViewById(R.id.elevator);
    SeekBar control = (SeekBar) findViewById(R.id.elevatorControl);

    control.setOnSeekBarChangeListener(new SeekBar.OnSeekBarChangeListener() {
        public void onProgressChanged(SeekBar seekBar,
        int progress, boolean fromUser) {
            raisable.setElevation(progress);
            raisable.setText(getString(R.string.raise_me) + " " + progress);
        }
        // Two methods from SeekBar.OnSeekBarChangeListener interface omitted
    });
}
```

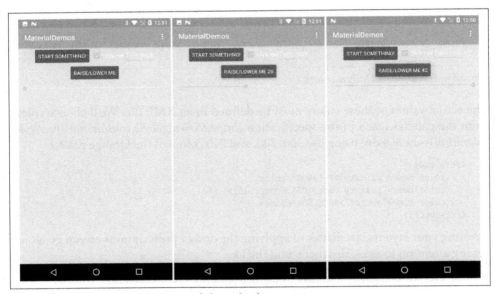

Figure 6-2. Elevation variation and drop shadow

Please refer to other recipes on using new features such as Card widgets (Recipe 6.13) and new versions of widgets such as the RecyclerView (Recipe 8.1) in place of the older ListView.

There are even new icons for Material Design. Quoting its download page (*http://google.github.io/material-design-icons/*):

> Material design system icons are simple, modern, friendly, and sometimes quirky. Each icon is created using our design guidelines to depict in simple and minimal forms the universal concepts used commonly throughout a UI. Ensuring readability and clarity at both large and small sizes, these icons have been optimized for beautiful display on all common platforms and display resolutions.

As if to emphasize that Material isn't just for Android, the icons are available in several forms, for web view (as images or as a web font), for Android, and even for iOS. See *https://design.google.com/icons/* for information on the Material Icons package.

See Also

Google's Android team has published, well, a lot of "material" on Material Design, including the following:

- The developer documentation on Material Design for Android (*https://developer.android.com/design/material/*)
- Material Design for Developers (*https://developer.android.com/training/material/*)
- Using the Material Theme (*https://developer.android.com/training/material/theme.html*)
- Creating Lists and Cards (*https://developer.android.com/training/material/lists-cards.html*)

As well, several good third-party discussions have been published, including these by Greg Nudelman:

- "7 Insights Every Serious Designer Needs to Know" (*http://www.designcaffeine.com/articles/visual-guide-to-android-l-material-design-7-insights-every-serious-designer-needs-to-know/*)
- "8 Mobile UX Trends You Can't Afford to Ignore" (*http://www.designcaffeine.com/articles/8-mobile-ux-trends-you-cant-afford-to-ignore-in-2015/?*)
- *The $1 Prototype Book* (*http://www.designcaffeine.com/overview-the-1-dollar-prototype/*) (DesignCaffeine Press)

6.3 Choosing a Layout Manager (a.k.a. ViewGroup) and Arranging Components

Ian Darwin

Problem

You want to know how to arrange your GUI components within your view.

Solution

Use one of the many layout managers or ViewGroups that are available.

Discussion

As in the case of Java SE and most other GUI packages, there are multiple components you can use to control the layout of individual GUI components. Java SE's AWT and Swing provide two classes that work together: Container and LayoutManager. A Container has a LayoutManager instance to perform layout calculations on its behalf. Android, having been conceived for smaller devices, combines these two functions into a single class, android.view.ViewGroup. There are many subclasses of ViewGroup intended for you to use. While LinearLayout is the most well-known, there are many others. There are also some subclasses that are not intended for use as arbitrary layout managers, such as the drop-down–like Spinner (see Recipe 6.14). The following table should help you get a handle on which one(s) to use.

Name	Basic idea
AbsoluteLayout	Absolute positioning; almost never the right choice!
FrameLayout	Multiple Views in a stack
GridLayout	Equal-sized Views in rows and columns
LinearLayout	Views in a row or column
RelativeLayout	Complex layouts, like HTML tables; more efficient than nesting
TableLayout	A set of rows, each with some number of columns[a]
TabHost	Tabbed view
SlidingDrawer (deprecated)	Vertical divide of the screen

[a] See also Recipe 1.25.

All modern IDEs for Android come with a built-in drag-and-drop visual layout editor that lets you drag and drop GUI components to arrange the layout as you want it. There also used to be a standalone GUI builder tool called DroidDraw, but it seems to have been abandoned by its original author, left behind when Google shut down GoogleCode. There have been multiple attempts to revive DroidDraw; you can find them with a GitHub search (*https://github.com/search?utf8=%E2%9C%93&q=droiddraw*) if you have some reason for not using the tools that come with your IDE.

6.4 Handling Configuration Changes by Decoupling the View from the Model

Alex Leffelman

Problem

When your device's configuration changes (most frequently due to an orientation change), your Activity is destroyed and re-created, making state information difficult to maintain.

Solution

Decouple your user interface from your data model so that the destruction of your Activity doesn't affect your state data.

Discussion

It's a situation that all Android developers (except those who read this part of this book in time) run into with their very first applications: "My application works great, but when I change my phone's orientation everything resets!"

By design, when a device's configuration (read: orientation) changes, the Android UI framework destroys the current Activity and re-creates it for the new configuration. This enables the designer to optimize the layout for different screen orientations and sizes. However, this causes a problem for the developer who wishes to maintain the state of the Activity as it was before the orientation change destroyed the screen. Attempting to address this problem can lead to many complicated solutions, some more graceful than others. But if we take a step back and design our applications wisely, we can write cleaner, more robust code that makes life easier for everyone.

A graphical user interface is exactly what its name describes. It is a graphical representation of an underlying data model that allows the user to interface with and manipulate the data. It is *not* the data model itself. Let's talk our way through an example to illustrate why that is an important point to make.

Consider a tic-tac-toe application. A simple main Activity for this would most likely include *at bare minimum* a GridView (with appropriate Adapter) to display the board and a TextView to tell the user whose turn it is. When the user clicks a square in the grid, an appropriate X or O is placed in that grid cell. As new Android developers, we find it logical to also include a two-dimensional array containing a representation of the board to store its data so that we can determine if the game is over, and if so, who won (see Example 6-3).

Example 6-3. First version of the TicTacToe Activity class

```
public class TicTacToeActivity extends Activity {

    private TicTacToeState[][] mBoardState;

    private GridView mBoard;
    private TextView mTurnText;

    @Override
    public void onCreate(Bundle savedInstanceState) {

        setContentView(R.layout.main);

        mBoardState = new TicTacToeState[3][3];

        mBoard = (GridView)findViewById(R.id.board);
        mTurnText = (TextView)findViewById(R.id.turn_text);

        // Set up Adapter, OnClickListeners, etc., for mBoard
    }
}
```

This is easy enough to imagine and implement, and everything works great—except that when you turn your phone sideways in the middle of an intense round of tic-tac-toe, you have a fresh board staring you in the face and your inevitable victory is postponed. As described earlier, the UI framework just destroyed your Activity and re-created it, calling onCreate() and resetting the board data.

While reading the code in Example 6-3, you might have said to yourself, "Hey, that Bundle savedInstanceState looks promising!" And you'd be right. For this painfully simple example, you could stick your board data into a Bundle and use it to reload your screen. There's even a pair of methods, onRetainNonConfigurationInstance() and getLastNonConfigurationInstance(), that let you pass any Object you want from your old, destroyed Activity to your newly created one. For this example you could just pass your mBoardState array to your new Activity, and you'd be all set. But you're going to be writing big, successful, amazing apps any day now, and that just doesn't scale well with complicated interfaces. We can do better!

This is why separating your GUI from your data model is so handy. Your GUI can be destroyed, re-created, and changed, but the underlying data can survive unharmed through as many UI changes as you can throw at it. Let's separate our game state out into a separate data class (see Example 6-4).

Example 6-4. The TicTacToe class divided

```java
public class TicTacToeGame {

    private TicTacToeState[][] mBoardState;

    public TicTacToeGame() {
        mBoardState = new TicTacToeState[3][3];
        // Initialize
    }

    public TicTacToeState getCellState(int row, int col) {
        return mBoardState[row][col];
    }
    public void setCellState(int row, int col, TicTacToeState state) {
        mBoardState[row][col] = state;
    }

    // Other methods to determine whose turn it is, if the game is over, etc.
}
```

This will not only help us maintain our application state but is generally just good object-oriented design.

Now that we have our data safely outside of the volatile Activity, how do we access it to build our interface? There are two common approaches: we can declare all variables in `TicTacToeGame` as `static` and access them through static methods; or we can design `TicTacToeGame` as a singleton, allowing access to one global instance to be used throughout our application.

I prefer the second option purely from a design perspective. We can turn `TicTacToeGame` into a singleton by making the constructor `private` and adding the following lines to the top of the class:

```java
private static TicTacToeGame instance = new TicTacToeGame();
public static TicTacToeGame getInstance() {
    return instance;
};
```

Now all we have to do is obtain the game data and set our UI elements to appropriately display the data. It's most useful to wrap this in its own function—`refreshUI()`, perhaps—so that it can be used whenever our Activity makes a change to the data. For example, when a user clicks a cell of the board, there need only be two lines of code in the listener: one call to modify the data model (via our `TicTacToeGame` singleton), and one call to refresh the UI.

It may be obvious, but it is worth mentioning that your data classes survive only as long as your application's process is running. If it is killed by the user or the system, naturally the data is lost. That situation necessitates more persistent storage through the filesystem or databases and is outside the scope of this recipe.

This approach very effectively decouples your visual representation of the data from the data itself, and makes orientation changes trivial. Simply calling `refreshUI()` in your `onCreate(Bundle)` method is enough to ensure that whenever your Activity is destroyed and re-created, it can access the data model and display itself correctly. And as an added bonus, you're now practicing better object-oriented design and will see your code base become cleaner, more scalable, and easier to maintain.

6.5 Controlling the Action Bar

Ian Darwin

Problem

The action bar is an important part of most modern Android applications. You need to know how to create, configure, and, when necessary, hide the action bar.

Solution

Use either a `Toolbar` or the older `ActionBar` in your layout, and use a mixture of XML and code to control the action bar's functionality.

Discussion

The action bar was introduced in Android Honeycomb (3.0, API 11) as a standard component for most normal applications. The one common use case for an app that doesn't have an action bar is full-screen applications such as cameras, photo display/editing apps, or video games.

The action bar consists of a full-width rectangle about 5% of the vertical size of the screen, with an icon and program name at the left, an "overflow menu" icon (replacing the hard Menu button present on older Android hardware) at the right (three dots in a vertical row), and optionally actions to the left of the overflow menu. A typical layout is shown in Figure 6-3.

There are several ways to get an `ActionBar`. Assuming you are targeting modern versions (4.0 and later), you will automatically have an action bar unless you provide an application theme that is not derived directly or indirectly from the Holo theme. This will be implemented by the "standard" `android.app.ActionBar` (*https://devel oper.android.com/reference/android/app/ActionBar.html*) class. One downside of this is that some features have been added since the time the `ActionBar` was introduced (Android 3.0), in modern versions such as Android 7.0; thus you may be calling methods that exist in modern versions but will not exist in the library on the user's device if the device is running an older version of Android. This would, of course, end badly.

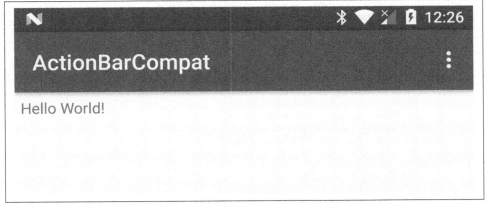

Figure 6-3. Action bar general layout

Accordingly, the current recommendation is to use the "v7 appcompat" library. This library provides two different ActionBar implementations, the appcompat ActionBar (*https://developer.android.com/reference/android/support/v7/app/ActionBar.html*) and the recommended appcompat ToolBar (*https://developer.android.com/reference/android/support/v7/widget/Toolbar.html*) class. The ToolBar is more general than the ActionBar and can be used in different places, though we'll only consider its use as an action bar here.

The recommended steps for your action bar are thus:

1. Ensure that v7 appcompat is included; the coordinates for this library as of API 24 are com.android.support:appcompat-v7:24.1.1. But use the latest one for the API you are targeting.

2. Make your Activities extend AppCompatActivity, not Activity.

3. In the *AndroidManifest.xml* file, set the application element to use a NoActionBar theme so you don't get a native ActionBar added (two action bars will not coexist well).

4. In the layout file, use an android.support.v7.widget.Toolbar (as in Example 6-5) and position it at the top of your layout so it will look like a standard action bar.

5. In your Activity startup code, set this toolbar as the action bar using setCompatActionBar().

Example 6-5 is the layout file with a ToolBar, as generated by Android Studio.

Example 6-5. XML layout using appcompat ToolBar as action bar

```
<?xml version="1.0" encoding="utf-8"?>
<android.support.design.widget.CoordinatorLayout
```

```xml
        xmlns:android="http://schemas.android.com/apk/res/android"
        xmlns:app="http://schemas.android.com/apk/res-auto"
        xmlns:tools="http://schemas.android.com/tools"
        android:layout_width="match_parent"
        android:layout_height="match_parent"
        android:fitsSystemWindows="true"
        tools:context="com.androidcookbook.actionbarcompat.MainActivity">

    <android.support.design.widget.AppBarLayout
        android:layout_width="match_parent"
        android:layout_height="wrap_content"
        android:theme="@style/AppTheme.AppBarOverlay">

        <android.support.v7.widget.Toolbar
            android:id="@+id/toolbar"
            android:layout_width="match_parent"
            android:layout_height="?attr/actionBarSize"
            android:background="?attr/colorPrimary"
            app:popupTheme="@style/AppTheme.PopupOverlay" />

    </android.support.design.widget.AppBarLayout>

    <LinearLayout
        android:orientation="vertical"
        android:layout_width="match_parent"
        android:layout_height="wrap_content"
        app:layout_behavior="@string/appbar_scrolling_view_behavior">

        <TextView
            android:layout_width="wrap_content"
            android:layout_height="wrap_content"
            android:text="Hello World!"
            android:padding="5dp"/>
    </LinearLayout>

</android.support.design.widget.CoordinatorLayout>
```

 The `CoordinatorLayout` is part of the appcompat library, and requires use of the `app:layout_behavior` attribute on its immediate children; without it, they are ignored.

Example 6-6 is the Activity code for this sample application.

Example 6-6. Activity code for appcompat ToolBar

```java
public class MainActivity extends AppCompatActivity {

    @Override
    protected void onCreate(Bundle savedInstanceState) {
        super.onCreate(savedInstanceState);
        setContentView(R.layout.activity_main);
```

```
    Toolbar toolbar = (Toolbar) findViewById(R.id.toolbar);
    setSupportActionBar(toolbar);
}
...
}
```

Once you have created your action bar, you can control it in various ways. To make your action bar disappear or reappear, you can use:

```
getCompatActionBar().hide()
getCompatActionBar().show()
```

In fact, any of the standard appcompat ActionBar methods can be used. The getCompatActionBar() method doesn't return the toolbar directly, but returns it wrapped in a ToolbarActionBar which, as the name implies, provides all the ActionBar methods.

In the first paragraphs of this recipe, I referred to the "overflow menu" without explaining that. The traditional Android Options menu (described in Recipe 7.3) appears in response to the "Menu button," but modern Android devices are not required to have a physical button for this purpose. Instead, the three dots at the right of the action bar (see Figure 6-3) call up the menu. However—and this is one of the original uses for the action bar—you can "promote" menu items from the Activity's menu to the action bar! All you have to do is add the showAsAction attribute in the menu.xml file. This attribute can take the value never (which is the default), ifRoom (whose meaning is obvious), or always (which is also obvious, but whose use is not recommended; you should use ifRoom in preference to this last choice).

Here is a Help menu item added to the default menu file:

```
<menu xmlns:android="http://schemas.android.com/apk/res/android"
    xmlns:app="http://schemas.android.com/apk/res-auto"
    xmlns:tools="http://schemas.android.com/tools"
    tools:context="com.androidcookbook.actionbarcompat.MainActivity">
    <item
        android:id="@+id/action_settings"
        android:orderInCategory="100"
        android:title="@string/action_settings"
        app:showAsAction="never"
        />
    <item
        android:id="@+id/action_help"
        android:title="Help"
        app:showAsAction="ifRoom"
        />
</menu>
```

This produces the layout shown in Figure 6-4.

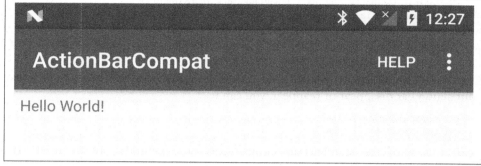

Figure 6-4. Action bar with menu item

As with other menu items, you can use text, icons, or both.

See Also

You will find more information in the official documentation (*https://devel oper.android.com/training/appbar/index.html*). The "Share action" in the action bar is treated specially, in Recipe 6.6.

Source Download URL

The source code for this example is in the Android Cookbook repository (*https:// github.com/IanDarwin/Android-Cookbook-Examples*), in the subdirectory *ActionBar-Compat* (see "Getting and Using the Code Examples" on page 18).

6.6 Adding a Share Action to Your Action Bar

Ian Darwin

Problem

You want to add the standard Share icon to your action bar and have it handle an application-provided Intent.

Solution

Use the `actionProviderClass` attribute in a menu item, set up an Intent for it to process, and pass the Intent into the `ActionProvider`. It really is that simple!

Discussion

Sharing information is one of the canonical uses of mobile and computing devices. Having one application use another to handle data is a prime feature of the Android platform. Android offers a "Share" menu that lets you pass text, images, or almost anything else off to any of a number of applications to be handled.

For example, let's examine how to export (share) a short string as "plain text"; this will be sharable to (acceptable by) quite a few applications, but Android will choose the "most popular" to put at the top of the Share menu.

We start by adding a menu item that will go into the `ActionBar`:

```
<menu xmlns:android="http://schemas.android.com/apk/res/android" >

    <item android:id="@+id/menu_item_share"
        android:showAsAction="ifRoom"
        android:title="@string/action_share"
        android:actionProviderClass="android.widget.ShareActionProvider" />
    ...
</menu>
```

In our `onCreate()` method, we create an Intent with an action of `ACTION_SEND`, a content type of plain text, and an `Extra` of the string we want to share. There is nothing special about text—this mechanism can share almost any kind of data, as long as there's at least one app that has registered with an Intent filter for the given content type:

```
@Override
protected void onCreate(Bundle savedInstanceState) {
    super.onCreate(savedInstanceState);
    setContentView(R.layout.activity_main);
    mShareIntent = new Intent();
    mShareIntent.setAction(Intent.ACTION_SEND);
    mShareIntent.setType("text/plain");
    mShareIntent.putExtra(Intent.EXTRA_TEXT,
    "From me to you, this text is new.");
}
```

Finally, in our menu creation method, we find the `MenuItem` by its ID and ask it for its `ActionProvider` (this is where API level 14 is required!). If we find that, we just add the share Intent to it:

```
@Override
public boolean onCreateOptionsMenu(Menu menu) {
    // Inflate the menu; this adds items to the action bar if it is present
    getMenuInflater().inflate(R.menu.main, menu);

    // Find the MenuItem that we know has the ShareActionProvider
    MenuItem item = menu.findItem(R.id.menu_item_share);

    // Get its ShareActionProvider
    mShareActionProvider = (ShareActionProvider) item.getActionProvider();

    // Connect the dots: give the ShareActionProvider its Share Intent
    if (mShareActionProvider != null) {
        mShareActionProvider.setShareIntent(mShareIntent);
    }
```

```
        // Return true so Android will know we want to display the menu
        return true;
}
```

That really is all there is to it.

When you first run the app, it looks like Figure 6-5.

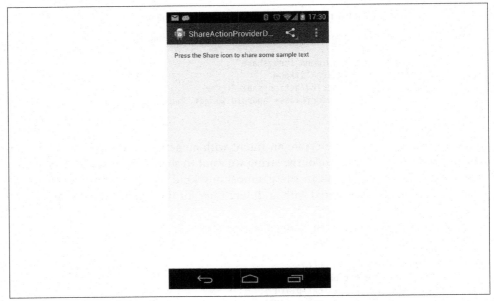

Figure 6-5. Share action in action

Tap the Share icon and the Share menu appears—all courtesy of the `ShareActionProvider`! As mentioned, the most likely apps are at the top of the list; the rest are delegated to the "See all" section (Figure 6-6).

I picked the Messaging app and, just as a quick reality check, sent it to myself, as in Figure 6-7.

Figure 6-6. Share menu

Figure 6-7. Sending a message to myself

The message arrives, as in Figure 6-8!

Figure 6-8. Message arrives

Note that if you later go back to the app that started the sharing, if there is room in the action bar, the app you chose to share with (in my case, Messaging) appears beside the Share icon—a neat optimization!

6.7 Building Modern UIs with the Fragment API

Ian Darwin

Problem

You want a more flexible arrangement of parts of your screen. Or, you need to use some newer APIs that only work with Fragments.

Solution

Use the `FragmentManager` and layouts to arrange `Fragment` views.

Discussion

Fragments were introduced with Android 3.0 and have become increasingly common since. It's possible to use them in a simple Activity, as in Example 6-7.

Example 6-7. Portion of MainActivity.java

```java
@Override
protected void onCreate(Bundle savedInstanceState) {
    super.onCreate(savedInstanceState);
    setContentView(R.layout.activity_main);
}
```

Surprisingly, for the simplest use of a single Fragment, there is no code needed. The work is done in the layout, as in Example 6-8.

Example 6-8. layout/activity_main.xml

```xml
<?xml version="1.0" encoding="utf-8"?>
<android.support.design.widget.CoordinatorLayout
    xmlns:android="http://schemas.android.com/apk/res/android"
    xmlns:app="http://schemas.android.com/apk/res-auto"
    xmlns:tools="http://schemas.android.com/tools"
    android:layout_width="match_parent"
    android:layout_height="match_parent"
    android:fitsSystemWindows="true"
    tools:context="com.androidcookbook.fragmentsimple.MainActivity">

    <android.support.design.widget.AppBarLayout
        android:layout_width="match_parent"
        android:layout_height="wrap_content"
        android:theme="@style/AppTheme.AppBarOverlay">

        <android.support.v7.widget.Toolbar
            android:id="@+id/toolbar"
            android:layout_width="match_parent"
            android:layout_height="?attr/actionBarSize"
            android:background="?attr/colorPrimary"
            app:popupTheme="@style/AppTheme.PopupOverlay" />
    </android.support.design.widget.AppBarLayout>

    <fragment
        android:id="@+id/fragment"
        android:name=".MainActivityFragment"
        android:layout_width="match_parent"
        android:layout_height="match_parent"
        app:layout_behavior="@string/appbar_scrolling_view_behavior"
        tools:layout="@layout/fragment_main" />

</android.support.design.widget.CoordinatorLayout>
```

Notice that unlike with regular Views (such as Button and TextView), where the name is the simple name of the class, the fragment element is not capitalized, but treated specially; you always subclass Fragment, so the actual class name must be provided by the android:name attribute.

The `Fragment` itself is a class in our application, so it exists as a Java class, shown in Example 6-9. And a `Fragment` has a `View`, so it has a layout XML file, shown in Example 6-10.

Example 6-9. Simple Fragment code

```java
public class MainActivityFragment extends Fragment {

    public MainActivityFragment() {
        // Constructor with arguments may be needed in more sophisticated apps
    }

    /** Like Menus, Fragments must be inflated by the developer */
    @Override
    public View onCreateView(
                LayoutInflater inflater, ViewGroup container,
                Bundle savedInstanceState) {
        return inflater.inflate(R.layout.fragment_main, container, false);
    }
}
```

Example 6-10. Simple Fragment layout

```xml
<RelativeLayout xmlns:android="http://schemas.android.com/apk/res/android"
    xmlns:tools="http://schemas.android.com/tools"
    android:layout_width="match_parent"
    android:layout_height="match_parent"
    tools:context="com.androidcookbook.fragmentsdemos.MainActivityFragment"
    tools:showIn="@layout/activity_main">

    <TextView
        android:layout_width="wrap_content"
        android:layout_height="wrap_content"
        android:text="Hello World!" />

</RelativeLayout>
```

In more sophisticated Activities, one will typically use the `FragmentManager` to load Fragments into the Activity dynamically. The `FragmentManager` is transaction-based; a simple use might be something like:

```java
Fragment frag = new MyDemoFragment();
FragmentTransaction tx = getFragmentManager();
tx.beginTransaction();
tx.add(container, frag); // Or: tx.replace(container, newFragment);
tx.commit();
```

This can also be written in a fluent API style, as:

```java
getFragmentManager().beginTransaction()
    .add(container, new MyDemoFragment())
    .commit();
```

In a support library–based Activity, use `getSupportFragmentManager()` instead of `getFragmentManager()`.

One main use of the `Fragment` subclasses is to have multiple views in place concurrently. Consider a list-detail application. In a small-screen device, or in a device that is narrow when in portrait mode, it makes sense to have a single view—either the list of items or the details of one item—onscreen at a time. However, on a tablet in landscape mode, where you have lots of width available, it makes sense to have the list and one item's details side-by-side (see Figure 6-9).

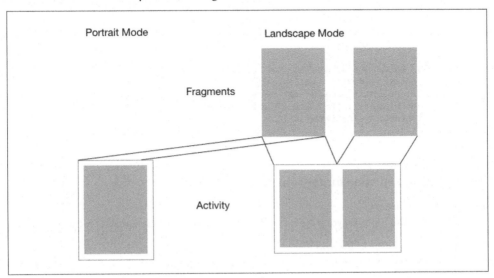

Figure 6-9. Portrait or landscape layout

As you can only have one Activity onscreen in an application, this would require a lot of shuffling around of `View` objects if you were to try to implement it using a single Activity. Using Fragments, however, makes it much easier.

Fragments can be thought of as mini-Activities in some ways, but they must reside within an actual Activity. In our list-detail example, we will have a `DisplayActivity`, with both a `ListFragment` and a `DetailFragment` contained within it. In portrait mode, only the `ListFragment` will be shown, but in landscape mode on any device of reasonable size, the two Fragments will display side-by-side. This is commonly performed by using different view configurations based on the resources system, and triggering on this in the code to either use the `FragmentManager` to install the second Fragment, or to start the detail view as an Activity so it appears in front of the List. In our demo we have a `TaskListActivity`, which is launched from the Tasks menu item in the action bar; `TaskListActivity` contains the code in Example 6-11 (slightly simplified).

Example 6-11. Showing the detail in either a Fragment or an Activity

```java
holder.mView.setOnClickListener(new View.OnClickListener() {
    @Override
    public void onClick(View v) {
        // This view will be created (but empty) on wide devices; show DetailFragment
        if (findViewById(R.id.task_detail_container) != null) {
            Bundle arguments = new Bundle();
            arguments.putString(TaskDetailFragment.ARG_ITEM_ID, holder.mItem.id);
            TaskDetailFragment fragment = new TaskDetailFragment();
            fragment.setArguments(arguments);
            // Replace the empty container with the actual DetailFragment
            getSupportFragmentManager().beginTransaction()
                    .replace(R.id.task_detail_container, fragment)
                    .commit();
        } else {
            // Not on a wide device, show the DetailActivity
            Context context = v.getContext();
            Intent intent = new Intent(context, TaskDetailActivity.class);
            intent.putExtra(TaskDetailFragment.ARG_ITEM_ID, holder.mItem.id);
            context.startActivity(intent);
        }
    }
});
```

The layout configuration for the container is as follows:

res/layout/task_list.xml

> Contains the List (RecyclerView; see Recipe 8.1) with no ViewGroup around it.

res/layout-w900dpi/task_list.xml

> Contains the List in a horizontal LinearLayout, which also has an empty FrameLayout with android:id="@+id/task_detail_container" and android:layout_width="0dp", the latter causing it not to show until it is replaced by the Fragment. The fact that task_detail_container only exists in the wide view is tested in the code to control the switch between Fragment and Activity, so the code will display correctly if the user switches the device orientation while the app is running.

Note that a Fragment is not an Activity. All the same life-cycle methods (Recipe 1.2) are available, but there are several additional ones. The following should be kept in mind:

- Call getActivity() in the Fragment for API calls that need a Context or Activity reference.

- Implement onCreateView() to connect your View with that of the Activity.

- Implement onActivityCreated() to be notified when your owning Activity is completely set up.

Note that onCreateView() (rather than onCreate()) is where you should create your View, *and* that you are responsible for inflating the View yourself. For example:

```
public View onCreateView(LayoutInflater inf, ViewGroup container) {
    return inf.inflate(R.layout.This_Fragment's_Layout, container, false);
}
```

Source Download URL

The source code for this example is in the Android Cookbook repository (*https://github.com/IanDarwin/Android-Cookbook-Examples*), in the subdirectory *Fragments-Demos* (see "Getting and Using the Code Examples" on page 18).

6.8 Creating a Button and Its Click Event Listener

Ian Darwin

Problem

You need to do something when the user presses a button.

Solution

Create a button in your layout, and use an OnClickListener implementation to make it perform the relevant action when clicked.

Discussion

Creating a button in your layout is simple. In the XML layout, you can create a button like so:

```
<Button android:id="@+id/start_button"
    android:text="@string/start_button_label"
    android:layout_width="wrap_content"
    android:layout_height="wrap_content"/>
```

In your Activity's onCreate() method, find the button by its ViewID (in this example, R.id.start_button). Call its setOnClickListener() method with an OnClickListener.

In the OnClickListener implementation, check for the ViewID and perform the relevant action:

```
public class MainActivity extends Activity implements OnClickListener {
    public void onCreate() {
        startButton = findViewById(R.id.start_button);
        startButton.setOnClickListener(this);
        ...
    }

    @Override
```

```
public void onClick(View v) {
    switch (v.getId()) {
    case R.id.start_button:
        // Start whatever it is the start button starts...
        ...
    case R.id.some_other_button:
        // etc.
    }
}
}
```

An experienced Java programmer would expect to use an anonymous inner class for the onClickListener, as has been done in AWT and Swing since Java 1.1. For performance reasons, early Android documentation recommended against this, suggesting instead that you have the Activity implement OnClickListener and check the ViewID (i.e., analogous to the Java 1.0 way of doing things). As with Swing, as the power of devices has increased such old-style ways of doing things are becoming less popular, though you will likely still see both styles in use for some time.

6.9 Enhancing UI Design Using Image Buttons

Rachee Singh

Problem

You want to enhance your UI design, but without adding a lot of descriptive text.

Solution

Use an image button. This requires less effort than a text view with descriptive text, since an image can explain the scenario much better than a lot of words can.

Discussion

Making your own image button requires defining the characteristics of the button in an XML file that should be placed in */res/drawable*. This file specifies the three states of an image button:

- Pressed state
- Focused state
- Other states (optional)

For instance:

```
<?xml version="1.0" encoding="utf-8"?>
<selector xmlns:android="http://schemas.android.com/apk/res/android">
    <item android:drawable="@drawable/play_pressed"
        android:state_checked="true" />
```

```
        <item android:drawable="@drawable/play" />
    </selector>
```

So, for each of these states, the ID of an image is specified (the image present in */res/drawable* as a *.png* file). When the button is pressed, the `play_pressed` image is displayed. There are two such buttons in the sample application: the Play button and the Settings button. In the *.java* file of the application, the `onClick` aspect of the buttons can be taken care of. In this recipe, a toast is displayed with some appropriate text. Programmers can start a new Activity from here, or broadcast an Intent, or do many other things based on their requirements.

In Figure 6-10, the left screenshot shows the Play button not pressed, and the right screenshot shows the Play button pressed.

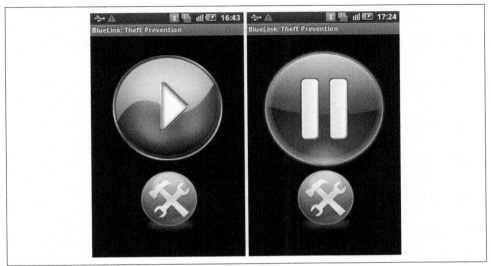

Figure 6-10. Play button not pressed (left) and pressed (right)

Source Download URL

The source code for this example is in the Android Cookbook repository (*https://github.com/IanDarwin/Android-Cookbook-Examples*), in the subdirectory *ImageButtonDemo* (see "Getting and Using the Code Examples" on page 18).

6.10 Using a FloatingActionButton

Ian Darwin

Problem

You want a round graphic button that will appear in front of your application (similar to the "Add" button found on many Google apps, such as the GMail app in Figure 6-11), and you want to respond to this button being pressed.

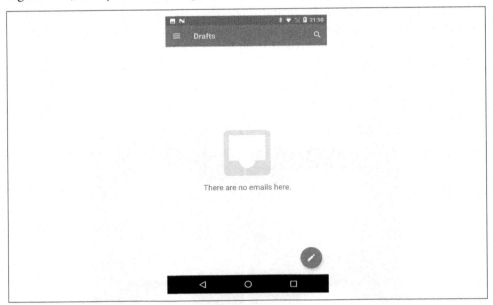

Figure 6-11. GMail "Add" floating action button

Solution

Use a FloatingActionButton.

Discussion

The FloatingActionButton appears in the lower right of your application window and is often used for a rounded "+" button with an associated action such as adding a contact, creating a new message to be sent, and so on. While there have always been ways to provide this functionality, it is now available as a supported component (in the support library; see Recipe 1.21) in Android. It is as easy to use as a regular button; just add it to your XML layout, like so:

```
<android.support.design.widget.FloatingActionButton
    android:id="@+id/floatingButton"
    android:layout_width="wrap_content"
    android:layout_height="wrap_content"
    android:layout_gravity="bottom|end"
    android:layout_margin="@dimen/fab_margin"
    android:src="@android:drawable/ic_dialog_info" />
```

Because this button is in the support library rather than in `android.widget`, we have to list its full class in the layout file. We give it an `id` so we can refer to it. The gravity and padding are recommended for the button to appear in the lower right. We use `src` to indicate the drawable to display inside the circular button (it's named as it is to remind us that we're not providing the complete drawable, unlike with an `ImageButton`), and use either `android:onClick` in the XML or `findViewById()` and `setOnclickListener()` in code to specify what to do when the button is tapped. This example uses `android:onClick="runMe"` in the XML and the following code:

```
public void runMe(View v) {
    final String msg = "You pressed my button";
    Log.d(TAG, msg);
    Toast.makeText(this, msg, Toast.LENGTH_SHORT).show();
}
```

The result is shown in Figure 6-12.

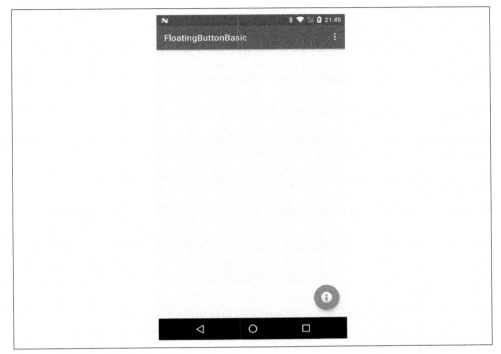

Figure 6-12. FloatingActionButton in action

See Also

The new `Snackbar` component, introduced at around the same time as the `FloatingActionButton`, is discussed in Recipe 7.1.

Android Studio's New Activity wizard includes a "Basic Activity" choice that provides a preconfigured FloatingActionButton, which out of the box shows a Snackbar.

Source Download URL

The source code for this example is in the Android Cookbook repository (*https://github.com/IanDarwin/Android-Cookbook-Examples*), in the subdirectory *Floating-ButtonSnackbarDemo* (see "Getting and Using the Code Examples" on page 18).

6.11 Wiring Up an Event Listener in Many Different Ways

Daniel Fowler

Problem

You need to be familiar with the different ways to code event handlers, both to know when to use which approach and because you will come across the various methods in this Cookbook and elsewhere.

Solution

When writing software, very rarely is there only one way to do things. This holds true when wiring up View events; half a dozen techniques are shown in this recipe.

Discussion

When a View fires an event, an application will not respond to it unless the app is listening for it. To detect the event, a listener is instantiated and assigned to the View. Take, for example, the onClick event, the most widely used event in Android apps. Nearly every View that can be added to an app screen will fire the event when the user taps it (on touch screens) or presses the trackpad/trackball when the View has focus. This event is listened to by a class implementing the OnClickListener interface. The class instance is then assigned to the required View using the View's setOnClickListener() method. In the following section, the HandleClick inner class sets the text of a TextView (textview1) when a Button (button1) is pressed.

Technique 1. The Member class

In Example 6-12, a nested class called HandleClick implementing OnClickListener is declared as a member of the Activity (main). This is useful when several listeners require similar processing that can be handled by a single class.

Example 6-12. The Member class

```java
public class MainActivity extends Activity {
    @Override
    public void onCreate(Bundle savedInstanceState) {
        super.onCreate(savedInstanceState);
        setContentView(R.layout.main);
        // Attach an instance of HandleClick to the Button
        findViewById(R.id.button1).setOnClickListener(new HandleClick());
    }
    private class HandleClick implements OnClickListener{
        public void onClick(View arg0) {
            Button btn = (Button)arg0;      // Cast view to a button
            // Get a reference to the TextView
            TextView tv = (TextView) findViewById(R.id.textview1);
            // Update the TextView text
            tv.setText("You pressed " + btn.getText());
        }
    }
}
```

A variation on this would involve making the inner class public and putting it in its own source file. In theory, any Activity that needed a copy of such a class could create its own instance thereof. It is relatively rare, however, that action listeners are generic enough to be shared in this way.

Technique 2. The interface type

In Java an interface can be used as a type. A variable is declared as an OnClickListener and assigned using new OnClickListener() {}, while behind the scenes Java is creating an object (an anonymous class) that implements OnClickListener. This has similar benefits to the first technique (see Example 6-13). When an instance is being saved, many Java developers (including this Cookbook's main author) consider it a good practice to use interface variables rather than the specific implementation type for the variable.

Example 6-13. The interface type

```java
public class MainActivity extends Activity {
    @Override
    public void onCreate(Bundle savedInstanceState) {
        super.onCreate(savedInstanceState);
        setContentView(R.layout.main);
        // Use the handleClick variable to attach the event listener
        findViewById(R.id.button1).setOnClickListener(handleClick);
    }
    private OnClickListener handleClick = new OnClickListener() {
            public void onClick(View arg0) {
            Button btn = (Button)arg0;
            TextView tv = (TextView) findViewById(R.id.textview1);
            tv.setText("You pressed " + btn.getText());
        }
```

```
    };
}
```

Technique 3. The anonymous inner class

Declaring the OnClickListener within the call to the setOnClickListener() method is common. This method is useful when each listener does not have functionality that could be shared with other listeners, though some novice developers find this type of code difficult to understand. Again, Java is creating an object that implements the interface behind the scenes for new OnClickListener() {} (see Example 6-14).

Example 6-14. The anonymous inner class

```
public class MainActivity extends Activity {
    @Override
    public void onCreate(Bundle savedInstanceState) {
        super.onCreate(savedInstanceState);
        setContentView(R.layout.main);
        findViewById(R.id.button1).setOnClickListener(new OnClickListener() {
            public void onClick(View arg0) {
                Button btn = (Button)arg0;
                TextView tv = (TextView) findViewById(R.id.textview1);
                tv.setText("You pressed " + btn.getText());
            }
        });
    }
}
```

Technique 4. Implementation in Activity

The Activity itself can implement the OnClickListener (see Example 6-15). Since the Activity object (main) already exists, this saves a small amount of memory by not requiring another object to host the onClick() method. It does make public a method that is unlikely to be used elsewhere, however, and implementing multiple events will make the declaration of main long.

Example 6-15. Implementation in Activity

```
public class MainActivity extends Activity implements OnClickListener{
    @Override
    public void onCreate(Bundle savedInstanceState) {
        super.onCreate(savedInstanceState);
        setContentView(R.layout.main);
        findViewById(R.id.button1).setOnClickListener(this);
    }
    public void onClick(View arg0) {
        Button btn = (Button)arg0;
        TextView tv = (TextView) findViewById(R.id.textview1);
        tv.setText("You pressed " + btn.getText());
    }
}
```

Technique 5. Lambda expression (requires the Java 8 toolchain)

In Android 7 and later, using an up-to-date SDK which should include the Java 8 tooling, you can use a lambda expression to shorten the code. Lambdas can be recognized by the -> syntax, introduced into the Java language with Java SE version 8. An example use of a lambda expression is shown in Example 6-16.

Example 6-16. Lambda expression

```
public class MainActivity extends Activity {
    @Override
    public void onCreate(Bundle savedInstanceState) {
        super.onCreate(savedInstanceState);
        setContentView(R.layout.main);
        View v = findViewById(R.id.button1);
        v.setOnClickListener(v->{
            Button btn = (Button)arg0;
            TextView tv = (TextView) findViewById(R.id.textview1);
            tv.setText("You pressed " + btn.getText());
        });
    }
}
```

One restriction is that a lambda expression can only be used to implement a functional interface—that is, an interface that has only a single abstract method in it—since the name of the method (as well as the name of the interface itself) is inferred by the compiler. Fortunately, most "action event" listener interfaces are functional.

Technique 6. Attribute in View layout for onClick events

The name of a method defined in the Activity can be assigned to the android:onClick attribute in a layout file (see Example 6-17). This can save you from having to write a lot of boilerplate code.

Example 6-17. Class named in manifest

```
public class MainActivity extends Activity {
    @Override
    public void onCreate(Bundle savedInstanceState) {
        super.onCreate(savedInstanceState);
        setContentView(R.layout.main);
    }
    public void handleClick(View arg0) {
        Button btn = (Button)arg0;
        TextView tv = (TextView) findViewById(R.id.textview1);
        tv.setText("You pressed " + btn.getText());
    }
}
```

In the layout file the Button would be declared with the android:onClick attribute:

```
<Button android:id="@+id/button1"
        android:layout_width="wrap_content"
        android:layout_height="wrap_content"
        android:text="Button 1"
        android:onClick="handleClick"/>
```

The first five techniques for handling events can be used with other event types (onLongClick, onKey, onTouch, onCreateContextMenu, onFocusChange). The technique described in this subsection only applies to the onClick event. The layout file in Example 6-18 declares an additional two buttons. Using the android:onClick attribute, you don't need an additional code is required than that defined earlier; that is, no additional findViewById() and setOnClickListener() method for each button. This should appear as in Figure 6-13.

Example 6-18. Multiple uses of android:onClick

```
<?xml version="1.0" encoding="utf-8"?>
<LinearLayout xmlns:android="http://schemas.android.com/apk/res/android"
    android:orientation="vertical"
    android:layout_width="fill_parent"
    android:layout_height="fill_parent">
  <TextView android:id="@+id/textview1"
            android:layout_width="fill_parent"
            android:layout_height="wrap_content"
            android:text="Click a button."
            android:textSize="20dp"/>
  <LinearLayout android:orientation="horizontal"
                android:layout_width="fill_parent"
                android:layout_height="wrap_content">
    <Button android:id="@+id/button1"
            android:layout_width="wrap_content"
            android:layout_height="wrap_content"
            android:text="Button 1"
            android:onClick="HandleClick"/>
    <Button android:id="@+id/button2"
            android:layout_width="wrap_content"
            android:layout_height="wrap_content"
            android:text="Button 2"
            android:onClick="HandleClick"/>
    <Button android:id="@+id/button3"
            android:layout_width="wrap_content"
            android:layout_height="wrap_content"
            android:text="Button 3"
            android:onClick="HandleClick"/>
  </LinearLayout>
</LinearLayout>
```

Deciding which technique to use to wire up a listener will depend on the functionality required, how much code is reusable across Views, and how easy the code will be for future maintainers to understand. Ideally the code should be succinct and easy to read.

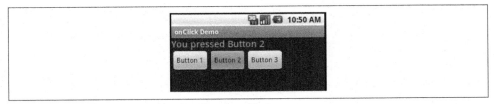

Figure 6-13. onClick event from android:onClick

6.12 Using CheckBoxes and RadioButtons

Blake Meike

Problem

You want to offer the user a set of choices that is more limited than a list.

Solution

Use CheckBoxes or RadioButtons as appropriate.

Discussion

These views are probably familiar to you from other user interfaces. They allow the user to choose from multiple options. CheckBox is typically used when you want to offer multiple selections with a yes/no or true/false choice for each. RadioButton is used when only one choice is allowed at a time. Android has adapted these familiar components to make them more useful in a touch-screen environment. Figure 6-14 shows these multiple-choice views laid out in an Android application.

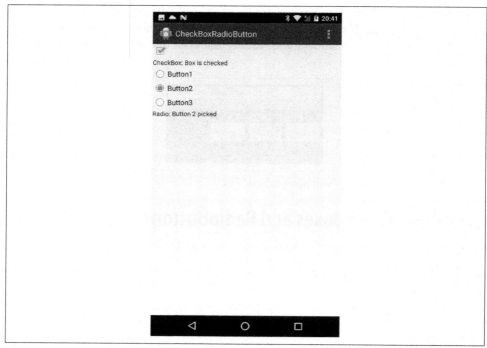

Figure 6-14. A checkbox and three radio buttons

The layout XML file that created the screen in Figure 6-14 looks like this:

```xml
<?xml version="1.0" encoding="utf-8"?>
<LinearLayout xmlns:android="http://schemas.android.com/apk/res/android"
    android:layout_width="fill_parent"
    android:layout_height="fill_parent"
    android:orientation="vertical" >

    <CheckBox
        android:id="@+id/cbxBox1"
        android:layout_width="32dp"
        android:layout_height="32dp"
        android:checked="false" />

    <TextView
        android:id="@+id/txtCheckBox"
        android:layout_width="fill_parent"
        android:layout_height="wrap_content"
        android:text="CheckBox: Not checked" />

    <RadioGroup
        android:id="@+id/rgGroup1"
        android:layout_width="fill_parent"
        android:layout_height="wrap_content"
        android:orientation="vertical" >
```

```
        <RadioButton
            android:id="@+id/RB1"
                        android:layout_width="fill_parent"
                        android:layout_height="wrap_content"
            android:text="Button1" />

        <RadioButton
            android:id="@+id/RB2"
                        android:layout_width="fill_parent"
                        android:layout_height="wrap_content"
            android:text="Button2" />

        <RadioButton
            android:id="@+id/RB3"
                        android:layout_width="fill_parent"
                        android:layout_height="wrap_content"
            android:text="Button3" />

    </RadioGroup>

    <TextView
        android:id="@+id/txtRadio"
        android:layout_width="fill_parent"
        android:layout_height="wrap_content"
        android:text="RadioGroup: Nothing picked" />

</LinearLayout>
```

The XML file just lists each view we want on the screen along with the attributes we want. A `RadioGroup` is also a `ViewGroup`, so it can contain the appropriate `RadioButton` views.

Example 6-19 is the Java file that responds to user clicks.

Example 6-19. The Chooser examples

```
package com.androidcookbook.checkboxradiobutton;

import android.app.Activity;
import android.os.Bundle;
import android.view.Menu;
import android.view.View;
import android.widget.CheckBox;
import android.widget.RadioButton;
import android.widget.RadioGroup;
import android.widget.TextView;

public class SelectExample extends Activity {
    private CheckBox checkBox;
    private TextView txtCheckBox, txtRadio;

    /** Called when the Activity is first created. */
    @Override
```

```
public void onCreate(Bundle savedInstanceState) {
    super.onCreate(savedInstanceState);
    setContentView(R.layout.activity_select_example);
    checkBox = (CheckBox) findViewById(R.id.cbxBox1);
    txtCheckBox = (TextView) findViewById(R.id.txtCheckBox);

    // React to events from the CheckBox
    checkBox.setOnClickListener(new CheckBox.OnClickListener() {
        public void onClick(View v) {
            if (checkBox.isChecked()) {
                txtCheckBox.setText("CheckBox: Box is checked");
            } else {
                txtCheckBox.setText("CheckBox: Not checked");
            }
        }
    });

    final RadioGroup rg = (RadioGroup) findViewById(R.id.rgGroup1);
    // React to events from the RadioGroup
    rg.setOnCheckedChangeListener(new RadioGroup.OnCheckedChangeListener() {
        @Override
        public void onCheckedChanged(RadioGroup group, int checkedId) {
            RadioButton rb =
                (RadioButton) findViewById(rg.getCheckedRadioButtonId());
            txtRadio.setText(rb.getText() + " picked");
        }
    });
    txtRadio = (TextView) findViewById(R.id.txtRadio);
}

@Override
public boolean onCreateOptionsMenu(Menu menu) {
    getMenuInflater().inflate(R.menu.activity_select_example, menu);
    return true;
}
}
```

These views work as follows:

CheckBox

> The CheckBox view takes care of flipping its state back and forth and displaying a checkmark when the state is true, but not when it is false. All you have to do is create an OnClickListener to catch click events, and you can add whatever code you want to react.

RadioGroup

> As mentioned earlier, the RadioGroup view is really a ViewGroup that contains any number of RadioButton views. The user can select only one of the buttons at a time, and you capture the selection either by setting a RadioGroup.OnCheckedChangeListener on the group *or* by setting OnClickListeners for each RadioButton.

RadioButton

A RadioButton is one of the buttons to be placed into a RadioGroup; it displays its given text as well as a circle to indicate which one of the buttons in the group is currently selected.

Taken together, these views let you provide a short set of choices and have the user select one or multiple choices from those offered.

6.13 Using Card Widgets

Ian Darwin

Problem

Card widgets are a relatively new form of UI control, and you want to learn when and how to use them.

Solution

Use a Card when you want self-contained ViewGroups with a nice border, commonly many of them in a ListView or a RecyclerView.

Discussion

Card is a new ViewGroup, subclassing FrameLayout, that provides a border and shadow. It is part of the compatibility package, so that it can work with old as well as new versions of Android. Card is easy to use as long as you remember that it *is* a FrameLayout (see Recipe 6.3). Items placed directly in a FrameLayout appear in a stack, and if they are different sizes, parts of various ones will be visible. In our example, which is drawn from a hypothetical real estate home listing project, we place a RelativeLayout with a photograph (ImageView) and some descriptive text (TextView) together in a Card, and place the Card in our main layout. We are using default shadow and border settings, but overriding the size and corner radius. The Card's layout file is shown in Example 6-20.

Example 6-20. Layout file for Card

```
<?xml version="1.0" encoding="utf-8"?>
<android.support.v7.widget.CardView
        xmlns:android="http://schemas.android.com/apk/res/android"
        xmlns:card_view="http://schemas.android.com/apk/res-auto"
        xmlns:tools="http://schemas.android.com/tools"
        android:id="@+id/card_view"
        android:layout_gravity="center"
        android:layout_width="300dp"
        android:layout_height="340dp"
        card_view:cardCornerRadius="6dp"
        tools:context="com.androidcookbook.carddemo.CardActivity">
```

```
<RelativeLayout
    android:layout_width="match_parent"
    android:layout_height="match_parent"
    android:orientation="vertical">

    <ImageView
        android:id="@+id/house_front_view"
        android:layout_alignParentTop="true"
        android:layout_width="match_parent"
        android:layout_height="wrap_content" />

    <TextView
        android:id="@+id/house_descr"
        android:layout_width="match_parent"
        android:layout_height="wrap_content"
        android:layout_alignParentBottom="true" />

</RelativeLayout>

</android.support.v7.widget.CardView>
```

The code that shows this Card's layout only populates one Card (see Example 6-21), but it would be easy to turn that into an adapter for use on a ListView or RecyclerView, and the layout file is also already suitable for such use.

Example 6-21. Java setup for Card

```
public class CardActivity extends AppCompatActivity {

    @Override
    protected void onCreate(Bundle savedInstanceState) {
        super.onCreate(savedInstanceState);
        setContentView(R.layout.card_layout);

        // Dynamically set the image and text

        ImageView img = (ImageView) findViewById(R.id.house_front_view);
        Drawable d = ContextCompat.getDrawable(this,R.drawable.fixer_upper_1);
        img.setImageDrawable(d);

        TextView descr = (TextView) findViewById(R.id.house_descr);
        descr.setText("Beautiful fixer-upper! Only used on weekends
                    by respectable Hobbit couple!");
    }
}
```

The results of these few lines of code can be seen in Figure 6-15.

Figure 6-15. CardDemo in action

See Also

The developer documentation on creating lists and cards (*https://devel
oper.android.com/training/material/get-started.html*).

Source Download URL

The source code for this example is in the Android Cookbook repository (*https://
github.com/IanDarwin/Android-Cookbook-Examples*), in the subdirectory *CardDemo*
(see "Getting and Using the Code Examples" on page 18).

6.14 Offering a Drop-Down Chooser via the Spinner Class

Ian Darwin

Problem

You want to offer a drop-down choice.

Solution

Use a `Spinner` object; you can pass the list of selections as an adapter.

Discussion

Generally known as a *combo box*, the spinner is the analog of the HTML `select` element or the Swing `JComboBox`. It provides a drop-down chooser whose values appear to float over the screen when the spinner is clicked. One item can be selected and the floating version will pop down, displaying the selection in the spinner (see Figure 6-16).

Like all standard components, the spinner can be created and customized in XML or in code. In this example, the term "context" or "reading context" is used to indicate when a patient's blood pressure reading was taken (after breakfast, after lunch, etc., as shown in Figure 6-16), so that the health care practitioner can understand the value *in context* of the patient's day. Here is an excerpt from *res/layout/main.xml*:

```
<Spinner  android:id="@+id/contextChooser"
          android:layout_height="wrap_content"
          android:layout_width="wrap_content"
          android:prompt="@string/context_choice"/>
```

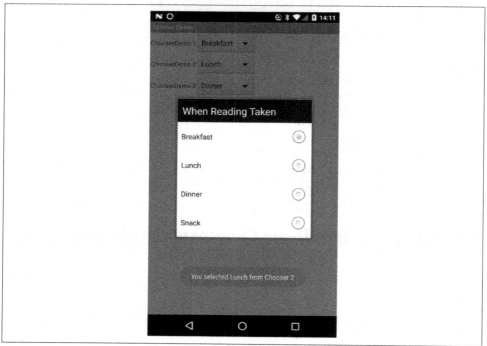

Figure 6-16. Spinner (drop-down) demonstration

Ideally the list of values will come from a resource file, so as to be internationalizable. Here is the file *res/values/contexts.xml* containing the XML values for the list of times to choose:

```
<?xml version="1.0" encoding="utf-8"?>
<resources>
    <string name="context_choice">When Reading Taken</string>
    <string-array name="context_names">
        <item>Breakfast</item>
        <item>Lunch</item>
        <item>Dinner</item>
        <item>Snack</item>
    </string-array>
</resources>
```

To tie the list of strings to the spinner at compile time, just use `<Spinner android:entries="@array/context_names" …>` in the layout file. This is the simplest way to hook the list into the spinner, and is used for "Chooser1" in the example code.

To tie the list of strings to the spinner at runtime, just look up the `Spinner` object and set the values, as shown in Example 6-22. You might want to do so if you need to modify any of the list entries at runtime, for example, or if the list is coming from a Java language `enum`. "Chooser2" in Example 6-22 gets the list from the XML, and "Chooser3" gets it from the Java enum.

Example 6-22. The Spinner code

```
// Spinner 1 gets its labels automatically from an XML array
Spinner contextChooser1 = (Spinner) findViewById(R.id.contextChooser1);
contextChooser1.setOnItemSelectedListener(listener);

// Spinner 2 gets its labels programmatically from the XML array
Spinner contextChooser2 = (Spinner) findViewById(R.id.contextChooser2);
ArrayAdapter<CharSequence> adapter2 = ArrayAdapter.createFromResource(this,
    R.array.reading_context_names, android.R.layout.simple_spinner_item);
contextChooser2.setAdapter(adapter2);
contextChooser2.setOnItemSelectedListener(listener);

// Spinner 3 gets its labels programmatically from a Java language enum
Spinner contextChooser3 = (Spinner) findViewById(R.id.contextChooser3);
ArrayAdapter<ReadingContext> adapter3 = new ArrayAdapter<ReadingContext>(
    this, android.R.layout.simple_spinner_item, ReadingContext.values());
contextChooser3.setAdapter(adapter3);
contextChooser3.setOnItemSelectedListener(listener);
```

That is all you need in order for the spinner to appear, and to allow the user to select items (see Figure 6-16). If you want to know the chosen value as soon as the user has selected it, you can send an `OnItemSelectedListener` instance to the `Spinner` class's `setOnItemSelectedListener()` method. This interface has two callback methods, `setItemSelected()` and `setNothingSelected()`. Both are called with the `Spinner` (but the argument is declared as a `ViewAdapter`); the former method is called with two integer arguments, the list position and the identity of the selected item, like so:

```
OnItemSelectedListener listener = new OnItemSelectedListener() {

    @Override
    public void onItemSelected(AdapterView<?> spinner, View arg1,
            int pos, long id) {
        Toast.makeText(SpinnerDemoActivity.this,
            "You selected " + spinner.getSelectedItem(),
            Toast.LENGTH_SHORT).show();
    }

    @Override
    public void onNothingSelected(AdapterView<?> spinner) {
        Toast.makeText(SpinnerDemoActivity.this,
            "Nothing selected.", Toast.LENGTH_SHORT).show();
    }
};
```

On the other hand, you may not need the value from the spinner until the user fills in multiple items and clicks a button. In this case, you can simply call the `Spinner` class's `getSelectedItem()` method, which returns the item placed in that position by the Adapter. Assuming you placed strings in the list, you can just call `toString()` to get back the given `String` value.

Source Download URL

The source code for this project is in the Android Cookbook repository (*https://github.com/IanDarwin/Android-Cookbook-Examples*), in the subdirectory *Spinner-Demo* (see "Getting and Using the Code Examples" on page 18).

6.15 Handling Long-Press/Long-Click Events

Ian Darwin

Problem

You want to listen for long-press/long-click events and react to them, without having to manually check for multiple events.

Solution

Use the `View` class's `setLongClickable()` and `setOnLongClickListener()` methods, and provide an `OnLongClickListener`.

Discussion

The `View` class has a method to enable/disable long-click support, `set LongClickable(boolean)`, and the corresponding `setOnLongClickListener(On LongClickListener)` method. In Example 6-23 we listen for long-clicks on a `View` and respond by popping up a `PopupMenu`, which will be modal and will appear in front of the `ListView`.

Example 6-23. A LongClickListener

```
final View myView = findViewById(R.id.myView);
...
myView.setOnLongClickListener(new OnLongClickListener() {
        @Override
        public boolean onLongClick(View view) {
            PopupMenu p = new PopupMenu(Main.this, view);
            p.getMenuInflater().inflate(
                R.layout.main_popup_menu, p.getMenu());
            p.show();
            return true;
        }
});
```

The pop-up menu will be dismissed when you click one of its items; the list of menu items comes from the XML file *res/menu/main_popup_menu.xml*, which just contains a series of `item` elements with the text for the menu items.

Note that calling `setOnLongClickListener()` has the side effect of calling `setLongClickEnabled(true)`.

Note also that adding an `OnClickListener` to a `ListView` (or other multi-item view) does not work as you might expect; the list items simply get dispatched as per a normal click. Instead, you must use the `setOnItemLongClickListener()` method that takes, unsurprisingly, an instance of `OnItemLongClickListener()`, which will be invoked when you long-press on an item in the list.

In fact, you can even simplify this for a `ListView` by preinflating your menu and passing it to the `Activity`'s `setContextMenu(view, menu)` method.

6.16 Displaying Text Fields with TextView and EditText

Ian Darwin

Problem

You want to display text on the screen, either read-only or editable.

Solution

Use a `TextView` when you want the user to have read-only access to text; this includes what most other GUI API packages call a `Label`, there being no explicit `Label` class in `android.widget`. Use an `EditText` when you want the user to have read/write access to text; this includes what other packages may call a `TextField` or a `TextArea`.

Discussion

`EditText` is a direct subclass of `TextView`. Note that `EditText` has many direct and indirect subclasses, many of which are GUI controls in their own right, such as `CheckBox`, `RadioButton`, and the like. A further subclass is the `AutoCompleteTextView`, which, as the name implies, allows for auto-completion when the user types the first few letters of some data item. As with the recipes in Chapter 8, there is an adapter to provide the completable text items.

Placing an `EditText` or `TextView` is trivial using the XML layout. Assigning the initial value to be displayed is also simple using XML. It is possible to set the value directly using the following:

```
<TextView android:text="Welcome!"/>
```

However, it is preferable to use a value like `"@string/welcome_text"` and define the string in *strings.xml* so that it can be changed and internationalized more readily.

Since `TextView` and `EditText` are used throughout this book, we do not have a sample application that uses them. One is provided with the Android API Examples, called `LabelView`, if you need it.

6.17 Constraining EditText Values with Attributes and the TextWatcher Interface

Daniel Fowler

Problem

You need to limit the range and type of values that users can input.

Solution

Use appropriate attributes on the `EditText` views in the layout XML and enhance them by implementing the `TextWatcher` interface.

Discussion

When an application needs input from a user, sometimes only a specific type of value is required; maybe a whole number, a decimal number, a number between two values, or words that are capitalized. When defining an EditText in a layout, attributes such as android:inputType can be used to constrain what the user is able to type. This automatically reduces the amount of code required later on because there are fewer checks to perform on the data that was entered. The TextWatcher interface is also useful for restricting values. In the following example an EditText only allows a value between 0 and 100—for example, to represent a percentage. There is no need to check the value because it is all done as the user types.

Here is a simple layout with one such EditText:

```xml
<?xml version="1.0" encoding="utf-8"?>
<LinearLayout xmlns:android="http://schemas.android.com/apk/res/android"
            android:orientation="vertical"
            android:layout_width="fill_parent"
            android:layout_height="fill_parent">
   <EditText android:layout_width="fill_parent"
            android:layout_height="wrap_content"
            android:id="@+id/percent"
            android:text="0"
            android:maxLength="3"
            android:inputType="number"/>
</LinearLayout>
```

The EditText is given a starting value of zero with android:text="0", and the number of characters that can be typed has been limited to three with android:maxLength="3" because the largest number we need, 100, only has three digits. Finally, the user is restricted to only positive numbers with android:inputType="number". It is a good idea to review the attributes that Android views support, because defining views in the XML layout can reduce the amount of code you need to write. For further details on the attributes supported by EditText see the Android documentation on the TextView (*https://developer.android.com/reference/android/widget/TextView.html*), from which EditText is subclassed.

Within Example 6-24's Activity class, an inner class can be used to implement the TextWatcher interface (or, for example, the Activity class itself could implement the interface). The afterTextChanged() method is overridden and will be called when the text changes as the user types. In this method the value being typed is checked to see if it is greater than 100. If so, it is set to 100. There is no need to check for values less than zero because they cannot be entered, because of the XML attributes. The try-catch is needed for when all the numbers are deleted, in which case the test for values greater than 100 would cause an exception (trying to parse an empty string).

TextWatcher also has a beforeTextChanged() and an onTextChanged() method that you can override, but they are not used in this example.

Example 6-24. The TextWatcher implementation

```
class CheckPercentage implements TextWatcher{
    @Override
    public void afterTextChanged(Editable s) {
        try {
            Log.d("Percentage", "input: " + s);
            if(Integer.parseInt(s.toString())>100)
                s.replace(0, s.length(), "100");
        }
        catch(NumberFormatException nfe) {
            // Empty
        }
    }
    @Override
    public void beforeTextChanged(CharSequence s, int start, int count, int after) {
        // Not used, details on text just before it changed
        // Used to track in detail changes made to text, e.g. to implement an undo
    }
    @Override
    public void onTextChanged(CharSequence s, int start, int before, int count) {
        // Not used, details on text at point change made
    }
}
```

Finally, in the onCreate() method for the Activity, the inner class implementing TextWatcher is connected to the EditText using its addTextChangedListener() method:

```
@Override
public void onCreate(Bundle savedInstanceState) {
    super.onCreate(savedInstanceState);
    setContentView(R.layout.main);
    EditText percentage=(EditText) findViewById(R.id.percent);
    percentage.addTextChangedListener(new CheckPercentage());
}
```

Note that it is fine to change the EditText value in afterTextChanged() as its internal Editable class is passed in. However, you cannot change it by altering the CharSequence passed into beforeTextChanged() and onTextChanged().

Running this example, with Logcat running, should show the values being set, as shown in Figure 6-17.

Also remember that if you change the value in the EditText, it will cause the afterTextChanged() method to be called again. Care must be taken to ensure that the code using TextWatcher does not result in endless looping.

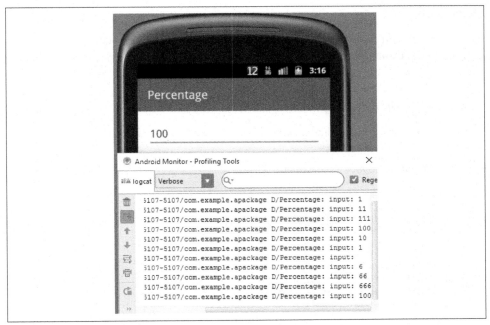

Figure 6-17. TextWatcher in action

See Also

The developer documentation on the TextView class (*https://developer.android.com/reference/android/widget/TextView.html*), EditText class (*https://developer.android.com/reference/android/widget/EditText.html*), and TextWatcher interface (*https://developer.android.com/reference/android/text/TextWatcher.html*).

6.18 Implementing AutoCompleteTextView

Rachee Singh

Problem

You want to save the user from typing entire words, and instead auto-complete entries based on the first few characters the user enters.

Solution

Use the AutoCompleteTextView widget that acts as a cross between an EditText and a Spinner, enabling auto-completion.

Discussion

The demo layout here includes a `TextView` that supports auto-completion. Auto-completion is done using an `AutoCompleteTextView` widget. Example 6-25 shows the layout XML code.

Example 6-25. The auto-completion layout

```
<LinearLayout xmlns:android="http://schemas.android.com/apk/res/android"
    android:orientation="vertical"
    android:layout_width="fill_parent"
    android:layout_height="fill_parent"
    >
    <TextView
    android:id="@+id/field"
    android:layout_width="fill_parent"
    android:layout_height="wrap_content"
    />
    <AutoCompleteTextView
    android:id="@+id/autocomplete"
    android:layout_width="fill_parent"
    android:layout_height="wrap_content"
    android:completionThreshold="2"/>

</LinearLayout>
```

The `completionThreshold` field in the `AutoCompleteTextView` sets the minimum number of characters that the user has to enter in the `TextView` so that auto-completion options corresponding to his input to show up.

The `Activity` in which we are implementing auto-completion should implement `TextWatcher` so that we can override the `onTextChanged()` method:

```
public class AutoComplete extends Activity implements TextWatcher {
```

We need to override the unimplemented methods: `onTextChanged()`, `beforeTextChanged()`, and `afterTextChanged()`. We also require three fields:

- A handle onto the `TextView`
- A handle onto the `AutoCompleteTextView`
- A list of `String` items from which the auto-completion will choose

These three items are shown here:

```
private TextView field;
private AutoCompleteTextView autocomplete;
String autocompleteItems [] = {"apple", "banana", "mango", "pineapple","apricot",
    "orange", "pear", "grapes"};
```

Our `onTextChanged()` method, shown next, simply copies the current value of the text field into another text field—this is not mandatory, but in this demo it will show you what values are being set in the auto-completion component:

```
@Override
public void onTextChanged(CharSequence arg0, int arg1, int arg2, int arg3) {
    field.setText(autocomplete.getText());
}
```

In the `onCreate()` method of the same `Activity`, we get a handle on the `TextView` and the `AutoCompleteTextView` components of the layout. We also set a `String` adapter for the `AutoCompleteTextView`:

```
setContentView(R.layout.main);
field = (TextView) findViewById(R.id.field);
autocomplete = (AutoCompleteTextView)findViewById(R.id.autocomplete);
autocomplete.addTextChangedListener(this);
autocomplete.setAdapter(new ArrayAdapter<String>(this,
    android.R.layout.simple_dropdown_item_1line, autocompleteItems));
```

Source Download URL

You can download the source code for this example from Google Docs (*https://docs.google.com/leaf?id=0B_rESQKgad5LYzVkOTdlOGUtODg5My00ZTRmLWIyN TYtMDdiMzA0NjhiNGRk&hl=en_US*).

6.19 Feeding AutoCompleteTextView Using a SQLite Database Query

Jonathan Fuerth

Problem

Although the Android documentation contains a complete working example of using `AutoCompleteTextView` with an `ArrayAdapter`, just substituting a `SimpleCursorAdapter` into the example does not work.

Solution

There are two extra twists to using `SimpleCursorAdapter` instead of `ArrayAdapter`:

- You need to tell the Adapter which column to use to fill the `TextView` after the user selects a completion.
- You need to tell the Adapter how to requery based on the user's latest input in the text field. Otherwise, it shows all rows returned by the cursor and the list never shrinks to include the items of actual interest.

Discussion

The following example code would typically be found in the onCreate() method of the Activity that contains the AutoCompleteTextView. It retrieves the AutoCompleteTextView from the Activity's layout, creates a SimpleCursorAdapter, configures that SimpleCursorAdapter to work with the AutoCompleteTextView, and then assigns the Adapter to the View.

The two important differences from the ArrayAdapter example in the Android Developers Guide are marked in Example 6-26.

Example 6-26. The onCreate() code

```
final AutoCompleteTextView itemName =
    (AutoCompleteTextView) findViewById(R.id.item_name_view);

SimpleCursorAdapter itemNameAdapter = new SimpleCursorAdapter(
        this, R.layout.completion_item, itemNameCursor, fromCol, toView);

itemNameAdapter.setStringConversionColumn(                          ❶
itemNameCursor.getColumnIndexOrThrow(GroceryDBAdapter.ITEM_NAME_COL));

itemNameAdapter.setFilterQueryProvider(new FilterQueryProvider() { ❷

    public Cursor runQuery(CharSequence constraint) {
        String partialItemName = null;
        if (constraint != null) {
            partialItemName = constraint.toString();
        }
        return groceryDb.suggestItemCompletions(partialItemName);
    }
});

itemName.setAdapter(itemNameAdapter);
```

❶ With ArrayAdapter, there is no need to specify how to convert the user's selection into a String. However, SimpleCursorAdapter supports using one column for the text of the suggestion, and a different column for the text that's fed into the text field after the user selects a suggestion. Although the most common case is to use the same text for the suggestion as you get in the text field after picking it, this is *not* the default. The default is, as is often the case in Java, to use toString(), e.g., to fill the text view with the toString() representation of your cursor—something like android.database.sqlite.SQLiteCursor@f00f00d0. That is not what you want!

❷ With ArrayAdapter, the system takes care of filtering the alternatives to display only those strings that start with what the user has typed into the text field so far. The SimpleCursorAdapter is more flexible, but again, the default behavior is not useful. If you fail to write a FilterQueryProvider for your adapter, the AutoCompleteTextView will simply show the initial set of suggestions no matter what the user types. With the `FilterQueryProvider`, the suggestions work as expected.

6.20 Turning Edit Fields into Password Fields

Rachee Singh

Problem

You need to designate an `EditText` as a password field so that characters the user types will not be visible to "shoulder surfers."

Solution

Android provides the `password` attribute on the `EditText` class, which provides the needed behavior.

Discussion

If your application requires the user to enter a password, the `EditText` being used should be special. It should hide the characters entered. This can be done by adding this property to the `EditText` in XML:

```
android:inputType="textPassword"
```

Figure 6-18 shows how the password `EditText` would look.

Figure 6-18. EditText with password

6.21 Changing the Enter Key to "Next" on the Soft Keyboard

Jonathan Fuerth

Problem

Several apps, including the Browser and Contacts apps, replace the Enter key on the onscreen keyboard with a Next key that gives focus to the next data entry view. You want to add this kind of polish to your own apps.

Solution

Set the appropriate input method editor (IME) attribute on the views in question.

Discussion

Figure 6-19 shows a simple layout with three text fields (EditText views) and a Submit button.

Figure 6-19. Three text fields and a Submit button

Note the Enter key at the bottom right. Pressing it causes the currently focused text field to expand vertically to accommodate another line of text. This is not what you normally want!

Here is the code for the layout in Figure 6-19:

```xml
<?xml version="1.0" encoding="utf-8"?>
<LinearLayout xmlns:android="http://schemas.android.com/apk/res/android"
    android:orientation="vertical"
    android:layout_width="fill_parent"
    android:layout_height="fill_parent">
<EditText
    android:layout_width="fill_parent"
    android:layout_height="wrap_content"
    android:text="Field 1" />
<EditText
    android:layout_width="fill_parent"
    android:layout_height="wrap_content"
    android:text="Field 2" />
<EditText
    android:layout_width="fill_parent"
    android:layout_height="wrap_content"
    android:text="Field 3" />
<Button
    android:layout_width="wrap_content"
    android:layout_height="wrap_content"
    android:layout_gravity="center_horizontal"
    android:text="Submit" />
</LinearLayout>
```

Figure 6-20 shows a better version of the same UI, with a Next key where Enter was.

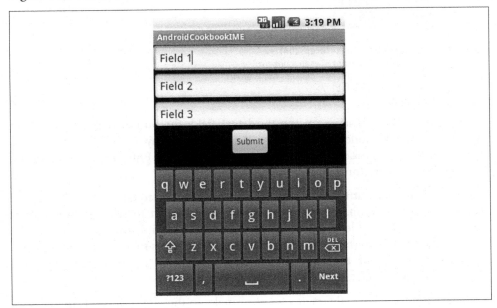

Figure 6-20. Improved UI: Next key

Besides being more convenient for users, this also prevents people from entering multiple lines of text into a field that was only intended to hold a single line.

Here's how to tell Android to display a Next button on your keyboard. Note the `android:imeOptions` attributes on each of the three `EditText` views:

```xml
<?xml version="1.0" encoding="utf-8"?>
<LinearLayout xmlns:android="http://schemas.android.com/apk/res/android"
    android:orientation="vertical"
    android:layout_width="fill_parent"
    android:layout_height="fill_parent">
<EditText
    android:layout_width="fill_parent"
    android:layout_height="wrap_content"
    android:text="Field 1"
    android:singleLine="true"
    android:imeOptions="actionNext" />
<EditText
    android:layout_width="fill_parent"
    android:layout_height="wrap_content"
    android:text="Field 2"
    android:singleLine="true"
    android:imeOptions="actionNext" />
<EditText
    android:layout_width="fill_parent"
    android:layout_height="wrap_content"
    android:text="Field 3"
    android:singleLine="true"
    android:imeOptions="actionDone" />
<Button
    android:layout_width="wrap_content"
    android:layout_height="wrap_content"
    android:layout_gravity="center_horizontal"
    android:text="Submit" />
</LinearLayout>
```

Finally, notice the `actionDone` on the third text field: the button that follows is not focusable in touch mode, and if it were, it wouldn't display a keyboard anyway. As you might guess, `actionDone` puts a Done button where the Enter key normally goes. Pressing the Done button simply hides the keyboard.

The `android:singleLine` attribute is required for the `imeOptions` to take effect. The official Android documentation says that this "constrains the text to a single horizontally scrolling line instead of letting it wrap onto multiple lines, and advances focus instead of inserting a newline when you press the enter key." This is marked as deprecated in the current SDK, but the replacement (`android:maxLines="1"`) does not cause the `imeOptions` to take effect.

There are a number of refinements you can make to the appearance of the software keyboard, including hints about the input type, suggested capitalization, and even select-all-on-focus behavior. They are all worth investigating. Every little touch can make your app more pleasurable to use.

See Also

The Android API documentation for TextView (*https://developer.android.com/refer ence/android/widget/TextView.html*), especially the section on imeOptions (*https://devel oper.android.com/reference/android/widget/TextView.html#attr_android:imeOptions*).

Source Download URL

The source code for this project is in the Android Cookbook repository (*https:// github.com/IanDarwin/Android-Cookbook-Examples*), in the subdirectory *SoftKey boardEnterNext* (see "Getting and Using the Code Examples" on page 18).

6.22 Processing Key-Press Events in an Activity

Rachee Singh

Problem

You want to intercept the keys pressed by the user and perform actions correspond ing to them.

Solution

Override the onKeyDown() method in an Activity.

Discussion

If the application must react differently to different key-presses, you need to override the onKeyDown() method in the Activity's Java code. This method takes the KeyCode as an argument so that, within a switch-case block, different actions can be carried out (see Example 6-27).

Example 6-27. The onKeyDown() method

```
public boolean onKeyDown(int keyCode, KeyEvent service) {
    switch(keyCode) {
        case KeyEvent.KEYCODE_HOME:
            keyType.setText("Home Key Pressed!");
            break;
        case KeyEvent.KEYCODE_DPAD_CENTER :
            keyType.setText("Center Key Pressed!");
            break;
        case KeyEvent.KEYCODE_DPAD_DOWN :
            keyType.setText("Down Key Pressed!");
            break;
        // And so on...
    }
}
```

Source Download URL

You can download the source code for this example from Google Docs (*https://docs.google.com/leaf?id=0B_rESQKgad5LMDdhMDllYmYtOWE5Mi00MDU0LWE4YWEtODkwNGYwMWVkOTNl&hl=en_US*).

6.23 Let Them See Stars: Using RatingBar

Ian Darwin

Problem

You want the user to choose from a number of identical GUI elements in a group to indicate a value such as a "rating" or "evaluation."

Solution

Use the `RatingBar` widget; it lets you specify the number of stars to appear and the default rating, notifies you when the user changes the value, and lets you retrieve the rating.

Discussion

`RatingBar` provides the now-familiar "rating" user interface experience, where a user is asked to rank or rate something using star classification (the `RatingBar` doesn't display the thing to be rated; that's up to the rest of your app). `RatingBar` is a subclass of `ProgressBar`, extended to display a whole number of icons (the stars) in the bar. Its primary properties are:

`numStars`
    The number of stars to display (`int`)

`rating`
    The user's chosen rating (`float`, because of `stepSize`)

`stepSize`
    The increment for selection (`float`; common values are 1.0 and 0.5, depending on how fine-grained you want the rating to be)

`isIndicator`
    A `boolean`, set to `true` to make this read-only

These properties are normally set in the XML:

```
<RatingBar
    android:id="@+id/serviceBar"
    android:gravity="center"
    android:layout_width="wrap_content"
```

```
        android:layout_height="wrap_content"
        android:numStars="5"
        android:rating="3"
        android:stepSize="1.0"
        android:isIndicator='false'
        />
```

The `RatingBar` maintains its rating value internally. You can find out how the user has rated the item in two ways:

- Invoke the `getRating()` method.
- Provide a change notification listener of type `OnRatingBarChangeListener`.

The `OnRatingBarChangeListener` has a single method, `onRatingChanged()`, called with three arguments:

`RatingBar rBar`
> The event source, a reference to the particular `RatingBar`

`float fRating`
> The rating that was set

`boolean fromUser`
> `true` if set by a user, `false` if set programmatically

Example 6-28 simulates a customer survey; it creates two `RatingBars`, one to rate service and another to rate price (the XML for both is identical except for the `android:id`). In the main program, an `OnRatingBarChangeListener` is created to display touchy-feely–sounding feedback for the given rating (the rating is converted to an `int` and a `switch` statement is used to generate a message for the toast).

Example 6-28. The RatingBar demo app

```
public class MainActivity extends Activity {
    /** Called when the Activity is first created. */
    @Override
    public void onCreate(Bundle savedInstanceState) {
        super.onCreate(savedInstanceState);
        setContentView(R.layout.main);
        OnRatingBarChangeListener barChangeListener =
            new OnRatingBarChangeListener() {
            @Override
            public void onRatingChanged(RatingBar rBar,
                float fRating, boolean fromUser) {
                int rating = (int) fRating;
                String message = null;
                switch(rating) {
                case 1: message = "Sorry you're really upset with us"; break;
                case 2: message = "Sorry you're not happy"; break;
                case 3: message = "Good enough is not good enough"; break;
                case 4: message = "Thanks, we're glad you liked it."; break;
```

```
            case 5: message = "Awesome - thanks!"; break;
            }
            Toast.makeText(Main.this,
                message,
                Toast.LENGTH_LONG).show();
        }
    };
    final RatingBar sBar = (RatingBar) findViewById(R.id.serviceBar);
    sBar.setOnRatingBarChangeListener(barChangeListener);
    final RatingBar pBar = (RatingBar) findViewById(R.id.priceBar);
    pBar.setOnRatingBarChangeListener(barChangeListener);

    Button doneButton = (Button) findViewById(R.id.doneButton);
    doneButton.setOnClickListener(new OnClickListener() {

        @Override
        public void onClick(View arg0) {
            String message = String.format(
                "Final Answer: Price %.0f/%d, Service %.0f/%d%nThank you!",
                sBar.getRating(), sBar.getNumStars(),
                pBar.getRating(), pBar.getNumStars()
                );
            // Thank the user
            Toast.makeText(Main.this,
                message,
                Toast.LENGTH_LONG).show();
            // And upload the numbers to a database, hopefully...

            // That's all for this Activity, and hence this App
            finish();
        }
    });
    }
}
```

There is more than one RatingBar, so we don't save the value in the listener, because an incomplete survey is not useful; in the Done button action listener we fetch both values and display them, and this would be the place to save them. Your mileage may vary: it may make more sense to save them in the OnRatingBarChangeListener.

If you're not used to printf-like formatting, the String.format call uses %.0f to format the float as an int, instead of casting it (since we have to do nice formatting anyway). Ideally the format message should be from the XML strings, but this is only a demo program.

The main UI is shown in Figure 6-21.

When the user clicks the Done button, she will see the Farewell message displayed in the desktop window (see Figure 6-22).

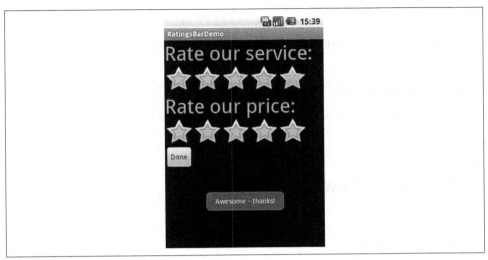

Figure 6-21. Displaying a feedback rating

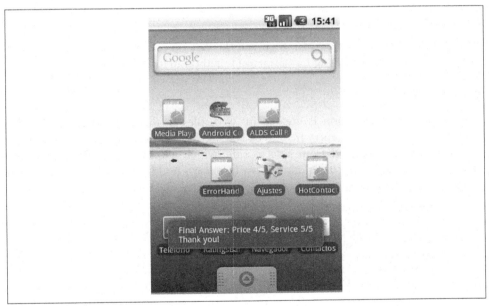

Figure 6-22. Completion of the rating/survey

When you wish to both display the current "average" or similar measure ratings from a community *and* allow users to enter their own ratings, it is customary to display the current ratings read-only and to create a pop-up dialog where a user can enter her particular rating. This is described on the Android Patterns website (*https://unitid.nl/androidpatterns/uap_pattern/rating-stars*).

See Also

The reference documentation page (*https://developer.android.com/reference/android/widget/RatingBar.html*).

Source Download URL

The source code for this project is in the Android Cookbook repository (*https://github.com/IanDarwin/Android-Cookbook-Examples*), in the subdirectory *RatingBarDemo* (see "Getting and Using the Code Examples" on page 18).

6.24 Making a View Shake

Ian Darwin

Problem

You want a View component to shake for a few seconds to catch the user's attention.

Solution

Create an animation in the XML, then call the View object's startAnimation() method, using the convenience routing loadAnimation() method to load the XML.

Discussion

The animation specification is created in XML files in the *anim* directory. In this example, we want the text entry field to be able to shake either left to right (to emulate a person shaking his head from side to side, which means "no" or "I disagree" in many parts of the world) or up and down (a person nodding in agreement). So, we create two animations, *horizontal.xml* and *vertical.xml*. Here is *horizontal.xml*:

```xml
<?xml version="1.0" encoding="utf-8"?>
<translate
    xmlns:android="http://schemas.android.com/apk/res/android"
    android:fromXDelta="0"
    android:toXDelta="10"
    android:duration="1000"
    android:interpolator="@anim/cycler"
    />
```

The file *vertical.xml* is identical except it uses fromYDelta and toYDelta.

The Interpolator—the function that drives the animation—is contained in another file, *cycler.xml*, shown here:

```xml
<?xml version="1.0"?>
<cycleInterpolator
```

```
xmlns:android="http://schemas.android.com/apk/res/android"
android:cycles="5"/>
```

To apply one of the two animations to a View component, you need a reference to it. You can, of course, use the common findViewById(R.id.*). You can also use the Activity method getCurrentFocus() if you are dealing with the current input (focused) View component; this avoids coupling to the name of a particular component, if you know that your animation will always apply to the current input object. In my code I know this is true because the animation startup is done in an onClick() method. Alternatively, you could use the View that is passed into the onClick() method, but that would make the button shake, not the text field.

I won't show the whole application, but here is the onClick() method that contains all the animation code (see Example 6-29).

Example 6-29. The animation code

```
@Override
public void onClick(View v) {
    String answer = answerEdit.getText().toString();
    if ("yes".equalsIgnoreCase(answer)) {
        getCurrentFocus().startAnimation(
        AnimationUtils.loadAnimation(getApplicationContext(),
        R.anim.vertical));
        return;
    }
    if ("no".equalsIgnoreCase(answer)) {
        getCurrentFocus().startAnimation(
        AnimationUtils.loadAnimation(getApplicationContext(),
        R.anim.horizontal));
        return;
    }
    Toast.makeText(this, "Try to be more definite, OK?",
        Toast.LENGTH_SHORT).show();
}
```

The shaking effect is convenient for drawing the user's attention to an input that is incorrect, but it can easily be overdone. Use judiciously!

6.25 Providing Haptic Feedback

Adrian Cowham

Problem

You want to provide haptic feedback with your application.

Solution

Use Android's haptic controls to provide instant physical feedback.

Discussion

Building confidence among users that their actions had an effect is a requirement for any app on any platform. The canonical example is displaying a progress bar to let users know an action is being processed. For touch interfaces this technique still applies, but the advantage of a touch interface is that developers have the opportunity to provide physical feedback, as users are capable of actually feeling the device react to their actions.

Android has some stock haptic controls, but if these don't satisfy your needs you can gain control of the device's vibrator for custom feedback.

Custom control of the device's vibrator requires permission. This is something you'll have to explicitly list in your *AndroidManifest.xml* file. If you're paranoid about asking for permission or if you already have a long list of permissions, you may want to use the stock Android haptic feedback options.

Also be aware that some devices don't have a vibrator; when you run the examples in this recipe on such devices, you will not receive haptic feedback.

I'll start by showing the more complicated example first, custom haptic feedback.

Custom haptic feedback using the device's vibrator

Your first step is to request the necessary permission. Add the following line to your *AndroidManifest.xml* file:

```
<uses-permission android:name="android.permission.VIBRATE" />
```

Now define a listener to respond to touch events. The CustomHapticListener shown in Example 6-30 is implemented as a private nonstatic inner class of the main Activity because it needs access to the Context method getSystemService().

Example 6-30. The haptic feedback listener implementation

```
private class CustomHapticListener implements View.OnClickListener {

    // Duration in milliseconds to vibrate
    private final int durationMs;

    public CustomHapticListener(int ms) {
        durationMs = ms;
    }
```

```
@Override
public void onClick(View v) {
    Vibrator vibe = (Vibrator) getSystemService(VIBRATOR_SERVICE);  ❶
    vibe.vibrate(durationMs);  ❷
}
}
```

❶ and ❷ are the important lines. ❶ gets a reference to the Vibrator service and ❷ vibrates the device. If you have not requested the vibrate permission, ❷ will throw an exception.

Now register the listener. In your Activity's onCreate() method, you'll need to get a reference to the GUI element you want to attach haptic feedback to and then register the OnClickListener defined earlier:

```
@Override
public void onCreate( Bundle savedInstance ) {
    Button customBtn = ( Button ) findViewById( R.id.btn_custom );
    customBtn.setOnTouchListener( new CustomHapticListener( 100 ) );
}
```

That's it; you're in control of the haptic feedback. Now we'll move on to using stock Android haptic feedback.

Stock haptic feedback events

First things first: to use stock Android haptic feedback events you must enable this on a view-by-view basis. That is, you must explicitly enable haptic feedback for each view. You can enable haptic feedback declaratively in your layout file or programmatically in Java. To enable haptic feedback in your layout, simply add the android:hapticFeedbackEnabled="true" attribute to your view(s). Here's an abbreviated example:

```
<button android:hapticFeedbackEnabled="true">
</button>
```

Here's how you do the same thing in code:

```
Button keyboardTapBtn = ( Button ) findViewById( btnId );
keyboardTapBtn.setHapticFeedbackEnabled( true );
```

Now that haptic feedback has been enabled, the next step is to register a listener in which to then perform the actual feedback. For this example we'll use a touch listener so that touch events will invoke the feedback; Example 6-31 shows how to register an OnTouchListener and perform haptic feedback when a user touches the view.

Example 6-31. Haptic feedback demo app

```
// Initialize some buttons with the stock Android haptic feedback values
private void initializeButtons() {
```

```
        // Initialize the buttons with the standard haptic feedback options
        initializeButton( R.id.btn_keyboardTap, HapticFeedbackConstants.KEYBOARD_TAP ); ❶
        initializeButton( R.id.btn_longPress,   HapticFeedbackConstants.LONG_PRESS );   ❷
        initializeButton( R.id.btn_virtualKey,  HapticFeedbackConstants.VIRTUAL_KEY );  ❸
    }

    // Helper method to initialize single buttons and register an OnTouchListener
    // to perform the haptic feedback
    private void initializeButton( int btnId, int hapticId ) {
        Button btn = ( Button ) findViewById( btnId );
        btn.setOnTouchListener( new HapticTouchListener( hapticId ) );
    }

    // Class to handle touch events and respond with haptic feedback
    private class HapticTouchListener implements OnTouchListener {

        private final int feedbackType;

        public HapticTouchListener( int type ) { feedbackType = type; }

        public int feedbackType() { return feedbackType; }

        @Override
        public boolean onTouch(View v, MotionEvent event) {
            // Only perform feedback when the user touches the view, as opposed
            // to lifting a finger off the view
            if( event.getAction() == MotionEvent.ACTION_DOWN ) {
                // Perform the feedback
                v.performHapticFeedback( feedbackType() );❹
            }
            return true;
        }
    }
}
```

You'll notice that in lines ❶ through ❸, I'm initializing three different buttons with three different haptic feedback constants. These are Android's stock values; two of the three seem to provide exactly the same feedback.

Example 6-31 is part of a test app I wrote to demonstrate haptic feedback, and I could not tell the difference between HapticFeedbackConstants.LONG_PRESS and HapticFeedbackConstants.KeyboardTap. HapticFeedbackConstants.VIRTUAL_KEY, when tested, does not appear to provide any feedback. ❹ is where the haptic feedback is performed. All in all, providing haptic feedback is pretty simple, but remember that if you want control of the device's vibrator you must request permission in your *AndroidManifest.xml* file. If you choose to use the stock Android haptic feedback options, make sure you enable haptic feedback for your views either in the layout or programmatically.

See Also

The blog post by the author of this recipe, entitled "Android's Haptic Feedback" (*http://mytensions.blogspot.com/2011/03/androids-haptic-feedback.html*).

Source Download URL

The source code for this project is in the Android Cookbook repository (*https://github.com/IanDarwin/Android-Cookbook-Examples*), in the subdirectory *HapticFeedback* (see "Getting and Using the Code Examples" on page 18).

6.26 Navigating Different Activities Within a TabView

Pratik Rupwal

Problem

You want to change from an Activity within a TabView to another Activity within the same tab.

Solution

Replace the content view of the tab with the new Activity you want to move to.

Discussion

When a "calling" Activity within a TabView calls another Activity through an Intent, the TabView gets replaced by the view of the called Activity. To show the called Activity within the TabView, we can replace the view of the calling Activity with the view of the called Activity so that the TabView remains stable. To achieve this we need to extend the calling Activity from ActivityGroup rather than Activity.

In Example 6-32 the Calling Activity extended from ActivityGroup has been set within a TabView.

Example 6-32. Replacing the Activity within a tab

```
// 'Calling' Activity
public class Calling extends ActivityGroup implements OnClickListener
{
    Button b1;
    Intent i1;
    /** Called when the Activity is first created. */
    @Override
    public void onCreate(Bundle savedInstanceState) {
        super.onCreate(savedInstanceState);
        setContentView(R.layout.calling);
        b1=(Button)findViewById(R.id.changeactivity);
```

```
            b1.setOnClickListener();
        }
    public void onClick(View view) {
        // Create an intent to call the 'Called' Activity
        i1=new Intent(this.getBaseContext(),Called.class);
        // Call the method to replace the view.
        replaceContentView("Called", i1);
    }
    // This replaces the view of the 'Calling' Activity with the 'Called' Activity.
    public void replaceContentView(String id, Intent newIntent) {
        // Obtain the view of the 'Called' Activity using its Intent 'newIntent'
        View view = getLocalActivityManager().startActivity(id,
            newIntent.addFlags(Intent.FLAG_ACTIVITY_CLEAR_TOP)) .getDecorView();
        // Set the above view to the content of the 'Calling' Activity.
        this.setContentView(view);
    }
}
```

The "called Activity" can also call another Activity (say `CalledSecond`), as shown here:

```
// 'Called Activity'
public class Called extends Activity implements OnClickListener
{
    Button b1;
    Intent i1;
    Calling caller;
    /** Called when the Activity is first created. */
    @Override
    public void onCreate(Bundle savedInstanceState) {
        super.onCreate(savedInstanceState);
        setContentView(R.layout.called);
        b1=(Button)findViewById(R.id.changeactivity);
        b1.setOnClickListener();
    }
    public void onClick(View view) {
        // Create an Intent to call the 'CalledSecond' Activity
        i1=new Intent(this.getBaseContext(),CalledSecond.class);
        /**
         * 'CalledSecond' can be any Activity, even
         * 'Calling' (in case backward navigation is required)
         */

        // Initialize the object of the 'Calling' class
        caller=(Calling)getParent();
        // Call the method to replace the view.
        caller.replaceContentView("CalledSecond", i1);
    }
}
```

6.27 Creating a Loading Screen that Will Appear Between Two Activities

Shraddha Shravagi

Problem

You are getting a black screen before loading an Activity.

Solution

Create a simple Activity that shows a loading image instead of a black screen.

Discussion

Sometimes it takes time for an Activity to fetch user-requested data from a database or the internet, and then to load the data onto the user's screen. In such cases, usually the screen goes black while the user waits for the data to load. The following scenario illustrates this:

ProfileList (the user selects one profile) → black screen → ProfileData

Instead of showing the user a black screen while she waits for the data to load, you can show an image, as illustrated in the following scenario:

ProfileList (the user selects one profile) → LoadingScreenActivity → ProfileData

In this recipe we will create a simple loading screen that appears for 2.5 seconds while the next Activity loads.

To do this, you need to start by creating a LoadingScreen layout file. This layout creates a screen that displays a "loading" message and a progress bar:

```
<LinearLayout
    xmlns:android="http://schemas.android.com/apk/res/android"
    android:layout_width="fill_parent"
    android:gravity="center" android:orientation="vertical"
    android:layout_height="fill_parent" android:background="#E5E5E5">

    <TextView android:text="Please wait while your data is being loaded..."
        android:layout_width="wrap_content" android:layout_height="wrap_content"
        android:textColor="#000000">
    </TextView>
    <ProgressBar android:id="@+id/mainSpinner1" android:layout_gravity="center"
        android:layout_width="wrap_content" android:layout_height="wrap_content"
        android:indeterminate="true"
        style="?android:attr/progressBarStyleInverse">
    </ProgressBar>

</LinearLayout>
```

Next, create a LoadingScreen class file (see Example 6-33).

Example 6-33. The LoadingScreen class

```
public class LoadingScreenActivity extends Activity {

    // Introduce a delay
    private final int WAIT_TIME = 2500;
    @Override
    protected void onCreate(Bundle savedInstanceState) {

        super.onCreate(savedInstanceState);
        System.out.println("LoadingScreenActivity  screen started");
        setContentView(R.layout.loading_screen);
        findViewById(R.id.mainSpinner1).setVisibility(View.VISIBLE);

        new Handler().postDelayed(new Runnable() {
            @Override
            public void run() {
                // Simulating a long-running task
                try {
                    Thread.sleep(1000);
                } catch (InterruptedException e) {
                    // Can't happen
                }
                System.out.println("Going to Profile Data");
                /* Create an Intent that will start the ProfileData Activity */
                Intent mainIntent =
                    new Intent(LoadingScreenActivity.this, ProfileData.class);
                LoadingScreenActivity.this.startActivity(mainIntent);
                LoadingScreenActivity.this.finish();
            }
        }, WAIT_TIME);
    }
}
```

This will load the next Activity once WAIT_TIME has elapsed.

Now all you need to do is to create an Intent to launch the loading screen Activity:

```
protected void onListItemClick(ListView l, View v, int position, long id) {
        super.onListItemClick(l, v, position, id);

    Intent intent = new Intent(ProfileList.this, LoadingScreenActivity.class);
        startActivity(intent);
}
```

6.28 Adding a Border with Rounded Corners to a Layout

Daniel Fowler

Problem

You need to put a border around an area of the screen or add interest to a user interface.

Solution

Define an Android shape in an XML file and assign it to a layout's `background` attribute.

Discussion

The *drawable* folder, under *res* in an Android project, is not restricted to bitmaps (PNG or JPG files); it can also hold shapes defined in XML files. These shapes can then be reused in the project. A shape can be used to put a border around a layout. This example shows how to make a rectangular border with curved corners.

Create a new file called *customborder.xml* in the *drawable* folder. Right-click on the *drawable* folder and select New → Drawable Resource File from the context menu (or, with that folder selected, use the File menu). In the New Drawable Resource File dialog, enter a filename of *customborder*. Set the "Root element" to shape, and click OK. Enter the following XML, defining the border shape, into the *customborder.xml* file:

```xml
<?xml version="1.0" encoding="UTF-8"?>
<shape xmlns:android="http://schemas.android.com/apk/res/android"
    android:shape="rectangle">
    <corners android:radius="20dp"/>
    <padding android:left="10dp" android:right="10dp"
        android:top="10dp" android:bottom="10dp"/>
    <solid android:color="#CCCCCC"/>
</shape>
```

The attribute `android:shape` is set to `rectangle` (shape files also support `oval`, `line`, and `ring`). `rectangle` is the default value, so you can leave out this attribute if you're defining a rectangle. For detailed information on shape files, refer to the Android documentation on shapes (*https://developer.android.com/guide/topics/resources/drawable-resource.html#Shape*).

The element `corners` sets the rectangle corners to be rounded; it is possible to set a different radius on each corner (see the Android reference).

The `padding` attributes are used to move the contents of the view to which the shape is applied, to prevent the contents from overlapping the border.

The border color here is set to a light gray (the hexadecimal RGB value #CCCCCC).

Shapes also support gradients, but that is not used in our example; again, see the Android documentation to see how a gradient is defined.

The shape is applied using `android:background="@drawable/customborder"`.

Within the layout other views can be added as usual. In this example a single `TextView` has been added, and the text is white (hexadecimal RGB value #FFFFFF). The background is set to blue, plus some transparency to reduce the brightness (hexadecimal alpha RGB value #A00000FF).

Finally, the layout is offset from the screen edge by placing it into another layout with a small amount of padding. The full layout file looks like this:

```xml
<?xml version="1.0" encoding="utf-8"?>
<LinearLayout xmlns:android="http://schemas.android.com/apk/res/android"
              android:orientation="vertical"
              android:layout_width="fill_parent"
              android:layout_height="fill_parent"
              android:padding="5dp">
    <LinearLayout android:orientation="vertical"
              android:layout_width="fill_parent"
              android:layout_height="fill_parent"
              android:background="@drawable/customborder">
    <TextView android:layout_width="fill_parent"
              android:layout_height="fill_parent"
              android:text="Text View"
              android:textSize="20dp"
              android:textColor="#FFFFFF"
              android:gravity="center_horizontal"
              android:background="#A00000FF" />
    </LinearLayout>
</LinearLayout>
```

This produces the result shown in Figure 6-23.

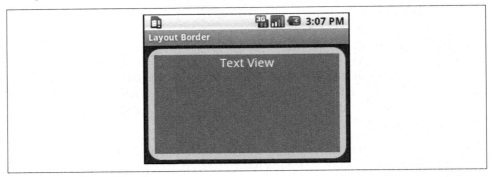

Figure 6-23. Curved border

See Also

The developer documentation on shapes (*https://developer.android.com/guide/topics/ resources/drawable-resource.html#Shape*).

Source Download URL

The source code for this project is in the Android Cookbook repository (*https:// github.com/IanDarwin/Android-Cookbook-Examples*), in the subdirectory *LayoutBorder* (see "Getting and Using the Code Examples" on page 18).

6.29 Detecting Gestures in Android

Pratik Rupwal

Problem

You want the user to be able to traverse through different screens using simple gestures, such as flipping/scrolling the page.

Solution

Use the GestureDetector class to detect simple gestures such as tapping, scrolling, swiping, or flipping.

Discussion

The sample application in this recipe has four views, each a different color. It also has two modes: SCROLL and FLIP. The application starts in FLIP mode. In this mode, when you perform the swipe/fling gesture in a left-to-right or top-to-bottom direction, the view changes back and forth. When a long-press is detected, the application changes to SCROLL mode, in which you can scroll the displayed view. While in this mode, you can double-tap the screen to bring the screen back to its original position. When a long-press is detected again, the application changes to FLIP mode.

This recipe focuses on gesture detection, hence the animation between those views is not discussed. Refer to Recipe 6.24 for an example of shaking a view using an animation, as well as the Android documentation for android.view.animation (*https://developer.android.com/reference/android/view/animation/package-summary.html*).

Example 6-34 provides an introduction to simple gesture detection in Android. Our GestureDetector class detects gestures using the supplied MotionEvent class. We use this class along with the onTouchEvent() method. Inside this method we call GestureDetector.onTouchEvent(). The GestureDetector class identifies the gestures or events that occurred and reports back to us using the GestureDetector.OnGestureListener callback interface. We create an instance of the GestureDetector class by passing the Context and GestureDetector.OnGestureListener listener. The double-tap event is not present in the GestureDetector.OnGestureListener callback interface; this event is reported using another callback interface, GestureDetector.OnDoubleTapListener. To use this callback interface we have to register a GestureDetector.OnDoubleTapListener for these events. The MotionEvent class contains all the values corresponding to a movement and touch event. This class holds values such as the *x*- and *y*- positions at which the event occurred, the timestamp at which the event occurred, and the mouse pointer index.

Example 6-34. Gesture detection

```
...
import android.view.GestureDetector;
...
import android.view.animation.OvershootInterpolator;
import android.view.animation.TranslateAnimation;

public class FlipperActivity extends Activity
        implements GestureDetector.OnGestureListener,
            GestureDetector.OnDoubleTapListener {

    final private int SWIPE_MIN_DISTANCE = 100;
    final private int SWIPE_MIN_VELOCITY = 100;

    private ViewFlipper flipper = null;
    private ArrayList<TextView> views = null;
    private GestureDetector gesturedetector = null;
    private Vibrator vibrator = null;
    int colors[] = { Color.rgb(255,128,128),
        Color.rgb(128,255,128),
        Color.rgb(128,128,255),
        Color.rgb(128,128,128) };

    private Animation animleftin = null;
    private Animation animleftout = null;

    private Animation animrightin = null;
    private Animation animrightout = null;

    private Animation animupin = null;
    private Animation animupout = null;

    private Animation animdownin = null;
    private Animation animdownout = null;

    private boolean isDragMode = false;
    private int currentview = 0;

/ ** Initializes the first screen and animation to be applied to the screen
    * after detecting the gesture. */

    @Override
    public void onCreate(Bundle savedInstanceState) {
        super.onCreate(savedInstanceState);

        flipper = new ViewFlipper(this);
        gesturedetector = new GestureDetector(this, this);
        vibrator = (Vibrator)getSystemService(VIBRATOR_SERVICE);
        gesturedetector.setOnDoubleTapListener(this);

        flipper.setInAnimation(animleftin);
        flipper.setOutAnimation(animleftout);
        flipper.setFlipInterval(3000);
        flipper.setAnimateFirstView(true);
```

```java
        prepareAnimations();
        prepareViews();
        addViews();
        setViewText();

        setContentView(flipper);
    }

    private void prepareAnimations() {
        animleftin = new TranslateAnimation(
          Animation.RELATIVE_TO_PARENT, +1.0f, Animation.RELATIVE_TO_PARENT, 0.0f,
          Animation.RELATIVE_TO_PARENT, 0.0f, Animation.RELATIVE_TO_PARENT, 0.0f);

        animleftout = new TranslateAnimation(
          Animation.RELATIVE_TO_PARENT, 0.0f, Animation.RELATIVE_TO_PARENT, -1.0f,
          Animation.RELATIVE_TO_PARENT, 0.0f, Animation.RELATIVE_TO_PARENT, 0.0f);

        animrightin = new TranslateAnimation(
          Animation.RELATIVE_TO_PARENT, -1.0f, Animation.RELATIVE_TO_PARENT, 0.0f,
          Animation.RELATIVE_TO_PARENT, 0.0f, Animation.RELATIVE_TO_PARENT, 0.0f);

        animrightout = new TranslateAnimation(
          Animation.RELATIVE_TO_PARENT,  0.0f, Animation.RELATIVE_TO_PARENT,  +1.0f,
          Animation.RELATIVE_TO_PARENT, 0.0f, Animation.RELATIVE_TO_PARENT, 0.0f);

        animupin = new TranslateAnimation(
          Animation.RELATIVE_TO_PARENT,  0.0f, Animation.RELATIVE_TO_PARENT, 0.0f,
          Animation.RELATIVE_TO_PARENT, +1.0f, Animation.RELATIVE_TO_PARENT, 0.0f);

        animupout = new TranslateAnimation(
          Animation.RELATIVE_TO_PARENT,  0.0f, Animation.RELATIVE_TO_PARENT, 0.0f,
          Animation.RELATIVE_TO_PARENT, 0.0f, Animation.RELATIVE_TO_PARENT, -1.0f);

        animdownin = new TranslateAnimation(
          Animation.RELATIVE_TO_PARENT,  0.0f, Animation.RELATIVE_TO_PARENT, 0.0f,
          Animation.RELATIVE_TO_PARENT, -1.0f, Animation.RELATIVE_TO_PARENT, 0.0f);

        animdownout = new TranslateAnimation(
          Animation.RELATIVE_TO_PARENT, 0.0f, Animation.RELATIVE_TO_PARENT, 0.0f,
          Animation.RELATIVE_TO_PARENT, 0.0f, Animation.RELATIVE_TO_PARENT, +1.0f);

        animleftin.setDuration(1000);
        animleftin.setInterpolator(new OvershootInterpolator());
        animleftout.setDuration(1000);
        animleftout.setInterpolator(new OvershootInterpolator());

        animrightin.setDuration(1000);
        animrightin.setInterpolator(new OvershootInterpolator());
        animrightout.setDuration(1000);
        animrightout.setInterpolator(new OvershootInterpolator());

        animupin.setDuration(1000);
        animupin.setInterpolator(new OvershootInterpolator());
        animupout.setDuration(1000);
        animupout.setInterpolator(new OvershootInterpolator());
```

```
animdownin.setDuration(1000);
animdownin.setInterpolator(new OvershootInterpolator());
animdownout.setDuration(1000);
animdownout.setInterpolator(new OvershootInterpolator());
}

private void prepareViews() {
        TextView view = null;

        views = new ArrayList<TextView>();

        for (int color: colors) {
                view = new TextView(this);

                view.setBackgroundColor(color);
                view.setTextColor(Color.BLACK);
                view.setGravity(
                    Gravity.CENTER_HORIZONTAL | Gravity.CENTER_VERTICAL);

                views.add(view);
        }
}

private void addViews() {
        for (int index=0; index<views.size(); ++index) {
                flipper.addView(views.get(index),index,
                                new LayoutParams(LayoutParams.FILL_PARENT,
                                LayoutParams.FILL_PARENT));

        }
}

private void setViewText() {
        String text = getString(isDragMode ? R.string.app_info_drag :
        R.string.app_info_flip);
        for (int index=0; index<views.size(); ++index) {
                views.get(index).setText(text);
        }
}

/** Gets invoked when a screen touch is detected. */
@Override
public boolean onTouchEvent(MotionEvent event) {
        return gesturedetector.onTouchEvent(event);
}

/** The onDown() method is called when the user first touches the screen;
 * the MotionEvent parameter represents the event that corresponds to
 * the touch event. */
@Override
public boolean onDown(MotionEvent e) {
        return false;
}

/** The onFling() method is called whenever the user swipes the screen
 * in any direction (i.e., touches the screen and immediately
 * moves the finger in any direction). */
```

```java
@Override
public boolean onFling(MotionEvent event1, MotionEvent event2,
float velocityX,float velocityY) {
        if(isDragMode)
                return false;

        final float ev1x = event1.getX();
        final float ev1y = event1.getY();
        final float ev2x = event2.getX();
        final float ev2y = event2.getY();
        final float xdiff = Math.abs(ev1x - ev2x);
        final float ydiff = Math.abs(ev1y - ev2y);
        final float xvelocity = Math.abs(velocityX);
        final float yvelocity = Math.abs(velocityY);

        if (xvelocity > this.SWIPE_MIN_VELOCITY &&
            xdiff > this.SWIPE_MIN_DISTANCE) {
                if(ev1x > ev2x) { // Swipe left
                        --currentview;

                        if (currentview < 0) {
                                currentview = views.size() - 1;
                        }

                        flipper.setInAnimation(animleftin);
                        flipper.setOutAnimation(animleftout);
                }
                else { // Swipe right
                        ++currentview;

                        if(currentview >= views.size()) {
                                currentview = 0;
                        }

                        flipper.setInAnimation(animrightin);
                        flipper.setOutAnimation(animrightout);
                }

                flipper.scrollTo(0,0);
                flipper.setDisplayedChild(currentview);
        }
        else if (yvelocity > this.SWIPE_MIN_VELOCITY &&
            ydiff > this.SWIPE_MIN_DISTANCE) {
                if(ev1y > ev2y) { // Swipe up
                        --currentview;

                        if(currentview < 0) {
                                currentview = views.size() - 1;
                        }

                        flipper.setInAnimation(animupin);
                        flipper.setOutAnimation(animupout);
                }
                else { // swipe down
                        ++currentview;
```

```
                        if(currentview >= views.size()) {
                                currentview = 0;
                        }
                        flipper.setInAnimation(animdownin);
                        flipper.setOutAnimation(animdownout);
                }

                flipper.scrollTo(0,0);
                flipper.setDisplayedChild(currentview);
        }

        return false;
}

/** The onLongPress() method is called when the user touches the screen
 * and holds it for a period of time. The MotionEvent parameter represents
 * the event that corresponds to the touch event. */
@Override
public void onLongPress(MotionEvent e) {
        vibrator.vibrate(200);
        flipper.scrollTo(0,0);

        isDragMode = !isDragMode;

        setViewText();
}

/** The onScroll() method is called when the user touches the screen
 * and moves their finger to another location on the screen. */
@Override
public boolean onScroll(MotionEvent e1, MotionEvent e2,
        float distanceX,float distanceY) {
        if(isDragMode)
                flipper.scrollBy((int)distanceX, (int)distanceY);

        return false;
}

/** The onShowPress() method is called when the user touches the screen,
 * before they lift or move their finger. This event is mostly used for
 * giving visual feedback to the user to show their action. */
@Override
public void onShowPress(MotionEvent e) {
}

/** The onSingleTapUp() method is called when the user taps the screen. */
@Override
public boolean onSingleTapUp(MotionEvent e) {
        return false;
}

/** The onDoubleTap() method is called when a double-tap event has occurred.
 * The only parameter, MotionEvent, corresponds to the double-tap
 * event that occurred. */
@Override
public boolean onDoubleTap(MotionEvent e) {
```

```
        flipper.scrollTo(0,0);

        return false;
    }

    /** The onDoubleTapEvent() method is called for all events that occurred
     * within the double-tap; i.e., down, move, and up events. */

    @Override
    public boolean onDoubleTapEvent(MotionEvent e) {
        return false;
    }

    /** The onSingleTapConfirmed() method is called when a single tap
    * has occurred and been confirmed, but this is not same as the
    * single-tap event in the GestureDetector.OnGestureListener. This
    * is called when the GestureDetector detects and confirms that
    * this tap does not lead to a double-tap. */
    @Override
    public boolean onSingleTapConfirmed(MotionEvent e) {
        return false;
    }
}
```

When the mode of the application changes the user is notified with a vibration. To use the Vibrator service, set the following permission in your application's *Android-Manifest.xml* file:

```
<uses-permission android:name="android.permission.VIBRATE"></uses-permission>
```

The application uses some strings, which are declared under *res/values/string.xml*:

```
<?xml version="1.0" encoding="utf-8"?>
<resources>
    <string name="app_info_drag">
    GestureDetector sample.\n\nCurrent Mode:
        SCROLL\n\nDrag the view using finger.\nLong press to change
    the mode to FLIP.\nDouble tap to reposition the view to normal.</string>
    <string name="app_name">Gesture Detector Sample</string>
    <string name="app_info_flip">
    GestureDetector sample.\n\nCurrent Mode: FLIP\n\nSwipe left, right, up, down
        to change the views\nLong
    press to change to mode to SCROLL</string>
</resources>
```

See Also

The documentation for the GestureOverlayView class (*https://developer.android.com/refer ence/android/gesture/GestureOverlayView.html*) for handling complex gestures in Android.

6.30 Creating a Simple App Widget

Catarina Reis

Problem

You want to enable users to more easily interact with your application.

Solution

Create an `Application` widget, which is a simple GUI control that appears on the Home screen and allows users to easily interact with an existing application (Activity and/or Service).

Discussion

In this recipe we will create a widget that starts a Service that updates its visual components. The widget, called `CurrentMoodWidget`, presents the user's current mood in the form of a text smiley. The current mood smiley changes to a random mood smiley whenever the user clicks the smiley image button. In Figure 6-24, the screenshot on the left shows the initial view, and the screenshot on the right shows the view after a random change.

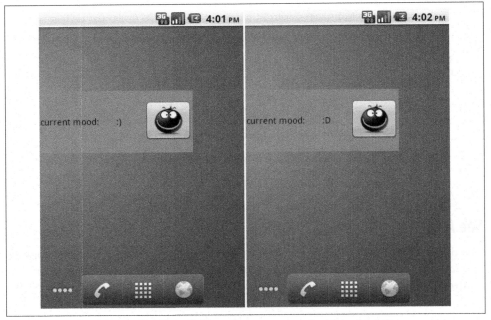

Figure 6-24. Initial mood widget (left) and current mood widget (right)

Here's how to create this simple app widget:

1. Start by creating a new Android project (`CurrentMoodWidgetProject`). Use "Current Mood" as the application name and "oreillymedia.cookbook.android.spikes" as the package name. Do not create an Activity. Set the minimum SDK version to anything modern (technically the minimum API level is 8, for Android 2.2, the version that introduced app widgets).

2. Add the string definitions for the widget in the file *res/values/string.xml*, according to the following name/value pairs:

   • `widgettext—current mood`

   • `widgetmoodtext—:)`

3. Add the images that will appear in the widget's button (*smile_icon.png*). Place these under the *res/drawable* structure.

4. Create a new layout file inside *res/layout*, under the project structure, that will define the widget layout (*widgetlayout.xml*) according to the following structure:

```
<TextView android:text="@string/widgettext"
    android:layout_width="0dp"
    android:layout_height="wrap_content"
    android:layout_weight="0.8"
    android:layout_gravity="center_vertical"
    android:textColor="#000000"></TextView>
<TextView android:text="@string/widgetmoodtext"
    android:id="@+id/widgetMood" android:layout_width="0dp"
    android:layout_height="wrap_content"
    android:layout_weight="0.3"
    android:layout_gravity="center_vertical"
    android:textColor="#000000"></TextView>
<ImageButton android:id="@+id/widgetBtn" android:layout_width="0dp"
    android:layout_height="wrap_content"
    android:layout_weight="0.5" android:src="@drawable/smile_icon"
    android:layout_gravity="center_vertical"></ImageButton>
```

5. Provide the widget provider setup configuration by first creating the *res/xml* folder under the project structure and then creating an XML file (*widgetprovider-info.xml*) with the following parameters:

```
<appwidget-provider
    xmlns:android="http://schemas.android.com/apk/res/android"
    android:minWidth="220dp"
    android:minHeight="72dp"
    android:updatePeriodMillis="86400000"
    android:initialLayout="@layout/widgetlayout">
</appwidget-provider>
```

6. Create the Service that reacts to the user interaction with the smiley image button (*CurrentMoodService.java*); see Example 6-35.

Example 6-35. Widget's Service implementation

```java
@Override
public int onStartCommand(Intent intent, int flags, int startId) {
    super.onStart(intent, startId);
    updateMood(intent);
    stopSelf(startId);
    return START_STICKY;
}

private void updateMood(Intent intent) {
    if (intent != null) {
        String requestedAction = intent.getAction();
        if (requestedAction != null &&  requestedAction.equals(UPDATEMOOD)) {
            this.currentMood = getRandomMood();
            int widgetId =
                intent.getIntExtra(AppWidgetManager.EXTRA_APPWIDGET_ID, 0);
            AppWidgetManager appWidgetMan = AppWidgetManager.getInstance(this);
            RemoteViews views =
                new RemoteViews(this.getPackageName(),R.layout.widgetlayout);
            views.setTextViewText(R.id.widgetMood, currentMood);
            appWidgetMan.updateAppWidget(widgetId, views);
        }
    }
}
```

7. Implement the widget provider class (*CurrentMoodWidgetProvider.java*); see Example 6-36.

Example 6-36. Widget provider class

```java
@Override
public void onUpdate(Context context, AppWidgetManager appWidgetManager,
        int[] appWidgetIds) {
    super.onUpdate(context, appWidgetManager, appWidgetIds);

    for (int i=0; i<appWidgetIds.length; i++) {
        int appWidgetId = appWidgetIds[i];
        RemoteViews views = new RemoteViews(context.getPackageName(),
            R.layout.widgetlayout);
        Intent intent = new Intent(context, CurrentMoodService.class);
        intent.setAction(CurrentMoodService.UPDATEMOOD);
        intent.putExtra(AppWidgetManager.EXTRA_APPWIDGET_ID,appWidgetId);
        PendingIntent pendingIntent =
            PendingIntent.getService(context, 0, intent, 0);
        views.setOnClickPendingIntent(R.id.widgetBtn, pendingIntent);
        appWidgetManager.updateAppWidget(appWidgetId, views);
    }
}
```

8. Finally, declare the Service and the app widget provider in the manifest file (*AndroidManifest.xml*):

```
<service android:name=".CurrentMoodService">
</service>
<receiver android:name=".CurrentMoodWidgetProvider">
    <intent-filter>
      <action android:name="android.appwidget.action.APPWIDGET_UPDATE"/>
    </intent-filter>
    <meta-data android:name="android.appwidget.provider"
               android:resource="@xml/widgetproviderinfo"/>
</receiver>
```

Source Download URL

The source code for this example is in the Android Cookbook repository (*https://github.com/IanDarwin/Android-Cookbook-Examples*), in the subdirectory *Current-MoodWidget* (see "Getting and Using the Code Examples" on page 18).

## CHAPTER 7

GUI Alerts: Menus, Dialogs, Toasts, Snackbars, and Notifications

User interface toolkits as diverse as Java Swing, the Apple Macintosh toolbox, Microsoft Windows, and browser JavaScript all feature the ubiquitous "pop-up menu," usually in the window-frame version and the context (in-window) form. Android follows this convention, with some variations to be expected due to the smaller screens used on many devices (e.g., pop-up or context menus cover a large portion of the screen).

Those other window systems also feature the ubiquitous "dialog," a window smaller than the main screen that pops up to notify you of some condition or occurrence and asks you to confirm your acceptance, or asks you to make one of several choices, provide some information, and so on.

Android provides a fairly standard dialog mechanism, as well as a smaller, lighter "pop-up" called a *toast*. This only appears on the screen for a few seconds, and fades away on its own. Intended for passive notification of low-importance events, it is often used for error notification, although I advise against this usage. There is also a Snackbar, which looks like an action bar at the bottom of the screen, but behaves like a toast—it pops up, and then disappears after a few seconds.

And it doesn't stop there. Android also provides a notification mechanism, which allows you to put text and/or an icon in the notifications bar (top left of the screen). A notification can optionally be accompanied by any combination of LED flashing, audio sounds, and device vibration.

Each of these interactive mechanisms is discussed in this chapter. The chapter proceeds in the same order as this introduction, from menus, to dialogs and toasts, to notifications.

7.1 Alerting the User with Toast and Snackbar

Ian Darwin

Problem

You want to notify the user of some occurrence, using a short-lived, onscreen notification mechanism.

Solution

Use a toast for a short notification that appears in front of your application, or a Snackbar for a short notification that occupies the bottom part of your application's screen.

Discussion

The toast mechanism is so basic that it is used everywhere. So named because its "pop up" action reminded an early developer of how an electric toaster pops up the bread when it's toasted, the toast was designed to be easy to use:

```
Toast.makeText(context, message, length).show();
```

The `Context` argument can be an Activity or a Service. The `message` argument is a `String` (or a `CharSequence`), or the `R.id` of a `String` resource. The `length` argument is an integer, with one of the values `Toast.LENGTH_SHORT` or `Toast.LENGTH_LONG`.

In older code you will often see the use of the nonfluent style:

```
Toast myTemporaryToastVariable = Toast.makeText(context, message, length);
myTemporaryToastVariable.show();
```

When I see code like this, I tend to ask: "But why create a temporary variable that's only ever used once? Do you get paid by the keystroke?" If you like this style, use it, but most developers will use the shorter style.

For a slightly neater effect, you may want to use a Snackbar. While the normal action bar appears at the top of an Activity, the Snackbar appears at the bottom. Like a toast, a Snackbar is normally used to indicate something that you want the user to see, but that's not *critical* for them to they see—if it's critical, and you want confirmation that they've seen it, you need them to make a choice, etc., then use a dialog instead (Recipe 7.6).

The Snackbar is used in a similar fashion to the toast, but the first argument is a `View`:

```
Snackbar.make(view, message, length).show();
```

It is common to set an `Action` with the Snackbar. This is not done using the normal `setOnClickListener()` but instead using `setAction()`, whose second argument is the familiar `OnClickListener` (here implemented as a lambda; see Recipe 1.18):

```
Snackbar.make(view, pickRandomMessage(), Snackbar.LENGTH_LONG)
    .setAction("Tap Me!", e->Log.d(TAG, "We should do something here"))
    .show();
```

The `message` argument, a `String` or `CharSequence`, is displayed at the end of the Snackbar, and if the user taps on it, the `OnClickListener` will be invoked. If the user does nothing, the entire Snackbar will disappear in a few seconds (based on the `length` argument).

Figure 7-1 shows our example Snackbar in action.

Figure 7-1. Snackbar in action

7.2 Customizing the Appearance of a Toast

Rachee Singh

Problem

You want to customize the look of toast notifications.

Solution

Define an XML layout for the toast and then inflate the view in Java.

Discussion

First, we will define the layout of the custom toast in an XML file, *toast_layout.xml*. It contains an `ImageView` and a `TextView`, as shown in Example 7-1.

Example 7-1. Toast layout in XML

```xml
<LinearLayout xmlns:android="http://schemas.android.com/apk/res/android"
              android:id="@+id/toast_layout_root"
              android:orientation="horizontal"
              android:layout_width="fill_parent"
              android:layout_height="fill_parent"
              android:padding="10dp"
              android:background="#f0ffef"
              >
    <ImageView android:id="@+id/image"
               android:layout_width="wrap_content"
               android:layout_height="fill_parent"
               android:layout_marginRight="10dp"
               />
    <TextView android:id="@+id/text"
              android:layout_width="wrap_content"
              android:layout_height="fill_parent"
              android:textColor="#000000"
              />
</LinearLayout>
```

Then, in the Java code, we inflate this view using `LayoutInflater`. We set the gravity and duration of the toast. The `setGravity()` method modifies the position at which the toast will be displayed. On the click of the `customToast` button, we show the toast (see Example 7-2).

Example 7-2. Inflating the view

```java
customToast = (Button)findViewById(R.id.customToast);
```

```
LayoutInflater inflater = getLayoutInflater();
View layout = inflater.inflate(R.layout.toast_layout,
    (ViewGroup) findViewById(R.id.toast_layout_root));

ImageView image = (ImageView) layout.findViewById(R.id.image);
image.setImageResource(R.drawable.icon);
TextView text = (TextView) layout.findViewById(R.id.text);
text.setText("Hello! This is a custom toast!");

final Toast toast = new Toast(getApplicationContext());
toast.setGravity(Gravity.CENTER_VERTICAL, 0, 0);
toast.setDuration(Toast.LENGTH_LONG);
toast.setView(layout);
customToast.setOnClickListener(new View.OnClickListener() {
    @Override
    public void onClick(View v) {
        toast.show();
    }
});
```

Source Download URL

The source code for this example is in the Android Cookbook repository (*https:// github.com/IanDarwin/Android-Cookbook-Examples*), in the subdirectory *Custom-Toast* (see "Getting and Using the Code Examples" on page 18).

7.3 Creating and Displaying a Menu

Rachee Singh

Problem

You want to show a menu when the user presses the Menu button on an Android device. On ancient versions of Android such as Gingerbread, most devices had a physical Menu button, whereas modern applications generally use an ActionBar (see Recipe 6.5), which exposes a "soft" Menu button consisting of three dots in a vertical stack.

Solution

Implement a menu by setting it up in the XML and attaching it to your Activity by overriding onCreateOptionsMenu().

Discussion

First, create a directory named *menu* in the *res* directory of the project. In the *menu* directory, create a *Menu.xml* file. Example 7-3 shows the code for *Menu.xml*.

Example 7-3. The menu definition

```
<menu xmlns:android="http://schemas.android.com/apk/res/android">
    <item android:id="@+id/icon1"
        android:title="One"
        android:icon="@drawable/first" />
    <item android:id="@+id/icon2"
        android:title="Two"
        android:icon="@drawable/second" />
    <item android:id="@+id/icon3"
        android:title="Three"
        android:icon="@drawable/three" />
    <item android:id="@+id/icon4"
        android:title="Four"
        android:icon="@drawable/four" />
</menu>
```

In this XML code, we add a menu and to it we add as many items as our application requires. We can also provide an image for each menu item (in this example, default images have been used).

Now, in the Java code for the Activity, override the `onCreateOptionsMenu()`:

```
@Override
public boolean onCreateOptionsMenu(Menu menu) {
    MenuInflater inflater = getMenuInflater();
    inflater.inflate(R.menu.menu, menu);
    return true;
}
```

Figure 7-2 shows how the menu should look.

Figure 7-2. The custom menu

7.4 Handling Choice Selection in a Menu

Rachee Singh

Problem

After creating a menu, you want to react when the user chooses a menu item.

Solution

Override the `onOptionsItemSelected()` method.

Discussion

In the Java Activity, we need to override `onOptionsItemSelected()`. This method takes in a `MenuItem` and checks for its ID. Based on the ID of the item that is clicked, a `switch-case` can be used. Depending on the `case` selected, an appropriate action can be taken. The custom menu might look something like Figure 7-2 from the previous recipe.

For this example, the code just displays one of several toasts indicating which menu item was selected. Here's the source code:

```
@Override
public boolean onOptionsItemSelected(MenuItem item) {
    switch (item.getItemId()) {
        case R.id.icon1:
            Toast.makeText(this, "Icon 1 Beep Bop!", Toast.LENGTH_LONG).show();
            break;
        case R.id.icon2:
            Toast.makeText(this, "Icon 2 Beep Bop!", Toast.LENGTH_LONG).show();
            break;
        case R.id.icon3:
            Toast.makeText(this, "Icon 3 Beep Bop!", Toast.LENGTH_LONG).show();
            break;
        case R.id.icon4 :
            Toast.makeText(this, "Icon 4 Beep Bop!", Toast.LENGTH_LONG).show();
            break;
    }
    return true;
}
```

Figure 7-3 shows the result.

Source Download URL

The source code for this project is in the Android Cookbook repository (*https://github.com/IanDarwin/Android-Cookbook-Examples*), in the subdirectory *MenuAction* (see "Getting and Using the Code Examples" on page 18).

Figure 7-3. Menu choice confirmed

7.5 Creating a Submenu

Rachee Singh

Problem

You want to display additional options to the user from within an existing menu, a sort of "nested menu."

Solution

Use a submenu implementation to provide additional options to the user.

Discussion

A submenu is a part of a menu that displays options in a hierarchical manner. On desktop operating systems, submenus appear to "cascade" down and to the side (usually to the right side). Android devices may not have room for that, so submenus appear like dialogs in that they float over the main screen of the application, rather like a spinner (see Recipe 6.14). You can create the menu hierarchy in the following ways:

- By inflating an XML layout
- By creating the menu items in the Java code

While the first approach is by far the most common, in this recipe we will follow the second approach to show that it's possible, creating the menu/submenu items in the onCreateOptionsMenu() method.

First we add the submenu to the menu using the addSubMenu() method. In order to prevent conflicts with other items in the menu, we explicitly provide the group ID and item ID to the submenu we are creating (specifying constants for the item ID and group ID). Then we set an icon for the header of the submenu with the seHeadertIcon() method and an icon for the submenu with setIcon() (see Example 7-4).

To add items to the submenu, we use the add() method. As arguments to the method, the group ID, item ID, position of the item in the submenu, and text associated with each item are specified:

```
private static final int OPTION_1 = 0;
private static final int OPTION_2 = 1;
private int GROUP_ID = 4;
private int ITEM_ID =3;
```

Example 7-4. The menu creation and listener methods

```
@Override
public boolean onCreateOptionsMenu(Menu menu) {
    MenuItem mi = menu.add("Main Menu, Option 1");
    mi.setShowAsAction(SHOW_AS_ACTION_IF_ROOM);
    SubMenu sub1 = menu.addSubMenu(GROUP_ID, ITEM_ID, Menu.NONE, R.string.submenu);
    sub1.setHeaderIcon(R.drawable.icon);
    sub1.setIcon(R.drawable.icon);
    sub1.add(GROUP_ID, OPTION_1, 0, "Submenu Option 1");
    sub1.add(GROUP_ID, OPTION_2, 1, "Submenu Option 2");
    return super.onCreateOptionsMenu(menu);
}


@Override
public boolean onOptionsItemSelected(MenuItem item) {
    switch (item.getItemId()) {
        case OPTION_1:
            Toast.makeText(this, "Submenu 1, Option 1", Toast.LENGTH_LONG).show();
            break;
        case OPTION_2:
            Toast.makeText(this, "Submenu 1, Option 2", Toast.LENGTH_LONG).show();
            break;
    }
    return true;
}
```

The onOptionItemSelected() method is called when an item on the menu/submenu is selected. In this method, using a switch-case we check for the item that is clicked and an appropriate message is displayed.

Figure 7-4 shows the application before and after you press the Menu button, then the message that appears when you click a submenu item (#2 in this screen capture).

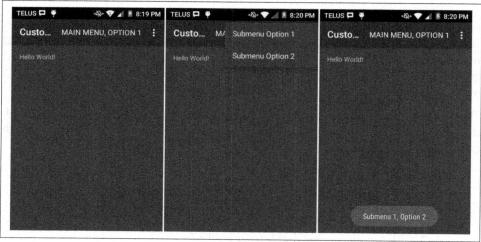

Figure 7-4. Custom submenu: Main menu active, submenu active, submenu item chosen

Source Download URL

The source code for this example is in the Android Cookbook repository (*https:// github.com/IanDarwin/Android-Cookbook-Examples*), in the subdirectory *Custom-SubMenu* (see "Getting and Using the Code Examples" on page 18).

7.6 Creating a Pop-up/Alert Dialog

Rachee Singh

Problem

You would like a way to prompt the user about things such as unsaved changes in the application through an alerting mechanism.

Solution

Use AlertDialog, a class that enables you to provide suitable options to the user. In the case of an "unsaved changes" scenario, for example, the options would be:

- Save
- Discard changes
- Cancel

Discussion

Through the `AlertDialog` class, you can provide the user with up to three options that can be used in any scenario:

- Positive reaction
- Neutral reaction
- Negative reaction

If the user has entered some data in an `EditText` and is then attempting to cancel that Activity, the application should prompt the user to either save his changes, discard them, or cancel the alert dialog, which should also cancel the cancellation of the Activity.

Here is the code that would implement this kind of `AlertDialog`, along with appropriate click listeners on each button on the dialog:

```
alertDialog = new AlertDialog.Builder(this)
  .setTitle(R.string.unsaved)
  .setMessage(R.string.unsaved_changes_message)
  .setPositiveButton(R.string.save_changes, new AlertDialog.OnClickListener() {
    public void onClick(DialogInterface dialog, int which) {
      saveInformation();
    }
})
  .setNeutralButton(R.string.discard_changes, new AlertDialog.OnClickListener() {
    public void onClick(DialogInterface dialog, int which) {
      finish();
    }
})
  .setNegativeButton(android.R.string.cancel_dialog,
    new AlertDialog.OnClickListener() {
    public void onClick(DialogInterface dialog, int which) {
      Dialog.cancel();
    }
})
  .create();
alertDialog.show();
```

7.7 Using a Timepicker Widget

Pratik Rupwal

Problem

You need to ask the user to enter the time for processing some element in the application. Accepting times in text boxes is not graceful, and requires validation.

Solution

You can use the standard Timepicker widget to accept a time from the user. It makes the app appear graceful and reduces the requirement of validation. The Datepicker widget works in a similar fashion for choosing dates.

Discussion

The code in Example 7-5 shows how to reveal the current time on the screen and shows a button that, when clicked, produces the Timepicker widget through which the user can accept the time.

Example 7-5. The main Activity

```
public class Main extends Activity {

    private TextView mTimeDisplay;
    private Button mPickTime;

    private int mHour;
    private int mMinute;

    static final int TIME_DIALOG_ID = 0;

    /** Called when the Activity is first created. */
    @Override
    public void onCreate(Bundle savedInstanceState) {
        super.onCreate(savedInstanceState);
        setContentView(R.layout.main);

        // Capture our View elements
        mTimeDisplay = (TextView) findViewById(R.id.timeDisplay);
        mPickTime = (Button) findViewById(R.id.pickTime);

        // Add a click listener to the button
        mPickTime.setOnClickListener(new View.OnClickListener() {
            public void onClick(View v) {
                showDialog(TIME_DIALOG_ID);
            }
        });
```

```
    // Get the current time
    final Calendar c = Calendar.getInstance();
    mHour = c.get(Calendar.HOUR_OF_DAY);
    mMinute = c.get(Calendar.MINUTE);

    // Display the current date
    updateDisplay();
}

// The overridden method shown below gets invoked when
// showDialog() is called inside the onClick() method defined
// for handling the click event of the "Change the time" button

@Override
protected Dialog onCreateDialog(int id) {
    switch (id) {
    case TIME_DIALOG_ID:
        return new TimePickerDialog(this,
                mTimeSetListener, mHour, mMinute, false);
    }
    return null;
}

// Update the time we display in the TextView
private void updateDisplay() {
    mTimeDisplay.setText(
        new StringBuilder()
                .append(pad(mHour)).append(":")
                .append(pad(mMinute)));
}

// The callback received when the user "sets" the time in the dialog
private TimePickerDialog.OnTimeSetListener mTimeSetListener =
        new TimePickerDialog.OnTimeSetListener() {
    public void onTimeSet(TimePicker view, int hourOfDay, int minute) {
            mHour = hourOfDay;
            mMinute = minute;
            updateDisplay();
    }
};

private static String pad(int c) {
    if (c >= 10)
        return String.valueOf(c);
    else
        return "0" + String.valueOf(c);
}
}
```

Figure 7-5 shows the timepicker that appears onscreen after the user clicks the "Change the time" button.

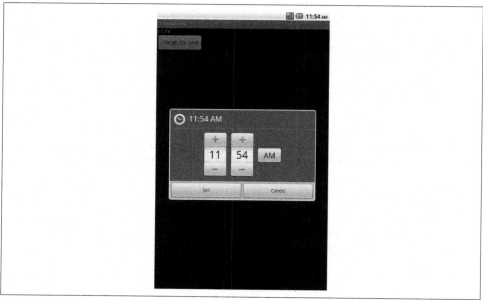

Figure 7-5. Setting the time

7.8 Creating an iPhone-like WheelPicker for Selection

Wagied Davids

Problem

You want a selection UI component similar to the iPhone's picker wheel.

Solution

Create a scroll-wheel picker with the third-party widget Android-Wheel, the iPhone-like picker wheel widget for Android.

Discussion

You can download Android-Wheel from the Google Code Archive (*https://code.google.com/archive/p/android-wheel*). Unfortunately, installation requires more than just installing a JAR file in your *libs* directory, because resources needed for drawing must be in the *res* directory. You can extract the *android-wheel-xx.zip* file and copy the *wheel/src* and *wheel/res* folders into your project. Alternatively, create a new Android project from the *wheel* subdirectory (Android will automatically make it an Android library project) and make your main project depend on that (see Recipe 1.19). Then you can add one or more WheelView objects to your Layout, using the full class name. This class and its friends are found in the kankan.wheel.widget package; the adapters subpackage provides the WheelViewAdapter interface and some implementations. The widget package provides two interfaces that follow the standard setListener pattern on the WheelView component:

- wheel.addChangingListener(OnWheelChangedListener)
- wheel.addScrollingListener(OnWheelScrollListener)

The code in Example 7-6, which comes from a medical app, lets you choose a body part and location (R or L for Right or Left, respectively). The choices are hardcoded here; in a real-world app, they would come from an XML file to allow for internationalization. The app should appear as shown in Figure 7-6. This code uses the "kankan" wheel components, whose Java top-level package is kankan.wheel.widget and whose Maven/Gradle coordinates are com.googlecode.android-wheel:datetime-picker:1.1.

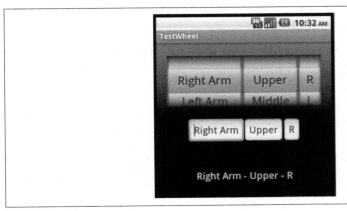

Figure 7-6. Picker wheel in action

Example 7-6. The ScrollWheel example code

```java
public class WheelDemoActivity extends Activity {

    private final static String TAG = "WheelDemo";

    private final static String[] wheelMenu1 = {
            "Right Arm", "Left Arm",
            "R-Abdomen", "L-Abdomen",
            "Right Thigh", "Left Thigh"
    };
    private final static String[] wheelMenu2 = {
            "Upper", "Middle", "Lower"
    };
    private final static String[] wheelMenu3 = {"R", "L"};

    // Wheel scrolled flag
```

```
    private boolean wheelScrolled = false;
    private TextView resultText;
    private EditText text1;
    private EditText text2;
    private EditText text3;

    @Override
    public void onCreate(Bundle savedInstanceState) {
        super.onCreate(savedInstanceState);
        setContentView(R.layout.activity_wheel_picker);
        initWheel(R.id.p1, wheelMenu1);
        initWheel(R.id.p2, wheelMenu2);
        initWheel(R.id.p3, wheelMenu3);
        text1 = (EditText) this.findViewById(R.id.r1);
        text2 = (EditText) this.findViewById(R.id.r2);
        text3 = (EditText) this.findViewById(R.id.r3);
        resultText = (TextView) this.findViewById(R.id.resultText);
    }

    /**
     * Wheel scrolled listener
     */
    OnWheelScrollListener scrolledListener = new OnWheelScrollListener() {
        @Override
        public void onScrollingStarted(WheelView wheel) {
            wheelScrolled = true;
        }
        @Override
        public void onScrollingFinished(WheelView wheel) {
            wheelScrolled = false;
            updateStatus();
        }
    };

    /**
     * Wheel changed listener
     */
    private final OnWheelChangedListener changedListener =
            new OnWheelChangedListener() {
        @Override
        public void onChanged(WheelView wheel, int oldValue, int newValue) {
            Log.d(TAG, "onChanged, wheelScrolled = " + wheelScrolled);
            if (!wheelScrolled) {
                updateStatus();
            }
        }
    };

    /**
     * Updates entered status
     */
    private void updateStatus() {
    text1.setText(wheelMenu1[((WheelView) findViewById(R.id.p1)).getCurrentItem()]);
    text2.setText(wheelMenu2[((WheelView) findViewById(R.id.p2)).getCurrentItem()]);
    text3.setText(wheelMenu3[((WheelView) findViewById(R.id.p3)).getCurrentItem()]);
    resultText.setText(
```

```
wheelMenu1[((WheelView) findViewById(R.id.p1)).getCurrentItem()] + " - " +
wheelMenu2[((WheelView) findViewById(R.id.p2)).getCurrentItem()] + " - " +
wheelMenu3[((WheelView) findViewById(R.id.p3)).getCurrentItem()]);
    }

    /**
     * Initializes one wheel
     * @param id
     * the wheel widget ID
     */
    private void initWheel(int id, String[] wheelMenu1) {
        WheelView wheel = (WheelView) findViewById(id);
        wheel.setViewAdapter(new ArrayWheelAdapter<String>(this, wheelMenu1));
        wheel.setVisibleItems(2);
        wheel.setCurrentItem(0);
        wheel.addChangingListener(changedListener);
        wheel.addScrollingListener(scrolledListener);
    }
}
```

Source Download URL

The source code for this example is in the Android Cookbook repository (*https://github.com/IanDarwin/Android-Cookbook-Examples*), in the subdirectory *WheelPickerDemo* (see "Getting and Using the Code Examples" on page 18).

7.9 Creating a Tabbed Dialog

Rachee Singh

Problem

You want to categorize the display of information in a custom dialog.

Solution

Use a tabbed layout within a custom dialog.

Discussion

The CustomDialog class extends the Dialog class:

```
public class CustomDialog extends Dialog
```

The constructor of the class has to be initialized:

```
public CustomDialog(final Context context) {
        super(context);

        setTitle("My First Custom Tabbed Dialog");
        setContentView(R.layout.custom_dialog_layout);
```

To create two tabs, insert the Example 7-7 code within the constructor: place tab_image1 and tab_image2 in /res/drawable. These images are placed on the tabs of the tabbed custom dialog.

Example 7-7. Constructor code to create and add the tabs

```
// Get our tabHost from the xml
TabHost tabHost = (TabHost)findViewById(R.id.TabHost01);
tabHost.setup();

// Create tab 1
TabHost.TabSpec spec1 = tabHost.newTabSpec("tab1");
spec1.setIndicator("Profile",
    context.getResources().getDrawable(R.drawable.tab_image1));
spec1.setContent(R.id.TextView01);
tabHost.addTab(spec1);
// Create tab2
TabHost.TabSpec spec2 = tabHost.newTabSpec("tab2");
spec2.setIndicator("Profile",
    context.getResources().getDrawable(R.drawable.tab_image2));
spec2.setContent(R.id.TextView02);
tabHost.addTab(spec2);
```

This is a simple tabbed dialog. It requires the addition of just a few lines to the constructor's code. To implement something like a list view, a list view adapter would be required. A variety of tabs can be inserted based on the application's requirements.

As shown in Example 7-8, the XML code for a tabbed dialog requires TabHost tags enclosing the entire layout. Within these tags you place the locations of various parts of the tabbed dialog. You must use a frame layout to place the content of the different tabs. In this case, we are creating two tabs, both with a scroll view containing text (stored in *strings.xml* and named *lorem_ipsum*).

Example 7-8. The custom_dialog_layout.xml file

```
<TabHost
    xmlns:android="http://schemas.android.com/apk/res/android"
    android:id="@+id/TabHost01"
    android:layout_width="fill_parent"
    android:layout_height="500dip">

    <LinearLayout
        android:orientation="vertical"
        android:layout_width="fill_parent"
        android:layout_height="wrap_content"
        android:padding="5dp">

        <TabWidget
        android:id="@android:id/tabs"
        android:layout_width="fill_parent"
        android:layout_height="wrap_content"/>
```

```
        <FrameLayout
    android:id="@android:id/tabcontent"
    android:layout_width="fill_parent"
    android:layout_height="wrap_content"
    android:padding="5dp">

        <ScrollView android:id="@+id/ScrollView01"
            android:layout_width="wrap_content"
            android:layout_height="200px">

        <TextView
            android:id="@+id/TextView01"
            android:text="@string/lorem_ipsum"
            android:layout_width="wrap_content"
            android:layout_height="wrap_content"
            android:gravity="center_horizontal"
            android:paddingLeft="15dip"
            android:paddingTop="15dip"
            android:paddingRight="20dip"
            android:paddingBottom="15dip"/>

        </ScrollView>

        <ScrollView android:id="@+id/ScrollView02"
            android:layout_width="wrap_content"
            android:layout_height="200px">

        <TextView
            android:id="@+id/TextView02"
            android:text="@string/lorem_ipsum"
            android:layout_width="wrap_content"
            android:layout_height="wrap_content"
            android:gravity="center_horizontal"
            android:paddingLeft="15dip"
            android:paddingTop="15dip"
            android:paddingRight="20dip"
            android:paddingBottom="15dip"/>

        </ScrollView>
    </FrameLayout>
    </LinearLayout>
</TabHost>
```

Source Download URL

The source code for this example is in the Android Cookbook repository (*https://github.com/IanDarwin/Android-Cookbook-Examples*), in the subdirectory *TabHost-Demo* (see "Getting and Using the Code Examples" on page 18).

7.10 Creating a ProgressDialog

Rachee Singh

Problem

You want to be able to alert the user of background processing occurring in the application.

Solution

Show a ProgressDialog while the processing is being carried out.

Discussion

In this recipe we will provide a button that shows a ProgressDialog when clicked. In the ProgressDialog we set the title as "Please Wait" and the content as "Processing Information." After this we create a new thread and start the thread's execution. In the run() method (which gets executed once the thread gets started) we call the sleep() method for four seconds. After these four seconds expire the ProgressDialog is dismissed and the text in the TextView gets changed:

```
complete = (TextView) this.findViewById(R.id.complete);
complete.setText("Press the Button to start Processing");
processing = (Button)findViewById(R.id.processing);
processing.setOnClickListener(new View.OnClickListener() {

    @Override
    public void onClick(View v) {
        progressDialog = ProgressDialog.show(ProgressDialogExp.this,
            "Please Wait", "Processing Information...", true,false);
        Thread thread = new Thread(ProgressDialogExp.this);
        thread.start();
    }
});
```

We use a Handler to update the UI once thread execution finishes. We send an empty message to the Handler after thread execution completes, and then in the Handler we dismiss the ProgressDialog and update the text of the TextView:

```
public void run() {
    try {
        Thread.sleep(4000);
    } catch (InterruptedException e) {
        e.printStackTrace();
    }
    handler.sendEmptyMessage(0);
}

private Handler handler = new Handler() {
```

```
        @Override
        public void handleMessage(Message msg) {
            progressDialog.dismiss();
            complete.setText("Processing Finished");
        }
    };
```

Source Download URL

The source code for this project is in the Android Cookbook repository (*https://github.com/IanDarwin/Android-Cookbook-Examples*), in the subdirectory *Progress-DialogDemo* (see "Getting and Using the Code Examples" on page 18).

7.11 Creating a Custom Dialog with Buttons, Images, and Text

Rachee Singh

Problem

Your application requires a dialog-like structure in place of a full-fledged Activity to show some information. Text, images, and a button are required on this custom dialog.

Solution

Create a custom dialog with tabs. Since everything can be squeezed into a dialog in place of an entire Activity, the application will seem more compact.

Discussion

The CustomDialog class can directly extend Dialog:

```
public class CustomDialog extends Dialog
```

The following lines of code in the CustomDialog class's onCreate() method add a title and get handles for the buttons in the dialog:

```
            setTitle("Dialog Title");
            setContentView(R.layout.custom_dialog_layout);
            // OnClickListeners for the buttons present in the Dialog
            Button button1 = (Button) findViewById(R.id.button1);
            Button button2 = (Button) findViewById(R.id.button2);
```

For the two buttons that are added, OnClickListeners are defined in the next lines of code. On being clicked, button1 dismisses the dialog and button2 starts a new Activity:

```
            button1.setOnClickListener(new View.OnClickListener() {

                @Override
```

```
            public void onClick(View v) {
                dismiss(); // To dismiss the Dialog
            }
        });

        button2.setOnClickListener(new View.OnClickListener() {

            @Override
            public void onClick(View v) {
                // Fire an Intent on click of this button
                Intent showQuickInfo =
                New Intent("com.android.oreilly.QuickInfo");
                showQuickInfo.setFlags(Intent.FLAG_ACTIVITY_NEW_TASK);
                context.startActivity(showQuickInfo);
            }
        });
```

Here is the XML layout of the dialog, present in */res/layout custom_dialog_layout.xml*. The entire code is enclosed in a LinearLayout. Within the LinearLayout, a RelativeLayout is used to position two buttons. Then, below the RelativeLayout is another RelativeLayout containing a scroll view. *android_button* and *thumbsup* are the names of the images in */res/drawable*:

```
<LinearLayout
        android:orientation="vertical"
        android:layout_width="fill_parent"
        android:layout_height="wrap_content"
        android:padding="5dp">

    <RelativeLayout
        android:layout_width="fill_parent"
        android:layout_height="wrap_content"
        android:paddingBottom="10dip">
            <Button
                android:id="@+id/button1"
                android:background="@drawable/android_button"
                android:layout_height="80dip"
                android:layout_width="80dip"
                android:layout_alignParentLeft="true"
                android:layout_marginLeft="10dip"
                android:gravity="center"/>

            <Button
                android:id="@+id/button2"
                android:background="@drawable/thumbsup"
                android:layout_height="80dip"
                android:layout_width="80dip"
                android:layout_alignParentRight="true"
                android:layout_marginRight="10dip"
                android:gravity="center"/>
    </RelativeLayout>

    <RelativeLayout
        android:layout_width="fill_parent"
        android:layout_height="wrap_content"
```

```
android:paddingBottom="10dip">

    <ScrollView android:id="@+id/ScrollView01"
        android:layout_width="wrap_content"
        android:layout_height="200px">

        <TextView
            android:id="@+id/TextView01"
            android:text="@string/lorem"
            android:layout_width="wrap_content"
            android:layout_height="wrap_content"
            android:gravity="center_horizontal"
            android:paddingLeft="15dip"
            android:paddingTop="15dip"
            android:paddingRight="20dip"
            android:paddingBottom="15dip"/>

    </ScrollView>
    </RelativeLayout>
</LinearLayout>
```

7.12 Creating a Reusable "About Box" Class

Daniel Fowler

Problem

About boxes are common in applications; it is useful not to have to recode them for each new app.

Solution

Write an AboutBox class that can be installed into any new app.

Discussion

Whatever the operating system, whatever the program, chances are it has an About option. This is useful for support:

> Customer: *"Hello, there is a problem with my application."*
> Help Desk: *"Hi, can you press 'About' and tell me the version number?"*

Since it is likely to be required again and again, it is worth having a ready-made AboutBox class that you can easily add to any new app that you develop. At a minimum, the About option should display a dialog with a title (such as About My App), the version name from the manifest, some descriptive text (loaded from a string resource), and an OK button.

The version name can be read from the PackageInfo class. (PackageInfo is obtained from PackageManager, which itself is available from the app's Context). Here is a method to read an app's version name string:

```
static String VersionName(Context context) {
    try {
        return context.getPackageManager().getPackageInfo(
            context.getPackageName(),0).versionName;
    }
    catch (NameNotFoundException e) {
        return "Unknown";
    }
}
```

PageInfo can throw a NameNotFoundException (for when the class is used to find information on other packages). The exception is unlikely to occur; here it is just consumed by returning an error string. (To return the version code, the app's internal version number, swap versionName for versionCode and return an integer.)

With an AlertDialog.Builder and the setTitle(), setMessage(), and show() methods, you will soon have an About option up and running; but you can improve the About option by using the Android Linkify class and a custom layout. In the About text, any web addresses (such as app help pages on the web) and email addresses (useful for a support email link) can be made clickable. The layout shown in Example 7-9 is the contents of the file *aboutbox.xml*.

Example 7-9. The aboutbox.xml file

```
<?xml version="1.0" encoding="utf-8"?>
<ScrollView xmlns:android="http://schemas.android.com/apk/res/android"
    android:id="@+id/aboutView"
    android:layout_width="fill_parent"
    android:layout_height="fill_parent">
    <LinearLayout android:id="@+id/aboutLayout"
    android:orientation="horizontal"
    android:layout_width="fill_parent"
    android:layout_height="fill_parent"
    android:padding="5dp">
    <TextView android:id="@+id/aboutText"
        android:layout_width="wrap_content"
        android:layout_height="fill_parent"
        android:textColor="#888"/>
    </LinearLayout>
</ScrollView>
```

A ScrollView is required for when the About text is long and the screens are small (e.g., QVGA; see Table 5-2).

The AboutBox class uses a Spannable to hold the text; the TextView containing the spanned text is be passed to android.text.util.Linkify. The layout is inflated, the About text is set, and then `AlertBuilder.Builder` is used to create the dialog. Example 7-10 shows the full code for the `AboutBox` class.

 You could also load the text from a static HTML file shipped with the application (see Recipe 10.3).

Example 7-10. The AboutBox class

```java
public class AboutBox {
    static String VersionName(Context context) {
        try {
            return context.getPackageManager().getPackageInfo(
                context.getPackageName(),0).versionName;
        }
        catch (NameNotFoundException e) {
            return "Unknown";
        }
    }

    public static void show(Activity callingActivity) {
        // Use a Spannable to allow for link highlighting
        SpannableString aboutText = new SpannableString("Version " +
            VersionName(callingActivity)+ "\n\n" +
            callingActivity.getString(R.string.about));
        // Generate views to pass to AlertDialog.Builder and to set the text
        View about;
        TextView tvAbout;
        try {
            // Inflate the custom view
            LayoutInflater inflater = callingActivity.getLayoutInflater();
            about = inflater.inflate(R.layout.aboutbox,
                (ViewGroup) callingActivity.findViewById(R.id.aboutView));
            tvAbout = (TextView) about.findViewById(R.id.aboutText);
        }
        catch(InflateException e) {
            // Unchecked exception - unlikely, but default to TextView if it occurs
            about = tvAbout = new TextView(callingActivity);
        }
        // Set the about text
        tvAbout.setText(aboutText);
        // Now Linkify the text
        Linkify.addLinks(tvAbout, Linkify.ALL);
        // Build and show the dialog
        new AlertDialog.Builder(callingActivity)
            .setTitle("About " + callingActivity.getString(R.string.app_name))
            .setCancelable(true)
            .setIcon(R.drawable.icon)
            .setPositiveButton("OK", null)
            .setView(about)
            .show();     // Builder method returns allow for method chaining
```

```
    }
}
```

The app's icon can be shown in the About box title using `setIcon(R.drawable.icon)`.

String resources for the About text can be placed in a separate file for easier maintenance, such as *res/values/about_strings.xml*. The name of this file is irrelevant, as string resources are identified by their ID:

```xml
<?xml version="1.0" encoding="utf-8"?>
<resources>
    <string name="about">This is our App, please see
    http://www.example.com. Email support at support@example.com.</string>
</resources>
```

Showing the About box requires only one line of code, shown here on a button click:

```java
public class Main extends Activity {
    @Override
    public void onCreate(Bundle savedInstanceState) {
        super.onCreate(savedInstanceState);
        setContentView(R.layout.main);
        findViewById(R.id.button1).setOnClickListener(new OnClickListener() {
            public void onClick(View v) {
                AboutBox.show(Main.this);
            }
        });
    }
}
```

The result should look something like Figure 7-7.

Figure 7-7. The About box in action

To reuse this About box, just copy the *aboutbox.xml* file into a project's *res/layout* folder, copy *about_strings.xml* to *res/values* (adjusting its text as needed), and copy the *AboutBox.java* file into the source folder (adjusting the package name as needed). Then call `AboutBox.show()` from a button or menu listener. Web addresses and email addresses highlighted in the text can be clicked and invoke the browser or email client, which makes it easier for the user to contact you using those means.

See Also

The developer documentation for `Linkify` (*https://developer.android.com/reference/ android/text/util/Linkify.html*) and dialogs (*https://developer.android.com/guide/ topics/ui/dialogs.html*).

Source Download URL

The source code for this project is in the Android Cookbook repository (*https:// github.com/IanDarwin/Android-Cookbook-Examples*), in the subdirectory *AboutBox-Demo* (see "Getting and Using the Code Examples" on page 18).

7.13 Creating a Notification in the Status Bar

Ian Darwin

Problem

You want to place a notification icon in the status bar to call the user's attention to an event that occurred, or to remind her of a Service that is running in the background.

Solution

Create a `Notification` object, and provide it with a `PendingIntent` that wraps a real `Intent` for what to do when the user selects the notification. At the same time you pass in the `PendingIntent` you also pass a title and text to be displayed in the notification area. You should set the `AUTO_CANCEL` flag unless you want to remove the notification from the status bar manually. Finally, find and ask the `NotificationManager` to display (notify) your notification, associating with it an ID so that you can refer to it later (e.g., to remove it).

Discussion

Notifications are normally used from a running `Service` class to notify (hence the name) the user of some fact, either because an event has occurred (receipt of a message, loss of contact with a server, or whatever) or just to remind the user that a long-running Service is still running. The notification is commonly used to start an Activity and is, in fact, the only recommended way for a background Service to start an Activity (Services should never start Activities directly!).

Create a Notification object; the constructor takes an Icon ID, the text to display briefly in the status bar, and the time at which the event occurred (a timestamp in milliseconds). Before you can show the notification, you have to provide it with a PendingIntent for what to do when the user selects the notification, and ask the NotificationManager to display your notification. Example 7-11 shows the notification code.

 The following menus code shows doing the right thing in the (usually) wrong place. Notifications are frequently shown from Services; this recipe just focuses on the Notification API.

Example 7-11. The notification code

```
public class Main extends Activity {

        private static final int NOTIFICATION_ID = 1;

        /** Called when the Activity is first created. */
        @Override
        public void onCreate(Bundle savedInstanceState) {
                super.onCreate(savedInstanceState);
                setContentView(R.layout.main);

                int icon = R.drawable.icon;  // Preferably a distinct icon

                // Create the notification itself
                String noticeMeText = getString(R.string.noticeMe);
                Notification n =
                        new Notification(
                        icon, noticeMeText, System.currentTimeMillis());

                // And the Intent of what to do when user selects notification
                Context applicationContext = getApplicationContext();
                Intent notifyIntent = new Intent(this, NotificationTarget.class);
                PendingIntent wrappedIntent =
                        PendingIntent.getActivity(this, 0,
                        notifyIntent, Intent.FLAG_ACTIVITY_NEW_TASK);

                // Condition the notification
                String title = getString(R.string.title);
                String message = getString(R.string.message);
                n.setLatestEventInfo(applicationContext, title,
                        message, wrappedIntent);
                n.flags |= Notification.FLAG_AUTO_CANCEL;

                // Now invoke the Notification service
                String notifService = Context.NOTIFICATION_SERVICE;
```

```
                NotificationManager mgr =
                        (NotificationManager) getSystemService(notifService);
                mgr.notify(NOTIFICATION_ID, n);
        }
}
```

The following is the file *strings.xml*:

```
<resources>
    <string name="app_name">NotificationDemo</string>
    <string name="hello">Hello World, Main!</string>
    <string name="noticeMe">Lookie Here!!</string>
    <string name="title">My Notification</string>
    <string name="message">This is my message</string>
    <string name="target_name">Notification Target</string>
    <string name="thanks">Thank you for selecting the notification.</string>
</resources>
```

The noticeMe string may appear briefly (only for a few seconds) in the status bar. Notification text and icons appear in the very upper left of the screen, as shown in Figure 7-8. The tiny Android logo is this application's icon.

When the user drags the status bar down, it expands to show the details, which include the icons and the title and message strings (see Figure 7-9). You can also use a custom view here; refer to the official Android documentation (*https://devel oper.android.com/guide/topics/ui/notifiers/notifications.html*).

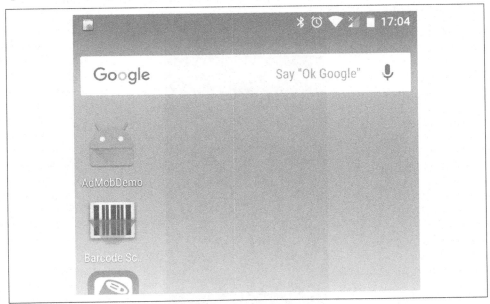

Figure 7-8. Notification demo

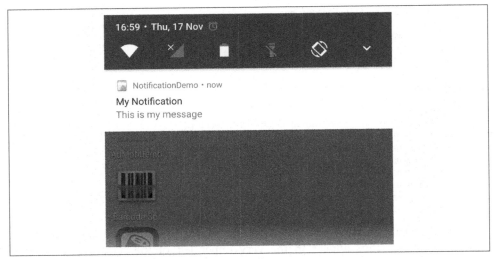

Figure 7-9. Notification "pulled down"

If you have auto-clear set, the notification will no longer appear in the status bar. If the user selects the notification box, the `PendingIntent` becomes current. Ours simply shows a basic "Thank you" notification (Figure 7-10). If the user clicks the Clear button, however, the Intent does not get run (even with auto-clear, which can leave you in a bit of a lurch).

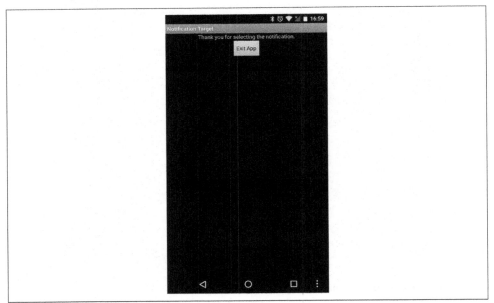

Figure 7-10. Response to choosing a notification

Sounds and other irritants

If the user's attention is needed right away, you can specify a sound to be played when the notification is first displayed. Or you can make the device vibrate, where supported.

The user's default notification sound can be played as follows:

```
notification.defaults |= Notification.DEFAULT_SOUND;
```

Alternatively, you can provide a `Uri` to a sound file, either on the SD card or in your application:

```
notification.sound = Uri.parse("file:///sdcard/mydata/annoy_the_user.mp3");
```

Note that if you both set `DEFAULT_SOUND` and provide a "sound" URI, only the default will be used.

To really annoy the user, you can make the sound play repeatedly; just add the flag `FLAG_INSISTENT` to the `flags` field:

```
notification.defaults |= Notification.FLAG_INSISTENT;
```

Invoking device vibration when your notification is displayed is as simple as:

```
notification.defaults |= Notification.DEFAULT_VIBRATE;
```

Lighting the LED

As a final flourish, on devices with a signaling LED (on most phones it's near the bottom of the physical screen or otherwise in the controls area), you can make the LED flash in various colors and patterns. At a bare minimum, you need:

```
notification.ledARGB = color;
notification.defaults |= Notification.FLAGS_SHOW_LIGHTS;
```

The +color+ is a four-byte integer containing, as the name suggests, alpha (transparency), red, green, and blue values. This is similar to traditional web color syntax, but for the transparency part; thus, `0xff0000ff` is bright blue (full opacity/no transparency; no red or green).

You can also specify a flashing pattern using `notification.ledOnMS` and `notification.ledOffMS`, which are the times in milliseconds for the LED to be on and off as it flashes. Again, if you set any of these values but don't specify `FLAGS_SHOW_LIGHTS`, nothing will happen.

See Also

The developer documentation on notifications (*https://developer.android.com/guide/topics/ui/notifiers/notifications.html*).

Source Download URL

The source code for this example is in the Android Cookbook repository (*https://github.com/IanDarwin/Android-Cookbook-Examples*), in the subdirectory *NotificationDemo* (see "Getting and Using the Code Examples" on page 18).

## CHAPTER 8

Other GUI Elements: Lists and Views

It may seem odd to have a separate chapter for the RecyclerView and ListView components. But these are, in fact, among the most important GUI components, being used in probably 80% of all Android applications. And these list components are very flexible; you can do a lot with them, but figuring out how to do it is sometimes not as intuitive as it could be.

In this chapter we cover topics from basic RecyclerView and ListView uses through to advanced uses.

So why are there two list components? ListView has been around since the beginning of Android time. RecyclerView was introduced around 2015 as a more modern replacement, but many applications still use the original ListView, so we discuss both.

A good overview of ListView can be found in a Google I/O 2010 talk that's available on Google's YouTube channel (*https://www.youtube.com/watch?v=wDBM6wVEO70*); this was presented by Google employees Romain Guy and Adam Powell, who work on the code for ListView.

8.1 Building List-Based Applications with RecyclerView

Ian Darwin

Problem

RecyclerView is a modern reinterpretation of the classical ListView. You want to learn when and how to use the new paradigm.

Solution

Use a RecyclerView.

Discussion

You could argue that `RecyclerView` is badly named. It should have been called `ListView2` or something similar, to tie it in to the `ListView`, which it aims to replace. Paraphrasing Dr. Seuss: "But they didn't, and now it's too late." It's called `RecyclerView` because it is better at recycling `View` objects than its predecessor. Thus, it is more efficient, especially for dealing with large lists.

To build a `RecyclerView` application, you need to do the following:

- Provide an `Activity` with a `RecyclerView` as part of its view layout.
- Provide a `RecyclerView.Adapter` implementation with several methods.
- Provide a `ViewHolder` class as part of your adapter implementation.

Our simple example has the following layout:

```
<RelativeLayout xmlns:android="http://schemas.android.com/apk/res/android"
    xmlns:tools="http://schemas.android.com/tools"
    android:layout_width="match_parent"
    android:layout_height="match_parent"
    android:paddingBottom="@dimen/activity_vertical_margin"
    android:paddingLeft="@dimen/activity_horizontal_margin"
    android:paddingRight="@dimen/activity_horizontal_margin"
    android:paddingTop="@dimen/activity_vertical_margin"
    tools:context="com.androidcookbook.recyclerviewdemo.ListActivity">

    <android.support.v7.widget.RecyclerView
        android:id="@+id/recyclerView"
        android:layout_width="match_parent"
        android:layout_height="match_parent"/>
</RelativeLayout>
```

The containing `RelativeLayout` is not needed, but you will usually have at least one other control in a real example.

Our simple `Activity` class using this layout contains the obvious imports and fields, and the following in its `onCreate()` method:

```
@Override
protected void onCreate(Bundle savedInstanceState) {
    super.onCreate(savedInstanceState);
    setContentView(R.layout.activity_list);

    mRecyclerView = (RecyclerView) findViewById(R.id.recyclerView);
    mAdapter =
        new MyListAdapter(getResources().getStringArray(R.array.foodstuffs));
    mRecyclerView.setAdapter(mAdapter);

    mLayoutManager = new LinearLayoutManager(this);
    mRecyclerView.setLayoutManager(mLayoutManager);
}
```

The Adapter class, like any other adapter, is responsible for converting data between its internal form in the application and the View components used to display it. The inheritance is different from the normal Adapter class, however. The RecyclerView.Adapter must implement the following:

```
public class MyListAdapter
        extends RecyclerView.Adapter<MyListAdapter.ViewHolder> {
    public ViewHolder onCreateViewHolder(ViewGroup parent, int viewType);
    public void onBindViewHolder(ViewHolder holder, int position);
    public int getItemCount();
}
```

The first method is called to actually create a new ViewHolder, which will usually encapsulate the actual View class to be used for one "row" in the list—it may be a ViewGroup of course, since a ViewGroup is a View.

The second method is where the "recycling" happens—in this method, we must populate a ViewHolder. Obviously it will be one that we previously created in onCreateViewHolder(), but we make no assumptions about whether it's previously been populated. All we know is that it's our time to populate it with the data at the supplied position within the list of data.

Of course, getItemCount() returns the size of our list. Our example is simple, just a list of String values which are statically allocated, so this method is trivial to implement.

Both ListView and RecyclerView need a separate XML layout to specify the View object(s) comprising the individual rows. Our example, like most introductory list recipes, contains just a TextView; the XML for this appears in Example 8-1.

Example 8-1. row_item.xml (complete)

```
<TextView xmlns:android="http://schemas.android.com/apk/res/android"
    xmlns:tools="http://schemas.android.com/tools"
    android:id="@+id/textview"
    android:layout_width="wrap_content"
    android:layout_height="wrap_content" />
```

Here is the actual code for these methods in our RecyclerView.Adapter implementation:

```
public class MyListAdapter
        extends RecyclerView.Adapter<MyListAdapter.ViewHolder> {

    private static final String TAG = "CustomAdapter";
    String[] mData;

    public MyListAdapter(String[] data) {
        mData = data;
    }

    @Override
    public ViewHolder onCreateViewHolder(ViewGroup viewGroup, int viewType) {
```

```
        final Context context = viewGroup.getContext();
        return new ViewHolder(context, LayoutInflater.from(context)
                .inflate(R.layout.row_item, viewGroup, false));
    }

    @Override
    public void onBindViewHolder(ViewHolder holder, int position) {
        Log.d(TAG, "onBindViewHolder(" + position + ")");
        TextView v = holder.getView();
        v.setText(mData[position]);
    }

    @Override
    public int getItemCount() {
        return mData.length;
    }
    ...
}
```

Finally, here is the code for our `ViewHolder` implementation, whose job is to hold onto a `View` on behalf of the `RecyclerView`. We pass the `Context` into our `ViewHolder` constructor only for use in generating a toast to show when the user taps an item (this is arguably not best practice, just an expedient to make the example shorter):

```
class ViewHolder extends RecyclerView.ViewHolder {

    private TextView mTextView; // The View we hold

    public ViewHolder(final Context context, View itemView) {
        super(itemView);
        itemView.setOnClickListener(new View.OnClickListener() {
            @Override
            public void onClick(View v) {
                Toast.makeText(context, "You clicked " + mData[getPosition()],
                Toast.LENGTH_SHORT).show();
            }
        });
        mTextView = (TextView) itemView.findViewById(R.id.textview);
    }

    public TextView getView() {
        return mTextView;
    }
}
```

See Also

The developer documentation on `RecyclerView` (*https://developer.android.com/refer ence/android/support/v7/widget/RecyclerView.html*).

8.2 Building List-Based Applications with ListView

Jim Blackler

Problem

Many mobile applications follow a similar pattern, allowing users to browse and interact with multiple items in a list. How can you use standard Android UI classes to quickly build an app that works the way users will expect, providing them a list-based view of their data?

Solution

Use a ListView, an extremely versatile control that is well suited to the screen size and control constraints of a mobile application, displaying information in a vertical stack of rows. This recipe shows how to set up a ListView, including rows that contain any combination of standard UI views.

Discussion

Many Android applications are based on the ListView control. It solves the problem of how to present a lot of information in a way that's easy for the user to browse, displaying information in a vertical stack of rows that the user can scroll through. As the user approaches the results at the end of the list, more results can be generated and added. This allows result paging in a natural and intuitive manner.

Android's ListView helps organize your code by separating browsing and editing operations into separate Activities. A ListView simply requires the user to press somewhere in the row, which works well on a small, finger-operated screen. When the row is clicked, a new Activity can be launched that can contain further options to manipulate the data shown in the row.

Another advantage of the ListView format is that it allows paging in an uncomplicated way. Paging is where all the information requested by a user cannot feasibly be shown at once. For instance, the user may be browsing his email inbox, which contains 2,000 messages; it would not be feasible to download all 2,000 from the email server, and nor would it be required, as the user will probably only scan the first 10 or so messages.

Most web applications handle this problem by segmenting the results into pages, and having controls in the footer that allow the user to navigate through them. With a ListView, the application can retrieve an initial batch of results, which are shown to the user in a list. When the user reaches the end of the list, a final row is seen, containing an indeterminate progress bar. As this comes into view, the application can fetch the next batch of results in the background. When they are ready to be shown, the last progress bar row is replaced with rows containing the new data. The user's view of the list is not interrupted, and new data is fetched purely on demand.

To implement a ListView in your Android application, you need an Activity layout to host it. This should contain a ListView control configured to take up most of the screen layout. This allows other elements such as progress bars and extra overlaid indicators to be included in the layout.

While many Android experts (including most of the other contributors to this chapter) recommend using the ListActivity, I personally do not recommend this. It supplies little extra logic over a plain Activity, but using it restricts the form of the inheritance tree your application's Activities can take. For instance, it is very common that all Activities will inherit from a single common Activity, such as ApplicationActivity, supplying common functionality such as an About box or Help menu. This pattern isn't possible if some Activities are inherited from ListActivity and some are directly inherited from Activity. That said, you will see most of the examples in this book doing it the "official" way. As with all such things, choose one way or the other, and try to stick with it.

An application controls the data added to a ListView by supplying a ListAdapter using the setListAdapter() method. There are 13 functions that a ListAdapter is expected to supply. However, if a BaseAdapter is used, this reduces the number of functions supplied to four, representing the minimum functionality that must be supplied. The adapter specifies the number of item rows in the list, and is expected to supply a View object to represent any item given its row number. It is also expected to return both an object and an object ID to represent any given row number. This is to aid advanced list features such as row selection (not covered in this recipe).

I suggest starting with the most versatile type of ListAdapter, the BaseAdapter (android.widget.BaseAdapter). This allows any layout to be specified for a row (multiple layouts can be matched to multiple row types). These layouts can contain any View elements that a layout would normally contain.

Rows are created on demand by the adapter as they come onto the screen. The adapter is expected to either inflate a view of the appropriate type, or recycle the existing view and then customize it to display a row of data.

This "recycling" is a technique employed by the Android OS to improve performance. When new rows come onscreen, Android will pass into the adapter method the View of a row that has moved offscreen. It is up to the method to decide whether it's appropriate to reuse that View to create the new row. For this to be the case, the View has to represent the layout of the new row. One way to check this is to write the layout ID into the Tag of each View inflated with setTag(). When checking to see whether it's appropriate to reuse a given View, use getTag() to determine whether the View was inflated with the correct type. If an application is able to recycle a view, the scrolling appears smoother because CPU time is saved inflating the view.

Another way to make scrolling smoother is to do as little as possible on the UI thread. This is the default thread that your getView() method will be invoked on. If time-intensive operations need to be invoked, these can be done on a new background thread created especially for the operation. Then, when the UI thread is required again so that controls can be updated, operations can be invoked on it with activity.runOnUiThread(Runnable) or using a handler (see the discussions of inter-thread communication in Chapter 4). Care must be taken to ensure that the View to be modified has not been recycled for another row. This can happen if the row has moved off the screen in the time it took the operation to complete; this is quite possible if the operation was a lengthy download operation.

Setting up a basic ListView

Use the Eclipse New Android Project wizard to create a new Android project with a starting Activity called MainActivity. In the *main.xml* layout, replace the existing TextView section with the following:

```
<ListView android:id="@+id/ListView01"
    android:layout_width="wrap_content"
    android:layout_height="fill_parent"/>
```

At the bottom of the MainActivity.onCreate() method, insert the code shown in Example 8-2. This will declare a dummy anonymous class extending BaseAdapter, and apply an instance of it to the ListView. The code in Example 8-2 illustrates the methods that need to be supplied in order to populate the ListView with data.

Example 8-2. The adapter implementation

```
ListView listView = (ListView) findViewById(R.id.ListView01);
listView.setAdapter(new BaseAdapter(){

  public int getCount() {
    return 0;
  }

  public Object getItem(int position) {
    return null;
  }

  public long getItemId(int position) {
    return 0;
  }

  public View getView(int position, View convertView, ViewGroup parent) {
    return null;
  }
});
```

By customizing the anonymous class members, you can modify the data shown by the control. However, before any data can be shown, a layout must be supplied to present the data in rows. Add a file called *list_row.xml* to your project's *res/layout* directory with the following content:

```
<LinearLayout xmlns:android="http://schemas.android.com/apk/res/android"
    android:layout_width="wrap_content" android:layout_height="wrap_content">
    <TextView android:text="@+id/TextView01" android:id="@+id/TextView01"
        android:layout_width="fill_parent" android:layout_height="wrap_content"/>
</LinearLayout>
```

In your `MainActivity`, add the following static array field containing just three strings:

```
static String[] words = {"one", "two", "three"};
```

Now customize your existing anonymous `BaseAdapter` as shown in Example 8-3, to display the contents of the `words` array in the `ListView`.

Example 8-3. The adapter implementation

```
listView.setAdapter(new BaseAdapter() {

  public int getCount() {
    return words.length;
  }

  public Object getItem(int position) {
    return words[position];
  }

  public long getItemId(int position) {
    return position;
  }

  public View getView(int position, View convertView, ViewGroup parent) {
    LayoutInflater inflater =
        (LayoutInflater) getSystemService(LAYOUT_INFLATER_SERVICE);
    View view = inflater.inflate(R.layout.list_row, null);
    TextView textView = (TextView) view.findViewById(R.id.TextView01);
    textView.setText(words[position]);
    return view;
  }
});
```

The `getCount()` method is customized to return the number of items in the list. Both `getItem()` and `getItemId()` supply the `ListView` with unique objects and IDs to identify the data in the rows. Finally, `getView()` creates and customizes an Android view to represent the row. This is the most complex step, so let's break down what's happening. First, the system `LayoutInflater` is obtained. This is the Service that creates views:

```
LayoutInflater inflater =
    (LayoutInflater) getSystemService(LAYOUT_INFLATER_SERVICE);
```

Next, the new layout we created earlier is inflated:

```
View view = inflater.inflate(R.layout.list_row, null);
```

Then the TextView is located:

```
TextView textView = (TextView) view.findViewById(R.id.TextView01);
```

and customized with the appropriate item in the words array:

```
textView.setText(words[position]);
```

This allows the user to view elements from the words array in a ListView:

```
return view;
```

Other recipes will discuss more details of ListView usage.

8.3 Creating a "No Data" View for ListViews

Rachee Singh

Problem

When a ListView has no items to show, the screen on an Android device is blank. You want to show an appropriate message, indicating the absence of data.

Solution

Use the "No Data" view from the XML layout.

Discussion

Often we need to use a ListView in an Android app. Before a user has loaded any data into the application, the list of data that the ListView shows is empty, generally resulting in a blank screen. In order to make the user feel more comfortable with the application, we might want to display an appropriate message (or even an image) stating that the list is empty. For this purpose, we can use a No Data view. This simply requires the addition of a few lines of code in the XML layout of the Activity that contains the ListView:

```xml
<?xml version="1.0" encoding="utf-8"?>
<RelativeLayout xmlns:android="http://schemas.android.com/apk/res/android"
    android:layout_width="fill_parent"
    android:layout_height="fill_parent"
    >

<TextView
    android:id="@+id/textView1"
    android:text="@string/app_name"
    android:layout_height="wrap_content"
    android:layout_width="match_parent"/>
```

```
<ListView
    android:id="@id/android:list"
    android:layout_width="fill_parent"
    android:layout_height="wrap_content"
    android:layout_below="@id/textView1"/>
    <TextView
        android:id="@id/android:empty"
        android:text = "@string/list_is_empty"
        android:layout_width="fill_parent"
        android:layout_height="fill_parent"
        android:layout_below = "@id/textView1"
        android:textSize="25sp"
        android:gravity="center_vertical|center_horizontal"/>
</RelativeLayout>
```

The important line is android:id="@id/android:empty". This line ensures that when the list is empty, the TextView with this ID will be displayed on the screen. In this TextView, the string "List is Empty" is displayed (see Figure 8-1).

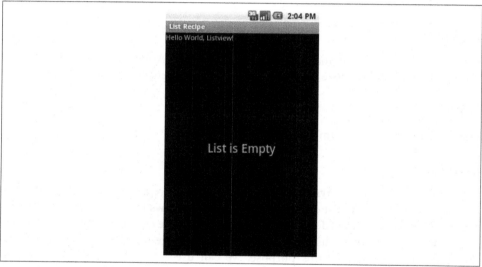

Figure 8-1. Empty list

A less important but interesting and relevant technique is the use of a RelativeLayout and the android:layout_below attribute to make the huge, empty text area appear directly below the tiny TextView at the top when the list is empty (effectively making the ListView and the "empty" message TextView the same size; only one will be visible at a time).

8.4 Creating an Advanced ListView with Images and Text

Marco Dinacci

Problem

You want to write a ListView that shows an image next to a string.

Solution

Create an Activity that inherits from ListActivity, prepare the XML resource files, and create a custom view adapter to load the resources into the view.

Discussion

The Android documentation says that the ListView widget is easy to use. This is true if you just want to display a simple list of strings, but as soon as you want to customize your list things become more complicated.

This recipe shows you how to write a ListView that displays a static list of images and strings, similar to the settings list on your phone. Figure 8-2 shows the final result.

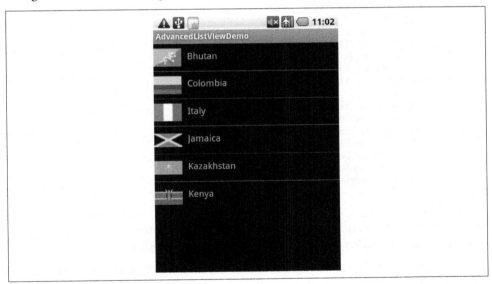

Figure 8-2. ListView with icons

Let's start with the Activity code. First, we inherit from ListActivity instead of Activity so that we can easily supply our custom adapter (see Example 8-4).

Example 8-4. The ListActivity implementation

```
public class AdvancedListViewActivity extends ListActivity {

    @Override
    public void onCreate(Bundle savedInstanceState) {
        super.onCreate(savedInstanceState);
        setContentView(R.layout.main);

        Context ctx = getApplicationContext();
        Resources res = ctx.getResources();

        String[] options = res.getStringArray(R.array.country_names);
        TypedArray icons = res.obtainTypedArray(R.array.country_icons);

        setListAdapter(new ImageAndTextAdapter(ctx,
            R.layout.main_list_item, options, icons));
    }
}
```

In the `onCreate()` method we also create an array of strings, which contains the country names, and a `TypedArray`, which will contain our `Drawable` flags. The arrays are created from an XML file. Here is the content of the *countries.xml* file:

```
<?xml version="1.0" encoding="utf-8"?>
<resources>
    <string-array name="country_names">
        <item>Bhutan</item>
        <item>Colombia</item>
        <item>Italy</item>
        <item>Jamaica</item>
        <item>Kazakhstan</item>
        <item>Kenya</item>
    </string-array>
    <array name="country_icons">
        <item>@drawable/bhutan</item>
        <item>@drawable/colombia</item>
        <item>@drawable/italy</item>
        <item>@drawable/jamaica</item>
        <item>@drawable/kazakhstan</item>
        <item>@drawable/kenya</item>
    </array>
</resources>
```

Now we're ready to create the adapter. The official documentation for `Adapter` (*https://developer.android.com/reference/android/widget/Adapter.html*) says:

> An Adapter object acts as a bridge between an `AdapterView` and the underlying data for that view. The Adapter provides access to the data items. The Adapter is also responsible for making a `View` for each item in the data set.

There are several subclasses of `Adapter`; we're going to extend `ArrayAdapter`, which is a concrete `BaseAdapter` that is backed by an array of arbitrary objects (see Example 8-5).

Example 8-5. The ImageAndTextAdapter class

```
public class ImageAndTextAdapter extends ArrayAdapter<String> {

    private LayoutInflater mInflater;

    private String[] mStrings;
    private TypedArray mIcons;

    private int mViewResourceId;

    public ImageAndTextAdapter(Context ctx, int viewResourceId,
            String[] strings, TypedArray icons) {
        super(ctx, viewResourceId, strings);

        mInflater = (LayoutInflater)ctx.getSystemService(
                Context.LAYOUT_INFLATER_SERVICE);

        mStrings = strings;
        mIcons = icons;

        mViewResourceId = viewResourceId;
    }

    @Override
    public int getCount() {
        return mStrings.length;
    }

    @Override
    public String getItem(int position) {
        return mStrings[position];
    }

    @Override
    public long getItemId(int position) {
        return 0;
    }

    @Override
    public View getView(int position, View convertView, ViewGroup parent) {
        convertView = mInflater.inflate(mViewResourceId, null);

        ImageView iv = (ImageView)convertView.findViewById(R.id.option_icon);
        iv.setImageDrawable(mIcons.getDrawable(position));

        TextView tv = (TextView)convertView.findViewById(R.id.option_text);
        tv.setText(mStrings[position]);

        return convertView;
    }
}
```

The constructor accepts a `Context`, the `id` of the layout that will be used for every row (more on this soon), an array of strings (the country names), and a `TypedArray` (our flags).

The `getView()` method is where we build a row for the list. We first use a `LayoutInflater` to create a `View` from XML, and then we retrieve the country flag as a `Drawable` and the country name as a `String`; we use them to populate the `ImageView` and `TextView` that we've declared in the layout. Here is the layout for the list rows:

```
<?xml version="1.0" encoding="utf-8"?>
<LinearLayout xmlns:android="http://schemas.android.com/apk/res/android">
    <ImageView
    android:id="@+id/option_icon"
    android:layout_width="48dp"
    android:layout_height="fill_parent"/>
    <TextView
        android:id="@+id/option_text"
        android:layout_width="fill_parent"
        android:layout_height="fill_parent"
        android:padding="10dp"
        android:textSize="16dp" >
    </TextView>
</LinearLayout>
```

And this is the content of the main layout:

```
<?xml version="1.0" encoding="utf-8"?>
<LinearLayout xmlns:android="http://schemas.android.com/apk/res/android"
    android:orientation="vertical"
    android:layout_width="fill_parent"
    android:layout_height="fill_parent"
    >
    <ListView android:id="@android:id/list"
    android:layout_height="wrap_content"
    android:layout_width="fill_parent"
    />
</LinearLayout>
```

Note that the `ListView` ID must be exactly `@android:id/list` or you'll get a `RuntimeException`.

Source Download URL

The source code for this example is in the Android Cookbook repository (*https://github.com/IanDarwin/Android-Cookbook-Examples*), in the subdirectory *ListViewAdvanced* (see "Getting and Using the Code Examples" on page 18).

8.5 Using Section Headers in ListViews

Wagied Davids

Problem

You want to display categorized items—for example, by time/day, by product category, or by sales/price.

Solution

Implement section headers yourself, using a custom list adapter, or use Jeff Sharkey's implementation to display a list with headers.

Discussion

The "do it yourself" technique consists of creating a custom list adapter, and having its createView() method return either the standard layout or the header layout, depending on which layout is appropriate. This method will also work with the newer RecyclerView. Tutorials are available on using this approach with ListView (*http://stack tips.com/tutorials/android/listview-with-section-header-in-android*) and RecyclerView (*https://androidtutorialmagic.wordpress.com/android-material-design-tutorial/ sectionheader-with-recyclerview-and-swipe-to-addeditdelete/*).

However, you may find it easier to use a packaged solution. Jeff Sharkey packaged his into a downloadable JAR file: the original section headers (*http://jsharkey.org/blog/ 2008/08/18/separating-lists-with-headers-in-android-09/*) solution has been around since Android 0.9, which is basically the beginning of time. The intention was to duplicate the look of the standard Settings app, which at the time featured a look similar to the following image, which we will develop in this recipe:

The reusable part of this application is Jeff's `SeparatedListAdapter` class, which implements the Composite design pattern by holding multiple adapters inside it and figuring out the correct one in its `getItem()` method.

We start with four XML files, one for the main layout (see Example 8-6) and three for the list entries. Jeff credited Romain Guy of Google with figuring out the built-in but rather occult styles used.

Example 8-6. main.xml

```xml
<?xml version="1.0" encoding="utf-8"?>
<LinearLayout
    xmlns:android="http://schemas.android.com/apk/res/android"
    android:orientation="vertical"
    android:layout_width="fill_parent"
    android:layout_height="fill_parent">

    <ListView
        android:id="@+id/add_journalentry_menuitem"
        android:layout_width="fill_parent"
        android:layout_height="wrap_content" />
    <ListView
        android:id="@+id/list_journal"
        android:layout_width="fill_parent"
        android:layout_height="wrap_content" />
</LinearLayout>
```

The `list_header` layout (see Example 8-7) is used for the smaller list separators (e.g., "Security").

Example 8-7. list_header.xml

```xml
<TextView
    xmlns:android="http://schemas.android.com/apk/res/android"
    android:id="@+id/list_header_title"
    android:layout_width="fill_parent"
    android:layout_height="wrap_content"
    android:paddingTop="2dip"
    android:paddingBottom="2dip"
    android:paddingLeft="5dip"
    style="?android:attr/listSeparatorTextViewStyle" />
```

The `list_item` and `list_complex` layouts are, of course, used for individual items (see Examples 8-8 and 8-9).

Example 8-8. list_item.xml

```xml
<?xml version="1.0" encoding="utf-8"?>
<TextView
    xmlns:android="http://schemas.android.com/apk/res/android"
    android:id="@+id/list_item_title"
```

```
    android:layout_width="fill_parent"
    android:layout_height="fill_parent"
    android:paddingTop="10dip"
    android:paddingBottom="10dip"
    android:paddingLeft="15dip"
    android:textAppearance="?android:attr/textAppearanceLarge"
    />
```

Example 8-9. list_complex.xml

```
<?xml version="1.0" encoding="utf-8"?>
<LinearLayout
    xmlns:android="http://schemas.android.com/apk/res/android"
    android:layout_width="fill_parent"
    android:layout_height="wrap_content"
    android:orientation="vertical"
    android:paddingTop="10dip"
    android:paddingBottom="10dip"
    android:paddingLeft="15dip"
    >
    <TextView
        android:id="@+id/list_complex_title"
        android:layout_width="fill_parent"
        android:layout_height="wrap_content"
        android:textAppearance="?android:attr/textAppearanceLarge"
        />
    <TextView
        android:id="@+id/list_complex_caption"
        android:layout_width="fill_parent"
        android:layout_height="wrap_content"
        android:textAppearance="?android:attr/textAppearanceSmall"
        />
</LinearLayout>
```

The add_journalentry_menuitem layout is used to add new entries, and is shown in action here (Example 8-10).

Example 8-10. add_journalentry_menuitem.xml

```
<?xml version="1.0" encoding="utf-8"?>
<!-- list_item.xml -->
<TextView
    xmlns:android="http://schemas.android.com/apk/res/android"
    android:id="@+id/list_item_title"
    android:gravity="right"
    android:drawableRight="@drawable/ic_menu_add"
    android:layout_width="fill_parent"
    android:layout_height="fill_parent"
    android:paddingTop="0dip"
    android:paddingBottom="0dip"
    android:paddingLeft="10dip"
    android:textAppearance="?android:attr/textAppearanceLarge" />
```

Finally, Example 8-11 contains the Java Activity code.

Example 8-11. ListSample.java

```java
public class ListSample extends Activity {

    public final static String ITEM_TITLE = "title";
    public final static String ITEM_CAPTION = "caption";

    // Section headers
    private final static String[] days =
        new String[]{"Mon", "Tue", "Wed", "Thur", "Fri"};

    // Section contents
    private final static String[] notes = new String[]
        {"Ate Breakfast", "Ran a Marathon ...yah really", "Slept all day"};

    // Menu - ListView
    private ListView addJournalEntryItem;

    // Adapter for ListView contents
    private SeparatedListAdapter adapter;

    // ListView contents
    private ListView journalListView;

    public Map<String, ?> createItem(String title, String caption) {
        Map<String, String> item = new HashMap<String, String>();
        item.put(ITEM_TITLE, title);
        item.put(ITEM_CAPTION, caption);
        return item;
    }

    @Override
    public void onCreate(Bundle icicle) {
        super.onCreate(icicle);

        // Sets the view layer
        setContentView(R.layout.main);

        // Interactive tools
        final ArrayAdapter<String> journalEntryAdapter =
          new ArrayAdapter<String>(this, R.layout.add_journalentry_menuitem,
          new String[]{"Add Journal Entry"});

        // addJournalEntryItem
        addJournalEntryItem = (ListView) this.findViewById(
            R.id.add_journalentry_menuitem);
        addJournalEntryItem.setAdapter(journalEntryAdapter);
        addJournalEntryItem.setOnItemClickListener(new OnItemClickListener() {
            @Override
            public void onItemClick(AdapterView<?> parent, View view,
                int position, long duration) {
                    String item = journalEntryAdapter.getItem(position);
                    Toast.makeText(getApplicationContext(), item,
```

```
                            Toast.LENGTH_SHORT).show();
            }
        });

        // Create the ListView adapter
        adapter = new SeparatedListAdapter(this);
        ArrayAdapter<String> listadapter = new ArrayAdapter<String>(this,
            R.layout.list_item, notes);

        // Add sections
        for (int i = 0; i < days.length; i++) {
                adapter.addSection(days[i], listadapter);
        }

        // Get a reference to the ListView holder
        journalListView = (ListView) this.findViewById(R.id.list_journal);

        // Set the adapter on the ListView holder
        journalListView.setAdapter(adapter);

        // Listen for click events
        journalListView.setOnItemClickListener(new OnItemClickListener() {
                @Override
                public void onItemClick(AdapterView<?> parent, View view,
                    int position, long duration) {
                        String item = (String) adapter.getItem(position);
                        Toast.makeText(getApplicationContext(), item,
                            Toast.LENGTH_SHORT).show();
                    }
        });
    }

}
```

Unfortunately, we could not get copyright clearance from Jeff Sharkey to include the code, so you will have to download his SeparatedListAdapter, which ties all the pieces together; the link appears in the following "See Also" section.

See Also

Jeff's original article on section headers (*http://jsharkey.org/blog/2008/08/18/ separating-lists-with-headers-in-android-09/*).

Source Download URL

The source code for this example is in the Android Cookbook repository (*https:// github.com/IanDarwin/Android-Cookbook-Examples*), in the subdirectory *ListView-SectionedHeader* (see "Getting and Using the Code Examples" on page 18).

8.6 Keeping the ListView with the User's Focus

Ian Darwin

Problem

You don't want to distract the user by moving the ListView to its beginning, away from what the user just did.

Solution

Keep track of the last thing you did in the List, and move the view there in onCreate().

Discussion

One of my biggest peeves is list-based applications that are always going back to the top of the list. Here are a few examples, some of which may have been fixed in recent years:

The standard Contacts manager
> When you edit an item, it forgets about it and goes back to the top of the list.

The OpenIntents File Manager
> When you delete an item from the bottom of a long list, it goes back to the top of the list to redisplay it, ignoring the fact that if I deleted an item, I may be cleaning up, and would like to keep working in the same area.

The HTC SenseUI for Tablets mail program
> When you select a large number of emails using the per-message checkboxes and then delete them as one, it leaves the scrolling list in its previous position, which is now typically occupied by mail from yesterday or the day before!

It's actually pretty simple to set the focus where you want it. Just find the item's index in the adapter (using theList.getAdapter(), if needed), and then call:

```
theList.setSelection(index);
```

This will scroll to the given item and select it so that it becomes the default to act upon, though it doesn't invoke the action associated with the item.

You can calculate this anyplace in your action code and pass it back to the main list view with Intent.putExtra(), or set it as a field in your main class and scroll the list in your onCreate() method or elsewhere.

8.7 Writing a Custom List Adapter

Alex Leffelman

Problem

You want to customize the content of a `ListView`.

Solution

In the Activity that will host your `ListView`, define a private class that extends Android's `BaseAdapter` class. Then override the base class's methods to display custom views that you define in an XML layout file.

Discussion

This code is lifted from a media application I wrote that allowed the user to build playlists from the songs on the SD card. We'll extend the `BaseAdapter` class inside my `MediaListActivity`:

```
private class MediaAdapter extends BaseAdapter {
    ...
}
```

Querying the phone for the media info is outside the scope of this recipe, but the data to populate the list was stored in a `MediaItem` class that kept standard artist, title, album, and track number information, as well as a Boolean field indicating whether the item was selected for the current playlist. In certain cases, you may want to continually add items to your list—for example, if you're downloading information and displaying it as it comes in—but in this recipe we're going to supply all the required data to the adapter at once in the constructor:

```
public MediaAdapter(ArrayList<MediaItem> items) {
    mMediaList = items;
    ...
}
```

If you're developing in Eclipse you'll notice that it wants us to override `BaseAdapter`'s abstract methods; if you're not, you'll find this out as soon as you try to compile the code without them. Let's take a look at those abstract methods:

```
public int getCount() {
    return mMediaList.size();
}
```

The framework needs to know how many views it needs to create in your list. It finds out by asking your adapter how many items you're managing. In our case we'll have a view for every item in the media list:

```
public Object getItem(int position) {
    return mMediaList.get(position);
}
public long getItemId(int position) {
    return position;
}
```

We won't really be using these methods, but for completeness, getItem(int) is what gets returned when the ListView hosting this adapter calls getItemAtPosition(int), which won't happen in our case. getItemId(int) is what gets passed to the ListView.onListItemClick(ListView, View, int, int) callback when you select an item. It gives you the position of the view in the list and the ID supplied by your adapter. In our case they're the same.

The real work of your custom adapter will be done in the getView() method. This method is called every time the ListView brings a new item into view. When an item goes out of view, it is recycled by the system to be used later. This is a powerful mechanism for providing potentially thousands of View objects to our ListView while using only as many views as can be displayed on the screen. The getView() method provides the position of the item it's creating, a view that may be not-null that the system is recycling for you to use, and the ViewGroup parent. You'll return either a new view for the list to display, or a modified copy of the supplied convertView parameter to conserve system resources. Example 8-12 shows the code.

Example 8-12. The getView() method

```
public View getView(int position, View convertView, ViewGroup parent) {
    View V = convertView;

    if(V == null) {
        LayoutInflater vi =
            (LayoutInflater)getSystemService(Context.LAYOUT_INFLATER_SERVICE);
        V = vi.inflate(R.layout.media_row, null);
    }

    MediaItem mi = mMediaList.get(position);
    ImageView icon = (ImageView)V.findViewById(R.id.media_image);
    TextView title = (TextView)V.findViewById(R.id.media_title);
    TextView artist = (TextView)V.findViewById(R.id.media_artist);

    if(mi.isSelected()) {
        icon.setImageResource(R.drawable.item_selected);
    }
    else {
        icon.setImageResource(R.drawable.item_unselected);
    }

    title.setText(mi.getTitle());
    artist.setText("by " + mi.getArtist());

    return V;
}
```

We start by checking whether we'll be recycling a view (which is a good practice) or need to generate a new view from scratch. If we weren't given a convertView, we'll call the LayoutInflater Service to build a view that we've defined in an XML layout file.

Using the view that we've ensured was built with our desired layout resource (or is a recycled copy of one we previously built), it's simply a matter of updating its UI elements. In our case, we want to display the song title, artist, and an indication of whether the song is in our current playlist. (I've removed the error checking, but it's a good practice to make sure any UI elements you're updating are not null—you don't want to crash the whole ListView if there was a small mistake in one item.) This method gets called for every (visible) item in the ListView, so in this example we have a list of identical View objects with different data being displayed in each one. If you wanted to get really creative, you could populate the list with different view layouts based on the list item's position or content.

That takes care of the required BaseAdapter overrides. However, you can add any functionality to your adapter to work on the data set it represents. In my example, I want the user to be able to click a list item and toggle it on/off for the current playlist. This is easily accomplished with a simple callback on the ListView and a short function in the adapter.

This function belongs to ListActivity:

```
protected void onListItemClick(ListView l, View v, int position, long id) {
    super.onListItemClick(l, v, position, id);

    mAdapter.toggleItem(position);
}
```

This is a member function in our MediaAdapter:

```
public void toggleItem(int position) {
    MediaItem mi = mMediaList.get(position);

    mi.setSelected(!mi.getSelected());
    mMediaList.set(position, mi);

    this.notifyDataSetChanged();
}
```

First we simply register a callback for when the user clicks an item in our list. We're given the ListView, the View, the position, and the ID of the item that was clicked, but we'll only need the position, which we simply pass to the MediaAdapter.toggleItem(int) method. In that method we update the state of the corresponding MediaItem and make an important call to notifyDataSetChanged(). This method lets the framework know that it needs to redraw the ListView. If we don't call it, we can do whatever we want to the data, but we won't see anything change until the next redraw (e.g., when we scroll the list).

When all is said and done, we need to tell the parent ListView to use our adapter to populate the list. That's done with a simple call in the ListActivity's onCreate(Bundle) method:

```
MediaAdapter mAdapter = new MediaAdapter(getSongsFromSD());
this.setListAdapter(mAdapter);
```

First we instantiate a new adapter with data generated from a private function that queries the phone for the song data, and then we tell the `ListActivity` to use that adapter to draw the list. And there it is—your own list adapter with a custom view and extensible functionality.

8.8 Using a SearchView to Search Through Data in a ListView

Ian Darwin

Problem

You want a search box (with a magnifying glass icon and an X to clear the text) to filter the content displayed in a `ListView`.

Solution

Use a `SearchView` in your layout. Call `setTextFilterEnabled(true)` on the `ListView`. Call `setOnQueryTextListener()` on the `SearchView`, passing an instance of `SearchView.OnQueryTextListener`. In the listener's `onQueryTextChanged()` method, pass the argument along to the `ListView`'s `setFilterText()`, and you're done!

Discussion

`SearchView` is a powerful control that is often overlooked in designing list applications. It has two modes: inline and Activity-based. In the inline mode, which we'll demonstrate here, the `SearchView` can be added to an existing list-based application with minimal disruption. In the Activity-based mode, a separate Activity must be created to display the results; that is not covered here but is in the official documentation (*https://developer.android.com/training/search/index.html*).

The `ListView` class has a filter mechanism built in. If you enable it and call `setFilterText("`*string*`")`, then only items in the list that contain +*string*+ will be visible. You can call this many times, e.g., as each character is typed, for a dynamic effect.

Assuming you have a working `ListView`-based application, you need to take the following steps:

1. Add a `SearchView` to the layout file and give it an `id` such as `searchView`.

2. In your list Activity's `onCreate()` method, find the `ListView` if needed, and call its `setTextFilterEnabled(true)` method.

---

3. In your list Activity's `onCreate()` method, find the `SearchView` by ID and call several methods on it, the important one being `setOnQueryTextListener()`.

4. In the `QueryTextListener`'s `onQueryTextChanged()` method, if the passed `CharSequence` is empty, clear the `ListView`'s filter text (so it will display all the entries). If the passed `CharSequence` is not empty, convert it to a `String` and pass it to the `ListView`'s `setFilterText()` method.

It really is that simple! The following code snippets are taken from a longer `ListView` example that was made to work with a `SearchView` by following this recipe.

In the Activity's `onCreate()` method:

```
// Tailor the adapter for the SearchView
mListView.setTextFilterEnabled(true);

// Tailor the SearchView
mSearchView = (SearchView) findViewById(R.id.searchView);
mSearchView.setIconifiedByDefault(false);
mSearchView.setOnQueryTextListener(this);
mSearchView.setSubmitButtonEnabled(false);
mSearchView.setQueryHint(getString(R.string.search_hint));
```

And in the Activity's implementation of `SearchView.OnQueryTextListener`:

```
public boolean onQueryTextChange(String newText) {
    if (TextUtils.isEmpty(newText)) {
        mListView.clearTextFilter();
    } else {
        mListView.setFilterText(newText.toString());
    }
    return true;
}

public boolean onQueryTextSubmit(String query) {
    return false;
}
```

The `ListView` does the work of filtering; we just need to control its filtering using the two methods called from `onQueryTextChange()`. There is a lot more to the `SearchView`, though; consult the Javadoc page or the developer documentation for more information.

See Also

The Android training guide on adding search functionality (*https://devel oper.android.com/training/search/index.html*), the developer documentation on `SearchView` (*https://developer.android.com/reference/android/widget/SearchView.html*).

Source Download URL

This code is in the `MainActivity` class of *TodoAndroid* (*https://github.com/IanDarwin/TodoAndroid.git*), a simple to-do list manager.

8.9 Handling Orientation Changes: From ListView Data Values to Landscape Charting

Wagied Davids

Problem

You want to react to orientation changes in layout-appropriate ways. For example, data values to be plotted are contained in a portrait list view, and upon device rotation to landscape, a graph of the data values in a chart/plot is displayed.

Solution

Do something in reaction to physical device orientation changes. A new `View` object is created on orientation changes. You can override the `Activity` method `onConfigurationChanged(Configuration newConfig)` to accommodate orientation changes.

Discussion

In this recipe, data values to be plotted are contained in a portrait list view. When the device/emulator is rotated to landscape, a new Intent is launched to change to a plot/charting View to graphically display the data values. Charting is accomplished using the free DroidCharts package (*https://code.google.com/archive/p/droidcharts*).

Note that for testing this in the Android emulator, the Ctrl-F11 key combination will result in a portrait to landscape (or vice versa) orientation change.

The most important trick is to modify the *AndroidManifest.xml* file (shown in Example 8-13) to allow for the following:

```
android:configChanges="orientation|keyboardHidden"
android:screenOrientation="portrait"
```

Example 8-13. AndroidManifest.xml

```
<?xml version="1.0" encoding="utf-8"?>
<manifest
    xmlns:android="http://schemas.android.com/apk/res/android"
    package="com.examples"
    android:versionCode="1"
    android:versionName="1.0">
    <application
        android:icon="@drawable/icon"
```

```
        android:label="@string/app_name"
        android:debuggable="true">
    <activity
        android:name=".DemoList"
        android:label="@string/app_name"
        android:configChanges="orientation|keyboardHidden"
        android:screenOrientation="portrait">
        <intent-filter>
            <action
                android:name="android.intent.action.MAIN" />
            <category
                android:name="android.intent.category.LAUNCHER" />
        </intent-filter>
    </activity>
    <activity
        android:name=".DemoCharts"
        android:configChanges="orientation|keyboardHidden"></activity>
</application>
</manifest>
```

The main Activity in this example is `DemoCharts`, shown in Example 8-14. It does the usual `onCreate()` stuff, but also—if a parameter was passed—it assumes our app was restarted from the `DemoList` class shown in Example 8-15 and sets up the data accordingly. (A number of methods have been elided here as they aren't relevant to the core issue, that of configuration changes. These are in the online source for this recipe.)

Example 8-14. DemoCharts.java

```
...
import net.droidsolutions.droidcharts.core.data.XYDataset;
import net.droidsolutions.droidcharts.core.data.xy.XYSeries;
import net.droidsolutions.droidcharts.core.data.xy.XYSeriesCollection;

public class DemoCharts extends Activity {
        private static final String tag = "DemoCharts";
        private final String chartTitle = "My Daily Starbucks Allowance";
        private final String xLabel = "Week Day";
        private final String yLabel = "Allowance";

        /** Called when the Activity is first created. */
        @Override
        public void onCreate(Bundle savedInstanceState) {
            super.onCreate(savedInstanceState);

            // Access the Extras from the Intent
            Bundle params = getIntent().getExtras();

            // If we get no parameters, we do nothing
            if (params == null) { return; }

            // Get the passed parameter values
            String paramVals = params.getString("param");
```

```java
            Log.d(tag, "Data Param:= " + paramVals);
            Toast.makeText(getApplicationContext(), "Data Param:= " +
                paramVals, Toast.LENGTH_LONG).show();

        ArrayList<ArrayList<Double>> dataVals = stringArrayToDouble(paramVals);

            XYDataset dataset =
                createDataset("My Daily Starbucks Allowance", dataVals);
            XYLineChartView graphView = new XYLineChartView(this, chartTitle,
                xLabel, yLabel, dataset);
            setContentView(graphView);
    }

    private String arrayToString(String[] data) {
        ...
    }

    private ArrayList<ArrayList<Double>> stringArrayToDouble(String paramVals) {
        ...
    }

    /**
     * Creates a sample data set.
     */
    private XYDataset createDataset(String title,
            ArrayList<ArrayList<Double>> dataVals) {

        final XYSeries series1 = new XYSeries(title);
        for (ArrayList<Double> tuple : dataVals) {
                double x = tuple.get(0).doubleValue();
                double y = tuple.get(1).doubleValue();

                series1.add(x, y);
            }

        // Create a collection to hold various data sets
        final XYSeriesCollection dataset = new XYSeriesCollection();
        dataset.addSeries(series1);
        return dataset;
    }

    @Override
    public void onConfigurationChanged(Configuration newConfig) {
        super.onConfigurationChanged(newConfig);
        Toast.makeText(this, "Orientation Change", Toast.LENGTH_SHORT);

        // Let's go to our DemoList view
        Intent intent = new Intent(this, DemoList.class);
        startActivity(intent);

        // Finish current Activity
        this.finish();
    }
}
```

The DemoList view is the portrait view. Its onConfigurationChanged() method passes control back to the landscape DemoCharts class if a configuration change occurs.

Example 8-15. DemoList.java

```java
public class DemoList extends ListActivity implements OnItemClickListener {
        private static final String tag = "DemoList";
        private ListView listview;
        private ArrayAdapter<String> listAdapter;

        // Want to pass data values as parameters to next Activity/View/Page
        private String params;

        // Our data for plotting
        private final double[][] data = {
            { 1, 1.0 }, { 2.0, 4.0 }, { 3.0, 10.0 }, { 4, 2.0 },
            { 5.0, 20 }, { 6.0, 4.0 }, { 7.0, 1.0 },
        };

        @Override
        public void onCreate(Bundle savedInstanceState) {
                super.onCreate(savedInstanceState);

                // Set the view layer
                setContentView(R.layout.data_listview);

                // Get the default declared ListView @android:list
                listview = getListView();

                // List for click events to the ListView items
                listview.setOnItemClickListener(this);

                // Get the data
                ArrayList<String> dataList = getDataStringList(data);

                // Create an adapter for viewing the ListView
                listAdapter = new ArrayAdapter<String>(this,
                    android.R.layout.simple_list_item_1, dataList);

                // Bind the adapter to the ListView
                listview.setAdapter(listAdapter);

                // Set the parameters to pass to the next view/page
                setParameters(data);
        }

        private String doubleArrayToString(double[][] dataVals) {
                ...
        }

        /**
         * Sets parameters for the Bundle
         * @param dataList
         */
```

```java
        private void setParameters(double[][] dataVals) {
                params = toJSON(dataVals);
        }

        public String getParameters() {
                return this.params;
        }

        /**
         * @param dataVals
         * @return
         */
        private String toJSON(double[][] dataVals) {

                ...

        }

        private ArrayList<String> getDataStringList(double[][] dataVals) {

                ...

        }

        @Override
        public void onConfigurationChanged(Configuration newConfig) {
                super.onConfigurationChanged(newConfig);

                // Create an Intent to switch view to the next page view
                Intent intent = new Intent(this, DemoCharts.class);

                // Pass parameters along to the next page
                intent.putExtra("param", getParameters());

                // Start the Activity
                startActivity(intent);

                Log.d(tag, "Orientation Change...");
                Log.d(tag, "Params: " + getParameters());
        }

        @Override
        public void onItemClick(AdapterView<?> parent, View view,
                int position, long duration) {

            // Upon clicking item in list, pop up a toast
            String msg = "#Item: " + String.valueOf(position) +
                " - " + listAdapter.getItem(position);
            Toast.makeText(getApplicationContext(), msg, Toast.LENGTH_LONG).show();
        }
}
```

The XYLineChartView class is not included here as it relates only to the plotting. It is included in the online version of the code, which you can download.

Source Download URL

The source code for this example is in the Android Cookbook repository (*https://github.com/IanDarwin/Android-Cookbook-Examples*), in the subdirectory *OrientationChanges* (see "Getting and Using the Code Examples" on page 18).

## CHAPTER 9

Multimedia

Android is a rich multimedia environment. The standard Android load includes music and video players, and most commercial devices ship with these or fancier versions as well as YouTube players and more. The recipes in this chapter show you how to control some aspects of the multimedia world that Android provides.

9.1 Playing a YouTube Video

Marco Dinacci

Problem

You want to play a video from YouTube on your device.

Solution

Given a URI to play the video, create an ACTION_VIEW Intent with it and start a new Activity.

Discussion

Example 9-1 shows the code required to start a YouTube video with an Intent.

For this recipe to work, the standard YouTube application (or one compatible with it) must be installed on the device.

Example 9-1. Starting a YouTube video with an Intent

```
public void onCreate(Bundle savedInstanceState) {
    super.onCreate(savedInstanceState);
    setContentView(R.layout.main);

    String video_path = "http://www.youtube.com/watch?v=opZ69P-OJbc";
    Uri uri = Uri.parse(video_path);

    // With this line the YouTube application, if installed, will launch immediately.
    // Without it you will be prompted with a list of applications to choose from.
    uri = Uri.parse("vnd.youtube:" + uri.getQueryParameter("v"));

    Intent intent = new Intent(Intent.ACTION_VIEW, uri);
    startActivity(intent);
}
```

The example uses a standard YouTube.com URL. The `uri.getQueryParameter("v")` is used to extract the video ID from the URI itself; in our example, the ID is `opZ69P-OJbc`.

9.2 Capturing Video Using MediaRecorder

Marco Dinacci

Problem

You want to capture video using the built-in device camera and save it to disk.

Solution

Capture a video and record it on the phone by using the `c` class provided by the Android framework.

Discussion

The `MediaRecorder` is normally used to perform audio and/or video recording. The class has a straightforward API, but because it is based on a simple state machine, the methods must be called in the proper order to avoid `IllegalStateExceptions` from popping up.

Create a new Activity and override the `onCreate()` method with the code shown in Example 9-2.

Example 9-2. The onCreate() method of the main Activity

```
@Override
public void onCreate(Bundle savedInstanceState) {
super.onCreate(savedInstanceState);
setContentView(R.layout.media_recorder_recipe);
```

```
// We shall take the video in landscape orientation
setRequestedOrientation(ActivityInfo.SCREEN_ORIENTATION_LANDSCAPE);

mSurfaceView = (SurfaceView) findViewById(R.id.surfaceView);
    mHolder = mSurfaceView.getHolder();
    mHolder.addCallback(this);
    mHolder.setType(SurfaceHolder.SURFACE_TYPE_PUSH_BUFFERS);

    mToggleButton = (ToggleButton) findViewById(R.id.toggleRecordingButton);
    mToggleButton.setOnClickListener(new OnClickListener() {
            @Override
            // Toggle video recording
            public void onClick(View v) {
                    if (((ToggleButton)v).isChecked())
                            mMediaRecorder.start();
                    else {
                            mMediaRecorder.stop();
                            mMediaRecorder.reset();
                            try {
                                    initRecorder(mHolder.getSurface());
                            } catch (IOException e) {
                                    e.printStackTrace();
                            }
                    }
            }
    });
}
```

The preview frames from the camera will be displayed on a SurfaceView. Recording is controlled by a toggle button. After the recording is over, we stop the MediaRecorder. Since the stop() method resets all the state machine variables in order to be able to grab another video, we reset the state machine and call our initRecorder() method once more. initRecorder() is where we configure the MediaRecorder and the camera, as shown in Example 9-3.

Example 9-3. Setting up the MediaRecorder

```
/* Init the MediaRecorder. The order the methods are called in is vital to
 * its correct functioning.
 */
private void initRecorder(Surface surface) throws IOException {
    // It is very important to unlock the camera before calling setCamera(),
    // or it will result in a black preview
    if(mCamera == null) {
        mCamera = Camera.open();
        mCamera.unlock();
    }

    if(mMediaRecorder == null)
        mMediaRecorder = new MediaRecorder();

    mMediaRecorder.setPreviewDisplay(surface);
```

```
mMediaRecorder.setCamera(mCamera);

mMediaRecorder.setVideoSource(MediaRecorder.VideoSource.CAMERA);
mMediaRecorder.setOutputFormat(MediaRecorder.OutputFormat.DEFAULT);
File file = createFile();

mMediaRecorder.setOutputFile(file.getAbsolutePath());

// No limit. Don't forget to check the space on disk.
mMediaRecorder.setMaxDuration(-1);
mMediaRecorder.setVideoFrameRate(15);

mMediaRecorder.setVideoEncoder(MediaRecorder.VideoEncoder.DEFAULT);

try {
    mMediaRecorder.prepare();
} catch (IllegalStateException e) {
    // This is thrown if the previous calls are not made in the
    // proper order
    e.printStackTrace();
}

mInitSuccesful = true;
}
```

It is important to create and unlock a Camera object before the creation of a MediaRecorder. setPreviewDisplay, and setCamera() must be called immediately after the creation of the MediaRecorder. The choice of the format and output file is obligatory. Other options, if present, must be called in the order outlined in Example 9-3.

The MediaRecorder is best initialized when the surface has been created. We register our Activity as a SurfaceHolder.Callback listener in order to be notified of this and override the surfaceCreated() method to call our initialization code:

```
@Override
public void surfaceCreated(SurfaceHolder holder) {
    try {
        if(!mInitSuccessful)
            initRecorder(mHolder.getSurface());
    } catch (IOException e) {
        e.printStackTrace();    // Better error handling?
    }
}
```

When you're done with the surface, don't forget to release the resources, as the Camera is a shared object and may be used by other applications:

```
private void shutdown() {
    // Release MediaRecorder and especially the Camera as it's a shared
    // object that can be used by other applications
    mMediaRecorder.reset();
    mMediaRecorder.release();
    mCamera.release();
```

```
    // Once the objects have been released they can't be reused
    mMediaRecorder = null;
    mCamera = null;
}
```

Override the `surfaceDestroyed()` method so that the preceding code can be called automatically when the user is done with the Activity:

```
@Override
public void surfaceDestroyed(SurfaceHolder holder) {
    shutdown();
}
```

Source Download URL

The source code for this project is in the Android Cookbook repository (*https://github.com/IanDarwin/Android-Cookbook-Examples*), in the subdirectory *MediaRecorderDemo* (see "Getting and Using the Code Examples" on page 18).

9.3 Using Android's Face Detection Capability

Wagied Davids

Problem

You want to find out whether a given image contains any human faces and, if so, where they're located.

Solution

Use Android's built-in face detection capability.

Discussion

This recipe illustrates how to implement face detection in images. Face detection is a cool and fun hidden API feature of Android. In essence, face detection is the act of recognizing the parts of an image that appear to be human faces. It is part of a machine learning technique of recognizing objects using a set of features.

Note that this is not face *recognition*; it detects the parts of the image that are faces, but does not tell you who the faces belong to. Android 4.0 and later feature face recognition for unlocking the phone.

The main Activity (see Example 9-4) creates an instance of our `FaceDetectionView`. In this example, we hardcode the file to be scanned, but in real life you would probably want to capture the image using the camera, or choose the image from a gallery.

Example 9-4. The main Activity

```
import android.app.Activity;
import android.os.Bundle;

public class Main extends Activity
{
    /** Called when the Activity is first created. */
    @Override
    public void onCreate(Bundle savedInstanceState)
    {
        super.onCreate(savedInstanceState);
        setContentView(new FaceDetectionView(this, "face5.JPG"));
    }
}
```

FaceDetectionView is our custom class used to manage the face detection code using android.media.FaceDetector. The init() method conditions some graphics used to mark the faces—in this example, we know where the faces are, and hope that Android will find them. The real work is done in detectFaces(), where we call the FaceDetector's findFaces() method, passing in our image and an array to contain the results. We then iterate over the found faces. Example 9-5 shows the code, and Figure 9-1 shows the result.

Example 9-5. FaceDetectionView.java

```
...
import android.media.FaceDetector;

public class FaceDetectionView extends View {
    private static final String tag = FaceDetectionView.class.getName();
    private static final int NUM_FACES = 10;
    private FaceDetector arrayFaces;
    private final FaceDetector.Face getAllFaces[] = new FaceDetector.Face[NUM_FACES];
    private FaceDetector.Face getFace = null;

    private final PointF eyesMidPts[] = new PointF[NUM_FACES];
    private final float eyesDistance[] = new float[NUM_FACES];

    private Bitmap sourceImage;

    private final Paint tmpPaint = new Paint(Paint.ANTI_ALIAS_FLAG);
    private final Paint pOuterBullsEye = new Paint(Paint.ANTI_ALIAS_FLAG);
    private final Paint pInnerBullsEye = new Paint(Paint.ANTI_ALIAS_FLAG);

    private int picWidth, picHeight;
    private float xRatio, yRatio;
    private ImageLoader mImageLoader = null;

    public FaceDetectionView(Context context, String imagePath) {
        super(context);
        init();
        mImageLoader = ImageLoader.getInstance(context);
```

```
        sourceImage = mImageLoader.loadFromFile(imagePath);
        detectFaces();
    }

    private void init() {
        Log.d(tag, "Init()...");
        pInnerBullsEye.setStyle(Paint.Style.FILL);
        pInnerBullsEye.setColor(Color.RED);
        pOuterBullsEye.setStyle(Paint.Style.STROKE);
        pOuterBullsEye.setColor(Color.RED);
        tmpPaint.setStyle(Paint.Style.STROKE);
        tmpPaint.setTextAlign(Paint.Align.CENTER);
        BitmapFactory.Options bfo = new BitmapFactory.Options();
        bfo.inPreferredConfig = Bitmap.Config.RGB_565;
    }

    private void loadImage(String imagePath) {
        sourceImage = mImageLoader.loadFromFile(imagePath);
    }

    @Override
    protected void onDraw(Canvas canvas) {
        Log.d(tag, "onDraw()...");

        xRatio = getWidth() * 1.0f / picWidth;
        yRatio = getHeight() * 1.0f / picHeight;
        canvas.drawBitmap(
            sourceImage, null, new Rect(0, 0, getWidth(), getHeight()), tmpPaint);
        for (int i = 0; i < eyesMidPts.length; i++) {
            if (eyesMidPts[i] != null) {
                pOuterBullsEye.setStrokeWidth(eyesDistance[i] / 6);
                canvas.drawCircle(eyesMidPts[i].x * xRatio,
                    eyesMidPts[i].y * yRatio, eyesDistance[i] / 2, pOuterBullsEye);
                canvas.drawCircle(eyesMidPts[i].x * xRatio,
                    eyesMidPts[i].y * yRatio, eyesDistance[i] / 6, pInnerBullsEye);
            }
        }
    }

    private void detectFaces() {
        Log.d(tag, "detectFaces()...");

        picWidth = sourceImage.getWidth();
        picHeight = sourceImage.getHeight();

        arrayFaces = new FaceDetector(picWidth, picHeight, NUM_FACES);
        arrayFaces.findFaces(sourceImage, getAllFaces);

        for (int i = 0; i < getAllFaces.length; i++) {
            getFace = getAllFaces[i];
            try {
                PointF eyesMP = new PointF();
                getFace.getMidPoint(eyesMP);
                eyesDistance[i] = getFace.eyesDistance();
                eyesMidPts[i] = eyesMP;
```

```
        Log.i("Face",
            i + " " + getFace.confidence() + " " +
            getFace.eyesDistance() + " " +
            "Pose: (" + getFace.pose(FaceDetector.Face.EULER_X) + "," +
            getFace.pose(FaceDetector.Face.EULER_Y) + "," +
            getFace.pose(FaceDetector.Face.EULER_Z) + ")" +
            "Eyes Midpoint: (" + eyesMidPts[i].x + "," +
            eyesMidPts[i].y + ")");
    } catch (Exception e) {
        Log.e("Face", i + " is null");
    }
    }
    }
    }
}
```

Figure 9-1. Face detection in action

Source Download URL

The source code for this example is in the Android Cookbook repository (*https://github.com/IanDarwin/Android-Cookbook-Examples*), in the subdirectory *FaceFinder* (see "Getting and Using the Code Examples" on page 18).

9.4 Playing Audio from a File

Marco Dinacci

Problem

You want to play an audio file stored on the device.

Solution

Create and properly configure a `MediaPlayer` and a `MediaController`, provide the path of the audio file to play, and enjoy the music.

Discussion

Playing an audio file is as easy as setting up a `MediaPlayer` and a `MediaController`. First, create a new Activity that implements the `MediaPlayerControl` interface (see Example 9-6).

Example 9-6. The MediaPlayerControl class header

```
public class PlayAudioActivity extends Activity implements MediaPlayerControl {
    private MediaController mMediaController;
    private MediaPlayer mMediaPlayer;
    private Handler mHandler = new Handler();
```

In the `onCreate()` method, we create and configure a `MediaPlayer` and a `MediaController`. The first is the object that performs the typical operations on an audio file, such as playing, pausing, and seeking. The second is a view containing the buttons that launch the aforementioned operations through our `MediaPlayerControl` class. Example 9-7 shows the `onCreate()` code.

Example 9-7. The MediaPlayer's onCreate() method

```
@Override
public void onCreate(Bundle savedInstanceState) {
    super.onCreate(savedInstanceState);
    setContentView(R.layout.main);

    mMediaPlayer = new MediaPlayer();
    mMediaController = new MediaController(this);
    mMediaController.setMediaPlayer(PlayAudioActivity.this);
    mMediaController.setAnchorView(findViewById(R.id.audioView));

    String audioFile = "" ;
    try {
        mMediaPlayer.setDataSource(audioFile);
        mMediaPlayer.prepare();
    } catch (IOException e) {
        Log.e("PlayAudioDemo",
            "Could not open file " + audioFile + " for playback.", e);
    }

    mMediaPlayer.setOnPreparedListener(new OnPreparedListener() {
```

```
        @Override
        public void onPrepared(MediaPlayer mp) {
                mHandler.post(new Runnable() {
                        public void run() {
                                mMediaController.show(10000);
                                mMediaPlayer.start();
                        }
                });
        }
    });
}
```

In addition to configuring our `MediaController` and `MediaPlayer`, we create an anonymous `OnPreparedListener` in order to start the player only when the media source is ready for playback. Remember to clean up the `MediaPlayer` when the Activity is destroyed (see Example 9-8).

Example 9-8. The MediaPlayer cleanup

```
@Override
protected void onDestroy() {
    super.onDestroy();
    mMediaPlayer.stop();
    mMediaPlayer.release();
}
```

Lastly, we implement the `MediaPlayerControl` interface. The code is straightforward, as shown in Example 9-9.

Example 9-9. The MediaPlayerControl implementation

```
@Override
public boolean canPause() {
    return true;
}

@Override
public boolean canSeekBackward() {
    return false;
}

@Override
public boolean canSeekForward() {
    return false;
}

@Override
public int getBufferPercentage() {
    return (mMediaPlayer.getCurrentPosition() * 100) / mMediaPlayer.getDuration();
}
```

```
    // Remaining methods just delegate to the MediaPlayer
}
```

As a final touch, we override the `onTouchEvent()` method in order to show the `MediaController` buttons when the user clicks the screen. Since we create our `MediaController` programmatically, the layout is very simple:

```xml
<?xml version="1.0" encoding="utf-8"?>
<LinearLayout xmlns:android="http://schemas.android.com/apk/res/android"
    android:orientation="vertical"
    android:layout_width="fill_parent"
    android:layout_height="fill_parent"
    android:id="@+id/audioView"
    >
</LinearLayout>
```

Source Download URL

The source code for this example is in the Android Cookbook repository (*https://github.com/IanDarwin/Android-Cookbook-Examples*), in the subdirectory *Media-PlayerInteractive* (see "Getting and Using the Code Examples" on page 18).

9.5 Playing Audio Without Interaction

Ian Darwin

Problem

You want to play an audio file with no interaction (e.g., no user-settable volume, pause/play controls, etc.).

Solution

All you need to do to play a file with no interaction is create a `MediaPlayer` for the file and call its `start()` method.

Discussion

This is the simplest way to play a sound file. In contrast with Recipe 9.4, this version offers the user no controls to interact with the sound. You should therefore usually offer at least a Stop or Cancel button, especially if the audio file is (or might be) long. If you're just playing a short sound effect within your application, no such control is needed.

You must have a MediaPlayer created for your file. The audio file may be on the SD card or in your application's *res/raw* directory. If the sound file is part of your application, store it under *res/raw*. Suppose it is in *res/raw/alarm_sound.3gp*; then the reference to it is R.raw.alarm_sound, and you can play it as follows:

```
MediaPlayer player = MediaPlayer.create(this, R.raw.alarm_sound);
player.start();
```

In the SD card case, use the following invocation:

```
MediaPlayer player = new MediaPlayer();
player.setDataSource(fileName);
player.prepare();
player.start();
```

There is also a convenience routine, MediaPlayer.create(Context, URI), that you can use; in all cases, create() calls prepare() for you.

To control the player from within your application, you can call the relevant methods such as player.stop(), player.pause(), and so on. If you want to reuse a player after stopping it, you must call prepare() again. To be notified when the audio is finished, use an OnCompletionListener:

```
player.setOnCompletionListener(new OnCompletionListener() {
        @Override
        public void onCompletion(MediaPlayer mp) {
                Toast.makeText(Main.this,
                        "Media Play Complete", Toast.LENGTH_SHORT).show();
        }
});
```

When you are truly done with any MediaPlayer instance, you should call its release() method to free up memory; otherwise, you will run out of resources if you create a lot of MediaPlayer objects.

See Also

To really use the MediaPlayer effectively, you should understand its various states and transitions, as this will help you to understand what methods are valid. The developer documentation (*https://developer.android.com/reference/android/media/MediaPlayer.html*) contains a complete state diagram for the MediaPlayer.

Source Download URL

The source code for this example is in the Android Cookbook repository (*https://github.com/IanDarwin/Android-Cookbook-Examples*), in the subdirectory *MediaPlayerDemo* (see "Getting and Using the Code Examples" on page 18).

9.6 Using Speech to Text

Corey Sunwold

Problem

You want to accept speech input and process it as text.

Solution

One of Android's unique features is native speech-to-text processing. This provides an alternative form of text input for the user, who in some situations might not have her hands free to type in information.

Discussion

Android provides an easy API for using its built-in voice recognition capability through the RecognizerIntent. Our example layout will be very simple (see Example 9-10). I've only included a TextView called speechText and a Button called getSpeechButton. The Button will be used to launch the voice recognizer, which will remain listening and recognizing until the user stops talking for a few seconds. When results are returned they will be displayed in the TextView.

Example 9-10. The speech recognizer demo program

```
public class Main extends Activity {

    private static final int RECOGNIZER_RESULT = 1234;

    /** Called when the Atctivity is first created. */
    @Override
    public void onCreate(Bundle savedInstanceState) {
        super.onCreate(savedInstanceState);
        setContentView(R.layout.main);

        Button startSpeech = (Button)findViewById(R.id.getSpeechButton);
        startSpeech.setOnClickListener(new OnClickListener() {

            @Override
            public void onClick(View v) {
             Intent intent = new Intent(RecognizerIntent.ACTION_RECOGNIZE_SPEECH);
             intent.putExtra(RecognizerIntent.EXTRA_LANGUAGE_MODEL,
                        RecognizerIntent.LANGUAGE_MODEL_FREE_FORM);
             intent.putExtra(RecognizerIntent.EXTRA_PROMPT, "Speech to text");
             startActivityForResult(intent, RECOGNIZER_RESULT);
            }

        });
```

```
    }

    /**
     * Handle the results from the recognition Activity.
     */
    @Override
    protected void onActivityResult(int requestCode, int resultCode, Intent data) {
        if (requestCode == RECOGNIZER_RESULT && resultCode == RESULT_OK) {
            ArrayList<String> matches = data.getStringArrayListExtra(
                    RecognizerIntent.EXTRA_RESULTS);

            TextView speechText = (TextView)findViewById(R.id.speechText);
            speechText.setText(matches.get(0).toString());
        }

        super.onActivityResult(requestCode, resultCode, data);
    }
}
```

See Also

The developer documentation on `RecognizerIntent` (*https://developer.android.com/refer ence/android/speech/RecognizerIntent.html*).

Source Download URL

The source code for this project is in the Android Cookbook repository (*https:// github.com/IanDarwin/Android-Cookbook-Examples*), in the subdirectory *SpeechRe- cognizerDemo* (see "Getting and Using the Code Examples" on page 18).

9.7 Making the Device Speak with Text-to-Speech

Ian Darwin

Problem

You want your application to pronounce words of text so that the user can perceive them without watching the screen (e.g., when driving).

Solution

Use the TextToSpeech API.

Discussion

The TextToSpeech (TTS) API is built into Android (though you may have to install the voice files, depending on the version you are using). To get started you just need a TextToSpeech object. In theory, you could simply do this:

```
private TextToSpeech myTTS = new TextToSpeech(this, this);
myTTS.setLanguage(Locale.US);
myTTS.speak(textToBeSpoken, TextToSpeech.QUEUE_FLUSH, null);
myTTS.shutdown();
```

However, to ensure success, you actually have to use a couple of Intents: one to check that the TTS data is available and install it if not, and another to start the TTS mechanism. So, in practice, the code needs to look something like Example 9-11. This quaint little application chooses one of half a dozen banal phrases to utter each time the Speak button is pressed.

Example 9-11. The text-to-speech demo program

```
public class Main extends Activity implements OnInitListener {

    private TextToSpeech myTTS;
    private List<String> phrases = new ArrayList<String>();

    public void onCreate(Bundle savedInstanceState) {

        phrases.add("Hello Android, Goodbye iPhone");
        phrases.add("The quick brown fox jumped over the lazy dog");
        phrases.add("What is your mother's maiden name?");
        phrases.add("Etaoin Shrdlu for Prime Minister");
        phrases.add(
            "The letter 'Q' does not appear in 'antidisestablishmentarianism')");
        super.onCreate(savedInstanceState);
        setContentView(R.layout.main);

        Button startButton = (Button) findViewById(R.id.start_button);
        startButton.setOnClickListener(new View.OnClickListener() {
            @Override
            public void onClick(View arg0) {
                Intent checkIntent = new Intent();
                checkIntent.setAction(TextToSpeech.Engine.ACTION_CHECK_TTS_DATA);
                startActivityForResult(checkIntent, 1);
            }
        });
    }

    protected void onActivityResult(int requestCode, int resultCode, Intent data) {
        if (requestCode == 1) {

            if (resultCode == TextToSpeech.Engine.CHECK_VOICE_DATA_PASS) {
                myTTS = new TextToSpeech(this, this);  ❶
                myTTS.setLanguage(Locale.US);
            } else {
                // TTS data not yet loaded, try to install it
                Intent ttsLoadIntent = new Intent();
                ttsLoadIntent.setAction(TextToSpeech.Engine.ACTION_INSTALL_TTS_DATA);
                startActivity(ttsLoadIntent);
            }
        }
    }
}
```

```
public void onInit(int status) {
    if (status == TextToSpeech.SUCCESS) {

        int n = (int)(Math.random() * phrases.size());
        myTTS.speak(phrases.get(n), TextToSpeech.QUEUE_FLUSH, null);

    } else if (status == TextToSpeech.ERROR) {
        myTTS.shutdown();
    }
}
}
```

❶ The first argument is a Context (the Activity) and the second is an OnInitListener, also implemented by the main Activity in this case. When the initialization of the TextToSpeech object is done, it calls the listener, whose onInit() method is meant to notify that the TTS is ready. In this trivial Speaker program, we simply do the speaking. In a longer example, you would probably want to start a thread or Service to do the speaking operation.

Source Download URL

The source code for this example is in the Android Cookbook repository (*https://github.com/IanDarwin/Android-Cookbook-Examples*), in the subdirectory *Speaker* (see "Getting and Using the Code Examples" on page 18).

Data Persistence

Data persistence is a wide subject area. In this chapter we focus on selected topics, including:

- Filesystem topics relating to the app-accessible parts of the filesystems (*/sdcard* and friends)—but we assume you know the basics of reading/writing text files in Java.

- Persisting data in a database, commonly but not exclusively SQLite.

- Reading data from the database, and doing various conversions on it.

- Reading and writing the Preferences data, used to store small per-application customization values.

- Some data format conversions (e.g., JSON and XML conversions) that don't fit naturally into any of the other chapters.

- The Android `ContentProvider`, which allows unrelated applications to share data in the form of a SQLite cursor. We'll focus specifically on the Android Contacts provider.

- Drag and drop, which might seem to be a GUI topic but typically involves using a `ContentProvider`.

- `FileProvider`, a simplification of the `ContentProvider` that allows unrelated applications to share individual files.

- The `SyncAdapter` mechanism, which allows data to be synchronized to/from a backend database; we discuss one example, that of synchronizing "todo list" items.

- Finally, we cover a new cloud database called Firebase from Google.

10.1 Reading and Writing Files in Internal and External Storage

Ian Darwin

Problem

You want to know how to store files in internal versus external storage. Files can be created and accessed in several different places on the device (notably, application private data and SD card–style data). You need to learn the APIs for dealing with these sections of the filesystem.

Solution

Use the `Context` methods `getFilesDir()`, `openFileInput()`, and `openFileOutput()` for "internal" storage, and use the methods `Context.getExternalFilesDir()` or `Environment.getExternalStoragePublicDirectory()` for shared storage.

Discussion

Every Android device features a fairly complete Unix/Linux filesystem hierarchy. Parts of it are "off-limits" for normal applications, to ensure that the device's integrity and functionality are not compromised. Storage areas available for reading/writing within the application are divided into "internal" storage, which is private per application, and "public" storage, which may be accessed by other applications.

Internal storage is always located in the device's "flash memory" area—part of the 8 GB or 32 GB of "storage" that your device was advertised with—under */data/data/ PKG_NAME/*. External storage may be on the SD card (which should technically be called "removable storage," as it might be a MicroSD card or even some other media type). However, there are several complications.

First, some devices don't have removable storage. On these, the external storage directory always exists—it is just in a different partition of the same flash memory storage as internal storage.

Second, on devices that do have removable storage, the storage might be removed at the time your application checks it. There's no point trying to write it if it's not there.

On these devices, as well, the storage might be "read-only" as most removable media memory devices have a "write-protect" switch that disables power to the write circuitry.

The Files API

Internal storage can be accessed using the Context methods openFileInput(String filename), which returns a FileInputStream object, or openFileOutput(String filename, int mode), which returns a FileOutputStream. The mode value should either be 0 for a new file, or Context.MODE_APPEND to add to the end of an existing file. Other mode values are deprecated and should not be used. Once obtained, these streams can be read using standard java.io classes and methods (e.g., wrap the FileInputStream in an InputStreamReader and a BufferedReader to get line-at-a-time access to character data). You should close these when finished with them.

Alternatively, the Context method getFilesDir() returns the root of this directory, and you can then access it using normal java.io methods and classes.

Example 10-1 shows a simple example of writing a file into this area and then reading it back.

Example 10-1. Writing and reading internal storage

```
try (FileOutputStream os =
        openFileOutput(DATA_FILE_NAME, Context.MODE_PRIVATE)) {
    os.write(message.getBytes());
    println("Wrote the string " + message + " to file " +
        DATA_FILE_NAME);
} catch (IOException e) {
    println("Failed to write " + DATA_FILE_NAME + " due to " + e);
}

// Get the absolute path to the directory for our app's internal storage
File where = getFilesDir();
println("Our private dir is " + where.getAbsolutePath());

try (BufferedReader is = new BufferedReader(
        new InputStreamReader(openFileInput(DATA_FILE_NAME)))) {
    String line = is.readLine();
    println("Read the string " + line);
} catch (IOException e) {
    println("Failed to read back " + DATA_FILE_NAME + " due to " + e);
}
```

Accessing the external storage is, predictably, more complicated. The mental model of external storage is a removable flash-memory card such as an SD card. Initially most devices had an SD card or MicroSD card slot. Today most do not, but some still do, so Android always treats the SD card as though it might be removable, or might be present but the write-protect switch might be enabled. You should not access it by the directory name */sdcard*, but rather through API calls. On some devices the path may change when an SD card is inserted or removed. And, Murphy's Law being what it is, a removable card can be inserted or removed at any time; the users may or may not know that they're supposed to unmount it in software before removing it. Be prepared for IOExceptions!

For external storage you will usually require the READ_EXTERNAL_STORAGE or WRITE_EXTERNAL_STORAGE permission (note that WRITE implies READ, so you don't need both):

```
<uses-permission android:name="android.permission.WRITE_EXTERNAL_STORAGE"/>
```

The first thing your application must do is check if the external storage is even available. The method static String Environment.getExternalStorageState() returns one of almost a dozen String values (*https://developer.android.com/reference/android/os/Environment.html*), but unless you are writing a File Manager–type application, you only care about two: MEDIA_MOUNTED and MEDIA_MOUNTED_READ_ONLY. Any other values imply that the external storage directory is not currently usable. You can verify this as follows:

```
String state = Environment.getExternalStorageState();
println("External storage state = " + state);
if (state.equals(Environment.MEDIA_MOUNTED_READ_ONLY)) {
    mounted = true;
    readOnly = true;
    println("External storage is read-only!!");
} else if (state.equals(Environment.MEDIA_MOUNTED)) {
    mounted = true;
    readOnly = false;
    println("External storage is usable");
} else {
    println("External storage NOT USABLE");
}
```

Once you've ascertained that the external storage is usable, you can create files and/or directories in it. The Environment class exposes a bunch of public directory types, such as DIRECTORY_MUSIC for playable music, DIRECTORY_RINGTONES for music files that should only be used as telephone ringtones, DIRECTORY_MOVIES for videos, and so on. If you use one of these your files will be placed in the correct directory for the stated purpose. You can create subdirectories here using File.mkdirs():

```
// Get the external storage folder for Music
final File externalStoragePublicDirectory =
        Environment.getExternalStoragePublicDirectory(
            Environment.DIRECTORY_MUSIC);
// Get the directory for the user's public pictures directory.
// We want to use it, for example, to create a new music album.
File albumDir = new File(externalStoragePublicDirectory, "Jam Session 2017");
albumDir.mkdirs();
if (!albumDir.isDirectory()) {
    println("Unable to create music album");
} else {
    println("Music album exists as " + albumDir);
}
```

You could then create files in the subdirectory that would show up as the "album" "Jam Session 2017."

The final category of files is "private external storage." This is just a directory with your package name in it, for convenience, and offers *zero* security—any application with the appropriate EXTERNAL_STORAGE permission can read or write to it. However, it has the advantage that it will be removed if the user uninstalls your app. This category is thus intended for use for configuration and data files that are specific to your application, and should *not* be used for files that logically "belong" to the user.

Directories in this category are accessed by passing null to the getExternalStorageDirectory() method, as in Example 10-2.

Example 10-2. Reading and writing "private" external storage

```
// Finally, we'll create an "application private" file on /sdcard,
// Note that these are accessible to all other applications!
final File privateDir = getExternalFilesDir(null);
File semiPrivateFile = new File(privateDir, "fred.jpg");
try (OutputStream is = new FileOutputStream(semiPrivateFile)) {
    println("Writing to " + semiPrivateFile);
    // Do some writing here...
} catch (IOException e) {
    println("Failed to create " + semiPrivateFile + " due to " + e);
}
```

The sample project *FilesystemDemos* includes all this code plus a bit more. Running it will produce the result shown in Figure 10-1.

See Also

For getting information about files, and directory listings, see Recipe 10.2. To read static files that are shipped (read-only) as part of your application, see Recipe 10.3. For more information on data storage options in Android, refer to the official documentation (*https://developer.android.com/guide/topics/data/data-storage.html*).

Source Download URL

The source code for this example is in the Android Cookbook repository (*https://github.com/IanDarwin/Android-Cookbook-Examples*), in the subdirectory *Filesystem-Demos* (see "Getting and Using the Code Examples" on page 18).

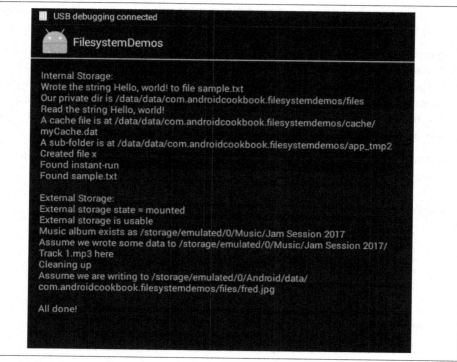

Figure 10-1. FilesystemDemos in action

10.2 Getting File and Directory Information

Ian Darwin

Problem

You need to know all you can about a given file "on disk," typically in internal memory or on the SD card, or you need to list the filesystem entries named in a directory.

Solution

Use a `java.io.File` object.

Discussion

The `File` class has a number of "informational" methods. To use any of these, you must construct a `File` object containing the name of the file on which it is to operate. It should be noted up front that creating a `File` object has no effect on the permanent filesystem; it is only an object in Java's memory. You must call methods on the `File` object in order to change the filesystem; there are numerous "change" methods, such as one for creating a new (but empty) file, one for renaming a file, and so on, as well as many informational methods. Table 10-1 lists some of the informational methods.

Table 10-1. File class informational methods

Return type	Method name	Meaning
boolean	exists()	True if something of that name exists
String	getCanonicalPath()	Full name
String	getName()	Relative filename
String	getParent()	Parent directory
boolean	canRead()	True if file is readable
boolean	canWrite()	True if file is writable
long	lastModified()	File modification time
long	length()	File size
boolean	isFile()	True if it's a file
boolean	isDirectory()	True if it's a directory (note: might be neither file nor directory)
String[]	list()	List contents if it's a directory
File[]	listFiles()	List contents if it's a directory

You cannot change the name stored in a `File` object; you simply create a new `File` object each time you need to refer to a different file.

Standard Java as of JDK 1.7 includes `java.nio.Files`, which is a newer replacement for the `File` class, but Android does not yet ship with this class.

Example 10-3 is drawn from desktop Java, but the `File` object operates the same in Android as in Java SE.

Example 10-3. A file information program

```java
import java.io.*;
import java.util.*;

/**
 * Report on a file's status in Java
 */
public class FileStatus {

    public static void main(String[] argv) throws IOException {
        // Ensure that a filename (or something) was given in argv[0]
        if (argv.length == 0) {
```

```java
            System.err.println("Usage: FileStatus filename");
            System.exit(1);
        }

        for (int i = 0; i < argv.length; i++) {
            status(argv[i]);
        }
    }

    public static void status(String fileName) throws IOException {
        System.out.println("---" + fileName + "---");

        // Construct a File object for the given file
        File f = new File(fileName);

        // See if it actually exists
        if (!f.exists()) {
            System.out.println("file not found");
            System.out.println(); // Blank line
            return;
        }

        // Print full name
        System.out.println("Canonical name " + f.getCanonicalPath());

        // Print parent directory if possible
        String p = f.getParent();
        if (p != null) {
            System.out.println("Parent directory: " + p);
        }

        // Check our permissions on this file
        if (f.canRead()) {
            System.out.println("File is readable by us.");
        }
        // Check if the file is writable
        if (f.canWrite()) {
            System.out.println("File is writable by us.");
        }

        // Report on the modification time
        Date d = new Date();
        d.setTime(f.lastModified());
        System.out.println("Last modified " + d);

        // See if file, directory, or other. If file, print size.
        if (f.isFile()) {
            // Report on the file's size
            System.out.println("File size is " + f.length() + " bytes.");
        } else if (f.isDirectory()) {
            System.out.println("It's a directory");
        } else {
            System.out.println("So weird, man! Neither a file nor a directory!");
        }

        System.out.println(); // Blank line between entries
```

```
        }
}
```

Take a look at the output produced when the program is run (on MS Windows) with
the three command-line arguments shown, it produces the output shown here:

```
C:\javasrc\dir_file> java FileStatus / /tmp/id /autoexec.bat
---/---
Canonical name C:\
File is readable.
File is writable.
Last modified Thu Jan 01 00:00:00 GMT 1970
It's a directory

---/tmp/id---
file not found

---/autoexec.bat---
Canonical name C:\AUTOEXEC.BAT
Parent directory: \
File is readable.
File is writable.
Last modified Fri Sep 10 15:40:32 GMT 1999
File size is 308 bytes.
```

As you can see, the so-called *canonical name* not only includes a leading directory
root of *C:*, but also has had the name converted to uppercase. You can tell I ran that
on an older version of Windows. On Unix, it behaves differently, as you can see here:

```
$ java FileStatus / /tmp/id /autoexec.bat
---/---
Canonical name /
File is readable.
Last modified October 4, 1999 6:29:14 AM PDT
It's a directory

---/tmp/id---
Canonical name /tmp/id
Parent directory: /tmp
File is readable.
File is writable.
Last modified October 8, 1999 1:01:54 PM PDT
File size is 0 bytes.

---/autoexec.bat---

file not found

$
```

This is because a typical Unix system has no *autoexec.bat* file. And Unix filenames
(like those on the filesystem inside your Android device, and those on a Mac) can
consist of upper- and lowercase characters: what you type is what you get.

The java.io.File class also contains methods for working with directories. For example, to list the filesystem entities named in the current directory, just write:

```
String[] list = new File(".").list()
```

To get an array of already constructed File objects rather than strings, use:

```
File[] list = new File(".").listFiles();
```

You can display the result in a ListView (see Recipe 8.2).

Of course, there's lots of room for elaboration. You could print the names in multiple columns across or down the screen in a TextView in a monospace font, since you know the number of items in the list before you print. You could omit filenames with leading periods, as does the Unix ls program, or you could print the directory names first, as some "file manager"–type programs do. By using listFiles(), which constructs a new File object for each name, you could print the size of each, as per the MS-DOS dir command or the Unix ls -l command. Or you could figure out whether each object is a file, a directory, or neither. Having done that, you could pass each directory to your top-level function, and you would have directory recursion (the equivalent of using the Unix find command, or ls -R, or the DOS DIR /S command). Quite the makings of a file manager application of your own!

A more flexible way to list filesystem entries is with list(FilenameFilter ff). FilenameFilter is a tiny interface with only one method: boolean accept(File inDir, String fileName). Suppose you want a listing of only Java-related files (*.java, *.class, *.jar, etc.). Just write the accept() method so that it returns true for these files and false for any others. Example 10-4 shows the Ls class warmed over to use a FilenameFilter instance.

Example 10-4. Directory lister with FilenameFilter

```
import java.io.*;

/**
 * FNFilter - directory lister modified to use FilenameFilter
 */
public class FNFilter {
 public static String[] getListing(String startingDir) {
 // Generate the selective list, with a one-use File object
 String[] dir = new java.io.File(startingDir).list(new OnlyJava());
 java.util.Arrays.sort(dir); // Sorts by name
 return dir;
}

/** FilenameFilter implementation:
 * The accept() method only returns true for .java , .jar, and .class files.
 */
class OnlyJava implements FilenameFilter {
 public boolean accept(File dir, String s) {
 if (s.endsWith(".java") || s.endsWith(".jar") || s.endsWith(".dex"))
```

```
 return true;
 // Others: projects, ... ?
 return false;
 }
}
```

We could make the `FilenameFilter` a bit more flexible; in a full-scale application, the list of files returned by the `FilenameFilter` would be chosen dynamically, possibly automatically, based on what you were working on. File chooser dialogs implement this as well, allowing the user to select interactively from one of several sets of files to be listed. This is a great convenience in finding files, just as it is here in reducing the number of files that must be examined.

For the `listFiles()` method, there is an additional overload that accepts a `FileFilter`. The only difference is that `FileFilter`'s `accept()` method is called with a `File` object, whereas `FileNameFilter`'s is called with a filename string.

See Also

See Recipe 8.2 to display the results in your GUI. Chapter 11 of *Java Cookbook*, written by me and published by O'Reilly, has more information on file and directory operations.

10.3 Reading a File Shipped with the App Rather than in the Filesystem

Rachee Singh

Problem

The standard file-oriented Java I/O classes can only open files stored on "disk," as described in Recipe 10.1. If you want to read a file that is a static part of your application (installed as part of the APK rather than downloaded), you can access it in one of two special places.

Solution

If you'd like to read a static file, you can place it either in the *assets* directory or in *res/ raw*. For *res/raw*, open it with the `getResources()` and `openRawResource()` methods, and then read it normally. For *assets*, you access the file as a filesystem entry (see Recipe 10.1); Android maps this directory to *file:///android_asset/* (note the triple slash and singular spelling of "asset").

Discussion

We wish to read information from a file packaged with the Android application, so we will need to put the relevant file in the *res/raw* directory or the *assets* directory (and probably create the directory, since it is often not created by default).

If the file is stored in *res/raw*, the generated R class will have an ID for it, which we pass into openRawResource(). Then we will read the file using the returned InputStreamReader wrapped in a BufferedReader. Finally, we extract the string from the BufferedReader using the readLine() method.

If the file is stored in *assets*, it will appear to be in the *file:///android_asset/* directory, which we can just open and read normally.

In both cases the IDE will ask us to enclose the readLine() function within a try-catch block since there is a possibility of it throwing an IOException.

For *res/$$raw* the file is named *samplefile* and is shown in Example 10-5.

Example 10-5. Reading a static file from res/raw

```
InputStreamReader is =
    new InputStreamReader(this.getResources().openRawResource(R.raw.samplefile));
BufferedReader reader = new BufferedReader(is);
StringBuilder finalText = new StringBuilder();
String line;
try {
    while ((line = reader.readLine()) != null) {
        finalText.append(line);
    }
} catch (IOException e) {
    e.printStackTrace();
}
fileTextView = (TextView)findViewById(R.id.fileText);
fileTextView.setText(finalText.toString());
```

After reading the entire string, we set it to the TextView in the Activity.

When using the *assets* folder, the most common use is for loading a web resource into a WebView. Suppose we have *samplefile.html* stored in the *assets* folder; the code in Example 10-6 will load it into a web display.

Example 10-6. Reading from assets

```
webView = (WebView)findViewById(R.id.about_html);
webview.loadUrl("file:///android_asset/samplefile.html");
```

Figure 10-2 shows the result of both the text and HTML files.

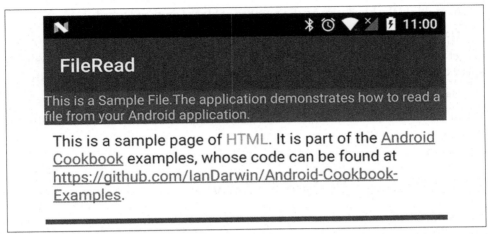

Figure 10-2. File read from application resource

Source Download URL

The source code for this example is in the Android Cookbook repository (*https://github.com/IanDarwin/Android-Cookbook-Examples*), in the subdirectory *StaticFileRead* (see "Getting and Using the Code Examples" on page 18).

10.4 Getting Space Information About the SD Card

Amir Alagic

Problem

You want to find out the amount of total and available space on the SD card.

Solution

Use the `StatFs` and `Environment` classes from the `android.os` package to find the total and available space on the SD card.

Discussion

Here is some code that obtains the information:

```
StatFs statFs = new StatFs(Environment.getExternalStorageDirectory().getPath());
double bytesTotal = (long) statFs.getBlockSize() * (long) statFs.getBlockCount();
double megTotal = bytesTotal / 1048576;
```

To get the total space on the SD card, use `StatFs` in the `android.os` package. Use `Environment.getExternalStorageDirectory().getPath()` as a constructor parameter.

Then, multiply the block size by the number of blocks on the SD card:

```
(long) statFs.getBlockSize() * (long) statFs.getBlockCount();
```

To get size in megabytes, divide the result by 1048576. To get the amount of available space on the SD card, replace statFs.getBlockCount() with statFs.getAvailableBlocks():

```
(long) statFs.getBlockSize() * (long) statFs.getAvailableBlocks();
```

If you want to display the value with two decimal places you can use a DecimalFormat object from java.text:

```
DecimalFormat twoDecimalForm = new DecimalFormat("#.##");
```

10.5 Providing a Preference Activity

Ian Darwin

Problem

You want to let the user specify one or more preferences values, and have them persisted across runs of the program.

Solution

Have your Preferences or Settings menu item or button load an Activity that subclasses PreferenceActivity; in its onCreate() method, load an XML PreferenceScreen.

Discussion

Android will happily maintain a SharedPreferences object for you in semipermanent storage. To retrieve settings from it, use:

```
sharedPreferences = PreferenceManager.getDefaultSharedPreferences(this);
```

This should be called in your main Activity's onCreate() method, or in the onCreate() of any Activity that needs to view the user's chosen preferences.

You do need to tell Android what values you want the user to be able to specify, such as name, Twitter account, favorite color, or whatever. You don't use the traditional view items such as ListView or Spinner, but instead use the special Preference items. A reasonable set of choices are available, such as Lists, TextEdits, CheckBoxes, and so on, but remember, these are *not* the standard View subclasses. Example 10-7 uses a List, a TextEdit, and a CheckBox.

Example 10-7. XML PreferenceScreen

```
<PreferenceScreen xmlns:android="http://schemas.android.com/apk/res/android">

    <ListPreference
```

```
        android:key="listChoice"
        android:title="List Choice"
        android:entries="@array/choices"
        android:entryValues="@array/choices"
        />

    <PreferenceCategory
        android:title="Personal">

        <EditTextPreference
            android:key="nameChoice"
            android:title="Name"
            android:hint="Name"
        />

        <CheckBoxPreference
            android:key="booleanChoice"
            android:title="Binary Choice"
        />

    </PreferenceCategory>

</PreferenceScreen>
```

The PreferenceCategory in the XML allows you to subdivide your panel into labeled sections. It is also possible to have more than one PreferenceScreen if you have a large number of settings and want to divide it into "pages." Several additional kinds of UI elements can be used in the XML PreferenceScreen; see the official documentation (*https://developer.android.com/reference/android/preference/PreferenceScreen.html*) for details.

The PreferenceActivity subclass can consist of as little as this onCreate() method:

```
@Override
protected void onCreate(Bundle savedInstanceState) {
    super.onCreate(savedInstanceState);
    addPreferencesFromResource(R.layout.prefs);
}
```

When activated, the PreferenceActivity looks like Figure 10-3.

When the user clicks, say, Name, an Edit dialog opens, as in Figure 10-4.

In the XML layout for the preferences screen, each preference setting is assigned a name or "key," as in a Java Map or Properties object. The supported value types are the obvious String, int, float, and boolean. You use this to retrieve the user's values, and you provide a default value in case the settings screen hasn't been put up yet or in case the user didn't bother to specify a particular setting:

```
String preferredName =
    sharedPreferences.getString("nameChoice", "No name");
```

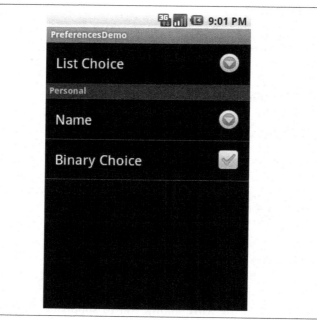

Figure 10-3. Preferences screen

Figure 10-4. String edit dialog

Since the preferences screen does the editing for you, there is little need to set preferences from within your application. There are a few uses, though, such as remembering that the user has accepted an end-user license agreement, or EULA. The code for this would be something like the following:

```
sharedPreferences.edit().putBoolean("accepted EULA", true).commit();
```

When writing, don't forget the `commit()`! And, for this particular use case, the EULA option should obviously not appear in the GUI, or the user could just set it there without having a chance to read and ignore the text of your license agreement.

Like many Android apps, this demo has no Back button from its preferences screen; the user simply presses the system's Back button. When the user returns to the main Activity, a real app would operate based on the user's choices. My demo app simply displays the values. This is shown in Figure 10-5.

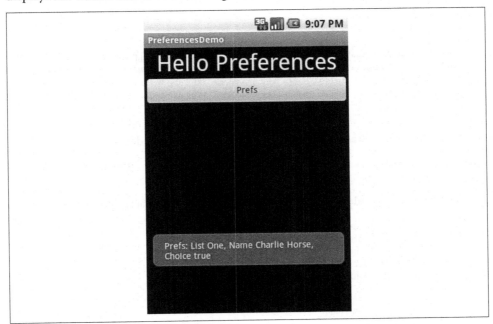

Figure 10-5. Values the main Activity uses

There is no "official" way to add a Done button to an XML `PreferenceScreen`, but some developers use a generic `Preference` item:

```
<Preference android:title="@string/done"
    android:key="settingsDoneButton"
    />
```

You can then make this work like a `Button` just by giving it an `OnClickListener` (from `Preference`, not the normal one from `View`):

```
// Set up our Done preference to function as a Button
Preference button = findPreference("settingsDoneButton"); // NOI18N
button.setOnPreferenceClickListener(
        new Preference.OnPreferenceClickListener() {
    @Override
    public boolean onPreferenceClick(Preference arg0) {
        finish();
        return true;
    }
});
```

When building a full-size application, I like to define the keys used as strings, for stylistic reasons and to prevent misspellings. I create a separate XML resource file for these strings called, say, *keys.xml*:

```
<?xml version="1.0" encoding="utf-8"?>
<resources>

<string translatable="false" name="key_enable_sync">KEY_ENABLE_SYNC</string>
<string translatable="false" name="key_sync_interval">KEY_SYNC_INTERVAL</string>
<string translatable="false" name="key_username">KEY_USERNAME</string>
<string translatable="false" name="key_password">KEY_PASSWORD</string>
...
</resources>
```

Note the use of `translatable="false"` to prevent translation accidents.

I can use these strings directly in the *prefs.xml* file, and in code using the `Activity` method `getString()`:

```
<PreferenceScreen xmlns:android="http://schemas.android.com/apk/res/android">

    <PreferenceCategory android:title="Synchronization">
        <CheckBoxPreference
            android:key="@string/key_enable_synch"
            android:title="Enable Sync"
            android:hint="Sync"
            />

        <EditTextPreference
            android:key="@string/key_sync_interval"
            android:title="Sync Interval (minutes)"
            android:inputType="number"
            android:defaultValue="60"
        />
    ...
    </PreferenceScreen>
```

Basically, that's all you need: an XML `PreferenceScreen` to define the properties and how the user sets them; a call to `getDefaultSharedPrefences()`; and calls to `getString()`, `getBoolean()`, and so on on the returned `SharedPreferences` object. It's easy to handle preferences this way, and it gives the Android system a feel of uniformity, consistency, and predictability that is important to the overall user experience.

10.6 Checking the Consistency of Default Shared Preferences

Federico Paolinelli

Problem

Android provides a very easy way to set up default preferences by defining a `PreferenceActivity` and providing it a resource file, as discussed in Recipe 10.5. What is not clear is how to perform checks on preferences given by the user.

Solution

You can implement the `PreferenceActivity` method `onSharedPreferenceChanged()`:

```
public void onSharedPreferenceChanged(SharedPreferences prefs, String key)
```

You perform your checks in this method's body. If the check fails you can restore a default value for the preference. Be aware that even though the `SharedPreferences` will contain the right value, you won't see it displayed correctly; for this reason, you need to reload the `PreferenceActivity`.

Discussion

If you have a default `PreferenceActivity` that implements `OnSharedPreferenceChangeListener`, your `PreferenceActivity` can implement the `onSharedPreferenceChanged()` method, as shown in Example 10-8.

Example 10-8. PreferenceActivity implementation

```
public class MyPreferenceActivity extends PreferenceActivity
        implements OnSharedPreferenceChangeListener {

    public void onCreate(Bundle savedInstanceState) {
        super.onCreate(savedInstanceState);
        Context context = getApplicationContext();
        prefs = PreferenceManager.getDefaultSharedPreferences(context);
        addPreferencesFromResource(R.xml.userprefs);
    }
}
```

The onSharedPreferenceChanged() method will be called after the change is committed, so every other change you perform will be permanent.

The idea is to check whether the value is appropriate, and if not replace it with a default value or disable it.

To arrange to have this method called at the appropriate time, you have to register your Activity as a valid listener. A good way to do so is to register in onResume() and unregister in onPause():

```
@Override
protected void onResume() {
    super.onResume();
    prefs.registerOnSharedPreferenceChangeListener(this);
}

@Override
protected void onPause() {
    super.onPause();
    prefs.unregisterOnSharedPreferenceChangeListener(this);
}
```

Now it's time to perform the consistency check. For example, if you have an option whose key is MY_OPTION_KEY, you can use the code in Example 10-9 to check and allow/ disallow the value.

Example 10-9. Checking and allowing/disallowing the supplied value

```
public void onSharedPreferenceChanged(SharedPreferences prefs, String key) {
    SharedPreferences.Editor prefEditor = prefs.edit();

    if(key.equals(MY_OPTION_KEY)) {
        String optionValue = prefs.getString(MY_OPTION_KEY, "");
        if(dontLikeTheValue(optionValue)) {
            prefEditor.putString(MY_OPTION_KEY, "Default value");
            prefEditor.commit();
            reload();
        }
    }
    return;
}
```

Of course, if the check fails the user will be surprised and will not know why you refused his option. You can then show an error dialog and perform the reload action after the user confirms the dialog (see Example 10-10).

Example 10-10. Explaining rejection

```
private void showErrorDialog(String errorString) {
    String okButtonString = context.getString(R.string.ok_name);
    AlertDialog.Builder ad = new AlertDialog.Builder(context);
    ad.setTitle(context.getString(R.string.error_name));
```

```
        ad.setMessage(errorString);
        ad.setPositiveButton(okButtonString,new OnClickListener() {
            public void onClick(DialogInterface dialog, int arg1) {
                reload();
            }
        } );
        ad.show();
        return;
}
```

In this way, the dontLikeTheValue() "if" becomes:

```
    if(dontLikeTheValue(optionValue)) {
        if(!GeneralUtils.isPhoneNumber(smsNumber)) {
            showErrorDialog("I dont like the option");
            prefEditor.putString(MY_OPTION_KEY, "Default value");
            prefEditor.commit();
        }
    }
```

What's still missing is the reload() function, but it's pretty obvious. It relaunches the Activity using the same Intent that fired it:

```
    private void reload() {
        startActivity(getIntent());
        finish();
    }
```

10.7 Using a SQLite Database in an Android Application

Rachee Singh

Problem

You want data you save to last longer than the application's run, and you want to access that data in a standardized way.

Solution

SQLite is a popular relational database using the SQL model that you can use to store application data. To access it in Android, create and use a class that subclasses SQLiteOpenHelper.

Discussion

SQLite is used in many platforms, not just Android. While SQLite provides an API, many systems (including Android) develop their own APIs for their particular needs.

Getting started

To use a SQLite database in an Android application, it is necessary to create a class that inherits from the SQLiteOpenHelper class, a standard Android class that arranges to open the database file:

```
public class SqlOpenHelper extends SQLiteOpenHelper {
```

It checks for the existence of the database file and, if it exists, it opens it; otherwise, it creates one.

The constructor for the parent SQLiteOpenHelper class takes in a few arguments—the context, the database name, the CursorFactory object (which is most often null), and the version number of your database schema:

```
public static final String DBNAME = "tasksdb.sqlite";
public static final int VERSION =1;
public static final String TABLE_NAME = "tasks";
public static final String ID= "id";
public static final String NAME="name";

public SqlOpenHelper(Context context) {
    super(context, DBNAME, null, VERSION);
}
```

To create a table in SQL, you use the CREATE TABLE statement. Note that Android's API for SQLite assumes that your primary key will be a long integer (long in Java). The primary key column can have any name for now, but when we wrap the data in a ContentProvider in a later recipe (Recipe 10.15) this column is *required* to be named _id, so we'll start on the right foot by using that name now:

```
CREATE TABLE some_table_name (
    _id INTEGER PRIMARY KEY AUTOINCREMENT NOT NULL,
    name TEXT);
```

The SQLiteOpenHelper method onCreate() is called to allow you to create (and possibly populate) the database. At this point the database file exists, so you can use the passed-in SQLiteDatabase object to invoke SQL commands, using its execSql(String) method:

```
public void onCreate(SQLiteDatabase db) {
    createDatabase(db);
}

private void createDatabase(SQLiteDatabase db) {
    db.execSQL("create table " + TABLE_NAME + "(" +
        ID + " integer primary key autoincrement not null, " +
        NAME + " text "
        + ");"
        );
}
```

The table name is needed to insert or retrieve data, so it is customary to identify it in a final String field named TABLE or TABLE_NAME.

To get a "handle" to write to or read from the SQL database you created, instantiate the SQLiteOpenHelper subclass, passing the Android Context (e.g., Activity) into the constructor, then call its getReadableDatabase() method for read-only access or getWritableDatabase() for read/write access:

```
SqlOpenHelper helper = new SqlOpenHelper(this);
SQLiteDatabase database= helper.getWritableDatabase();
```

Inserting data

Now, the SQLiteDatabase database methods can be used to insert and retrieve data. To insert data, we'll use the SQLiteDatabase insert() method and pass an object of type ContentValues.

ContentValues is similar to a Map<String,Object>, a set of key/value pairs. Android does not provide an object-oriented API to the database; you must decompose your object into a ContentValues. The keys must map to the names of columns in the database. For example, NAME could be a final string containing the key (the name of the "Name" column), and Mangoes could be the value. We could pass this to the insert() method to insert a row in the database with the value Mangoes in it. SQLite returns the ID for the newly created row in the database (id):

```
ContentValues values = new ContentValues();
values.put(NAME, "Mangoes");
long id = (database.insert(TABLE_NAME, null, values));
```

Reading data

Now we want to retrieve data from the existing database. To query the database, we use the query() method along with appropriate arguments, most importantly the table name and the column names for which we are extracting values (see Example 10-11). We'll use the returned Cursor object to iterate over the database and process the data.

Example 10-11. Querying and iterating over results

```
ArrayList<Food> foods = new ArrayList();
Cursor listCursor = database.query(TABLE_NAME,
    new String [] {ID, NAME},
    null, null, null, null, NAME);
while (listCursor.moveToNext()) {
    Long id = listCursor.getLong(0);
    String name= listCursor.getString(1);
    Food t = new Food(name);
    foods.add(t);
}
listCursor.close();
```

The moveToNext() method moves the Cursor to the next item and returns true if there is such an item, rather like the JDBC ResultSet.next() in standard Java (there is also moveToFirst() to move back to the first item in the database, a moveToLast() method, and so on). We keep checking until we have reached the end of the database Cursor. Each item of the database is added to an ArrayList. We close the Cursor to free up resources.

There is considerably more functionality available in the query() method, whose most common signature is:[1]

```
Cursor query(String tableName, String[] columns, String selection,
    String[] selectionArgs, String groupBy, String having, String orderBy)
```

The most important of these are the selection and orderBy arguments. Unlike in standard JDBC, the selection argument is just the selection part of the SELECT statement. However, it does use the ? syntax for parameter markers, whose values are taken from the following selectionArgs parameter, which must be an array of Strings regardless of the underlying column types. The orderBy argument is the ORDER BY part of a standard SQL query, which causes the database to return the results in sorted order instead of making the application do the sorting. In both cases, the keywords (SELECT and ORDER BY) must be omitted as they will be added by the database code. Likewise for the SQL keywords GROUP BY and HAVING, if you are familiar with those; their values without the keywords appear as the third-to-last and second-to-last arguments, which are usually null. For example, to obtain a list of customers aged 18 or over living in the US state of New York, sorted by last name, you might use something like this:

```
Cursor custCursor =
    db.query("customer", "age > ? AND state = ? and COUNTRY = ?",
    new String[] { Integer.toString(minAge), "NY", "US" },
    null, null, "lastname ASC");
```

I've written the SQL keywords in uppercase in the query to identify them; this is not required as SQL keywords are not case-sensitive.

10.8 Performing Advanced Text Searches on a SQLite Database

Claudio Esperanca

Problem

You want to implement an advanced "search" capability, and you need to know how to build a data layer to store and search text data using SQLite's full-text search extension.

---

1 There are other signatures; see the official documentation (*https://developer.android.com/reference/android/database/sqlite/SQLiteDatabase.html#pubmethods*) for details.

Solution

Use a SQLite Full-Text Search 3 (FTS3) virtual table and the MATCH function from SQLite to build such a mechanism.

Discussion

By following these steps, you will be able to create an example Android project with a data layer where you will be able to store and retrieve some data using a SQLite database:

1. Create a new Android project (AdvancedSearchProject) targeting a current API level.

2. Specify AdvancedSearch as the application name.

3. Use com.androidcookbook.example.advancedsearch as the package name.

4. Create an Activity with the name AdvancedSearchActivity.

5. Create a new Java class called DbAdapter within the package com.androidcookbook.example.advancedsearch in the *src* folder.

To create the data layer for the example application, enter the Example 10-12 source code in the created file.

Example 10-12. The DbAdapter class

```java
public class DbAdapter {
    public static final String APP_NAME = "AdvancedSearch";
    private static final String DATABASE_NAME = "AdvancedSearch_db";
    private static final int DATABASE_VERSION = 1;
    // Our internal database version (e.g., to control upgrades)
    private static final String TABLE_NAME = "example_tbl";
    public static final String KEY_USERNAME = "username";
    public static final String KEY_FULLNAME = "fullname";
    public static final String KEY_EMAIL = "email";
    public static long GENERIC_ERROR = -1;
    public static long GENERIC_NO_RESULTS = -2;
    public static long ROW_INSERT_FAILED = -3;
    private final Context context;
    private DbHelper dbHelper;
    private SQLiteDatabase sqlDatabase;

    public DbAdapter(Context context) {
        this.context = context;
    }

    private static class DbHelper extends SQLiteOpenHelper {
        private boolean databaseCreated=false;
        DbHelper(Context context) {
            super(context, DATABASE_NAME, null, DATABASE_VERSION);
        }
```

```java
    @Override
    public void onCreate(SQLiteDatabase db) {
        Log.d(APP_NAME, "Creating the application database");

        try {
            // Create the FTS3 virtual table
            db.execSQL(
                "CREATE VIRTUAL TABLE ["+TABLE_NAME+"] USING FTS3 (" +
                    "["+KEY_USERNAME+"] TEXT," +
                    "["+KEY_FULLNAME+"] TEXT," +
                    "["+KEY_EMAIL+"] TEXT" +
                ");"
            );
            this.databaseCreated = true;
        } catch (Exception e) {
            Log.e(APP_NAME,
            "An error occurred while creating the database: " + e.toString(), e);
            this.deleteDatabaseStructure(db);
        }
    }
    public boolean databaseCreated() {
        return this.databaseCreated;
    }
    private boolean deleteDatabaseStructure(SQLiteDatabase db) {
        try {
            db.execSQL("DROP TABLE IF EXISTS ["+TABLE_NAME+"];");
            return true;
        } catch (Exception e) {
            Log.e(APP_NAME,
            "An error occurred while deleting the database: " + e.toString(), e);
        }
        return false;
    }
}

/**
 * Open the database; if the database can't be opened, try to create it
 *
 * @return {@link Boolean} true if database opened/created OK, false otherwise
 * @throws {@link SQLException] if an error occurred
 */
public boolean open() throws SQLException {
    try {
        this.dbHelper = new DbHelper(this.context);
        this.sqlDatabase = this.dbHelper.getWritableDatabase();
        return this.sqlDatabase.isOpen();
    } catch (SQLException e) {
        throw e;
    }
}

/**
 * Close the database connection
 * @return {@link Boolean} true if the connection was terminated, false otherwise
 */
public boolean close() {
```

```java
    this.dbHelper.close();
    return !this.sqlDatabase.isOpen();
}

/**
 * Check if the database was opened
 *
 * @return {@link Boolean} true if it was, false otherwise
 */
public boolean isOpen() {
    return this.sqlDatabase.isOpen();
}

/**
 * Check if the database was created
 *
 * @return {@link Boolean} true if it was, false otherwise
 */
public boolean databaseCreated() {
    return this.dbHelper.databaseCreated();
}

/**
 * Insert a new row i3n the table
 *
 * @param username {@link String} with the username
 * @param fullname {@link String} with the fullname
 * @param email {@link String} with the email
 * @return {@link Long} with the row ID or ROW_INSERT_FAILED (value < 0) on error
 */
public long insertRow(String username, String fullname, String email) {
    try{
        // Prepare the values
        ContentValues values = new ContentValues();
        values.put(KEY_USERNAME, username);
        values.put(KEY_FULLNAME, fullname);
        values.put(KEY_EMAIL, email);

        // Try to insert the row
        return this.sqlDatabase.insert(TABLE_NAME, null, values);
    }catch (Exception e) {
        Log.e(APP_NAME,
            "An error occurred while inserting the row: "+e.toString(), e);
    }
    return ROW_INSERT_FAILED;
}

/**
 * The search() method uses the FTS3 virtual table and
 * the MATCH function from SQLite to search for data.
 * @see http://www.sqlite.org/fts3.html to know more about the syntax.
 * @param search {@link String} with the search expression
 * @return {@link LinkedList} with the {@link String} search results
 */
public LinkedList<String> search(String search) {
```

```
        LinkedList<String> results = new LinkedList<String>();
        Cursor cursor = null;
        try {
            cursor = this.sqlDatabase.query(true, TABLE_NAME, new String[] {
                KEY_USERNAME, KEY_FULLNAME, KEY_EMAIL }, TABLE_NAME + " MATCH ?",
                new String[] { search }, null, null, null, null);

            if(cursor!=null && cursor.getCount()>0 && cursor.moveToFirst()) {
                int iUsername = cursor.getColumnIndex(KEY_USERNAME);
                int iFullname = cursor.getColumnIndex(KEY_FULLNAME);
                int iEmail = cursor.getColumnIndex(KEY_EMAIL);

                do {
                    results.add(
                        new String(
                            "Username: "+cursor.getString(iUsername) +
                            ", Fullname: "+cursor.getString(iFullname) +
                            ", Email: "+cursor.getString(iEmail)
                        )
                    );
                } while(cursor.moveToNext());
            }
        } catch(Exception e) {
            Log.e(APP_NAME,
                "An error occurred while searching for "+search+": "+e.toString(), e);
        } finally {
            if(cursor!=null && !cursor.isClosed()) {
                cursor.close();
            }
        }

        return results;
    }
}
```

Now that the data layer is usable, the AdvancedSearchActivity can be used to test it.

To define the application strings, replace the contents of the *res/values/strings.xml* file with the following:

```
<?xml version="1.0" encoding="utf-8"?>
<resources>
    <string name="label_search">Search</string>
    <string name="app_name">AdvancedSearch</string>
</resources>
```

The application layout can be set within the file *res/layout/main.xml*. This contains the expected EditText (named etSearch), a Button (named btnSearch), and a TextView (named tvResults) to display the results, all in a LinearLayout.

Finally, Example 10-13 shows the *AdvancedSearchActivity.java* code.

Example 10-13. AdvancedSearchActivity.java

```java
public class AdvancedSearchActivity extends Activity {
    private DbAdapter dbAdapter;
    @Override
    public void onCreate(Bundle savedInstanceState) {
        super.onCreate(savedInstanceState);
        setContentView(R.layout.main);

        dbAdapter = new DbAdapter(this);
        dbAdapter.open();

        if(dbAdapter.databaseCreated()) {
            dbAdapter.insertRow("test", "test example", "example_test@example.com");
            dbAdapter.insertRow("lorem", "lorem ipsum", "lorem.ipsum@example2.com");
            dbAdapter.insertRow("jdoe", "Jonh Doe", "j.doe@example.com");
        }

        Button button = (Button) findViewById(R.id.btnSearch);
        final EditText etSearch = (EditText) findViewById(R.id.etSearch);
        final TextView tvResults = (TextView) findViewById(R.id.tvResults);
        button.setOnClickListener(new View.OnClickListener() {
            public void onClick(View v) {
                LinkedList<String> results =
                    dbAdapter.search(etSearch.getText().toString());

                if(results.isEmpty()) {
                    tvResults.setText("No results found");
                } else {
                    Iterator<String> i = results.iterator();
                    tvResults.setText("");
                    while(i.hasNext()) {
                        tvResults.setText(tvResults.getText()+i.next()+"\n");
                    }
                }
            }
        });
    }
    @Override
    protected void onDestroy() {
        dbAdapter.close();
        super.onDestroy();
    }
}
```

See Also

See the SQLite website (*http://www.sqlite.org/fts3.html*) to learn more about the Full-Text Search 3 extension module's capabilities, including the search syntax, and localizeandroid (*https://github.com/cesperanc/localizeandroid*) to learn about a project with an implementation of this search mechanism.

10.9 Working with Dates in SQLite

Jonathan Fuerth

Problem

Android's embedded SQLite3 database supports date and time data directly, including some useful date and time arithmetic. However, getting these dates out of the database is troublesome: there is no `Cursor.getDate()` in the Android API.

Solution

Use SQLite's `strftime()` function to convert between the SQLite timestamp format and the Java API's "milliseconds since the epoch" representation.

Discussion

This recipe demonstrates the advantages of using SQLite timestamps over storing raw millisecond values in your database, and shows how to retrieve those timestamps from your database as `java.util.Date` objects.

Background

The usual representation for an absolute timestamp in Unix is `time_t`, which historically was just an alias for a 32-bit integer. This integer represented the date as the number of seconds elapsed since UTC 00:00 on January 1, 1970 (the Unix *epoch*). On systems where `time_t` is still a 32-bit integer, the clock will roll over partway through the year 2038.

Java adopted a similar convention, but with a few twists. The epoch remains the same, but the count is always stored in a 64-bit signed integer (the native Java `long` type) and the units are milliseconds rather than seconds. This method of timekeeping will not roll over for another 292 million years.

Android example code that deals with persisting dates and times tends to simply store and retrieve the raw *milliseconds since the epoch* values in the database. However, by doing this, it misses out on some useful features built into SQLite.

The advantages

There are several advantages to storing proper SQLite timestamps in your data: you can default timestamp columns to the current time using no Java code at all; you can perform calendar-sensitive arithmetic such as selecting the first day of a week or month, or adding a week to the value stored in the database; and you can extract just the date or time components and return those from your data provider.

All of these code-saving advantages come with two added bonuses: first, your data provider's API can stick to the Android convention of passing timestamps around as `long` values; second, all of this date manipulation is done in the natively compiled SQLite code, so the manipulations don't incur the garbage collection overhead of creating multiple `java.util.Date` or `java.util.Calendar` objects.

The code

Without further ado, here's how to do it.

First, create a table that defines a column of type `timestamp`:

```
CREATE TABLE current_list (
        item_id INTEGER NOT NULL,
        added_on TIMESTAMP NOT NULL DEFAULT current_timestamp,
        added_by VARCHAR(50) NOT NULL,
        quantity INTEGER NOT NULL,
        units VARCHAR(50) NOT NULL,
        CONSTRAINT current_list_pk PRIMARY KEY (item_id)
);
```

Note the default value for the `added_on` column. Whenever you insert a row into this table, SQLite will automatically fill in the current time, accurate to the second, for the new record (this is shown here using the command-line SQLite program running on a desktop; we'll see later in this recipe how to get these into a database under Android):

```
sqlite> insert into current_list (item_id, added_by, quantity, units)
   ...> values (1, 'fuerth', 1, 'EA');
sqlite> select * from current_list where item_id = 1;
1|2020-05-14 23:10:26|fuerth|1|EA
sqlite>
```

See how the current date was inserted automatically? This is one of the advantages you get from working with SQLite timestamps.

How about the other advantages?

Select just the date part, forcing the time back to midnight:

```
sqlite> select item_id, date(added_on,'start of day')
   ...> from current_list where item_id = 1;
1|2020-05-14
sqlite>
```

Or adjust the date to the Monday of the following week:

```
sqlite> select item_id, date(added_on,'weekday 1')
   ...> from current_list where item_id = 1;
1|2020-05-17
sqlite>
```

Or the Monday before:

```
sqlite> select item_id, date(added_on,'weekday 1','-7 days')
   ...> from current_list where item_id = 1;
1|2020-05-10
sqlite>
```

These examples are just the tip of the iceberg. You can do a lot of useful things with your timestamps once SQLite recognizes them as such.

Last, but not least, you must be wondering how to get these dates back into your Java code. The trick is to press another of SQLite's date functions into service—this time strftime(). Here is a Java method that fetches a row from the current_list table we've been working with:

```
Cursor cursor = database.rawQuery(
        "SELECT item_id AS _id," +
        " (strftime('%s', added_on) * 1000) AS added_on," +
        " added_by, quantity, units" +
        " FROM current_list", new String[0]);
long millis = cursor.getLong(cursor.getColumnIndexOrThrow("added_on"));
Date addedOn = new Date(millis);
```

That's it: using strftime()'s %s format, you can select timestamps directly into your Cursor as Java *milliseconds since the epoch* values. Client code will be none the wiser, except that your content provider will be able to do date manipulations for free that would otherwise take significant amounts of Java code and extra object allocations.

See Also

SQLite's documentation for its date and time functions (*http://www.sqlite.org/lang_datefunc.html*).

10.10 Exposing Non-SQL Data as a SQL Cursor

Ian Darwin

Problem

You have non-SQL data, such as a list of files, and want to present it as a Cursor.

Solution

Subclass AbstractCursor and implement various required methods.

Discussion

It is common to have data in a form other than a Cursor, but to want to present it as a Cursor for use in a ListView with an Adapter or a CursorLoader.

The `AbstractCursor` class facilitates this. While `Cursor` is an interface that you could implement directly, there are a number of routines therein that are pretty much the same in every implementation of `Cursor`, so they have been abstracted out and made into the `AbstractCursor` class.

In this short example we expose a list of filenames with the following structure:

- `_id` is the sequence number.
- `filename` is the full path.
- `type` is the filename extension.

This list of files is hardcoded to simplify the demo. We will expose this as a `Cursor` and consume it in a `SimpleCursorAdapter`. First, the start of the `DataToCursor` class:

```
/**
 * Provide a Cursor from a fixed list of data
 * column 1 - _id
 * column 2 - filename
 * column 3 - file type
 */
public class DataToCursor extends AbstractCursor {

    private static final String[] COLUMN_NAMES = {"_id", "filename", "type"};

    private static final String[] DATA_ROWS = {
        "one.mpg",
        "two.jpg",
        "tre.dat",
        "fou.git",
    };
```

As you can see, there are two arrays: one for the column names going across, and one for the rows going down. In this simple example we don't have to track the ID values (since they are the same as the index into the `DATA_ROWS` array) or the file types (since they are the same as the filename extension).

There are a few structural methods that are needed:

```
@Override
public int getCount() {
    return DATA.length;
}

@Override
public int getColumnCount() {
    return COLUMN_NAMES.length;
}

@Override
public String[] getColumnNames() {
    return COLUMN_NAMES;
}
```

The `getColumnCount()` method's value is obviously derivable from the array, but since it's constant, we override the method for efficiency reasons—probably not necessary in most applications.

Then there are some necessary get methods, notably `getType()` for getting the type of a given column (whether it's numeric, string, etc.):

```
@Override
public int getType(int column) {
    switch(column) {
    case 0:
        return Cursor.FIELD_TYPE_INTEGER;
    case 1:
    case 2:
        return Cursor.FIELD_TYPE_STRING;
    default: throw new IllegalArgumentException(Integer.toString(column));
    }
}
```

The next methods have to do with getting the value of a given column in the current row. Nicely, the `AbstractCursor` handles all the `moveToRow()` and related methods, so we just have to call the inherited (and protected) method `getPosition()`:

```
/**
 * Return the _id value (the only integer-valued column).
 * Conveniently, rows and array indices are both 0-based.
 */
@Override
public int getInt(int column) {
    int row = getPosition();
    switch(column) {
        case 0: return row;
        default: throw new IllegalArgumentException(Integer.toString(column));
    }
}

/** SQLite _ids are actually long, so make this work as well.
 * This direct equivalence is usually not applicable; do not blindly copy.
 */
@Override
public long getLong(int column) {
    return getInt(column);
}

@Override
public String getString(int column) {
    int row = getPosition();
    switch(column) {
        case 1: return DATA_ROWS[row];
        case 2: return extension(DATA_ROWS[row]);
        default: throw new IllegalArgumentException(Integer.toString(column));
    }
}
```

The remaining methods aren't interesting; methods like getFloat(), getBlob(), and so on merely throw exceptions as, in this example, there are no columns of those types.

The main Activity shows nothing different than the other ListView examples in Chapter 8: the data from the Cursor is loaded into a ListView using a SimpleCursorAdapter (this overload of which is deprecated, but works fine for this example).

The result is shown in Figure 10-6.

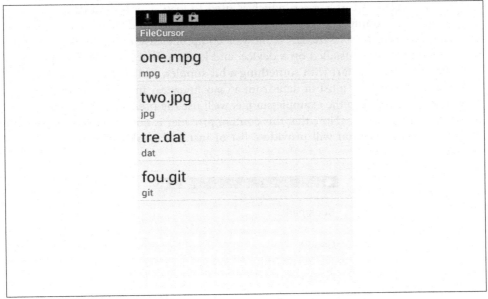

Figure 10-6. Main Activity with synthetic Cursor data

We have successfully shown this proof-of-concept of generating a Cursor without using SQLite. It would obviously be straightforward to turn this into a more dynamic file-listing utility, even a file manager. You'd want to use a CursorLoader instead of a SimpleCursorAdapter to make it complete, though; CursorLoader is covered in the next recipe.

10.11 Displaying Data with a CursorLoader

Ian Darwin

Problem

You need to fetch information via a database Cursor and display it in a graphical user interface with correct use of threads to avoid blocking the UI thread.

Solution

Use a `CursorLoader`.

Discussion

`Loader` is a top-level class that provides a basic capability for loading almost any type of data. `AsyncTaskLoader<T>` provides a specialization of `Loader` to handle threading. Its important subclass is `CursorLoader`, which is used to load data from a database `Cursor` and, typically in conjunction with a Fragment or Activity, to display it. The Android documentation for `AsyncTaskLoader<T>` shows a comprehensive example of loading the list of all applications installed on a device, and keeping that information up-to-date as it changes. We will start with something a bit simpler, which reads (as `CursorLoader` classes are expected to) a list of data from a `ContentProvider` implementation, and displays it in a list. To keep the example simple, we'll use the preinstalled Browser Bookmarks content provider. (Note that this content provider is not available in Android 7 or later). The application will provide a list of installed bookmarks, similar to that shown in Figure 10-7.

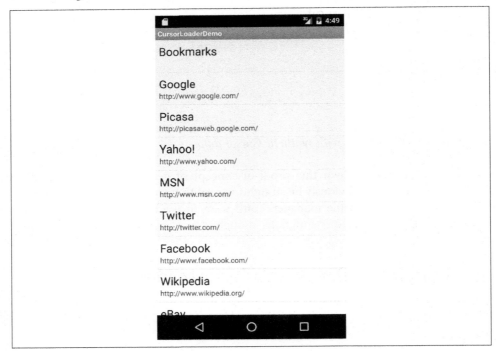

Figure 10-7. CursorLoader showing Browser Bookmarks

To use the `Loader`, you have to provide an implementation of the `LoaderManager.LoaderCallbacks<T>` interface, where `T` is the type you want to load from; in our case, `Cursor`. While most examples have the Activity or Fragment directly implement this, we'll make it an inner class just to isolate it, and make more of the argument types explicit.

We start off in `onCreate()` or `onResume()` by creating a `SimpleCursorAdapter`. The constructor for this adapter—the mainstay of many a list-based application in prior releases of Android—is now deprecated, but calling it with an additional `flags` argument (the final 0 argument here) for use with the `Loader` family is not deprecated. Other than the final `flags` arg, and passing `null` for the `Cursor`, the code is largely the same as our non-Loader-based example, *ContentProviderBookmarks*, which has been left in the Android Cookbook repository to show "the old way." With the extra `flags` argument the `Cursor` may be `null`, as we will provide it later, in the `LoaderCallbacks` code (Example 10-14):

```
@Override
protected void onCreate(Bundle savedInstanceState) {
    super.onCreate(savedInstanceState);
    setContentView(R.layout.activity_main);

    String[] fromFields = new String[] {
            Browser.BookmarkColumns.TITLE,
            Browser.BookmarkColumns.URL
    };
    int[] toViews = new int[] { android.R.id.text1, android.R.id.text2 };
    mAdapter = new SimpleCursorAdapter(this, android.R.layout.simple_list_item_2,
            null, fromFields, toViews, 0);
    setListAdapter(mAdapter);

    // Prepare the loader: reconnects an existing one or reuses one
    getLoaderManager().initLoader(0, null, new MyCallbacks(this));
}
```

Note also the last line, which will find a `Loader` instance and associate our callbacks with it. The callbacks are where the actual work gets done. There are three required methods in the `LoaderCallbacks` object:

`onCreateLoader()`
Called to create an instance of the actual loader; the framework will start it, which will perform a `ContentProvider` query

`onLoadFinished()`
Called when the loader has finished loading its data, to set its cursor to the one from the query

`onLoaderReset()`
Called when the loader is done, to disassociate it from the view (by setting its cursor back to `null`)

Our implementation is fairly simple. As we want all the columns and don't care about the order, we only need to provide the bookmarks Uri, which is predefined for us (see Example 10-14).

Example 10-14. The LoaderCallbacks implementation

```
class MyCallbacks implements LoaderCallbacks<Cursor> {
    Context context;

    public MyCallbacks(Activity context) {
        this.context = context;
    }

    @Override
    public Loader<Cursor> onCreateLoader(int id, Bundle stuff) {
        Log.d(TAG, "MainActivity.onCreateLoader()");
        return new CursorLoader(context,
                // Normal CP query: url, proj, select, where, having
                Browser.BOOKMARKS_URI, null, null, null, null);
    }

    @Override
    public void onLoadFinished(Loader<Cursor> loader, Cursor data) {
        // Load has finished, swap the loaded cursor into the view
        mAdapter.swapCursor(data);
    }

    @Override
    public void onLoaderReset(Loader<Cursor> loader) {
        // The end of time: set cursor to null to prevent bad ending
        mAdapter.swapCursor(null);
    }
}
```

The Loader family is quite sophisticated; it lets you load a Cursor in the background then adapt it to the GUI. The AsyncTaskLoader<T>, as the name implies, uses an AsyncTask (see Recipe 4.10) to do the data loading on a background thread and runs the updating on the UI thread. Its subclass, the CursorLoader, is now the tool of choice for loading lists of data.

Source Download URL

The source code for this example is in the Android Cookbook repository (*https://github.com/IanDarwin/Android-Cookbook-Examples*), in the subdirectory *CursorLoaderDemo* (see "Getting and Using the Code Examples" on page 18).

10.12 Parsing JSON Using JSONObject

Rachee Singh

Problem

JavaScript Object Notation (JSON) is a simple text format for data interchange. Many websites provide data in JSON, and many applications need to parse and provide JSON data.

Solution

While there are a couple of dozen Java APIs for JSON listed on the JSON website (*http://json.org/*), we'll use the built-in JSONObject class to parse JSON and retrieve the data values contained in it.

Discussion

For this recipe, we will use a method to generate JSON code. In a real application you would likely obtain the JSON data from some web service. In this method we make use of a JSONObject class object to put in values and then to return the corresponding string (using the toString() method). Creating an object of type JSONObject can throw a JSONException, so we enclose the code in a try-catch block (see Example 10-15).

Example 10-15. Generating mock data in JSON format

```java
private String getJsonString() {
    JSONObject string = new JSONObject();
    try {
        string.put("name", "John Doe");
        string.put("age", new Integer(25));
        string.put("address", "75 Ninth Avenue, New York, NY 10011");
        string.put("phone", "8367667829");
    } catch (JSONException e) {
        e.printStackTrace();
    }
    return string.toString();
}
```

We need to instantiate an object of class JSONObject that takes the JSON string as an argument. In this case, the JSON string is being obtained from the getJsonString() method. We extract the information from the JSONObject and print it in a TextView (see Example 10-16).

Example 10-16. Parsing the JSON string and retrieving values

```java
try {
    String jsonString = getJsonString();
    JSONObject jsonObject = new JSONObject(jsonString);
    String name = jsonObject.getString("name");
    String age = jsonObject.getString("age");
    String address = jsonObject.getString("address");
```

```
        String phone = jsonObject.getString("phone");
        String jsonText = name + "\n" + age + "\n" + address + "\n" + phone;
        json = (TextView)findViewById(R.id.json);
        json.setText(jsonText);
    } catch (JSONException e) {
        // Display the exception...
    }
```

See Also

For more information on JavaScript Object Notation, see the JSON website (*http://json.org/*).

There are about two dozen JSON APIs for Java alone. One of the more powerful ones —which includes a data-binding package that will automatically convert between Java objects and JSON—is JackSON (*https://github.com/FasterXML/jackson*).

Source Download URL

The source code for this project is in the Android Cookbook repository (*https://github.com/IanDarwin/Android-Cookbook-Examples*), in the subdirectory *JSONParsing* (see "Getting and Using the Code Examples" on page 18).

10.13 Parsing an XML Document Using the DOM API

Ian Darwin

Problem

You have data in XML, and you want to transform it into something useful in your application.

Solution

Android provides a fairly good clone of the standard DOM API used in the Java Standard Edition. Using the DOM API instead of writing your own parsing code is clearly the more efficient approach.

Discussion

Example 10-17 is the code that parses the XML document containing the list of recipes in this book, as discussed in Recipe 12.1. The input file has a single recipes root element, followed by a sequence of recipe elements, each with an id and a title with textual content.

The code creates a DOM DocumentBuilderFactory, which can be tailored, for example, to make schema-aware parsers. In real code you could create this in a static initializer instead of re-creating it each time. The DocumentBuilderFactory is used to create a document builder, a.k.a. parser. The parser expects to be reading from an InputStream, so we convert the data that we have in string form into an array of bytes and construct a ByteArrayInputStream. Again, in real life you would probably want to combine this code with the web service consumer so that you could simply get the input stream from the network connection and read the XML directly into the parser, instead of saving it as a string and then wrapping that in a converter as we do here.

Once the elements are parsed, we convert the document into an array of data (the singular of data is datum, so the class is called Datum) by calling tDOM API methods such as getDocumentElement(), getChildNodes(), and getNodeValue(). Since the DOM API was not invented by Java people, it doesn't use the standard Collections API but has its own collections, like NodeList. In DOM's defense, the same or similar APIs are used in a really wide variety of programming languages, so it can be said to be as much a standard as Java's Collections.

Example 10-17 shows the code.

Example 10-17. Parsing XML code

```java
/** Convert the list of Recipes in the String result from the
 * web service into an ArrayList of Datum objects.
 * @throws ParserConfigurationException
 * @throws IOException
 * @throws SAXException
 */
public static ArrayList<Datum> parse(String input) throws Exception {

    final ArrayList<Datum> results = new ArrayList<Datum>(1000);
    final DocumentBuilderFactory dbFactory =
        DocumentBuilderFactory.newInstance();
    final DocumentBuilder parser = dbFactory.newDocumentBuilder();

    final Document document =
        parser.parse(new ByteArrayInputStream(input.getBytes()));

    Element root = document.getDocumentElement();
    NodeList recipesList = root.getChildNodes();
    for (int i = 0; i < recipesList.getLength(); i++) {
        Node recipe = recipesList.item(i);
        NodeList fields = recipe.getChildNodes();
        String id = ((Element) fields.item(0)).getNodeValue();
        String title =
            ((Element) fields.item(1)).getNodeValue();
        Datum d = new Datum(Integer.parseInt(id), title);
        results.add(d);
    }
    return results;
}
```

In converting this code from Java SE to Android, the only change we had to make was to use `getNodeValue()` in the retrieval of `id` and `title` instead of Java SE's `getTextContent()`, so the API really is very close.

See Also

The web service is discussed in Recipe 12.1. There is much more in the XML chapter of my *Java Cookbook* (O'Reilly).

Should you wish to process XML in a streaming mode, you can use the XMLPull-Parser, documented in the online version of this Cookbook (*https://androidcook book.com/r/2217*).

10.14 Storing and Retrieving Data via a Content Provider

Ian Darwin

Problem

You want to read from and write to a `ContentProvider` such as Contacts.

Solution

One way is to create a `Content Uri` using constants provided by the `ContentProvider` and use `Activity.getContentResolver().query()`, which returns a SQLite `Cursor` object. Another way, useful if you want to select one record such as a single contact, is to create a `PICK Uri`, open it in an Intent using `startActivityForResult()`, extract the URI from the returned Intent, then perform the query as just described.

Discussion

This is part of the contact selection code from TabbyText, my SMS-over-WiFi text message sender (the rest of its code is in Recipe 10.17).

First, the main program sets up an `OnClickListener` to use the Contacts app as a chooser, from a Find Contact button:

```
b.setOnClickListener(new View.OnClickListener() {
    @Override
    public void onClick(View arg0) {
        Uri uri = ContactsContract.Contacts.CONTENT_URI;
        System.out.println(uri);
        Intent intent = new Intent(Intent.ACTION_PICK, uri);
        startActivityForResult(intent, REQ_GET_CONTACT);
    }
});
```

The URI is predefined for us; it actually has the value `content://com.android.contacts/contacts`. The constant `REQ_GET_CONTACT` is arbitrary; it's just there to associate this Intent start-up with the handler code, since more complex apps will often start more than one Intent and they need to handle the results differently. Once this button is pressed, control passes from our app out to the Contacts app. The user can then select a contact she wishes to send an SMS message to. The Contacts app then is backgrounded and control returns to our app at the `onActivityResult()` method, to indicate that the Activity we started has completed and delivered a result.

The next bit of code shows how the `onActivityResult()` method converts the response from the Activity into a SQLite cursor (see Example 10-18).

Example 10-18. onActivityResult()

```
@Override
protected void onActivityResult(int requestCode, int resultCode, Intent data) {
    if (requestCode == REQ_GET_CONTACT) {
        switch(resultCode) {
        case Activity.RESULT_OK:
        // The Contacts API is about the most complex to use.
        // First retrieve the Contact, as we only get its URI from the Intent.
        Uri resultUri = data.getData(); // E.g., content://contacts/people/123
        Cursor cont = getContentResolver().query(resultUri, null, null, null, null);
        if (!cont.moveToNext()) {     // Expect exactly one row
            Toast.makeText(this, "Cursor has no data", Toast.LENGTH_LONG).show();
            return;
        }
        ...
```

There are a few key things to note here. First, make sure the `request Code` is the one you started, and the `resultCode` is `RESULT_OK` or `RESULT_CANCELED` (if not, pop up a warning dialog). Then, extract the URL for the response you picked—the Intent data from the returned Intent—and use that to create a query, using the inherited `Activity` method `getContentResolver()` to get the `ContentResolver` and its `query()` method to make up a SQLite cursor.

We expect the user to have selected one contact, so if that's not the case we error out. Otherwise, we'd go ahead and use the SQLite cursor to read the data. The exact formatting of the Contacts database is a bit out of scope for this recipe, so it's been deferred to Recipe 10.17.

To insert data, we need to create a `ContentValues` object and populate it with the fields. Once that's done, we use the `ContentContracts`-provided base `Uri` value, along with the `ContentValues`, to insert the values, somewhat like the following:

```
mNewUri = getContentResolver().
    insert(ContactsContract.Contacts.CONTENT_URI, contentValues);
```

You could then put the `mNewUri` into an Intent and display it.

This is shown in more detail in Recipe 10.16.

10.15 Writing a Content Provider

Ashwini Shahapurkar, Ian Darwin

Problem

You want to expose data from your application without giving direct access to your application's database.

Solution

Write a ContentProvider that will allow other applications to access data contained in your app.

Discussion

ContentProviders allow other applications to access the data generated by your app. A custom ContentProvider is effectively a wrapper around your existing application data (typically but not necessarily contained in a SQLite database; see Recipe 10.7). Remember that just because you *can* do so doesn't mean that you *should*; in particular, you generally do not need to write a ContentProvider just to access your data from within your application.

To make other apps aware that a ContentProvider is available, we need to declare it in *AndroidManifest.xml* as follows:

```
<application ...>
    <activity .../>
    <provider
        android:authorities="com.example.contentprovidersample"
        android:name="MyContentProvider" />
</application>
```

The android:authorities attribute is a string used throughout the system to identify your ContentProvider; it should also be declared in a public static final String variable in your provider class. The android:name attribute refers to the class MyContentProvider, which extends the ContentProvider class. We need to override the following methods in this class:

```
onCreate();
getType(Uri);

insert(Uri, ContentValues);
query(Uri, String[], String, String[], String);
update(Uri, ContentValues, String, String[]);
delete(Uri, String, String[]);
```

The onCreate() method is for setup, as in any other Android component. Our example just creates a SQLite database in a field:

```
mDatabase = new MyDatabaseHelper(this);
```

The getType() method assigns MIME types to incoming Uri values. This method will typically use a statically allocated UriMatcher to determine whether the incoming Uri refers to a list of values (does not end with a numeric ID) or a single value (ends with a / and a numeric ID, indicated by "/#" in the pattern argument). The method must return either ContentResolver.CURSOR_ITEM_BASE_TYPE + "/" + MIME_VND_TYPE for a single item or ContentResolver.CURSOR_DIR_BASE_TYPE + "/" + MIME_VND_TYPE for a multiplicity, where MIME_VND_TYPE is an application-specific MIME type string; in our example that's "vnd.example.item". It must begin with "vnd," which stands, throughout this paragraph, for "Vendor," as these values are not provided by the official MIME type committee but by Android. The UriMatcher is also used in the four data methods shown next to sort out singular from plural requests. Example 10-19 contains the declarations and code for the matcher and the getType() method.

Example 10-19. Declarations and code for the UriMatcher and the getType() method

```
public class MyContentProvider extends ContentProvider {

    /** The authority name. MUST be as listed in
     * <provider android:authorities=...> in AndroidManifest.xml
     */
    public static final String AUTHORITY = "com.example.contentprovidersample";

    public static final String MIME_VND_TYPE = "vnd.example.item";

    private static final UriMatcher matcher = new UriMatcher(UriMatcher.NO_MATCH);

    private static final int ITEM = 1;
    private static final int ITEMS = 2;
    static {
        matcher.addURI(AUTHORITY, "items/#", ITEM);
        matcher.addURI(AUTHORITY, "items", ITEMS);
    }

    @Override
    public String getType(Uri uri) {
        int matchType = matcher.match(uri);
        Log.d("ReadingsContentProvider.getType()", uri + " --> " + matchType);
        switch (matchType) {
        case ITEM:
            return ContentResolver.CURSOR_ITEM_BASE_TYPE + "/" + MIME_VND_TYPE;
        case ITEMS:
            return ContentResolver.CURSOR_DIR_BASE_TYPE + "/" + MIME_VND_TYPE;
        default:
            throw new IllegalArgumentException("Unknown or Invalid URI " + uri);
        }
    }
}
```

The last four methods are usually wrapper functions for SQL queries on the SQLite database; note that they have the same parameter lists as the like-named SQLite methods, with the insertion of a Uri at the front of the parameter list. These methods typically parse the input parameters, do some error checking, and forward the operation on to the SQLite database, as shown in Example 10-20.

Example 10-20. The ContentProvider: data methods

```
/** The C of CRUD: insert() */
@Override
public Uri insert(Uri uri, ContentValues values) {
    Log.d(Constants.TAG, "MyContentProvider.insert()");
    switch(matcher.match(uri)) {
    case ITEM: // Fail
        throw new RuntimeException("Cannot specify ID when inserting");
    case ITEMS: // OK
        break;
    default:
        throw new IllegalArgumentException("Did not recognize URI " + uri);
    }

    long id = mDatabase.getWritableDatabase().insert(
            TABLE_NAME, null, values);
    uri = Uri.withAppendedPath(uri, "/" + id);
    getContext().getContentResolver().notifyChange(uri, null);
    return uri;
}

/** The R of CRUD: query() */
@Override
public Cursor query(Uri uri, String[] projection, String selection,
        String[] selectionArgs, String sortOrder) {
    Log.d(Constants.TAG, "MyContentProvider.query()");
    switch(matcher.match(uri)) {
    case ITEM: // OK
        selection = "_id = ?";
        selectionArgs = new String[]{ Long.toString(ContentUris.parseId(uri)) };
        break;
    case ITEMS: // OK
        break;
    default:
        throw new IllegalArgumentException("Did not recognize URI " + uri);
    }
    // Build the query with SQLiteQueryBuilder
    SQLiteQueryBuilder qBuilder = new SQLiteQueryBuilder();
    qBuilder.setTables(TABLE_NAME);

    // Query the database and get result in cursor
    final SQLiteDatabase db = mDatabase.getWritableDatabase();
    Cursor resultCursor = qBuilder.query(db,
            projection, selection, selectionArgs, null, null, sortOrder,
            null);
    resultCursor.setNotificationUri(getContext().getContentResolver(), uri);
```

```
        return resultCursor;
    }
}
```

The remaining methods, `update()` and `delete()`, are parallel in structure and so have been omitted from this book to save space, but the online example is fully fleshed out.

Providing a `ContentProvider` lets you expose your data without giving other developers direct access to your database and also reduces the chances of database inconsistency.

Source Download URL

The source code for this recipe is in the Android Cookbook repository (*https://github.com/IanDarwin/Android-Cookbook-Examples*), in the subdirectory *Content-ProviderSample* (see "Getting and Using the Code Examples" on page 18).

10.16 Adding a Contact Through the Contacts Content Provider

Ian Darwin

Problem

You have a person's contact information that you want to save for use by the Contacts application and other apps on your device.

Solution

Set up a list of operations for batch insert, and tell the persistence manager to run it.

Discussion

The `Contacts` database is, to be sure, "flexible." It has to adapt to many different kinds of accounts and contact management uses, with different types of data. And it is, as a result, somewhat complicated.

> The classes named `Contacts` (and, by extension, all their inner classes and interfaces) are deprecated, meaning "don't use them in new development." The classes and interfaces that take their place have names beginning with the somewhat cumbersome and tongue-twisting `ContactsContract`.

We'll start with the simplest case of adding a person's contact information. We want to insert the following information, which we either got from the user or found on the network someplace:

Name	Jon Smith
Home Phone	416-555-5555
Work Phone	416-555-6666
Email	jon@jonsmith.domain

First we have to determine which Android account to associate the data with. For now we will use a fake account name (*darwinian* is both an adjective and my name, so we'll use that).

For each of the four fields, we'll need to create an account operation.

We add all five operations to a List, and pass that into getContentResolver().applyBatch().

Example 10-21 shows the code for the addContact() method.

Example 10-21. The addContact() method

```
private void addContact() {
    final String ACCOUNT_NAME = "darwinian"
    String name = "Jon Smith";
    String homePhone = "416-555-5555";
    String workPhone = "416-555-6666";
    String email = "jon@jonsmith.domain";

    // Use new-style Contacts batch operations.
    // Build List of ops, then call applyBatch().
    try {
        ArrayList<ContentProviderOperation> ops =
            new ArrayList<ContentProviderOperation>();
        AuthenticatorDescription[] types = accountManager.getAuthenticatorTypes();
        ops.add(ContentProviderOperation.newInsert(
            ContactsContract.RawContacts.CONTENT_URI).withValue(
                ContactsContract.RawContacts.ACCOUNT_TYPE, types[0].type)
                .withValue(ContactsContract.RawContacts.ACCOUNT_NAME, ACCOUNT_NAME)
                .build());
        ops.add(ContentProviderOperation
            .newInsert(ContactsContract.Data.CONTENT_URI)
            .withValueBackReference(ContactsContract.Data.RAW_CONTACT_ID, 0)
            .withValue(ContactsContract.Data.MIMETYPE,
                ContactsContract.CommonDataKinds.StructuredName.CONTENT_ITEM_TYPE)
                .withValue
                    (ContactsContract.CommonDataKinds.StructuredName.DISPLAY_NAME,name)
                .build());
        ops.add(ContentProviderOperation.newInsert(
            ContactsContract.Data.CONTENT_URI).withValueBackReference(
                ContactsContract.Data.RAW_CONTACT_ID, 0).withValue(
```

```
            ContactsContract.Data.MIMETYPE,
            ContactsContract.CommonDataKinds.Phone.CONTENT_ITEM_TYPE)
            .withValue(ContactsContract.CommonDataKinds.Phone.NUMBER,
            homePhone).withValue(
                    ContactsContract.CommonDataKinds.Phone.TYPE,
                    ContactsContract.CommonDataKinds.Phone.TYPE_HOME)
        .build());
    ops.add(ContentProviderOperation.newInsert(
        ContactsContract.Data.CONTENT_URI).withValueBackReference(
            ContactsContract.Data.RAW_CONTACT_ID, 0).withValue(
            ContactsContract.Data.MIMETYPE,
            ContactsContract.CommonDataKinds.Phone.CONTENT_ITEM_TYPE)
            .withValue(ContactsContract.CommonDataKinds.Phone.NUMBER,
                workPhone).withValue(
                    ContactsContract.CommonDataKinds.Phone.TYPE,
                    ContactsContract.CommonDataKinds.Phone.TYPE_WORK)
        .build());
    ops.add(ContentProviderOperation.newInsert(
        ContactsContract.Data.CONTENT_URI).withValueBackReference(
            ContactsContract.Data.RAW_CONTACT_ID, 0).withValue(
            ContactsContract.Data.MIMETYPE,
            ContactsContract.CommonDataKinds.Email.CONTENT_ITEM_TYPE)
            .withValue(ContactsContract.CommonDataKinds.Email.DATA,email)
            .withValue(ContactsContract.CommonDataKinds.Email.TYPE,
                    ContactsContract.CommonDataKinds.Email.TYPE_HOME)
        .build());

    getContentResolver().applyBatch(ContactsContract.AUTHORITY, ops);

    Toast.makeText(this, getString(R.string.addContactSuccess),
        Toast.LENGTH_LONG).show();
} catch (Exception e) {

    Toast.makeText(this, getString(R.string.addContactFailure),
        Toast.LENGTH_LONG).show();
    Log.e(LOG_TAG, getString(R.string.addContactFailure), e);
    }
}
```

The resultant contact shows up in the Contacts app, as shown in Figure 10-8. If the new contact is not initially visible, go to the main Contacts list page, press Menu, select Display Options, and select Groups until it does appear. Alternatively, you can search in All Contacts and it will show up.

Source Download URL

The source code for this project is in the Android Cookbook repository (*https://github.com/IanDarwin/Android-Cookbook-Examples*), in the subdirectory *AddContact* (see "Getting and Using the Code Examples" on page 18).

Figure 10-8. Contact added

10.17 Reading Contact Data Using a Content Provider

Ian Darwin

Problem

You need to extract details, such as a phone number or email address, from the Contacts database.

Solution

Use an Intent to let the user pick one contact. Use a `ContentResolver` to create a SQLite query for the chosen contact, and use SQLite and predefined constants in the confusingly named `ContactsContract` class to retrieve the parts you want. Be aware that the Contacts database was designed for generality, not for simplicity.

Discussion

The code in Example 10-22 is from TabbyText, my SMS/text message sender for tablets. The user has already picked the given contact (using the Contactz app; see Recipe 10.14). Here we want to extract the mobile number and save it in a text field in the current Activity, so the user can post-edit it if need be, or even reject it, before actually sending the message, so we just set the text in an `EditText` once we find it.

Finding it turns out to be the hard part. We start with a query that we get from the `ContentProvider`, to extract the ID field for the given contact. Information such as phone numbers and email addresses are in their own tables, so we need a second query to feed in the ID as part of the "select" part of the query. This query gives a list of the contact's phone numbers. We iterate through this, taking each valid phone number and setting it on the `EditText`.

A further elaboration would restrict this to only selecting the mobile number (some versions of Contacts allow both home and work numbers, but only one mobile number).

Example 10-22. Getting the contact from the Intent query's ContentResolver

```java
@Override
protected void onActivityResult(int requestCode, int resultCode, Intent data) {
    if (requestCode == REQ_GET_CONTACT) {
        switch(resultCode) {
        case Activity.RESULT_OK:
            // The Contacts API is about the most complex to use.
            // First we have to retrieve the Contact, since
            // we only get its URI from the Intent.
            Uri resultUri = data.getData(); // E.g., content://contacts/people/123
            Cursor cont =
                getContentResolver().query(resultUri, null, null, null, null);
            if (!cont.moveToNext()) {    // Expect 001 row(s)
                Toast.makeText(this,
                    "Cursor contains no data", Toast.LENGTH_LONG).show();
                return;
            }
            int columnIndexForId =
                cont.getColumnIndex(ContactsContract.Contacts._ID);
            String contactId =
                cont.getString(columnIndexForId);
            int columnIndexForHasPhone =
                cont.getColumnIndex(ContactsContract.Contacts.HAS_PHONE_NUMBER);
            boolean hasAnyPhone =
                Boolean.parseBoolean(cont.getString(columnIndexForHasPhone));
            if (!hasAnyPhone) {
                Toast.makeText(this,
                    "Selected contact seems to have no phone numbers ",
                    Toast.LENGTH_LONG).show();
            }

            // Now we have to do another query to actually get the numbers!
            Cursor numbers = getContentResolver().query(
                    ContactsContract.CommonDataKinds.Phone.CONTENT_URI,
                    null,
                    ContactsContract.CommonDataKinds.Phone.CONTACT_ID +
                    "=" + contactId, // "selection",
```

```
                null, null);
    // Could further restrict to mobile number...
    while (numbers.moveToNext()) {
        String aNumber = numbers.getString(numbers.getColumnIndex(
            ContactsContract.CommonDataKinds.Phone.NUMBER));
        System.out.println(aNumber);
        number.setText(aNumber);
    }
    if (cont.moveToNext()) {
        System.out.println(
            "WARNING: More than 1 contact returned by picker!");
    }
    numbers.close();
    cont.close();
    break;
case Activity.RESULT_CANCELED:
    // Nothing to do here
    break;
default:
    Toast.makeText(this, "Unexpected resultCode: " + resultCode,
        Toast.LENGTH_LONG).show();
    break;
    }
  }
  super.onActivityResult(requestCode, resultCode, data);
}
```

Source Download URL

You can download the source code for this example from GitHub (*https://github.com/ IanDarwin/TabbyText.git*).

10.18 Implementing Drag and Drop

Ian Darwin

Problem

You want to implement drag-and-drop, similar to what the Home screen/launcher does when you long-press on an application icon.

Solution

Use the drag and drop API, supported since Android 3.0 and even in the appcompat library. Register a drag listener on the drop target. Start the drag in response to a UI event in the drag source.

Discussion

The normal *use* of drag-and-drop is to request a change, such as uninstalling an application, removing an item from a list, and so on. The normal *operation* of a drag is to communicate some user-chosen data from one View to another; i.e, both the source of the drag and the target of the drop must be View objects. To pass information from the source View (e.g., the list item from where you start the drag) to the drop target, there is a special wrapper object called a ClipData. The ClipData can either hold an Android URI representing the object to be dropped, or some arbitrary data. The URI will usually be passed to a ContentProvider for processing.

The basic steps in a drag and drop are:

1. Implement an OnDragListener; its only method is onDrag(), in which you should be prepared for the various action events such as ACTION_DRAG_STARTED, ACTION_DRAG_ENTERED, ACTION_DRAG_EXITED, ACTION_DROP, and ACTION_DRAG_ENDED.

2. Register this listener on the drop target, using the View's setOnDragListener() method.

3. In a listener attached to the source View, usually in an onItemLongClick() or similar method, start the drag.

4. For ACTION_DRAG_STARTED and/or ACTION_DRAG_ENTERED on the drop target, highlight the View to direct the user's attention to it as a target, by changing the background color, the image, or similar.

5. For ACTION_DROP, in the drop target, perform the action.

6. For ACTION_DRAG_EXITED and/or ACTION_DRAG_ENDED, do any cleanup required (e.g., undo changes made in the ACTION_DRAG_STARTED and/or ACTION_DRAG_ENTERED case).

In this example (Figure 10-9) we implement a very simple drag-and-drop scenario: a URL is passed from a button to a text field. You start the drag by long-pressing on the button at the top, and drag it down to the text view at the bottom. As soon as you start the drag, the drop target's background changes to yellow, and the "drag shadow" (by default, an image of the source View object) appears to indicate the drag position. At this point, if you release the drag shadow outside the drop target, the drag shadow will find its way back to the drag source, and the drag will end (the target turns white again). On the other hand, if you drag into the drop target, its color changes to red. If you release the drag shadow here, it is considered a successful drop, and the listener is called with an action code of ACTION_DROP; you should perform the corresponding action (our example just displays the Uri in a toast to prove that it arrived).

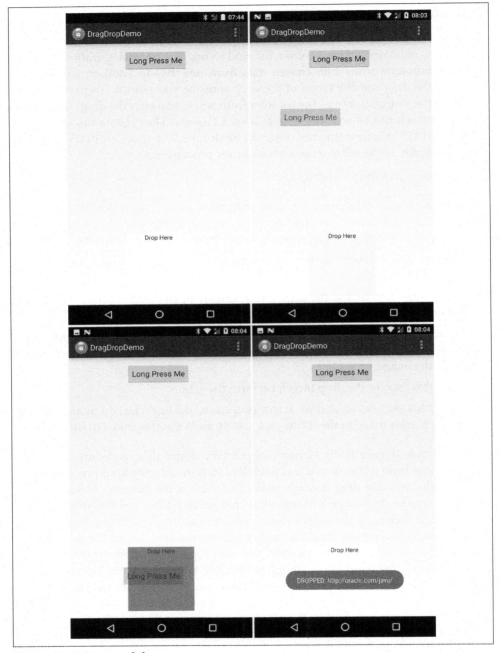

Figure 10-9. Drag and drop sequence

Example 10-23 shows the code in `onCreate()` to start the drag in response to a long-press on the top button.

Example 10-23. Starting the drag-and-drop operation

```java
// Register the long-click listener to START the drag
Button b = (Button) findViewById(R.id.button);
b.setOnLongClickListener(new View.OnLongClickListener() {

    @Override
    public boolean onLongClick(View v) {
        Uri contentUri = Uri.parse("http://oracle.com/java/");
        ClipData cd = ClipData.newUri(getContentResolver(), "Dragging", contentUri);
        v.startDrag(cd, new DragShadowBuilder(v), null, 0);
        return true;
    }
});
```

This version passes a `Uri` through the `ClipData`. To pass arbitrary information, you can use another factory method such as:

```java
ClipData.newPlainText(String label, String data)
```

Then you need to register your `OnDragListener` with the target `View`:

```java
target = findViewById(R.id.drop_target);
target.setOnDragListener(new MyDrag());
```

The code for our `OnDragListener` is shown in Example 10-24.

Example 10-24. Drag-and-drop listener

```java
public class MyDrag implements View.OnDragListener {
    @Override
    public boolean onDrag(View v, DragEvent e) {
        switch (e.getAction()) {
        case DragEvent.ACTION_DRAG_STARTED:
            target.setBackgroundColor(COLOR_TARGET_DRAGGING);
            return true;
        case DragEvent.ACTION_DRAG_ENTERED:
            Log.d(TAG, "onDrag: ENTERED e=" + e);
            target.setBackgroundColor(COLOR_TARGET_ALERT);
            return true;
        case DragEvent.ACTION_DRAG_LOCATION:
            // Nothing to do but MUST consume the event
            return true;
        case DragEvent.ACTION_DROP:
            Log.d(TAG, "onDrag: DROP e=" + e);
            final ClipData clipItem = e.getClipData();
            Toast.makeText(DragDropActivity.this,
                "DROPPED: " + clipItem.getItemAt(0).getUri(),
                Toast.LENGTH_LONG).show();
            return true;
        case DragEvent.ACTION_DRAG_EXITED:
```

```
            target.setBackgroundColor(COLOR_TARGET_NORMAL);
            return true;
        case DragEvent.ACTION_DRAG_ENDED:
            target.setBackgroundColor(COLOR_TARGET_NORMAL);
            return true;
        default:                    // Unhandled event type
            return false;
        }
    }
}
```

In the `ACTION_DROP` case, you would usually pass the `Uri` to a `ContentResolver`; for example:

```
getContentResolver().delete(event.getClipData().getItemAt(0).getUri());
```

 In some versions of Android, you must consume the `DragEvent.ACTION_DRAG_LOCATION` event as shown, or you will get a strange `ClassCastException` with the stack trace down in the `View` class.

If you are maintaining compatibility with ancient legacy versions of Android (anything pre-Honeycomb), you must protect the calls to this API with a code guard; it will compile for those older releases with the compatibility library, but calls will cause an application failure.

10.19 Sharing Files via a FileProvider

Ian Darwin

Problem

You want to share internal-storage files (see Recipe 10.1) with another app, without the bother of putting the data into a `Cursor` and creating a `ContentProvider`.

Solution

The `FileProvider` class allows you to make files available to another application, usually in response to an Intent. It is simpler to set up than a `ContentProvider` (Recipe 10.15), but is actually a subclass of `ContentProvider`.

Discussion

This example exposes a *secrets.txt* file from one application to another. For this example I have created an Android Studio project called *FileProviderDemo*, which contains two different applications in two different packages, `providerapp` and `requestingapp`. We'll start by discussing the Provider app since it contains the actual `FileProvider`. However, you have to run the Requester application first, as it will start the Provider app. Figure 10-10 shows the sequence of the Requester app, then the Provider app, and finally the Requester app with its request satisfied.

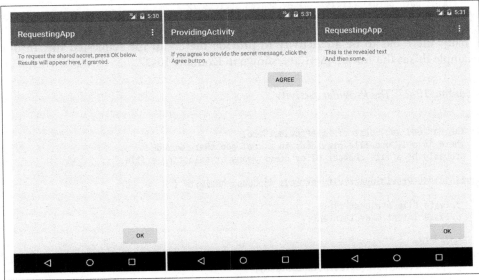

Figure 10-10. FileProviderDemo in action: request, confirmation, completion

Unlike the ContentProvider case, you rarely have to write code for the provider itself; instead, use the FileProvider class directly as a provider in your *AndroidManifest.xml* file, as shown in Example 10-25.

Example 10-25. The provider definition

```
<provider
    android:name="android.support.v4.content.FileProvider"
    android:authorities="com.darwinsys.fileprovider"
    android:grantUriPermissions="true"
    android:exported="false">
    <meta-data
        android:name="android.support.FILE_PROVIDER_PATHS"
        android:resource="@xml/filepaths" />
</provider>
```

The provider does not have to be exported for this usage, but must have the ability to grant Uri permissions as shown. The meta-data element gives the name of a simple mapping file, which is required to map "virtual paths" to actual paths, as shown in Example 10-26.

Example 10-26. The filepaths file

```
<paths>
    <files-path path="secrets/" name="shared_secrets"/>
</paths>
```

Finally, there has to be an Activity to provide the Uri to the requested file. In our example this is the ProvidingActivity, shown in Example 10-27.

Example 10-27. The Provider Activity

```java
/**
 * The backend app, part of FileProviderDemo.
 * There is only one file provided; in a real app there would
 * probably be a file chooser UI or other means of selecting a file.
 */
public class ProvidingActivity extends AppCompatActivity {

    private File mRequestFile;
    private Intent mResultIntent;

    @Override
    protected void onCreate(Bundle savedInstanceState) {
        super.onCreate(savedInstanceState);

        mResultIntent = new Intent("com.darwinsys.fileprovider.ACTION_RETURN_FILE");
        setContentView(R.layout.activity_providing);
        Toolbar toolbar = (Toolbar) findViewById(R.id.toolbar);
        setSupportActionBar(toolbar);

        // The Layout provides a text field with text like
        // "If you agree to provide the file, press the Agree button"

        Button button = (Button) findViewById(R.id.button);
        button.setOnClickListener(new View.OnClickListener() {
            @Override
            public void onClick(View view) {
                provideFile();
            }
        });

        mRequestFile = new File(getFilesDir(), "secrets/demo.txt");

        // On first run of application, create the "hidden" file in internal storage
        if (!mRequestFile.exists()) {
            mRequestFile.getParentFile().mkdirs();
            try (PrintWriter pout = new PrintWriter(mRequestFile)) {
                pout.println("This is the revealed text");
                pout.println("And then some.");
            } catch (IOException e) {
                e.printStackTrace();
            }
        }
    }
```

```
/**
 * The provider application has to return a Uri wrapped in an Intent,
 * along with permission to read that file.
 */
private void provideFile() {

    // The approved target is one hardcoded file in our directory
    mRequestFile = new File(getFilesDir(), "secrets/demo.txt");
    Uri fileUri = FileProvider.getUriForFile(this,
            "com.darwinsys.fileprovider",
            mRequestFile);

    // The requester is in a different app so can't normally read our files!
    mResultIntent.addFlags(Intent.FLAG_GRANT_READ_URI_PERMISSION);

    mResultIntent.setDataAndType(fileUri, getContentResolver().getType(fileUri));

    // Attach that to the result Intent
    mResultIntent.setData(fileUri);

    // Set the result to be "success" + the result
    setResult(Activity.RESULT_OK, mResultIntent);
    finish();
    }
}
```

The important part of this code is in the `provideFile()` method, which:

- Creates a `Uri` for the actual file (in this trivial example there is only one file, with a hardcoded filename)
- Adds flags to the result Intent to let the receiving app read this one file (only) with our permissions
- Sets the MIME type of the result
- Adds the file `Uri` as data to the result Intent
- Sets the result Intent, and the "success" flags `Activity.RESULT_OK`, as the result of this Activity
- Calls `finish()` to end the Activity

Note that this Activity is not meant to be invoked by the user directly, so it does not have LAUNCHER in its *AndroidManifest* entry. Thus when you "run" it, you will get an error message, "Could not identify launch activity: Default Activity not found." *This error is normal and expected.* If it bothers you, build the application and install it, but don't try to run it. Or, you could add a dummy Activity with a trivial message onscreen.

Remember that the point of the `FileProvider` is to share files from one *application* to another, running with different user permissions. Our second application also has only one Activity, the "requesting" Activity. Most of this is pretty standard boilerplate code. In `onCreate()`, we create the requesting Intent:

```
mRequestFileIntent = new Intent(Intent.ACTION_PICK);
mRequestFileIntent.setType("text/plain");
```

The main part of the UI is a text area, which initially suggests that you request a file by pressing the button. That button's action listener is only one line:

```
startActivityForResult(mRequestFileIntent, ACTION_GET_FILE);
```

This will, as discussed in Recipe 4.5, result in a subsequent call to `onActivityComplete()`, which is shown in Example 10-28.

Example 10-28. The Requester Activity: onActivityResult()

```
public class RequestingActivity extends AppCompatActivity {

    private static final int ACTION_GET_FILE = 1;
    private Intent mRequestFileIntent;

    ...

    @Override
    protected void onActivityResult(int requestCode,
    int resultCode, Intent resultIntent) {
        if (requestCode == ACTION_GET_FILE) {
            if (resultCode == Activity.RESULT_OK) {
                try {
                    // get the file
                    Uri returnUri = resultIntent.getData();
                    final InputStream is =
                        getContentResolver().openInputStream(returnUri);
                    final BufferedReader br =
                        new BufferedReader(new InputStreamReader(is));
                    String line;
                    TextView fileViewTextArea =
                        (TextView) findViewById(R.id.fileView);
                    fileViewTextArea.setText(""); // reset each time
                    while ((line = br.readLine()) != null) {
                        fileViewTextArea.append(line);
                        fileViewTextArea.append("\n");
                    }
                } catch (IOException e) {
                    Toast.makeText(this, "IO Error: " + e, Toast.LENGTH_LONG).show();
                }
            } else {
                Toast.makeText(this,
                    "Request denied or canceled", Toast.LENGTH_LONG).show();
            }
            return;
        }
    }
```

```
        // For any other Activity, we can do nothing...
        super.onActivityResult(requestCode, resultCode, resultIntent);
    }
}
```

Assuming that the request succeeds, you will get called here with `requestCode` set to the only valid action, `RESULT_OK`, and the `resultIntent` being the one that the providing Activity set as the Activity result—that is, the Intent wrapping the `Uri` that we need in order to read the file! So we just get the `Uri` from the Intent and open that as an input stream, and we can read the "secret" file from the providing application's otherwise-private internal storage. Just to show that we got it, we display the "secret" file in a text area, shown in the righthand screenshot in Figure 10-10.

See Also

The official documentation on sharing files (*https://developer.android.com/training/ secure-file-sharing/index.html*).

10.20 Backing Up Your SQLite Data to the Cloud with a SyncAdapter

Problem

You want your SQLite or `ContentProvider` data to be bidirectionally synchronized with a database running on a server.

Solution

Use a `SyncAdapter`, which lets you synchronize in both directions, providing the infra-structure to run a "merge" algorithm of your own devising.

Discussion

Assuming that you have decided to go the `SyncAdapter` route, you will first need to make some design decisions:

- How will you access the remote service? (A REST API, as in Recipe 12.1? Volley, as in Recipe 12.2? Custom socket code?)
- How will you package the remote service code? (`ContentProvider`, as in Recipe 10.15? DAO? Other?)
- What algorithm will you use for ensuring that all the objects are kept up-to-date on the server and on one (or more!) mobile devices? (Don't forget to handle inserts, updates, and deletions originating from either end!)

Then you need to prepare (design and code) the following:

1. A ContentProvider (see Recipe 10.15. You'll need this even if you aren't using one to access your on-device data, but if you already have one, you can certainly use it.

2. An AuthenticatorService, which is boilerplate code, to start the Authenticator.

3. An Authenticator class, since you must have an on-device "account" to allow the system to control syncing.

4. A SyncAdapterService, which is boilerplate code, to start the SyncAdapter.

5. And finally, the actual SyncAdapter, which can probably subclass AbstractThreadedSyncAdapter.

The following code snippets are taken from my working todo list manager, Todo-More (*https://github.com/IanDarwin/TodoMore/*), which exists as an Android app, a JavaServer Faces (JSF) web application, a JAX-RS REST service used by the Android app, and possibly others. Each is its own GitHub module, so you can git clone just the parts you need.

In your main Activity's onCreate() method you need to tell the system that you want to be synchronized. This consists mainly of creating an Account (the first time; after that, finding it) and requesting synchronization using this Account. You can start this in your main Activity's onCreate() method by calling two helper methods shown in Example 10-29. Note that accountType is just a unique string, such as "MyTodoAccount".

Example 10-29. Sync setup code in main Activity class

```
public void onCreate(Bundle savedInstanceState) {
    // ...
    mAccount = createSyncAccount(this);
    enableSynching(mPrefs.getBoolean(KEY_ENABLE_SYNC, true));
}

Account createSyncAccount(Context context) {
    AccountManager accountManager =
            (AccountManager) context.getSystemService(ACCOUNT_SERVICE);
    Account[] accounts = accountManager.getAccountsByType(
            getString(R.string.accountType));     // Our account type
    if (accounts.length == 0) {                   // Haven't created one?
        // Create the account type and default account
        Account newAccount =
                new Account(ACCOUNT, getString(R.string.accountType));
        /*
         * Add the account and account type; no password or user data yet.
         * If successful, return the Account object; else report an error.
         */
        if (accountManager.addAccountExplicitly(
                newAccount, "top secret", null)) {
            Log.d(TAG, "Add Account Explicitly: Success!");
            return newAccount;
```

```
        } else {
            throw new IllegalStateException("Add Account failed...");
        }
    } else {                        // Or we already created one, so use it
        return accounts[0];
    }
}

void enableSynching(boolean enable) {
    String authority = getString(R.string.datasync_provider_authority);
    if (enable) {
        ContentResolver.setSyncAutomatically(mAccount, authority, true);

        // Force immediate syncing at startup - optional feature
        Bundle immedExtras = new Bundle();
        immedExtras.putBoolean("SYNC_EXTRAS_MANUAL", true);
        ContentResolver.requestSync(mAccount, authority, immedExtras);

        Bundle extras = new Bundle();
        long pollFrequency = SYNC_INTERVAL_IN_MINUTES;
        ContentResolver.addPeriodicSync(
                mAccount, authority, extras, pollFrequency);
    } else {
        // Disabling, so cancel all outstanding syncs until further notice
        ContentResolver.cancelSync(mAccount, authority);
    }
}
```

The Authority is that of your ContentProvider, which is why you need one of those even if you are accessing your data through a DAO (Data Access Object) that, for example, calls SQLite directly. The Extras that you put in your call to requestSync() control some of the optional behavior of the SyncAdapter. You can just copy my code for now, but you'll want to read the full documentation at some point.

Let's turn now to the most interesting (and complex) part, the SyncAdapter itself, which subclasses AbstractThreadedSyncAdapter and whose central mover and shaker is the onPerformSync() method:

```
public class MySyncAdapter extends AbstractThreadedSyncAdapter {

    public void onPerformSync(Account account,
            Bundle extras,
            String authority,
            ContentProviderClient provider,
            SyncResult syncResult) {
        // Do some awesome work here
        syncResult.clear();          // Indicate success
    }
}
```

This one method is called automatically by the synchronization subsystem when the specified interval has elapsed, or when you call requestSync() for an immediate sync (which is optional, but you probably want to do it at application startup, as we did in our onCreate()).

As the method signature states, it is called with an Account (which you created earlier), a Bundle for arguments, your Authority string again, a ContentProvider wrapper called a ContentProviderClient, and a SyncResult (which you have to use to inform the framework whether your operation succeeded or failed).

When it comes to writing the body of this method, you're completely on your own. I did something like the following in my todo list application:

1. Fetch the previous update timestamp.
2. Delete remotely any Tasks that were deleted locally.
3. Get a list of all the Remote tasks.
4. Get a list of all the Local tasks.
5. Step through each list, determining which Tasks need to be sent to the other side (remote Tasks to local database, local Tasks to remote database), by such criteria as whether they have a Server ID yet, whether their modification time is later than the previous update timestamp, etc.
6. Save any new/modified remote Tasks into the local database.
7. Save any new/modified local Tasks into the remote database.
8. Update the timestamp.

The core of this operation is #5, "step through each list." Because this does all the decision making, I extracted it to a separate method, unimaginatively called algorithm(), which does no I/O or networking, but just works on lists that are passed in. This was done for testability: I can easily unit test this part without invoking any Android or networking functionality. It gets passed the remote list and the local list from steps 3 and 4, and populates two more lists (which are passed in empty) to contain the to-be-copied tasks.

The algorithm() method is called in the middle of the onPerformSync() method—after steps 1–4 have been completed—to prepare the lists for use in steps 6 and 7, in which the code in onPerformSync() has to do the actual work of updating the local and remote databases. Here you can use almost any database access method for the local database (such as a ContentProvider, a DAO, direct use of SQLite, etc.), and almost any network method to add, update, and remove remote objects (URLConnection to the REST service, the deprecated HttpClient, perhaps Volley, etc.). I don't even show the code for onPerformSync() or my inner algorithm() method, as this is something you'll have to work out on your own; it is in the sample GitHub download if you want to look at mine. I will say that I used a DAO locally and a URLConnection to the REST service for remote access.

You must have a ContentProvider, even if you're not using it but are instead using SQLite directly, as mentioned. A dummy ContentProvider just has to exist, it doesn't have to do anything if you don't use it. All the methods can in fact be dummied out, as long as your dummy content provider in fact subclasses ContentProvider:

```
public class TodoContentProvider extends ContentProvider {
    /*
     * Always return true, indicating success
     */
    @Override
    public boolean onCreate() {
        return true;
    }

    /*
     * Return no type for MIME type
     */
    @Override
    public String getType(Uri uri) {
        return null;
    }

    /*
     * query() always returns no results
     */
    @Override
    public Cursor query(
            Uri uri,
            String[] projection,
            String selection,
            String[] selectionArgs,
            String sortOrder) {
        return null;
    }
    // Other methods similarly return null
    // or could throw UnsupportedOperationException(?)
}
```

You will also need a Service to start your SyncAdapter. This is pretty basic; my version just gets the SharedPreferences because they are needed in the adapter, and passes that to the constructor. The onBind() method is called by the system to connect things up:

```
public class TodoSyncService extends Service {

    private TodoSyncAdapter mSyncAdapter;
    private static final Object sLock = new Object();

    @Override
    public void onCreate() {
        super.onCreate();
        SharedPreferences prefs =
            PreferenceManager.getDefaultSharedPreferences(getApplication());
        synchronized(sLock) {
            if (mSyncAdapter == null) {
                mSyncAdapter =
```

```
                            new TodoSyncAdapter(getApplicationContext(), prefs, true);
                }
            }
        }

        @Override
        public IBinder onBind(Intent intent) {
            return mSyncAdapter.getSyncAdapterBinder();
        }
    }
```

We also need an `AccountAuthenticator`, which can be dummied out:

```
    public class TodoDummyAuthenticator extends AbstractAccountAuthenticator {

        private final static String TAG = "TodoDummyAuthenticator";
        public TodoDummyAuthenticator(Context context) {
            super(context);
        }

        @Override
        public Bundle editProperties(
                AccountAuthenticatorResponse response, String accountType) {
            throw new UnsupportedOperationException();
        }

        @Override
        public Bundle addAccount(
                AccountAuthenticatorResponse response, String accountType,
                String authTokenType, String[] requiredFeatures, Bundle options) {
            Log.d(TAG, "TodoDummyAuthenticator.addAccount()");
            return null;
        }

        @Override
        public Bundle confirmCredentials(
            AccountAuthenticatorResponse response, Account account, Bundle options) {
            return null;
        }

        @Override
        public Bundle getAuthToken(
                AccountAuthenticatorResponse response, Account account,
                String authTokenType, Bundle options) {
            throw new UnsupportedOperationException();
        }

        @Override
        public String getAuthTokenLabel(String authTokenType) {
            throw new UnsupportedOperationException();
        }

        @Override
        public Bundle updateCredentials(
                AccountAuthenticatorResponse response, Account account,
                String authTokenType,
```

```
        Bundle options) {
      throw new UnsupportedOperationException();
  }

  @Override
  public Bundle hasFeatures(
        AccountAuthenticatorResponse response, Account account,
        String[] features) {
      throw new UnsupportedOperationException();
  }
}
```

And as with the SyncAdapter itself, you need a Service class to start this, which is pretty simple:

```
public class TodoDummyAuthenticatorService extends Service {

    // Instance field that stores the authenticator object,
    // so we only create it once for multiple uses
    private TodoDummyAuthenticator mAuthenticator;

    @Override
    public void onCreate() {
        // Create the Authenticator object
        mAuthenticator = new TodoDummyAuthenticator(this);
    }
    /*
     * Called when the system binds to this Service to make the IPC call;
     * just return the authenticator's IBinder
     */
    @Override
    public IBinder onBind(Intent intent) {
        return mAuthenticator.getIBinder();
    }
}
```

The Services that expose the SyncAdapter and the Authenticator, as well as the ContentProvider, are Android components, so they must all be listed in the Android manifest:

```
<!-- Sync Adapter-->
<service
        android:name=".sync.TodoSyncService"
        android:exported="true"
        android:process=":sync">
    <intent-filter>
        <action android:name="android.content.SyncAdapter"/>
    </intent-filter>
    <meta-data
        android:name="android.content.SyncAdapter"
        android:resource="@xml/synchadapter" />
</service>
<!-- Dummy authenticator - needed by SyncAdapter -->
<service
    android:name=".sync.TodoDummyAuthenticatorService">
    <!-- Required filter used by the system to launch our account service. -->
```

```
        <intent-filter>
            <action android:name="android.accounts.AccountAuthenticator" />
        </intent-filter>
        <!-- This points to an XML file which describes our account service. -->
        <meta-data android:name="android.accounts.AccountAuthenticator"
                    android:resource="@xml/authenticator" />
    </service>
    <!-- Dummy ContentProvider also "needed" -->
    <provider
            android:name="TodoContentProvider"
            android:authorities="@string/datasync_provider_authority"
            android:exported="false"
            android:syncable="true" />
```

With all the pieces in place, you should see your account type showing up in Settings
→ Accounts, and selecting it should allow you to trigger a sync, enable/disable syncing, see the time of the last sync, and so on (see Figure 10-11).

Figure 10-11. SyncAdapter's user interface: Settings app

See Also

The official documentation on transferring data using sync adapters (*https://devel
oper.android.com*).

Sample Code

The sample code is available on GitHub (*https://github.com/IanDarwin/TodoAndroid/*). To use it as a distributed system you would have to set up your own server (possibly using the TodoREST repository), then configure the server, credentials, etc. in the Settings Activity and test it out.

SyncAdapter Versus Firebase

The ContentProvider (see Recipe 10.14 and related recipes) and the SyncAdapter (see Recipe 10.20) have long been the traditional way of saving data on a device and in the cloud, respectively. Recently Google has begun offering a "database as a service" called Firebase (see Recipe 10.21, also *https://firebase.google.com*). It has some advantages and some disadvantages compared to the traditional methods.

First, Firebase is a cost center at Google. It is free to use in development and for very small organizations—up to 100 users of a given application. Beyond that, the charges start. Rates may vary over time so I won't detail them here; they're quite reasonable when starting off and get more expensive as you scale up. Using a SyncAdapter requires that you have a server on the internet, but if you already have one and it can scale, you may save money by using that with a SyncAdapter instead of using Firebase.

Of course this means that with a SyncAdapter, you are in charge of running the server, doing data backups, etc. This imposes work and resource usage on your organization, but means you have full control over how your data is used and where it is stored (including what jurisdiction it is subject to government inspection in/control over), all of which is "looked after" by Google when you use Firebase.

There is no doubt that using Firebase requires a lot less code, and it's simply far easier to work with. The Firebase version of my Todo application (*https://github.com/IanDarwin/TodoAndroidFirebase/*) taps in at under 600 lines of Java code. The SyncAdapter version (*https://github.com/IanDarwin/TodoAndroid/*) weighs in at a more corpulent 1,800 lines (figures as of April 2016; the two versions are not completely feature-identical, but the SyncAdapter version even uses MetaWidget to reduce the amount of hand-maintained user interface code). That's about a third as much coding, testing, debugging, and polishing to get your app out the door!

Firebase is also more cross-platform–friendly. It includes a Java/Android runtime, which can be used on Java SE, Java EE, and so on. Plus there's an iOS version, so you can use the same Firebase backend from Objective C when building Apple apps. But wait! There's more! There is also a JavaScript version, usable with Ember, Angular, and other popular JavaScript frameworks. Finally, there's a web-based developer console that lets you configure your application, as well as view, enter, and modify data.

The Android service underlying the SyncAdapter works hard to conserve battery life by batching updates from multiple SyncAdapters (in case you didn't know, a big con-

---

sumer of battery power is turning the radio modem on every time you start transmitting; even though you see 2, 3, or 4 "bars of service" on your phone's display, it's actually not connected much of the time, except of course when on a voice call).

Firebase, by contrast, works hard to ensure immediate updating. In my experience on a relatively slow home internet connection, changes made in my app would typically reflect on the developer web console, and vice versa, in a fraction of a second. I do not know if this will become a battery hog, but my todo app only needs updating when you think of something else you have to do or when you get something done and check it off, so the battery life won't be an issue for this app.

With the SyncAdapter, you have to provide authentication. It's common to use HTTP Basic Authentication, as we did in our SyncAdapter example. Firebase provides multiple authentication schemes, including Google login (of course!), OAuth2, and several others.

The SyncAdapter lets you do full SQL-style queries including a WHERE clause and get the results back. Firebase of course does not use SQL syntax, and offers only a single "where" field per query.

The SyncAdapter lets you do synchronization in whatever order you like, and lets you write code to deal with duplicate entries, records that get modified in multiple places at the same time, and so on. Firebase manages concurrency itself, and seems to get by without the need for a complex synchronization step.

Both work correctly when the device is moving between online and offline. But the SyncAdapter has a slight advantage, since the local database gives it at least an always reasonably up-to-date list. The Firebase client's use of a data change listener means the Firebase app will be behind until reconnection. This is not the only way to write the Firebase code, but it's the simplest and probably the most common.

In the end both techniques are useful, and both should be considered when designing an app that needs to share data with a server.

10.21 Storing Data in the Cloud with Google Firebase

Ian Darwin

Problem

You need to store data from your app users' devices into the cloud, and don't have time to write a SyncAdapter. You want to have access to your cloud data from Apple iOS devices and/or a web application.

Solution

While the SyncAdapter is fine in its own way, it is a complex beast to use. Firebase, a Google commercial product, makes it easier to develop your application.

Discussion

Firebase is far from the first solution in this area, but it is the one that Android recommends—unsurprisingly, since Google offers it as a commercial service. We discuss it here not to say that it's the best or only way to do things, but because it really is the path of least resistance to getting an Android cloud-based database up and running, and it's a good example of how such things work.

A brief summary of the steps are:

1. Create an account on the Firebase website (*https://firebase.google.com*), which will give you a unique URL to use, of the form *https://nnn.firebase.com/* (the *nnn* will be provided when you register).

2. Decide how to structure the data.

3. Add the Firebase library coordinates to your *pom.xml* or *build.gradle* file (or download the JAR and add it to your project the hard way, or use Android Studio to add the Firebase library to your project).

4. Write code in the onCreate() method of your Activity or application (see Recipe 2.3) to create a Firebase object using your unique URL.

5. To receive the data, add a listener to the Firebase object.

6. To insert, query, update, or delete, invoke methods on the Firebase object, some of which have additional listeners to notify you of completion and/or results.

In this example we will explore a simple "todo list" application, with data stored only in Firebase. This is an alternate implementation of the example used in the SyncAdapter recipe (Recipe 10.20); both are part of my "TodoMore" application family, but the two use different backends at this point. The Firebase version shown here can be downloaded from GitHub (*https://github.com/IanDarwin/TodoAndroidFirebase/*).

Creating an account is just a matter of using the website signup. It's free to sign up and develop your app; see the Pricing page for the various plans available.

My data is quite simple; it consists of a list of Todo Task items for each user. The Firebase data is basically a hierarchy of data, effectively in JSON format. The Task class in Java maps directly to the fields of the database. As you can see in Figure 10-12, there are fields like name (a one-liner describing the item), description (a longer discussion if needed, may be null), creationDate (when you entered the task, stored as a lightweight custom Data class, not a java.util.Date), modified (simple timestamp format), priority and status (which are enums in the Java code but represented as Strings in the JSON), and id (a long integer used as a primary key in the relational database, but not used here).

Figure 10-12. Developer console showing data

Initializing the database is done in the onCreate() method of the Application class, so the database will be available to any Activity classes that need it:

```
private String mBaseUrl; // Loaded from a config file
private Firebase mDatabase; // The database connection, has a get method

@Override
public void onCreate() {
    super.onCreate();
    Firebase.setAndroidContext(this);
    String baseUrl = getBaseUrl() + TaskListActivity.mCurrentUser + "/tasks/";
    mDatabase = new Firebase(baseUrl);
}
```

With that out of the way, we can add a Listener to receive the data. In the Todo application we want to download this user's complete list of tasks at the start of the application. If you had a larger database and didn't want it all on the device, you'd use a Query, discussed in Recipe 10.7. This is done in the onCreate() method of the main Activity:

```
((ApplicationClass)getApplication()).getDatabase().
    addValueEventListener(new ValueEventListener() {
    @Override
```

```
public void onDataChange(DataSnapshot snapshot) {
    System.out.println("
        There are " + snapshot.getChildrenCount() + " Todo Tasks(s)");
    ApplicationClass.sTasks.clear();
    for (DataSnapshot dnlSnapshot: snapshot.getChildren()) {
        Task task = dnlSnapshot.getValue(Task.class);
        System.out.println(task.getName() + " - " + task.getDescription());
        String jsonKey = dnlSnapshot.getKey();
        ApplicationClass.sTasks.add(new KeyValueHolder<>(jsonKey, task));
    }
    Collections.sort(ApplicationClass.sTasks, tasksComparator);
    mAdapter.notifyDataSetChanged();
}
@Override public void onCancelled(FirebaseError error) {
    Toast.makeText(getBaseContext(),
        "Task read cancelled!! " + error, Toast.LENGTH_LONG).show();
}
});
```

The DataSnapshot object is vaguely analogous to a SQLite Cursor or a JDBC ResultSet. We iterate over its children, which are magically turned into Task objects when we call getValue(Task.class). Normally that's all you'd have to do—it really is that simple!

Except, we will later (to update or delete) need the objects' Firebase key values—i.e., the -KFq... strings at the top level of each Task. We don't want to store these inside the Task class, because otherwise they'd be persisted as fields inside the object as well as the keys. So we introduce a wrapper class, the KeyValueHolder (part of our application, not the Firebase API), to map the Firebase key and the Task object. We want the data in List format, both for speed and to preserve order; otherwise, the keys and values could be put in a Map. Speaking of order, once we've added them to the list (a field in the Application class, again to share with other Activities), we sort the list using Collections.sort(), and notify our list adapter (see Chapter 8) that its data has changed, so the list will now show the latest data.

When I was starting I didn't have a save() method yet and wasn't quite sure how the data would look, so I created the first few entries using the "+" button in the developer's console, to add hierarchical objects. The "+" and "×" buttons allow you to insert and remove data at any node in the tree. If you do make changes this way after your app has been set up—even with just the code we've shown so far—the list view on the device will reflect the changes almost instantly. Nice! That's also why the first entry has a "1" for its key instead of the longer strings that Firebase likes to use for its keys. Those longer keys are generated client-side, by the way, to allow you to generate them even if the device is offline, but they have more randomness than the standard UUID format so pretty much guarantee unique key values on the server.

What about updates and deletes? Well, yes. They work, and they're pretty simple. Let's take a look at the update and delete code. This is in the EditActivity; the startup code gets the task to edit by getting its key passed in the Intent. There is a modelToView() method that puts it into text fields and so on in the UI, and of course viewToModel()

does the inverse. The `doSave()` method is called from a `Button`, and `doDelete()`—hopefully less common—is called from a menu:

```java
private String mKey;
private Task mTask;
private EditText nameTF, descrTF;

@Override
protected void onCreate(Bundle savedInstanceState) {
    super.onCreate(savedInstanceState);

    int index = getIntent().getIntExtra(TaskDetailFragment.ARG_ITEM_INDEX, 0);
    KeyValueHolder<String, Task> taskWrapper =
        ApplicationClass.sTasks.get(index);
    mKey = taskWrapper.key;
    mTask = taskWrapper.value;

    setContentView(R.layout.activity_task_edit);
    nameTF = (EditText) findViewById(R.id.nameEditText);
    descrTF = (EditText) findViewById(R.id.descrEditText);

    FloatingActionButton fab = (FloatingActionButton) findViewById(R.id.fab);
    fab.setOnClickListener(new View.OnClickListener() {
        @Override
        public void onClick(View view) {
            viewToModel();
            doSave();
        }
    });

    modelToView();     // Copies fields from mTask to the UI components
}

void doSave() {
    viewToModel();
    ((ApplicationClass)getApplication()).getDatabase().
        child(mKey).setValue(mTask);
    finish();
}

void doDelete() {
    ((ApplicationClass)getApplication()).getDatabase().child(mKey).removeValue();
    finish();
}
```

Figure 10-13 shows how the application looks in action.

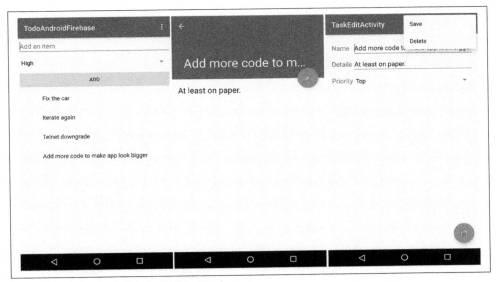

Figure 10-13. Simple "todo list" in Firebase

See Also

There are more capabilities in Firebase. The most important one that we didn't explore is authentication; Google provides a complete and powerful authentication API along with an Access Control–based permissions scheme that you'll certainly want to enable before you make your app-specific data available to the world. This and other features are documented on the Firebase website (*https://fire base.google.com/*).

## CHAPTER 11

Telephone Applications

Android began as a platform for cellular telephone handsets, so it is no surprise that Android apps are very capable of dealing with the phone. You can write apps that dial the phone, or that guide the user to do so. You can write apps that verify or modify the number the user is calling (e.g., to add a long-distance dialing prefix). You can also write apps that send and receive SMS (Short Message Service) messages, a.k.a. text messages, assuming the device is telephony-equipped. Nowadays, a great many Android tablets are WiFi-only, and do not have 4G, 3G, or even 2G telephone/SMS capabilities. For these devices, other capabilities such as SMS via internet and VoIP (Voice over IP, usually using SIP) have to be used.

This chapter covers most of these topics; a few are discussed elsewhere in this book.

11.1 Doing Something When the Phone Rings

Johan Pelgrim

Problem

You want to act on an incoming phone call and do something with the incoming number.

Solution

You can implement a broadcast receiver and then listen for a `TelephonyManager.ACTION_PHONE_STATE_CHANGED` action.

Discussion

If you want to do something when the phone rings you have to implement a broadcast receiver, which listens for the TelephonyManager.ACTION_PHONE_STATE_CHANGED Intent action. This is a broadcast Intent action indicating that the call state (cellular) on the device has changed. Example 11-1 shows the code for the incoming call interceptor, and Example 11-2 shows the incoming call interceptor's layout file.

Example 11-1. The incoming call interceptor

```
package nl.codestone.cookbook.incomingcallinterceptor;

import android.content.BroadcastReceiver;
import android.content.Context;
import android.content.Intent;
import android.telephony.TelephonyManager;
import android.widget.Toast;

public class IncomingCallInterceptor extends BroadcastReceiver {          ❶

    @Override
    public void onReceive(Context context, Intent intent) {              ❷
        String state = intent.getStringExtra(TelephonyManager.EXTRA_STATE);   ❸
        String msg = "Phone state changed to " + state;

        if (TelephonyManager.EXTRA_STATE_RINGING.equals(state)) {        ❹
            String incomingNumber = intent.getStringExtra(
            TelephonyManager.EXTRA_INCOMING_NUMBER);  ❺
            msg += ". Incoming number is " + incomingNumber;

            // This is where you have to "Do something when the phone rings" ;-)

            Toast.makeText(context, msg, Toast.LENGTH_LONG).show();
        }

    }
}
```

❶ Create an IncomingCallInterceptor class that extends BroadcastReceiver.

❷ Override the onReceive() method to handle incoming broadcast messages.

❸ The EXTRA_STATE Intent extra in this case indicates the new call state.

❹ If (and only if) the new state is RINGING, a second Intent extra, EXTRA_INCOMING_NUMBER, provides the incoming phone number as a string.

❺ Extract the number information from the EXTRA_INCOMING_NUMBER Intent extra.

Additionally, you can act on a state change to OFFHOOK or IDLE when the user picks up the phone or ends/rejects the phone call, respectively.

Example 11-2. The incoming call interceptor's AndroidManifest() file

```xml
<?xml version="1.0" encoding="utf-8"?>
<manifest xmlns:android="http://schemas.android.com/apk/res/android"
        package="nl.codestone.cookbook.incomingcallinterceptor"
        android:versionCode="1"
        android:versionName="1.0">
    <uses-sdk android:minSdkVersion="3" />

    <application android:icon="@drawable/icon"
                android:label="Incoming Call Interceptor">

        <receiver android:name="IncomingCallInterceptor">          ❶
            <intent-filter>                                         ❷
                <action android:name="android.intent.action.PHONE_STATE"/> ❸
            </intent-filter>
        </receiver>

    </application>

    <uses-permission android:name="android.permission.READ_PHONE_STATE"/>  ❹

</manifest>
```

❶ We register our IncomingCallInterceptor as a receiver within the application element.

❷ We register an intent-filter ...

❸ And an action value that registers our receiver to listen for TelephonyManager.ACTION_PHONE_STATE_CHANGED broadcast messages.

❹ Finally, we register a uses-permission so that we are allowed to listen to phone state changes.

If all is well, you should see something like Figure 11-1 when the phone rings.

Figure 11-1. Incoming call intercepted

What happens if two receivers listen for phone state changes?

In general, a broadcast message is just that: a message that is sent out to many receivers at the same time. This is the case for a *normal broadcast*, which is used to send out the ACTION_PHONE_STATE_CHANGED Intent as well. All receivers of the broadcast are run in an undefined order, often at the same time, and for that reason order is not applicable.

In other cases the system sends out an *ordered broadcast*, which is described in more detail in Recipe 11.2.

Final notes

When your BroadcastReceiver does not finish the processing in its onMessage() method within 10 seconds, the Android framework will show the infamous Application Not Responding (ANR) dialog, giving your users the ability to kill your program.

It is common for a BroadcastReceiver to simply start a Service. Since a BroadcastReceiver has no user interface, it can either start an Activity (using the inherited startActivity() method) or create and show a Notification (see Recipe 7.13).

See Also

Recipe 11.2, the developer documentation on `BroadcastReceiver` (*https://devel oper.android.com/reference/android/content/BroadcastReceiver.html*) and `ACTION_ PHONE_STATE_CHANGED` (*https://developer.android.com/reference/android/telephony/Telepho nyManager.html#ACTION_PHONE_STATE_CHANGED*).

Source Download URL

The source code for this project is in the Android Cookbook repository (*https:// github.com/IanDarwin/Android-Cookbook-Examples*), in the subdirectory *CallInter-ceptorIncoming* (see "Getting and Using the Code Examples" on page 18).

11.2 Processing Outgoing Phone Calls

Johan Pelgrim

Problem

You want to block certain calls, or alter the phone number about to be called.

Solution

Listen for the `Intent.ACTION_NEW_OUTGOING_CALL` broadcast action and set the result data of the broadcast receiver to the new number.

Discussion

If you want to intercept a call before it is placed, you can implement a broadcast receiver and listen for the `Intent.ACTION_NEW_OUTGOING_CALL` action. This recipe is similar to Recipe 11.1, but it is more interesting since we can actually manipulate the phone number in this case!

Example 11-3 shows the code.

Once the broadcast is finished, the result data is used as the actual number to call. If the result data is `null`, no call will be placed at all!

Example 11-3. The outgoing call interceptor (a BroadcastReceiver)

```
package nl.codestone.cookbook.outgoingcallinterceptor;

import android.content.BroadcastReceiver;
import android.content.Context;
import android.content.Intent;
import android.widget.Toast;
```

```
public class OutgoingCallInterceptor extends BroadcastReceiver {           ❶

    @Override
    public void onReceive(Context context, Intent intent) {                ❷
        final String oldNumber = intent.getStringExtra(Intent.EXTRA_PHONE_NUMBER); ❸
        this.setResultData("0123456789");                                  ❹
        final String newNumber = this.getResultData();
        String msg = "Intercepted outgoing call. Old number " +
                oldNumber + ", new number " + newNumber;
        Toast.makeText(context, msg, Toast.LENGTH_LONG).show();
    }

}
```

❶ Create an `OutgoingCallInterceptor` class that extends `BroadcastReceiver`.

❷ Override the `onReceive()` method.

❸ Extract the phone number that the user originally intended to call via the `Intent.EXTRA_PHONE_NUMBER` Intent extra.

❹ Replace this number by calling `setResultData()` with the new number as the `String` argument.

Example 11-4 shows the code in the outgoing call interceptor's *AndroidManifest.xml* file.

Example 11-4. The outgoing call interceptor's AndroidManifest.xml file

```
<?xml version="1.0" encoding="utf-8"?>
<manifest xmlns:android="http://schemas.android.com/apk/res/android"
    package="nl.codestone.cookbook.outgoingcallinterceptor"
    android:versionCode="1" android:versionName="1.0">
    <uses-sdk android:minSdkVersion="3" />

    <application android:icon="@drawable/icon"
        android:label="Outgoing Call Interceptor">

        <receiver android:name="OutgoingCallInterceptor">           ❶
            <intent-filter android:priority="1">                    ❷
                <action android:name="android.intent.action.NEW_OUTGOING_CALL" />  ❸
            </intent-filter>
        </receiver>

    </application>

    <uses-permission android:name="android.permission.PROCESS_OUTGOING_CALLS" />  ❹

</manifest>
```

❶ We register our `OutgoingCallInterceptor` as a receiver within the `application` element.

❷ We add an `intent-filter` element within this `receiver` declaration and set an `android:priority` of 1.

❸ We add an `action` element within the `intent-filter`, to only receive `Intent.ACTION_NEW_OUTGOING_CALL` Intent actions.

❹ We have to hold the `PROCESS_OUTGOING_CALLS` permission to receive this intent, so we register a `uses-permission` to `PROCESS_OUTGOING_CALLS` right below the `application` element.

Now, when you try to dial the number 11111 you will actually be forwarded to 0123456789 instead! (See Figure 11-2.)

Figure 11-2. Outgoing call intercepted

What happens if two receivers process outgoing calls?

The `Intent.ACTION_NEW_OUTGOING_CALL` is an *ordered broadcast* and is a protected intent that can only be sent by the system. Compared to normal broadcast messages, ordered broadcast messages have three additional features:

- You can use the `intent-filter` element's `android:priority` attribute to influence your position in the sending mechanism. The `android:priority` is an integer indicating which parent (receiver) has higher priority in processing the incoming broadcast message. The higher the number, the higher the priority and the sooner that receiver can process the broadcast message.

- You can propagate a result to the next receiver by calling the `setResultData()` method.

- You can completely abort the broadcast by calling the `abortBroadcast()` method so that it won't be passed to other receivers.

Note that, according to the API, any `BroadcastReceiver` receiving the `Intent.ACTION_NEW_OUTGOING_CALL` must *not* *abort* the broadcast by calling the `abortBroadcast()` method. Doing so does not present any errors, but apparently some system receivers still want to have a go at the broadcast message. Emergency calls *cannot* be intercepted using this mechanism, and other calls cannot be modified to call emergency numbers using this mechanism.

It is perfectly acceptable for multiple receivers to process the outgoing call in turn: for example, a parental control application might verify that the user is authorized to place the call at that time, and then a number-rewriting application might add an area code if one was not specified.

If two receivers are defined with an equal `android:priority` attribute they will be run in an arbitrary order (according to the API). However, in practice, when they both reside in the same *AndroidManifest.xml* file it appears that the order in which the receivers are defined determines the order in which they will receive the broadcast message.

Furthermore, if two receivers are defined with an equal `android:priority` attribute but they are defined in different *AndroidManifest.xml* files (i.e., they belong to different applications), it appears that the broadcast receiver that was *installed* first is *registered* first and thus will be the one that is allowed to process the message first. But again, don't count on it!

If you want to have a shot at being the very first to process a message, you can set the priority to the maximum integer value (2147483647). Even though using this feature of the API still does not guarantee you will be first, you will have a pretty good chance!

Also, other applications could have intercepted the phone number before your app. If you are pretty sure you want to take action on the original number, you can use the `EXTRA_PHONE_NUMBER` Intent extra as described earlier and completely ignore the result from the receiver before you. If you simply want to fall in line and pick up where another broadcast receiver has left off, you can retrieve the intermediary phone number via the `getResultData()` method.

For consistency, any receiver whose purpose is to prohibit phone calls should have a priority of 0, to ensure that it will see the final phone number to be dialed. Any receiver whose purpose is to rewrite phone numbers to be called should have a *positive* priority. Negative priorities are reserved for the system for this broadcast; using them may cause problems.

See Also

Recipe 11.1; , the developer documentation on ACTION_NEW_OUTGOING_CALL (*https://devel oper.android.com/reference/android/content/Intent.html#ACTION_NEW_OUTGO ING_CALL*).

Source Download URL

The source code for this project is in the Android Cookbook repository (*https:// github.com/IanDarwin/Android-Cookbook-Examples*), in the subdirectory *CallInterceptorOutgoing* (see "Getting and Using the Code Examples" on page 18).

11.3 Dialing the Phone

Ian Darwin

Problem

You want to dial the phone from within an application, without worrying about details of telephony.

Solution

Start an Intent to dial the phone.

Discussion

One of the beauties of Android is the ease with which applications can reuse other applications, without being tightly coupled to the details (or even names) of the other programs, using the Intent mechanism. For example, to dial the phone, you only need to create and start an Intent with an action of DIAL and a URI of "tel:" + the number you want to dial. Thus, a basic dialer can be as simple as Example 11-5.

Example 11-5. Simple dialer Activity

```
public class Main extends Activity {
    String phoneNumber = "555-1212";
    String intentStr = "tel:" + phoneNumber;

    /** Standard creational callback.
```

```
    * Just dial the phone.
    */
@Override
public void onCreate(Bundle savedInstanceState) {
    super.onCreate(savedInstanceState);
    setContentView(R.layout.main);

    Intent intent = new Intent("android.intent.action.DIAL",
            Uri.parse(intentStr));

    startActivity(intent);
    }
}
```

You need to have the permission android.permission.CALL_PHONE to use this code. The user will see the screen shown in Figure 11-3; users know to press the green phone button to let the call proceed.

Figure 11-3. Simple dialer

Typically, in real life, you would not hardcode the number. In other circumstances you might want the user to call a number from the phone's Contacts list.

Source Download URL

The source code for this example is in the Android Cookbook repository (*https://github.com/IanDarwin/Android-Cookbook-Examples*), in the subdirectory *Simple-Dialer* (see "Getting and Using the Code Examples" on page 18).

11.4 Sending Single-part or Multipart SMS Messages

Colin Wilcox

Problem

You want a simple way to send either a single-part or a multipart SMS/text message from a single entry point.

Solution

Use `SmsManager`.

Discussion

SMS messages, also called text messages, have been part of cellular technology for years. The Android API allows you to send an SMS message either by an Intent or in code; we're only covering the code approach here.

SMS messages are limited to about 160 characters, depending on the carrier (in case you ever wondered where Twitter got the idea for 140-character messages). Text messages above this size must be broken into chunks. To give you control over this, the `SmsManager` class allows you to break a message into "parts," and returns a list of them.

 For information about how the division of longer messages into parts works "under the hood," see *https://en.wikipedia.org/wiki/Concatenated_SMS*.

If there is only one part, the message is short enough to send directly, so we use the `sendTextMessage()` method. Otherwise, we have to send the list of parts, so we pass the list back into the `sendMultipartTextMessage()` method. The actual sending code is shown in Example 11-6. The downloadable code features a trivial Activity to invoke the sending code.

Example 11-6. The SMS sender

```
package com.example.sendsms;
import java.util.ArrayList;
```

```
import android.telephony.SmsManager;
import android.util.Log;

/** The code for dealing with the SMS manager;
 * called from the GUI code.
 */
public class SendSMS {
    static String TAG = "SendSMS";
    SmsManager mSMSManager = null;
    /* The list of message parts our message
     * gets broken up into by SmsManager */
    ArrayList<String> mFragmentList = null;
    /* Service Center - not used */
    String mServiceCentreAddr = null;

    SendSMS() {
        mSMSManager = SmsManager.getDefault();
    }

    /* Called from the GUI to send one message to one destination */
    public boolean sendSMSMessage(
            String aDestinationAddress,
            String aMessageText) {

        if (mSMSManager == null) {
            return (false);
        }

        mFragmentList = mSMSManager.divideMessage(aMessageText);
        int fragmentCount = mFragmentList.size();
        if (fragmentCount > 1) {
            Log.d(TAG, "Sending " + fragmentCount + " parts");
            mSMSManager.sendMultipartTextMessage(aDestinationAddress,
                    mServiceCentreAddr,
                    mFragmentList, null, null);
        } else {
            Log.d(TAG, "Sending one part");
            mSMSManager.sendTextMessage(aDestinationAddress,
                    mServiceCentreAddr,
                    aMessageText, null, null);
        }

        return true;
    }
}
```

Although sent as three parts, it arrives as a single message, as shown in Figure 11-4.

As you might expect, the application needs the android.permission.SEND_SMS permission in its *AndroidManifest.xml* file.

See Also

For information on the `SmsManager`, see the official documentation (*https://devel oper.android.com/reference/android/telephony/SmsManager.html*).

Figure 11-4. The multipart message arrived

Source Download URL

The source code for this example is in the Android Cookbook repository (*https:// github.com/IanDarwin/Android-Cookbook-Examples*), in the subdirectory *SendSMS* (see "Getting and Using the Code Examples" on page 18).

11.5 Receiving an SMS Message

Rachee Singh

Problem

You wish to enable your application to receive incoming SMS messages.

Solution

Use a broadcast receiver to listen for incoming SMS messages and then extract the messages.

Discussion

When an Android device receives a message, a broadcast Intent is fired (the Intent also includes the SMS message that was received). The application can register to receive these Intents.

The Intent has an action, `android.provider.Telephony.SMS_RECEIVED`. The application designed to receive SMS messages should include the `RECEIVE_SMS` permission in the manifest:

```
<uses-permission android:name="android.permission.RECEIVE_SMS"/>
```

When a message is received, the `onReceive()` method is called. Within this method, you can process the message. From the Intent that is received, the SMS message has to be extracted using the `get()` method. The `BroadcastReceiver` with the code for extracting the message part looks like Example 11-7. The code makes a `Toast` to display the contents of the received SMS message.

Example 11-7. The SMS BroadcastReceiver

```
public class InvitationSmsReceiver extends BroadcastReceiver {

    public void onReceive(Context context, Intent intent) {

        Bundle bundle = intent.getExtras();
        SmsMessage[] msgs = null;
        String message = "";
        if (bundle != null) {
            Object[] pdus = (Object[]) bundle.get("pdus");
            msgs = new SmsMessage[pdus.length];

            for (int i=0; i<msgs.length;i++) {
                msgs[i] = SmsMessage.createFromPdu((byte[]) pdus[i]);
                message = msgs[i].getMessageBody();
                Toast.makeText(context,message,Toast.LENGTH_SHORT).show();
            }
        }
    }
}
```

To register the `InvitationSmsReceiver` class for receiving the SMS messages, add the following to the manifest:

```
<receiver android:name=".InvitationSmsReceiver"
          android:enabled="true">
    <intent-filter>
```

```
        <action android:name="android.provider.Telephony.SMS_RECEIVED"/>
        <category android:name="android.intent.category.DEFAULT"/>
    </intent-filter>
</receiver>
```

Source Download URL

The source code for this project is in the Android Cookbook repository (*https:// github.com/IanDarwin/Android-Cookbook-Examples*), in the subdirectory *SMSReceiver* (see "Getting and Using the Code Examples" on page 18).

11.6 Using Emulator Controls to Send SMS Messages to the Emulator

Rachee Singh

Problem

To interactively test an SMS message–based application before loading it onto a device, you need to be able to send an SMS message to the emulator.

Solution

Emulator control in the DDMS perspective of Eclipse allows sending SMS messages to the emulator.

Discussion

To test whether your application responds to incoming SMS messages, you need to send an SMS message to the emulator. The DDMS perspective of Eclipse or the Android Device Monitor of Android Studio provides this function. (You may wish to maximize the Emulator Control window as otherwise the important parts of it may be hidden and require both vertical and horizontal scrolling to access.) In the Emulator Control tab, go to Telephony Actions and provide a phone number. This number can be any number that you want the message to appear to come from. Select the SMS radio button. In the Message box, type the message you wish to send. Finally, press the Send button below the message text. See Figure 11-5.

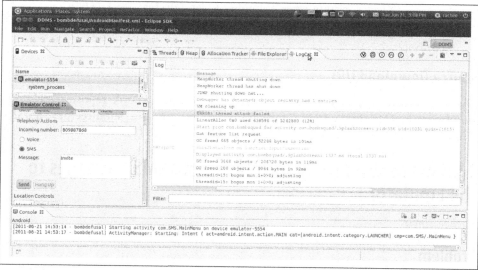

Figure 11-5. Emulator control sending an SMS message

11.7 Using Android's TelephonyManager to Obtain Device Information

Pratik Rupwal

Problem

You want to obtain network-related and telephony information about the user's device.

Solution

Use Android's standard TelephonyManager to obtain statistics about network status and telephony information.

Discussion

Android's TelephonyManager provides information about the Android telephony system. It assists in collecting information such as cell location, International Mobile Equipment Identity (IMEI) number, and network provider.

The program in Example 11-8 is long and covers most of the facilities provided by the Android TelephonyManager. It is unlikely you will need all of these in a single application, but they are consolidated here to provide a comprehensive example.

Example 11-8. The phone state sample Activity

```
...
import android.telephony.CellLocation;
import android.telephony.NeighboringCellInfo;
import android.telephony.PhoneStateListener;
import android.telephony.ServiceState;
import android.telephony.TelephonyManager;
import android.telephony.gsm.GsmCellLocation;

public class PhoneStateSample extends Activity {

        private static final String APP_NAME = "SignalLevelSample";
        private static final int EXCELLENT_LEVEL = 75;
        private static final int GOOD_LEVEL = 50;
        private static final int MODERATE_LEVEL = 25;
        private static final int WEAK_LEVEL = 0;

        // These are used to store Strings into an array for display
        private static final int INFO_SERVICE_STATE_INDEX = 0;
        private static final int INFO_CELL_LOCATION_INDEX = 1;
        private static final int INFO_CALL_STATE_INDEX = 2;
        private static final int INFO_CONNECTION_STATE_INDEX = 3;
        private static final int INFO_SIGNAL_LEVEL_INDEX = 4;
        private static final int INFO_SIGNAL_LEVEL_INFO_INDEX = 5;
        private static final int INFO_DATA_DIRECTION_INDEX = 6;
        private static final int INFO_DEVICE_INFO_INDEX = 7;

        // These are the IDs of the displays; must keep in sync with above constants
        private static final int[] info_ids= {
                R.id.serviceState_info,
                R.id.cellLocation_info,
                R.id.callState_info,
                R.id.connectionState_info,
                R.id.signalLevel,
                R.id.signalLevelInfo,
                R.id.dataDirection,
                R.id.device_info
        };

        @Override
        public void onCreate(Bundle savedInstanceState) {
            super.onCreate(savedInstanceState);
            setContentView(R.layout.main);
            startSignalLevelListener();
            displayTelephonyInfo();
        }

        @Override
        protected void onPause() {
                super.onPause();
                stopListening();
        }

        @Override
        protected void onResume() {
```

```
        super.onResume();
        startSignalLevelListener();
}

@Override
protected void onDestroy() {
        stopListening();
        super.onDestroy();
}

private void setTextViewText(int id,String text) {
        ((TextView)findViewById(id)).setText(text);
}
private void setSignalLevel(int id,int infoid,int level) {
        int progress = (int) ((((float)level)/31.0) * 100);
        String signalLevelString =getSignalLevelString(progress);
        ((ProgressBar)findViewById(id)).setProgress(progress);
        ((TextView)findViewById(infoid)).setText(signalLevelString);
        Log.i("signalLevel ","" + progress);
}

private String getSignalLevelString(int level) {
        String signalLevelString = "Weak";
        if(level > EXCELLENT_LEVEL)     signalLevelString = "Excellent";
        else if(level > GOOD_LEVEL)     signalLevelString = "Good";
        else if(level > MODERATE_LEVEL) signalLevelString = "Moderate";
        else if(level > WEAK_LEVEL)     signalLevelString = "Weak";
        return signalLevelString;
}

private void stopListening() {
        TelephonyManager tm =
            (TelephonyManager) getSystemService(TELEPHONY_SERVICE);
        tm.listen(phoneStateListener, PhoneStateListener.LISTEN_NONE);
}

private void setDataDirection(int id, int direction) {
        int resid = getDataDirectionRes(direction);
        ((ImageView)findViewById(id)).setImageResource(resid);
}
private int getDataDirectionRes(int direction) {
        int resid = R.drawable.data_none;

        switch(direction) {
                case TelephonyManager.DATA_ACTIVITY_IN:
                    resid = R.drawable.data_in; break;
                case TelephonyManager.DATA_ACTIVITY_OUT:
                    resid = R.drawable.data_out; break;
                case TelephonyManager.DATA_ACTIVITY_INOUT:
                    resid = R.drawable.data_both; break;
                case TelephonyManager.DATA_ACTIVITY_NONE:
                    resid = R.drawable.data_none; break;
                default: resid = R.drawable.data_none; break;
        }
        return resid;
}
```

```
    private void startSignalLevelListener() {
    TelephonyManager tm =
        (TelephonyManager) getSystemService(TELEPHONY_SERVICE);
    int events = PhoneStateListener.LISTEN_SIGNAL_STRENGTH |
                 PhoneStateListener.LISTEN_DATA_ACTIVITY |
                 PhoneStateListener.LISTEN_CELL_LOCATION|
                 PhoneStateListener.LISTEN_CALL_STATE |
                 PhoneStateListener.LISTEN_CALL_FORWARDING_INDICATOR |
                 PhoneStateListener.LISTEN_DATA_CONNECTION_STATE |
                 PhoneStateListener.LISTEN_MESSAGE_WAITING_INDICATOR |
                 PhoneStateListener.LISTEN_SERVICE_STATE;
        tm.listen(phoneStateListener, events);
    }
    ...
```

Much of the information-gathering in this program is done by the various listeners. One exception is the method displayTelephonyInfo(), shown in Example 11-9, which simply gathers a large number of information bits directly from the TelephonyManager and adds them to a long string, which is displayed in the TextView.

Example 11-9. The phone state Activity (continued)

```
...

private void displayTelephonyInfo() {
        TelephonyManager tm = (TelephonyManager)getSystemService(TELEPHONY_SERVICE);
        GsmCellLocation loc = (GsmCellLocation)tm.getCellLocation();
        int cellid = loc.getCid();
        int lac = loc.getLac();
        String deviceid = tm.getDeviceId();
        String phonenumber = tm.getLine1Number();
        String softwareversion = tm.getDeviceSoftwareVersion();
        String operatorname = tm.getNetworkOperatorName();
        String simcountrycode = tm.getSimCountryIso();
        String simoperator = tm.getSimOperatorName();
        String simserialno = tm.getSimSerialNumber();
        String subscriberid = tm.getSubscriberId();
        String networktype = getNetworkTypeString(tm.getNetworkType());
        String phonetype = getPhoneTypeString(tm.getPhoneType());
        logString("CellID: " + cellid);
        logString("LAC: " + lac);
        logString("Device ID: " + deviceid);
        logString("Phone Number: " + phonenumber);
        logString("Software Version: " + softwareversion);
        logString("Operator Name: " + operatorname);
        logString("SIM Country Code: " + simcountrycode);
        logString("SIM Operator: " + simoperator);
        logString("SIM Serial No.: " + simserialno);
        logString("Sibscriber ID: " + subscriberid);
        String deviceinfo = "";
        deviceinfo += ("CellID: " + cellid + "\n");
        deviceinfo += ("LAC: " + lac + "\n");
        deviceinfo += ("Device ID: " + deviceid + "\n");
        deviceinfo += ("Phone Number: " + phonenumber + "\n");
```

```
        deviceinfo += ("Software Version: " + softwareversion + "\n");
        deviceinfo += ("Operator Name: " + operatorname + "\n");
        deviceinfo += ("SIM Country Code: " + simcountrycode + "\n");
        deviceinfo += ("SIM Operator: " + simoperator + "\n");
        deviceinfo += ("SIM Serial No.: " + simserialno + "\n");
        deviceinfo += ("Subscriber ID: " + subscriberid + "\n");
        deviceinfo += ("Network Type: " + networktype + "\n");
        deviceinfo += ("Phone Type: " + phonetype + "\n");
        List<NeighboringCellInfo> cellinfo =tm.getNeighboringCellInfo();
        if(null != cellinfo) {
                for(NeighboringCellInfo info: cellinfo) {
                        deviceinfo += ("\tCellID: " +
                        info.getCid() +", RSSI: " + info.getRssi() + "\n");
                }
        }
        setTextViewText(info_ids[INFO_DEVICE_INFO_INDEX],deviceinfo);
    }

    private String getNetworkTypeString(int type) {
        String typeString = "Unknown";
        switch(type) {
                case TelephonyManager.NETWORK_TYPE_EDGE:
                    typeString = "EDGE"; break;
                case TelephonyManager.NETWORK_TYPE_GPRS:
                    typeString = "GPRS"; break;
                case TelephonyManager.NETWORK_TYPE_UMTS:
                    typeString = "UMTS"; break;
                default:
                    typeString = "UNKNOWN"; break;
        }
        return typeString;
    }

    private String getPhoneTypeString(int type) {
        String typeString = "Unknown";
        switch(type) {
                case TelephonyManager.PHONE_TYPE_GSM:
                    typeString = GSM"; break;
                case TelephonyManager.PHONE_TYPE_NONE:
                    typeString = UNKNOWN"; break;
                default:typeString = "UNKNOWN"; break;
        }
        return typeString;
    }

    private int logString(String message) {
        return Log.i(APP_NAME,message);
    }

    private final PhoneStateListener phoneStateListener = new PhoneStateListener() {

        @Override
        public void onCallForwardingIndicatorChanged(boolean cfi) {
                Log.i(APP_NAME, "onCallForwardingIndicatorChanged " +cfi);
                super.onCallForwardingIndicatorChanged(cfi);
        }
```

```java
        @Override
        public void onCallStateChanged(int state, String incomingNumber) {
                String callState = "UNKNOWN";
                switch(state) {
                        case TelephonyManager.CALL_STATE_IDLE:
                                callState = "IDLE"; break;
                        case TelephonyManager.CALL_STATE_RINGING:
                                callState = "Ringing (" + incomingNumber + ")"; break;
                        case TelephonyManager.CALL_STATE_OFFHOOK:
                                callState = "Offhook"; break;
                }
                setTextViewText(info_ids[INFO_CALL_STATE_INDEX],callState);
                Log.i(APP_NAME, "onCallStateChanged " + callState);
                super.onCallStateChanged(state, incomingNumber);
        }
        @Override
        public void onCellLocationChanged(CellLocation location) {
                String locationString = location.toString();
                setTextViewText(
                    info_ids[INFO_CELL_LOCATION_INDEX],locationString);

                Log.i(APP_NAME, "onCellLocationChanged " + locationString);
                super.onCellLocationChanged(location);
        }

        @Override
        public void onDataActivity(int direction) {
                String directionString = "none";
                switch (direction) {
                        case TelephonyManager.DATA_ACTIVITY_IN:
                            directionString = "IN"; break;
                        case TelephonyManager.DATA_ACTIVITY_OUT:
                            directionString = "OUT"; break;
                        case TelephonyManager.DATA_ACTIVITY_INOUT:
                            directionString = "INOUT"; break;
                        case TelephonyManager.DATA_ACTIVITY_NONE:
                            directionString = "NONE"; break;
                        default: directionString = "UNKNOWN: " + direction; break;
                }
                setDataDirection(info_ids[INFO_DATA_DIRECTION_INDEX],direction);
                Log.i(APP_NAME, "onDataActivity " + directionString);
                super.onDataActivity(direction);
        }

        @Override
        public void onDataConnectionStateChanged(int state) {
                String connectionState = "Unknown";
                switch(state) {
                        case TelephonyManager.DATA_CONNECTED:
                            connectionState = "Connected"; break;
                        case TelephonyManager.DATA_CONNECTING:
                            connectionState = "Connecting"; break;
                        case TelephonyManager.DATA_DISCONNECTED:
                            connectionState = "Disconnected"; break;
                        case TelephonyManager.DATA_SUSPENDED:
```

```
                connectionState = "Suspended"; break;
            default:
                connectionState = "Unknown: " + state; break;
        }

        setTextViewText(
            info_ids[INFO_CONNECTION_STATE_INDEX], connectionState);

        Log.i(APP_NAME,
            "onDataConnectionStateChanged " + connectionState);

        super.onDataConnectionStateChanged(state);
    }

    @Override
    public void onMessageWaitingIndicatorChanged(boolean mwi) {
        Log.i(APP_NAME, "onMessageWaitingIndicatorChanged " + mwi);
        super.onMessageWaitingIndicatorChanged(mwi);
    }

    @Override
    public void onServiceStateChanged(ServiceState serviceState) {
        String serviceStateString = "UNKNOWN";
        switch(serviceState.getState()) {
            case ServiceState.STATE_IN_SERVICE:
                serviceStateString = "IN SERVICE"; break;
            case ServiceState.STATE_EMERGENCY_ONLY:
                serviceStateString = "EMERGENCY ONLY"; break;
            case ServiceState.STATE_OUT_OF_SERVICE:
                serviceStateString = "OUT OF SERVICE"; break;
            case ServiceState.STATE_POWER_OFF:
                serviceStateString = "POWER OFF"; break;
            default:
                serviceStateString = "UNKNOWN"; break;
        }

        setTextViewText(
            info_ids[INFO_SERVICE_STATE_INDEX], serviceStateString);

        Log.i(APP_NAME, "onServiceStateChanged " + serviceStateString);

        super.onServiceStateChanged(serviceState);
    }

    @Override
    public void onSignalStrengthChanged(int asu) {
        Log.i(APP_NAME, "onSignalStrengthChanged " + asu);
        setSignalLevel(info_ids[INFO_SIGNAL_LEVEL_INDEX],
            info_ids[INFO_SIGNAL_LEVEL_INFO_INDEX],asu);
        super.onSignalStrengthChanged(asu);
    }
};
}
```

The *main.xml* layout, shown next, consists of a variety of nested linear layouts so that all the information gathered in the preceding code can be displayed neatly:

```xml
<?xml version="1.0" encoding="utf-8"?>
<ScrollView xmlns:android="http://schemas.android.com/apk/res/android"
            android:layout_width="fill_parent"
            android:layout_height="wrap_content"
            android:orientation="vertical"
            android:scrollbarStyle="insideOverlay"
            android:scrollbarAlwaysDrawVerticalTrack="false">
    <LinearLayout
            android:orientation="vertical"
            android:layout_width="fill_parent"
            android:layout_height="fill_parent">
        <LinearLayout
                android:layout_width="fill_parent"
                android:layout_height="wrap_content"
                android:orientation="horizontal">
                <TextView android:text="Service State"
                        style="@style/labelStyleRight"/>
                <TextView android:id="@+id/serviceState_info"
                        style="@style/textStyle"/>
        </LinearLayout>
        <LinearLayout
                android:layout_width="fill_parent"
                android:layout_height="wrap_content"
                android:orientation="horizontal">
                <TextView android:text="Cell Location"
                        style="@style/labelStyleRight"/>
                <TextView android:id="@+id/cellLocation_info"
                        style="@style/textStyle"/>
        </LinearLayout>
        <LinearLayout
                android:layout_width="fill_parent"
                android:layout_height="wrap_content"
                android:orientation="horizontal">
                <TextView android:text="Call State"
                        style="@style/labelStyleRight"/>
                <TextView android:id="@+id/callState_info"
                        style="@style/textStyle"/>
        </LinearLayout>
        <LinearLayout
                android:layout_width="fill_parent"
                android:layout_height="wrap_content"
                android:orientation="horizontal">
                <TextView android:text="Connection State"
                        style="@style/labelStyleRight"/>
                <TextView android:id="@+id/connectionState_info"
                        style="@style/textStyle"/>
        </LinearLayout>
        <LinearLayout
                android:layout_width="fill_parent"
                android:layout_height="wrap_content"
                android:orientation="horizontal">
                <TextView android:text="Signal Level"
```

```
                                    style="@style/labelStyleRight"/>
                        <LinearLayout
                                android:layout_width="fill_parent"
                                android:layout_height="wrap_content"
                                android:layout_weight="0.5"
                                android:orientation="horizontal">
                                <ProgressBar android:id="@+id/signalLevel"
                                             style="@style/progressStyle"/>
                                <TextView android:id="@+id/signalLevelInfo"
                                          style="@style/textSmallStyle"/>
                        </LinearLayout>
                </LinearLayout>
                <LinearLayout
                        android:layout_width="fill_parent"
                        android:layout_height="wrap_content"
                        android:orientation="horizontal">
                        <TextView android:text="Data"
                                  style="@style/labelStyleRight"/>
                        <ImageView android:id="@+id/dataDirection"
                                   style="@style/imageStyle"/>
                </LinearLayout>
                <TextView android:id="@+id/device_info"
                          style="@style/labelStyleLeft"/>
        </LinearLayout>
    </ScrollView>
```

Our code uses some UI styles, which are declared in this file, named *styles.xml*:

```
<?xml version="1.0" encoding="utf-8"?>
<resources>
        <style name="labelStyleRight">
                <item name="android:layout_width">fill_parent</item>
                <item name="android:layout_height">wrap_content</item>
                <item name="android:layout_weight">0.5</item>
                <item name="android:textSize">15dip</item>
                <item name="android:textStyle">bold</item>
                <item name="android:layout_margin">10dip</item>
                <item name="android:gravity">center_vertical|right</item>
        </style>

        <style name="labelStyleLeft">
                <item name="android:layout_width">fill_parent</item>
                <item name="android:layout_height">wrap_content</item>
                <item name="android:layout_weight">0.5</item>
                <item name="android:textSize">15dip</item>
                <item name="android:textStyle">bold</item>
                <item name="android:layout_margin">10dip</item>
                <item name="android:gravity">center_vertical|left</item>
        </style>

        <style name="textStyle">
                <item name="android:layout_width">fill_parent</item>
                <item name="android:layout_height">wrap_content</item>
                <item name="android:layout_weight">0.5</item>
                <item name="android:textSize">15dip</item>
                <item name="android:textStyle">bold</item>
```

```
                <item name="android:layout_margin">10dip</item>
                <item name="android:gravity">center_vertical|left</item>
        </style>

        <style name="textSmallStyle">
                <item name="android:layout_width">fill_parent</item>
                <item name="android:layout_height">fill_parent</item>
                <item name="android:layout_weight">0.5</item>
                <item name="android:textSize">10dip</item>
                <item name="android:layout_margin">10dip</item>
                <item name="android:gravity">center_vertical|left</item>
        </style>

        <style name="progressStyle">
                <item name="android:layout_width">fill_parent</item>
                <item name="android:layout_height">wrap_content</item>
                <item name="android:layout_margin">10dip</item>
                <item name="android:layout_weight">0.5</item>
                <item name="android:indeterminateOnly">false</item>
                <item name="android:minHeight">20dip</item>
                <item name="android:maxHeight">20dip</item>
                <item name="android:progress">15</item>
                <item name="android:max">100</item>
                <item name="android:gravity">center_vertical|left</item>
                <item name="android:progressDrawable">
                    @android:drawable/progress_horizontal</item>
                <item name="android:indeterminateDrawable">
                    @android:drawable/progress_indeterminate_horizontal</item>
        </style>

        <style name="imageStyle">
                <item name="android:layout_width">fill_parent</item>
                <item name="android:layout_height">wrap_content</item>
                <item name="android:layout_weight">0.5</item>
                <item name="android:src">@drawable/icon</item>
                <item name="android:scaleType">fitStart</item>
                <item name="android:layout_margin">10dip</item>
                <item name="android:gravity">center_vertical|left</item>
        </style>
    </resources>
```

The application uses the ACCESS_COARSE_LOCATION permission (to get the approximate location from the cell radio service), which needs to be added to your project's *AndroidManifest.xml* file:

```
<uses-permission android:name="android.permission.ACCESS_COARSE_LOCATION" />
```

The application also uses some images for indicating the data communication state as no data communication, incoming data communication, outgoing data communication, or both-ways data communication. These images are, respectively, named *data_none.png*, *data_in.png*, *data_out.png*, and *data_both.png*. Please add some icons with the aforementioned names in the *res/drawable* folder of your project structure.

Figure 11-6 shows the result.

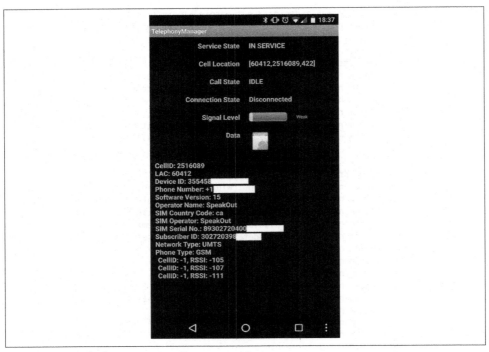

Figure 11-6. TelephonyManagerDemo in action

Source Download URL

The source code for this example is in the Android Cookbook repository (*https://github.com/IanDarwin/Android-Cookbook-Examples*), in the subdirectory *Telephony-Manager* (see "Getting and Using the Code Examples" on page 18).

## CHAPTER 12

Networked Applications

Networking—one could talk about it for hours. In the context of Android, it is primarily about web services, which are services accessed by another program (your Android app) over the HTTP ("web") protocol. Web services come in two flavors: XML/SOAP and RESTful. XML/SOAP web services are more formal and thus have significantly more overhead, both at development time and at runtime, but offer more capabilities. RESTful services are more lighterweight, and are not tied to XML: this chapter covers using JSON (JavaScript Object Notation) and other formats with web services.

Finally, while it's not traditionally thought of as networking, Android also offers a more general "remote procedure" (technically an inter-process Communication or IPC) mechanism layered on AIDL (the Android Interface Definition Language) that is actually used for communication among processes on the same "machine" (Android device); a recipe describing that is at the end of this chapter.

Choose your protocol wisely

While Java makes it easy to create network connections on any protocol, experience shows that HTTP (and HTTPS) is the most universal. If you use a custom protocol to talk to your own server, there are some users who will not be able to access your server. Bear in mind too that in some countries high-speed data is either not yet available or very expensive, whereas GPRS/EDGE is less expensive and more widely available. Most GPRS service providers only allow HTTP/HTTPS connections, often through a proxy. That being said, there may be things you need to do that can't be done via HTTP—for example, because the protocol demands a different port number (e.g., SIP over port 5000). But do try to make HTTP your first choice when you can— you'll include more customers.

All recipes in this chapter require that you add the android.permission.INTERNET permission to your *AndroidManifest.xml* file in order to be able to open network connections:

```
<uses-permission
    android:name="android.permission.INTERNET"/>
```

12.1 Consuming a RESTful Web Service Using a URLConnection

Ian Darwin

Problem

You need to access a RESTful web service.

Solution

You can either use the "standard" Java URL and URLConnection objects, or use the Android-provided Apache HttpClient library to code at a slightly higher level or to use HTTP methods other than GET and POST.

Discussion

REST (Representational State Transfer) was originally intended as an architectural description of the early web, in which GET requests were used and the URL fully specified (represented) the state of the request. Today, RESTful web services are those that eschew the overhead of XML, SOAP, WSDL, and (usually) XML Schema, and simply send URLs that contain all the information needed to perform the request (or almost all of it, as there is often a POST body sent for some types of requests). For example, to support an Android client that allows offline editing of recipes for this book, there is a (draft) web service that lets you view the list of recipes (you send an HTTP GET request ending in /recipe/list), view the details of one recipe (using an HTTP GET ending in /recipe/NNN, where NNN is the primary key of the entry, gotten from the requested list of recipes), and later upload your revised version of the recipe using an HTTP POST to /recipe/NNN, with the POST body containing the revised recipe in the same XML document format as the "get recipe" operation downloads it.

The RESTful service used by these examples is implemented in server-side Java using the Java EE standard JAX-RS API, provided by the RestEasy (*http://www.jboss.org/resteasy*) implementation.

Using URL and URLConnection

Android's developers wisely preserved a lot of the Java Standard API, including some widely used classes for networking, so as to make it easy to port existing code. The `converse()` method shown in Example 12-1 uses a `URL` and `URLConnection` from java.net to do a GET, and is extracted from an example in the networking chapter of my *Java Cookbook* (*http://shop.oreilly.com/product/9780596007010.do*), published by O'Reilly. Comments in this version show what you'd need to change to do a POST.

Example 12-1. The RESTful web service client—URLConnection version

```
public static String converse(String host, int port, String path)
        throws IOException {
    URL url = new URL("http", host, port, path);
    URLConnection conn = url.openConnection();
    // This does a GET; to do a POST, add conn.setDoOutput(true);
    conn.setDoInput(true);
    conn.setAllowUserInteraction(true); // Useless but harmless

    conn.connect();

    // To do a POST, you'd write to conn.getOutputStream();

    StringBuilder sb = new StringBuilder();
    BufferedReader in = new BufferedReader(
        new InputStreamReader(conn.getInputStream()));
    String line;
    while ((line = in.readLine()) != null) {
        sb.append(line);
    }
    in.close();
    return sb.toString();
}
```

The invocation of this method can be as simple as the following, which gets the list of recipes from this book, as long as you don't try this on the main thread:

```
String host = "androidcookbook.com";
String path = "/seam/resource/rest/recipe/list";
String ret = converse(host, 80, path);
```

Note that the `path` value is expected to change to just "/rest/recipe/list" sometime in 2017.

Using HttpClient (deprecated)

Android used to support the Apache HttpClient library, but has now deprecated it (and removed it, as of Android 6, meaning you have to add it as a project dependency if you want to use it in projects compiled for Android 6 or later). HttpClient is widely used in the Java world at large for communicating at a slightly higher level than the `URLConnection`. I've used it in my PageUnit web test framework (*https://pageunit.darwin*

sys.com/). HttpClient also lets you use other HTTP methods that are common in RESTful services, such as PUT and DELETE. Example 12-2 shows the same converse() method coded for a GET using HttpClient.

Example 12-2. The RESTful web service client—Apache HttpClient version

```
public static String converse(String host, int port, String path,
        String postBody) throws IOException {
    HttpHost target = new HttpHost(host, port);
    HttpClient client = new DefaultHttpClient();
    HttpGet get = new HttpGet(path);
    HttpEntity results = null;
    try {
        HttpResponse response=client.execute(target, get);
        results = response.getEntity();
        return EntityUtils.toString(results);
    } catch (Exception e) {
        throw new RuntimeException("Web Service Failure");
    } finally {
        if (results!=null)
            try {
                results.consumeContent();
            } catch (IOException e) {
                // Empty, checked exception but don't care
            }
    }
}
```

Usage will be exactly the same as for the URLConnection-based version.

The results

In the present version of the web service, as discussed in this recipe, the return value comes back as an XML document, which you'd need to parse to display in a List. We will probably add a JSON version as well, triggering on the standard content-type header.

The output of either form should look something like the page displayed in Figure 12-1, where we access the REST URL using a browser (a common exploration technique for very simple, GET-based REST services).

See Also

Recipe 10.13.

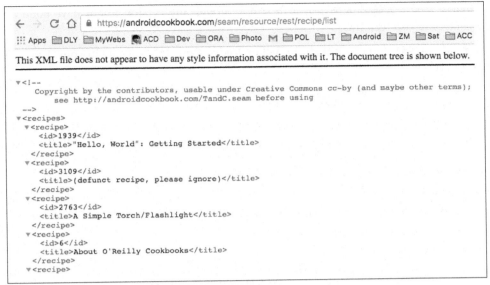

Figure 12-1. Android Cookbook contents via REST

12.2 Consuming a RESTful Web Service with Volley

Ian Darwin

Problem

You want an easy way to access a REST service and have heard that Volley might be the answer.

Solution

Using Volley (*https://github.com/google/volley*), create a `RequestQueue`, and submit a URL with two "callbacks": a success listener and a failure listener.

Discussion

Volley, a semi-official Google library, really does make it easy to use REST networking. We call it "semi-official" because it's not part of the standard Android system, but is hosted on Google's official source repository (if you wish to examine the library's internals you can git `clone https://android.googlesource.com/platform/frameworks/volley`) and documented on the official Android documentation site (*https://devel oper.android.com/training/volley/*).

To use Volley in your app, first you have to add the Volley library to your project, as it is not part of the standard Android distribution. At the time of this writing, the coordinates were `com.android.volley:volley:1.0.0`, though the version might have gone up by the time you read this.

With that done, you can initialize a Volley "request queue," typically in your Activity's `onCreate()` method:

```
// Set up the Volley queue for REST processing
queue = Volley.newRequestQueue(this);
```

Assuming that you want to fetch data in response to a button press or similar event, you will have a `View` handler to create and queue up the request. Along with the URL, the request will contain a callback handler that Volley will run on the UI thread to display the results, and a failure listener to handle errors.

In this example we use the well-known Google Suggest service, which the Chrome browser uses to make suggestions when you start typing in the browser's search box:

```
public void fetchResults(View v) {

    String host = "https://suggestqueries.google.com/";
    // Amusingly, client=firefox makes the output come back in JSON
    String baseUrl = "complete/search?output=toolbar&hl=en&client=firefox&q=";
    String listUrl = mSearchBox.getText().toString();

    // Some error handling here...

    // Create a String request to get information from the provided URL
    String requestUrl = host + baseUrl + listUrl;
    JsonArrayRequest request = new JsonArrayRequest(
            requestUrl, successListener, failListener);

    // Queue the request to do the sending and receiving
    queue.add(request);
}
```

We ask for the data in JSON as that's the common format for REST services. As with any JSON-based service, you need to know the format, so feel free to explore the REST responses using your favorite REST client (if you don't have one, we suggest PostMan for Chrome or REST Client for Firefox). The results will be processed by the `SuccessListener` defined here (for simplicity we display the strings in a large `TextView` instead of a `ListView`; elaborating that is an obvious "exercise for the reader"):

```
/**
 * What we get back from this particular web service is a JSON array
 * containing:
 * 0) A JSON String containing the query string
 * 1) A JSON Array of strings with the results
 */
final Response.Listener<JSONArray> successListener =
  new Response.Listener<JSONArray>() {
    @Override
    public void onResponse(JSONArray response) {
        try {
```

```
            String query = response.getString(0);
            mTextView.append("Original query: " + query + "\n");
            JSONArray rest = response.getJSONArray(1);
            mTextView.setText("We got " + rest.length() + " results:\n");
            for (int i = 0; i < rest.length(); i++) {
                mTextView.append(rest.getString(i) + "\n");
            }
        } catch (JSONException e) {
            mTextView.append("\n);");
            mTextView.append("FAIL: " + e);
            e.printStackTrace();
        }
    }
};
```

See Also

The official documentation on using Volley (*https://developer.android.com/training/volley/index.html*).

Source Download URL

The source code for this project is in the Android Cookbook repository (*https://github.com/IanDarwin/Android-Cookbook-Examples*), in the subdirectory *VolleyDemo* (see "Getting and Using the Code Examples" on page 18).

12.3 Notifying Your App with Google Cloud Messaging "Push Messaging"

Ian Darwin

Problem

You want to get "push" notifications sent asynchronously from a server, without setting up your own complex infrastructure. This can be used to send short data (up to about 4 KB), or to send a "ping" notification that will cause the app to download new data from your server.

Solution

Consider using Google Cloud Messaging (GCM).

> GCM has just been upgraded to "Firebase Cloud Messaging," and its documentation is now at *https://firebase.google.com/docs/cloud-messaging/*.

Discussion

GCM is a free service offered to Android developers to deliver small messages direct to your application running on an Android device. This avoids your application having to poll a server, which would be either not very responsive, or very bad for battery life. The basic operation of GCM is:

particular user's device (e.g., new or changed data available). .You send a message to the GCM server. .The GCM server sends the message to the user's device, where it is passed to a BroadcastReceiver in your app. .You do something with the information.

There are other solutions, such as intercepting incoming SMS messages (see Recipe 11.5). GCM has the advantage that it's free, and the disadvantage that it takes a bit longer to set up than other solutions. Note that prior to API 4.0.4, the user was required to have a Google sign-in in order to receive GCM push messages.

The basic steps in building a GCM application are:

1. Sign up with Google to use GCM.
2. Set up your development environment for GCM.
3. Configure ProGuard to preserve GCM services in your APK.
4. Configure your client's *AndroidManifest.xml*.
5. Initialize GCM in your startup code.
6. Create a BroadcastReceiver to handle the incoming notifications.
7. Configure your backend server to notify the GCM server when it has data to send (or to send a notice to tell the client to download new data, a form of distributed MVC).

The following sections elaborate on these steps.

Sign up with Google to use GCM

Assuming that you have a Google Play Developer account (if not, see "Signing up" in Recipe 21.2), go to your Developer Console (*https://console.cloud.google.com/*). If this is your first time here, or you need to make a new project, click Create Project; otherwise, select the project. In either case, jot down the Project Number, which appears in the URL and at the top of the page. This number is used as your GCM Sender ID.

At the left of the page, select APIs. Then set "Google Cloud Messaging for Android" to ON. You have to accept a license. The API will disappear from the list and reappear at the top, with the status set to ON.

Back at the left, under "APIs & auth," click Credentials, then "Create new Key" (*not* "Create new Client ID"). Then select "Server key" (*not* "Android key"). Click Create, and put in your server's IP address (you can enter as many as you need). Click OK.

The reason you need a server key is that your app server will be the one contacting GCM, not your client app.

Save the API key that is generated; you will need it in your server. This is further described in the GCM documentation (*https://developer.android.com/google/gcm/*).

Set up your development environment for GCM

Ensure you have the Google Play Services SDK installed (use the Android SDK Manager in your IDE, or the `android sdk` command-line tool). Then select Google Play Services, under Extras.

If this is your first use of Google Play Services, you'll have to install the library project from */extras/google/google_play_services/libproject/google-play-services_lib/* to a source folder. If you're using Eclipse, then import it using File → Import → Android → Existing Android Code. If, like me, you prefer to keep everything in your workspace, you can point the Import at the library project path above, but be sure to check the "Copy files into Workspace" checkbox.

Then you need to make your client app project depend upon this library using Project → Properties → Android → Library → Add (it is a common mistake to use Project → Build Path → Add Library → Project instead; this does not work).

Configure ProGuard to preserve GCM Services in your APK

If you're using ProGuard (see Recipe 21.5), add the following to your *proguard-project.txt* file:

```
-keep class * extends java.util.ListResourceBundle {
protected Object[][] getContents();
}

-keep public class
com.google.android.gms.common.internal.safeparcel.SafeParcelable {
public static final *** NULL;
}

-keepnames @com.google.android.gms.common.annotation.KeepName class *
-keepclassmembernames class * {
@com.google.android.gms.common.annotation.KeepName *;
}

-keepnames class * implements android.os.Parcelable {
public static final ** CREATOR;
}
```

Configure your client's AndroidManifest.xml

There are several pieces to go in your *AndroidManifest.xml* file. First, add the permissions `android.permission.INTERNET` and `com.google.android.c2dm.permission.RECEIVE`. Also, add `android.permission.WAKE_LOCK` if you want to keep the device from sleeping between receipt of a message and its processing. And add `android.permission.GET_ACCOUNTS` if the device API is lower than 4.0.4.

You also have to build your own permission, in order to prevent other apps from stealing your messages. Create and give yourself the permission `applicationPackage.permission.C2D_MESSAGE` (for example, `com.example.gcmplay.permission.C2D_MESSAGE`). You must use this exact name for your custom permission. This might look like the following:

```
<permission android:name="com.example.gcmplay.permission.C2D_MESSAGE"
        android:protectionLevel="signature" />
<uses-permission android:name="com.example.gcmplay.permission.C2D_MESSAGE" />
```

Inside the `application` element, add:

```
<meta-data android:name="com.google.android.gms.version"
        android:value="@integer/google_play_services_version" />
```

Configure a `BroadcastReceiver` to receive the GCM Intent, protected by the GCM permission. This might look like the following:

```
<receiver android:name=".GcmplayBroadcastReceiver"
        android:permission="com.google.android.c2dm.permission.SEND" >
    <intent-filter>
        <action android:name="com.google.android.c2dm.intent.RECEIVE" />
        <category android:name="com.example.gcm" />
    </intent-filter>
</receiver>
```

Last but not least, you'll probably want an `IntentService` to receive the messages from the receiver and get them into the app:

```
<service android:name=".GcmIntentService"/>
```

Initialize GCM in your startup code

In your app's startup code (e.g., in `onCreate()` or `onResume()`), check to see that Google Play Services are available using the static method `GooglePlayServicesUtil.isGooglePlayServicesAvailable(Context ctx)`. For example:

```
boolean checkForGcm() {
    int ret = GooglePlayServicesUtil.isGooglePlayServicesAvailable(this);
    if (ConnectionResult.SUCCESS == ret) {
        return true;
    } else {
        if (GooglePlayServicesUtil.isUserRecoverableError(ret)) {
            GooglePlayServicesUtil.getErrorDialog(ret, this,
                PLAY_SERVICES_RESOLUTION_REQUEST).show();
        } else {
```

```
                        Toast.makeText(this,
                            "Google Message Not Supported on this device",
                            Toast.LENGTH_LONG).show();
                }
            return false;
            }
        }
```

At this point you have to decide whether you are going to use HTTP or XMPP to communicate from the server to your client. XMPP (the Extensible Messaging and Presence Protocol, a chat protocol now used by Google Talk) allows bidirectional messages, whereas HTTP is simpler to set up but is only one-way. While the official documentation uses XMPP, we'll use HTTP because it is simpler; you can later refer to the official documentation if you want to use XMPP.

Create a BroadcastReceiver to handle the incoming notification

The BroadcastReceiver gets the message via an Intent, and hands it off to another class (the IntentService) to handle it. The only change it makes to the incoming Intent is to change it to explicitly have the class name of the Service in order to pass it along. Reusing the Intent this way causes the Intent extra—which contains the actual data from the server—to be passed along.

The use of WakefulBroadcastReceiver (shown in the following code) is optional; if you don't care about the device possibly going to sleep before the Service has finished, you can just use a plain BroadcastReceiver (and remove the call to completeWakefulIntent() in the Service):

```
public class GcmReceiver extends WakefulBroadcastReceiver {
    /**
     * Called when a message is received from GCM for this app
     */
    @Override
    public void onReceive(Context context, Intent intent) {
        Log.d(GcmMainActivity.TAG, "GcmReceiver.onReceive()");
        // Recycle "intent" into an explicit Intent for the handler.
        ComponentName comp =
                new ComponentName(context.getPackageName(),
                                  GcmService.class.getName());
        intent.setComponent(comp);

        // Pass control to the handler. Using startWakefulService() will keep the
        // device awake so the user has a good chance of seeing the message;
        // the WakeLock is released at the end of the handler. Reusing
        // the incoming Intent this way lets us pass along Intent extras, etc.
    startWakefulService(context, intent);

        // If we didn't throw an exception yet, life is good.
    setResultCode(Activity.RESULT_OK);
    }
}
```

The last bit of client code is the IntentService, also known as the "do what you want with the result" section. This trivial example merely displays the result in the LogCat output, but that is enough to show that our "Hello, World" application is receiving messages and handling them (a better example would show the result in a notification, and an even *better* example would update the GUI in the main Activity; these are left as an exercise for the reader):

```java
/**
 * A very simple program which pretends to be a "server" in that it sends
 * a notification to the Google Cloud Messaging Server to cause it to send
 * a message to our GCM Client.
 * @author Ian Darwin, http://androidcookbook.com/
 */
public class GcmMockServer {
    /** Confidential Server API key gotten from the Google Dev Console
     * -> Credentials -> Create new Key -> Server key */
    final static String AUTH_KEY;

    final static String POST_URL = "https://android.googleapis.com/gcm/send";

    public static void main(String[] args) throws Exception {

        final  String[][]  MESSAGE_HEADERS = {
            {"Content-Type", "application/json"},
            {"Authorization", "key=" + AUTH_KEY}
        };

        String regIdFromClientApp = "Paste GCM Client App Google ID here";
        String jsonMessage =
                "{\n" +
                "    \"registration_ids\" : [\""+ regIdFromClientApp + "\"],\n" +
                "    \"data\" : {\n" +
                "        \"message\": \"See your doctor ASAP!\"\n" +
                "    }\n" +
                "}\n";

        // Dump out the HTTP send for debugging
        for (String[] hed : MESSAGE_HEADERS) {
            System.out.println(hed[0] + "=>" + hed[1]);
        }
        System.out.println(jsonMessage);

        // Actually send it
        sendMessage(POST_URL, MESSAGE_HEADERS, jsonMessage);
    }

    private static void sendMessage(String postUrl, String[][] messageHeaders,
            String jsonMessage) throws IOException {
        HttpURLConnection conn =
                (HttpURLConnection) new URL(postUrl).openConnection();
        for (String[] h : messageHeaders) {
            conn.setRequestProperty(h[0], h[1]);
        }
        System.out.println("Connected to " + postUrl);
```

```
        conn.setDoOutput(true);
        conn.setDoInput(true);
        conn.setUseCaches(false);          // Ensure response always from server

        PrintWriter pw = new PrintWriter(
                new OutputStreamWriter(conn.getOutputStream()));

        pw.print(jsonMessage);
        pw.close();

        System.out.println("Connection status code " + conn.getResponseCode());
    }

    /** Static initializer, just load API key so it doesn't appear
     * in the commit history */
    static {
            InputStream is = null;
            try {

                is = GcmMockServer.class.getResourceAsStream("keys.properties");
                if (is == null) {
                    throw new RuntimeException("could not open keys files");
                    "maybe copy keys.properties.sample "
                    "to keys.properties in resource?");
                }
                Properties p = new Properties();
                p.load(is);
                AUTH_KEY = p.getProperty("GCM_API_KEY");
                if (AUTH_KEY == null) {
                    String message = "Could not find GCM_API_KEY in props";
                    throw new ExceptionInInitializerError(message);
                }

            } catch (Exception e) {
                String message = "Error loading properties: " + e;
                throw new ExceptionInInitializerError(message);
            } finally {
                if (is != null) {
                    try {
                        is.close();
                    } catch (IOException e) {
                        // What a useless exception
                    }
                }
            }
        }
    }
}
```

Configure your backend server to notify the GCM server when it has data

Instead of writing a full server, here we just show a standalone main program containing the code that your server would use to send a message to the client. It just uses a Java HttpUrlConnection to talk to the Google server.

In real life your app would need to send its registration ID string to your server, which would use it as a token to identify the client to receive this particular message. The registration ID is a unique identifier for a version of your app installed at a particular instant on a particular device; uninstall and reinstall the same app and you get a different client ID.

Your server also needs the API key we generated near the outset of this recipe in order to authenticate itself. *Keep this key confidential*, as it will allow anybody who finds it to send messages to your clients.

Here's the code from my GcmMockServer application:

```
/**
 * A very simple Java SE program which pretends to be a "server" in that it sends
 * a notification to the Google Cloud Messaging Server to cause it to send
 * a message to our GCM Client.
 * @author Ian Darwin, http://androidcookbook.com/
 */
public class GcmMockServer {

    /** Confidential Server API key gotten from the Google Dev Console ->
     * Credentials -> Create new Key -> Server key */
    final static String AUTH_KEY; // Set in a static initializer, not shown

    final static String POST_URL = "https://android.googleapis.com/gcm/send";

    public static void main(String[] args) throws Exception {

        final String[][] MESSAGE_HEADERS = {
            {"Content-Type", "application/json"},
            {"Authorization", "key=" + AUTH_KEY}
            };

        String regIdFromClientApp = null; // Has to be set somehow!
        String jsonMessage =
            "{\n" +
            " \"registration_ids\" : [\""+ regIdFromClientApp + "\"],\n" +
            " \"data\" : {\n" +
            " \"message\": \"See your doctor ASAP!\"\n" + // THE ACTUAL MESSAGE
            " }\n" +
            "}\n";

        // Dump out the HTTP send for debugging
        for (String[] hed : MESSAGE_HEADERS) {
            System.out.println(hed[0] + "=>" + hed[1]);
        }
        System.out.println(jsonMessage);

        // Actually send it
        sendMessage(POST_URL, MESSAGE_HEADERS, jsonMessage);
    }

    private static void sendMessage(String postUrl, String[][] messageHeaders,
            String jsonMessage) throws IOException {
```

```
        HttpURLConnection conn =
        (HttpURLConnection) new URL(postUrl).openConnection();
    for (String[] h : messageHeaders) {
        conn.setRequestProperty(h[0], h[1]);
    }
    System.out.println("Connected to " + postUrl);
    conn.setDoOutput(true);
    conn.setDoInput(true);
    conn.setUseCaches(false); // Ensure response always from server

    PrintWriter pw = new PrintWriter(
            new OutputStreamWriter(conn.getOutputStream()));

    pw.print(jsonMessage);
    pw.close();

    System.out.println("Connection status code " + conn.getResponseCode());
    }
}
```

So, does it all work? If everything has been set up just so, and you run the client in a device (or maybe it will work in an emulator), and then you copy the `RegistrationId` string into the server (`logcat` is your friend here!), and then you run the GcmMock-Server as a Java application, and the winds are blowing from the south, then you will see the following, or something very like it, in the `logcat` output:

```
D/com.darwinsys.gcmdemo( 7496): GcmReceiver.onReceive()
D/com.darwinsys.gcmdemo( 7496): Got a message of type gcm
D/com.darwinsys.gcmdemo( 7496): MESSAGE = 'See your doctor ASAP!'
    (Bundle[{from=117558675814, message=See your doctor ASAP!,
     android.support.content.wakelockid=2,
      collapse_key=do_not_collapse}])
```

See Also

The official GCM documentation (*https://developer.android.com/google/gcm/index.html*).

Source Download URL

The source code for the client part of project is in the Android Cookbook repository (*https://github.com/IanDarwin/Android-Cookbook-Examples*), in the subdirectory *GcmClient* (see "Getting and Using the Code Examples" on page 18). The mock server is in the subdirectory *GcmMockServer*.

12.4 Extracting Information from Unstructured Text Using Regular Expressions

Ian Darwin

Problem

You want to get information from another organization, but the organization doesn't make it available as information, only as a viewable web page.

Solution

Use `java.net` to download the HTML page, and use regular expressions to extract the information from the page.

Discussion

If you aren't already a big fan of regular expressions, well, you should be. Maybe this recipe will help interest you in learning regex technology.

Suppose that I, as a published author, want to track how my book is selling in comparison to others. I can obtain this information for free just by clicking the page for my book on any of the major bookseller sites, reading the sales rank number off the screen, and typing the number into a file—but that's too tedious. As I wrote in one of my earlier books, "computers get paid to extract relevant information from files; people should not have to do such mundane tasks."

The program shown in Example 12-3 uses the Regular Expressions API and, in particular, newline matching to extract a value from an HTML page on the Amazon.com website. It also reads from a URL object (see Recipe 12.1). The pattern to look for is something like this (bear in mind that the HTML may change at any time, so I want to keep the pattern fairly general):

```
(bookstore name here) Sales Rank:
# 26,252
```

As the pattern may extend over more than one line, I read the entire web page from the URL into a single long string using a private convenience routine, `readerToString()`, instead of the more traditional line-at-a-time paradigm. The value is extracted from the regular expression, converted to an integer value, and returned. The longer version of this code in *Java Cookbook* would also plot a graph using an external program. The complete program is shown in Example 12-3.

Example 12-3. Part of class BookRank

```java
public static int getBookRank(String isbn) throws IOException {
    // The RE pattern - digits and commas allowed.
    final String pattern = "Rank:</b> #([\\d,]+)";
    final Pattern r = Pattern.compile(pattern);

    // The url -- must have the "isbn=" at the very end, or otherwise
    // be amenable to being appended to.
    final String url = "http://www.amazon.com/exec/obidos/ASIN/" + isbn;

    // Open the URL and get a Reader from it.
    final BufferedReader is = new BufferedReader(new InputStreamReader(
        new URL(url).openStream()));
    // Read the URL looking for the rank information, as
    // a single long string, so can match RE across multiple lines.
    final String input = readerToString(is);

    // If found, append to sales data file.
    Matcher m = r.matcher(input);
    if (m.find()) {
        // Group 1 is digits (and maybe ','s) that matched; remove comma
        return Integer.parseInt(m.group(1).replace(",",""));
    } else {
        throw new RuntimeException(
            "Pattern not matched in `" + url + "'!");
    }
}
```

It should be noted that in general you cannot parse arbitrary HTML using regular expressions; the reasons have to do with complexity and have been well covered online, both seriously (*http://stackoverflow.com/questions/6751105/why-its-not-possible-to-use-regex-to-parse-html-xml-a-formal-explanation-in-la*) and humorously (*http://stackoverflow.com/questions/1732348/regex-match-open-tags-except-xhtml-self-contained-tags/1732454#1732454*).

See Also

As mentioned, using the regex API is vital to being able to deal with semistructured data that you will meet in real life. Chapter 4 of *Java Cookbook*, written by me and published by O'Reilly, is all about regular expressions, as is Jeffrey Friedl's comprehensive *Mastering Regular Expressions*, also published by O'Reilly.

Source Download URL

You can download the source code for this example from GitHub (*https://github.com/IanDarwin/javasrc/blob/master/src/main/java/regex/BookRank.java*).

12.5 Parsing RSS/Atom Feeds Using ROME

Wagied Davids

Problem

You want to parse RSS/Atom feeds, which are commonly used to provide an updated list of news articles on websites and often identified by the "news" icon:

Solution

This recipe shows an RSS/Atom feed parser based on ROME (*http://rome tools.github.io/rome/*), a Java-based RSS syndication feed parser. It has some useful features such as HTTP conditional GETs, ETags, and Gzip compression. It also covers a wide range of formats, including RSS 0.90, RSS 2.0, and Atom 0.3 and 1.0. The web site for the Rome project is *http://rometools.github.io/rome/*.

Discussion

The basic steps for parsing an RSS/Atom feed with a ROME-based parser are as follows:

1. Modify your *AndroidManifest.xml* file to have INTERNET permission to allow for Internet browsing.

2. Create an Android project. Set the layout file to be the contents of Example 12-4.

3. Add the dependency rome:rome:1.0 in your build file. Or, manually download the *rome-1.0.jar* and *jdom-1.0.jar* files and add them to your project.

4. Create the Activity shown in Example 12-5. In particular, the getRSS() method demonstrates the use of the ROME API to parse the XML RSS feed and display the results.

When run with the given feed URL (*http://rss.cbc.ca/lineup/topstories.xml*), the output should look like Figure 12-2, except with newer news items.

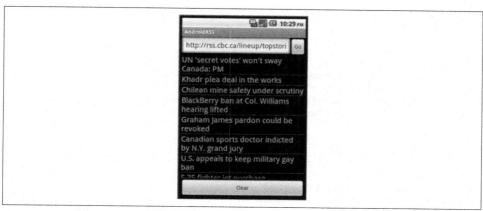

Figure 12-2. RSS feed in ListView

The layout is shown in Example 12-4, and the Java code in Example 12-5.

Example 12-4. main.xml

```xml
<?xml version="1.0" encoding="utf-8"?>
<LinearLayout
    xmlns:android="http://schemas.android.com/apk/res/android"
    android:orientation="vertical"
    android:layout_width="fill_parent"
    android:layout_height="fill_parent">

    <TableLayout
        android:id="@+id/table"
        android:layout_width="fill_parent"
        android:layout_height="wrap_content"
        android:stretchColumns="0">
    <TableRow
        android:id="@+id/top_add_entry_row"
        android:layout_height="wrap_content"
        android:layout_width="fill_parent">

        <EditText
            android:id="@+id/rssURL"
            android:hint="Enter RSS URL"
            android:singleLine="true"
            android:maxLines="1"
            android:maxWidth="220dp"
            android:layout_width="wrap_content"
            android:layout_height="wrap_content">
        </EditText>
        <Button
            android:id="@+id/goButton"
            android:text="Go"
            android:layout_width="fill_parent"
            android:layout_height="wrap_content">
        </Button>
```

```
            </TableRow>
    </TableLayout>

    <!-- Mid Panel -->
    <ListView
        android:id="@+id/ListView"
        android:layout_weight="1"
        android:layout_width="fill_parent"
        android:layout_height="wrap_content">
    </ListView>

    <Button
        android:id="@+id/clearButton"
        android:text="Clear"
        android:layout_width="fill_parent"
        android:layout_height="wrap_content">
    </Button>
</LinearLayout>
```

Example 12-5. AndroidRss.java

```java
import java.io.IOException;
import java.net.MalformedURLException;
import java.net.URL;
import java.util.ArrayList;
import java.util.Iterator;
import java.util.List;

import android.app.Activity;
import android.os.Bundle;
import android.util.Log;
import android.view.View;
import android.view.View.OnClickListener;
import android.widget.AdapterView;
import android.widget.ArrayAdapter;
import android.widget.Button;
import android.widget.EditText;
import android.widget.ListView;
import android.widget.Toast;
import android.widget.AdapterView.OnItemClickListener;

import com.sun.syndication.feed.synd.SyndEntry;
import com.sun.syndication.feed.synd.SyndFeed;
import com.sun.syndication.io.FeedException;
import com.sun.syndication.io.SyndFeedInput;
import com.sun.syndication.io.XmlReader;

public class AndroidRss extends Activity {
    private static final String tag="AndroidRss ";
    private int selectedItemIndex = 0;
    private final ArrayList list = new ArrayList();
    private EditText text;
    private ListView listView;
    private Button goButton;
    private Button clearButton;
```

```java
        private ArrayAdapter adapter = null;

        @Override
        public void onCreate(Bundle savedInstanceState) {
                super.onCreate(savedInstanceState);
                setContentView(R.layout.main);

                text = (EditText) this.findViewById(R.id.rssURL);
                goButton = (Button) this.findViewById(R.id.goButton);
                goButton.setOnClickListener(new OnClickListener() {
                        @Override
                        public void onClick(View v) {
                                String rss = text.getText().toString().trim();
                                getRSS(rss);
                        }
                });

                clearButton = (Button) this.findViewById(R.id.clearButton);
                clearButton.setOnClickListener(new OnClickListener() {
                        @Override
                        public void onClick(View v) {
                                adapter.clear();
                                adapter.notifyDataSetChanged();
                        }
                });

                listView = (ListView) this.findViewById(R.id.ListView);
                listView.setOnItemClickListener(new OnItemClickListener() {
                        @Override
                        public void onItemClick(AdapterView parent, View view,
                        int position, long duration) {
                                selectedItemIndex = position;
                                Toast.makeText(getApplicationContext(),
                                    "Selected " + adapter.getItem(position) +
                                    " @ " + position, Toast.LENGTH_SHORT).show();
                        }
                });

                adapter = new ArrayAdapter(this, R.layout.dataview, R.id.ListItemView);
                listView.setAdapter(adapter);

        }

        private void getRSS(String rss) {

                URL feedUrl;
                try {
                        Log.d("DEBUG", "Entered:" + rss);
                        feedUrl = new URL(rss);

                        SyndFeedInput input = new SyndFeedInput();
                        SyndFeed feed = input.build(new XmlReader(feedUrl));
                        List entries = feed.getEntries();
                        Toast.makeText(this,
                            "#Feeds retrieved: " + entries.size(),
                            Toast.LENGTH_SHORT).show();
```

```
                Iterator iterator = entries.listIterator();
                while (iterator.hasNext()) {
                        SyndEntry ent = (SyndEntry) iterator.next();
                        String title = ent.getTitle();
                        adapter.add(title);
                }
                adapter.notifyDataSetChanged();

        }
        catch (Exception e) {
                e.printStackTrace();
        }
    }

    private void clearTextFields() {
            Log.d(tag, "clearTextFields()");
            this.text.setText("");
    }
}
```

Source Download URL

The source code for this example is in the Android Cookbook repository (*https://github.com/IanDarwin/Android-Cookbook-Examples*), in the subdirectory *AndroidRss* (see "Getting and Using the Code Examples" on page 18).

12.6 Using MD5 to Digest Clear Text

Colin Wilcox

Problem

Sometimes you need to convert clear text to a nonreadable form before saving or transmitting it.

Solution

Android provides a standard Java MD5 class to allow plain text to be replaced with an MD5 digest of the original text. This is a one-way digest that is not believed to be easily reversible (if you need that, use *Java Cryptography* (O'Reilly)).

Discussion

Example 12-6 is a simple function that takes a clear-text string and digests it using MD5, returning the encrypted string as a return value.

Example 12-6. MD5 hash

```
public static String md5(String s) {
    try {
        // Create MD5 hasher
        MessageDigest digest = java.security.MessageDigest.getInstance("MD5");
        digest.update(s.getBytes());
        byte messageDigest[] = digest.digest();
        // Create hex string
        StringBuffer hexString = new StringBuffer();
        for (int i = 0; i < messageDigest.length; i++) {
            hexString.append(Integer.toHexString(0xFF & messageDigest[i]));
        }
        return hexString.toString();
    }
    catch (NoSuchAlgorithmException e) {
        e.printStackTrace();
    }
    return "";     // Or give the user an Exception...
}
```

12.7 Converting Text into Hyperlinks

Rachee Singh

Problem

You need to turn web page URLs into hyperlinks in a `TextView` of your Android app.

Solution

Use the `autoLink` property for a `TextView`.

Discussion

Say you are setting the URL *www.google.com* as part of the text in a `TextView`, but you want this text to be a hyperlink so that the user can open the web page in a browser by clicking it. To achieve this, add the `autoLink` property to the `TextView`:

```
android:autoLink = "all"
```

Now, in the Activity's code, you can set any text to the `TextView` and all the URLs will be converted to hyperlinks! See Figure 12-3.

```
linkText = (TextView)findViewById(R.id.link);
linkText.setText("The link is: www.google.com");
```

Figure 12-3. TextView with links auto-converted

12.8 Accessing a Web Page Using a WebView

Rachee Singh

Problem

You want to download and display a web page within your application.

Solution

Embed the standard WebView component in the layout and invoke its loadUrl() method to load and display the web page.

Discussion

WebView is a View component that can be placed in an Activity. Its primary use is, as its name implies, to handle web pages for you. Since WebViews usually need to access remote web page(s), don't forget to add the INTERNET permission into the manifest file:

```
<uses-permission android:name="android.permission.INTERNET" />
```

Then you can add the WebView to your XML layout:

```
<WebView
    android:id="@+id/webview"
    android:layout_height="fill_parent"
    android:layout_width="fill_parent"/>
```

In the Java code for the Activity that displays the web page, we obtain a handle onto the `WebView` using the `findViewById()` method. On the `WebView` we use the `loadUrl()` method to provide it the URL of the website we wish to open in the application:

```
WebView webview = (WebView)findViewById(R.id.webview);
webview.loadUrl("http://google.com");
```

Source Download URL

You can download the source code for this example from Google Docs (*https://docs.google.com/leaf?id=0B_rESQKgad5LN2JhMDFjZTUtY2IwZS00NzkyLWFlNjItMzhiZWRlYTQxMWNm&hl=en_US*).

12.9 Customizing a WebView

Rachee Singh

Problem

You need to customize the `WebView` opened by your application.

Solution

Use the `WebSettings` class to access built-in functions for customizing the browser.

Discussion

As discussed in Recipe 12.8, to open a web page in an Android application, we use a `WebView` component. Then, to load a URL in the `WebView`, we use, for example:

```
webview.loadUrl("http://www.google.com/");
```

We can do many things to customize the browser to suit users' needs. To customize the view, we need an instance of the `WebSettings` class, which we can get from the `WebView` component:

```
WebSettings webSettings = webView.getSettings();
```

Here are some of the things we can do using `WebSettings`:

- Tell the `WebView` to block network images:
  ```
  webSettings.setBlockNetworkImage(true);
  ```
- Set the default font size in the browser:
  ```
  webSettings.setDefaultFontSize(25);
  ```
- Control whether the `WebView` supports zoom:
  ```
  webSettings.setSupportZoom(true);
  ```

- Tell the `WebView` to enable JavaScript execution:

    `webSettings.setJavaScriptEnabled(true);`

- Control whether the `WebView` will save passwords:

    `webSettings.setSavePassword(false);`

- Control whether the `WebView` will save form data:

    `webSettings.setSaveFormData(false);`

Many more methods of this kind are available. For more information, see the developer documentation on the `WebView` class (*https://developer.android.com/reference/android/webkit/WebView.html*).

12.10 Writing an Inter-Process Communication Service

Rupesh Chavan

Problem

You want to know how to write an IPC service and access it from another application.

Solution

Android provides an AIDL-based programming interface that both the client and the service agree upon in order to communicate with each other using inter-process communication (IPC).

Discussion

IPC is a key feature of the Android programming model. It provides the following two mechanisms:

- Intent-based communication
- Remote service–based communication

In this recipe we will concentrate on the remote service–based communication approach. This Android feature allows you to make method calls that look "local" but are executed in another process. This is somewhat similar to standard Java's Remote Method Invocation (RMI), and involves use of the Android Interface Definition Language (AIDL). The service has to declare a service interface in an AIDL files and then the AIDL tool will automatically create a Java interface corresponding to the AIDL file. The AIDL tool also generates a stub class that provides an abstract implementation of the service interface methods. You have to provide a `Service` class, which will extend this stub class to provide the real implementation of the methods exposed through the interface.

The service clients will invoke the onBind() method of the Service in order to connect to the service. The onBind() method returns an object of the stub class to the client. Example 12-7 shows the code-related snippets.

Example 12-7. IMyRemoteService.aidl

```
package com.demoapp.service;

interface IMyRemoteService {
    String getMessage();
}
```

Note that the AIDL file in Example 12-7 looks like Java code but must be stored with a filename extension of *.aidl* in order to be processed correctly. Either Eclipse or Android Studio will automatically generate (in the generated sources directory, since you don't need to modify it) the remote interface corresponding to your AIDL file; the generated interface will also provide an abstract member class named Stub, which must be implemented by the RemoteService class. The stub class implementation within the service class is shown in Example 12-8.

Example 12-8. Remote service stub

```
public class MyService extends Service {
    private IMyRemoteService.Stub myRemoteServiceStub = new IMyRemoteService.Stub() {
        public int getMessage() throws RemoteException {
            return "Hello World!";
        }
    };
    // The onBind() method in the service class:
    public IBinder onBind(Intent arg0) {
        Log.d(getClass().getSimpleName(), "onBind()");
        return myRemoteServiceStub;
    }
}
```

Now, let's quickly look at the meat of the service class before we move on to how the client connects to this class. Our MyService class consists of one method, which just returns a string. Example 12-9 shows the overridden onCreate(), onStart(), and onDestroy() methods. The onCreate() method of the service will be called only once in a service life cycle. The onStart() method will be called every time the service is started. Note that the resources are all released in the onDestroy() method (see Example 12-9). Since these just call super() and log their presence, they could be omitted from the service class.

Example 12-9. Service class onCreate(), onStart(), and onDestroy() methods

```
public void onCreate() {
    super.onCreate();
    Log.d(getClass().getSimpleName(),"onCreate()");
}
public void onStart(Intent intent, int startId) {
    super.onStart(intent, startId);
    Log.d(getClass().getSimpleName(), "onStart()");
}
public void onDestroy() {
    super.onDestroy();
    Log.d(getClass().getSimpleName(),"onDestroy()");
}
```

Let's discuss the client class. For simplicity, I placed the start, stop, bind, release, and invoke methods all in the same client, and will discuss each method in turn. In reality, though, one client may start and another can bind to the already started service.

There are five buttons, one each for the start, stop, bind, release, and invoke actions, each with an obvious listener method to invoke one of the five corresponding methods.

A client needs to bind to a service before it can invoke any method on the service, so we begin with Example 12-10, which shows the start method. In our simplified example, the code from Example 12-10 (which starts the service) to the end of this Recipe is all in the main Activity class; in a "real" application, the service would be started in a separate application.

Example 12-10. The startService() method

```
private void startService() {
    if (started) {
        Toast.makeText(RemoteServiceClient.this, "Service already started",
            Toast.LENGTH_SHORT).show();
    } else {
        Intent i = new Intent(this, MyRemoteService.class);
        startService(i);
        started = true;
        updateServiceStatus();
        Log.d( getClass().getSimpleName(), "startService()" );
    }
}
```

An explicit Intent is created and the service is started with the Context.startService(i) method. The rest of the code updates some status on the UI. There is nothing specific to a remote service invocation here; it is in the bindService() method that we see the difference from a local service (see Example 12-11).

Example 12-11. The bindService() method

```
private void bindService() {
    if(conn == null) {
        conn = new RemoteServiceConnection();
        Intent i = new Intent(this, MyRemoteService.class);
        bindService(i, conn, Context.BIND_AUTO_CREATE);
        updateServiceStatus();
        Log.d( getClass().getSimpleName(), "bindService()" );
    } else {
        Toast.makeText(RemoteServiceClient.this,
            "Cannot bind - service already bound", Toast.LENGTH_SHORT).show();
    }
}
```

Here we get a connection to the remote service through the RemoteServiceConnection class, which implements the ServiceConnection interface. The connection object is required by the bindService() method—an intent, a connection object, and the type of binding are to be specified. So, how do we create a connection to the RemoteService? Example 12-12 shows the implementation.

Example 12-12. The ServiceConnection implementation

```
class RemoteServiceConnection implements ServiceConnection {
    public void onServiceConnected(ComponentName className,
            IBinder boundService ) {
        remoteService = IMyRemoteService.Stub.asInterface((IBinder)boundService);
        Log.d( getClass().getSimpleName(), "onServiceConnected()" );
    }

    public void onServiceDisconnected(ComponentName className) {
        remoteService = null;
        updateServiceStatus();
        Log.d( getClass().getSimpleName(), "onServiceDisconnected" );
    }
};
```

The Context.BIND_AUTO_CREATE ensures that a service is created if one did not exist, although the onStart() method will be called only on explicit start of the service.

Once the client is bound to the service and the service has already started, we can invoke any of the methods that are exposed by the service. In our interface and its implementation (see Example 12-7 and Example 12-8), there is only one method, getMessage(). In this example, the invocation is done by clicking the Invoke button. That will return the text message and update it below the button. Example 12-13 shows the invoke method.

Example 12-13. The invokeService() method

```
private void invokeService() {
    if(conn == null) {
        Toast.makeText(RemoteServiceClient.this,
            "Cannot invoke - service not bound", Toast.LENGTH_SHORT).show();
    } else {
        try {
            String message = remoteService.getMessage();
            TextView t = (TextView)findViewById(R.id.R.id.output);
            t.setText( "Message: "+message );
            Log.d( getClass().getSimpleName(), "invokeService()" );
        } catch (RemoteException re) {
            Log.e( getClass().getSimpleName(), "RemoteException" );
        }
    }
}
```

Once we use the service methods, we can release the service. This is done as shown in Example 12-14 (by clicking the Release button).

Example 12-14. The releaseService() method

```
private void releaseService() {
    if(conn != null) {
        unbindService(conn);
        conn = null;
        updateServiceStatus();
        Log.d( getClass().getSimpleName(), "releaseService()" );
    } else {
        Toast.makeText(RemoteServiceClient.this,
            "Cannot unbind - service not bound",
            Toast.LENGTH_SHORT).show();
    }
}
```

Finally, we can stop the service by clicking the Stop button. After this point, no client can invoke this service. Example 12-15 shows the relevant code.

Example 12-15. The stopService() method

```
private void stopService() {
    if (!started) {
        Toast.makeText(RemoteServiceClient.this, "Service not yet started",
            Toast.LENGTH_SHORT).show();
    } else {
        Intent i = new Intent(this, MyRemoteService.class);
        stopService(i);
        started = false;
        updateServiceStatus();
        Log.d( TAG, "stopService()" );
    }
}
```

If the client and the service are using different package structures, then the client has to include the AIDL file along with the package structure, just like the service does.

These are the basics of working with a remote service on the Android platform.

Source Download URL

The source code for this example is in the Android Cookbook repository (*https:// github.com/IanDarwin/Android-Cookbook-Examples*), in the subdirectory *IPCDemo* (see "Getting and Using the Code Examples" on page 18).

## CHAPTER 13

Gaming and Animation

Gaming is an important activity that people used to perform on "computers" and now perform on mobile devices. Android is a perfectly capable contender in the graphics arena, providing support for OpenGL ES.

If you want to use some advanced gaming features without having to write a lot of code, you're in luck, as there are many game-development frameworks in existence today. Many of them are primarily or exclusively for desktops. The ones shown in Table 13-1 are known to be usable on Android; if you find others, please add a comment on this book's website (*https://androidcookbook.com/r/1816*), and we will incorporate it into the online version and eventually into a future revision of the published book.

Table 13-1. Android game frameworks

Name	Open source?	Cost	URL
AndEngine	Y	Free	*http://www.andengine.org/*
Box2D	Y	Free	*http://www.box2d.org*
Corona SDK	N	Free and Enterprise editions available	*https://coronalabs.com/*
Flixel-gdx	Y	Free	*http://flixel-gdx.com/*
libgdx	Y	Free	*https://github.com/libgdx/libgdx/*
PlayN	Y	Free	*https://github.com/playn/playn*
rokon	Y	Free	*https://code.google.com/archive/p/rokon*
ShiVa3D	N	Free, basic, and advanced licenses available	*http://www.shiva-engine.com/*
Unity	N	Free and paid plans available	*https://unity3d.com/unity/multiplatform/*

A list of Android-compatible game frameworks is also maintained on this book's website (*https://androidbookcook.com/gameframeworks.html*).

You will need to compare the functions that each offers before choosing one for your project.

13.1 Building an Android Game Using flixel-gdx

Wagied Davids

Problem

You want to build an Android game using a high-level framework.

Solution

Use the flixel-gdx (*http://flixel-gdx.com/html*) framework.

Discussion

The original Flixel framework (*http://flixel.org/*) was an Adobe ActionScript-based game framework developed by Adam ("Atomic") Saltsman. This was ported by "Wing Eraser" to make flixel-gdx, a Java-based port that closely resembles the AS3-based Flixel in terms of programming paradigm. Flixel-gdk on its own was not released in distribution form, but required you to merge its source code and resources into your project. It was then modified to use the *libgdx* graphics framework, and made more suitable for distribution; in the process, it gained desktop support, so it is possible to run your games on Android, or on the desktop using either Java SE or HTML5. Documentation on flixel-gdk is available at *http://flixel-gdx.com/documentation/*, and the source code is available on GitHub (*https://github.com/flixel-gdx/flixel-gdx*).

Due to the fact that Android doesn't use the standard Java classpath mechanism for "resources" such as drawables, so flixel-gdx must provide drawable and other resources, it is not a single-JAR solution, and there are no public Maven or Gradle artifacts. Instead, flixel-gdx provides a setup JAR file that creates three Eclipse projects (sorry Gradle fans): one for common code, one for Android code, and one for Java Desktop code; see Figure 13-1.

Note that after you select "Open the generation screen," on the next screen you will see a Launch button. When you click this button, the setup program will download some files and create the projects. When it is all done, the text area in the upper left will end with the words "All done":

```
Finding required files... done
Decompressing projects... done
Decompressing libraries... done
Configuring libraries... done
Post-processing files... done
Copying projects... done
```

```
Cleaning... done
All done!
```

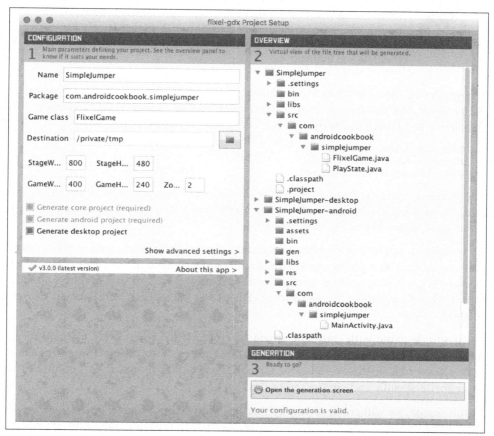

Figure 13-1. The flixel-gdx project installer

You then need to import the projects into Eclipse, or just "open" them in Eclipse (by selecting File → New Java Project) if you have created them at the top level of your workspace. You could presumably import them into Android Studio, but I haven't tested this. Note that the two UI projects have a "-" in their name, which isn't valid in Eclipse, so I renamed them, e.g., from SimpleJumper-android to SimpleJumper.android.

At this point you can run the Android and desktop applications. The desktop version is much quicker to start up (no need to deploy to a device or AVD) and so is useful for quick tests, even if you don't plan to release a desktop edition of your game.

The desktop version (either of the default app or of our app) works; the Android version works on ARM-based ("armeabi") devices (most real devices) but crashes with a missing GDX runtime library on the Intel-based emulators because the GDX library is only precompiled for ARM. If you need Intel support, you could download the code and build it.

The generated files, like most Flixel games, provide a few little classes for starting up the program, then a PlayState class (which must have an extends FlxState clause). This class has several main methods:

```
@Override public void create();
@Override public void update();
@Override public void destroy();
```

The purpose of create() and destroy() are obvious. The update() method is called periodically, and each call represents either a clock tick or a user interaction such as pressing an arrow key to move the player.

As well, there can be any number of ancillary classes. Each object that moves around the screen, such as a player, an enemy, and so on, will have its own class, which will extend FlxSprite (a *sprite* is a small graphic that moves around in a graphics application, such as a player in a video game). The player classes can also have an update() method.

For a simple game with only one sprite-type object, the main body of the update() method can be in either the PlayState class or the Sprite class. For a larger game, it makes sense to have the overall game logic in the PlayState class's update() method, and some sprite-specific code in the Sprite class.

In this recipe, we will create a simple "jumper" game (think Mario™ (*https://en.wikipe dia.org/wiki/Mario*)). We'll do this by replacing code in the core and Android projects created by the setup JAR. We'll need a few entities, a Droid (FlxSprite subclass) to move around, a pusher, and a few elevators. Each entity is declared as a separate class containing its own asset resources and listeners for digital touchpad events. Example 13-1 shows the code for the Flixel-based game Activity, from the SimpleJumper.android project.

Example 13-1. The Flixel-based game Activity

```
public class MainActivity extends FlxAndroidApplication {

    public MainActivity() {
            super(new FlixelGame());
    }

    @Override
    public void onCreate(Bundle savedInstanceState) {
```

```
        super.onCreate(savedInstanceState);

        getWindow().setFlags(WindowManager.LayoutParams.FLAG_FULLSCREEN,
        WindowManager.LayoutParams.FLAG_FULLSCREEN);

        // ORIENTATION
        // setRequestedOrientation(ActivityInfo.SCREEN_ORIENTATION_PORTRAIT);
        setRequestedOrientation(ActivityInfo.SCREEN_ORIENTATION_LANDSCAPE);
    }
}
```

Example 13-2 shows the code for the Flixel-based PlayState class, where we add a label in the upper right and start an animation.

Example 13-2. The Flixel-based PlayState class

```
public class PlayState extends FlxState {
        @Override
        public void create() {
                add(new FlxText(0, 0, 200, "SimpleJumper 0.0"));
                add(new Droid(50, 50));
        }
}
```

Example 13-3 shows the code for the Flixel-based Sprite class.

Example 13-3. Droid.java, a FlxSprite implementation

```
public class Droid extends FlxSprite {
    private final FlxSound sound = new FlxSound();

    public Droid(int X, int Y) {
        super(X, Y);
        // loadGraphic("player", true, true);
        maxVelocity.x = 100; // Walking speed
        acceleration.y = 10; // Gravity
        drag.x = maxVelocity.x * 4; // Deceleration (sliding to a stop)

        // Tweak the bounding box for better feel
        width = 8;
        height = 10;

        offset.x = 3;
        offset.y = 3;

        addAnimation("idle", new int[] { 0 }, 0, false);
        addAnimation("walk", new int[] { 1, 2, 3, 0 }, 12);
        addAnimation("walk_back", new int[] { 3, 2, 1, 0 }, 10, true);
        addAnimation("flail", new int[] { 1, 2, 3, 0 }, 18, true);
        addAnimation("jump", new int[] { 4 }, 0, false);
    }

    @Override
```

```java
public void update() {
        // Smooth slidey walking controls
        acceleration.x = 0;
        if (FlxG.keys.LEFT)
                acceleration.x -= drag.x;
        if (FlxG.keys.RIGHT)
                acceleration.x += drag.x;

        if (isTouching(FLOOR)) {
                // Jump controls
                if (FlxG.keys.UP) {
                        // sound.loadEmbedded(R.raw.jump);
                        // sound.play();

                        velocity.y = -acceleration.y * 0.51f;
                        play("jump");

                } // Animations
                else if (velocity.x > 0) {
                        play("walk");
                } else if (velocity.x < 0) {
                        play("walk_back");
                } else
                        play("idle");
        } else if (velocity.y < 0)
                play("jump");
        else
                play("flail");

    // Default object physics update
    //super.update();
    }
}
```

Source Download URL

The source code for this example is in the Android Cookbook repository (*https://github.com/IanDarwin/Android-Cookbook-Examples*), in the subdirectory *Simple-Jumper* (see "Getting and Using the Code Examples" on page 18).

13.2 Building an Android Game Using AndEngine

Wagied Davids

Problem

You want to design an Android game using the AndEngine game framework.

Solution

AndEngine (*http://www.andengine.org/*) is a game engine framework designed for producing games on Android. Originally developed by Nicholas Gramlich, it has some advanced features for producing awesome games.

Discussion

For this recipe, I have designed a simple pool game with physics capabilities, such that the effects of the accelerometer are taken into account, as are touch events. As a result, touching a specific billiard ball and pulling down on it will cause it to shoot into other balls, with the collision detection taken care of. Example 13-4 shows the code for the AndEngine-based game Activity.

Example 13-4. The AndEngine-based game Activity

```
import org.anddev.andengine.engine.Engine;
import org.anddev.andengine.engine.camera.Camera;
import org.anddev.andengine.engine.options.EngineOptions;
import org.anddev.andengine.engine.options.EngineOptions.ScreenOrientation;
import org.anddev.andengine.engine.options.resolutionpolicy.RatioResolutionPolicy;
import org.anddev.andengine.entity.Entity;
import org.anddev.andengine.entity.primitive.Rectangle;
import org.anddev.andengine.entity.scene.Scene;
import org.anddev.andengine.entity.scene.Scene.IOnAreaTouchListener;
import org.anddev.andengine.entity.scene.Scene.IOnSceneTouchListener;
import org.anddev.andengine.entity.scene.Scene.ITouchArea;
import org.anddev.andengine.entity.shape.Shape;
import org.anddev.andengine.entity.sprite.AnimatedSprite;
import org.anddev.andengine.entity.sprite.Sprite;
import org.anddev.andengine.entity.util.FPSLogger;
import org.anddev.andengine.extension.physics.box2d.PhysicsConnector;
import org.anddev.andengine.extension.physics.box2d.PhysicsFactory;
import org.anddev.andengine.extension.physics.box2d.PhysicsWorld;
import org.anddev.andengine.extension.physics.box2d.util.Vector2Pool;
import org.anddev.andengine.input.touch.TouchEvent;
import org.anddev.andengine.opengl.texture.Texture;
import org.anddev.andengine.opengl.texture.TextureOptions;
import org.anddev.andengine.opengl.texture.region.TextureRegion;
import org.anddev.andengine.opengl.texture.region.TextureRegionFactory;
import org.anddev.andengine.opengl.texture.region.TiledTextureRegion;
import org.anddev.andengine.sensor.accelerometer.AccelerometerData;
import org.anddev.andengine.sensor.accelerometer.IAccelerometerListener;
import org.anddev.andengine.ui.activity.BaseGameActivity;

import android.hardware.SensorManager;
import android.util.DisplayMetrics;

import com.badlogic.gdx.math.Vector2;
import com.badlogic.gdx.physics.box2d.Body;
import com.badlogic.gdx.physics.box2d.BodyDef.BodyType;
import com.badlogic.gdx.physics.box2d.FixtureDef;
```

```java
public class SimplePool extends BaseGameActivity
    implements IAccelerometerListener, IOnSceneTouchListener, IOnAreaTouchListener {

    private Camera mCamera;
    private Texture mTexture;
    private Texture mBallYellowTexture;
    private Texture mBallRedTexture;
    private Texture mBallBlackTexture;
    private Texture mBallBlueTexture;
    private Texture mBallGreenTexture;
    private Texture mBallOrangeTexture;
    private Texture mBallPinkTexture;
    private Texture mBallPurpleTexture;
    private Texture mBallWhiteTexture;

    private TiledTextureRegion mBallYellowTextureRegion;
    private TiledTextureRegion mBallRedTextureRegion;
    private TiledTextureRegion mBallBlackTextureRegion;
    private TiledTextureRegion mBallBlueTextureRegion;
    private TiledTextureRegion mBallGreenTextureRegion;
    private TiledTextureRegion mBallOrangeTextureRegion;
    private TiledTextureRegion mBallPinkTextureRegion;
    private TiledTextureRegion mBallPurpleTextureRegion;
    private TiledTextureRegion mBallWhiteTextureRegion;

    private Texture mBackgroundTexture;
    private TextureRegion mBackgroundTextureRegion;

    private PhysicsWorld mPhysicsWorld;

    private float mGravityX;
    private float mGravityY;
    private Scene mScene;

    private final int mFaceCount = 0;

    private final int CAMERA_WIDTH = 720;
    private final int CAMERA_HEIGHT = 480;

    @Override
    public Engine onLoadEngine() {
        DisplayMetrics dm = new DisplayMetrics();
        getWindowManager().getDefaultDisplay().getMetrics(dm);

        this.mCamera = new Camera(0, 0, CAMERA_WIDTH, CAMERA_HEIGHT);
        return new Engine(new EngineOptions(true, ScreenOrientation.LANDSCAPE,
            new RatioResolutionPolicy(CAMERA_WIDTH, CAMERA_HEIGHT), this.mCamera));
    }

    @Override
    public void onLoadResources() {
        this.mTexture =
            new Texture(64, 64, TextureOptions.BILINEAR_PREMULTIPLYALPHA);
        this.mBallBlackTexture =
            new Texture(64, 64, TextureOptions.BILINEAR_PREMULTIPLYALPHA);
```

```
this.mBallBlueTexture =
    new Texture(64, 64, TextureOptions.BILINEAR_PREMULTIPLYALPHA);
this.mBallGreenTexture =
    new Texture(64, 64, TextureOptions.BILINEAR_PREMULTIPLYALPHA);
this.mBallOrangeTexture =
    new Texture(64, 64, TextureOptions.BILINEAR_PREMULTIPLYALPHA);
this.mBallPinkTexture =
    new Texture(64, 64, TextureOptions.BILINEAR_PREMULTIPLYALPHA);
this.mBallPurpleTexture =
    new Texture(64, 64, TextureOptions.BILINEAR_PREMULTIPLYALPHA);
this.mBallYellowTexture =
    new Texture(64, 64, TextureOptions.BILINEAR_PREMULTIPLYALPHA);
this.mBallRedTexture =
    new Texture(64, 64, TextureOptions.BILINEAR_PREMULTIPLYALPHA);
this.mBallWhiteTexture =
    new Texture(64, 64, TextureOptions.BILINEAR_PREMULTIPLYALPHA);

TextureRegionFactory.setAssetBasePath("gfx/");
mBallYellowTextureRegion =
  TextureRegionFactory.createTiledFromAsset(this.mBallYellowTexture, this,
  "ball_yellow.png", 0, 0, 1, 1); // 64x32
mBallRedTextureRegion =
  TextureRegionFactory.createTiledFromAsset(this.mBallRedTexture, this,
  "ball_red.png", 0, 0, 1, 1); // 64x32
mBallBlackTextureRegion =
  TextureRegionFactory.createTiledFromAsset(this.mBallBlackTexture, this,
  "ball_black.png", 0, 0, 1, 1); // 64x32
mBallBlueTextureRegion =
  TextureRegionFactory.createTiledFromAsset(this.mBallBlueTexture, this,
  "ball_blue.png", 0, 0, 1, 1); // 64x32
mBallGreenTextureRegion =
  TextureRegionFactory.createTiledFromAsset(this.mBallGreenTexture, this,
  "ball_green.png", 0, 0, 1, 1); // 64x32
mBallOrangeTextureRegion =
  TextureRegionFactory.createTiledFromAsset(this.mBallOrangeTexture, this,
  "ball_orange.png", 0, 0, 1, 1); // 64x32
mBallPinkTextureRegion =
  TextureRegionFactory.createTiledFromAsset(this.mBallPinkTexture, this,
  "ball_pink.png", 0, 0, 1, 1); // 64x32
mBallPurpleTextureRegion =
  TextureRegionFactory.createTiledFromAsset(this.mBallPurpleTexture, this,
  "ball_purple.png", 0, 0, 1, 1); // 64x32
mBallWhiteTextureRegion =
  TextureRegionFactory.createTiledFromAsset(this.mBallWhiteTexture, this,
  "ball_white.png", 0, 0, 1, 1); // 64x32

this.mBackgroundTexture = new Texture(512, 1024,
  TextureOptions.BILINEAR_PREMULTIPLYALPHA);
this.mBackgroundTextureRegion =
  TextureRegionFactory.createFromAsset(this.mBackgroundTexture, this,
  "table_bkg.png", 0, 0);

this.enableAccelerometerSensor(this);

mEngine.getTextureManager().loadTextures(mBackgroundTexture,
  mBallYellowTexture,
```

```
        mBallRedTexture, mBallBlackTexture, mBallBlueTexture,
        mBallGreenTexture, mBallOrangeTexture,
        mBallPinkTexture, mBallPurpleTexture);
    }

    @Override
    public Scene onLoadScene() {
        this.mEngine.registerUpdateHandler(new FPSLogger());

        this.mPhysicsWorld = new PhysicsWorld(
            new Vector2(0, SensorManager.GRAVITY_EARTH), false);

        this.mScene = new Scene();
        this.mScene.attachChild(new Entity());

        this.mScene.setBackgroundEnabled(false);
        this.mScene.setOnSceneTouchListener(this);
        Sprite background = new Sprite(0, 0, this.mBackgroundTextureRegion);
        background.setWidth(CAMERA_WIDTH);
        background.setHeight(CAMERA_HEIGHT);
        background.setPosition(0, 0);
        this.mScene.getChild(0).attachChild(background);

        final Shape ground = new Rectangle(0, CAMERA_HEIGHT, CAMERA_WIDTH, 0);
        final Shape roof = new Rectangle(0, 0, CAMERA_WIDTH, 0);
        final Shape left = new Rectangle(0, 0, 0, CAMERA_HEIGHT);
        final Shape right = new Rectangle(CAMERA_WIDTH, 0, 0, CAMERA_HEIGHT);

        final FixtureDef wallFixtureDef =
            PhysicsFactory.createFixtureDef(0, 0.5f, 0.5f);
        PhysicsFactory.createBoxBody(
            mPhysicsWorld, ground, BodyType.StaticBody, wallFixtureDef);
        PhysicsFactory.createBoxBody(
            mPhysicsWorld, roof, BodyType.StaticBody, wallFixtureDef);
        PhysicsFactory.createBoxBody(
            mPhysicsWorld, left, BodyType.StaticBody, wallFixtureDef);
        PhysicsFactory.createBoxBody(
            mPhysicsWorld, right, BodyType.StaticBody, wallFixtureDef);

        this.mScene.attachChild(ground);
        this.mScene.attachChild(roof);
        this.mScene.attachChild(left);
        this.mScene.attachChild(right);

        this.mScene.registerUpdateHandler(this.mPhysicsWorld);
        this.mScene.setOnAreaTouchListener(this);

        return this.mScene;
    }

    @Override
    public void onLoadComplete() {
        setupBalls();
    }

    @Override
```

```java
public boolean onAreaTouched(
    final TouchEvent pSceneTouchEvent, final ITouchArea pTouchArea,
    final float pTouchAreaLocalX, final float pTouchAreaLocalY) {
    if (pSceneTouchEvent.isActionDown()) {
        final AnimatedSprite face = (AnimatedSprite) pTouchArea;
        this.jumpFace(face);
        return true;
    }
    return false;
}

@Override
public boolean onSceneTouchEvent(
    final Scene pScene, final TouchEvent pSceneTouchEvent) {
    if (this.mPhysicsWorld != null) {
        if (pSceneTouchEvent.isActionDown()) {
            // this.addFace(pSceneTouchEvent.getX(),
            // pSceneTouchEvent.getY());
            return true;
        }
    }
    return false;
}

@Override
public void onAccelerometerChanged(final AccelerometerData pAccelerometerData) {
    this.mGravityX = pAccelerometerData.getX();
    this.mGravityY = pAccelerometerData.getY();

    final Vector2 gravity = Vector2Pool.obtain(this.mGravityX, this.mGravityY);
    this.mPhysicsWorld.setGravity(gravity);
    Vector2Pool.recycle(gravity);
}

private void setupBalls() {
    final AnimatedSprite[] balls = new AnimatedSprite[9];

    final FixtureDef objectFixtureDef =
        PhysicsFactory.createFixtureDef(1, 0.5f, 0.5f);

    AnimatedSprite redBall =
        new AnimatedSprite(10, 10, this.mBallRedTextureRegion);
    AnimatedSprite yellowBall =
        new AnimatedSprite(20, 20, this.mBallYellowTextureRegion);
    AnimatedSprite blueBall =
        new AnimatedSprite(30, 30, this.mBallBlueTextureRegion);
    AnimatedSprite greenBall =
        new AnimatedSprite(40, 40, this.mBallGreenTextureRegion);
    AnimatedSprite orangeBall =
        new AnimatedSprite(50, 50, this.mBallOrangeTextureRegion);
    AnimatedSprite pinkBall =
        new AnimatedSprite(60, 60, this.mBallPinkTextureRegion);
    AnimatedSprite purpleBall =
        new AnimatedSprite(70, 70, this.mBallPurpleTextureRegion);
    AnimatedSprite blackBall =
        new AnimatedSprite(70, 70, this.mBallBlackTextureRegion);
```

```
        AnimatedSprite whiteBall =
            new AnimatedSprite(70, 70, this.mBallWhiteTextureRegion);

        balls[0] = redBall;
        balls[1] = yellowBall;
        balls[2] = blueBall;
        balls[3] = greenBall;
        balls[4] = orangeBall;
        balls[5] = pinkBall;
        balls[6] = purpleBall;
        balls[7] = blackBall;
        balls[8] = whiteBall;

        for (int i = 0; i < 9; i++) {
            Body body = PhysicsFactory.createBoxBody(this.mPhysicsWorld, balls[i],
                BodyType.DynamicBody, objectFixtureDef);
            mPhysicsWorld.registerPhysicsConnector(new PhysicsConnector(balls[i],
                body, true, true));

            balls[i].animate(new long[] { 200, 200 }, 0, 1, true);
            balls[i].setUserData(body);
            this.mScene.registerTouchArea(balls[i]);
            this.mScene.attachChild(balls[i]);
        }
    }

    private void jumpFace(final AnimatedSprite face) {
        final Body faceBody = (Body) face.getUserData();

        final Vector2 velocity =
            Vector2Pool.obtain(this.mGravityX * -50, this.mGravityY * -50);
        faceBody.setLinearVelocity(velocity);
        Vector2Pool.recycle(velocity);
    }
}
```

Source Download URL

The source code for this example is in the Android Cookbook repository (*https://github.com/IanDarwin/Android-Cookbook-Examples*), in the subdirectory *SimplePool* (see "Getting and Using the Code Examples" on page 18).

13.3 Processing Timed Keyboard Input

Kurosh Fallahzadeh

Problem

You want to determine whether a user-generated action, such as a key-press/release, has occurred within a certain time interval. This can be useful in game input handling and elsewhere.

Solution

Put the thread to sleep for the time interval and use a handler to determine whether a key-press/release has occurred.

Discussion

The interval is a long integer that represents time in milliseconds. In Example 13-5, we override the onKeyUp() method so that when the user releases a key, Android will invoke our taskHandler methods, which basically continue to repeatedly execute task A as long as the user continues to press/release any key within the one-second interval; otherwise, they execute task B.

Example 13-5. The keyboard input timing code

```
// In the main class...

private long interval = 1000; // 1-second time interval

private taskHandler myTaskHandler = new TaskHandler();

class TaskHandler extends Handler {

    @Override
    public void handleMessage(Message msg) {
        MyMainClass.this.executeTaskB();
    }

    public void sleep(long timeInterval) {
      // Remove previous keyboard message in queue
        this.removeMessages(0);
        // Enqueue current keyboard message to execute after timeInterval
        sendMessageDelayed(obtainMessage(0), timeInterval);
    }
}

@Override
public boolean onKeyUp(int keyCode, KeyEvent event) {
```

```
    // Execute TaskA and call handler to execute TaskB if
    / Key release message arrives after 'interval' has elapsed
    executeTaskA();
    myTaskHandler.sleep(interval);

 return true;
}

public void executeTaskA() {
...
}

public void executeTaskB() {
...
}
```

## CHAPTER 14

Social Networking

In the second decade of this century, nobody writing about the internet would underestimate the importance of social networking. Dominated as it is by a few major sites —Facebook and Twitter being the biggest of the big—social networking provides both an opportunity for developers and a missed opportunity for the developer community as a whole. Certainly there are still opportunities for creative use of social networking. But what is missing (despite valiant efforts) is a single "open social networking" API that includes authorization, messaging, and media interchange.

This chapter provides a few how-tos for accessing sites such as Facebook and Twitter, using plain HTTP (they all originated as web-based sites just before the explosion of mobile apps) and using more comprehensive (but more specific) APIs.

14.1 Authenticating Users with OAUTH2

Ian Darwin

Problem

Most of the popular social networks use OAuth2 for authentication, so you will probably need to connect to it sometime.

Solution

There are many APIs available for OAuth2. Here's a short list:

- The Android code in the built-in `AccountManager` (*https://developer.android.com/training/id-auth/authenticate.html*)
- The Google Play Android code in the `GoogleAuthUtil` class (*https://developers.google.com/android/guides/http-auth*) in the Google Play library

- The open source *android-oauth-client* library (*https://github.com/wuman/android-oauth-client*)

- A commercial toolkit from Auth0 (*https://auth0.com/docs/quickstart/native/android*)

We'll use the first of these in this recipe, and the third in Recipe 14.3.

Discussion

OAuth2 is the second version of the Open Authentication protocol, the core of many sites' user-authentication strategies. It is a multistep protocol with several variations, so you should probably learn a bit about it. If you are new to OAuth, there's plenty of background reading available. For a textbook, refer to Ryan Boyd's *Getting Started with OAuth 2.0* (O'Reilly). For online information, start with this search query (*https://www.google.ca/search?q=understanding+oauth*) or Mitchell Anicas's introduction to OAuth 2 (*https://www.digitalocean.com/community/tutorials/an-introduction-to-oauth-2*).

For our example, we'll take the Tasks (todo list) API, which is a Google-hosted, OAuth2-authenticated service. There is a user interface to this service in the GMail web client (Figure 14-1), and some Android applications use it (although Google Keep doesn't).

Figure 14-1. GMail Tasks interface

Because authorization with OAuth2 requires network traffic, any API for use on Android must be written to be asynchronous, and any application that uses it must have INTERNET permission.

We'll use the AccountManager to handle OAuth2. Using OAuth2 requires:

- Identifying your application (using a clientId and a clientSecret previously obtained from the server)
- Getting permission from the user for the identified application to work on his behalf on the server
- An "authentication token" that represents the combination of the previous two items

In addition, for Google APIs, you need a Google API key, also obtained from the server (the Google API web console).

Once you've obtained the authentication token (we'll show how to get it in Example 14-1), you send it with the request you want to authorize, along with the other information. In the case of HTTP/HTTPS, the authentication is sent as HTTP headers, using something like this:

```
public void fetchTasks() {
    // Following code must not run on UI thread
    URL url = new URL(
        "https://www.googleapis.com/tasks/v1/users/@me/lists/@default/tasks?key=" +
        our_api_key);
    Map<String,String> headers = new HashMap<>();
    headers.put("accept", "text/json");
    headers.put("authorization", "OAuth " + authToken);
    headers.put("client_id", our_client_id);
    headers.put("client_secret", our_client_secret);
    final String result = ConversationURL.converse(url, null, headers);
    // Convert to List<Task> using some JSON API
    // Display list in a RecyclerView or ListView
}
```

Of course, before we can run that code, we have to get the auth token (Example 14-1). Since we aren't writing a Google app (only Google can do that!) but we want to use a Google service, we need the GET_ACCOUNTS Android permission to be able to view arbitrary accounts on the device. On Android 6 or later we will have to request this permission (see Recipe 2.2).

Example 14-1. Requesting the OAuth token

```
public void getTasks() {

    // Code to request GET_ACCOUNTS permission not shown...

    // Find the Google account - other AccountManager calls would
    //   let you choose by type
    final Account[] accounts = am.getAccounts();
    if (accounts.length == 0) {
        Toast.makeText(this,
            "Please create a Google account before using this app",
            Toast.LENGTH_LONG).show();
        finish();
        return;
    }
    for (Account acct : accounts) {
        Log.d(TAG, "Account " + acct.name + "(" + acct.type + ")");
        if (acct.type.equals("com.google")) {

            // Since the credential often expires, just get a new one
            am.invalidateAuthToken(acct.type, authToken);

            // Get the authToken. Async: doesn't return token;
            // find it in the callbacks.
            am.getAuthToken(
                    // Android "Account" for Google access:
                    acct,
                    // Google-provided auth scope for viewing tasks:
                    AUTHDOM_RO,
                    // If any authenticator-specific options needed:
                    new Bundle(),
                    MainActivity.this,
                    // Success callback:
                    new OnTokenAcquired(),
                    Failure callback:
                    new Handler(new OnError())));
            break;
        }
    }
}
```

As mentioned, this is all asynchronous. The call to getAuthToken() will contact the server's OAuth code and get the auth token for us to use. If it succeeds, it will call our success callback:

```
/**
 * Success callback indicates that OAuth2 authenticator has gotten an auth
 * token for us, so save it in a field for use in the REST service code,
 * and invoke same.
 */
private class OnTokenAcquired implements AccountManagerCallback<Bundle> {
    @Override
```

```
public void run(AccountManagerFuture<Bundle> result) {
    Log.d(TAG, "OnTokenAcquired.run()");
    // Get the result of the operation from the AccountManagerFuture
    try {
        Bundle bundle = result.getResult();

        // The authToken arrives in the bundle, named KEY_AUTHTOKEN

        authToken = bundle.getString(AccountManager.KEY_AUTHTOKEN);

        Log.d(TAG, "Got this authToken: " + authToken);

        doFetchTasks();      // Near start of this recipe

    } catch (OperationCanceledException | IOException e) {
        // Handle this error...
    } catch (AuthenticatorException e) {
        // Handle this error...
    }
  }
}
```

 A vulnerability in how some mobile apps use OAuth2 was discovered just as the second edition of this book was going to press; see the original paper (*http://www.blackhat.com/docs/eu-16/materials/eu-16-Yang-Signing-Into-Billion-Mobile-Apps-Effortlessly-With-OAuth20-wp.pdf*) for details.

See Also

There is some official documentation (*https://developer.android.com/training/id-auth/authenticate.html*) on the techniques in this recipe. For a more general (non-Android) API, see Google OAuth2 client library for Java (*https://developers.google.com/api-client-library/java/google-api-java-client/oauth2*). This library is open sourced on GitHub (*https://github.com/google/google-api-java-client*).

Source Download URL

The source code for this project is in the Android Cookbook repository (*https://github.com/IanDarwin/Android-Cookbook-Examples*), in the subdirectory *OAuth2Demo* (see "Getting and Using the Code Examples" on page 18).

14.2 Integrating Social Networking Using HTTP

Shraddha Shravagi

Problem

You need a basic level of social networking support in your app.

Solution

Instead of diving into the API, you can simply add social networking support. For Facebook, Twitter, and LinkedIn integration, just follow three simple steps to get started:

1. Download the logos for Facebook, Twitter, and LinkedIn.

2. Create image buttons for each of them.

3. Implement an event handler that, when the user presses the button, passes control to the relevant site and displays the results in a browser window.

Discussion

Here is a simple approach to adding basic social networking.

Step 1: Get the logos

Download the logos from their respective websites, or use a web search engine.

Step 2: Create image buttons for each logo

The layout shown in Example 14-2 provides image buttons for each of the social networking sites. Figure 14-2 shows the buttons.

Example 14-2. The main layout

```
<!-- Facebook button -->
<ImageView android:src="@drawable/icon_facebook"
    android:layout_width="28dip"
    android:layout_height="28dip" android:id="@+id/facebookBtn"
    android:clickable="true"
    android:onClick="facebookBtnClicked" />

<!-- Twitter button -->
<ImageView android:src="@drawable/icon_twitter"
    android:clickable="true"
    android:layout_width="30dip" android:layout_height="28dip"
    android:id="@+id/twitterBtn" android:layout_marginLeft="3dp"
    android:layout_marginRight="3dp" android:onClick="twitterBtnClicked"
    />

<!-- LinkedIn button -->
<ImageView android:src="@drawable/icon_linkedin"
    android:layout_width="28dip"
```

```
android:layout_height="30dip" android:clickable="true"
android:id="@+id/linkedinBtn"
android:onClick="linkedinBtnClicked"
/>
```

Figure 14-2. Social networking buttons

Step 3: Implement the click event

The code in Example 14-3 provides a series of listeners, each of which will open an Intent to the respective social networking website. These are added as OnClickListeners by use of android:onClick attributes in the layout in Example 14-2, so the main Activity code is fairly short.

Example 14-3. The social networking action handling code

```
/* The URL used here is for the application I want the user to redirect to,
 * and a comment about it. For example, here I am using http://goo.gl/eRAD9
 * as the URL, but you can use the URL of your app. Take the URL from
 * Google Play and shorten it with bit.ly or the Google URL shortener.
 */

public void facebookBtnClicked(View v) {
    Toast.makeText(this,
        "Facebook Loading...\n +
        "Please make sure you are connected to the internet.",
        Toast.LENGTH_SHORT).show();
```

```
    String url="http://m.facebook.com/sharer.php?u=http%3A%2F%2Fgoo.gl%2FeRAD9";
    Intent i = new Intent(Intent.ACTION_VIEW);
    i.setData(Uri.parse(url));
    startActivity(i);
}

public void twitterBtnClicked(View v) {
    Toast.makeText(this,
        "Twitter Loading... \n Please make sure you are connected to the internet.",
        Toast.LENGTH_SHORT).show();
    String url = "http://www.twitter.com/share?text=
        Checkout+This+Demo+http://goo.gl/eRAD9+";
    Intent i = new Intent(Intent.ACTION_VIEW);
    i.setData(Uri.parse(url));
    startActivity(i);
}

public void linkedinBtnClicked(View v) {
    Toast.makeText(this,
        "LinkedIn Loading... \n Please make sure you are connected to the internet",
        Toast.LENGTH_SHORT).show();
    String url="http://www.linkedin.com/shareArticle?url=
        http%3A%2F%2Fgoo.gl%2FeRAD9&mini=
        true&source=SampleApp&title=App+on+your+mobile";
    Intent intent=new Intent(Intent.ACTION_VIEW);
    intent.setData(Uri.parse(url));
    startActivity(intent);
}
```

This is how, in three simple steps, you can get a social networking feature for your application. Here we used Intents to start the site in the user's browser; you could also use a `WebView` as shown in Recipe 12.8.

14.3 Loading a User's Twitter Timeline Using HTML or JSON

Rachee Singh, Ian Darwin

Problem

You want to load a user's Twitter timeline (list of tweets) into an Android application.

Solution

Since timeline information is public, you don't necessarily have to deal with Twitter's authentication. You can use a `WebView` or an Intent to launch a Twitter search for the user's screen name to get an HTML page without authenticating. Or, you can authenticate using OAuth2 (see Recipe 14.1) and use a REST API to obtain the data from the user's Twitter page in JSON format.

Discussion

If you just want to view a given user's Twitter feed, for example, you can use a URL like *https://twitter.com/search?q=%40androidcook*, which searches for the `@AndroidCook` user. You could load this into a `WebView` object:

```
String url = "https://twitter.com/search?q=%40androidcook";
WebView wv = (WebView)findViewById(R.id.webview);
wv.loadUrl(url);
```

Or, to have the URL show up in its own window, just open an Intent for it:

```
startActivity(new Intent(url));
```

What if you want to be able to process the results yourself? HTML is notoriously difficult to extract useful information from. Due to Twitter's current permissions scheme, the URL method described in this recipe in the first edition of this book no longer works:

```
String url = "http://twitter.com/statuses/user_timeline/androidcook.json";
```

If you open the preceding URL today, the result comes back in JSON as:

```
{"errors":[{"message":"Sorry, that page does not exist","code":34}]}
```

Instead, you have to authenticate using OAuth2 and use the REST API to get results back in JSON format. One of the best libraries around appears to be the *wuman* OAuth library, which supports OAuth versions 1 and 2, the latter with various types of authorization. It is also noteworthy as it ships with sample applications for Flickr, Foursquare, GitHub, Instagram, LinkedIn, Twitter, and more, all in open source. This API requires an external dependency:

```
<dependency>
  <groupId>com.wu-man</groupId>
  <artifactId>android-oauth-client</artifactId>
  <version>0.4.5</version>
</dependency>
```

The code is more complicated than our previous OAuth recipe, and rather than repeat the sample application, we will just direct your attention to the project website (*https://github.com/wuman/android-oauth-client*). The *library* folder contains the library, and the *samples* folder contains the applications for the social sites previously listed. The *wuman* library is licensed under the Apache Software License v2 so you can pretty much use it for any purpose.

## CHAPTER 15

Location and Map Applications

Not that long ago, GPS devices were either unavailable, expensive, or cumbersome. Today, almost every smartphone has a GPS receiver, and many digital cameras do, too. GPS is well on its way to becoming truly ubiquitous in devices. The organizations that provide map data are well aware of this trend. Indeed, OpenStreetMap (*http://openstreetmap.org/*) exists and provides its "free, editable map of the world" in part because of the rise of consumer GPS devices; most of its map data was provided by enthusiasts. Google gets much of its data from commercial mapping services, but in Android, Google has been very driven by the availability of GPS receivers in Android devices. This chapter thus concentrates on the ins and outs of using Google Maps and OpenStreetMap in Android devices.

15.1 Getting Location Information

Ian Darwin

Problem

You want to know where you are.

Solution

Use Android's built-in location providers.

Discussion

Android provides two levels of location detection. If you need to know fairly precisely where you are, you can use the FINE resolution, which is GPS-based. If you only need to know roughly where you are, you can use the coarse resolution, which is based on the location of the cell tower(s) your phone is talking to or in range of. The FINE resolution is usually accurate to a few meters; the coarse resolution may be accurate down to the building or city block in densely built-up areas, or to the nearest 5 or 10 kilometers in very lightly populated areas with cell towers maximally spaced out.

Example 15-1 shows the setup portion of the code that gets location data. This is part of JPSTrack (*http://www.darwinsys.com/jpstrack/*), a mapping application for OpenStreetMap. For mapping purposes the GPS is a must, so I only ask for the FINE resolution.

Example 15-1. Getting location data

```
// Part of JPSTrack Main.java
LocationManager mgr =
    (LocationManager) getSystemService(LOCATION_SERVICE);
for (String prov : mgr.getAllProviders()) {
    Log.i(LOG_TAG, getString(R.string.provider_found) + prov);
}

// GPS setup
Criteria criteria = new Criteria();
criteria.setAccuracy(Criteria.ACCURACY_FINE);
List<String> providers = mgr.getProviders(criteria, true);
if (providers == null || providers.size() == 0) {
    Log.e(JPSTRACK, getString(R.string.cannot_get_gps_service));
    Toast.makeText(this, "Could not open GPS service",
        Toast.LENGTH_LONG).show();
    return;
}
String preferred = providers.get(0); // first == preferred
```

After this setup, when you actually want to start the GPS sending you location data, you have to call LocationManager.requestLocationUpdates() with the name of the provider you looked up previously, the minimum time between updates (in milliseconds), the minimum distance between updates (in meters), and an instance of the LocationListener interface. You should stop updates by calling removeUpdates() with the previously passed-in LocationListener; doing so will reduce overhead and save battery life. In JPSTrack, the code looks like Example 15-2.

Example 15-2. Suspend and resume location updates

```
@Override
protected void onResume() {
    super.onResume();
    if (preferred != null) {
        mgr.requestLocationUpdates(preferred,
            MIN_SECONDS * 1000,
            MIN_METRES, this);
    }
}
```

```
@Override
protected void onPause() {
    super.onPause();
    if (preferred != null) {
        mgr.removeUpdates(this);
    }
}
```

Finally, the `LocationListener`'s `onLocationChanged()` method is called when the location changes, and this is where you do something with the location information:

```
@Override
public void onLocationChanged(Location location) {
    long time = location.getTime();
    double latitude = location.getLatitude();
    double longitude = location.getLongitude();
    // Do something with latitude and longitude (and time?)...
}
```

The remaining few methods in `LocationListener` can be stub methods.

What you do with the location data depends on your application, of course. In JPSTrack, I save it into a track file with handwritten XML-writing code. Commonly you would use it to update your position on a map, or upload it to a location service. There's no limit to what you can do with it.

Source Download URL

You can download the source code for this example from GitHub (*https://github.com/ IanDarwin/jpstrack.android*).

15.2 Accessing GPS Information in Your Application

Pratik Rupwal

Problem

You need access to the GPS location in a class of your application.

Solution

Add a class that implements the `LocationListener` interface. Create an instance of this class where you want to access the GPS information and retrieve the data.

Discussion

In Example 15-3, the `MyLocationListener` class implements `LocationListener`.

Example 15-3. LocationListener implementation

```java
public class MyLocationListener implements LocationListener {

    @Override
    public void onLocationChanged(Location loc) {
        loc.getLatitude();
        loc.getLongitude();
    }

    @Override
    public void onProviderDisabled(String provider) {
        // Empty
    }
    @Override
    public void onProviderEnabled(String provider) {
        // Empty
    }
    @Override
    public void onStatusChanged(String provider, int status, Bundle extras) {
        // Empty
    }
} // End of class MyLocationListener
```

Add the class file in Example 15-3 in the package of your application; you can use its instance as shown in Example 15-4 to access GPS information in any class.

Example 15-4. Class that uses the LocationListener

```java
public class AccessGPS extends Activity {

    // Declaration of required objects

    LocationManager mlocManager;
    LocationListener mlocListener;
    Location lastKnownLocation;
    Double latitude,longitude;
    ...
    ...

protected void onCreate(Bundle savedInstanceState) {

    ...
    ...
        // Instantiating objects for accessing GPS information

        mlocListener = new MyLocationListener();

        // Request for location updates

        mlocManager.requestLocationUpdates(
        LocationManager.GPS_PROVIDER, 0, 0, mlocListener);
        locationProvider=LocationManager.GPS_PROVIDER;
        ...
```

```
...
// Access the last identified location

lastKnownLocation = mlocManager.getLastKnownLocation(locationProvider);

// The above object can be used for accessing GPS data as below

latitude=lastKnownLocation.getLatitude();
longitude=lastKnownLocation.getLongitude();

// The above GPS data can be used to carry out operations
//  specific to the location
...
...

    }
}
```

You can use the Location object loc in onLocationChanged() to access GPS information; however, it is not always possible in an application to perform all the GPS information–related tasks in this overridden method due to issues such as data accessibility. For example, in an application providing information on shopping malls near the user's current location, the app accesses the names of malls according to the user's location and displays them; when the user chooses a mall, the app displays the different stores in that mall. In this example, the application uses the user's location to determine which mall names to fetch from the database through a database handler that is a private member of the class hosting the view to the display list of malls; hence that database handler cannot be accessible in this overridden method, and therefore this operation cannot be carried out.

15.3 Mocking GPS Coordinates on a Device

Emaad Manzoor

Problem

You need to demonstrate your application, but you're scared it might choke when trying to triangulate your GPS coordinates. Or you'd like to simulate being in a place you're not.

Solution

Attach a mock location provider to your LocationManager object, and then attach mock coordinates to the mock location provider.

Discussion

The Android `LocationManager` has support for testing in code. While it will often be used in testing (see Chapter 3), we will use it directly in the application in Example 15-5 to set mock GPS coordinates on the device.

Example 15-5. Setting mock GPS coordinates

```
private void setMockLocation(double latitude, double longitude, float accuracy) {
    // This coding style is a way of handling a long list of boolean parameters
    lm.addTestProvider (LocationManager.GPS_PROVIDER,
                        "requiresNetwork" == "",
                        "requiresSatellite" == "",
                        "requiresCell" == "",
                        "hasMonetaryCost" == "",
                        "supportsAltitude" == "",
                        "supportsSpeed" == "",
                        "supportsBearing" == "",
                         android.location.Criteria.POWER_LOW,
                         android.location.Criteria.ACCURACY_FINE);

    Location newLocation = new Location(LocationManager.GPS_PROVIDER);

    newLocation.setLatitude(latitude);
    newLocation.setLongitude(longitude);
    newLocation.setAccuracy(accuracy);
    newLocation.setTime(System.currentTimeMillis());

    lm.setTestProviderEnabled(LocationManager.GPS_PROVIDER, true);

    lm.setTestProviderStatus(LocationManager.GPS_PROVIDER,
                        LocationProvider.AVAILABLE,
                        null,System.currentTimeMillis());

    lm.setTestProviderLocation(LocationManager.GPS_PROVIDER, newLocation);

}
```

In Example 15-5, we add a mock provider using the `addTestProvider()` method of the `LocationManager` class. Then we create a new location using the `Location` object, which allows us to set latitude, longitude, and accuracy.

We activate the mock provider by first setting a mock-enabled `value` for the `LocationManager` using its `setTestProviderEnabled()` method; then we set a mock `status`, and finally a mock `location`.

To use the `setMockLocation()` method, you must create a `LocationManager` object as you usually would, and then invoke the method with your coordinates (see Example 15-6).

Example 15-6. Mocking location

```
LocationManager lm = (LocationManager)getSystemService(Context.LOCATION_SERVICE);

lm.requestLocationUpdates(LocationManager.GPS_PROVIDER, 0, 0, new LocationListener(){
        @Override
        public void onStatusChanged(String provider, int status, Bundle extras){}
        @Override
        public void onProviderEnabled(String provider){}
        @Override
        public void onProviderDisabled(String provider){}
        @Override
        public void onLocationChanged(Location location){}
});

/* Set a mock location for debugging purposes */
setMockLocation(15.387653, 73.872585, 500);
```

- In your *AndroidManifest.xml* file, you'll have to add the permission `<uses-permission android:name="android.permission.ACCESS_MOCK_LOCATION>`.
- To run on a real device (as opposed to an AVD emulator), you must also enable → "Developer options" → "Allow mock locations" or the newer Settings → "Developer options" → "Select mock location app" (see Entering Developer Mode on a real device if you don't yet have a "Developer options" item under Settings).

You may need to restart the device after using the mock GPS to reenable the real GPS.

Example application usage

Find Me X is an Android application that takes in a search query of the form `place_type` in `locality`, `city` and returns results augmented with their distance from the user. Regardless of the chosen location, the location in this application is mocked to be BITS–Pilani Goa Campus, Goa, India.

See Also

Recipe 15.1, the developer documentation on the `LocationManager` (*https://developer.android.com/reference/android/location/LocationManager.html*) and `Location` (*https://developer.android.com/reference/android/location/Location.html*) classes.

Source Download URL

The source code for this project is in the Android Cookbook repository (*https://github.com/IanDarwin/Android-Cookbook-Examples*), in the subdirectory *FindMeX* (see "Getting and Using the Code Examples" on page 18).

15.4 Using Geocoding and Reverse Geocoding

Nidhin Jose Davis

Problem

You want to geocode (convert an address to its coordinates) and reverse geocode, (convert coordinates to an address).

Solution

Use the built-in Geocoder class.

Discussion

Geocoding is the process of finding the geographical coordinates (latitude and longitude) of a given address or location. *Reverse geocoding* is the opposite: taking a latitude and longitude pair and converting it into an address or location. In order to geocode or reverse geocode the first thing to do is to import the Geocoder class:

```
import android.location.Geocoder;
```

The geocoding or reverse geocoding should not be done on the UI thread as it may involve server access, and thus might cause the system to display an Application Not Responding (ANR) dialog to the user. The work has to be done in a separate thread. Example 15-7 shows the code for geocoding, and Example 15-8 shows the code for reverse geocoding.

Example 15-7. To geocode

```
Geocoder gc = new Geocoder(context);

if(gc.isPresent()) {
  List<Address> list =
      gc.getFromLocationName("1600 Amphitheatre Parkway, Mountain View, CA", 1);

  Address address = list.get(0);

  double lat = address.getLatitude();
  double lng = address.getLongitude();
}
```

Example 15-8. To reverse geocode

```
Geocoder gc = new Geocoder(context);

if(gc.isPresent()) {
  List<Address> list = gc.getFromLocation(37.42279, -122.08506,1);

  Address address = list.get(0);

  StringBuffer str = new StringBuffer();
  str.append("Name: " + address.getLocality() + "\n");
  str.append("Sub-Admin Areas: " + address.getSubAdminArea() + "\n");
  str.append("Admin Area: " + address.getAdminArea() + "\n");
  str.append("Country: " + address.getCountryName() + "\n");
  str.append("Country Code: " + address.getCountryCode() + "\n");

  String strAddress = str.toString();
}
```

15.5 Getting Ready for Google Maps API V2 Development

Ian Darwin

Problem

You want to get set up to use the current (V2) Google Maps API.

Solution

Download Google Play Services, get an API key, import a project or two, and start coding! Android Studio will do most of this work for you; this recipe guides you through the process.

Discussion

This recipe describes only the V2 API. The V1 API is deprecated; you can still code to it, but unless you have an API key already, you will not be able to run your application, as new API keys are no longer being issued. We no longer discuss use of the V1 API, since you would be unable to get a key for your application were you to use that API. (This highlights one drawback of using a proprietary Maps API: you are dependent upon Google for API key access. The OpenStreetMap API, covered starting in Recipe 15.7, doesn't have this problem; it is entirely open source and open data.)

Note that the V2 API can only be used on devices that have Google Play installed (e.g., official, Google-branded devices) and which have OpenGL ES 2.0 or later (almost all devices do). Note further that this API carries a *mandatory* "Attribution" requirement, which we'll cover in Recipe 15.6.

Adding maps support to a project

You can either make a new project with Maps support, or add Maps support to an existing project. To make a new project with Maps support using Android Studio, choose File → New → Project, configure the project, and choose Google Maps Activity on the "Add an activity to Mobile" screen of the Create New Project wizard. To add Maps V2 support to an existing project using Android Studio, just create a new Google Maps Activity as shown in Figure 15-1.

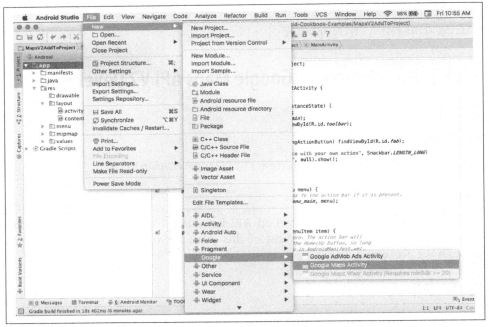

Figure 15-1. Adding a Google Maps Activity to an existing project

Whichever of these two ways you add Maps support, *doing so will automatically do the following*:

- Add the dependency `com.google.android.gms:play-services:9.4.0` (or later) to your *build.gradle* file.
- Create a string resources file named *src/debug/res/values/google_maps_api.xml*, shown in Example 15-9, in which you have to enter your API key.

- Create a reference to the string resource defined in *google_maps_api.xml* as a `meta-data` element in your `application` element, so that Google Maps can find it at runtime.

Example 15-9. The auto-created google_maps_api.xml file

```
<resources>
    <!--
    TODO: Before you run your application, you need a Google Maps API key.

    To get one, follow this link, follow the directions and press "Create":

    https://console.developers.google.com/flows/enableapi?apiid=maps_android_backend&
    keyType=CLIENT_SIDE_ANDROID&r=5F:21:CC:9B:77:00:4D:4E:37:F4:98:5D:C2:A4:47:70:1F:27
    :1D:DA%3Bcom.androidcookbook.mapsv2addtoproject

    You can also add your credentials to an existing key, using this line:
    5F:21:CC:9B:77:00:4D:4E:37:F4:98:5D:C2:A4:47:70:1F:27:1D:DA;com.androidcookbook.
    mapsv2addtoproject

    Alternatively, follow the directions here:
    https://developers.google.com/maps/documentation/android/start#get-key

    Once you have your key (it starts with "AIza"), replace the "google_maps_key"
    string in this file.
    -->
    <string name="google_maps_key" templateMergeStrategy="preserve"
            translatable="false">
        YOUR_KEY_HERE
    </string>
</resources>
```

This string resource is in a file all by itself, so that if you are sharing your source code you can choose whether to give out your API key along with the code.

Follow the link (to *console.developers.google.com*) in Example 15-9 and you will be asked to create a project (Figure 15-2).

Then you will be asked to create credentials (see Figure 15-3). Note that the "Create credentials" screen already has one package name and key hash filled in—the only one you need for development and debugging—courtesy of the URL provided in Example 15-9.

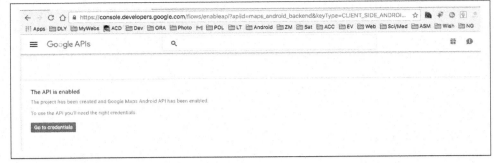

Figure 15-2. Starting a project

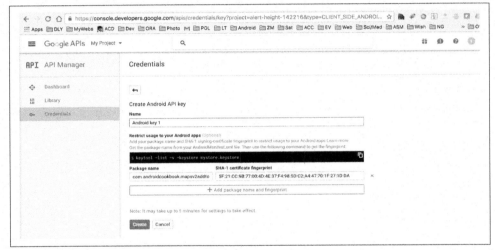

Figure 15-3. Creating credentials

Then you will be presented with your API key (Figure 15-4). Paste it into the *google_maps_api.xml* file, replacing the string YOUR_KEY_HERE and (optionally) removing the comments at the same time. Your file should now look like Example 15-10.

Example 15-10. The updated google_maps_api.xml file, with API key installed

```
<resources>
<string name="google_maps_key" templateMergeStrategy="preserve"
        translatable="false">
AIzaSyBgNZndPB67egfGMRukE1dVc_te1869Zkk
</string>
</resources>
```

Figure 15-4. Maps project

Finally, with all these steps completed, you can run the application. It should look something like Figure 15-5.

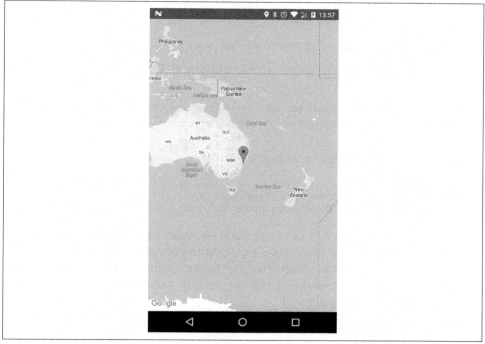

Figure 15-5. Default map application running

Note, however, that when you want to ship your application to the Google Play Store or some other production environment, you will need to obtain a new API key, since the one generated in this recipe is based on your debug signing key.

To create an API key, you need to provide the package name and a certificate signature; the "signature" is in the form of a SHA1 hash of the actual production signing key. You will typically have two signing certificates. The one for development and debug is called *debug.keystore*, and lives in *~/.android* (or in *C:\Users\your_user_name\.android* on current Windows systems). After you cd to the correct *.android* directory path, you can extract its SHA1 hash using the following:

```
keytool -list -v -keystore debug.keystore -alias androiddebugkey \
    -storepass android -keypass android
```

The debug key hash was provided for you earlier in this recipe; see Figure 15-3.

For your production signing key, neither the filename, the alias, nor the keystore password is standard, so getting the hash takes a bit more work:

```
keytool -list keystore YOUR_KEYSTORE
```

```
keytool -v -list -keystore YOUR_KEYSTORE -alias THE_LISTED_ALIAS
```

For both invocations of keytool, you will need to enter the keystore password when prompted.

In either case, once you have done the -list with -alias, you will see lines like those in Example 15-11 (except there will be hex digits where I have all zeros).

Example 15-11. Partial output from keytool -list

```
Certificate fingerprints:
    MD5: 4D:00:00:00:00:00:00:00:00:00:00:00:00:00:00:00
    SHA1 0F:00:00:00:00:00:00:00:00:00:00:00:00:00:00:00:00:00:00:00
```

To create your production API key, copy the SHA1 value and repeat the process starting from the beginning of this recipe, replacing the hexadecimal digits in the URL with the SHA1 hash for your production signing key. This API key will be placed in *src/main/res/values/google_maps_api.xml*. See more on publishing your application to the Google Play Store in Chapter 21.

We will discuss the Maps API V2 in more detail in Recipe 15.6.

Source Download URL

The source code for this project is in the Android Cookbook repository (*https://github.com/IanDarwin/Android-Cookbook-Examples*), in the subdirectory *MapsV2AddToProject* (see "Getting and Using the Code Examples" on page 18).

15.6 Using the Google Maps API V2

Ian Darwin

Problem

Now that you've set up your environment as described in Recipe 15.5, you want to do something with the Maps API.

Solution

This recipe will show some of the useful things you can do using the Maps API V2.

Discussion

The main class through which you generally interact with a map is the GoogleMap class. There is a wealth of functionality in this class. In this recipe we will show you how to:

- Add one or more Google Maps–style markers to the map.
- Move the map to a given location.
- Display the (mandatory!) internationalized attribution text.
- Add some extra UI elements.

Add markers and center the map position

First, we need to get the GoogleMap controller from the layout, in onCreate(). The MapFragment that we used in the layout file in Recipe 15.5 has a getMap() method that returns the GoogleMap:

```
map = ((MapFragment) getFragmentManager().findFragmentById(R.id.map)).getMap();
```

To add markers ("map pins") to the map, create a LatLng object and call the GoogleMap class's addMarker() method. This is a "fluent API" with each call returning the object operated upon, supporting what some Java people call "method call chaining," so you can call map.addMarker().setTitle().setSnippet() and so on. The code looks like Example 15-12.

Example 15-12. Adding a map marker in Maps API V2

```
LatLng location = new LatLng(markerLat, markerLng);
map.addMarker(new MarkerOptions()
    .position(location)
    .title(markerTitle)
    .snippet(markerSnippet));
```

The "title" and "snippet" are the title and detail text that pop up when the user taps the map marker.

The map can be moved and zoomed to give a convenient starting view. The Google Maps API V2 uses the notion of a "camera" or view position, which we set with moveCamera() (see Example 15-13).

Example 15-13. Moving and zooming the view ("camera") in Maps API V2

```
// Move the "camera" (view position) to our center point with a zoom of 15
final LatLng CENTER = new LatLng(lat, lng);
map.moveCamera(CameraUpdateFactory.newLatLng(CENTER));
// Zoom in, animating the camera
map.animateCamera(CameraUpdateFactory.zoomTo(15), 1000, null);
```

Example 15-14 shows a complete example of creating a map with half a dozen marker pins, taken from data stored in an array. This data originally came from a Google Map I prepared on the Google Maps website for a computer conference at the University of Toronto. A better way of getting the data—actually used in the conference app—is to download the KML file from Google Maps and parse it yourself, or to host the data in a simple JSON format on a server and parse that.

Example 15-14. Code for Maps API V2 demo

```
import com.google.android.gms.maps.CameraUpdateFactory;
import com.google.android.gms.maps.GoogleMap;
import com.google.android.gms.maps.MapFragment;
import com.google.android.gms.maps.model.LatLng;
import com.google.android.gms.maps.model.MarkerOptions;

public class MapsActivity extends Activity {

    public static final String TAG = MainActivity.TAG;
    private GoogleMap map;
    final LatLng CENTER = new LatLng(43.661049, -79.400917);

    class Data {
        public Data(float lng, float lat, String title, String snippet) {
            super();
            this.lat = (float)lat;
            this.lng = (float)lng;
            this.title = title;
            this.snippet = snippet;
        }
        float lat;
        float lng;
        String title;
        String snippet;
    }

    Data[] data = {
```

```
                new Data(-79.400917f,43.661049f, "New New College Res",
                        "Residence building (new concrete high-rise)"),
                new Data(-79.394524f,43.655796f, "Baldwin Street",
                        "Here be many good restaurants!"),
                new Data(-79.402206f,43.657688f, "College St",
                        "Many discount computer stores if you forgot a cable
                        or need to buy hardware."),
                new Data(-79.390381f,43.659878f, "Queen's Park Subway",
                        "Quickest way to the north-south (Yonge-University-Spadina)
                        subway/metro line"),
                new Data(-79.403732f,43.666801f, "Spadina Subway",
                        "Quickest way to the east-west (Bloor-Danforth)
                        subway/metro line"),
                new Data(-79.399696f,43.667873f, "St. George Subway back door",
                        "Token-only admittance, else use Spadina or
                        Bedford entrances!"),
                new Data(-79.384163f,43.655083f, "Eaton Centre (megamall)",
                        "One of the largest indoor shopping centres in eastern
                        Canada. Runs from Dundas to Queen."),
        };

        @Override
        protected void onCreate(Bundle savedInstanceState) {
            Log.d(TAG, "MapsActivity.onCreate()");
            super.onCreate(savedInstanceState);
            setContentView(R.layout.activity_main);
            map = ((MapFragment) getFragmentManager()
                .findFragmentById(R.id.map)).getMap();

            if (map==null) {
                String message = "Map Fragment Not Found or no Map in it!";
                Log.e(TAG, message);
                Toast.makeText(this, message, Toast.DURATION_LONG).show();
                return;
            }

            for (Data d : data) {
                LatLng location = new LatLng(d.lat, d.lng);
                map.addMarker(new MarkerOptions().position(location)
                    .title(d.title)
                    .snippet(d.snippet));
            }

            // Let the user see indoor maps if available
            map.setIndoorEnabled(true);

            // Enable my-location stuff
            map.setMyLocationEnabled(true);

            // Set the "camera" (view position) to our center point, then animate motion
            map.moveCamera(CameraUpdateFactory.zoomTo(14));
            map.animateCamera(CameraUpdateFactory.newLatLng(CENTER), 1750, null);
        }
}
```

The resulting map page looks something like Figure 15-6.

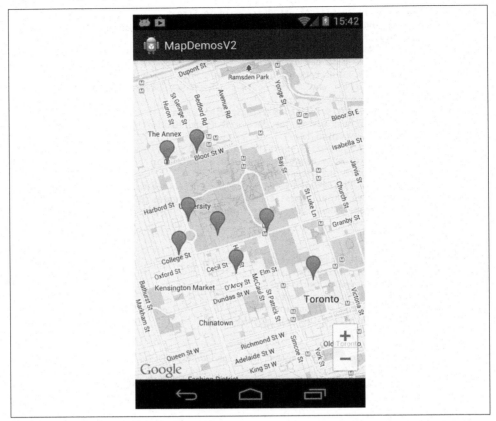

Figure 15-6. The map demo in action

Attribution text

The Google Android Maps API's terms of use (which you agreed to when you got your API key; see Recipe 15.5) require you to display the attribution text, which at present is basically the Apache 2 License. You can get the (hopefully internationalized) version of the required text by calling the convenience method `GooglePlayServicesUtil.getOpenSourceSoftwareLicenseInfo(Context)`.

The `AboutActivity` for this app contains an HTML file in a `WebView` (loaded from the *assets* folder), with a `TextView` below that for the attribution text. The code for this is shown in Example 15-15.

Example 15-15. Code to display app-specific text along with Google attribution

```
public void onCreate(Bundle savedInstanceState) {
    super.onCreate(savedInstanceState);
    setContentView(R.layout.about_activity);
    WebView aboutView = (WebView)findViewById(R.id.about_content);
    aboutView.loadUrl("file:///android_asset/about.html");
    TextView tv = (TextView)findViewById(R.id.about_version_tv);
    tv.setText(GooglePlayServicesUtil.getOpenSourceSoftwareLicenseInfo(this));
}
```

Everything else

There is quite a bit more that you can do with the Android Maps API V2. Among other things, you can:

- Add or remove various UI controls.
- Add polygons or polylines to the map.
- Add a `GroundOverlay` (anchored to the map) or `TileOverlay` (floating above it); in these, you can do any kind of drawing.
- Add various kinds of event listeners.

This is a new API and more features may be added. For example, there are several GUI controls that can be shown (Example 15-14 enables the "My Location" button), but there is not yet a way to enable the "Map Type" control. You can set the map type initially or programmatically, but you'd have to provide your own GUI for it. Nonetheless, it is quite a capable API. I urge you to explore it on your own until we get more recipes added or updated.

See Also

The official Maps documentation (*https://developers.google.com/maps/*).

Source Download URL

The source code for this project is in the Android Cookbook repository (*https://github.com/IanDarwin/Android-Cookbook-Examples*), in the subdirectory *MapDemosV2* (see "Getting and Using the Code Examples" on page 18).

15.7 Displaying Map Data Using OpenStreetMap

Rachee Singh

Problem

You want to use OpenStreetMap (OSM) map data in your application in place of Google Maps.

Solution

Use the third-party *osmdroid* library to interact with OpenStreetMap data.

Discussion

OpenStreetMap (*https://www.openstreetmap.org*) is a free, editable map of the world. osmdroid is "a (almost) full/free replacement for Android's `MapView` (v1 API) class."

To use OSM map data in your Android app, you need to include two JARs in the Android project, namely *osmdroid-android-x.xx.jar* and *slf4j-android-1.x.x.jar*. osmdroid is a set of tools for OpenStreetMap data; SLF4J is (yet another) simplified logging facade. You can add the JAR files to your Maven project using this dependency:

```
<dependency>
  <groupId>org.osmdroid</groupId>
  <artifactId>osmdroid-android</artifactId>
  <version>${osmdroid.version}</version>
</dependency>
```

The version should be 4.2 to compile the examples in this chapter. The current version as of this writing is 5.2, but there are several incompatible changes, including the removal (not just deprecation) of the `DefaultResourceProxyImpl` class and the switch from providing JAR files to proving AAR files (requiring the extra `<type>aar</type>` element). On the other hand, using 5.0 or later does eliminate the need for the extra SLF4J logging API.

If you prefer not to use a build tool to manage dependencies, you'll need to download the following:

- osmdroid (*https://repo1.maven.org/maven2/org/osmdroid/osmdroid-android/4.2/osmdroid-android-4.2.jar*).

- If using a version of osmdroid prior to 5.0, you will also need *slf4j-android-1.7.5.jar* (*http://www.slf4j.org/download.html*). When using slf4j, you need both its API JAR file (e.g., slf4j-1.x.x.jar) as well as one "implementation" JAR file (such as slf4j-android-1.x.x.jar) Note that the file on the download page is a ZIP file, which you will have to extract the files from (slf4j-1.7.25/slf4j-api-1.7.25.jar and slf4j-android-1.7.25.jar).

- If using SLF4J and you want to get logging output from osmdroid, you will also need an implementation JAR such as *slf4j-jdk14*, from the same source and the same version number.

See Recipe 1.20 for more information on using external libraries in your Android project.

After adding the JARs to the project you can start coding. You need to add an OSM MapView to your XML layout, like so:

```
<LinearLayout xmlns:android="http://schemas.android.com/apk/res/android"
    android:orientation="vertical"
    android:layout_width="fill_parent"
    android:layout_height="fill_parent">
  <org.osmdroid.views.MapView
      android:layout_width="fill_parent"
      android:layout_height="fill_parent"
      android:id="@+id/mapview">
  </org.osmdroid.views.MapView>
</LinearLayout>
```

Remember that you need to include the INTERNET permission in the *AndroidManifest.xml* file for any app that downloads information over the internet. The osmdroid code also needs the ACCESS_NETWORK_STATE permission:

```
<uses-permission android:name="android.permission.ACCESS_NETWORK_STATE" />
<uses-permission android:name="android.permission.INTERNET" />
```

Now you can use this MapView in the Activity code. The process is similar to the case of using Google Maps (see Example 15-16).

Example 15-16. Using the MapView in the application

```
private MapView mapView;
private MapController mapController;
mapView = (MapView) this.findViewById(R.id.mapview);
mapView.setBuiltInZoomControls(true);
mapView.setMultiTouchControls(true);
mapController = this.mapView.getController();
mapController.setZoom(2);
```

Figure 15-7 shows how the application should look on initial startup, and Figure 15-8 shows how it might look after the user has touched the zoom controls.

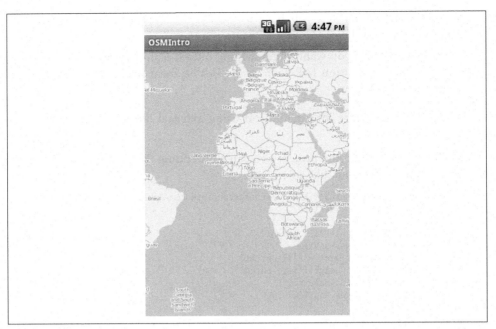

Figure 15-7. An OSM map

Figure 15-8. OSM map zoomed in

Source Download URL

The source code for this project is in the Android Cookbook repository (*https://github.com/IanDarwin/Android-Cookbook-Examples*), in the subdirectory *OSMIntro* (see "Getting and Using the Code Examples" on page 18).

15.8 Creating Overlays in OpenStreetMap Maps

Rachee Singh

Problem

You want to display graphics such as map markers on your OpenStreetMap view.

Solution

Instantiate an `Overlay` class and add the overlay to the point you wish to demarcate on the map.

Discussion

To get started with OpenStreetMap, see Recipe 15.7.

To add overlays, first we need to get a handle on the `MapView` defined in the XML layout of the Activity:

```
mapView = (MapView) this.findViewById(R.id.mapview);
```

Then we enable zoom controls on the `MapView` using the `setBuiltInZoomControls` method, and set the zoom level to a reasonable value:

```
mapView.setBuiltInZoomControls(true);
mapController = this.mapView.getController();
mapController.setZoom(12);
```

Now we create two `GeoPoints`. The first one (`mapCenter`) is to center the OSM map around the point where the application starts, and the second (`overlayPoint`) is where the overlay will be placed:

```
GeoPoint mapCenter = new GeoPoint(53554070, -2959520);
GeoPoint overlayPoint = new GeoPoint(53554070 + 1000, -2959520 + 1000);
mapController.setCenter(mapCenter);
```

Note that this `GeoPoint` constructor uses a `long` value, which the osmdroid API uses; this represents the latitude or longitude multiplied by `1e6` and cast to `long`. There is also a constructor overload that takes "normal" lat/long values as doubles; e.g., `new GeoPoint(53.5547, -29.59520);`.

To add the overlay, we create an `ArrayList` of `OverlayItems`. To this list, we will add the overlays we wish to add to the OSM map:

```
ArrayList<OverlayItem> overlays = new ArrayList<OverlayItem>();
overlays.add(new OverlayItem("New Overlay", "Overlay Description",
    overlayPoint));
```

To create the overlay item, we need to instantiate the ItemizedIconOverlay class (along with appropriate arguments specifying the point at which the overlay has to be placed, resource proxy, etc.). Then we add the overlay to the OSM map:

```
resourceProxy = new DefaultResourceProxyImpl(getApplicationContext());
this.myLocationOverlay = new ItemizedIconOverlay<OverlayItem>(
    overlays, null, resourceProxy);
this.mapView.getOverlays().add(this.myLocationOverlay);
```

Then, if we are updating values after onCreate(), a call to the invalidate() method is needed to update the MapView so that the user will see the changes we made to it:

```
mapView.invalidate();
```

The end result should look like Figure 15-9, and Figure 15-10 after zooming.

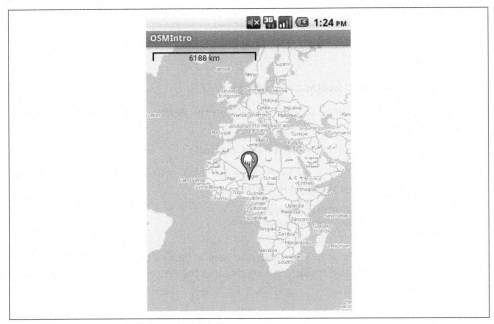

Figure 15-9. OSM map with marker overlay

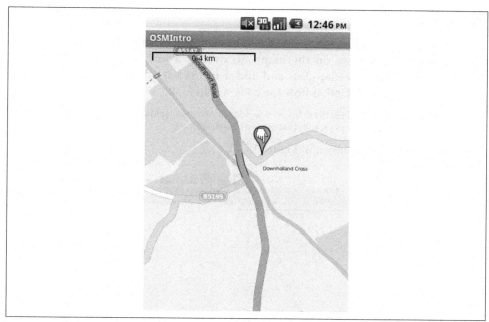

Figure 15-10. OSM map with marker overlay after zooming

Source Download URL

The source code for this project is in the Android Cookbook repository (*https://github.com/IanDarwin/Android-Cookbook-Examples*), in the subdirectory *OSMOverlay* (see "Getting and Using the Code Examples" on page 18).

15.9 Using a Scale on an OpenStreetMap Map

Rachee Singh

Problem

You need to show a map scale on your OSM map to indicate the zoom level on the MapView.

Solution

You can add a scale on the OSM map as an overlay using the osmdroid ScaleBarOverlay class.

Discussion

Putting a scale on your `MapView` helps the user keep track of the map's zoom level (as well as estimate distances on the map). To overlay a scale on your OSM `MapView`, instantiate the `ScaleBarOverlay` class and add it to the list of overlays in your `MapView` using the `add()` method. Here is how the code would look:

```
ScaleBarOverlay myScaleBarOverlay = new ScaleBarOverlay(this);
this.mapView.getOverlays().add(this.myScaleBarOverlay);
```

The scale bar overlay is shown in Figure 15-11.

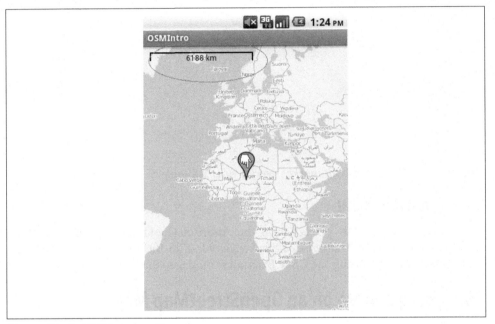

Figure 15-11. OSM map with scale

15.10 Handling Touch Events on an OpenStreetMap Overlay

Rachee Singh

Problem

You need to perform actions when the overlay on an OpenStreetMap map is tapped.

Solution

Override the methods of the OnItemGestureListener class for single-tap events and long-press events.

Discussion

To address touch events on the map overlay, we modify the way we instantiate an overlay item (for more details on using overlays in OSM, refer back to Recipe 15.8). While instantiating the OverlayItem, we make use of an anonymous object of the OnItemGestureListener class as an argument and provide our own implementation of the onItemSingleTapUp() and onItemLongPress() methods. In these methods, we simply display a toast depicting which action took place—single-tap or long-press—and the title and description of the overlay touched. Example 15-17 shows the code for this.

Example 15-17. Code for touch events in OSM

```
ArrayList<OverlayItem> items = new ArrayList<OverlayItem>();
items.add(
    new OverlayItem("New Overlay", "Overlay Sample Description", overlayPoint));

resourceProxy = new DefaultResourceProxyImpl(getApplicationContext());

this.myLocationOverlay = new ItemizedIconOverlay<OverlayItem>(items,
        new ItemizedIconOverlay.OnItemGestureListener<OverlayItem>() {
            @Override
            public boolean onItemSingleTapUp(
                final int index, final OverlayItem item) {
                Toast.makeText( getApplicationContext(), "Overlay Titled: " +
                item.mTitle + " Single Tapped" + "\n" + "Description: " +
                item.mDescription, Toast.LENGTH_LONG).show();
                return true;
            }
            @Override
            public boolean onItemLongPress(
                final int index, final OverlayItem item) {
                Toast.makeText( getApplicationContext(), "Overlay Titled: " +
                item.mTitle + " Long pressed" + "\n" + "Description: " +
                item.mDescription ,Toast.LENGTH_LONG).show();
                return false;
            }
        }, resourceProxy);
this.mapView.getOverlays().add(this.myLocationOverlay);
mapView.invalidate();
```

After a single-tap of the overlay, the application should look like Figure 15-12.

Figure 15-13 shows how the application might look after a long-press of the overlay.

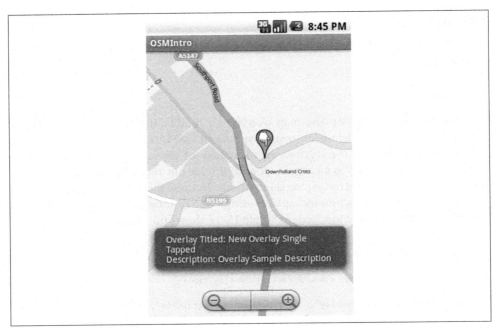

Figure 15-12. OSM map with touch event

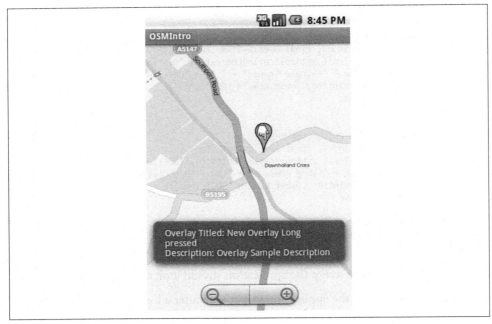

Figure 15-13. Long-press overlay reaction

Source Download URL

The source code for this project is in the Android Cookbook repository (*https:// github.com/IanDarwin/Android-Cookbook-Examples*), in the subdirectory *OSMTouchEvents* (see "Getting and Using the Code Examples" on page 18).

15.11 Getting Location Updates with OpenStreetMap Maps

Rachee Singh

Problem

You need to react to changes in the device's location and move the map to display the new location.

Solution

Using `LocationListener`, you can make an application request location updates (see Recipe 15.1) and then react to these changes in location by moving the map.

Discussion

The Activity that includes the OSM `MapView` needs to implement `LocationListener` to be able to request changes in the device's location. An Activity implementing `LocationListener` will also need to add the unimplemented (abstract) methods from the `LocationListener` interface (Eclipse will do this for you). We set the center of the map to the `GeoPoint` named `mapCenter` so that the application starts with the map focused on that point.

Now we need to get an instance of `LocationManager` and use it to request location updates using the `requestLocationUpdates()` method.

In one of the overridden methods (which were abstracted in the `LocationListener` interface), named `onLocationChanged()`, we can write the code that we want to be executed when the location of the device changes.

In the `onLocationChanged()` method we obtain the latitude and longitude of the new location and set the map's center to the new `GeoPoint`. Example 15-18 shows the relevant code.

Example 15-18. Managing location changes with OSM

```
public class LocationChange extends Activity implements LocationListener {
    private LocationManager myLocationManager;
    private MapView mapView;
```

```java
    private MapController mapController;

    @Override
    public void onCreate(Bundle savedInstanceState) {
        super.onCreate(savedInstanceState);
        setContentView(R.layout.main);
        mapView = (MapView)findViewById(R.id.mapview);
        mapController = this.mapView.getController();
        mapController.setZoom(15);
        GeoPoint mapCenter = new GeoPoint(53554070, -2959520);
        mapController.setCenter(mapCenter);
        myLocationManager = (LocationManager) getSystemService(LOCATION_SERVICE);
        myLocationManager.requestLocationUpdates(
            LocationManager.GPS_PROVIDER, 1000, 100, this);
    }

    @Override
    public void onLocationChanged(Location location) {
        int latitude = (int) (location.getLatitude() * 1E6);
        int longitude = (int) (location.getLongitude() * 1E6);
        GeoPoint geopoint = new GeoPoint(latitude, longitude);
        mapController.setCenter(geopoint);
        mapView.invalidate();

    }

    @Override
    public void onProviderDisabled(String arg0) {

    }

    @Override
    public void onProviderEnabled(String arg0) {

    }

    @Override
    public void onStatusChanged(String arg0, int arg1, Bundle arg2) {

    }
}
```

When the application starts, the map is centered on the mapCenter GeoPoint. Since the application is listening to location changes, the icon in the top bar of the phone is visible (see Figure 15-14).

Now, using the emulator controls, new GPS coordinates (−122.094095, 37.422006) are sent to the emulator. The application reacts to this and centers the map on the new coordinates (see Figure 15-15).

Similarly, different GPS coordinates are given from the emulator controls and the application centers the map on the new location (see Figure 15-16).

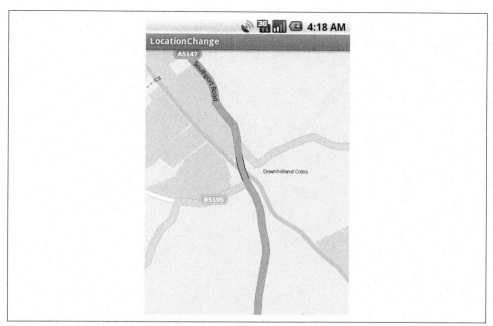

Figure 15-14. Moving the map, start of move

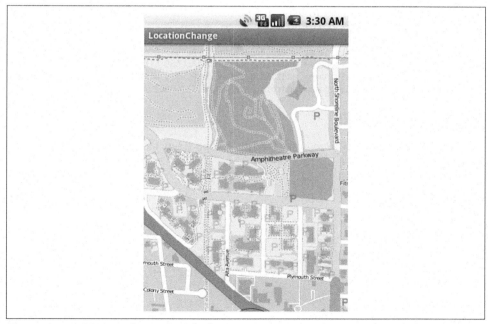

Figure 15-15. Moving the map, end of move

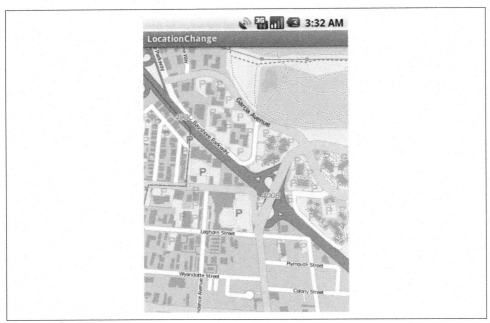

Figure 15-16. Changing the location via the emulator

Also, to allow the application to listen for location changes, include the following permissions in the *AndroidManifest.xml* file:

```
<uses-permission android:name="android.permission.ACCESS_COARSE_LOCATION"/>
<uses-permission android:name="android.permission.ACCESS_FINE_LOCATION"/>
<uses-permission android:name="android.permission.ACCESS_NETWORK_STATE"/>
<uses-permission android:name="android.permission.INTERNET"/>
```

Source Download URL

You can download the source code for this recipe from Google Drive (*http://bit.ly/156rruq*).

## CHAPTER 16

Accelerometer

Accelerometers are one of the more interesting bits of hardware in smartphones. Earlier devices such as the Openmoko Neo FreeRunner smartphone and the original Apple iPhone included them. Before Android was released I was advocating for Openmoko at open source conferences.

One of my favorite imaginary applications was private key generation. Adhering to the theory that "When privacy is outlawed, only outlaws will have privacy," several people were talking about this as early as 2008 (when I presented the idea at the Ontario Linux Fest). The idea is: if you can't or don't want to exchange private keys over a public channel, you meet on a street corner and shake hands—with each hand having a cell phone concealed in the palm. The devices are touching each other, thus their sensors should record exactly the same somewhat random motions. With a bit of mathematics to filter out the leading and trailing motion of the hands moving together, both devices should have quite a few bits' worth of identical, random data that nobody else has—just what you need for crypto key exchange. I've yet to see anybody implement this, but I must admit I still hope somebody will come through.

Meanwhile, we have many other recipes on accelerometers and other sensors in this chapter...

16.1 Checking for the Presence or Absence of a Sensor

Rachee Singh

Problem

You want to use a given sensor. Before using an Android device for a sensor-based application, you should ensure that the device supports the required sensor.

Solution

Check for the availability of the sensor on the Android device.

Discussion

The `SensorManager` class is used to manage the sensors available on an Android device. So we require an object of this class:

```
SensorManager deviceSensorManager =
    (SensorManager) getSystemService(SOME_SENSOR_SERVICE);
```

Then, using the `getSensorList()` method, we check for the presence of sensors of any type (accelerometer, gyroscope, pressure, etc.). If the list returned contains any elements, this implies that the sensor is present. A `TextView` is used to show the result: either "`Sensor present!`" or "`Sensor absent.`" Example 16-1 shows the code.

Example 16-1. Checking for the accelerometer

```
List<Sensor> sensorList =
        deviceSensorManager.getSensorList(Sensor.TYPE_ACCELEROMETER);

if (sensorList.size() > 0) {
    sensorPresent = true;
    sensor = sensorList.get(0);

}
else
    sensorPresent = false;

/* Set the face TextView to display sensor presence */
face = (TextView) findViewById(R.id.face);

if (sensorPresent)
    face.setText("Sensor present!");
else
    face.setText("Sensor absent.");
```

16.2 Using the Accelerometer to Detect Shaking

Thomas Manthey

Problem

Sometimes it makes sense to evaluate not only onscreen input, but also gestures like tilting or shaking the phone. You need to use the accelerometer to detect whether the phone has been shaken.

Solution

Register with the accelerometer and compare the current acceleration values on all three axes to the previous ones. If the values have repeatedly changed on at least two axes and those changes exceed a high enough threshold, you can clearly determine shaking.

Discussion

Let's first define *shaking* as a fairly rapid movement of the device in one direction followed by a further movement in another direction, typically (but not necessarily) the opposite one. If we want to detect such a shake motion in an Activity, we need a connection to the hardware sensors; those are exposed by the class SensorManager. Furthermore, we need to define a SensorEventListener and register it with the SensorManager. So the source of our Activity starts as shown in Example 16-2.

Example 16-2. ShakeActivity—getting accelerometer data

```
public class ShakeActivity extends Activity {
    /* The connection to the hardware */
    private SensorManager mySensorManager;

    /* The SensorEventListener lets us wire up to the real hardware events */
    private final SensorEventListener mySensorEventListener =
            new SensorEventListener() {

        public void onSensorChanged(SensorEvent se) {
            /* We will fill this one later */
        }

        public void onAccuracyChanged(Sensor sensor, int accuracy) {
            /* Can be ignored in this example */
        }
    };

    ....
```

In order to implement SensorEventListener, we have to implement two methods: onSensorChanged(SensorEvent se) and onAccuracyChanged(Sensor sensor, int accuracy). The first one gets called whenever new sensor data is available, and the second one whenever the accuracy of the measurement changes—for example, when the location service switches from GPS to network-based. In our example, we just need to cover onSensorChanged().

Before we continue, let's define some more variables, which will store the information about values of acceleration and some state (see Example 16-3).

Example 16-3. Variables for acceleration

```
/* Here we store the current values of acceleration, one for each axis */
private float xAccel;
private float yAccel;
private float zAccel;

/* And here the previous ones */
private float xPreviousAccel;
private float yPreviousAccel;
private float zPreviousAccel;

/* Used to suppress the first shaking */
private boolean firstUpdate = true;

/* What acceleration difference would we assume as a rapid movement? */
private final float shakeThreshold = 1.5f;

/* Has a shaking motion been started (one direction)? */
private boolean shakeInitiated = false;
```

I hope that the names and comments explain enough about what is stored in these variables; if not, it will become clearer in the next steps.

Now let's connect to the hardware sensors and wire up their events. onCreate() is the perfect place to do so (see Example 16-4).

Example 16-4. Initializing for accelerometer data

```
@Override
public void onCreate(Bundle savedInstanceState) {
    super.onCreate(savedInstanceState);
    setContentView(R.layout.main);
    mySensorManager = (SensorManager)getSystemService(Context.SENSOR_SERVICE); ❶
    mySensorManager.registerListener(mySensorEventListener, mySensorManager
            .getDefaultSensor(Sensor.TYPE_ACCELEROMETER),
            SensorManager.SENSOR_DELAY_NORMAL); ❷
}
```

❶ We get a reference to Android's sensor service.

❷ We register the previously defined SensorEventListener with the service. More precisely, we register only for events of the accelerometer and for a normal update rate; this could be changed if we needed to be more precise.

Now let's define what we want to do when new sensor data arrives. We have defined a stub for the SensorEventListener's method onSensorChanged(), so now we will fill it with some life (see Example 16-5).

Example 16-5. Using the sensor data

```
public void onSensorChanged(SensorEvent se) {
    updateAccelParameters(se.values[0], se.values[1], se.values[2]); ❶
    if ((!shakeInitiated) && isAccelerationChanged()) { ❷
    shakeInitiated = true;
    } else if ((shakeInitiated) && isAccelerationChanged()) { ❸
        executeShakeAction();
    } else if ((shakeInitiated) && (!isAccelerationChanged())) { ❹
        shakeInitiated = false;
}
}
```

❶ We copy the values of acceleration that we received from the SensorEvent into our state variables. The corresponding method is declared like this:

```
/* Store acceleration values from sensor */
private void updateAccelParameters(float xNewAccel, float yNewAccel,
        float zNewAccel) {
    /* We have to suppress the first change of acceleration,
     * it results from first values being initialized with 0 */
    if (firstUpdate) {
        xPreviousAccel = xNewAccel;
        yPreviousAccel = yNewAccel;
        zPreviousAccel = zNewAccel;
        firstUpdate = false;
    } else {
        xPreviousAccel = xAccel;
        yPreviousAccel = yAccel;
        zPreviousAccel = zAccel;
    }
    xAccel = xNewAccel;
    yAccel = yNewAccel;
    zAccel = zNewAccel;
}
```

❷ We test for a rapid change of acceleration and whether any has happened before; if not, we store the information that now has been gathered.

❸ We test again for a rapid change of acceleration, this time with the information from before. If this test is true, we can assume a shaking movement according to our definition and commence action.

❹ Finally, we reset the shake status if we detected shaking before but don't get a rapid change of acceleration anymore.

To complete the code, we add the last two methods. The first is the isAccelerationChanged() method (see Example 16-6).

Example 16-6. The isAccelerationChanged() method

```
/* If the values of acceleration have changed on at least two axes,
   we are probably in a shake motion */
private boolean isAccelerationChanged() {
    float deltaX = Math.abs(xPreviousAccel - xAccel);
    float deltaY = Math.abs(yPreviousAccel - yAccel);
    float deltaZ = Math.abs(zPreviousAccel - zAccel);
    return (deltaX > shakeThreshold && deltaY > shakeThreshold)
            || (deltaX > shakeThreshold && deltaZ > shakeThreshold)
            || (deltaY > shakeThreshold && deltaZ > shakeThreshold);
}
```

Here we compare the current values of acceleration with the previous ones, and if at least two of them have changed above our threshold, we return true.

The last method is executeShakeAction(), which does whatever we wish to do when the phone is being shaken:

```
private void executeShakeAction() {
    /* Save the cheerleader, save the world
       or do something more sensible... */
}
```

Source Download URL

The source code for this project is in the Android Cookbook repository (*https://github.com/IanDarwin/Android-Cookbook-Examples*), in the subdirectory *SensorShakeDetection* (see "Getting and Using the Code Examples" on page 18).

16.3 Checking Whether a Device Is Facing Up or Down

Rachee Singh

Problem

You want to check for the orientation (facing up/facing down) of the Android device.

Solution

Use a SensorEventListener to check for appropriate accelerometer values.

Discussion

To implement a SensorEventListener, the onSensorChanged() method is called when sensor values change. Within this method, we check to see if the values lie within a particular range for the device to be facing down or facing up. Here is the code to obtain the sensor object for an accelerometer:

```
List<android.hardware.Sensor> sensorList =
    deviceSensorManager.getSensorList(Sensor.TYPE_ACCELEROMETER);
sensor = sensorList.get(0);
```

Example 16-7 shows the `SensorEventListener` implementation.

Example 16-7. The SensorEventListener implementation

```
private SensorEventListener accelerometerListener = new SensorEventListener() {
    @Override
    public void onSensorChanged(SensorEvent event) {
        float z = event.values[2];
        if (z >9 && z < 10)
            face.setText("FACE UP");
        else if (z > -10 && z < -9)
            face.setText("FACE DOWN");
    }

    @Override
    public void onAccuracyChanged(Sensor arg0, int arg1) {

    }
};
```

After implementing the listener along with the methods required, we need to register the listener for a particular sensor (which in our case is the accelerometer). `sensor` is an object of the `Sensor` class; it represents the sensor being used in the application (the accelerometer):

```
deviceSensorManager.registerListener(accelerometerListener, sensor, 0, null);
```

Source Download URL

The source code for this project is in the Android Cookbook repository (*https://github.com/IanDarwin/Android-Cookbook-Examples*), in the subdirectory *SensorUpOrDown* (see "Getting and Using the Code Examples" on page 18).

16.4 Reading the Temperature Sensor

Rachee Singh

Problem

You need to get temperature values using the temperature sensor.

Solution

Use `SensorManager` and `SensorEventListener` to track changes in temperature values detected by the temperature sensor.

Discussion

We need to create an object of the SensorManager class to use sensors in an application. Then we register a listener with the type of sensor we require. To register the listener we provide the name of the listener, a Sensor object, and the type of delay (in this case, SENSOR_DELAY_FASTEST) to the registerListener() method. In this listener, within the overridden onSensorChanged() method, we can print the temperature value into a TextView named tempVal:

```
SensorManager sensorManager = (SensorManager)getSystemService(SENSOR_SERVICE);
sensorManager.registerListener(temperatureListener,
    sensorManager.getDefaultSensor(Sensor.TYPE_TEMPERATURE),
    SensorManager.SENSOR_DELAY_FASTEST);
```

Example 16-8 shows the SensorEventListener implementation.

Example 16-8. The SensorEventListener implementation

```
private final SensorEventListener temperatureListener = new SensorEventListener() {
    @Override
    public void onAccuracyChanged(Sensor sensor, int accuracy) {}
    @Override
    public void onSensorChanged(SensorEvent event) {

        tempVal.setText("Temperature is:"+event.values[0]);

    }
};
```

See Also

Recipe 16.1.

## CHAPTER 17

Bluetooth

Bluetooth technology allows users to connect a variety of peripherals to a computer, tablet, or phone. Headsets, speakers, keyboards, and printers; medical devices such as glucometers and ECG machines; these are only some of the numerous types of devices that can be connected via Bluetooth. Some, such as headsets, are supported automatically by Android; more esoteric ones will require some programming. Some of these other devices use the Serial Port Protocol (SPP), which is basically an unstructured protocol that requires you to write code to format data yourself.

This chapter has recipes on how to ensure that Bluetooth is turned on, how to make your device discoverable, how to discover other devices, and how to read from and write to another device over a Bluetooth connection.[1]

A future edition of this work will provide coverage of the Bluetooth Health Device Profile (HDP) standardized by the Continua Health Alliance.

17.1 Enabling Bluetooth and Making the Device Discoverable

Rachee Singh

Problem

The application requires that the Bluetooth adapter be switched on, so you need to check if this capability is enabled. If it isn't, you need to prompt the user to enable

---

[1] Bluetooth is a trademark of the Bluetooth Special Interest Group (*https://www.bluetooth.org/*).

Bluetooth. To allow remote devices to detect the host device, you must make the host device discoverable.

Solution

Use Intents to prompt the user to enable Bluetooth and make the device discoverable.

Discussion

Before performing any action with an instance of the `BluetoothAdapter` class, you should check whether the Bluetooth adapter is enabled on the device using the `isEnabled()` method. If the method returns `false`, the user should be prompted to enable Bluetooth:

```
BluetoothAdapter BT = BluetoothAdapter.getDefaultAdapter();
if (!BT.isEnabled()) {
    // Request user's permission to switch the Bluetooth adapter on.
    Intent enableIntent = new Intent(BluetoothAdapter.ACTION_REQUEST_ENABLE);
    startActivityForResult(enableIntent, REQUEST_ENABLE_BT);
}
```

The preceding code will show an `AlertDialog` to the user prompting her to enable Bluetooth (see Figure 17-1).

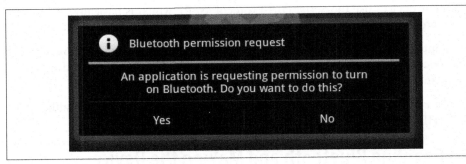

Figure 17-1. Bluetooth enable prompt

On returning to the Activity that started the Intent, `onActivityResult()` is called, in which the name of the host device and its MAC address can be extracted (see Example 17-1).

Example 17-1. Getting the device and its Bluetooth MAC address

```
protected void onActivityResult(int requestCode, int resultCode, Intent data) {
    if(requestCode==REQUEST_ENABLE_BT && resultCode==Activity.RESULT_OK) {
        BluetoothAdapter BT = BluetoothAdapter.getDefaultAdapter();
        String address = BT.getAddress();
        String name = BT.getName();
        String toastText = name + " : " + address;
```

```
        Toast.makeText(this, toastText, Toast.LENGTH_LONG).show();
    }
```

To request the user's permission to make the device discoverable to other Bluetooth-enabled devices in the vicinity, you can use the following lines of code:

```
// Request user's permission to make the device discoverable for 120 secs
Intent discoverableIntent =
    new Intent(BluetoothAdapter.ACTION_REQUEST_DISCOVERABLE);
startActivity(discoverableIntent);
```

The preceding code will show an `AlertDialog` to the user prompting her to make her device discoverable by other devices for 120 seconds (Figure 17-2).

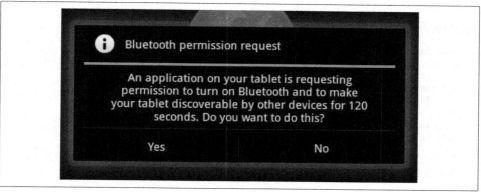

Figure 17-2. Bluetooth configuration

17.2 Connecting to a Bluetooth-Enabled Device

Ashwini Shahapurkar

Problem

You want to connect to another Bluetooth-enabled device and communicate with it.

Solution

Use the Android Bluetooth API to connect to the device using sockets. The communication will be over the socket streams.

Discussion

For any Bluetooth application, you need to add these two permissions to the *Android-Manifest.xml* file:

```
<uses-permission android:name="android.permission.BLUETOOTH_ADMIN" />
<uses-permission android:name="android.permission.BLUETOOTH" />
```

You will create the socket connection to the other Bluetooth device using some variation of the createRfcommSocket() API, as shown in Example 17-2. Then you should continuously listen for the data from the socket stream in a thread. You can write to the connected stream outside the thread. The Bluetooth socket connection is a blocking call and returns only if a connection is successful or an exception occurs while connecting to the device. With Bluetooth device discovery being a heavy process, this may slow down the connection, so it is a good practice to cancel the device discovery before trying to connect to the other device.

The BluetoothConnection will, once instantiated, create the socket connection to the other device and start listening to the data from the connected device.

Example 17-2. Reading from and writing to a Bluetooth device

```
private class BluetoothConnection extends Thread {
    private final BluetoothSocket mmSocket;
    private final InputStream mmInStream;
    private final OutputStream mmOutStream;
    byte[] buffer;

    // Unique UUID for this application, you should use a different one
    private static final UUID MY_UUID = UUID
            .fromString("fa87c0d0-afac-11de-8a39-0800200c9a66");

    public BluetoothConnection(BluetoothDevice device) {

        BluetoothSocket tmp = null;

        // Get a BluetoothSocket for a connection with the given BluetoothDevice
        try {
            tmp = device.createRfcommSocketToServiceRecord(MY_UUID);
        } catch (IOException e) {
            e.printStackTrace();
        }
        mmSocket = tmp;

        // Now make the socket connection in separate thread to avoid FC
        Thread connectionThread  = new Thread(new Runnable() {

            @Override
            public void run() {
                // Always cancel discovery because it will slow down a connection
                mAdapter.cancelDiscovery();

                // Make a connection to the BluetoothSocket
                try {
                    // This is a blocking call and will only return on a
                    // successful connection or an exception
                    mmSocket.connect();
                } catch (IOException e) {
                    // Connection to device failed, so close the socket
                    try {
```

```
                    mmSocket.close();
                } catch (IOException e2) {
                    e2.printStackTrace();
                }
            }
        }
    });

    connectionThread.start();

    InputStream tmpIn = null;
    OutputStream tmpOut = null;

    // Get the BluetoothSocket input and output streams
    try {
        tmpIn = socket.getInputStream();
        tmpOut = socket.getOutputStream();
        buffer = new byte[1024];
    } catch (IOException e) {
        e.printStackTrace();
    }

    mmInStream = tmpIn;
    mmOutStream = tmpOut;
}

public void run() {

    // Keep listening to the InputStream while connected
    while (true) {
        try {
            // Read the data from socket stream
            mmInStream.read(buffer);
            // Send the obtained bytes to the UI Activity
        } catch (IOException e) {
            // An exception here marks connection loss
            // Send message to UI Activity
            break;
        }
    }
}

public void write(byte[] buffer) {
    try {
        // Write the data to socket stream
        mmOutStream.write(buffer);
    } catch (IOException e) {
        e.printStackTrace();
    }
}

public void cancel() {
    try {
        mmSocket.close();
    } catch (IOException e) {
        e.printStackTrace();
```

```
            }
        }
    }
```

See Also

Recipe 17.4.

17.3 Accepting Connections from a Bluetooth Device

Rachee Singh

Problem

You want to create a listening server for Bluetooth connections.

Solution

Before two Bluetooth devices can interact, one of the communicating devices must act like a server. It obtains a `BluetoothServerSocket` instance and listens for incoming requests.

Discussion

The `BluetoothServerSocket` instance is obtained by calling the `listenUsingRfcommWithServiceRecord()` method on the Bluetooth adapter. With this instance, we can start listening for incoming requests from remote devices through the `start()` method. Listening is a blocking process, so we have to make a new thread and call it within the thread; otherwise, the UI of the application becomes unresponsive. Example 17-3 shows the relevant code.

Example 17-3. Creating a Bluetooth server and accepting connections

```
// Make the host device discoverable
startActivityForResult(new Intent(BluetoothAdapter.ACTION_REQUEST_DISCOVERABLE),
    DISCOVERY_REQUEST_BLUETOOTH);
  @Override
  protected void onActivityResult(int requestCode, int resultCode, Intent data) {
      if (requestCode == DISCOVERY_REQUEST_BLUETOOTH) {
          boolean isDiscoverable = resultCode > 0;
          if (isDiscoverable) {
              UUID uuid = UUID.fromString("a60f35f0-b93a-11de-8a39-08002009c666");
              String serverName = "BTserver";
              final BluetoothServerSocket bluetoothServer =
               bluetoothAdapter.listenUsingRfcommWithServiceRecord(serverName, uuid);

              Thread listenThread = new Thread(new Runnable() {

                  public void run() {
```

```
        try {
            BluetoothSocket serverSocket = bluetoothServer.accept();
            myHandleConnectionWith(serverSocket);
        } catch (IOException e) {
            Log.d("BLUETOOTH", e.getMessage());
        }
    }
});
listenThread.start();
        }
    }
}
```

17.4 Implementing Bluetooth Device Discovery

Shraddha Shravagi

Problem

You want to display a list of Bluetooth devices that are within communication range of your device.

Solution

Create an XML file to display the list, create a class file to load the list, and then edit the manifest file. It's that simple.

For security reasons, devices to be discovered must be in "discoverable" mode (also known as "pairing"); for Android devices there is a Discoverable setting in the Bluetooth settings, while for "conventional" Bluetooth devices you may need to refer to the device's instruction manual.

Discussion

Use the following code to create the XML file to display the list:

```
<ListView
    android:id="@+id/pairedBtDevices"
    android:layout_width="fill_parent"
    android:layout_height="wrap_content"
/>
```

The code in Example 17-4 creates a class file to load the list.

Example 17-4. Activity with BroadcastReceiver for connections

```
// IntentFilter will match the action specified
IntentFilter filter = new IntentFilter(BluetoothDevice.ACTION_FOUND);
```

```
// Broadcast receiver for any matching filter
this.registerReceiver(mReceiver, filter);

// Attach the adapter
ListView newDevicesListView = (ListView)findViewById(R.id.pairedBtDevices);
newDevicesListView.setAdapter(mNewDevicesArrayAdapter);

filter = new IntentFilter(BluetoothAdapter.ACTION_DISCOVERY_FINISHED);
this.registerReceiver(mReceiver, filter);

// Create a receiver for the Intent
private final BroadcastReceiver mReceiver = new BroadcastReceiver() {

    @Override
    public void onReceive(Context context, Intent intent) {

        String action = intent.getAction();

        if(BluetoothDevice.ACTION_FOUND.equals(action)) {
            BluetoothDevice btDevice =
                intent.getParcelableExtra(BluetoothDevice.EXTRA_DEVICE);

            if(btDevice.getBondState() != BluetoothDevice.BOND_BONDED) {
                mNewDevicesArrayAdapter.add(btDevice.getName()+"\n"+
                btDevice.getAddress());
            }
        }
        else
            if(BluetoothAdapter.ACTION_DISCOVERY_FINISHED.equals(action)) {
                setProgressBarIndeterminateVisibility(false);
                setTitle(R.string.select_device);
                if(mNewDevicesArrayAdapter.getCount() == 0) {
                    String noDevice =
                        getResources().getText(R.string.none_paired).toString();
                    mNewDevicesArrayAdapter.add(noDevice);
                }
            }

    }
};
```

Source Download URL

The source code for this example is in the Android Cookbook repository (*https://github.com/IanDarwin/Android-Cookbook-Examples*), in the subdirectory *Bluetooth-Demo* (see "Getting and Using the Code Examples" on page 18).

## CHAPTER 18

System and Device Control

Android provides a good compromise between the needs of the carriers for control and the needs of developers for device access. This chapter looks at some of the informational and control APIs that are publicly available that allow Android developers to explore and control the extensive hardware facilities provided by the system and to deal with the wide range of hardware it runs on, from 2-inch cell phones to 10-inch tablets and netbooks.

18.1 Accessing Phone Network/Connectivity Information

Amir Alagic

Problem

You want to find information about the device's current network connectivity.

Solution

Determine whether your phone is connected to the network, the type of connection, and whether it's in roaming territory using the `ConnectivityManager` class and a `NetworkInfo` object.

Discussion

Often you need to know whether the device you are running on can currently connect to the internet, and, since roaming can be expensive, it is also very useful if you can tell the user whether he is roaming. To do this and more we can use the `NetworkInfo` class in the `android.net` package, as in Example 18-1.

Example 18-1. Getting network information

```
ConnectivityManager connManager =
    (ConnectivityManager)this.getSystemService(Context.CONNECTIVITY_SERVICE);
NetworkInfo ni = connManager.getActiveNetworkInfo();
/* Indicates whether network connectivity is possible.
A network is unavailable when a persistent or semi-persistent
condition prevents the possibility of connecting to
that network. */
boolean available = ni.isAvailable();
/* Indicates whether network connectivity exists */
boolean connected = ni.isConnected();
/* Indicates whether the device is currently roaming */
boolean roaming = ni.isRoaming();
/* Reports the type of network (currently mobile or WiFi) to which the info
   in this object pertains; will be one of ConnectivityManager.TYPE_MOBILE,
   ConnectivityManager.TYPE_WIFI, ... */
int networkType = ni.getType();              // See also String ni.getTypeName();
```

See Also

The developer documentation for the `NetworkInfo` class (*https://developer.android.com/ reference/android/net/NetworkInfo.html*).

18.2 Obtaining Information from the Manifest File

Colin Wilcox

Problem

You want to obtain project settings (e.g., app version) data from the *AndroidManifest.xml* file during program execution.

Solution

Use the `PackageManager`.

Discussion

Rather than hardcoding values into the application that need to be changed each time the application is modified, it is easier to read the version number from the manifest file. Other settings can be read in a similar manner.

The `PackageManager` is fairly straightforward to use. The two `imports` in the following code need to be added to the Activity:

```
import android.content.pm.PackageInfo;
import android.content.pm.PackageManager;
```

The main part of the code is shown in Example 18-2.

Example 18-2. Code to get information from the manifest

```
// In the main Activity...
public String readVersionNameFromManifest() {
    PackageInfo packageInfo = null;

    // Read package name and version number from manifest
    try {
        // Load the package manager for the current context
        PackageManager packageManager = this.getPackageManager();

        // Get the package info structure and pick out the fields you want
        packageInfo = packageManager.getPackageInfo(this.getPackageName(), 0);
    } catch (Exception e) {
        Log.e(TAG, "Exception reading manifest version " + e);
    }
    return (packageInfo.versionName);
}
```

18.3 Changing Incoming Call Notification to Silent, Vibrate, or Normal

Rachee Singh

Problem

You need to set the Android device to silent, vibrate, or normal mode.

Solution

Use Android's AudioManager system service to set the phone to normal, silent, or vibrate mode.

Discussion

This recipe presents a simple application that has three buttons to change the phone mode to Silent, Vibrate, and Normal, as shown in Figure 18-1.

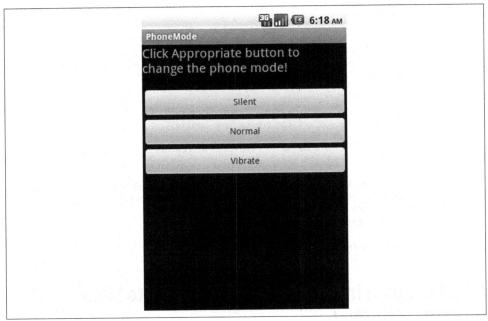

Figure 18-1. Setting phone notification mode

We instantiate the AudioManager class to be able to use the setRingerMode() method. For each of these buttons (silentButton, normalButton, and vibrateButton) we have OnClickListeners defined in which we use the AudioManager object to set the ringer mode. We also display a toast notifying the user of the mode change. See Example 18-3.

Example 18-3. Setting the audio mode

```
am = (AudioManager) getBaseContext().getSystemService(Context.AUDIO_SERVICE);
silentButton = (Button)findViewById(R.id.silent);
normalButton = (Button)findViewById(R.id.normal);
vibrateButton = (Button)findViewById(R.id.vibrate);

// For Silent mode
silentButton.setOnClickListener(new View.OnClickListener() {
    @Override
    public void onClick(View arg0) {
        am.setRingerMode(AudioManager.RINGER_MODE_SILENT);
        Toast.makeText(getApplicationContext(), "Silent Mode Activated.",
        Toast.LENGTH_LONG).show();
    }
});

// For Normal mode
normalButton.setOnClickListener(new View.OnClickListener() {
    @Override
    public void onClick(View arg0) {
```

```
        am.setRingerMode(AudioManager.RINGER_MODE_NORMAL);
        Toast.makeText(getApplicationContext(),
            "Normal Mode Activated", Toast.LENGTH_LONG).show();
    }
});

// For Vibrate mode
vibrateButton.setOnClickListener(new View.OnClickListener() {
    @Override
    public void onClick(View arg0) {
        am.setRingerMode(AudioManager.RINGER_MODE_VIBRATE);
        Toast.makeText(getApplicationContext(),
            "Vibrate Mode Activated", Toast.LENGTH_LONG).show();
    }
});
```

Figure 18-2 shows the application when the Silent button is clicked (notice also the silent icon in the phone's status bar).

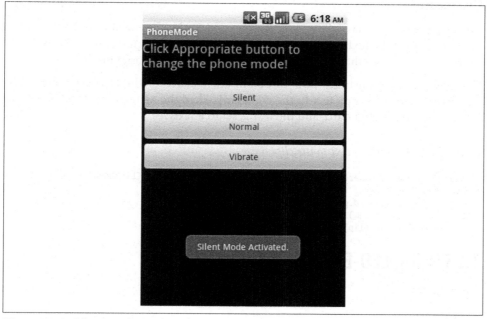

Figure 18-2. Silent mode activated

18.4 Copying Text and Getting Text from the Clipboard

Rachee Singh

Problem

You need to copy text to the clipboard and access the text stored on the clipboard; this allows you to provide full copy-and-paste functionality for text.

Solution

With the help of the ClipboardManager class, you can access the items stored on the clipboard of an Android device.

Discussion

The ClipboardManager class allows you to copy text to the clipboard using the setText() method and get the text stored on the clipboard using the getText() method. getText() returns a charSequence that is converted to a String by the toString() method.

Example 18-4 demonstrates how to obtain an instance of the ClipboardManager class and how to use it to copy text to the clipboard. Then the getText() method is used to get the text on the clipboard, and the text is set to a TextView.

Example 18-4. Copying text to the clipboard

```
ClipboardManager clipboard = (ClipboardManager)getSystemService(CLIPBOARD_SERVICE);
clipboard.setText("Using the clipboard for the first time!");
String clip = clipboard.getText().toString();
clipTextView = (TextView) findViewById(R.id.clipText);
clipTextView.setText(clip);
```

18.5 Using LED-Based Notifications

Rachee Singh

Problem

Most Android devices are equipped with an LED for notification purposes. You want to flash different colored lights using the LED.

Solution

Using the NotificationManager and Notification classes allows you to provide notifications using the LED on the device.

Discussion

As in the case of all notifications, we begin by obtaining a reference to the NotificationManager for our app. Then we create a Notification object. Using the method ledARGB() we can specify the color of the LED light. The constant ledOnMS is used to specify the duration (in milliseconds) that the LED will be on; ledOffMS specifies the time (in milliseconds) that the LED is off. The notify() method starts the notification process. Example 18-5 shows the code corresponding to the actions just described.

Example 18-5. Making the LED flash blue

```
NotificationManager notificationManager =
    (NotificationManager)getSystemService(NOTIFICATION_SERVICE);
Notification notification = new Notification();
notification.ledARGB = 0xff0000ff;        // Blue color light flash
notification.ledOnMS = 1000;              // LED is on for 1 second
notification.ledOffMS = 1000;             // LED is off for 1 second
notification.flags = Notification.FLAG_SHOW_LIGHTS;
notificationManager.notify(0, notification);
```

18.6 Making the Device Vibrate

Rachee Singh

Problem

You wish to notify the user of some event by means of device vibration.

Solution

Use notifications to set a vibration pattern.

Discussion

To allow device vibration, include this permission in the *AndroidManifest.xml* file:

```
<uses-permission android:name="android.permission.VIBRATE"/>
```

In the Java code, we need to get an instance of the NotificationManager class and of the Notification class:

```
NotificationManager notificationManager =
    (NotificationManager) getSystemService(NOTIFICATION_SERVICE);
Notification notification = new Notification();
```

To set a pattern for the vibration, we assign a sequence of long value pairs (time in milliseconds) to the Notification's vibrate property. This sequence represents the duration that the device will be silent and that it will vibrate. There should be an even number of values in the array. For instance, the pattern used in this example will cause the device to wait for one second and then vibrate for one second, then repeat this pattern two more times, then stop:

```
notification.vibrate =
    new long[]{ 1000, 1000, 1000, 1000, 1000, 1000 };
notificationManager.notify(0, notification);
```

Source Download URL

You can download the source code for this example from the Android Cookbook repository (*https://github.com/IanDarwin/Android-Cookbook-Examples*), in the subdirectory *Vibrate* (see "Getting and Using the Code Examples" on page 18).

18.7 Determining Whether a Given Application Is Running

Colin Wilcox

Problem

You want to know whether a certain app is running.

Solution

The system activity manager maintains a list of all active tasks. This provides the names of all running tasks and can be interrogated for various system-specific information.

Discussion

The code in Example 18-6 takes the name of an application and returns true if the ActivityManager thinks it is currently running.

Example 18-6. Checking for a running app

```
import android.app.ActivityManager;
import android.app.ActivityManager.RunningAppProcessInfo;

public boolean isAppRunning (String aApplicationPackageName)
{
    ActivityManager activityManager =
            (ActivityManager) this.getSystemService(ACTIVITY_SERVICE);
    if (activityManager == null) {
        return false; // Should report: can't get Activity Manager
    }

    List<RunningAppProcessInfo> procInfos =
            activityManager.getRunningAppProcesses();
    for(int idx = 0; idx < procInfos.size(); idx++) {
```

```java
        if (procInfos.get(i).processName.equals(aApplicationPackageName)) {
            return true;
        }
    }

    return false;
}
```

## CHAPTER 19

All the World's Not Java: Other Programming Languages and Frameworks

Developing new programming languages is a constant process in this industry. Several new (or not-so-new) languages have become popular recently. These include JVM languages like Groovy, Kotlin, Clojure, Scala as well as non-JVM languages such as Scheme, Erlang, C#, F#, Haskell, and more. Android encourages the use of many languages. You can write your app in pure Java using the SDK, of course—that's the subject of most of the rest of this book. You can also mix some C/C++ code into Java using Android's NDK for native code (see Recipe 19.3). People have made most of the major compiled languages work, especially (but not exclusively) the JVM-based ones. You can write using a variety of scripting languages such as Perl, Python, and Ruby (see Recipe 19.4). And there's more…

If you want a very high-level, drag-and-drop development process, look at Android App Inventor, a Google-originated environment for building applications easily using the drag-and-drop metaphor and "blocks" that snap together. App Inventor is now maintained at MIT (*http://appinventor.mit.edu*).

If you are a web developer used to working your magic in HTML, JavaScript, and CSS, there is a route for you to become an Android developer using the tools you already know. There are, in fact, five or six technologies that go this route, including AppCelerator Titanium, PhoneGap/Cordova (see Recipe 19.10), and more. These generally use CSS to build a style that looks close to the native device toolkit, JavaScript to provide actions, and W3 standards to provide device access such as GPS. Most of these work by packaging up a JavaScript interpreter along with your HTML and CSS into an APK file. Many have the further advantage that they can be packaged to run on iPhone, BlackBerry, and other mobile platforms. The risk I see with these is that, since they're not using native toolkit items, they may easily provide strange-looking user interfaces that don't conform either to the Android Guidelines or to users' expectations of how apps should behave on the Android platform. That is certainly something to be aware of if you are using one of these toolkits.

One of the main design goals of Android was to keep it as an open platform. The wide range of languages that you can use to develop Android apps testifies that this openness has been maintained.

19.1 Learning About Cross-Platform Solutions

Ian Darwin

Problem

There is no central list of the various "other" environments and languages available to build Android apps.

Discussion

There are many paths to cross-platform development that allow you to develop applications that run both on Android and on iOS, and possibly other less-used platforms. One thing to beware of is that many of these paths do not give the full native experience. Android's user interface is not the same as that of iOS, for example, and it's difficult to reconcile them; the basics are easy, but the nuances are hard. Some cross-platform apps don't even have the Android "Back button" working correctly! However, on the plus side, some of these development approaches also generate desktop apps for Microsoft Windows, macOS, or desktop Java versions. Table 19-1 lists some of the better-known tools at the time of this writing. Before using any of these, study it well.

Table 19-1. Cross-platform development tools

Name	Language	URL	Notes
Appcelerator Platform	JavaScript	http://www.appcelerator.com/mobile-app-development-products/	
App Inventor	Blocks (Logo)	http://www.appinventor.org/	Visual, no-code solution
Application Craft	HTML5	https://www.applicationcraft.com/	Cloud-based development; uses Cordova for Mobile
B4A (formerly Basic4android)	BASIC	https://www.b4x.com/	
Cordova	HTML5	https://cordova.apache.org/	See Recipe 19.10
Corona	Lua	https://coronalabs.com/	

Name	Language	URL		Notes
Gluon Mobile	Java	http://gluonhq.com/products/mobile/		Own Java API for device/hardware features; FOSS version
Intel XDK	HTML5	https://software.intel.com/en-us/html5/tools		Uses Cordova for Mobile
Monkey X	BASIC	http://www.monkeycoder.co.nz/		Focus on 2D games
Kivy	Python	https://kivy.org/#home		
MonoGame	C#	http://www.monogame.net/		
NDK	C/C++	-		Standard Android toolset for using native code; see Recipe 19.3
NSB/AppStudio	BASIC	https://www.nsbasic.com/		
PhoneGap	HTML5	Now known as Cordova; see above		
RFO BASIC!	BASIC	http://laughton.com/basic/		
RhoMobile Suite	Ruby	https://rms.rhomobile.com		
Xamarin	C#	https://www.xamarin.com/		Acquired by Microsoft

Of these, Cordova/PhoneGap is covered in Recipe 19.10 and Xamarin is covered in Recipe 19.9.

19.2 Running Shell Commands from Your Application

Rachee Singh

Problem

You need to run a Unix/Linux command (command-line program) or shell script from within your application (e.g., `pwd`, `ls`, etc.).

Solution

Determine the path of the program you wish to run. Use the `exec()` method of the `Runtime` class, passing in the command (and any arguments) that you wish to run. Sometimes you will need to read results back from the program; to do that, use classes from `java.io`.

Discussion

The `Runtime` class is a part of standard Java (Java SE), and works the same here as it does in Java SE. Your applications cannot create an instance of the `Runtime` class, but rather can get an instance by invoking the static `getRuntime()` method. Using this instance you call the `exec()` method, which executes the specified program in a separate native process. It takes the name of the program to execute as an argument. The exec() method returns the new Process object that represents the native process.

Usually standard Unix/Linux programs live in *system/bin*, but this path does vary on some versions or some distributions; you can explore the paths to find commands using a file manager application, or using adb ls. As an example, we will run the ps command that lists all the processes running on the system. The full location of this command (*system/bin/ps*) is specified as an argument to exec().

We get the output of the command and return the string. Then process.waitFor() is used to wait for the command to finish executing. See Example 19-1.

Example 19-1. Running a shell command

```java
private String runShellCommand() {
  try {
    Process process = Runtime.getRuntime().exec("/system/bin/ps");
    InputStreamReader reader = new InputStreamReader(process.getInputStream());
    BufferedReader bufferedReader = new BufferedReader(reader);
    int numRead;
    char[] buffer = new char[5000];
    StringBuffer commandOutput = new StringBuffer();
    while ((numRead = bufferedReader.read(buffer)) > 0) {
      commandOutput.append(buffer, 0, numRead);
    }
    bufferedReader.close();
    process.waitFor();

    return commandOutput.toString();
  } catch (IOException e) {
    throw new RuntimeException(e);
  } catch (InterruptedException e) {
    throw new RuntimeException(e);
  }
}
```

Figure 19-1 shows the output of the ps command displayed in a TextView.

You could, of course, capture the output of any system command back into your program and either parse it for display in, for example, a ListView, or display it as text in a TextView as was done here.

Source Download URL

The source code for this project is in the Android Cookbook repository (*https://github.com/IanDarwin/Android-Cookbook-Examples*), in the subdirectory *ShellCommand* (see "Getting and Using the Code Examples" on page 18).

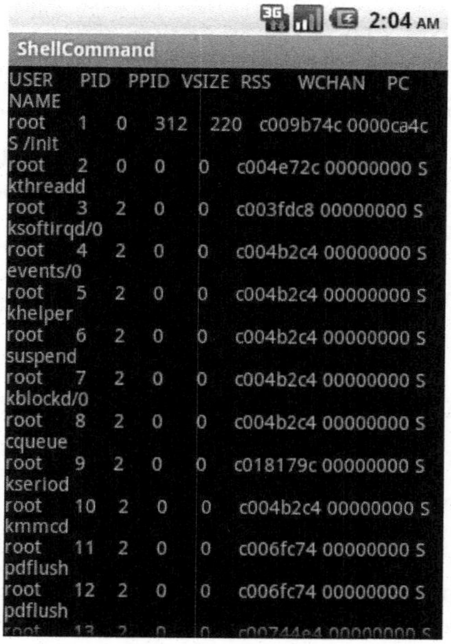

Figure 19-1. Android ps(1) command output

19.3 Running Native C/C++ Code with JNI on the NDK

Ian Darwin

Problem

You need to run parts of your application natively in order to use existing C/C++ code or, possibly, to improve performance of CPU-intensive code.

Solution

Use JNI (Java Native Interface) via the NDK, the Android Native Development Kit (*https://developer.android.com/sdk/ndk/*).

Discussion

Standard Java has always allowed you to load native or compiled code into your Java program, and the Android Runtime supports this in a way that is pretty much identical to the original. Why would you as a developer want to do such a thing? One reason might be to access OS-dependent functionality. Another is speed: native code will likely run faster than Java, at least at present, although there is some contention as to how much of a difference this really makes. Search the web for conflicting answers.

The native code language bindings are defined for code that has been written in C or C++. If you need to access a language other than C/C++, you could write a bit of C/C++ and have it pass control to other functions or applications, but you should also consider using the Scripting Layer for Android (see Recipe 19.4).

For this example I use a simple numeric calculation, computing the square root of a double using the Newton–Raphson iterative method. The code provides both a Java and a C version, to compare the speeds.

Ian's basic steps: Java calling native code

To call native code from Java, follow these steps:

1. Install the NDK in addition to the Android Development Kit (ADK).
2. Write Java code that declares and calls a native method.
3. Compile this Java code.
4. Create an .h header file using javah.
5. Write a C function that includes this header file and implements the native method to do the work.
6. Prepare the *Android.mk* (and optionally *Application.mk*) configuration file.
7. Compile the C code into a loadable object using $NDK/ndk-build.
8. Package and deploy your application, and test it.

We will now walk through the details of each of these steps. The preliminary step is to download the NDK (*https://developer.android.com/tools/sdk/ndk/*) as a TAR or ZIP file. Extract it someplace convenient, and set the environment variable NDK to the full path where you've installed it, for referring back to the NDK install. You'll want this to read documentation as well as to run the tools.

The next step is to write Java code that declares and calls a native method (see Example 19-2). Use the keyword native in the method declaration to indicate that the method is native. To use the native method, no special syntax is required, but your application—typically in the main Activity—must provide a static code block that loads your native method using System.loadLibrary(), as shown in Example 19-3. (The dynamically loadable module will be created in step 6.) Static blocks are executed when the class containing them is loaded; loading the native code here ensures that it is in memory when needed!

Object variables that your native code may modify should carry the volatile modifier. In my example, *SqrtDemo.java* contains the native method declaration (as well as a Java implementation of the algorithm).

Example 19-2. The Java code (SqrtDemo.java)

```
public class SqrtDemo {

    public static final double EPSILON = 0.05d;

    public static native double sqrtC(double d);

    public static double sqrtJava(double d) {
        double x0 = 10.0, x1 = d, diff;
        do {
            x1 = x0 - (((x0 * x0) - d) / (x0 * 2));
            diff = x1 - x0;
            x0 = x1;
        } while (Math.abs(diff) > EPSILON);
        return x1;
    }
}
```

Example 19-3. The Activity class Main.java uses the native code

```
// In the Activity class, outside any methods:
static {
    System.loadLibrary("sqrt-demo");
}

// In a method of the Activity class where you need to use it:
double d = SqrtDemo.sqrtC(123456789.0);
```

The next step is simple: just build the project normally, using your usual build process.

Next, you need to create a C-language *.h* header file that provides the interface between the JVM and your native code. Use javah to produce this file. javah needs to read the class that declares one or more native methods, and will generate an *.h* file specific to the package and class name (in the following example, *foo_ndkdemo_SqrtDemo.h*):

```
$ mkdir jni # Keep everything JNI-related here
$ javah -d jni -classpath bin foo.ndkdemo.SqrtDemo
```

The *.h* file produced is a "glue" file, not really meant for human consumption and particularly not for editing. But by inspecting the resultant *.h* file, you'll see that the C method's name is composed of the name "Java,"" the package name, the class name, and the method name:

```
JNIEXPORT jdouble JNICALL Java_foo_ndkdemo_SqrtDemo_sqrtC
  (JNIEnv *, jclass, jdouble);
```

Now create a C function that does the work. You must import the *.h* file and use the same function signature as is used in the *.h* file.

This function can do whatever it wishes. Note that it is passed two arguments before any declared arguments: a JVM environment variable and a "this" handle for the invocation context object. Table 19-2 shows the correspondence between Java types and the C types (JNI types) used in the C code.

Table 19-2. Java and JNI types

Java type	JNI	Java array type	JNI
byte	jbyte	byte[]	jbyteArray
short	jshort	short[]	jshortArray
int	jint	int[]	jintArray
long	jlong	long[]	jlongArray
float	jfloat	float[]	jfloatArray
double	jdouble	double[]	jdoubleArray
char	jchar	char[]	jcharArray
boolean	jboolean	boolean[]	jbooleanArray
void	jvoid		
Object	jobject	Object[]	jobjectArray
Class	jclass		
String	jstring		
array	jarray		
Throwable	jthrowable		

Example 19-4 shows the complete C native implementation. It simply computes the square root of the input number, and returns the result. The method is static, so the "this" pointer is not used.

Example 19-4. The C code

```
// jni/sqrt-demo.c

#include <stdlib.h>

#include "foo_ndkdemo_SqrtDemo.h"

JNIEXPORT jdouble JNICALL Java_foo_ndkdemo_SqrtDemo_sqrtC(
    JNIEnv *env, jclass clazz, jdouble d) {

    jdouble x0 = 10.0, x1 = d, diff;
    do {
        x1 = x0 - (((x0 * x0) - d) / (x0 * 2));
        diff = x1 - x0;
        x0 = x1;
    } while (labs(diff) > foo_ndkdemo_SqrtDemo_EPSILON);
```

```
    return x1;
}
```

The implementation is basically the same as the Java version. Note that javah even maps the final double EPSILON from the Java class SqrtDemo into a #define for use within the C version.

The next step is to prepare the file *Android.mk*, also in the *jni* folder. For a simple shared library, Example 19-5 will suffice.

Example 19-5. An Android.mk makefile example

```
# Android.mk

LOCAL_PATH := $(call my-dir)

include $(CLEAR_VARS)

LOCAL_MODULE     := sqrt-demo
LOCAL_SRC_FILES := sqrt-demo.c

include $(BUILD_SHARED_LIBRARY)
```

Finally, you compile the C code into a loadable object. In desktop Java, the details depend on the platform, compiler, and so on. However, the NDK provides a build script to automate this. Assuming you have set the NDK variable to the install root of the NDK download from step 1, you only need to type the following:

```
$ $NDK/ndk-build  # For Linux, Unix, macOS?
> %NDK%/ndk-build # For MS-Windows

Compile thumb  : sqrt-demo <= sqrt-demo.c
SharedLibrary : libsqrt-demo.so
Install        : libsqrt-demo.so => libs/armeabi/libsqrt-demo.so
```

And you're done! Just package and run the application normally. The output should be similar to Figure 19-2. The full download example for this chapter includes buttons to run the sqrt function a number of times in either Java or C and compare the times. Note that at present it does this work on the event thread, so large numbers of repetitions will result in Application Not Responding (ANR) errors, which will mess up the timing.

Congratulations! You've called a native method. Your code may run slightly faster. However, you will have to do extra work for portability; as Android begins to run on more hardware platforms, you will have to (at least) add them to the *Application.mk* file. If you have used any assembly language (machine-specific) code, the problem is much worse.

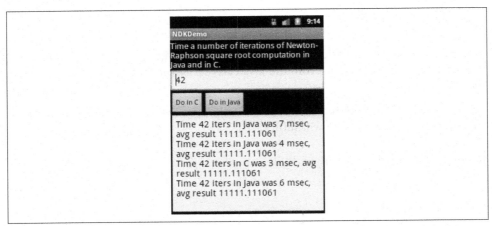

Figure 19-2. NDK demonstration output

Beware that problems with your native code can and will crash the runtime process right out from underneath the Java Virtual Machine. The JVM can do nothing to protect itself from poorly written C/C++ code. Memory must be managed by the programmer; there is no automatic garbage collection of memory obtained by the system runtime allocator. You're dealing directly with the operating system and sometimes even the hardware, so "Be careful. Be very careful."

See Also

There is a recipe in Chapter 26 of my *Java Cookbook* (*http://shop.oreilly.com/product/9780596007010.do*), published by O'Reilly, that shows variables from the Java class being accessed from within the native code. The official documentation for Android's NDK is found on the Android Native SDK information page (*https://developer.android.com/sdk/ndk/*). Considerable documentation is included in the *docs* folder of the NDK download. If you need more information on Java native methods, you might be interested in the comprehensive treatment found in *Essential JNI: Java Native Interface* by Rob Gordon (Prentice Hall), originally written for desktop Java.

Source Download URL

The source code for this example is in the Android Cookbook repository (*https://github.com/IanDarwin/Android-Cookbook-Examples*), in the subdirectory *NdkDemo* (see "Getting and Using the Code Examples" on page 18).

19.4 Getting Started with SL4A, the Scripting Layer for Android

Ian Darwin

Problem

You want to write your application in one of several popular scripting languages, or you want to program interactively on your phone.

Solution

One of the best approaches is to use the Scripting Layer for Android (SL4A).

 The original developers of SL4A appear to have abandoned it, but there are several alternative builds still available; you can find these by searching for "sl4a" on GitHub (*https://github.com/search?utf8= %E2%9C%93&q=sl4a*).

Here's how to get started:

1. Download the Scripting Layer for Android (formerly Android Scripting Environment) from GitHub (*https://github.com/damonkohler/sl4a*).
2. Add the interpreter(s) you want to use.
3. Type in your program.
4. Run your program immediately—no compilation or packaging steps are needed!

Discussion

SL4A provides support for several popular scripting languages (including Python, Perl, Lua, and BeanShell). An `Android` object is provided that gives access to most of the underlying Android APIs from this language. This recipe shows how to get started; several of the following recipes explore particular aspects of using SL4A. The SL4A application is not in the Google Play Store, so you have to visit the website and download it (there is a QR code for downloading on the website referenced in step 1, so start there, in your laptop or desktop browser). Before doing that, you'll have to go into Settings and allow applications from "Unknown sources." Also note that since you are not downloading via the Play Store, you will not be notified if the Google project releases a new binary.

Once you have the SL4A binary installed, you must start it and download the particular interpreter you want to use. The following are available as of this writing:

- Python
- Perl
- JRuby
- Lua
- BeanShell
- JavaScript
- Tcl
- Unix shell

Some of the interpreters (e.g., JRuby) run in the Android VM, while others (e.g., Python) run the "native" version of the language under Linux on your device. Communication happens via a little server that is started automatically when needed or can be started from the Interpreters menu bar.

The technique for downloading new interpreters isn't very intuitive. When you start the SL4A application it shows a list of scripts, if you have any. Click the Menu button, then go to the View menu and select Interpreters (while here, notice that you can also view the LogCat, the system exception logfile). From the Interpreters list, clicking Menu *again* will get you a menu bar with an Add button, and this lets you add another interpreter.

Pick a language (Python)

Suppose you think Python is a great language (which it is).

Once your interpreter is installed, go back to the SL4A main page and click the Menu button, then Add (in this context, Add creates a new file, not another interpreter). Select the installed interpreter and you'll be in Edit mode. We're trying Python, so type in this canonical "Hello, World" example:

```
import android
droid = android.Android()
droid.makeToast("Hello, Android")
```

Click the Menu button, and choose "Save and Run" if enabled, or "Save and Exit" otherwise. The former will run your new app; the latter will return you to the list of scripts, in which case you want to tap your script's name. In the resultant pop-up, the choices are (left to right):

- Run (DOS box icon)
- Disabled

- Edit (pencil icon)
- Save (1980s floppy disk icon)
- Delete (trash can icon)

If you long-press a filename, a pop-up gives you the choice of Rename or Delete.

When you run this trivial application, you will see the toast near the bottom of your screen.

Source editing

If you want to keep your scripts in a source repository, and/or if you prefer to edit them on a laptop or desktop with a traditional keyboard, just copy the files back and forth (if your phone is rooted, you can probably run your repository directly on the phone). Scripts are stored in *sl4a/scripts* on the SD card. If you have your phone mounted on your laptop's */mnt* folder, for example, you might see the code shown in Example 19-6 (on Windows it might be *E:* or *F:* instead of */mnt*).

Example 19-6. List of scripting files

```
laptop$ ls /mnt/sl4a/
Shell.log demo.sh.log dialer.py.log hello_world.py.log ifconfig.py.log
notify_weather.py.log phonepicker.py.log say_chat.py.log say_time.py.log
say_weather.py.log scripts/ sms.py.log speak.py.log take_picture.py.log
test.py.log
laptop$ ls /mnt/sl4a/scripts
bluetooth_chat.py demo.sh dialer.py foo.sh hello_world.py ifconfig.py
notify_weather.py phonepicker.py say_chat.py say_time.py say_weather.py
sms.py speak.py take_picture.py test.py weather.py weather.pyc
laptop$
```

19.5 Creating Alerts in SL4A

Rachee Singh

Problem

You need to create an alert box or pop-up dialog using Python in the Scripting Layer for Android.

Solution

You can create many kinds of alert dialogs using Python in SL4A. They can have buttons, lists, and other features.

Discussion

Begin by starting the SL4A app on your emulator/device (see Recipe 19.4). Then add a new Python script by clicking the Menu button and choosing Add (see Figure 19-3).

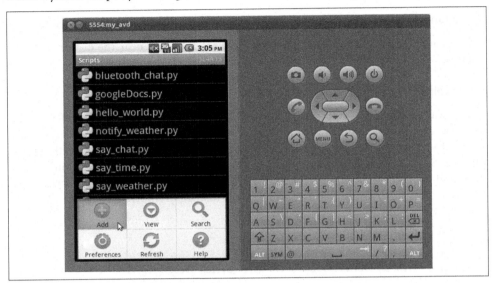

Figure 19-3. Starting to add a new script

Choose the Python 2.x option from the submenu that appears, as shown in Figure 19-4.

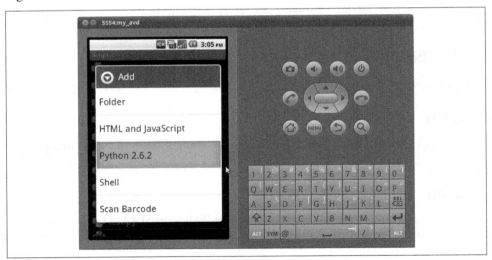

Figure 19-4. Choosing the language

This opens an editor, with the first two lines (shown in Figure 19-5) already filled in for you. Enter the name of the script (I have named mine *alertdialog.py*).

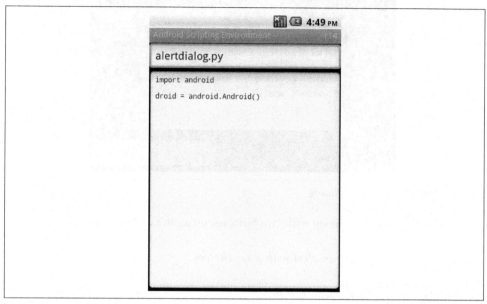

Figure 19-5. Composing the script

Now we are ready to enter the code to create the alert dialogs. Type in the code shown in Example 19-7.

Example 19-7. A simple SL4A Python script

```
title = 'Sample Alert Dialog'
text = 'Alert Dialog Type 1!'
droid.dialogCreateAlert(title, text)
droid.dialogSetPositiveButtonText('Continue')
droid.dialogShow()
```

Press the Menu button and choose "Save and Run" from the menu. This runs the script. The alert dialog should look like Figure 19-6.

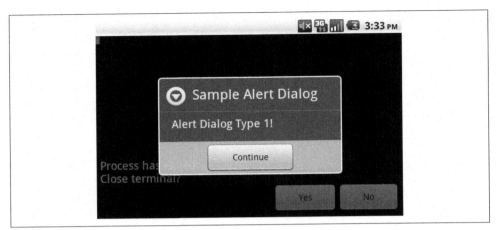

Figure 19-6. Sample alert dialog

Now let's create an alert dialog with two buttons, using the code in Example 19-8.

Example 19-8. Composing an alert with three choices

```
title = 'Sample Alert Dialog'
text = 'Alert Dialog Type 2 with buttons!'
droid.dialogCreateAlert(title, text)
droid.dialogSetPositiveButtonText('Yes')
droid.dialogSetNegativeButtonText('No')
droid.dialogSetNeutralButtonText('Cancel')
droid.dialogShow()
```

Figure 19-7 shows how this alert dialog looks.

Figure 19-7. Alert dialog with two choices in action

Now try the code in Example 19-9 to create an alert dialog with a list.

Example 19-9. Another approach to composing an alert with three choices

```
title = 'Sample Alert Dialog'
droid.dialogCreateAlert(title)
droid.dialogSetItems(['mango', 'apple', 'strawberry'])
droid.dialogShow()
```

Figure 19-8 shows how this alert dialog looks.

Figure 19-8. Dialog with three choices

19.6 Fetching Your Google Documents and Displaying Them in a ListView Using SL4A

Rachee Singh

Problem

You need to get the details of your Google documents after logging in to Google with your Google ID and password.

Solution

Google Docs is a widely used document editing and sharing service. Using the library *gdata.docs.service*, we can log in (getting the username and password from the user) and then get the "Google documents feed" or list of documents.

Discussion

Fire up the Scripting Layer for Android on your device (or emulator). Open a new Python script and add to the script the code shown in Example 19-10. If you have not worked in Python before, be aware that indentation, rather than braces, is used for statement grouping, so you must be very consistent about leading spaces.

Example 19-10. Composing a script to fetch Google documents

```python
import android
import gdata.docs.service

droid = android.Android()

client =  gdata.docs.service.DocsService()

username = droid.dialogGetInput('Username').result
password = droid.dialogGetPassword('Password', 'For ' _username).result

def truncate(content, length=15, suffix='...'):
    if len(content) <=length:
        return content
    else:
        return content[:length] + suffix
try:
    client.ClientLogin(username, password)
except:
    droid.makeToast("Login Failed")

docs_feed = client.GetDocumentListFeed()

documentEntries = []

for entry in docs_feed.entry:
    documentEntries.append('%-18s %-12s %s' %
        (truncate(entry.title.text.encode('UTF-8')), ❶
    entry.GetDocumentType(), entry.resourceId.text))

droid.dialogCreateAlert('Documents:')
droid.dialogSetItems(documentEntries)
droid.dialogShow()
```

❶   Note these two lines should be entered as one long line.

Figure 19-9 shows how the editor should look after you have finished entering the code.

In this Python code, we use the gdata.docs.service.DocsService() method to connect to the Google account of a user. The username and password are taken from the user. Once the login is done successfully, the GetDocumentListFeed() method is used to get the feed list of the Google documents. We format the details of each entry and append

---

them to a list named `documentEntries`. This list is then passed as an argument to the alert dialog, which displays all the entries in a list.

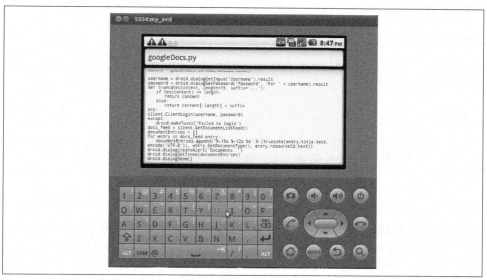

Figure 19-9. Google document fetcher in action

Figure 19-10 shows how my own document list looks.

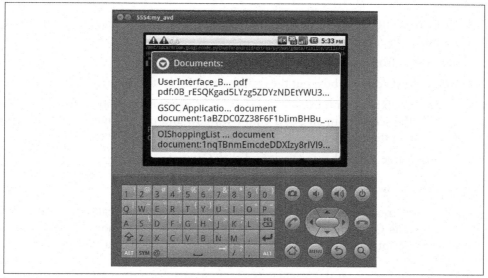

Figure 19-10. List of Google documents

19.7 Sharing SL4A Scripts in QR Codes

Rachee Singh

Problem

You have a neat/useful SL4A script and want to distribute it packed in a Quick Response (QR) code.

Solution

Use a tool such as ZXing's QR Code Generator (*http://zxing.appspot.com/generator/*) to generate a QR code that contains your entire script in the QR code graphic, and share this image.

Discussion

Most people think of QR codes as a convenient way to share URL-type links. But the QR code format is quite versatile, and can be used to package all sorts of things, like VCard (name and address) information. Here we use it to wrap the "plain text" of an SL4A script so that another Android user can get the script onto his device without retyping it. QR codes are a great way to share your scripts if they are short (QR codes can only encode 4,296 characters of content). Follow these simple steps to generate a QR code for your script:

1. Visit the QR Code Generator (*http://zxing.appspot.com/generator/*) in your mobile device's browser.
2. Select Text from the Contents drop-down menu.
3. In the "Text content" box, put the script's name in the first line.
4. From the next line onward, enter the script. (Or, as an alternative to steps 3 and 4, copy the script from an SL4A editor window and paste it into the "Text content" box in the browser).
5. Choose Large for the barcode size and click Generate.

Figure 19-11 shows how this looks in action.

Many QR code readers are available for Android. Any such application can decipher the text that the QR code encrypts. For example, with the common ZXing Barcode Scanner, the script is copied to the clipboard (this is controlled by a "When a Barcode is found…" entry in the Settings). Then start the SL4A editor, pick a name for your script (ideally the same as the original, if you know it—depending on how it was pasted into the QR code generator it may appear as the first line) then long-press in the body area and select Paste. You are now ready to save the script and run it! It should look like Figure 19-12.

Figure 19-11. Barcode generated from the SL4A script

Figure 19-12. The script, downloaded

I was able to run the script from the QR code with no further work other than commenting out the script name in the body and typing it into the filename field, then clicking "Save and Run" (see Figure 19-13).

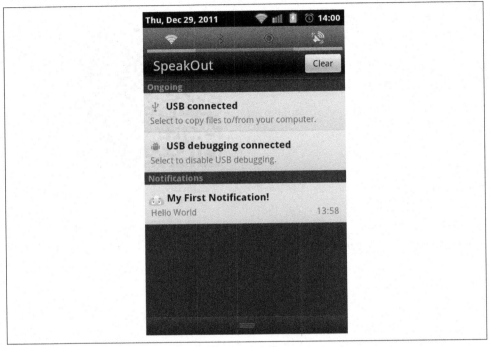

Figure 19-13. The script running, showing a notification

19.8 Using Native Handset Functionality from a WebView via JavaScript

Colin Wilcox

Problem

The availability of HTML5 as a standard feature in many browsers means that developers can exploit the features of the HTML5 standard to create applications much more quickly than they can in native Java. This sounds great for many applications, but alas, not all of the cool functionality on the device is accessible through HTML5 and JavaScript. Webkits attempt to bridge this gap, but they may not provide all the functionality needed in all cases.

Solution

You can invoke Java code in response to JavaScript events using a bridge between the JavaScript and Java environments.

Discussion

The idea is to tie up events within the JavaScript embedded in an HTML5 web page and handle the event on the Java side by calling native code.

The following code creates a button in HTML5 embedded in a WebView which, when clicked, causes the Contacts application to be invoked on the device through the Intent mechanism.

First, we write some thin bridge code in Java, as shown in Example 19-11.

Example 19-11. The bridge code

```
public class JavaScriptInterface
{
    private static final String TAG = "JavaScriptInterface";
    Context iContext = null;

    /** Instantiate the interface and set the context */
    JavaScriptInterface(Context aContext) {
        // Save the local content for later use
        iContext = aContext;
    }

    public void launchContacts(); {
        iContext.startActivity(contactIntent);
        launchNativeContactsApp ();
    }
}
```

The Java code to actually launch the Contacts app is shown in Example 19-12.

Example 19-12. Java code to launch contacts

```
private void launchNativeContactsApp()
{
    String packageName = "com.android.contacts";
    String className = ".DialtactsContactsEntryActivity";
    String action = "android.intent.action.MAIN";
    String category1 = "android.intent.category.LAUNCHER";
    String category2 = "android.intent.category.DEFAULT";

    Intent intent = new Intent();
    intent.setComponent(new ComponentName(packageName, packageName + className));
    intent.setAction(action);
    intent.addCategory(category1);
```

```
        intent.addCategory(category2);
        startActivity(intent);
}
```

The JavaScript that ties this all together is shown in the following snippet. In this case the call is triggered by a click event:

```
<input type="button" value="Say hello" onClick="showAndroidContacts())" />
<script type="text/javascript">
    function showAndroidContacts() {
        Android.launchContacts();
    }
</script>
```

The only preconditions are that the web browser has JavaScript enabled and the interface is known. This is done by:

```
WebView iWebView = (WebView) findViewById(R.id.webview);
iWebView.addJavascriptInterface(new JavaScriptInterface(this), "Android");
```

19.9 Building a Cross-Platform App with Xamarin

Ian Darwin

Problem

You want to build an app that can run on any major platform: Android, iOS, Windows Phone, etc.

Solution

One solution is to use Xamarin (*https://xamarin.com/*).

Discussion

I have always contended—and it is a main theme of this book—that you should write Android apps using the Android SDK, because if you write them in a generic way, the user will not have a great experience with your app as generic interfaces don't know about Activities, Services, the Android Back button behavior, etc.

Xamarin is a toolchain and set of libraries that allows you to build apps in the C# or F# programming language. Xamarin-based apps can run on Android, iOS, Windows, and a few other platforms. Xamarin depends on the open source Mono implementation of the .NET runtime. Xamarin Inc. began life as an independent company but was acquired by Microsoft in March 2016 as a way to get developers up to speed on Microsoft's Java clone C# and on the Microsoft .NET environment.

Note that Xamarin is not a cross-platform UI toolkit. You write real Android UI code using the Xamarin API, as shown in Example 19-13. The cross-platform aspect comes in when Xamarin is able to share business logic, persistence API, and other code that you write in C# across platforms. On Android it can import existing Java libraries (JAR files); on other platforms it can import those platforms' equivalent compiled code.

Example 19-13. A "Hello, World" Android application in Xamarin

```
using Android.App;
using Android.Widget;
using Android.OS;

namespace HelloXamarin {
        [Activity(Label = "HelloXamarin",
          MainLauncher = true, Icon = "@mipmap/icon")]
        public class MainActivity : Activity {
                int count = 1;

                protected override void OnCreate(Bundle savedInstanceState) {
                        base.OnCreate(savedInstanceState);

                        // Set our view from the "main" layout resource
                        SetContentView(Resource.Layout.Main);

                        // Get our button from the layout resource,
                        // and attach an event to it
                        Button button = FindViewById<Button>(Resource.Id.myButton);

                        button.Click += delegate {
                                button.Text = string.Format("{0} clicks!", count++);
                        };
                }
        }
}
```

If you've read this far in the book, you can figure out what this code is doing: read extends for ":" in a class definition, super for base, and a lambda expression or anonymous class for delegate; lowercase the first letter of the method names; use the odd-looking type parameter as a typecast instead; and so on. The general shape is quite recognizable—unsurprising, since historically C# began as a way to get around Java's licensing.

When getting started with Xamarin you have your choice of two IDEs:

Xamarin Studio
Its own IDE, which stores files in a format that Visual Studio can use

Visual Studio
Xamarin plug-in-based extension to Microsoft Visual Studio

For this example we used the free Community edition of Xamarin Studio (*https://www.xamarin.com/download*). Note that this edition is only "free" in the sense that you don't have to pay to license it if you are an indie developer or "small team"; for "enterprise" players, there is a licensing fee. The underlying mono toolkit is open source on GitHub (*https://github.com/mono/mono*), but most of the tooling is not open source.

Installing Xamarin Studio is a bit quirky: it correctly detected that I had the Intel HAXM emulator installed, but wasn't able to find the several Android SDK installations on my hard drive. Cue up some music to listen to while waiting for the 4 GB download (see Figure 19-14).

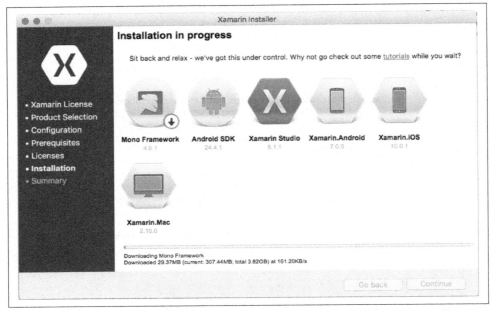

Figure 19-14. Xamarin download

Once the download finished, the installation was standard, and it placed Xamarin in the standard */Applications* folder on macOS. Once run, it offered the choice to start a new project ("solution"), then to create one of several types of Android applications (see Figure 19-15).

The next few steps are pretty similar to using a Java IDE: give your application a name, choose the Java package name, choose a version (see Figure 19-16), click Next, and then click Finish.

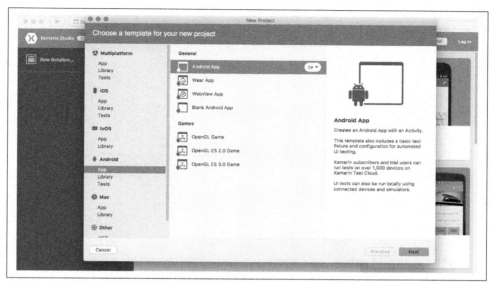

Figure 19-15. Xamarin creating an Android project

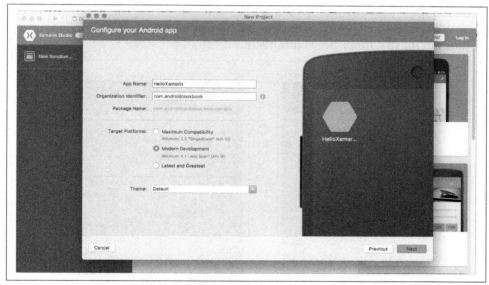

Figure 19-16. Xamarin Android version

Once the project is configured and set up, you will see a fairly standard IDE editing screen (Figure 19-17).

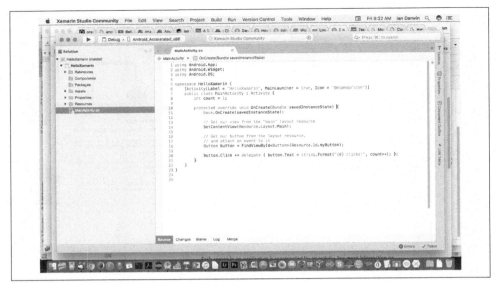

Figure 19-17. Xamarin project view

Press the Run button in the top toolbar and Xamarin will start an emulator and run your application (this took two tries the first time I ran it; the communication seemed to time out the first time). See Figure 19-18.

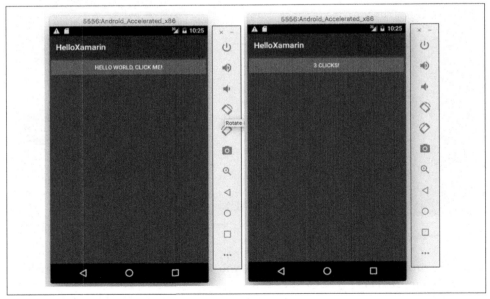

Figure 19-18. Xamarin app running

I did not take the time to learn macOS or Windows Phone UI coding, so this example doesn't show the cross-platform aspect of Xamarin, but it does show that you can use Xamarin Studio to build UI code and build runnable apps with it. A large amount of documentation and many startup videos and longer examples are available on the Xamarin website (*https://xamarin.com/*).

19.10 Creating a Cross-Platform App Using PhoneGap/Cordova

Shraddha Shravagi and Ian Darwin

Problem

You want an application to run on different platforms, such as iOS, Android, Black-Berry, Bada, Symbian, and Windows Phone.

Solution

Cordova (better known as PhoneGap) is an open source mobile development framework. If you plan to develop an application for multiple platforms, PhoneGap is one good solution—so much so that Oracle and BlackBerry, among others, either endorse it or base products on it. PhoneGap does not use traditional platform GUI controls; rather, you write a web page with buttons—made to approximate the native look of Android (and other platforms) by careful use of CSS—and PhoneGap runs this "mobile app" for you.

PhoneGap was written by Nitobi, a small company that Adobe Systems Inc. acquired in fall 2011. Adobe has donated the framework source code to the Apache Software Foundation, where its development continues under the name "Cordova." However, Adobe has continued to develop tooling for it under the name PhoneGap, and says that "Apache Cordova is… the engine that powers PhoneGap, much like WebKit is the engine that powers many modern web browsers. It's the robust tools that sets PhoneGap apart, including: our command line interface, the PhoneGap Desktop app, the PhoneGap developer app, and PhoneGap Build."

Cordova supports many platforms, including Android, iOS, Microsoft Windows (and Windows Phone), BlackBerry 10, Ubuntu, and (because Cordova apps are web apps) Firefox, and more. A matrix of supported environments versus features supported on each is provided on the Cordova website (*http://cordova.apache.org/docs/en/latest/guide/support/*).

Discussion

We will start with an Android application. We don't use the normal Android layouts, nor any Java code, nor the notion of "one activity per screen"; instead, we create HTML and JavaScript files, which can run on different platforms. In fact, the app is mostly a "mobile web app" that is packaged as an Android app.

 There are two slightly different versions of the setup, depending on whether you want to use the Adobe tooling or the Apache tooling. We'll use the latter here.

1. You must have NPM (the Node Package Manager) installed. NPM itself is command-line based. If it's not installed, visit the Node.js npm installer (*https://www.npmjs.com/package/cordova/tutorial*) and follow the steps there for major operating systems. Or go straight to Node.js (*https://https://nodejs.org/en/*) and download and install Node and npm. As of May 1, 2017, the recommended version is v6.10.2 LTS.

   After installation, check it:

   ```
   $ node -v
        v6.10.2
   $
   ```

2. Install cordova itself: `npm install -g cordova`

   You either have to do this as root, or arrange to install it in your own directory. This will run for a long time as it downloads most of the internet: 620 packages at last check. It will print a tree of the dependencies, looking something like this (but about 600 lines longer):

   ```
   $ sudo npm install -g cordova
   npm WARN deprecated node-uuid@1.4.8: Use uuid module instead
   /usr/local/bin/cordova -> /usr/local/lib/node_modules/cordova/bin/cordova
   /usr/local/lib
   ▦▦▦ cordova@6.5.0
     ▦▦▦ cordova-common@2.0.0
     ▦ ▦▦▦ ansi@0.3.1
     ▦ ▦▦▦ bplist-parser@0.1.1
     ▦ ▦ ▦▦▦ big-integer@1.6.22
     ▦ ▦▦▦ cordova-registry-mapper@1.1.15
     ...
   $
   ```

3. Create a project and configure it:

   ```
   $ cd SomePlaceNice
   $ cordova create CordovaDemo
   Creating a new cordova project.
   $ cd CordovaDemo
   ```

```
$ cordova platform add android
Adding android project...
Creating Cordova project for the Android platform:
    Path: platforms/android
    Package: io.cordova.hellocordova
    Name: HelloCordova
    Activity: MainActivity
    Android target: android-25
Subproject Path: CordovaLib
Android project created with cordova-android@6.1.2
Discovered plugin "cordova-plugin-whitelist" in config.xml. Adding it to the
    project
Fetching plugin "cordova-plugin-whitelist@1" via npm
Installing "cordova-plugin-whitelist" for android
$
```

4. Run your demo project:

```
$ cordova run android
```

If you get the following message:

```
Error: Could not find gradle wrapper within Android SDK. Might need to update your
    Android SDK.
Looked here: /Users/YOURNAME/android-sdk-macosx/tools/templates/gradle/wrapper
```

this is because your Android SDK is newer than the cordova you've installed (newer versions no longer feature this *templates* directory). Try this workaround:

```
$ cordova platform update android@6.2.1
Updating android project...
Subproject Path: CordovaLib
Android project updated with cordova-android@6.2.1
```

And try the run again:

```
$ cordova run android
ANDROID_HOME=/Users/ian/android-sdk-macosx
JAVA_HOME=/Library/Java/JavaVirtualMachines/jdk1.8.0.jdk/Contents/Home
Starting a Gradle Daemon (subsequent builds will be faster)
:wrapper
BUILD SUCCESSFUL
Total time: 10.935 secs
Subproject Path: CordovaLib
Starting a Gradle Daemon (subsequent builds will be faster)
Download https://jcenter.bintray.com/com/android/tools/build/gradle/2.2.3/
    gradle-2.2.3.pom
Download https://jcenter.bintray.com/com/android/tools/build/gradle-core/2.2.3/
    gradle-core-2.2.3.pom
Download https://jcenter.bintray.com/com/android/tools/build/builder/2.2.3/
    builder-2.2.3.pom
Download https://jcenter.bintray.com/com/android/tools/lint/lint/25.2.3/
    lint-25.2.3.pom
```

Again, it may take a time-out to download another half of the Internet.

Finally it should end up building an APK: CordovaDemo/platforms/android/build/outputs/apk/android-debug.apk

It will run it if there is an emulator running or a device connected that's usable by ADB, or else it will error out at this point.

5. You can build your app for any of the other supported applications just by using `cordova platform add platname` followed by `cordova run platname`.

6. Now that the structure is in place, you can build out your JavaScript application, starting with the "main program" web page file `www/index.html` and JavaScript file `www/js/index.js`. That is not detailed here since this is not a JavaScript book, but we'll give a brief example.

   In the body of this HTML page, change the `h1` element to read:

   ```
   <h1> Hello World </h1>
   ```

   You can add all your HTML/jQuery mobile code in the div element named *app* in the HTML file. For example, to add a button:

   ```
   <a data-role="button" data-icon="grid" data-theme="b"
       onClick="showAlert()">
   Click Me!!!</a>
   ```

7. In this JavaScript file you can add all your jQuery mobile and JavaScript code:

   ```
   function showAlert() {
       alert('Hello World from Cordova using JavaScript!!! ');
   }
   ```

That's it. You should be able to run the application.

See Also

http://cordova.apache.org/ is the current home page for the Apache Cordova project.

http://phonegap.com/ is the current home page for the Adobe PhoneGap tooling for Cordova.

Also, *Building Android Apps with HTML, CSS, and JavaScript* by Jonathan Stark (O'Reilly) gives slightly older PhoneGap-centric coverage of these "background" technologies as well as more information on PhoneGap development.

Source Download URL

The source code for this example is in the Android Cookbook repository (*https://github.com/IanDarwin/Android-Cookbook-Examples*), in the subdirectory *Cordova-Demo* (see "Getting and Using the Code Examples" on page 18).

## CHAPTER 20

All the World's Not English: Strings and Internationalization

"All the world's a stage," wrote William Shakespeare. But not all the players on that great and turbulent stage speak the great Bard's native tongue. To be usable on a global scale, your software needs to communicate in many different languages. The menu labels, button strings, dialog messages, title bar/action bar titles, and error messages must be settable to the user's choice of language. This is the topic of *internationalization and localization*. (Because the words "internationalization" and "localization" take a long time to say and write, they're often abbreviated using their first and last letters and the count of omitted letters: I18N and L10N.)

If you've got your strings in a separate XML file, as we advised in Chapter 1, you have already done part of the work of internationalizing your app. Aren't you glad you followed our advice?

Android provides a `Locale` class to discover/control the internationalization settings. A default `Locale` is inherited from the user's language settings when your app starts up. As a best practice, your app should never ask the users to choose a language, because they'll already have chosen one when setting up the device.

Note that if you know internationalization from desktop Java, it's pretty much the same here. We'll explain as we go along, with examples, in this chapter.

Ian's basic steps: Internationalization

Internationalization and localization consist of:

Sensitivity training (internationalization or I18N)
> Making your software sensitive to the issues introduced in the first paragraph of this recipe.

Language lessons (localization or L10N)
    Writing text mapping files for each language.

Culture lessons (optional)
    Customizing the presentation of numbers, fractions, dates, and message formatting. Images and colors, for example, can mean different things in different cultures.

This chapter's recipes provide examples of doing all three.

See also

Wikipedia has a good article on internalization and localization (*https://en.wikipedia.org/wiki/Internationalization_and_localization*). See also *Java Internationalization* by Andy Deitsch and David Czarnecki (O'Reilly).

Microsoft's *The GUI Guide: International Terminology for the Windows Interface* (*http://www.amazon.com/dp/1556155387*) was, despite the title, less about UI design than about internationalization; it came with a 3.5-inch floppy disk holding suggested translations of common Microsoft Windows GUI element names into a dozen or so common languages. This book is rather dated today, but it might be a start for translating simple texts into some common languages. It can often be found on the usual used-book websites.

20.1 Internationalizing Application Text

Ian Darwin

Problem

You want the text of your buttons, labels, and so on to appear in the user's chosen language.

Solution

Create or update the file *strings.xml* in the *res/values* subdirectory of your application. Translate the string values into the given language.

Discussion

Every Android project created with the SDK has a file called *strings.xml* in the *res/values* directory. This is where you are advised to place your application's strings, from the application title through to the button text and even down to the contents of dialogs. You can refer to a string by name in the following two ways:

- By a reference in a layout file, to apply the correct version of the string directly to a GUI component; for example, `android:text="@string/hello"`
- If you need the value in Java code, by using a lookup such as `getString(R.string.hello)` to look up the string's value from the file

To make all of these strings available in a different language, you need to know the correct ISO-639 language code; a few common ones are shown in Table 20-1.

Table 20-1. Common languages and codes

Language	Code
Chinese (traditional)	cn-tw
Chinese (simplified)	cn-zh
English	en
French	fr
German	de
Italian	it
Japanese	jp
Spanish	es

With this information, you can create a new subdirectory, *res/values-LL* (where *LL* is replaced by the ISO language code). In this directory you create a copy of *strings.xml*, and in it you translate the individual string values (but not the names). For example, a simple application might have the following in *strings.xml*:

```
<?xml version="1.0" encoding="utf-8"?>
<resources>
    <string name="app_name">MyAndroid</string>
    <string name="hello">Hello Android</string>
</resources>
```

You might create *res/values-es/strings.xml* containing the following Spanish text (see Figure 20-1):

```
<?xml version="1.0" encoding="utf-8"?>
<resources>
    <string name="app_name">MiAndroid</string>
    <string name="hello">Hola Android</string>
</resources>
```

You might also create the file *res/values-fr/strings.xml* containing the following French text:

```
<?xml version="1.0" encoding="utf-8"?>
<resources>
    <string name="hello">Bonjour Android</string>
    <string name="app_name">MonAndroid</string>
</resources>
```

Note that the order of entries within this file does not matter.

Now when you look up the string `"hello"` using either of the methods described earlier, you will get the version based on the user's language choice. If the user selects a language that you don't have a L10N file for, the app will still work, but it will get the value from the default file—the one in the *values* directory with no language code.

This lookup is done per string, so if there is a string that's not defined in a language-specific file, the app will find the version of it in the default *strings.xml* file.

Is it really that simple?

Yes. Just package your application and deploy it as usual. Go into the Settings app of your emulator or device, choose Language, select French or Spanish, and the program title and window contents should reflect the change (Figure 20-1).

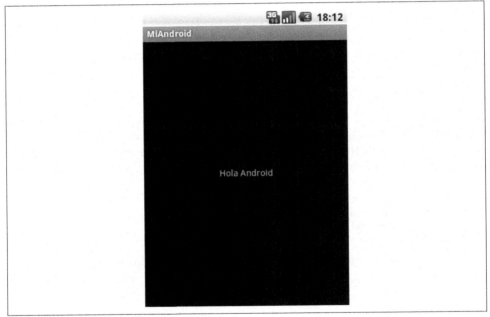

Figure 20-1. Hello app in Spanish

You just have to remember to keep all the versions of *strings.xml* in sync with the "master" copy.

Regional variants

OK, so it's not *quite* that simple. There are also regional variations within a language. In English there are, for example, UK English (a.k.a. "the real thing" to some, or "the Queen's/King's English"), US English, Canadian, Australian, and so on. These, fortu-

---

nately, have tended to use the same vocabulary for technical terms, so using the regional variations is not as important for English. On the other hand, French and Spanish, to name two that I am familiar with, are languages where there is significant variation in vocabulary from one region to another. Parisian French and Canadian French have used different vocabularies for many words coined since the 1500s, when the exodus to Canada began. The many Spanish colonies were likewise largely isolated from hearing and reading one another's words for hundreds of years—from the time of their founding until the age of radio—and they have diverged even more than French. So you may want to create "variant" files for these languages, as for any other that has significant regional variation.

Android's practice here diverges slightly from Java's, in that Android uses a letter *r* to denote regional variations; for example, you'd create a directory named *values-fr-rCA* for Canadian French. Note that, as in Java, language codes are in lowercase and variations (which are usually the two-letter ISO 3166-1 alpha-2 country codes) are written in capital letters (except for the leading *r*). So, for example, we might wind up with the set of files listed in Table 20-2.

Table 20-2. L10N directory examples

Directory	Meaning
values	English - default
values-es	Spanish - Castilian, generic
values-es-rCU	Spanish - Cuban
values-es-rCL	Spanish - Chilean
values-fr	French - generic
values-fr-rCA	French - Canadian

See Also

There is a bit more detail in the official Android localization documentation (*https://developer.android.com/guide/topics/resources/localization.html*).

20.2 Finding and Translating Strings

Ian Darwin

Problem

You need to find all the strings in your application, internationalize them, and translate them.

Solution

Use one of the several good tools for finding string literals, as well as collaborative and commercial services that translate text files.

Discussion

Suppose you have a mix of old and new Java code in your app; the new code was written specifically for Android, while the older code may have been used in some other Java environment. You need to find every string literal, isolate them into a *Strings.xml* file, and translate it into any necessary languages.

Current versions of Android Studio and Eclipse plug-ins will warn about strings that are not internationalized, when you use them inside your app. Android Lint (see Recipe 3.13) will do a stronger job of this.

The Android Localizer from ArtfulBits (*http://artfulbits.com/products/free/ailocal izer.aspx*) is a free and open source tool that you can use to handle both finding and translating strings.

Imagine a slightly different scenario: suppose your organization has a "native" (Objective-C) application from iOS and you are building the "native" Java version for Android. Here, the properties files are in very different formats—on iOS there is a Java properties-like file, but with the default (probably English) strings on the left and the translations on the right. No names are used, just the actual strings, so you might find something like the following:

```
You-not us-are responsible=You-not us-are responsible
```

You cannot translate this directly into XML, since the "name" is used as an identifier in the generated R (Resources) class, and the hyphen (-) and straight quotes (") characters are not valid in Java identifiers. Doing it manually, you might come up with something like this:

```
<string name="you_not_us_are_responsible">You-not us-are responsible</string>
```

Stack Overflow user johnthuss has developed a version of a Java program that performs such translations from iOS to Android format (*http://stackoverflow.com/ques tions/3141118/are-there-any-tools-to-convert-an-iphone-localized-string-file-to-a-string-resou/5838915#5838915*), handling characters that are not valid identifiers.

Now you are ready to begin translating your master resource file into other languages. While it may be tempting to scrimp on this part of the work, it is generally worthwhile to engage the services of a professional translation service skilled in the particular language(s) you target. Google offers an outsourced translation service through the Google Play Developer Console. Alternatively, you may wish to investigate the commercial collaborative translation service Crowdin (*https://crowdin.com/page/android-localization*).

When using any third-party translation service, especially for languages with which you or your staff are not personally "first or second childhood language" familiar, you should *get a second opinion*. Embarrassing errors in software shipped with "bad" translations can be very expensive.

A quick web search will find many commercial services that will perform translations for you, as well as some that can help with the internationalization part of the work.

20.3 Handling the Nuances of strings.xml

Daniel Fowler

Problem

On most occasions, entering text in the *strings.xml* file is easy enough, but sometimes peculiar results crop up.

Solution

Understanding how some text strings and characters work in *strings.xml* will prevent strange results.

Discussion

When some text is required on a screen, it can be declared in a layout file, as shown in the following android:text attribute:

```
<TextView android:id="@+id/textview1"
    android:layout_width="fill_parent"
    android:layout_height="wrap_content"
    android:text="This is text"/>
```

The text can also be set in code:

```
TextView tview = (TextView) findViewById(R.id.textview1);
tview.setText("This is text");
```

However, hardcoding strings like this is not recommended, because it reduces maintainability. Changing text at a later date may mean hunting down declarations across several Java source files and layout files. Instead, text in a project can be centralized into a *strings.xml* file. The file is located in the project's *res/values* folder. Centralizing text means that, if you need to change it, you only need to do so in one place. It also makes localization much easier (see Recipe 20.1}. Here is an example of a *strings.xml* file:

```
<?xml version="1.0" encoding="utf-8"?>
<resources>
    <string name="app_name">Strings XML</string>
    <string name="text1">This is text</string>
```

```
      <string name="text2">And so is this</string>
   </resources>
```

To access the declared string from another project's XML file, use `@string/<string_name>`. Using the preceding example, the text for two `TextViews` is set with the following layout XML file:

```xml
<LinearLayout xmlns:android="http://schemas.android.com/apk/res/android"
              android:orientation="vertical"
              android:layout_width="fill_parent"
              android:layout_height="fill_parent">
   <TextView android:id="@+id/textview1"
             android:layout_width="fill_parent"
             android:layout_height="wrap_content"
             android:text="@string/text1"
             android:textSize="16dp"/>
   <TextView android:id="@+id/textview2"
             android:layout_width="fill_parent"
             android:layout_height="wrap_content"
             android:text="@string/text2"
             android:textSize="16dp"/>
</LinearLayout>
```

When the *strings.xml* file is saved in the IDE, the `R.string` class is generated (see *R.java* in the generated sources folder for the project). This provides a `static int` that can be used to reference the string in code:

```java
tview = (TextView) findViewById(R.id.textview1);
    tview.setText(R.string.text1);
```

The `R` class should never be edited, because it is generated by the SDK and any changes you do make will be overwritten. In Android Studio the text attribute of a textual `View` object can be accessed via the Properties pane. The ellipsis button to the right of the name field allows an existing resource to be chosen or a new one generated (see Figure 20-2).

Figure 20-2. Assigning a string resource to the Text property of a View

In the *strings.xml* file, an entry can duplicate another string by referencing it the same way as a layout file:

```
<string name="text1">This is text</string>
<string name="text2">@string/text1</string>
```

This results in:

Since @ is used to indicate another string resource, trying to set the text to a single @ using `<string name="text1">@</string>` will not work. Nor will text that starts with an @, such as `<string name="text2">@mytwittername</string>`:

The first @ needs to be *escaped* with a \ (backslash), as in \@ and \@mytwittername:

If the @ does not start a string or is being set in code, it does not need to be escaped; you can use `android:text=Twitter:@mytwittername` or `tview.setText("@mytwittername");`, for example. This problem of @ as the first character, or only character, also applies to the ? (question mark). If it appears at the start of a string, it also needs escaping, as in `android:text=\?`. An alternative to escaping the @ or ? is to use quotes (speech marks); the closing quote mark is optional:

```
<string name="text1">"@"</string>
<string name="text2">"?"</string>
```

In fact, any number of quotes and any whitespace before and after the text will be dropped. The two lines in the preceding code snippet produce an identical result to these two lines:

```
<string name="text1">""""""""""@"""""""</string>
<string name="text2">          "?"          </string>
```

There is, however, a character for which this approach will not work:

```
<string name="text1">War & Peace</string>
<string name="text2">War and Peace</string>
```

The first line will result in an error because of the &. This is because of the XML file format itself. XML requires balanced pairs of tags—for example, <string> and </string>—and each start tag and end tag is enclosed in opening (<) and closing (>) angle brackets. Once a start tag is encountered, the editor is on the lookout for the opening bracket of the end tag. This produces a problem if the content of the XML tags contains the open angle bracket itself:

```
<string name="question">Is 5 < 6?</string>
```

This will not work. The solution is to use an XML internal entity; this is similar to using an escape character but is in a specific format for XML. The format is an ampersand, &, followed by the entity name and then a semicolon. For the open angle bracket, or less-than symbol, the name is lt, and therefore the full entity is < as in:

```
<string name="question">Is 5 &lt; 6?</string>
```

Depending on what is required in an XML file at a particular point, there are five internal entities defined for XML that can be used, as this table shows:

Entity	Name	Usage
The left angle bracket (<)	lt	&lt;
The right angle bracket (>)	gt	&gt;
The ampersand (&)	amp	&amp;
The single quote or apostrophe (')	apos	&apos;
The double quote (")	quot	&quot;

Now we can see why the ampersand causes us a problem. It is used to define an internal entity, and thus when one is required, the amp entity itself must be used. Therefore, <string name="text1">War & Peace</string> becomes <string name="text1">War & Peace</string>:

However, the XML internal entity apos, while valid for XML, is reported as an error when the file is saved:

```
<string name="text1">This isn't working</string>
<string name="text2">This isn&apos;t working either</string>
```

This is another character that requires escaping or wrapping in quotes:

```
<string name="text1">This\'ll work</string>
<string name="text2">"This'll work as well"</string>
```

To use quotes (speech marks) themselves—even the XML internal entity version—escape them:

```
<string name="text1">Quote: \"to be, or not to be\"</string>
<string name="text2">Quote: \&quot;to be, or not to be\&quot;</string>
```

Either form will work, so these two lines display identically:

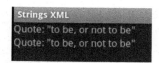

When defining a string that requires space before or after it, again use quotes:

```
<string name="text1"> No spaces before and after </string>
<string name="text2">"  Two spaces before and after  "</string>
```

The strings will support a newline by escaping the letter n:

```
<string name="text1">Split over\ntwo lines</string>
<string name="text2">2 TextViews\n4 Lines</string>
```

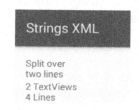

Escaping a t adds a tab to the defined string:

```
<string name="text1">Tab stops\ta\t\tb</string>
<string name="text2">\t\t\t\tc\t\td</string>
```

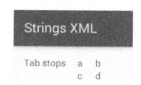

To see the escape character (backslash), use two of them:

```
<string name="text1">Backlash:\\</string>
<string name="text2">Slash:/</string>
```

The android:textstyle attribute of a TextView in a layout file can be used to set the text to bold or italic (or both):

```
android:textStyle="bold"
android:textStyle="italic"
android:textStyle="bold|italic"
```

This can be achieved in the *strings.xml* file using a bold (<b>) or italic (<i>) tag. It also supports an underline tag (<u>). However, instead of applying the formatting to the whole text of the TextView, it can be used for individual portions of the text:

```
<string name="text1">Hey look:<b>bold</b> and <i>italic</i>.</string>
<string name="text2">And look: <u>underline</u> and <b><i><u>bold
 italic underline
</u></i></b>.</string>
```

This results in:

Strings XML

Hey look: **bold** and *italic*.
And look: underline and ***bold italic underline***.

See Also

The developer documentation on string resources (*https://developer.android.com/ guide/topics/resources/string-resource.html*).

Source Download URL

The source code for this project is in the Android Cookbook repository (*https:// github.com/IanDarwin/Android-Cookbook-Examples*), in the subdirectory *StringsXML* (see "Getting and Using the Code Examples" on page 18).

## CHAPTER 21

Packaging, Deploying, and Distributing/Selling Your App

The success of Android has led to a proliferation of application markets. But the official Google Play Store remains the largest marketplace for distributing your app, so we will cover that here, along with information on preparing your app, making it harder to reverse-engineer, and other information you may need along the way.

21.1 Creating a Signing Certificate and Using It to Sign Your Application

Zigurd Mednieks

Problem

You want to publish an application, and you need a "signing key" to complete the process. You then want to sign your application prior to uploading it to the Google Play Store.

Solution

Use the standard JDK tool `keytool` to generate a self-signed certificate. An APK file is a standard Java Archive (JAR) file, so you just use the standard JDK tool `jarsigner`.

Discussion

Google has stated that one of its intentions with Android was to minimize the hassle of getting applications signed. You don't have to go to a central signing authority to get a signing certificate; you can create the certificate yourself. Once you generate the certificate, you can sign your application using the jarsigner tool that comes with the Java JDK. Once again, you don't need to apply for or get anyone's approval. As you'll see, it's about as straightforward as signing can be.

In this recipe, we are going to create an encrypted signing certificate and use it to sign an application. You can sign every Android application you develop with the same signing certificate. You can create as many signing certificates as you want, but you really only need one for all your applications. And using one certificate for all your applications lets you do some things that you couldn't do otherwise:

Simplify upgrades
> Signing certificates are tied to the application package name, so if you change the signing certificate you use with subsequent versions of your application, you'll have to change the package name, too. Changing certificates is manageable, but messy.

Run multiple applications per user ID
> When all your applications share the same signing certificate, they can run in the same Linux process. You can use this to separate your application into smaller modules (each one an Android application) that together make up the larger application. If you were to do that, you could update the modules separately and they could still communicate freely.

Share code/data
> Android lets you enable or restrict access to parts of your application based on the requester's signing certificate. If all your applications share the same certificate, it's easy for you to reuse parts of one application in another.

When you generate a key pair and certificate, you'll be asked for the validity period you desire for the certificate. Although usual practice in website development is to use 1 or 2 years, Google recommends that you set the validity period to at least 25 years, and in fact, if you're going to use the Google Play Store to distribute your application, it requires that your certificate be valid at least until October 22, 2033 (25 years to the day from when Google opened the Play Store, then known as the Android Market).

Generating a key pair (public and private keys) and a signing certificate

To generate a pair of public/private keys, use a tool called keytool, which came with the Sun JDK when you installed it onto your development computer. keytool asks you for some information and uses that to generate the pair of keys:

- A private key that will be kept in a keystore on your computer, secured with passwords. You will use this key to sign your application, and if you need a Maps API key for your application, you will use the MD5 fingerprint of the signing certificate to generate that key.

- A public key that Android can use to decrypt your signing certificate. You will send this key along with your published application so that it can be made available in the runtime environment. Signing certificates are actually checked only at install time, so once installed your application is good to run, even if the certificate or keys expire.

keytool is pretty straightforward. From your operating system's command line, enter something like the following:

```
$ keytool -genkey -v -keystore myapp.keystore -alias myapp -keyalg RSA
  -validity 10000
```

This asks keytool to generate a key pair and self-signed certificate (-genkey) in verbose mode (-v), so you get all the information, and put it in a keystore called myapp.keystore (-keystore). It also says that in the future you want to refer to that key by the name myapp (-alias), and that keytool should use the RSA algorithm for generating public/private key pairs (-keyalg). Finally, it says that you'd like the key to be valid for 10,000 days (-validity), or about 27 years.

keytool will prompt you for some information it uses to build the key pair and certificate:

- A password to be used in the future when you want to access the keystore
- Your first and last names
- Your organizational unit (the name for your division of your company, or something like "self" if you aren't developing for a company)
- Your organization's name (the name of your company, or anything else you want to use)
- The name of your city or locality
- The name of your state or province
- The two-letter country code where you are located

keytool will then echo all this information back to you to make sure it's accurate, and if you confirm the information it will generate the key pair and certificate. It will then ask you for another password to use for the key itself (and give you the option of using the same password you used for the keystore). Using that password, keytool will store the key pair and certificate in the keystore.

Signing your application

Having created a key pair, and a Maps API key if needed, you are almost ready to sign your application—but first you need to create an unsigned version that you can sign with your digital certificate. To do that, in the Package Explorer window of Eclipse, right-click your project name. You'll get a long pop-up menu; toward the bottom, click Android Tools. You should see another menu that includes the item you want: Export Unsigned Application Package. This item takes you to a dialog box where you can pick a place to save the unsigned version of your APK file. It doesn't matter where you put it, just pick a spot you can remember.

Now that you have an unsigned version of your APK file, you can go ahead and sign it using jarsigner. Open a terminal or command window in the directory where you stored the unsigned APK file. To sign MyApp, using the key you generated earlier, enter this command:

```
$ jarsigner -verbose -keystore myapp.keystore MyApp.apk myapp
```

You should now have a signed version of your application that can be loaded and run on any Android device. But before you send it in to the Google Play Store, there's one more intervening step: you have rebuilt the application, so you must test it again, on real devices. If you don't have a real device, get one. If you only have one, get more, or make friends with somebody who owns a device from a different manufacturer.

Note that in the current version of the IDE, there is an Export Signed Application Package option that will allow you to create the keys and sign your application all from one wizard. This option is available in the project's context menu in the Android Tools submenu and also in the File menu under Export, where it is known simply as Export Android Project.

 This action is so convenient that it probably makes it more likely that you will forget where you put the keystore. Don't do that! In fact, you must not lose either your keystore file or the keyphrase used to unlock it, or you will *never* be able to update your application. There is *no recovery* from this failure mode; it is not possible to reverse-engineer your key from your application (or else the bad guys would be able to do it, and install malware versions of your app!).

See Also

If you're not familiar with the algorithms used here, such as RSA and MD5, you don't actually need to know much. Assuming you've a modicum of curiosity, you can find out all you need to know about them with any good web search engine.

You can get more information about security, key pairs, and the keytool utility on the Java website (*http://docs.oracle.com/javase/1.5.0/docs/tooldocs/#security*).

21.2 Distributing Your Application via the Google Play Store

Zigurd Mednieks

Problem

You want to give away or sell your application via Google Play, the app store formerly known as Android Market.

Solution

Submit your app to the Google Play Store.

Discussion

 The original Android Market was combined with Google Books and other services to create the Play Store shortly after the first edition of this book went to press.

After you're satisfied that your application runs as expected on real Android devices, you're ready to upload it to the Play Store, Google's service for publishing and downloading Android applications. The procedure is pretty straightforward:

1. Sign up as an Android developer (if you haven't done so already).
2. Upload your signed application.

Signing up as an Android developer

Go to Google's website (*https://play.google.com/apps/publish*), and fill out the forms provided. You will be asked to:

- Use your Google account to log in (if you don't have a Google account, you can get one for free by following the Create Account link on the login page),
- Agree to the Google Play Developer distribution agreement.
- Pay a one-time fee of $25 (payable by credit card via Google Checkout; again, if you don't have an account set up, you can do so quickly).
- If the game is being charged for, specify your payment processor (again, you can easily sign up for a Google Payments account).

The forms ask for a minimal amount of information—your name, phone number, and so on. Once you provide that info, you're signed up.

Uploading your application

Now you can upload your application (*https://play.google.com/apps/publish*). To identify and categorize your application, you will be asked for the following:

Application APK filename and location
> This refers to the APK file of your application, signed with your private signing certificate.

Title and description
> These are very important, because they are the core of your marketing message to potential users. Try to make the title descriptive and catchy, and describe the application in a way that will make your target market want to download it.

Application type
> There are currently two choices: Applications or Games.

Category
> The list of categories varies depending on application type. The currently available categories for apps include items such as Business, Communications, Education, Entertainment, Finance, Lifestyle, Maps & Navigation, Productivity, Shopping, Social, Tools, Travel & Local, Video Players & Editors, and Weather. For games, the available categories include Action, Arcade, Card, Casino, Puzzle, Role Playing, Sports, and more.

Price
> This can be Free or a fixed price. Refer to the agreement you agreed to earlier to see what percentage you actually get to keep.

Distribution
> You can limit where your application is available, or make it available everywhere.

Finally, you are asked to confirm that your application meets the Android Content Ratings Guidelines and that it does not knowingly violate any export laws. After that, you can upload your APK file, and within a few hours your application will appear on the Google Play online catalog, accessible from any connected Android device. To view your application, just open Google Play on your device and use its Search box, or load in the device's browser a file with a URL of the form *market://details?id=com.yourorg.yourprog*, but with your application's actual package name. You can also visit the Play Store (*https://play.google.com/*) in a desktop browser and view your app's details page.

Then what?

Sit back and watch the fame or money—and the support emails—roll in. Be patient with end users, for they do not think as we do.

21.3 Distributing Your Application via Other App Stores

Ian Darwin

Problem

There are many Android stores now. Where should you publish your app?

Discussion

To use any "unofficial" source, the user will have to enable "Unknown sources" in the Settings app, which comes with a security warning. "Unofficial source" means an app store that is not shipped by default with the device. For the vast majority of devices, Google Play is the official store. However, for Amazon Kindle devices, Google Play is not even available, and the Amazon Appstore is the only official app store. Black-Berry maintains its own market as well, also without Google Play. There may be some other devices that ship with a different app store, particularly in Asia. Google does a really good job of vetting apps for security problems; it is not known to what extent these other stores do so (well, actually it is, but we can't say it here; just do a web search for which app stores have the worst security track record).

 Apps using Google Maps or other Google Play Services will not succeed in marketplaces that do not support Google Play.

From a developer point of view, you of course want to reach as many consumers as possible, so getting your app into multiple stores makes sense. Google Play and the Amazon Appstore are the two largest stores, so start there. To get your app into one of the others, start with the URL from Table 21-1, look at the store carefully, and see if you want to be associated with it. If so, look around for the "developer" or "partner" or "publisher" link, and sign up.

Table 21-1. The Main Android app stores

Name	Comments	URL
Google Play	Formerly Android Market	*https://play.google.com/apps/*
Amazon Appstore	Most Android apps can run unchanged	*https://developer.amazon.com/apps-and-games*
Barnes & Noble	Discontinued	N/A

Name	Comments	URL
BlackBerry World	Most Android apps run unchanged	https://appworld.blackberry.com
F-Droid	Free (open source) apps only!	https://f-droid.org/
GetJar	Not limited to Android	http://www.getjar.com/
Samsung Galaxy Apps	Included in Galaxy devices	http://www.samsung.com/global/galaxy/apps/galaxy-apps/
SlideME		http://slideme.org/

See Also

Table 21-1, although focused only on the major stores, will probably always be out of date, but updates are welcome. A web search on "alternative android market" will find some smaller/newer app stores. A fairly comprehensive list can be found on the AlternativeTo website (*http://alternativeto.net/software/android-market/*).

21.4 Monetizing Your App with AdMob

Enrique Diaz, Ian Darwin

Problem

You want to monetize your free app by showing advertisements within it.

Solution

Using AdMob libraries, you can display ads in your free app, getting money each time a user taps/clicks an ad.

Discussion

AdMob, which is owned by Google, is one of the world's largest mobile advertising networks. You can get more information and download the SDK for various platforms from the AdMob website (*https://www.google.com/admob/*).

The AdMob Android SDK contains the code necessary to install AdMob ads in your application.

You can manually perform all the steps involved in integrating AdMob, but it's easier to let Android Studio add the code for you. Just create a project whose main Activity already includes the AdMob code, or add an AdMob Activity to your existing app. Figure 21-1 shows how to select the AdMob Activity.

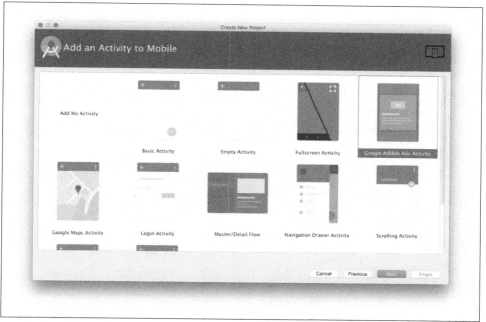

Figure 21-1. Creating the AdMob Activity

Figure 21-2 shows how to customize the Activity. The main choice that's ad-specific is the Ad Format. You can choose from one of the following (only the first two are supported in this AdMob Activity wizard):

Interstitial
 Interstitial means "in the spaces between." Interstitial ads appear in their own Activity so they cover up the rest of the app, forcing the user to interact.

Banner
 Banner ads appear at the top or bottom of the regular Activity; the user is more free to ignore them.

Video
 These are videos that play to drive the user to the advertiser's site.

Native
 These are graphics that are placed inside your Activity; supported with Firebase AdMob integration.

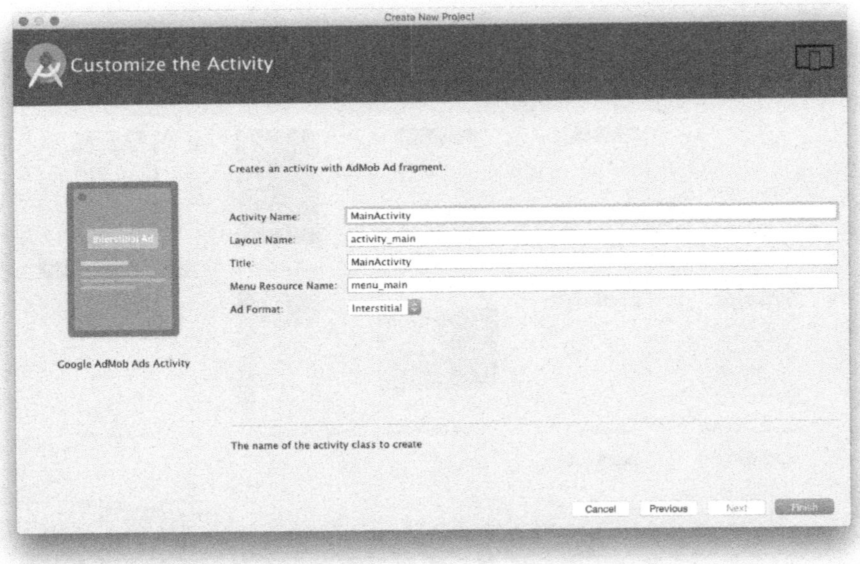

Figure 21-2. Configuring the Activity

Since the code is different for each type of ad, and because interstitials are usually more profitable (even though they are more annoying), this recipe will just show the interstitial type.

In this example, the New Activity wizard creates an app with two Activity classes, one that simulates a game with multiple levels, and another that shows the actual ads (initially a dummy ad) so you can get on with developing the rest of your application. Notice the following Toast text:

```
public class MainActivity extends Activity {
    // Remove the following line after defining your own ad unit ID
    private static final String TOAST_TEXT = "Test ads are being shown. "
            + "To show live ads, replace the ad unit ID in "
            + "res/values/strings.xml with your own ad unit ID.";
```

The string TOAST_TEXT is displayed in the sample application; you can remove it after you've installed your real application key, as discussed later in this recipe.

This basic Activity will work out of the box, as shown in the first image of Figure 21-3. When the user presses the Next Level button, the ad is imposed on the screen ahead of the next-level Activity, as shown in the second image of Figure 21-3. The user can either press the X in the upper left to ignore the ad and go on to the next level (third image), or tap anywhere in the ad and get taken to the ad's website (fourth image).

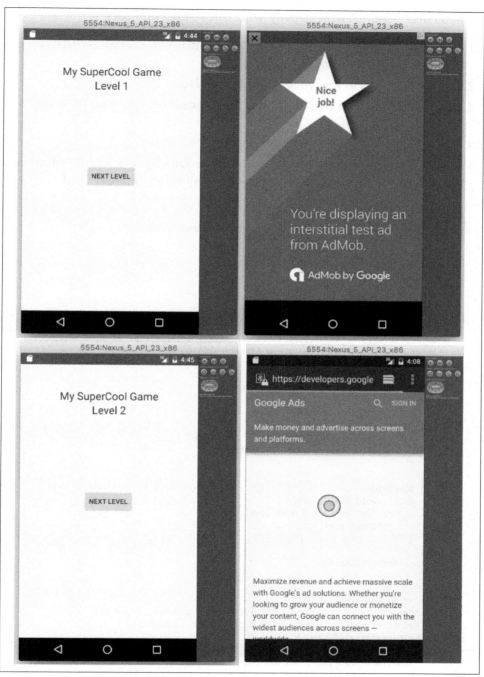

Figure 21-3. AdMob basic Activity running

If you'd rather perform all the steps by hand, here's a brief summary:

1. Add the Google Play "Ad Services" dependency (com.google.android.gms:play-services-ads:10.0.1) to your build file.

2. Add an AdActivity to your *AndroidManifest.xml* file.

3. Add the INTERNET and ACCESS_NETWORK_STATE permissions to your *AndroidManifest.xml* file.

4. Add a field of type InterstitialAd to your main Activity.

5. Add code to instantiate the InterstitialAd, configure it, and load it in the background with a listener to record completed loading (see Example 21-1).

Example 21-1. Code from main Activity to manage interstitial ad

```
// In onCreate():
mInterstitialAd = newInterstitialAd();
loadInterstitial();

// Method to get a new ad
private InterstitialAd newInterstitialAd() {
    InterstitialAd interstitialAd = new InterstitialAd(this);
    interstitialAd.setAdUnitId(getString(R.string.interstitial_ad_unit_id));
    interstitialAd.setAdListener(new AdListener() {
        @Override
        public void onAdLoaded() {
            mNextLevelButton.setEnabled(true);
        }

        @Override
        public void onAdFailedToLoad(int errorCode) {
            mNextLevelButton.setEnabled(true);
        }

        @Override
        public void onAdClosed() {
            // Proceed to the next level
            goToNextLevel();
        }
    });
    return interstitialAd;
}

private void showInterstitial() {
    // Show the ad if it's ready; otherwise toast and reload the ad
    if (mInterstitialAd != null && mInterstitialAd.isLoaded()) {
        mInterstitialAd.show();
    } else {
        Toast.makeText(this, "Ad did not load", Toast.LENGTH_SHORT).show();
        goToNextLevel();
    }
```

```
    }

    private void loadInterstitial() {
        // Disable the next level button and load the ad
        mNextLevelButton.setEnabled(false);
        AdRequest adRequest = new AdRequest.Builder()
                .setRequestAgent("android_studio:ad_template").build();
        mInterstitialAd.loadAd(adRequest);
    }
```

For this code to compile, you must also provide the goToNextLevel() method, which is highly application-dependent, but should at least have these two calls:

```
mInterstitialAd = newInterstitialAd(); // Get the next ad to be displayed
loadInterstitial();                     // Start the ad loading
```

When your application is complete and you are ready to ship it and display ads and generate revenue, you must open an AdMob account, which in turn requires an AdWords account. To get these accounts, go to *https://admob.com*, click the signup button, and follow the steps to create an account and set up an Android interstitial ad.

When you have your "ad unit" set up, copy and paste the "Ad Unit ID"—a long string that begins with ca-app-pub-—over top of the fake one ("ca-app-pub-3940256099942544/1033173712") in the provided *strings.xml*.

This string resource can be put into a file all by itself, so that if you are sharing your source code you can choose whether to give out your map key along with the code.

Note that even with a live ID, the software will always show fake test ads when run on the emulator. Also, do not click live ads, as that would generate false pay-per-click statistics and can result in suspension of your AdMob account.

See Also

There is much more to AdMob, including other types of ads, monitoring, Firebase integration, and more. See the website (*https://admob.com*) for details on these topics.

For more on interstitial ads and the Firebase integration (*https://firebase.google.com/docs/admob/android/interstitial*), see the Firebase documentation. For a comparison of mobile ad options, see Brittany Fleit's blog post on the topic (*http://blog.kiip.me/developers/mobile-ad-options/*). You may also want to join AdMob Publisher Discuss (*https://groups.google.com/d/forum/admob-publisher-discuss*), the official support forum for AdMob.

Source Download URL

The source code for this project is in the Android Cookbook repository (*https://github.com/IanDarwin/Android-Cookbook-Examples*), in the subdirectory *AdMob-Demo* (see "Getting and Using the Code Examples" on page 18).

21.5 Obfuscating and Optimizing with ProGuard

Ian Darwin

Problem

You want to obfuscate your code, or optimize it for speed or size, or all of the above.

Solution

The optimization and obfuscation tool ProGuard is supported by the build script provided with the Android New Project Wizard in the IDEs, needing only to be enabled.

Discussion

Obfuscation of code is the process of trying to hide information (such as compile-time names visible in the binary) that would be useful in reverse-engineering your code. If your application contains commercial or trade secrets, you probably want to obfuscate it. If your program is open source, there is probably no need to obfuscate the code. You decide.

Optimization of code is analogous to refactoring at the source level, but it usually aims to make the code either *faster*, *smaller*, or both.

The normal development cycle involves compilation to standard Java bytecode and then conversion to the Android-specific DEX format. DEX is the Dalvik Executable format (Dalvik being the old version of the Android Runtime). With Eclipse, the compilation is done by the built-in compiler (Eclipse being a full IDE). With Android Studio and other tools, a compiler (presumably javac) is invoked as part of the build. In either case, the Android SDK tool dex or dx is invoked; the current usage clause from dx explains that it is used to "Convert a set of classfiles into a dex file." Current versions of Android Studio provide an alternate build chain called Jack, which supports the latest version of Java, Java 8, providing both compilation and translation to DEX.

ProGuard (*http://proguard.sourceforge.net/*) is Eric Lafortune's open source, free software program for optimizing and obfuscating Java bytecode. ProGuard is not Android-specific; it works with console-mode applications, applets, Swing applications, Java ME midlets, Android applications, and just about any type of Java program. ProGuard works on compiled Java (*.class* format), so it must be interposed in the development cycle before conversion to DEX. This is most readily achieved using the standard Java build tool Ant. Most build chains (see Chapter 1) include support for ProGuard. If using the older ant process, for example, you only need to edit the file *build.properties* to include the following line, which gives the name of the configuration file:

```
proguard.config=proguard.cfg
```

When using Maven, the command mvn android:proguard will run ProGuard.

At present it does not appear possible to use ProGuard with the Java 8 compiler Jack (described in Recipe 1.18).

Configuration file

Regardless of your build process, the actual operation of ProGuard is controlled by the configuration file (normally called *proguard.cfg*), which has its own syntax. Basically, keywords begin with a - in the first character position, followed by a keyword, followed by optional parameters. Where the parameters reference Java classes or members, the syntax somewhat mimics Java syntax to make your life easier. Here is a minimal ProGuard configuration file for an Android application:

```
-injars     bin/classes
-outjars    bin/classes-processed.jar
-libraryjars /usr/local/android-sdk/platforms/android-19/android.jar

-dontpreverify
-repackageclasses ''
-allowaccessmodification
-optimizations !code/simplification/arithmetic

-keep public class com.example.MainActivity
```

The first section specifies the paths of your project, including a temporary dir3ectory for the optimized classes.

The Activity class (in this example com.example.MainActivity) must be present in the output of the optimization and obfuscation process, since it is the main Activity and is referred to by name in the *AndroidManifest.xml* file. This would also apply to any components mentioned by name in *AndroidManifest.xml*.

A full working *proguard.cfg* file will normally be generated for you by the Eclipse New Android Project wizard. Example 21-2 is one such configuration file.

Example 21-2. Example proguard.cfg file

```
-optimizationpasses 5
-dontusemixedcaseclassnames
-dontskipnonpubliclibraryclasses
-dontpreverify
-verbose
-optimizations !code/simplification/arithmetic,!field/*,!class/merging/*

-keep public class * extends android.app.Activity
-keep public class * extends android.app.Application
-keep public class * extends android.app.Service
-keep public class * extends android.content.BroadcastReceiver
-keep public class * extends android.content.ContentProvider
-keep public class * extends android.app.backup.BackupAgentHelper
-keep public class * extends android.preference.Preference
-keep public class com.android.vending.licensing.ILicensingService

-keepclasseswithmembernames class * {
    native <methods>;
}

-keepclasseswithmembernames class * {
    public <init>(android.content.Context, android.util.AttributeSet);
}

-keepclasseswithmembernames class * {
    public <init>(android.content.Context, android.util.AttributeSet, int);
}

-keepclassmembers enum * {
    public static **[] values();
    public static ** valueOf(java.lang.String);
}

-keep class * implements android.os.Parcelable {
    public static final android.os.Parcelable$Creator *;
}
```

The prolog is mostly similar to the earlier example. The `keep`, `keepclasseswithmembernames`, and `keepclassmembers` entries specify particular classes that must be retained. These are mostly obvious, but the `enum` entries may not be: the Java 5 enum methods `values()` and `valueOf()` are sometimes used with the Reflection API, so they must remain visible, as must any classes that you access via the Reflection API.

The `ILicensingService` entry is only needed if you are using Android's License Validation Tool (LVT):

```
-keep class com.android.vending.licensing.ILicensingService
```

See Also

The ProGuard Reference Manual (*https://www.guardsquare.com/en/proguard/manual/introduction*) has many more details. There is also information on optimization in at the Android Studio User Guide (*https://developer.android.com/guide/developing/tools/proguard.html*). Finally, Matt Quigley has written a helpful article titled "Optimizing, Obfuscating, and Shrinking your Android Applications with ProGuard" on the Android Engineer Blog (*http://www.androidengineer.com/2010/07/optimizing-obfuscating-and-shrinking.html*).

21.6 Hosting Your App on Your Own Server

Ian Darwin

Problem

While it may not be prudent to host your own email server, you want to host your own application on a server.

Solution

Just put your APK up on a web server, and get users to download it from the browser on their devices.

Discussion

You can host an application yourself on your own web server or a web server you can upload files to. Just install the APK file and tell users to visit that URL in their device's browser. The browser will give the usual security warnings, but will usually allow the user to install the application.

Hopefully most users will be skeptical of the security implications of downloading an app from some website they've never heard of, but for internal-only use, this approach is simpler than setting up an account on a major app store.

This will be especially interesting to enterprise users where it isn't necessary or desirable to put an internal-use application out into a public marketplace like Google Play.

Here is the formula to upload an APK to a web server using scp, the secure copy program (use of the old unencrypted ftp being generally considered hopelessly insecure in this day and age):

```
$ scp bin/*.apk testuser@myserver.com:/www/tmp
Enter password for testuser:
ShellCommand.apk           100%   15KB  14.5KB/s   00:00
$
```

For this example we just reused the *ShellCommand* APK from Recipe 19.2.

Then you can visit the site in a browser on your device (Chrome, in this example) and ask for the file by its full URL, e.g., *https://myserver.com/tmp/ShellCommand.apk*. You'll get the expected security warning (see Figure 21-4), but if you click OK, the app will install.

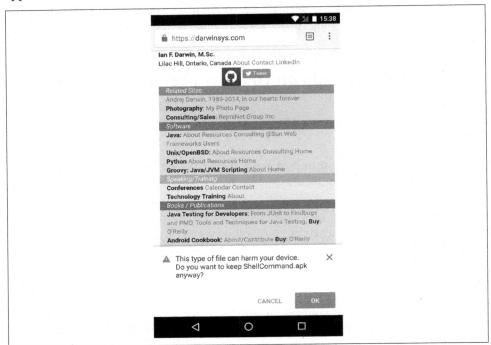

Figure 21-4. The security warning

Then you can open the app like any other app.

This whole process could be automated by having some other application open an Intent for the URL, but that begs the question of how you would get that app onto the users' devices.

Because it is not in an app store, this app will not get updates automatically. You can simply tell users to fetch it again, or you can use the fancier technique described in Recipe 21.7.

21.7 Creating a "Self-Updating" App

Problem

Your app is not in Google Play or another full-featured market, but you still want users to get updates when you improve the app.

Solution

You can find the last time your app was updated by use of the package manager. And you can usually get the last time the APK on the web server was updated just by sending an HTTP HEAD request. Compare the two timestamps, and if the web file is newer, open an Intent for the same URI used in the HTTP HEAD, and let the browser handle things from there.

Discussion

If you are hosting your app yourself, as discussed in Recipe 21.6, you almost certainly want a way to notify users when you update the app. Sending emails doesn't scale well unless you have a scheme for capturing users' email addresses with each download. And even then, many users will be too busy to update the app manually. Automating this task makes sense.

The package manager knows when it last updated the app, and the web server knows when you last updated the file containing the app. You just have to ask them both and compare the timestamps. If the web file is newer, you have an install candidate; start your UpdateActivity to ask the user if it's OK to update. If she says yes, open the browser via a URI back to the web server file. For a slightly better experience, send her to a page about the update. The browser will ultimately prompt the user for the final install. You will need to convince your users that it's OK to accept the somewhat scary warning about installing a non–Play Store app in this way, but they will have already needed to enable the Settings option to download from unknown sources to get your app installed in the first place.

This code in the *AutoUpdater* project uses a background Service (Recipe 4.6) to check once a day for an updated APK on the web server:

```
protected void onHandleIntent(Intent intent) {

    Log.d(TAG, "Starting One-time Service Runner");

    /* Now the simple arithmetic: if web package was updated after
     * last time app was updated, then it's time
     * again to update!
     */
    final long appUpdatedOnDevice = getAppUpdatedOnDevice();
    final long webPackageUpdated = getWebPackageUpdated();
```

```
        if (appUpdatedOnDevice == -1 || webPackageUpdated == -1) {
            return; // FAIL, try another day
        }
        if (webPackageUpdated > appUpdatedOnDevice) {
            triggerUpdate();
        }
    }

    public long getAppUpdatedOnDevice() {
        PackageInfo packageInfo = null;
        try {
            packageInfo = getPackageManager()
                .getPackageInfo(getClass().getPackage().getName(),
                    PackageManager.GET_PERMISSIONS);
        } catch (NameNotFoundException e) {
            Log.d(TAG, "Failed to get package info for own package!");
            return -1;
        }
        return packageInfo.lastUpdateTime;
    }

    protected void triggerUpdate() {
        Log.d(TAG, "UpdateService.triggerUpdate()");
        final Intent intent = new Intent(this, UpdateActivity.class);
        intent.setData(Uri.parse("http://" + SERVER_NAME + PATH_TO_APK));
        intent.setFlags(Intent.FLAG_ACTIVITY_NEW_TASK);
        startActivity(intent);
    }
```

The code of getWebPackageUpdated() is not shown, but it basically sends a HEAD request for the same URL handled in triggerUpdate(), and extracts the value of the Last-Modified header from the HTTP response.

A better way to get the installer to open your file is to save it locally yourself and to open it via an Intent. The *AppDownloader* project downloads the API to a local file in an AsyncTask (Recipe 4.10) and does the following to install the file:

```
// Do the install
notifyFromBackground("Installing...");
Intent promptInstall = new Intent(Intent.ACTION_VIEW)
        .setDataAndType(Uri.fromFile(outputFile),
                "application/vnd.android.package-archive");
startActivity(promptInstall);
```

See Also

https://dzone.com/articles/12-dev-tools-to-update-your-app-instantly-skip-the discusses several other methods for updating your app without going back to the Play market.

21.8 Providing a Link to Other Published Apps in the Google Play Store

Daniel Fowler

Problem

Your developed app is running on a device; you want a link to your other apps on the Play Store to encourage users to try them.

Solution

Use an Intent and a URI that contains your publisher name or the package name.

Discussion

Android's Intent system is a great way for your application to leverage functionality that has already been written by other developers. The Google Play application, which is used to browse and install apps, can be called from an application using an Intent. This allows an existing app to link to other apps on Google Play, thus allowing app developers and publishers to encourage users to try their other apps.

To view an app in the Google Play app, the standard Intent mechanism is used, as described in Recipe 4.1. The uniform resource identifier (URI) used is `market://search? q=search_term`, where *search_term* is replaced with the appropriate text, such as the program name or keyword. The Intent action is `ACTION_VIEW`.

The URI can also point directly to the Google Play details page for a package by using `market://details?id=package_name`, where *package_name_* is replaced with the unique *package_name* for the app.

The program shown in this recipe (and whose output is shown in Figure 21-5) will allow a text search of Google Play or show the details page for a given app. Example 21-3 is the layout.

Example 21-3. The main layout

```
<LinearLayout xmlns:android="http://schemas.android.com/apk/res/android"
    android:orientation="vertical"
    android:layout_width="fill_parent"
    android:layout_height="fill_parent">
    <EditText android:id="@+id/etSearch"
        android:layout_width="fill_parent"
        android:layout_height="wrap_content"
        android:textSize="20sp"
        android:singleLine="true"/>
    <RadioGroup android:layout_width="wrap_content"
```

```
            android:layout_height="wrap_content">
        <RadioButton android:id="@+id/rdSearch"
            android:layout_height="wrap_content"
            android:layout_width="wrap_content"
            android:checked="true"
            android:text="search"
            android:textSize="20sp"/>
        <RadioButton android:id="@+id/rdDetails"
            android:layout_height="wrap_content"
            android:layout_width="wrap_content"
            android:text="details"
            android:textSize="20sp"/>
    </RadioGroup>
    <Button android:id="@+id/butSearch"
        android:layout_width="wrap_content"
        android:layout_height="wrap_content"
        android:textSize="20sp"
        android:text="Search Google Play"/>
</LinearLayout>
```

An `EditText` allows entry of the search term, and a `RadioButton` can be used to choose to do a straight search or show an app's details page (provided the full package name is known). The `Button` starts the search.

Figure 21-5. Google Play search

The important point to notice in the code shown in Example 21-4 is that the search term is URL-encoded.

Example 21-4. The main Activity

```
public class Main extends Activity {
    RadioButton publisherOption;      // Option for straight search or details
    @Override
    public void onCreate(Bundle savedInstanceState) {
        super.onCreate(savedInstanceState);
        setContentView(R.layout.main);
        // Search button press processed by inner class HandleClick
        findViewById(R.id.butSearch).setOnClickListener(new OnClickListener() {
        public void onClick(View arg0) {
```

```
String searchText;
// Reference search input
EditText searchFor=(EditText)findViewById(R.id.etSearch);
try {
    // URL encoding handles spaces and punctuation in search term
    searchText = URLEncoder.encode(searchFor.getText().toString(),"UTF-8");
} catch (UnsupportedEncodingException e) {
    searchText = searchFor.getText().toString();
}
Uri uri; // Stores Intent Uri
// Get search option
RadioButton searchOption=(RadioButton)findViewById(R.id.rdSearch);
if(searchOption.isChecked()) {
    uri=Uri.parse("market://search?q=" + searchText);
} else {
    uri=Uri.parse("market://details?id=" + searchText);
}
Intent intent = new Intent(Intent.ACTION_VIEW, uri);
try {
    main.this.startActivity(intent);
} catch (ActivityNotFoundException anfe) {
    Toast.makeText(main.this, "Please install the Google Play App",
    Toast.LENGTH_SHORT);
}
}
});
}
}
```

A straight text search is simply the text appended to the URI `market://search?q=`. To search by publisher name use the `pub:` qualifier; that is, append the publisher's name to `market://search?q=pub:`.

The regular search is not case-sensitive; however, the `pub:` search qualifier *is* case-sensitive. Thus, `market://search?q=pub:IMDb` returns a result but `market://search?q=pub:imdb` does not.

It's also possible to search for a specific application (if the package name is known) by using the `id:` qualifier. So, if an app has a package name of `com.example.myapp`, the search term will be `market://search?q=id:com.example.myapp`. Even better is to go straight to the app's details page with `market://details?q=id:com.example.myapp`. For example, O'Reilly has a free app, the details of which can be shown using `market://details?id=com.aldiko.android.oreilly.isbn9781449388294`.

Figure 21-6 shows the output of the search entered in Figure 21-5.

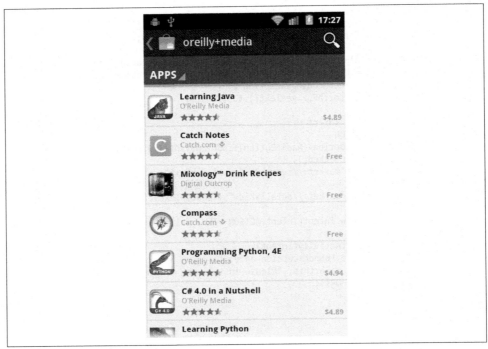

Figure 21-6. Google Play search results

Using these techniques, it is very easy to put a button or menu option on a screen to allow users to go directly to other apps that you've published.

See Also

The developer documentation on launch checklists (*https://developer.android.com/guide/publishing/publishing.html#marketintent*).

Source Download URL

The source code for this project is in the Android Cookbook repository (*https://github.com/IanDarwin/Android-Cookbook-Examples*), in the subdirectory *MarketSearch* (see "Getting and Using the Code Examples" on page 18).

Index

tabbed layout, 383
vs. Toasts, 367
DigitsKeyListener class, 135
directional pads (D-pads), 236
discoverability (Bluetooth), 645, 651
displays (see also graphics; GUI alerts; GUI
    development; text)
    hints vs. tool tips, 144
    launcher icon files, 255
    pinch-to-zoom capability, 280
    running background Services, 207
    scaling images, 269
    screen captures, 74
    screen size and density, 98
    scrolling/swiping capability, 355
    signaling LED, 397, 658
    splash screens, 113
distribution (see application distribution)
DocumentBuilderFactory, 486
doInBackground, 213
doInBackground(Params… params);, 213
DOM API, 486
Done buttons, 338
Donut, 6
Double.toString(), 124
drag-and-drop API, 498, 663
drawable folders, 255
drawing (see graphics)
DroidCharts package, 424
DroidDraw, 290
drop-down menus, 324
drop-shadow effects, 286
dynamic testing, 147, 189

E

Eclair, 6
Eclipse
    benefits and drawbacks of, 15
    build.gradle files, xviii
    converting projects to Android Studio, 30
    "Hello World" creation with, 46
    installing for Java development, 40
    JUnit testing, 155
    LogCat window, 171
    Marketplace Client (MPC), 51
    preserving history while converting to Stu-
        dio, 34
    providing Eclipse and Gradle build files, 36
    setting up with AndMore plugin, 39

sharing Java classes using, 59
    SWT GUI layer, 283
    upgrading projects to AndMore, 53
EditText class
    limiting input range and type, 328
    read-write access, 328
elevation, in Material Design, 286
emails
    emailing text from a view, 198
    sending attachments with, 201
emulators (see Android Virtual Device (AVD);
    Dalvik Debug monitor Server (DDMS))
Enter keys, 336
Environment class, 459
Epoch calendar, 222
errata, xxi
Espresso, 166
evaluation stars, 340
exception handling
    Android mechanisms, 101
    checked exceptions, 103
    exception translation, 102
    Java categories, 101
    reporting exceptions, 103
    where to catch exceptions, 102
exec(), 665
Experitest, 155
Export Signed Application Package, 710
external file storage
    getting space information about, 459
    reading/writing files in, 448

F

face detection, 435
face recognition, 435
FC (Force Close), 148
feature availability, 99
field errors, 178
FileProvider class, 502
Files API
    informational methods, 452
    reading/writing files in, 449
fileSaver object, 111
FindBugs, 147
FINE resolution (locational position), 605
Firebase (database as a service), 515-521
first-run preferences, 122, 460
flixel-gdx framework, 582
floating action buttons, 310

Focused state, 308
fonts, creating custom, 229
Fragments
    building modern UIs with, 302
    defined, 5
frame-anchored menus, 367
freehand bezier curves, 239
Froyo, 6, 67
Full Text Search 3 (FTS3), 471

G

gaming and animation
    AndEngine framework, 586
    flixel-gdx framework, 582
    game-development frameworks, 581
    raster animation, 277
    shaking View components, 344
    timed keyboard input handling, 593
gdata.docs.service library, 679
Geocoder class, 612
GeoPoint, 633
gesture detection, 355
getExtras(), 203
getFilesDir(), 448
getIntent(), 203
getLastNonConfigurationInstance(), 109
getResources(), 457
getRuntime(), 665
getSensorList(), 638
getString(), 203
getText(), 658
getting started (see development environment)
Gingerbread, 6, 67, 371
global data access, 107
Gluon Mobile, 664
Google Analytics, 119
Google Cloud Messaging (GCM), 555
Google Code Archive, 380
Google Docs, fetching/displaying, 679
Google Maps API V2
    additional features, 623
    attribution text, 622
    map pins and map centering, 619
    marketplace support for, 713
    setup, 613
Google Play Store
    Android Content Ratings Guidelines, 712
    app distribution via, 711
    input hardware declarations, 99

linking to other published apps, 727
    signing certificates, 707
Google ZXing barcode scanner, 250
GoogleAuthUtil class, 595
GPRS/EDGE data services, 549
GPS devices, 605
    (see also location and map applications)
Gradle format
    HelloGradle project, 12
    project creation, 10
    providing Eclipse and Gradle build files, 36
graphics
    charts and graphs, 253, 273, 424
    in custom dialogs, 387
    custom fonts, 229
    defined, 229
    freehand drawing smooth curves, 239
    launcher icons
        design considerations, 255
        with Inkscape, 257
        with Paint.NET, 262
    in OpenStreetMap maps, 627
    picture taking
        using android.media.Camera, 246
        using Intents, 244
    pinch-to-zoom capability, 280
    raster animation, 277
    scaling images, 269
    scanning barcodes/QR Codes, 250, 682
    spinning cubes
        controlling movement, 236
        creating, 232
graphs and charts
    using AndroidPlot, 253
    using RGraph, 273
GUI alerts
    about boxes, 389
    Android vs. other interfaces, 367
    background processing alerts, 386
    Bluetooth enable prompts, 646
    creating in SL4A, 675
    dialogs with buttons, images, and text, 387,
        675
    menu choice selection, 373
    menu creation and display, 371
    pop-up/alert dialog, 376
    revealing/accepting time and dates, 378
    scroll-wheel picker creation, 380
    status bar notifications, 393

onCreate(Bundle savedInstanceState), 4
onCreateOptionsMenu(), 371
onDestroy(), 4
onDraw(), 239
OnItemGestureListener, 631
onKeyDown, 339
onLocationChanged(), 607, 609, 633
OnLongClickListener, 326
onOptionsItemSelected(), 373
onPause(), 4
OnRatingBarChangeListener, 341
onRestart(), 4
onResume(), 4
onRetainNonConfigurationInstance(), 109
onSaveInstanceState(), 4, 109
onSensorChanged(), 639, 642
onSharedPreferenceChanged, 465
OnSharedPreferenceChangeListener, 465
onStart(), 4
onStop(), 4
onTouchEvent(), 239
OnTouchListener, 239
Open Authentication protocol, 596
OpenClipArt.org
    and Inkscape, 257
    and Paint.NET, 262
    raster animation, 277
openFileInput(), 448
openFileOutput(), 448
OpenGL ES
    animation using D-pads, 236
    basic application creation, 232
OpenMoko, 637
openRawResource(), 457
OpenStreetMap
    getting location updates with, 633
    handling touch events on overlays, 630
    JPStrack mapping application, 606
    overlay creation, 627
    scale and zoom level, 629
    user-supplied data in, 605
    using, 624
optimization, 720
ordered broadcast messages, 526, 529
orientation, determining, 642
OS-dependent functionality, 667
osmdroid library, 624
OTF (OpenTypeFace), 230
outgoing phone calls, 527, 531

Overlay class, 627, 631

P

PackageManager, 654, 725
packaging and deployment (see application distribution)
paging, 403
Paint.NET, 262
pairing (Bluetooth), 645, 651
parameters, passing into Activities during launch, 203
password fields, 335
Paused state, 4
Perfecto Mobile, 155
permission for code use, xx
permissions, requesting at run time, 104
phone calls (see telephone applications)
PhoneGap, 663, 664, 691
physical feedback, 345
pictures/photos (see also video)
    accessing raw image data, 246
    face detection, 435
    using android.media.Camera, 246
    using Intents, 244
pinch-in and pinch-out movements, 280
ping notifications, 555
Platform Editions, installing and updating, 21
Please Wait alerts, 386
plug-ins, installing, 51
plural words, correct formatting of, 128
PMD, 147
PNG (Portable Network Graphics), 255, 257
pop-up windows (see GUI alerts)
portrait list views, 424
PostMan, 554
Preference items, 460
PreferenceActivity class, 460, 465
Pressed state, 308
printf-like formatting, 124, 342
private external storage, 451
programming languages and frameworks (see also Java language)
    cross-platform solutions, 664, 686, 691
    native C/C++ code, 667
    overview of, 663
    PhoneGap/Cordova, 691
    shell commands, 665
    SL4A
        creating alerts in, 675

download and use, 673
  fetching/displaying Google Docs, 679
  sharing scripts in QR codes, 682
WebView, native handset functionality
    using, 684
Xamarin, 686
progress bars
  background processing, 212
  creating ProgressDialog, 386
  haptic feedback, 346
  RatingBar subclass, 340
  splash screens, 113
ProgressDialog, 212, 386
ProGuard, 720
project creation
  using Android Studio, 25
  using Apache Maven, 13
  using Eclipse, 46
  Gradle format, 10
  IDE selection, 15
  old format, 9
  providing Eclipse and Gradle build files, 36
  reusing Java classes, 59
  sample programs to examine, 68, 76, 79
project layout, xix, 16, 29
public/private keys, 708
push notifications, 555
pushFxn(), 205

Q

QR codes
  scanning, 250
  sharing SL4A scripts in, 682
questions and comments, xx
QVGA (Quarter VGA), 267

R

radio buttons, 317
raster images, 277
RatingBar widget, 340
ratings/evaluation stars, 340
read-write access, 327
readLine method, 458
RecognizerIntent, 443
RecyclerView
  list-based applications using, 399
  using Section Headers in, 413
referenced projects, 59
regional language variations, 698

Registration ID, 562
regular expressions (regex), 564
release cycles, 5, 21, 67
Remote Methods Invocation (RMI), 574
removable storage, 448
RequestQueue class, 553
res/raw directory, 457
resources, accessing dangerous, 104
REST Client, 554
RESTful web services
  access via URLConnection, 550
  access via Volley, 553
  Twitter timeline loading, 602
returnValuesFxn(), 206
reverse geocoding, 612
reverse-engineering, avoiding, 720
revision control history
  loss of in Android Studio, 32
  preserving, 34
  sharing Java classes and, 61
RFO Basic, 664
RGraph, 273
RhoMobile Suite, 664
roaming, 653
Roboelectric, 163
ROME feed parser, 566
rounded-corner borders, 352
RSS/Atom feeds, 566
Runtime class, 665, 665

S

sample programs
  in Android SDK, 68
Scalable Vector Graphics (SVG), 257
ScaleBarOverlay class, 629
scaling images, 269
screen captures, 70
screen size and density, 98
screen video captures, 74
Scripting Layer for Android (SL4A)
  creating alerts in, 675
  download and use, 673
  fetching/displaying Google Docs, 679
  interpreters available, 674
  Python example, 674
  sharing scripts in QR codes, 682
  source editing, 675
scroll-wheel pickers, 380
scrolling/swiping capability, 355

finding and translating strings, 699
MD5 digest of clear-text strings, 570
pushing string values using Intent, 203
string handling, 701
time/date calculations, 133
time/date formatting, 130
translating application text, 696
subactivities, retrieving data from, 204
submenus, 374
Submit buttons, 336
Swing, 283, 290
SWT GUI layer, 283
SyncAdapter class, 2, 507
system activity manager, 660
system and device control
   copying to and from clipboards, 658
   determining active tasks and apps, 660
   device vibration, 659
   LED-based notifications, 658
   obtaining network-related and telephony
      information, 538, 653
   obtaining project settings information, 654
   silent, vibrate, or normal notifications, 655

T

TabView, 349
target markets, 712
telephone applications
   acting on incoming phone calls, 523
   calls and text messages testing, 191
   obtaining network-related and telephony
      information, 538, 653
   outgoing phone call blocking/altering, 527
   overview of, 523
   phone dialing, 531
   silent, vibrate, or normal notifications, 655
   SMS messages
      receiving, 535
      sending single- or multi-part, 533
      sending to the emulator, 537
      testing, 191
TelephonyManager class, 538
temperature values, 643
test-hosting companies, 154
testing (see application testing)
text
   advanced text searches in SQLite, 470
   auto-completion implementation, 331
   auto-completion using SQLite queries, 333

copying to and from clipboards, 658
   in custom dialogs, 387
   extracting information from unstructured,
      564
   help text, 144
   hyperlinked text, 571
   limiting input range and type, 328, 338
   MD5 digest of clear-text strings, 570
   password fields, 335
   plurals formatting, 128
   read-only vs. editable fields, 327
   special effects, 229
   speech-to-text, 443
   string handling and localization, 695-706
   text-to-speech, 444
   translating into user's language, 696
text messages
   receiving, 535
   sending single- or multi-part, 533
   sending to the emulator, 537
   testing, 191
TextKeyListener, 137
TextView class, 328, 571
TextWatcher interface, 328
themes, in Material Design, 286
threads/threading
   Android Development Guide, 213
   vs. AsyncTask processing, 195, 213
   avoiding crashes with, 212
   creating responsive applications with, 211
   pool-based implementation, 211
   sending messages between threads, 195, 220
3D graphics, 232
time/date formatting
   in SQLite database, 476
   using DateFormat class, 130
   using java.time API, 133
Timepicker widget, 378
timestamp format, 476
Tipster (tip calculator program), 79
Titanium, 663, 664
titling/shaking detection, 638
Toasts
   creating, 368
   customizing appearance of, 370
   in exception handling, 104
   intended uses for, 367
tool tips vs. hints, 144
toString(), 658

touch events, 239, 631
TrackService class, 208
translation (see strings and localization)
TTF (TrueType Fonts), 230
12-key layout, 137
Twitter timelines, 602
Typeface.create(), 230
typographical conventions, xvii

U

unit testing, 147
unsaved changes alerts, 376
UpdateActivity, 725
updates, 21, 123, 725
URLConnection objects, 550

V

versioning
    Android releases, 5, 67
    obtaining project settings information, 654
vibration
    creating device vibrations, 397
    for incoming calls, 655
    setting up vibration pattern, 659
    stock haptic controls, 346
video
    screen captures, 74
    video capture using MediaRecorder, 432
    YouTube videos, 431, 431
View events
    Activity implementation technique, 314
    anonymous inner class technique, 314
    attribute in View layout, 315
    interface type technique, 313
    lambda expression technique, 315
    Member class technique, 312
    overview of, 312
ViewGroups, 290
vocabulary, localization of, 698

voice recognition, 443
Volley library, 553

W

WakefulBroadcastReceiver, 559
WAP proxies, 549
watermarks, 145
web servers, 723
web-based app testing services, 154
WebSettings class, 573
WebView
    accessing web pages via, 572
    customizing appearance of, 573
    native handset functionality via JavaScript, 684
wheel pickers, 380
widgets
    Android-Wheel, 380
    AutoCompleteTextView, 331
    BaseAdapter, 404
    card widgets, 321
    Datepicker, 378
    GUI controls vs. app widgets, 284, 362
    RatingBar, 340
    Timepicker, 378
    widget toolkit (AWT), 283, 290

X

Xamarin, 664, 686
XDA Developers groups, 7
XML documents, 486

Y

YouTube videos, 431

Z

zoom-in and zoom-out operations, 280
ZXing barcode scanner, 250

About the Author

Ian Darwin has worked in the computer field for "quite a while" and has worked with Java since before the release of JDK 1.0. He's the author of several other O'Reilly works, including the well-known *Java Cookbook* and the new video series "Java Testing for Developers: From JUnit to Findbugs and PMD; Tools and Techniques for Java Testing." Ian holds an MSc in Computing from Staffordshire University and has done software development for various organizations in the Toronto area. He and his wife live north of the city, surrounded by acres of hills and trees.

Colophon

The animal on the cover of the *Android Cookbook* is a marine iguana (*Amblyrhynchus cristatus*). These lizards are found exclusively in the Galapagos (with a subspecies particular to each island). They are believed to be descended from land iguanas carried to the islands on log rafts from mainland South America.

The marine iguana is the only type of lizard that feeds in the water. Darwin found the reptiles unattractive and awkward, labeling them "disgusting clumsy lizards" and "imps of darkness," but these streamlined large animals (up to 5 or 6 feet long) are graceful in the water, with flattened tails designed for swimming.

These lizards feed on seaweed and marine algae. They can dive deeply (as far as 50 feet), though their dives are usually shallow, and they can stay underwater for up to an hour (though 5 to 10 minutes is more typical). Like all reptiles, marine iguanas are cold-blooded and must regulate their body temperature by basking in the sun; their black or gray coloration maximizes their heat absorption when they come out of the cold ocean. Though these harmless herbivores often allow humans to approach them closely, they can be aggressive when cold.

Marine iguanas have specialized nasal glands that filter ocean salt from their blood. They sneeze up the excess salt, which often accumulates on their heads or faces, creating a distinctive white patch or "wig." These iguanas are vulnerable to predation by introduced species (including dogs and cats), as well as to ocean pollution and fluctuations in their food supply caused by weather events such as El Niño.

Many of the animals on O'Reilly covers are endangered; all of them are important to the world. To learn more about how you can help, go to *animals.oreilly.com*.

The cover image is from *Wood's Animate Creation*. The cover fonts are URW Typewriter and Guardian Sans. The text font is Adobe Minion Pro; the heading font is Adobe Myriad Condensed; and the code font is Dalton Maag's Ubuntu Mono.